Dwayne and Janice Smith 4/98

THE ENCYCLOPEDIA OF THE VICTORIAN WORLD

THE

ENCYCLOPEDIA OF THE *Victorian World*

A Reader's Companion to the People, Places, Events, and Everyday Life of the Victorian Era

Melinda Corey and George Ochoa

A Roundtable Press Book

A Henry Holt Reference Book
Henry Holt and Company ❦ New York

A Henry Holt Reference Book
Henry Holt and Company, Inc.
Publishers since 1866
115 West 18th Street
New York, New York 10011

Henry Holt® is a registered
trademark of Henry Holt and Company, Inc.

Published in Canada by Fitzhenry & Whiteside Ltd.,
195 Allstate Parkway, Markham, Ontario L3R 4T8.

Library of Congress Cataloging-in-Publication Data
The encyclopedia of the Victorian world: an A to Z guide
to the people, places, events, and everyday life
of the Victorian era / Melinda Corey and George Ochoa, editors.
p. cm.—(A Henry Holt reference book)
Includes bibliographical references.

ISBN 0-8050-2622-3 (alk. paper)

1. Great Britain—History—Victoria, 1837–1901—Encyclopedias.
2. Great Britain—Civilization—19th century—Encyclopedias.
I. Corey, Melinda. II. Ochoa, George. III. Series.
DA550.E53 1996 95-21077
941.081'03—dc20 CIP

Henry Holt books are available for special promotions
and premiums. For details contact: Director, Special Markets.

A Roundtable Press Book

First Edition—1996

Designed by Betty Lew

Printed in the United States of America
All first editions are printed on acid-free paper.∞
1 3 5 7 9 10 8 6 4 2

To Martha,

born at another *fin de siècle*

Contents

List of Contributors *xi*

Acknowledgments *xiii*

Introduction *xv*

Entries A to Z *1*

Bibliography *513*

Editors

Melinda Corey

George Ochoa

Contributors

Kerry Benson

Paul Borysewicz

Tom Brown

John Cameli

Gregory Galloway

Jill Herbers

Richard Kaye

Catherine Park

Beth Passaro

Pam Thomas

Timothy Wright

Acknowledgments

We thank our contributors who brought their individual knowledge, wit, and style to bear in helping to research and write the book. We also thank Marsha Melnick and Susan Meyer of Roundtable Press, who encouraged us to develop the idea, reviewed the manuscript, and gathered the illustrations. Finally, we thank our editors at Henry Holt and Company, Ken Wright and Kevin Ohe.

Introduction

The Encyclopedia of the Victorian World is a detailed portrait of a period of amazing achievement and change: the reign of Great Britain's Queen Victoria from 1837 to 1901. While focused on Britain, the book's scope is worldwide, with alphabetically arranged entries representing nearly every nation and region and nearly every area of human endeavor—politics, art, literature, music, science, thought, war, business, recreation, architecture, design, and everyday life—a format that reflects both the preeminence of Britain during this period and its status as one of many interconnected places in which the modern world was being invented.

The Victorian Age was a time when colonial empires swelled, linked by railroads, steamships, and telegraphs. It was a time when ancient societies were reordered around steam-powered factories. It was a time when wars became bloodier and medicine more effective. It was a time when the British Empire grew to encompass a quarter of the world's land area and population, when the United States expanded from Missouri to California, when the modern nations of Germany and Italy were founded. It was a time when Western explorers penetrated Antarctica and Africa, and when scientists developed the germ theory of disease, harnessed electricity, and discovered radioactivity. It was a time when reformers struggled against slavery, created new systems of public education and health, and gave birth to the modern labor and woman's rights movements. It was the time when the twentieth century, with all its ills, achievements, and obsessions, was born.

The era produced more than its share of genius in every field. Its political leaders included William Gladstone, Benjamin Disraeli, Abraham Lincoln, and Otto von Bismarck; its scientists, Charles Darwin, Gregor Mendel, James Clerk Maxwell, the Curies, and Louis Pasteur; its thinkers, Karl Marx, John Stuart Mill, Friedrich Nietzsche, and Sigmund Freud; its novelists, Charles Dickens, the Brontë sisters, Herman Melville, Gustave Flaubert, Fyodor Dostoevsky, and Leo Tolstoy; its poets, Alfred, Lord Tennyson, Emily Dickinson, Walt Whitman, Charles Baudelaire, and Aleksandr Pushkin; its playwrights, Henrik Ibsen, Anton Chekhov, Oscar Wilde, and George Bernard Shaw; its musicians, Johannes Brahms, Richard Wagner, Frédéric Chopin, and Pyotr Tchaikovsky; and its artists, Edouard Manet, Claude Monet, Paul Cézanne, Vincent Van Gogh, and Auguste Rodin. More astonishing still is that these are only a sampling of the Victorian personalities whose achievements are still common knowledge.

The unifying symbol of the age was the queen of Great Britain and Ireland, Victoria. During her sixty-four-year reign, the longest in British history, Britain was the greatest of the great powers—its empire the largest, its industry the wealthiest, its navy the strongest. People the world over, from Asia to America, imitated British architecture, fashion, design, and literary forms. They made use of British technology and adopted British moral values and prejudices.

At the same time, other nations competed with or surpassed Britain in many respects. Paris remained the world center of the visual arts, while central and eastern Europe produced most of the era's greatest musicians. France and Russia pursued intense geopolitical rivalries with Britain. By century's end the United States, Germany, and Japan had begun preparing their bids for economic, military, and cultural preeminence in the next century.

The Encyclopedia of the Victorian World emphasizes the people, events, and daily life of Great Britain and its far-flung empire, from Canada to India, from Australia to Hong Kong. But a large number of entries deal with the great European powers and the growing United States. There are also numerous entries on the rest of the world—Africa, Latin America, the Ottoman Empire, China, and Japan. By the Victorian Age it was becoming difficult for any part of the globe to remain in isolation from the other parts. The world as a whole is therefore represented in these pages.

In subject matter, the entries range from the broadly general—industrialization, fashion, Romanticism—to the minutely particular—whist, cameos, fireplace tools. The personalities range from the still renowned, such as novelist George Eliot and designer William Morris, to the lesser known, such as playwright Dion Boucicault and painter Augustus Leopold Egg. The book includes those who were finishing their careers in the early Victorian Age, such as William Wordsworth, and those who were just starting in the late Victorian Age, such as William Butler Yeats. There are entries on people, countries, wars, laws, institutions, inventions, discoveries, objects, trends, styles, and ideas. A randomly selected series of entries encompasses Crazy Horse, cribbage, cricket, Crimean War, crinoline, and Cro-Magnon man. As that series makes clear, topics have been selected with a view to both the pleasures of browsing and the virtues of comprehensiveness.

No single volume could give a fully exhaustive picture of the world during such a creative and eventful period. In the interest of conserving space, many potential subjects have not received separate entries. For example, relatively few literary works enjoy individual treatment, although there are entries on all major authors and many minor ones. The texture of daily life in every country could not be represented fully, although such an effort has been made for Britain and more particularly for London. The individual political leaders and events of non-Western countries are not presented in as many entries as are those of Britain,

Europe, and the United States. Yet, though it is impossible for every topic to have its own entry, cross-references, which appear in small caps within entries, have been provided as an aid in locating information. Readers looking up abolitionism, ice ages, or Elias Howe will be directed to slavery, Louis Agassiz, and sewing machine, respectively. Where several different phrases might be used to refer to one topic, cross-references are also in place (for example, at *Sepoy Mutiny,* the reader is directed to *Indian Mutiny*).

We hope that *The Encyclopedia of the Victorian World* will be a valuable reference tool for all students and aficionados of the age, whether their interests lie in decorative style, parliamentary reform, the U.S. Civil War, the scramble for Africa, Irish politics, Dickensian street life, steam power, workhouses, or salons. We hope it will illuminate the complexities of the age that gave rise to our own, and we hope it will be a lot of fun. Like the Gothic setting of many a nineteenth-century novel, the Victorian Age is an estate with many chambers, porches, gardens, wild places, and hidden corners. The landscape of the age is charted and celebrated in this book.

THE ENCYCLOPEDIA OF THE
VICTORIAN WORLD

Abbas II (1874–1944) Last KHEDIVE of EGYPT, 1892–1914. When he came to power in 1892, the British had occupied Egypt for ten years. Actual power was held by Lord CROMER, the British consul-general, though Abbas was the nominal ruler under the nominal suzerainty of the OTTOMAN EMPIRE. Abbas made attempts to break the British hold on Egypt but failed, and was deposed in 1914 at the beginning of World War I when the Ottoman Empire joined the Central Powers and Egypt officially became a British protectorate.

Abbe, Cleveland (1838–1916) American meteorologist. A pioneer in weather forecasting, Abbe began publishing bulletins and maps forecasting storms in the Great Lakes in the 1860s. In 1871 he joined the first U.S. weather bureau, then a part of the U.S. Army; he was in charge of the bureau when it became a separate department in 1891. Abbe was also instrumental in advocating the adoption of time zones in 1883.

Abbott, Edwin A. (1838–1926) English clergyman, educator, and Shakespeare scholar. A headmaster who wrote several books on literature and theology, he had a taste for mathematics. This emerged in his best known work, a satirical mathematical fantasy called FLATLAND: A ROMANCE OF MANY DIMENSIONS (1884).

Abdur Rahman Khan (1844?–1901) Emir of Afghanistan, reigned from 1880 to 1901. A grandson of dynastic founder DOST MUHAMMAD, Abdur Rahman took power after his uncle Shere Ali was forced to abandon the Afghan throne to the British during the second of the ANGLO-AFGHAN WARS. Playing the British off against the Russians, Abdur Rahman allowed the British to maintain influence in Afghan affairs while keeping his country from becoming a British colony. Abdur Rahman settled several border disputes and was the first in the dynasty to achieve physical control over all of Afghanistan. He was succeeded by Habibullah Khan (reigned 1901–19).

Abel, Sir Frederick Augustus (1827–1902) English chemist. In 1889, with Scottish chemist Sir JAMES DEWAR, he invented CORDITE, a smokeless explosive used to cut down on the clouds of obscuring smoke prevalent in nineteenth-century battlefields. Chemist to the War Department (1854–88), Abel wrote several works on explosives.

Aberdeen, George Hamilton-Gordon, 4th Earl of (1784–1860) British foreign secretary and prime minister. Born in Edinburgh as George Gordon, he was orphaned as a boy and inherited the earldom of Aberdeen from his grandfather in 1801 when still in his teens. He added his deceased first wife's surname Hamilton to his own in 1818. Lord Aberdeen held several high government posts from the 1820s to the 1840s. A Tory, he served as chancellor of the duchy of Lancaster (1828) and as foreign secretary (1828–30) during the ministry of the Duke of Wellington. Under Sir ROBERT PEEL, he was secretary for war and the colonies (1834–35) and later foreign secretary (1841–46). During the latter assignment he was responsible for the WEBSTER-ASHBURTON TREATY (1842), which settled eastern boundary disputes between Canada and the United States, and the OREGON TREATY (1846), which settled a similar dispute in the West.

After Peel's death in 1850, Aberdeen became the leader of the Peel faction. He was elected to serve as prime minister at the head of a coalition government in 1852. He was successful on domestic issues but was blamed for the mishandled diplomacy that brought GREAT BRITAIN into the unpopular CRIMEAN WAR with Russia (1853–56). Aberdeen was forced to resign in 1855, one of many statesmen and generals disgraced by the bloody conflict. He was succeeded by Lord PALMERSTON and died five years later.

abolitionism See SLAVERY.

acid rain Environmental condition. First described in the 1850s, acid rain consists of rain, snow, or other precipitation containing relatively high levels of sulfuric or nitric acid. Hazardous to plant and aquatic life, acid rain is brought on by the reaction of moisture in the atmosphere with sulfur dioxide and nitrogen oxides from such sources as industrial emissions and engine exhausts.

acoustics Study of sound and sound waves. Though philosophers and scientists have studied the phenomenon of sound since ancient times, particularly as it related to music, the modern science of acoustics was founded in the late nineteenth century. In 1877 the British scientist J. W. STRUTT, Lord RAYLEIGH, summarized and extended what was then known about acoustics in the landmark work *The Theory of Sound.* In 1896, American physicist Wallace Clement Ware Sabine completed a study of a Harvard lecture room plagued by excessive reverberations. Sabine developed mathematical equations showing how the sound-absorption qualities of various materials and the volume of the room affected the amount of reverberations. In so doing he founded the science of architectural acoustics.

Acton, Sir John [Emerich Edward Dalberg], 1st Baron Acton (1834–1902) English historian. The son of Sir Ferdinand Acton, Sir John was born in Naples and educated in Paris, Oscott, Edinburgh, and Munich. He was elected as a Whig member of Parliament for Carlow in 1859 and named Baron Acton in 1869 on the recommendation of WILLIAM GLADSTONE. A liberal and a Roman Catholic, he combined the two strands in his writing and teaching, as with his arguments against papal infallibility in *Letters from Rome on the Council,* 1870, sometimes getting into trouble with the Church as a result. He helped found the *English Historical Review* in 1886 and was appointed Regius Professor of Modern History at Cambridge in 1895. He also planned the *Cambridge Modern History* and served as its first editor (1899–1900).

Although Acton never completed a book, his influence was felt as a teacher, essayist, and editor. His lectures on modern history (1906) and the French Revolution (1910) were published after his death.

Acton, William (1813–1875) British surgeon and writer. After studies at St. Bartholomew's Hospital, London, and the Venereal Hospitals, Paris, he was qualified as a surgeon and apothecary and practiced in London beginning in the 1830s. In 1841 he published *A Complete Practical Treatise on Venereal Diseases;* this successful work went through several editions and changes of title throughout his lifetime. He also wrote *Prostitution: Considered in Its Moral, Social and Sanitary Aspects* (1857). Acton's medical writings relied heavily on the research of other practitioners but gained him fame nonetheless. He is remembered today as an exemplar of Victorian sexual repression, detailing the dangers of masturbation, and writing, "I should say that the majority of women (happily for society) are not very much troubled with sexual feeling of any kind." However, other Victorian physicians, notably James Paget (1814–1889), took a more moderate and medically sound view of sexuality.

Adam, Adolphe Charles (1803–1856) French composer, critic, and teacher. Composer of more than fifty stage works including the ballet *Giselle* (1841) and the comic opera *Le Postillon de Longjumeau* (1836).

Adam Bede (1859) English novel. The first full-length novel by GEORGE ELIOT, it is set in rural England and recounts the doomed love of a carpenter named Adam Bede for Hetty Sorel, who is seduced and abandoned by a squire, Arthur Donnithorne. Adam and Hetty agree to wed, but she flees when she discovers she is pregnant by Arthur. She is found guilty of the murder of her child and transported for life. In the end, Adam marries Dinah Morris, a Methodist preacher who comforted Hetty in her ordeal.

Adams, Henry [Brooks] (1838–1918) American historian and man of letters. A member of Boston's cultured elite, he was the great-grandson of John Adams and the grandson of JOHN QUINCY ADAMS, both presidents of the United States.

After graduating from Harvard and spending a winter attending lectures in law in Berlin, Adams served as private secretary to his father, then minister to England, which gave him access to sensitive diplomacy during the U.S. Civil War and its aftermath. He also began publishing historical articles and reviews.

In 1868, after returning to the United States, Adams wrote many essays, exposing corruption in politics and arguing in favor of the silver standard and civil service reform. From 1870 to 1877 he taught medieval history at Harvard and was the first American to use the seminar method. He also edited the *North American Review.* In 1872 he married Marian (Clover) Hooper. They settled in Washington, D.C., in 1877 while Adams edited the papers of Albert Gallatin, Jefferson's secretary of the Treasury. The Adams household became the apex of Washington society, with Adams at the center of an important sphere of influence.

Adams's work as a historian produced two biographies, *The Life of Albert Gallatin* (1879) and *John Randolph* (1882), along with his acclaimed nine-volume *History of the United States of America* (1889–91). His novel *Democracy* (1880), published anonymously, was a widely read tale of political disillusionment. In 1884, Adams wrote the novel *Esther* under a pseudonym. The novel is about the loss of religious faith.

In 1885 his wife committed suicide. Soon afterward the grieving Adams traveled extensively, through the South Sea Islands, Asia, the Middle East, and Europe. He remained interested in the medieval period as "a fixed point . . . from which he might measure motion down to his own time." His masterpiece of MEDIEVALISM, *Mont-Saint-Michel and Chartres* (printed privately, 1904; published 1913), described the period's architecture as reflecting a coherent ideological unity, focused in reverence for the Virgin Mary, "the ideal of human perfection." The two cathedrals in the book's title expressed "an emotion, the deepest man ever felt—the struggle of his own littleness to grasp the infinite." In contrast he found the twentieth century dominated by multiplicity, symbolized by the electric generator, or dynamo, he had seen in 1900 at the Paris Exposition. He elaborated on this view in his autobiography, *The Education of Henry Adams* (printed privately, 1906; published 1918). His best known work, the *Education* won a posthumous Pulitzer Prize and is considered by many one of the most thoughtful of American autobiographies. Adams uses himself as a model to explore his theory of history, patterned on physics, as a dynamic process influenced by competing forces and the tendency of human institutions to disintegrate.

In his last years Adams edited the papers of his friend John Hay, a diplomat, and wrote several essays and a biography, *The Life of George Cabot Lodge* (1911).

Adams, John Couch (1819–1892) English astronomer and mathematician. The son of a tenant farmer in the East Cornwall town of Launceston, Adams taught himself calculus and number theory. In 1841, while studying mathematics at Cambridge University, he began working on a solution to the problem of mysterious irregularities in the orbit of Uranus. By 1845, now a fellow at St. John's College, Cambridge, he had completed his solution and was able to predict where a previously unknown planet could be found.

He was unable to get astronomers interested in confirming his prediction. French astronomer URBAIN JEAN JOSEPH LEVERRIER, working independently, was the first to publish calculations leading to the discovery of NEPTUNE in 1846. Adams and Leverrier now share credit for the discovery.

Adams also studied the great meteor shower of 1866 and made contributions to our knowledge of the moon's motions and the earth's magnetic field.

Adams, John Quincy (1767–1848) Sixth president of the UNITED STATES. Born in Massachusetts, the son of the second president John Adams, he served as foreign minister to the Netherlands, Prussia, Russia, and England, and as U.S. senator. As President James Monroe's secretary of state, he was a principal architect of the Monroe Doctrine, which prohibited new European colonization in the Western Hemisphere. From 1825 to 1829, Adams served a single term as president. Defeated for a second term by Andrew Jackson, Adams entered the House of Representatives in 1831. He fought the extension of SLAVERY and helped repeal the "gag rule" that prohibited the House from considering antislavery petitions. He died after falling ill on the House floor. His best known work is his twelve-volume *Memoirs,* published posthumously in 1874–77. He was the father of railroad executive and historian Charles Francis

Adams (1835–1915), who served as president of the Union Pacific Railroad from 1884 to 1890, and grandfather of historian and memoirist HENRY ADAMS.

Adams, Sarah Flower (1805–1848) English poet and hymnist. She is best known for the hymn "Nearer, My God, to Thee." A member of a circle of radicals that also included Harriet Taylor, later HARRIET HARDY TAYLOR MILL and HARRIET MARTINEAU, she contributed to the periodical the *Monthly Repository* (1832–36) and wrote *Vivia Perpetua* (1841), a poetic drama about a woman martyr.

Addams, Jane Laura (1860–1935) American social reformer. Born in Cedarville, Illinois, she was influenced in young adulthood by English social reformers who effected change by living among the poor. In 1889 she and a college friend, Allen Gates Starr, opened Hull House, a settlement house, in Chicago's South Halsted Street slum area. There she and other social reformers worked to establish housing for young working women and advocated the abolition of child labor and the improvement of working conditions. Believing that war dissipated movements toward domestic reform, she actively opposed American involvement in World War I. In 1920 she helped found the American Civil Liberties Union; in 1931 she was awarded the Nobel Peace Prize. Her first autobiography, *Twenty Years at Hull House,* was published in 1910.

Aden See YEMEN.

Adventures of Tom Sawyer, The (1876) American novel. Written by MARK TWAIN (Samuel Clemens), the novel concerns Tom Sawyer, who lives in the Mississippi River town of St. Petersburg, Missouri, a fictionalized version of Twain's own hometown. A mischievous orphan, Tom resides with his very proper and often forgiving aunt Polly. On a midnight jaunt, Tom and his friend Huck Finn witness a grave robbing and a murder by Injun Joe. Unhappy and fearful of Injun Joe, Tom runs away, with Joe Harper and Huck, to a blissful island. But the boys observe the town's search parties and sneak back to attend their own joint funeral. Tom later testifies in the murder trial, and Injun Joe spectacularly escapes. During a picnic, Tom and his sweetheart Becky Thatcher get lost for three days in a cave near the river; searching for an exit, Tom sights Injun Joe hiding a chest Tom knows to contain a treasure. Eventually Injun Joe dies of starvation in the cave, and Tom returns with Huck to retrieve the chest. The two boys become rich, and the homeless Huck is adopted and civilized by the Widow Douglas.

While *Tom Sawyer* was very popular in its day and remains one of the most popular books among American children, its literary reputation has been superseded by its sequel, *The Adventures of Huckleberry Finn.*

advertising Announcements intended to promote sales of products. During the Victorian Age, the practice of persuading the public to buy a given product changed from an unrespectable act to a socially accepted one. Aimed squarely at the middle classes, advertising helped establish the modern consumer society. The rise of mass production and a growing urban populace in both Great Britain and the United States saw the proliferation of commercial household goods and services, which could reach their audience best through advertising.

Among the first products to employ advertising successfully in the United States and Britain were home remedies such as patent medicines. One of the earliest brand-name campaigns was for Lydia Pinkham's Vegetable

An advertisement for Cadbury's Cocoa reflects the dawn of the "consumer century." Photo courtesy of Topham/Image Works.

Compound. Called "the positive cure for all female complaints," the herb-and-alcohol creation became a household word in the United States through newspaper advertising in the 1870s. Its popularity grew in 1879 when a likeness of inventor Mrs. Pinkham in Quaker garb appeared in the advertisements. Saturation advertisement—the placement of ads in large numbers in a given geographical area—also brought success in England to Lipton Tea and Beecham's Pills, and in the United States to Sapolio Soap, Royal Baking Powder, and the air-filled Ivory Soap, whose slogan, "99 44/100 percent pure," is still used today.

Beginning in the 1880s, the union of American advertising maven J. Walter Thompson and American publisher Cyrus H. N. Curtis made advertising in PERIODICALS commonplace. An array of middle-class products—Kodak film, Pabst beer, Prudential insurance—were sold in Curtis's magazines, *Ladies' Home Journal* and *Saturday Evening Post.* Advertising space that had once been relegated to the back of the magazine and aimed at the elite carriage trade now spanned the entire magazine and concentrated on products for a much wider clientele. Such practices not only increased sales of the products but also broadened the audience for the more exclusive magazines.

Advertising agencies were born and also transformed during the Victorian era. The first advertising agency was opened by Volney Palmer in Philadelphia, Pennsylvania, in 1841. Rather than creating advertising campaigns, Palmer's primary service lay in acting as an agent selling the space of publishers to advertisers. In 1868, Francis Wayland Ayer revolutionized advertising agencies with the founding of N. W. Ayer & Son in Philadelphia. He set up the "open contract" between agent and advertiser, bringing the two together in a partnership, with the agent receiving a commission. Not until 1891 was the first full-service advertising agency opened, in New York by George Batten. He offered "service contracts" with companies that relieved their need for a self-run advertising department.

The popularity of advertising also affected advertising law. In Britain, for example, while the repeal of the duty on advertising in 1853 opened up the possibility for advertising on a wider scale, the end of the century saw the formation of advocacy organizations to protect citizens against dangerous excesses. In 1893 the Society for Checking the Abuses of Public Advertising (SCAPA) was founded. With other advocacy groups it helped to bring about parliamentary action through the Advertisements Regulation Act (1907), which allowed for local regulation of public advertising.

From the 1860s to the close of the century, advertising volume in the United States grew tenfold, from $50 million to $500 million. Substantial though less spectacular gains were made in England. In both countries, advertising had become an art, a business, a subject of law, even a science. By the close of the Victorian Age, the consumer century had begun.

aestheticism British artistic movement. Practicing the doctrine of ART FOR ART'S SAKE, aestheticism reached its peak in the 1870s through the 1890s. Aesthetes strove to express their individual sense of beauty, divorced from moral or social purpose, and felt free to use any subject matter, even the sexual or perverse. Among its chief spokesmen were WALTER PATER and OSCAR WILDE; among the artists associated with it were JAMES ABBOTT MCNEILL WHISTLER and Sir EDWARD BURNE-JONES. Characteristic works were exhibited at the opening of the Grosvenor Gallery in London in 1877. Influenced by the mid-century PRE-RAPHAELITES, it blended into the DECADENCE of the 1890s. It also had an impact on reform of household decoration. Aestheticism was ridiculed by *PUNCH* and in GILBERT AND SULLIVAN's operetta *Patience* (1881).

Afghanistan Nation in south central Asia. Bordered by Iran, Pakistan, China, Tajikistan, Uzbekistan, and Turkmenistan, and strategically located on the main route to India, it was the target of the bitter nineteenth-century rivalry between Great Britain and Russia for control of central Asia known as "THE GREAT GAME." Site of the ANGLO-AFGHAN WARS of 1838–42 and 1878–80, it was ruled by the dynasty founded by DOST MUHAMMAD in 1826 but remained subject to British influence until 1919 when Britain recognized Afghan independence. In popular Victorian imagination, the conflicts in Afghanistan yielded many stories of military derring-do, such as the 1880 march of Major-General FREDERICK SLEIGH ROBERTS from KABUL to KANDAHAR. The British also admired the martial virtues of the Afghans, who were called by British officer Vincent Eyre "perhaps the best marksmen in the world."

Africa The world's second-largest continent. Africa was the birthplace of humanity and home of one of the most ancient civilizations, that of EGYPT, which emerged before 3000 B.C. Historically, the continent's most significant boundary has been the Sahara, the world's largest desert, which marks the division between North Africa and sub-Saharan Africa. With ports on the Mediterranean Sea, North Africa has been in continuous contact with Europe and Asia from antiquity to the present. From the seventh century, the region was Islamic in character; by the seventeenth century much of it—including present-day ALGERIA, Tunisia, Libya, and Egypt—was part of the OTTOMAN EMPIRE. In the Victorian era, Europe dismembered the region, with France taking Algeria in 1848 and Tunisia in 1881, and Great Britain assuming administrative control of Egypt in 1882. Britain's interests had much to do with the SUEZ CANAL, completed in 1869; it created a direct water route from the Mediterranean Sea to the Red Sea, thereby facilitating east-west trade and increasing Egypt's strategic importance. Farther west, Libya remained Ottoman throughout the Victorian Age, while the kingdom of Morocco retained independent status, though it was the object of much European rivalry, particularly between France and Spain.

Parts of sub-Saharan Africa—the vast region south of the desert—were known to Muslim traders and conquerors since the Middle Ages, but the region was virtually unknown to Europeans until the fifteenth and sixteenth centuries when Portuguese explorers established trading stations in coastal areas, especially in the west. From the late sixteenth to the nineteenth century, Africa was the site of a flourishing slave trade, masterminded first by the Portuguese and later by the Spanish, British, Dutch, and others. Captured in the interior, often by fellow Africans, slaves were transported to European buyers on the coast and from there by ship to the New World. In 1833, Britain abolished SLAVERY throughout the empire, and most other nations followed suit later in the century. Eradication of the last vestiges of the slave trade was a major goal for humanitarians in Africa.

From the 1840s to the 1880s, British explorers such as DAVID LIVINGSTONE, Sir HENRY MORTON STANLEY, Sir RICHARD FRANCIS BURTON, and JOHN HANNING SPEKE led expeditions that mapped the African interior, bringing in their wake spiritual and secular missionaries who were convinced that Africans would benefit from European civilization. The explorers were also followed by people with more frankly commercial interests, whether it was in agricultural products, such as palm oil or cotton, or mineral ones, such as the diamonds from southern Africa that made the fortune of British colonizer CECIL RHODES.

By 1880, European nations had acquired a number of outposts in sub-Saharan Africa. In West Africa, Britain controlled Gambia, SIERRA LEONE, the Gold Coast (now Ghana), and Lagos (now part of Nigeria), while France occupied Senegal and Gabon. Portugal possessed Portuguese Guinea (now Guinea-Bissau) in West Africa, and in southern Africa, ANGOLA on the west coast and MOZAMBIQUE on the east coast. At the continent's southern tip, Britain possessed the Cape Colony—originally settled by the Dutch and still containing a number of their descendants, the BOERS—and adjoining it the TRANSVAAL and Natal, in what is now SOUTH AFRICA. Still, the vast bulk of the African interior remained independent, ruled by indigenous kings and chiefs in a complex network of states and villages, representing many languages and traditions. In the 1880s that independence began to come to an end as proponents of European IMPERIALISM embarked on what is known as "the scramble for Africa."

International political rivalry was the primary fuel for this frantic grab for colonies. In the early 1880s, King Leopold II of BELGIUM established a personal claim to the central African region of the Congo, later known as the Belgian Congo, which had been explored by Stanley. France countered by establishing a claim in the region just west, known as the French Congo. Meanwhile, German chancellor OTTO VON BISMARCK spurred the establishment of German colonies in East Africa, West Africa, and Southwest Africa. Alarmed by the entry of the new imperialist powers, Portugal called for an international conference to determine a process of legitimizing colonial claims in Africa. The resulting Conference of Berlin (1884–85), hosted by Bismarck and attended by all the interested European parties along with the United States and the Ottoman Empire, set the stage for the partition of Africa. The conferees declared the basins of the Congo and Niger rivers free trade areas and asserted the intention of suppressing slavery. They also agreed that colonial claims had to be backed by actual occupation. It therefore became imperative for the imperial powers to stake claims and place colonists there before their rivals did.

By 1914 all of the African continent except Liberia and Ethiopia had been divided among imperialist foreign powers. Much of that partitioning had taken place or been started by the end of the Victorian era. Typically, indigenous Africans were persuaded to sign treaties ceding territories or leasing their use; armed conflict followed when colonists abused or transgressed the treaty terms. In numerous battles between Europeans armed with MACHINE GUNS and indigenous fighters, resistance was overcome, territories annexed, and rebellions crushed. Europeans brought what they called progress: railroads, bridges, telegraph lines, roads, modern buildings, mining operations, and plantation farming. Their progress was often achieved by forced African labor, exacted as a form of taxation.

British conflicts with indigenous peoples included four Ashanti Wars in 1824–31, 1873–74, 1893–94, and 1895–96 with the Ashanti tribal confederation in the Gold Coast, clashes with the MASHONA and MATABELE of RHODESIA, and the KAFFIR WARS and ZULU WAR in South Africa.

At the turn of the century, the situation in sub-Saharan Africa stood as follows:

In West Africa, the French were dominant. French West Africa, organized in 1895, included Dahomey (now Benin), French Guinea (now Guinea), French Sudan (now Mali), Ivory Coast, Mauritania, Senegal, Upper Volta (now Burkina Faso), and Niger. The French were also moving into what is now Chad. The British extended their possessions in West Africa, notably southern and northern Nigeria, while the Germans maintained Togoland (now Togo) and Cameroon. Liberia, which had been founded as a home for freed American slaves in 1821, became an independent republic in 1847 and remained so throughout the scramble for Africa.

In central Africa, King Leopold of Belgium continued to rule what was known as the Congo Free State (now Zaire), while the French Congo (now Gabon and Congo) continued to expand. The French founded the colony of Ubangi-Shari, which later became part of French Equatorial Africa and still later became the Central African Republic. Spain possessed Spanish Sahara (now Western Sahara, occupied by Morocco) in West Africa and Spanish Guinea (now Equatorial Guinea) in Central Africa.

In East Africa, the British possessed what are now KENYA, UGANDA, and ZANZIBAR, while GERMAN EAST AFRICA included the mainland portion of modern Tanzania, along with Rwanda and Burundi.

In southwest Africa, Germany possessed what is now NAMIBIA.

In southern Africa, driven by Cecil Rhodes, the British presence spread into BECHUANALAND (now Botswana), BASUTOLAND (now Lesotho), SWAZILAND, and Rhodesia (now ZAMBIA and Zimbabwe), while the BOER WAR (1899–1902) established firm British control over all of modern South Africa.

On the horn of Africa, Italy possessed Eritrea but was unable to subdue the ancient kingdom of Ethiopia. Somaliland (now Djibouti and Somalia) was split among the British, French, and Italians.

Portugal remained in possession of Portuguese Guinea, Angola, and Mozambique.

Following World War II, most of the African colonies gained their independence.

Agassiz, [Jean] Louis [Rodolphe] (1807–1873) Swiss-born American naturalist. After graduating from the universities of Erlangen and Munich, and studying with anatomist Georges Cuvier (1769–1832), Agassiz became professor of natural history at the University of Neuchâtel in 1832. There his studies of fish resulted in the multivolume series *Research on Fossil Fish, 1833–44*. In 1837 he began his studies of glacial movements, following the work of Swiss geologist I. Venetz (1788–1859), who postulated that glaciers were once much more extensive than now. Through his work, Agassiz came to believe that ice sheets had once covered not only mountainous areas but lowlands throughout Europe and North America. From this he constructed his theory of the Ice Ages, past periods when millions of square miles of land over several continents were covered with ice sheets. At first rejected by many scientists, his concept of Ice Ages was eventually accepted. While on a lecture tour in the United States, Agassiz settled at Harvard University, where he taught for twenty-five years, and helped found the National Academy of Sciences.

Aguinaldo, Emilio (1869–1964) Philippine political leader. In 1896 he led a revolution to end Spanish rule of the Philippines, fighting from his base in his native province of Cavite. The revolution was suppressed and he was exiled to Hong Kong, but he returned in 1898 with U.S. backing during the SPANISH-AMERICAN WAR. The Philippines were declared independent, and Aguinaldo became president in 1899. He then fought against the attempt by the United States to take Spain's place as colonial ruler; he was captured and forced to swear allegiance to the United States in 1901.

Ainsworth, William Harrison (1805–1882) English novelist and editor. Born in Manchester, the son of a lawyer, he left the study of law to write poems and stories for magazines and to publish novels, the first of which was *Sir John Chiverton* (1826). The novel *Rockwood* (1834) was his first major success, followed by *Crichton* (1837). Beginning in 1839, he edited *Bentley's Miscellany*, a magazine he later owned for a time. He also founded *Ainsworth's Magazine* in 1842 and edited *New Monthly Magazine* beginning in 1845. At the same time he continued to write novels, many on historical subjects, such as *The Tower of London* (1840). A popular and prolific writer, he was a prominent member of London society and a friend to CHARLES DICKENS, WILLIAM WORDSWORTH, WILLIAM MAKEPEACE THACKERAY, Walter Scott and others. His novels, however, are little read today.

air brake Device using compressed air to stop a train. Invented in 1868 by American engineer GEORGE WESTINGHOUSE, it has become standard for passenger trains. The system operates by forcing compressed air through a cylinder and activating brakes on the wheels.

***Alabama*, C.S.S.** Confederate warship. The *Alabama* was the most famous of several warships built for the CONFEDERACY in British shipyards during the U.S. CIVIL WAR. Between September 1862 and April 1864 the *Alabama* captured or destroyed seventy-one Union vessels in every quarter of the globe. The raider also inflicted huge costs on Union naval commerce through increased insurance rates and cargo spoilage. The Union navy's search for the ship strained its resources until the U.S.S. *Kearsarge* sank it off the coast of France.

After the war the United States sought damages from Great Britain. The negotiations, often acrimonious, sputtered on until 1872 when an international arbitration commission awarded the United States between $14.5 and $15.5 million. Charles Francis Adams (1835–1915), son of JOHN QUINCY ADAMS, was the chief American negotiator at the final meetings.

Albert, places named Geographical sites around the world were named for Prince ALBERT, consort of Britain's Queen VICTORIA. (See also VICTORIA, PLACES NAMED.) These include:

- Lake ALBERT (MOBUTU SESE SEKO), Africa
- Lake Albert, Australia
- Albert Canyon, Canada
- Albert Nile River, Africa
- Albert Town, Bahamas
- Alberta, Canada (province)
- Albertinia, South Africa
- Alberton, Canada
- Mount Albert Edward, Papua New Guinea
- Albert Edward Range, Australia

Albert Bridge Structure over the Thames River in London. Named for the late Prince ALBERT, it was designed in 1873 by R. M. Ordish and reflected the Victorian taste for lacy cast-iron ornamentation.

Albert Hall, Royal Performing arts theater. Opened in 1871, it was dedicated to the late Prince ALBERT. With a seating capacity of five thousand two hundred, it was one of the largest auditoriums in the world and is now frequently the site of sports as well as music events.

Albert (Mobutu Sese Seko), Lake One-hundred-mile-long body of water in East Africa between Uganda and Zaire. It was named for Prince ALBERT as a companion to the nearby Lake VICTORIA NYANZA. The Victoria Nile River flows through here before becoming the Albert Nile.

Albert Memorial The most famous of Queen VICTORIA's many monuments to her late husband Prince ALBERT. Designed by Sir GEORGE GILBERT SCOTT, it was built in 1863–72 and is located in Kensington Gardens, London.

Albert of Saxe-Coburg-Gotha, Prince (1819–1861) Prince consort of Great Britain's Queen VICTORIA. A member of the Germanic Wettin dynasty, he accepted his first cousin Victoria's proposal of marriage in 1839, two years after her accession as queen of the United Kingdom. The marriage, which was championed by Leopold I, king of Belgium and uncle to Albert and Victoria, took place in 1840. Albert became Victoria's closest advisor, and their loving marriage helped the young queen adjust to her office. Active in foreign affairs, he provided the Foreign Office with information from his continental

Prince Albert's diplomatic abilities and devotion to Victoria were underappreciated by the British until after his death. Photo courtesy of The Bettman Archive.

relatives. In 1861 he toned down the wording of a British complaint to the United States over the removal of two Confederate commissioners from a British ship during the U.S. CIVIL WAR. His influence in this matter, known as the TRENT AFFAIR, helped the two countries avoid war.

Despite his devotion to Victoria and the stability of the royal marriage, Albert was not very popular during his lifetime. Many aristocrats resented his seriousness and his elevated moral tone, while some government officials bridled at his interest in foreign affairs. An amateur musician, painter, architect, and designer, he was an art collector and an influential patron of the arts. He helped design Osborne House, the royal residence on the Isle of Wight, and oversaw the GREAT EXHIBITION OF 1851, the profits from which were used to endow the VICTORIA AND ALBERT MUSEUM. In 1857, Victoria gave him the title prince consort. He died of typhoid fever in 1861 while planning another exhibition. Heartbroken, Victoria largely withdrew from public life for several years after his death, commemorating her deceased spouse in many monuments, including the ALBERT MEMORIAL. It was only after Albert's death that his subjects came to appreciate his talents and contributions to public affairs.

alcoholic beverages Due to the risk of disease from unsanitary drinking water, alcoholic beverages were widely consumed in Victorian England. Gin was the preferred spirit of the lower class, while wine and brandy were imbibed by the more comfortable citizenry. Sherry was a favorite drink near midday or with soup at dinner, while port and brandy were reserved for after dinner. By the end of the century, however, whiskey became the dominant after-dinner drink.

In an attempt to dissuade the poor from drinking too much gin, the Wellington Beer House Act of 1830 provided cheap licenses for public houses (pubs) serving beer. Beer production grew from 14 million barrels in 1830 to 37 million barrels in 1900. Ale continued to be the preferred malt beverage in England, while the rest of the world switched to lagers between 1840 and 1880.

Beer and whiskey were the drinks of choice in the United States, but mixed drinks also saw a rise in prominence. The martini first appeared sometime around 1870, although the early versions called for as much as a wineglass of vermouth. Saloons and bartenders were both creations of nineteenth-century America. The era's most famous bartender, Jerry Thomas of New York City, is responsible for the invention of numerous drinks. He published the recipes for ten cocktails in 1862, while his 1877 collection contained 140 drinks, including ones familiar today, such as the Manhattan and the Tom Collins, and obscure ones such as the Dead Beat, the Fiscal Agent, and the Vox Populi. An American bar was on display at the Paris Exposition of 1867, further promoting the panoply of cocktails available at the time.

It was also in the nineteenth century that alcoholism was recognized as a serious and growing problem. Temperance movements opposed to the unrestricted sale and consumption of alcoholic beverages were founded during this period in Britain, America, and continental Europe.

Alcott, [Amos] Bronson (1799–1888) American educator, transcendentalist philosopher, and social reformer. Born in Walcott, Connecticut, he had little formal education and made an early living as a peddler before becoming known for his support of dominant nineteenth-century reform movements such as women's rights and abolitionism. In 1834 he established the Temple School in Boston, Massachusetts, which operated mixed-race classes following the ideals of TRANSCENDENTALISM by attempting to nurture the potential of each individual student. The school met with some scorn and limited success; however, Alcott was able to effect reform in the Concord, Massachusetts, public schools as superintendent from 1859 to 1865. With William T. Harris he founded the Concord School of Philosophy in 1879 and directed it until the end of his life. The author of influential works on education, including *The Doctrine and Discipline of Human Culture* (1836) and *Observations on the Principles and Methods of Infant Instruction* (1830), he was also a frequent contributor to the transcendentalist periodical *The Dial.* He was the father of LOUISA MAY ALCOTT.

Alcott, Louisa May (1832–1888) American novelist. She was born in Germantown, Pennsylvania, to the financially strapped household of Abigail and BRONSON ALCOTT, the social reformer and adherent of TRANSCENDENTALISM whose many failed utopian plans rendered the family penurious. After the family moved to Concord, Massachusetts, Alcott contributed to family funds by working as a seamstress. Following her girlhood dream and hoping that it would make more money than menial labor, she started writing, publishing her first story in 1852; *Flower Fables,* a book of fairy tales, in 1854; and in 1863, *Hospital Sketches,* a book of letters written while a nurse during the Civil War. A regular contributor to *Atlantic Monthly,* she also wrote Gothic novels and tales for popular periodicals such as *Frank Leslie's Illustrated Newspaper,* anonymously or under the pseudonym A. N. Barnard. Great success came with the publication of *Little Women* in 1868, the semiautobiographical novel influenced by her own childhood with three sisters. Popular sequels included *Little Men* (1871) and *Jo's Boys* (1886). Among her many other novels of young life were *An Old-Fashioned Girl* (1870) and the six-volume *A Garland for Girls* (1888). Adult novels, including *Work* (1873), were less successful. A friend since her youth to the Concord-based transcendentalist thinkers RALPH WALDO EMERSON, HENRY DAVID THOREAU, and MARGARET FULLER, she became involved in forward-thinking causes in her adulthood, including abolition and women's rights.

Alexander II (1818–1881) Czar of RUSSIA (1855–81). The son of Czar NICHOLAS I, he negotiated an end to the CRIMEAN WAR (1854–56). He introduced reforms in military and government administration, including limited local self-rule, and emancipated the serfs (1861). He crushed a revolt in Poland (1863–64) and led the nation during the RUSSO-TURKISH WAR of 1877–78. His liberal reforms did not silence his many opponents, some of whom turned to terrorism. In response, Alexander introduced repressive measures that inspired more terrorism. Assassinated by a bomb, he was succeeded by his son ALEXANDER III.

Alexander III (1845–1894) Czar of RUSSIA (1881–94). Reversing the liberal reforms of his father, Czar ALEXANDER II, he increased repression, promoted fidelity to Russian language and culture, and persecuted minorities, particularly Jews. He forged a secret alliance with France and, through his advances into Central Asia, raised tensions with Great Britain. He was succeeded by his son NICHOLAS II.

Alger, Horatio, Jr. (1832–1899) American writer. Born in Revere, Massachusetts, he attended Harvard College and Harvard Divinity School, then traveled to Paris where he lived a bohemian life for several years. Returning to the United States, he became a Unitarian minister in 1864, a profession that led in 1866 to his chaplaincy at the Newsboys' Lodging House in New York. He fulfilled that charge with enthusiasm for most of the rest of his life. At the same time, he became famous for his fiction. Though his novels for adults were generally unsuccessful, the more than one hundred books he wrote for boys were extremely popular. Appearing first in serial form, they bore such titles as *Ragged Dick* (1867), *Luck and Pluck* (1869), and *Tattered Tom* (1871). Almost always the heroes of these novels rose from rags to riches through hard work and strong moral fiber. Supporting as they did the American ethos of self-reliance and the more general Victorian ideal of character, the novels won a wide audience. His biographies, such as *From Canal Boy to President* (1881), the story of Abraham Lincoln, offered similar accounts of men born into humble circumstances who triumphed through self-reliance. The phrase "Horatio Alger story" became a synonym for this type of tale.

Algeria North African country. A colony of FRANCE throughout the Victorian era, Algeria was populated by a mixture of Arabs and Berbers, nearly all of them Muslim. The country had previously been under the nominal control of the Ottoman Empire, but had become virtually independent, governed by a loose confederation of town governors and nomadic chiefs.

French involvement in Algeria arose out of a dispute with the *dey* (governor) of Algiers over debts owed to French merchants and the *dey*'s tolerance of piracy, an important source of income for the Algerians. After a blockade and prolonged negotiations, a large French expeditionary force captured Algiers in July 1830. The government of LOUIS-PHILIPPE initially tried to restrict involvement in Algeria to occupation of the coastal cities and suppression of piracy, but then a major campaign was mounted to subdue the interior plateau, a task accomplished by 1847. Sporadic fighting continued against the Turaeg tribes in the Sahara into the twentieth century.

Large numbers of French colonists began to emigrate to Algeria, settling mostly in towns and outposts as merchants and administrators. Under the SECOND REPUBLIC and the SECOND EMPIRE, these colonists had no political rights, and Algeria was governed by the military. Under the THIRD REPUBLIC, the colonists were given the vote and representatives in Paris. The result was a worsening of conditions for the indigenous population; high taxes were imposed on them, and the settlers were granted arbitrary judicial powers. Attempts to reform the situation were defeated by the settler lobby. A settler-led secessionist movement was headed off with further concessions and greater restrictions on Muslims in the 1880s and 1890s.

The French population of Algeria continued to grow throughout the period, but the Muslim population grew much more quickly. Algeria served as a base for further French colonization of North Africa and a source of manpower and material. An Algerian independence movement did not develop until the twentieth century; independence was proclaimed in 1962.

Alice's Adventures in Wonderland (1865; rev. 1886, 1897) Fantasy by English author LEWIS CARROLL. A classic of children's literature, it recounts the adventures of a little girl who falls down a rabbit hole into a bizarre dream world. Growing too large and then too

The Mad Hatter's tea party, a famous scene from Lewis Carroll's Alice's Adventures in Wonderland. *Private Collection.*

small, sitting in on a mad tea party, and witnessing a croquet match at which the Queen of Hearts repeatedly shouts "Off with his head!" Alice engages in wild illogic with such characters as the White Rabbit, the Cheshire Cat, the Mad Hatter, the March Hare, the Mock Turtle, and the Dormouse. The author's mathematical training is evident in the play of illogic, and parodies and puns abound. Carroll created this world for children, particularly a little girl of his acquaintance named Alice Liddell, but the book's good-humored lunacy, suggestive social satire, and commonsensical heroine have enchanted adults as well.

all-red route Term for an uninterrupted line of communication from Great Britain's imperial possessions to the capital, London. On British maps, the far-flung British possessions were colored in red; an "all-red" route indicated that messages, trade goods, and troops could travel along land and sea routes entirely controlled by the British. CECIL RHODES tried unsuccessfully to establish from the CAPE TO CAIRO an all-red route through the interior of Africa.

alpha and beta rays Byproducts of RADIOACTIVITY. The positively charged alpha particle is a helium nucleus, consisting of two protons and two neutrons; a beta particle is a negatively charged, high-speed electron, or sometimes a positron, the positively-charged antiparticle of an electron. Alpha and beta rays were first detected in uranium radiation by British physicist Ernest Rutherford in 1897, who named them after the first two letters of the Greek alphabet. GAMMA RAYS are another component of radiation, though unlike alpha and beta rays, they are waves of electromagnetic energy, not particles of matter.

Altamira cave paintings Prehistoric artwork. Discovered on the ceiling and walls of Altamira Cave in northern Spain by Spanish archeologist Marcellino de Sautuola in 1879, the artistically accomplished red and black paintings of bison, deer, and other animals, dating from about fourteen thousand years ago, were the first evidence that prehistoric people were capable of painting. Painting is now believed to have begun even earlier, as demonstrated by artwork from Namibia, Africa, dating from twenty-six thousand to nineteen thousand years ago.

Altgeld, John Peter (1847–1902) American politician. Born in Germany, he grew up in Ohio and fought for the Union in the American Civil War. He entered politics as a Democratic county attorney in Missouri. He then moved to Chicago, where he acquired wealth as a builder before becoming a county judge in 1886 and then state governor of Illinois (1892–96). A defender of liberal causes, he incurred vocal opposition when he pardoned the anarchists convicted for the HAYMARKET SQUARE RIOT (1886) and protested the use of federal troops to end the PULLMAN STRIKE (1894). At the 1896 Democratic national convention, he led the side of free silver (unlimited coinage of silver) against incumbent president GROVER CLEVELAND, whom he regarded as a tool of corporate interests. Altgeld won the party over to his side, but its presidential candidate, WILLIAM JENNINGS BRYAN, lost to Republican WILLIAM MCKINLEY. Altgeld himself was defeated that year for reelection as governor, and he returned to his law practice until his death.

amendments See U.S. CONSTITUTION, AMENDMENTS.

amusement parks See CONEY ISLAND.

analytical engine Forerunner of the modern digital computer. This calculating machine was designed and partially constructed by English mathematician CHARLES BABBAGE, who began working on it in 1834. The machine was to respond to punched-card instructions, store information for later retrieval, and print out results. With only mechanical gears and levers at his disposal and without techniques for precision construction of parts, Babbage was unable to finish the machine. It was described by one of its champions, Augusta Ada, Lady LOVELACE, daughter of Lord Byron, and is preserved in the Science Museum of London.

Andersen, Hans Christian (1805–1875) Danish writer. The son of a cobbler, he was raised in poverty and left his native Odense at fourteen for Copenhagen, where he worked as an actor with the Royal Theatre. From 1827 to 1828 he attended Copenhagen University. In 1835 he published *The Improvisatore,* the first of six autobiographical novels, and *Tales Told for Children,* which contained his first four fairy tales: "The Tinderbox," "Little Claus and Big Claus," "The Princess and the Pea," and "Little Ida's Flowers." Unlike the Brothers GRIMM, whom he admired, Andersen was not primarily a collector of folklore but a writer of original stories in the folk tale and fairy tale traditions. His 168 tales for children, published mostly in booklets of four from 1835 to 1872, combined serious themes and dark irony with elements of fantasy and fun. They included "Inchelina," "The Little Mermaid," "The Emperor's New Clothes," "The Steadfast Tin Soldier," "The Ugly Duckling," "The Snow Queen," "The Red Shoes," "The Little Fir Tree," "The Little Match Girl," and "The Sandman." Translated into many languages, the collected tales first appeared in an English edition in 1869–71. Andersen also wrote plays, poems, and travel narratives. His autobiographical *Fairy Tale of My Life* was published in 1855.

Anderson, Elizabeth Garrett (1836–1917) British physician and activist who worked to open medical education to women. Born in London, she decided to become a doctor after meeting with pioneering American physician ELIZABETH BLACKWELL. After being rejected by medical schools in London, Edinburgh, and Saint Andrew's, she obtained a license to practice from the Apothecaries' Hall in 1865. One year later she became a general medical attendant at St. Mary's Dispensary in London, where she served during the city's CHOLERA epidemic. When women were granted the right in France to become physicians, Anderson received her M.D. degree there in 1870. From 1886 to 1892 she helped to staff the

New Hospital for Women, the teaching institution connected to the London School for Medicine for Women. Active in the final years of her life in community affairs, she became the first woman to be elected mayor of an English town in 1908 when she presided over the town of Aldeburgh, Suffolk. In 1918 the New Hospital was renamed the Elizabeth Garrett Anderson Hospital. Anderson's sister was suffragist Dame MILLICENT GARRETT FAWCETT.

anesthesia Loss of sensation induced by drugs and used to relieve or eliminate pain. The practical use of anesthetic agents began in earnest during the mid-nineteenth century, effectively dividing the history of surgery into the pre- and post-anesthetic eras. As early as 1800, British chemist Sir Humphrey Davy (1778–1829) discovered and experimented with nitrous oxide. In 1842, American surgeon Crawford Williamson Long (1815–1878) first used ETHER as a general anesthetic during a tumor removal. But it was not until October 16, 1846, that Boston surgeon William Thomas Green Morton (1819–1868) successfully demonstrated to the world the use of ether as a surgical anesthetic, in removing a neck tumor from a patient at Massachusetts General Hospital. Two months later American dentist Horace Wells (1815–1848) published the results of his two years' experience in administering nitrous oxide as an anesthetic in dentistry.

Ether quickly made its way to England; in December 1846 prominent London surgeon Robert Liston (1794–1847) performed the first leg amputation under ether inhalation. In 1847, Scottish obstetrician James Young Simpson (1811–1870) published his discovery of the anesthetic property of CHLOROFORM, which he favored over ether because he found it less likely to irritate the nose and throat.

Though it revolutionized medicine, anesthesia was not without opposition. Fearing physical and moral side effects, some physicians, clergymen, and other commentators argued that patients, particularly women in childbirth, should tolerate pain unaided. English obstetrician Tyler Smith wrote extensively against anesthesia, asserting that it incited sexual passion in female patients under its influence. Most objections in Britain were dispelled after the effective use of chloroform by physician JOHN SNOW in the 1853 delivery of Queen Victoria's son Leopold. From then on the use of anesthetics became accepted practice in surgery and obstetrics. Mortality during surgery continued to be high, however, until the introduction of ANTISEPSIS later in the century.

Anglo-Afghan Wars Conflicts between AFGHANISTAN and GREAT BRITAIN. Anxious to protect its empire in INDIA against Russian designs, Britain attempted in these two wars to impose its authority on India's neighbor Afghanistan, which had strategic importance because it guarded the land route to India, via the ancient KHYBER PASS.

The First Afghan War (1838–42) began when LORD AUCKLAND, governor-general of India, issued the Simla Manifesto in 1838, announcing his intention to invade. The British deposed the Afghan ruler, DOST MUHAMMAD, and installed an unpopular Afghan noble named Shah Shuja as a puppet ruler. A rebellion broke out in 1841, resulting in a massacre of British troops retreating from Kabul in January 1842. General Sir Robert Sale gained fame defending the British outpost of Tellalabad, and Kabul was recaptured by the army of Major-General George Pollock, which had forced its way across the Khyber Pass, becoming the first army in history to do so successfully. Even so, the British were forced to relent, and Dost Muhammad was restored to power in 1842.

The Second Afghan War (1878–80) began when the British issued an ultimatum to Shere Ali, son of Dost Muhammad, ordering him to allow the British to establish a diplomatic mission in Kabul as the Russians had. Shere Ali refused, and the British invaded from India on November 21, 1878. After several battles, including a daring night march by Major-General FREDERICK SLEIGH ROBERTS against the Afghan army at Peiwar Kobal, Shere Ali fled, leaving his son Yakub Khan in charge. The Treaty of Gondornul in May 1879 temporarily ended the war, as the Afghans agreed to permit British hegemony over their country.

The peace was broken in September 1879 when the Afghans massacred the members of the British mission in Kabul. Roberts led a British force to victory against the Afghans at Charasia, retook Kabul, and hanged several Afghans convicted of murdering the British mission on December 22–23. Roberts held Kabul against an Afghan siege at his fortress of Sherpur, and Major-General Sir Donald Stewart arrived with reinforcements on May 5, 1880. However, the Afghans won a major victory at Maiwand in southern Afghanistan, and Roberts had to relieve Major-General James Primrose near Kandahar in a battle on September 1, 1880, after making a long march in August from KABUL TO KANDAHAR that was commemorated in a medal struck after the war. Despite military victories, the British decided they could not hold the country against Afghan resistance. ABDUR RAHMAN KHAN, a nephew of Shere Ali, took the amir's throne. The British continued to exercise influence in Kabul, though not to occupy it.

British involvement in Afghan affairs persisted until the Third Afghan War in 1919 when Britain was forced to recognize Afghan independence.

Anglo-Burmese Wars See SOUTHEAST ASIA.

Angola Republic located on the south Atlantic coast of Africa. It borders Zaire on the north and Namibia on the south. In Victorian times, Angola was a colony of Portugal. Portuguese navigator Diego Cao discovered it in 1482, and the first Portuguese colony was founded in 1575 at what is now the capital, the coastal port of Luanda. For centuries Angola profited from slavery, exporting slaves to another Portuguese colony, Brazil, but Brazil gained its independence in 1822 and abolished slavery in 1888.

After Angola's borders were fixed by the CONFERENCE OF BERLIN in 1885, the interior of the colony became a source of agricultural and mineral wealth, financed by British and Portuguese investors. The Mbundu kingdom in central Angola resisted colonial rule for decades but was conquered in 1902.

Angolan independence was declared on November 11, 1975.

Anna and the King of Siam See LEONOWENS, ANNA.

Antarctica The fifth largest continent (5.2 million square miles) surrounds the South Pole and is encompassed by the southern sections of the Pacific, Atlantic, and Indian oceans, sometimes collectively called the Antarctic Ocean. Most of the land mass is a plateau lying under about one-and-a-half miles of snow accumulated over the centuries. Captain Nathaniel Palmer, an American seal hunter, claimed to have been the first to reach the Antarctica Peninsula in 1830. This is disputed by British historians who argue that either Edward Bransfield or John Biscoe should be credited with the discovery at around the same time. By the 1840s the exploration and mapping by American CHARLES WILKES and Englishman JAMES

CLARK ROSS verified the existence of a continent. In 1895, Leonard Kristensen of Norway led the first team to land on the continent proper. It was not until the start of the twentieth century that scientific expeditions began to reach the interior of Antarctica. The Norwegian explorer Roald Amundsen reached the Pole in December 1911, one month ahead of the Englishman Robert Scott whose team perished after reaching its goal.

Anthony, Susan Brownell (1820–1906) American social reformer. This pioneer in the WOMAN SUFFRAGE movement was born in Adams, Massachusetts. She worked as a schoolteacher and fought for parity of pay in the profession. She also became active in movements for temperance, abolition, and higher education for women. A tireless crusader for women's political rights, she cofounded the National Woman Suffrage Association, later the National American Woman Suffrage Association, with ELIZABETH CADY STANTON in 1869 and began to campaign for a constitutional amendment granting women the vote. Her newspaper *Revolution* bore the motto, "Men, their rights and nothing more; women, their rights and nothing less." In 1871 she and other feminists were arrested in Rochester, New York, for attempting to vote. Along with Stanton and Matilda Joslyn Gage, she is the author of the six-volume *History of Woman Suffrage* (1881–1922).

Anti–Corn Law League Reform movement. The league originated in 1838 to fight for the repeal of the CORN LAWS, which regulated grain import to Great Britain. Comprised of manufacturers, radicals, and journalists, it represented a wide spectrum of society, all united in the belief that free trade, rather than protectionism, would best foster economic growth. Acting as a tool of public enlightenment, the league educated through pamphlets, petitions, and meetings; it also worked to elect pro–free trade members of Parliament. The combination of indirect and direct political force helped to effect the repeal of the Corn Laws in 1846, during the administration of Prime Minister ROBERT PEEL.

Antietam, Battle of Battle during the U.S. CIVIL WAR. It was fought along Antietam Creek, near Sharpsburg, Maryland; The Confederates called it the Battle of Sharpsburg. After winning the second battle of Manassas, or Bull Run, General ROBERT E. LEE advanced the Confederate Army into Maryland. On September 5, 1862, he crossed the Potomac River with 51,844 men, dividing his troops and sending General Thomas "Stonewall" Jackson to Harpers Ferry. President ABRAHAM LINCOLN placed General GEORGE MCCLELLAN in command of the 75,316 Union troops. McClellan advanced so slowly toward the Confederate troops, however, that Lee had enough time to reunite his army and take a position on Antietam Creek.

McClellan attacked on the morning of September 17, 1862, and after five Union attacks, neither side could claim victory. Each side suffered heavy losses; by day's end Lee had lost 13,533 men, and McClellan had lost 12,469.

Although 10,000 fresh troops arrived to assist McClellan, he made no move to attack the next day, and Lee took the opportunity to withdraw his army across the Potomac. While failing to secure a victory, McClellan and his army were able to stop the first and one of the greatest Confederate advances on Washington, D.C.

antimacassar White doily. Pinned to the back of a chair or sofa to protect furniture from the oil in a seated person's hair, it was named for macassar oil, a hair dressing used by Victorian men.

antisepsis The medical use of chemical agents, called antiseptics, that prevent or stop the growth of microorganisms, decreasing the risk of infection. The term is also used synonymously with asepsis, the maintenance of an environment free of disease-causing microorganisms. Just as the introduction of ANESTHESIA during the Victorian Age did much to reduce the pain of surgery, the introduction of antisepsis during the same period did much to reduce surgical mortality rates. In the 1860s, English surgeon JOSEPH LISTER became acquainted with the GERM THEORY OF DISEASE then being advanced by French biochemist LOUIS PASTEUR, and with Pasteur's suggestion that chemical agents could destroy bacteria. Knowing that carbolic acid or phenol, also known as German creosote, had been used successfully in urban sewage disinfection, Lister began disinfecting surgical and traumatic wounds with a solution of phenol. From 1871 to 1877, Lister administered the phenic acid spray in his surgery. He successfully demonstrated a reduction of almost 50 percent in the death rate from major amputations.

Although Lister's discovery and use of phenol in infection control remains his lasting contribution to medicine, he is also remembered for stressing antisepsis in its broader sense of asepsis, or techniques intended to keep an environment free of germs. His finding that wound suppuration, the discharge of pus, could be treated by antiseptics strengthened acceptance of the need for clean hands, surgical instruments, and operating rooms.

Apologia pro vita sua (1864) Autobiography. Written by English essayist and Catholic convert JOHN HENRY NEWMAN, it was published in serial form with the subtitle "Being a Reply to a Pamphlet Entitled: 'What, Then, Does Dr. Newman Mean?'" and originated as a response to an attack on Newman by militant Anglican Charles Kingsley. In a review of J. A. Froude's *History of England* published in *Macmillan's* magazine in January 1864, Kingsley observed: "Truth for its own sake has never been a virtue of the Roman clergy. Father Newman informs us that it need not and on the whole ought not to be." Kingsley's suggestion of intellectual dishonesty inspired Newman to justify his early career as an Anglican clergyman and subsequent conversion to Roman Catholicism. When it appeared in volume form in 1865, Newman detached the sections dealing with the original controversy and added a new subtitle: "Being a History of His Religious Opinions." What began as a polemical reply became a lucid, moving defense of the consistency and sincerity of Newman's views. An influential text for modern Catholicism, it is also an important source for information on the OXFORD MOVEMENT and a classic of spiritual autobiography.

Appomattox Court House Town in Virginia. The U.S. CIVIL WAR ended here, at the site of the Wilmer McLean house, where General ROBERT E. LEE surrendered to General ULYSSES S. GRANT on April 9, 1865. Lee evacuated Petersburg, Virginia, on April 2, 1865, after ten months and headed west in an attempt to join the army of General Joseph E. Johnston in North Carolina. Union forces led by General Philip H. Sheridan pursued the Confederate troops, however, and successfully blocked Lee's path. The Confederates lost heavily in two engagements, on April 6 and 7, and after a brief fight at Appomattox Station, surrounded by a large number of Union troops, Lee agreed to surrender.

Appomattox Court House was deserted in 1892 with the emergence of the new town of Appomattox. The site was made a national historical monument in 1940 and restored to its 1865 condition. In 1954 the area was designated a historical park.

archaeopteryx Prehistoric animal. One of paleontology's most famous fossil finds, the archaeopteryx, or "ancient feather," was unearthed by German quarry workers in 1861. The fossil had the bony tail of a reptile and other reptilian characteristics, but it also displayed distinct avian features including the clear impression of feathers. This creature is now believed to have lived about 150 million years ago, during the Jurassic period.

The discovery immediately became a bone of contention between scientists who supported the theory by CHARLES DARWIN of the evolution of species and those who questioned it. Published in 1859, Darwin's *THE ORIGIN OF SPECIES* argued that individuals within species evolved over time into new species. Darwin had to admit, however, that the fossil record had not yet yielded any clear examples of species in intermediate phases of evolution. His critics demanded to see a "missing link" between any two classes of living things.

Anti-Darwinians such as Sir Richard Owen (1804–1892), director of the natural history department of the BRITISH MUSEUM from 1856 to 1884, labeled archaeopteryx an ancient bird and denied that it represented a link between birds and ancient reptiles. THOMAS HUXLEY argued that it did represent such a link and that it supported Darwin's theory of evolution. Subsequent discoveries in the same German quarry strengthened the Darwinian view.

Armenia Republic in the southern Caucasus. Bound by Georgia to the north, Azerbaijan to the east, Iran to the south, and Turkey to the west, the present-day republic represents one part of a larger region of Armenia, also called Greater Armenia, that also includes northeast Turkey and parts of Iranian Azerbaijan. From the sixth century B.C. to the sixteenth century A.D., this region passed through many hands, being controlled at various times by Persia (Iran), Macedon, Syria, Rome, the Byzantine Empire, the Seljuk Turks, and the Mongols, with relatively brief periods as an independent kingdom. In the sixteenth century the Ottoman Turks, who were Muslims, made Armenia, which was Christian, part of their empire. Eastern Armenia remained disputed between the OTTOMAN EMPIRE and Persia (Iran); in 1828, Persia ceded to Russia its claim to the territory.

Beginning in 1894, Sultan Abd al-Hamid II, ruler of the Ottoman Empire from 1876 to 1909, put into effect a plan to exterminate the Armenians within the empire's borders. The genocidal plan culminated in the massacre of 1915, during World War I. As for Russian Armenia, it was briefly independent in 1918–20, following World War I, but was annexed by the Soviet Union in 1920. It won its independence in 1991.

Armour, Philip Danforth (1832–1901) American businessman. The founder of the Armour and Company meat-packing plant and developer of the Chicago stockyards was born in Stockbridge, Massachusetts. He was a farmer, grocer, and miner by trade when he entered the meat-packing business in 1870. In 1875 he founded Armour and Company in Chicago, Illinois. During his twenty-six-year tenure he developed many improvements in meat-packing techniques, including the use of Chicago as a central receiving point for cattle to be slaughtered and the purchasing of his own refrigerator cars for shipment of beef.

Two years before his death he and other meat packers were charged with selling chemically tainted meat to the armed services.

Arnold, Matthew (1822–1888) English poet and critic. The foremost literary critic in Victorian Britain, he was also one of its greatest poets and perhaps the most representative spokesperson for its intellectual conflicts. The son of THOMAS ARNOLD, headmaster of RUGBY SCHOOL, he was born at Laleham, Middlesex, and educated at Winchester, Rugby, and Balliol College, Oxford. While at Oxford he won the Newdigate Prize for his poem "Cromwell." Like his friend, poet ARTHUR HUGH CLOUGH, he was elected to a fellowship at Oriel College, Oxford (1845), but left to serve as private secretary to the Marquis of Lansdowne. During travels in Switzerland in the late 1840s, he met the woman named Marguerite who appears in some of his early poems.

In 1849, Arnold published his first book of poetry, *The Strayed Reveller and Other Poems.* Other volumes followed: *Empedocles on Etna and Other Poems* (1852), *Poems* (1853), *Poems Second Series* (1855), *Merope* (1858), and *New Poems* (1867). The poems, often characterized by melancholy, anxiety, and alienation, based on classical and modern material alike, include such famous works as the dramatic poem "Empedocles on Etna" (1852); "Switzerland" (1853), containing the Marguerite lyrics; the lyric "Philomela" (1853); the elegiac "The Scholar-Gipsy" (1853); the elegiac "Stanzas from the Grande Chartreuse" (1855); the narrative "Balder Dead" (1855); "Thyrsis" (1866), a memorial to his late friend Clough; and the lyric "Dover Beach" (1867).

In their prevailing melancholy, the poems express the condition of the intellectual Victorian "wandering between two worlds, one dead,/The other powerless to be born" (from "Stanzas from the Grande Chartreuse"). In "Dover Beach," Arnold used the metaphor of the sea to depict Christian faith ebbing under the pull of modern skepticism and materialism, leaving mankind stranded. His poetry offered no satisfactory substitute for the authority he considered lost. Yet in his literary and social criticism, Arnold presented a confident, optimistic view of how society could transcend its difficulties and divisions. Arnold's solution was the propagation of culture, which he defined both as a body of work, "the best that has been known and said in the world," and as a quality of mind, the ability to respond to experience in accordance with what is true and valuable.

Arnold propounded his critical and social ideas in books, essays, and lectures while serving as professor of poetry at Oxford (1857–67) and inspector of schools (1851–86). A master of clear, articulate prose, he published such works as *On Translating Homer* (1861); *Essays in Criticism* (first series, 1865; second series, 1888); his greatest prose work *CULTURE AND ANARCHY* (1869), which introduced such ideas as the "Philistine" middle class and the aesthetic poles of "Hebraism" and "Hellenism"; *St. Paul and Protestantism* (1870); *Literature and Dogma* (1873); and *Discourses in America* (1885). He argued that an appreciation of great literature or poetry—defined broadly as "nothing less than the most perfect speech of man"—purified and integrated a reader's sensibilities, making for a better society. Claiming that great poetry was marked by the "noble and profound application of ideas to life," he developed the idea of using isolated lines of great poetry as "touchstones" by which to evaluate other poems.

Arnold was highly influential in defending the value of humanistic studies, in making cosmopolitan ideas available to British critics and readers, and in establishing Victorian standards of poetic taste. He was also important as an educator who critiqued elementary and secondary education, and promoted national instruction. In Great Britain and the United States he was the most important literary critic since the time of Samuel Taylor Coleridge (1772–1834) and up to the time of T. S. Eliot (1888–1965).

Arnold, Thomas (1795–1842) English educator. Arnold's reforms as headmaster of the RUGBY SCHOOL influenced the English system of public schools. A classical scholar, Arnold was a fellow of Oriel College, Oxford, from 1815 to 1819. He was ordained an Anglican priest and became headmaster of Rugby in 1828, a position he retained until the year of his death. Late in life he was elected Regius Professor of History at Oxford.

Arnold added mathematics, modern languages, and modern history to the classical curriculum at Rugby. Convinced of the importance of character formation, he established a code of conduct based on Christian ethics and strengthened the role of the older boys in student government. Under his system of competitive houses, older boys were responsible as house monitors for younger boys.

The author of the three-volume *History of Rome* (1838–43), Arnold is best remembered as the father of poet and critic MATTHEW ARNOLD.

Aroostook War (1838–1839) Conflict between the UNITED STATES and CANADA. The conflict arose over the rival claims of Maine (U.S.) and New Brunswick (Canada) to the Aroostook Valley. Bloodshed was averted by an agreement in March 1839, and the border was settled by the WEBSTER-ASHBURTON TREATY (1842).

Arrow War See OPIUM WARS.

art for art's sake Artistic credo. The doctrine that art exists for the sake of its own beauty and need serve no external moral purpose appears to have been first used (in its French form, *l'art pour l'art*) by French philosopher Victor Cousin (1792–1867) in *Le Vrai, le beau et le bien* (1818, first published 1836). It became the central doctrine of AESTHETICISM in France and England in the late nineteenth century.

Art Nouveau Design style. The exaggerated asymmetrical style of decoration and architecture was popular throughout Europe and the United States in the 1890s and early 1900s. Also called "Modern Style," its roots lay in the ARTS AND CRAFTS MOVEMENT of Victorian England and SYMBOLISM in France. The style received its best known appellation from the French Maison de l'Art Nouveau, a gallery for interior decoration that opened in Paris in 1896 and sold objects of "original" as opposed to "period" style. The same style in Germany is called Jugendstil after a magazine called *Die Jugend;* in Austria, Sezessionstil (see VIENNA SECESSION); and in Italy, Floreale, or Liberty, after the London store.

Rejecting nineteenth-century historicism, Art Nouveau was based on linear patterns of undulating forms derived from the sinuous curves of tendrils or plant stems. The decorative motifs were used in portraying flames, waves, and the flowing hair of stylized female figures. The influence of Art Nouveau could be seen in wrought-iron work such as the entrance to Paris métro stations designed by Hector Guimard as well as in the line drawings of graphic artist AUBREY VINCENT BEARDSLEY. Both the French artist Emile Galle and LOUIS TIFFANY in the United States adopted Art Nouveau forms for their furniture and glassware.

In architecture, the Art Nouveau movement was led by the Scotsman Charles Rennie Mackintosh and the Spanish artist ANTONIO GAUDI Y CORNET, whose Casa Mila shows a fantastic avoidance of all flat surfaces, straight lines, and symmetry. Henry van de Velde, one of the Belgian founding fathers of Art Nouveau, demonstrated the style's emphasis on structural clarity through his interior decorations. Art Nouveau had a profound effect on public taste, including even women's fashions, up through the first decade of the twentieth century.

Arthur, Chester Alan (1830–1886) Twenty-first president of the UNITED STATES. He was born in Vermont, graduated from Union College in upstate New York, and established a law practice in New York City. He supported the growing REPUBLICAN PARTY in the 1850s, and in 1871, President ULYSSES S. GRANT rewarded his party service by appointing him collector of customs for the port of New York. Arthur held this widely desired patronage plum during one of the most corrupt eras in American history.

President RUTHERFORD B. HAYES, bent on reforming the civil service, fired him in 1878. Arthur responded by backing Grant's bid for a third-term presidential nomination in 1880. The Republican convention of 1880 nominated Arthur for vice president, running with JAMES A. GARFIELD for president, in an effort to heal the party's divisions.

The Republican ticket won the election, and on July 2, 1881, after only a few months in office, Arthur became president when Garfield was assassinated by a disappointed office seeker. President Arthur shocked his longtime party supporters by embracing the principles of civil service reform and running an honest administration. This conversion cost Arthur the nomination in 1884. He retired from politics and died two years later in New York City.

Arts and Crafts Movement English movement promoting craftsmanship in the decorative arts. It was named for the Arts and Crafts Exhibition Society founded in England in the 1880s. Its roots were in the attempts by AUGUSTUS PUGIN and JOHN RUSKIN to reform the decorative arts, encouraging the GOTHIC REVIVAL in architecture, emphasizing handmade objects as opposed to mass-produced ones, and stressing the potential for good social and moral influence. Ruskin's support of the craft aesthetic in "On the Nature of Gothic," a chapter in the second volume of *The Stones of Venice* (1853), was especially influential. WILLIAM MORRIS was the movement's primary practitioner in trying to return to the purity of hand craftsmanship over the machine. He revived the crafts of hand weaving, cabinetmaking, metalwork, stained glass, and even the hand-printed and illuminated manuscript. Like the PRE-RAPHAELITES, he idealized the aesthetics and ethos of the Middle Ages (see MEDIEVALISM). Other members of the movement included Walter Crane and C. R. Ashbee; organizations associated with it included the Art Workers' Guild, founded in 1884.

By the early twentieth century the movement spread to the United States, Germany, Belgium, and Austria. The work of the Belgian artist and architect Henry van de Velde is especially notable, particularly his graphic arts and later furniture designs. The movement foundered because of the economic impossibility of producing craft goods as cheaply as mass-produced ones, but it influenced future industrial design and inspired generations of potters, weavers, and other artisans to keep alive the craft tradition.

Ashanti Wars See AFRICA.

Ashburton, Alexander Baring, 1st Baron (1774–1848) British statesman and banker. A member of the powerful BARING financial family, he became head of John & Francis Baring & Co. in 1810 and greatly expanded its operations in the United States. As a member of Parliament (1806–35) he opposed the REFORM BILL OF 1832. Prime Minister ROBERT PEEL made him president of the Board of Trade during his first administration.

In 1842, Ashburton went to the United States to settle boundary disputes with Canada. He and U.S. Secretary of State DANIEL WEBSTER negotiated the WEBSTER-ASHBURTON TREATY. It fixed the Maine–New Brunswick border, an area so hotly disputed that war had almost broken out there three years earlier. The treaty also settled borders in New York, Vermont, and Minnesota. In addition, the United States agreed to participate in combined naval operations against the slave trade.

aspirin Man-made analgesic and anti-inflammatory drug. It is derived from a substance that occurs naturally in the bark of willow trees, salicylic acid, which was first isolated by English clergyman Edward Stone in 1763 as a possible cure for fever and rheumatism. Acetylsalicylic acid was first synthesized in 1853 by Alsatian chemist Karl Frederick Gerhardt, but it was not until forty years later that it was put into widespread use, after German chemists Felix Hoffman and Hermann Dreser rediscovered the drug in 1893. It was first marketed as a prescription drug in 1899 in the form of a loose powder; it was sold in tablet form by the Farbenfabriken Bayer drug firm of Düsseldorf, Germany, in 1915. Bayer is said to have derived the name "aspirin" from "a" for acetyl, "spir" from the Latin term for the plant *Spiraea ulmaria,* from which it is produced, and "in," a common suffix for drugs.

assegai Hardwood spear or javelin. Often tipped with iron and used by indigenous peoples in southern Africa, the assegai was encountered by nineteenth-century British soldiers in such colonies as RHODESIA.

Atget, Eugène [Jean-Eugène-Auguste] (1857–1927) French documentary photographer. After holding a variety of jobs that included actor and sailor, he became a photographer at age forty-two, making his subject matter the streets and people of Paris. The nuanced, straightforward works that sprang from the studio identified with the sign "Atget—Documents for Artists" came in time to be championed by modern artists such as Picasso and Man Ray but were largely unappreciated in Atget's time. In the early twentieth century Atget's work was introduced to the public by American photographer Berenice Abbott. Atget is now acknowledged as one of PHOTOGRAPHY's most masterful artists.

Auckland, George Eden, Earl of (1784–1849) English politician. He served as a Whig member of Parliament (1810–12, 1813–14) before being appointed president of the Board of Trade (1830–34) and then First Lord of the Admiralty (1834). In 1836, Prime Minister Lord MELBOURNE appointed him governor-general of India with orders to cultivate the goodwill of countries that buffered India from Russian encroachment. After trade negotiations with Afghanistan broke down, Auckland deposed Afghan ruler DOST MOHAMMAD and replaced him with the more pliant Shah Shoja. Auckland's reform policies and reduction of tribal subsidies led to the first of the ANGLO-AFGHAN WARS. He was recalled in 1842 after some five thousand British troops were killed or captured during a retreat from the city of Kabul in 1841.

Despite the military setbacks during his tenure, the Earl of Auckland's stewardship is noted for effective famine relief, expanded professional training, and enlarged irrigation projects. He served again as First Lord of the Admiralty from 1846 until his death.

Audubon, John James (1785–1851) American painter, writer, and naturalist. He was born in Haiti and moved to France as a young man where he received his art training. He moved to the United States in 1803 and began painting the birds around his home near Philadelphia.

Audubon settled in New Orleans and failed at several businesses. Unable to find an American publisher for his avian drawings, he went to London where he solicited orders for *The Birds of America* (1827–38), a collection of color prints that depicted some five hundred species, although not always with scientific accuracy. Robert Havell did the engraving, and William MacGillivray wrote the text. His original drawings have disappeared, and it is not clear how much Havell's engraving contributed to the quality of the work. Audubon prepared another edition, in seven volumes, for the United States (1840–44).

His work acclaimed, Audubon lived the rest of his life on his estate near New York City where he continued to study and paint birds. His writings were later published as *Delineations of American Scenery and Character* (1926) and *Audubon's America* (1940). A *Journal* appeared in 1929 and *Letters* in 1930.

Australia Island continent. Surrounded by the Indian and Pacific oceans and lying southeast of mainland Asia, this European settlement began in the early seventeenth century. English colonization of the area called New South Wales in southeastern Australia began with a penal colony in 1788 at what is now Sydney. This settlement was the first in a series of colonies that would later unite to form modern Australia: Tasmania (originally Van Diemen's Land, (1825), Western Australia (1829), South Australia (1834), Victoria (1851), and Queensland (1859).

Australia underwent rapid political and economic changes during the Victorian era. Four of the six states were founded between 1830 and 1860. Although convicts continued to be sent to Australia (about sixty thousand in 1830), a systematic program of colonization, organized along lines proposed by EDWARD GIBBON WAKEFIELD, was instituted to attract middle-class settlers. The system involved selling land at a price sufficient to discourage indigent settlers, entice those with means, and finance future emigration. In southern Australia the result was a colony of austere, well-behaved subjects, many of them Nonconformists in religion; their capital, Adelaide, became known as the "city of churches."

Relations with Britain grew strained over tax policies and the ending of free land grants, but no effective independence movements emerged. Most of the colonies established democratic governments with nearly universal white male suffrage. Colonists strongly protested against the continued transportation of convicts, and it stopped by 1868. An estimated 160,000 convicts, many of whom were not major felons, had migrated to Australia.

The greatest Australian economic boom occurred during the early Victorian Age. Sheep raising for wool production became a major industry, forcing the indigenous Aborigines further inland. Copper was discovered in the 1840s, and a major gold strike in 1851 attracted a flood of settlers into southeastern Australia.

Wool and minerals were the mainstays of the economy through the latter part of the century. Settlers converted vast tracts of land into grazing fields for sheep and cattle. This expansion spurred the rapid development of railroads, with over ten thousand miles of track laid down by the 1890s. New discoveries of copper, silver, and gold continued to fuel economic development. Growth in these primary industries accelerated the development of manufacturing and construction, and of further emigration to the continent. The Australian cities of Sydney and Melbourne became two of the world's largest population centers.

Politics was marked by liberal policies that resulted in factory laws, universal public education, and other social reforms. A strong labor movement developed in the 1870s and 1880s, with political parties emerging from the unions.

The movement toward unification of the colonies dominated Australia's politics toward the end of the century. Fear of foreign incursions and a desire to restrict Asian immigration helped the movement develop. Constitutional conventions convened in the 1890s, a referendum approved their recommendations, and the Commonwealth of Australia, with domestic self-government and continuing allegiance to the British crown, came into being in 1901.

A settler literature and culture began to develop in the 1830s. *Geoffrey Hamlyn* (1859) by Henry Kingsley is considered the first major Australian novel. Other notable novels include Marcus Clarke's *For the Term of His Natural Life* (1874) and Joseph Furpy's *Such Is Life* (1903). Several Australian opera singers of the period (notably Dame NELLIE MELBA) gained international reputations.

Austria Empire in central and eastern Europe. Austria comprised at its greatest extent the modern states of Austria, Hungary, the Czech Republic, Slovakia, Slovenia, Bosnia, Croatia, and portions of Poland, ROMANIA, and northern ITALY. Its population was extremely diverse ethnically and religiously, though dominated by the German-speaking minority. Successor to the Holy Roman Empire, which was dissolved in 1806, the domain was often called the Austro-Hungarian empire or Austria-Hungary because the emperor received a separate coronation as king of Hungary.

Throughout the nineteenth century Austria was governed by the Hapsburg dynasty, Europe's oldest ruling house, from the thirteenth century in Austria proper. The Hapsburg government's main preoccupation was to hold the disparate holdings together in the face of growing nationalism among the empire's ethnic minorities. In the years following the Napoleonic Wars (1803–15), Austria, under the leadership of KLEMENS VON METTERNICH, the foreign minister, was one of the main guarantors of the stability of conservative monarchical governments throughout Europe. The dominant member of the GERMAN CONFEDERATION, Austria wielded considerable influence in Italy beyond its own possessions there. The government generally restricted freedom of expression and political activity. Economically, the empire was mostly agrarian, though large cities such as Vienna, Prague, and Budapest had begun to industrialize.

Austria faced small local revolts in Italy in the 1830s. More threatening were the REVOLUTIONS OF 1848 when, after a series of food shortages throughout Europe, students and workers revolted in Vienna, Hungarian nationalists declared virtual independence, and uprisings in Prague, Milan, and Venice succeeded in temporarily driving out Austrian forces. In Vienna the emperor refused to order his troops to fire on the crowd. Metternich was forced to resign and went into exile while the emperor promised a liberal constitution and allowed a national guard to be formed. A subsequent outbreak of violence forced the imperial court to flee Vienna, and a reformist assembly took over the capital, but it had difficulty enacting a concrete agenda. In the fall of 1848, after the Prague rebellion had been suppressed, the army moved back into Vienna and ruthlessly put down the revolution there. The Italian rebellion was also defeated. Finally, in 1849, with Russian help, the Hungarian nationalist rebellion was ended. Following these revolts, Vienna took direct control over most of the empire, in particular abolishing Hungary's autonomous institutions. At the same time, all internal tariff barriers were eliminated, and other measures were taken to stimulate the Austrian economy.

In the 1850s, Austria, fearful of more revolts, tried to steer a neutral course. FRANZ JOSEPH, the new emperor, who succeeded his father Ferdinand I in December 1848, moved to reassert Austrian supremacy in the German Confederation. By sending an "army of observation" to the BALKANS during the CRIMEAN WAR (1853–56), the empire made a direct confrontation there between Russia and the Ottoman Empire impossible, but it refused to join Great Britain and France in their attack on Russia.

Austria faced its stiffest challenge in Italy where the kingdom of Piedmont-Sardinia was making a bid to become the leader of an independent unified Italy. In 1859, Piedmont gained the backing of NAPOLEON III of France and maneuvered Austria into a confrontation. The Austrians were defeated by the French and Piedmontese forces in a bloody campaign and were forced to concede Lombardy, retaining Venice.

Austria was next confronted with the rising power of Prussia under the leadership of OTTO VON BISMARCK. A series of quarrels over leadership in the German Confederation led to war in 1866. Austria expected an easy victory since it possessed a larger army and the support of most of the smaller German states, but the SEVEN WEEKS' WAR was a disastrous Austrian defeat. The German Confederation was dissolved, and the Hapsburgs lost any chance of heading a Germanic nation in central Europe. Austria also lost Venice to Italy, which had fought on Prussia's side.

Following these defeats, Vienna instituted sweeping changes in the administration of the empire. The most important was the Ausgleich ("settlement") with the Hungarians in 1867. Under the Ausgleich, the empire was declared a dual monarchy, attempts at Germanizing the Hungarian population were abandoned, and Hungary was given a separate constitution and domestic government that was dominated by the Hungarian nobility. In the other regions of the empire, all nationalities were declared equal and were granted political rights such as limited suffrage and local assemblies. The emperor retained control of finance, foreign policy, and war but in other respects acted as a constitutional monarch. The nationalities question, however, remained a source of continual tension within the empire, exacerbated by Vienna's occasional attempts to play one group off against another. A move to grant universal male suffrage in 1893, on the belief that it would curtail nationalist agitation, was roundly defeated.

In the years following 1866, the Austrian economy underwent a cycle of boom and bust. Certain areas of the empire, most notably Bohemia, began to industrialize much more rapidly than the rest. The government, fearful of socialist revolution, made some efforts to create a social welfare policy, but these were largely ineffective. The late nineteenth century saw the phenomenal rise of the Christian Socialist movement, especially in Vienna, which offered a nonviolent nationalistic alternative to international socialism. Culturally, Vienna, with its diversity and relative openness, became a magnet for talented members of the avant-garde in literature, painting, and music.

In foreign policy, Austria soon reached a *rapprochement* with the newly unified German Empire, and alliance with Germany became a persistent feature of Austrian policy. Franz Joseph joined the German emperor William I and the Russian emperor Alexander II in the THREE EMPERORS LEAGUE in 1873 (renewed in 1881 and 1884). Austria remained concerned over Russia's attempts to expand into the Balkans at the expense of the Ottoman Empire, and relations with Russia gradually worsened. Austria itself took the opportunity to occupy Bosnia in 1878, incurring the enmity of Serbian irredentists. Further tension with SERBIA and Russia, Serbia's guarantor, ultimately pushed Austria into World War I, leading to the dissolution of the empire.

Austro-Prussian War See SEVEN WEEKS' WAR.

automobile Self-propelled wheeled vehicle for transportation on roads. Its power generally comes from an INTERNAL COMBUSTION ENGINE using gasoline or diesel fuel as an energy source; however, STEAM and ELECTRIC POWER have also been used. Although the automobile is considered a child of the twentieth century, it was conceived in the nineteenth century after several hundred years of tinkering. Steam power was experimented with extensively in Europe and North America in the eighteenth century, and by 1804 both Englishman Richard Trevithick and American Oliver Evans had built workable steam-powered passenger-carrying vehicles. By 1840 steam-powered passenger cars carrying twelve to sixteen passengers could be seen on British and Continental roads, though rail, water, and horse-drawn transport remained preferable. The steam-powered vehicles were slow, large, bulky, and required a flagman to walk ahead of them so that they did not frighten passing horses. Not until the internal combustion engine was perfected did the "horseless carriage" become viable.

No person or country can claim credit for inventing the internal combustion engine. In 1860 a Frenchman, Jean-Joseph-Etienne Lenoir, devised an internal combustion engine that ran on illuminating gas. Later in the century, automotive research continued in the United States, Austria, and Germany, with particular credit going to Germans KARL FRIEDRICH BENZ and Gottlieb Daimler. In 1891 the French devised what became the standard automotive layout: an engine mounted in front of the chassis, with rear-wheel drive and a gearbox in the middle. In 1895, Americans Charles E. and J. Frank Duryea established the first automobile manufacturing company in the United States. By 1900, however, world automobile production totaled only about ninety-five hundred vehicles, and the automobile was still generally considered a toy. Still, the automobile industry had been born and would grow into a giant in less than twenty years.

Babbage, Charles (1792–1871) English mathematician and inventor. He conceived the principles behind the modern digital computer over a century before they were put into successful operation. Born in Teignmouth, Devonshire, the son of a banker, Babbage attended Cambridge, where he later served as Lucasian Professor of Mathematics (1827–39). In 1815 he helped found the Analytic Society, which was dedicated to bringing Continental developments in mathematics to Great Britain. In 1816 he was elected to the Royal Society of London, a group he attacked as moribund in 1830 in his controversial book *Reflections on the Decline of Science in England.* The book resulted in the formation of the British Association for the Advancement of Science.

In 1833, Babbage published his most influential book, *On the Economy of Machinery and Manufactures,* which outlined an early version of "operations research"—the modern field of mathematics, developed during World War II, in which mathematical applications are used to formulate and solve complex practical problems. In 1840, Babbage's work helped to establish modern POSTAL SERVICES in England. Babbage also compiled the first reliable actuarial tables and invented the first speedometer. His other inventions included skeleton keys, the locomotive cowcatcher, and an early ophthalmoscope.

Babbage's greatest legacy was also his greatest disappointment. Troubled by the human errors that marred tables of logarithms, he speculated that machines could do the job better. He invented a small calculator that could perform mathematical computations to eight decimals, and in 1823 he obtained British government funding for a machine that could calculate to twenty decimals. He scrapped that machine in 1834, however, and began work on a much more ambitious project: the analytical engine.

Despite years of work, much of his own fortune, and the support of Augusta Ada, Countess of LOVELACE and daughter of Lord Byron, the analytical engine was never finished. With only mechanical, not electronic, devices to rely on, Babbage was hampered by the lack of precision techniques for fabricating metal parts to close tolerances. His design was forgotten until 1937 when his unpublished notebook was discovered. His unfinished analytical engine is still preserved in the Science Museum in London.

Babism Religious sect. Founded in Persia, it grew originally out of Shiite Islam and became the basis for BAHAISM. Babism was founded by Mirza Ali Muhammad of Shiraz, who proclaimed himself the Bab, meaning the gate or prophet, in 1844. The ascetic sect included elements of Shiite, Sufi, and Gnostic doctrines. Persecution of Babists began in 1845, and the movement seceded from Islam in 1848. After members of the sect rebelled against the Persian shah, the Babists were massacred in Teheran and the Bab was executed in 1850. His successor, BAHA ALLAH, fled Persia and founded the religion of Bahaism in 1863.

babu Hindi form of address for a gentleman. Similar to "Mr.", in Victorian times the term was applied, often with disdain, to an Indian educated in English, particularly a clerk writing in English.

badminton Game. Badminton is played by two to four players. A shuttlecock, a small cork hemisphere with feathers, is hit over a net by light, long-handled rackets. Similar to tennis, the game is believed to have originated in India as a sport called poona. British officers in India picked it up about 1870; the duke of Beaufort introduced it to England in 1873 at his estate, Badminton, hence the modern name. The game spread quickly: The Bath Badminton Club formed in 1887 and was replaced in 1893 by the Badminton Association of England, which formulated the existing rules. The first U.S. badminton club began in New York City in 1878.

For singles, the court is 17 feet by 44 feet; for doubles the court is 3 feet wider. The top of the net is 5 feet 1 inch from the court surface. A server scores when the opponent lets the shuttle fall or commits a fault. In doubles or men's singles, 15 or 21 points wins; in women's singles it is 11 points.

Bagehot, Walter (1826–1877) English political thinker, social scientist, and literary critic. With R. H. Hutton, a friend from college who would edit some of his later works, he served as joint editor of *The National Review* in 1855. From 1860 to 1877, Bagehot edited the influential *The Economist.* Noted for his shrewd, lively, and idiosyncratic style, he wrote a classic work on the British parliamentary system, *The English Constitution* (1867), in which he speaks approvingly of the reliance on class deference in British politics and warns against the rising tide of democratization. In 1872 he published *Physics or Politics: Thoughts on the Application of the Principles of "Natural Selection" and "Inheritance" to Political Society.* With this work, which applied principles from biology to a theory of civilization, Bagehot became an influential thinker in the growing field of SOCIAL DARWINISM.

Bagehot applied his intellect to the money market and commerce in two works: *Lombard Street* (1873), a study of the English banking system, and *Economic Studies* (1880). He also ventured into literary criticism with *Estimates of Some Englishmen and Scotchmen* (1858) and *Literary Studies* (1879).

Baha Allah (Baha Ullah) (1817–1892) Persian founder of the religion BAHAISM. Originally named Mirza Husayn Ali Nuri, Baha Allah was an early disciple of the Shiite sect called BABISM. In 1863, shortly before being forced to leave Persia for Constantinople, he founded Bahaism when he declared himself to be the Promised One awaited by the Babists. He wrote the sacred scripture of Bahaism, *Kitabi Ikan* (*The Book of Certitude*).

Bahaism Religion. Bahaism was founded in 1863 by BAHA ALLAH as an offshoot of the Persian Shiite sect BABISM when Baha Allah declared himself the "Promised One," or manifestation of God, through whom alone God could be known. His son and successors carried on the tradition. Bahaism teaches charity, simplicity, the unity of all religions, the equality of the sexes, and the need for world peace and world government.

Bahrain Archipelago in the Persian Gulf between the Qatar Peninsula and Saudi Arabia. The two main oil-rich islands are Bahrain and Al Muharraq. Ruled by Portugal from the 1500s to 1602, and by Persia after 1602. In 1783 it became a sheikhdom, ruled by a Kuwaiti sheikh. In 1861 it became a British protectorate, which it remained until independence in 1971.

Baily, Edward Hodges (1788–1867) English sculptor. The son of a carver of ships' figureheads, he became a successful producer of portrait busts and public sculpture, including the statues at the top of Nelson's Column in TRAFALGAR SQUARE (1843) and Grey's Monument in Newcastle upon Tyne (1837).

Balaklava, Battle of (October 25, 1854) Battle of the CRIMEAN WAR in which Russian forces failed to break the siege of the port of Sebastopol in the Crimea but inflicted heavy losses on the British. Remembered in TENNYSON's poem "THE CHARGE OF THE LIGHT BRIGADE."

Balfour, Arthur James (1848–1930) Scottish statesman. Born at Whittingeham, Scotland, he was educated at Trinity College in Cambridge and entered the House of Commons as a Conservative in 1874. Four years later he served as secretary to his uncle Lord SALISBURY at the Foreign Office in Berlin.

In 1885, Lord Salisbury became prime minister, and during the formation of his second administration in July 1886, Balfour held the post of secretary for Scotland.

Balfour was an opponent of Irish HOME RULE, and he suppressed the Irish insurrection with such zeal that he was dubbed "Bloody Balfour." On the resignation of his uncle in 1902, Balfour became prime minister. He worked hard for reforms in education and defense, and secured an entente with France; a split in the CONSERVATIVE PARTY over tariff reform, however, led to Balfour's resignation in 1905 and the rise of the Liberal Party.

Balfour remained very active in British politics throughout his life and was especially active during World War I. He was made a Knight of the Garter in March 1922, and in May he was named "1st Earl of Balfour and Viscount Traprain." He served as lord president under Prime Minister Stanley Baldwin from 1925 to 1929.

Balkans Peninsula in southeast Europe. It is bounded by the Adriatic, Aegean, and Black seas. The population is extremely mixed, with several languages spoken and three main religious groups: Orthodox, Muslim, and Catholic. Fragmented among rival states, the Balkans was a source of instability and an arena for great power rivalry throughout the Victorian era. The region was often called the "powder keg of Europe."

The main feature of the political history of the region during the Victorian era was the gradual decline of the OTTOMAN EMPIRE, which had ruled virtually the entire peninsula. Claiming the role of protector of the Slavs and the Orthodox Church, Russia sought to fill the vacuum and was often resisted by the other great powers.

GREECE gained independence from the Ottoman Empire in 1832. SERBIA gained autonomy in 1830. Following the RUSSO-TURKISH WAR (1877–78), BULGARIA and ROMANIA gained independence. The new Balkan governments were generally marked by instability, intrigue, and corruption. The new states were also involved in intense rivalries to acquire more territory from the Ottoman Empire and each other. Several wars were fought in the region, culminating in World War I, which broke out in 1914 over a dispute between Serbia and Austria-Hungary.

balloon Aircraft. Shortly after the Montgolfier brothers invented the first practical hot-air balloon in 1783, practical applications and manned travel in the lighter-than-air craft began to be explored. In 1844, American writer EDGAR ALLAN POE published a fictitious account of a balloon's crossing of the Atlantic Ocean after a seventy-two-hour voyage. Poe's hoax proved to be an embarrassment for the newspaper, but the writer proved prophetic when the Atlantic was finally conquered by a balloon flight in 1919, in just four minutes less time than Poe had allotted.

Actual flights were less spectacular. Françoise Arban flew the first successful balloon flight across the Alps in 1849, from Marseilles, France, to Turin, Italy. Ten years later John Wise flew from St. Louis, Missouri, to Henderson, New York, covering a distance of more than eight hundred miles in less than twenty hours.

The first military use of balloons occurred in 1849 when Austria sent pilotless hot-air balloons to bomb Venice. During the Civil War, both the Union and Confederate armies used balloons to observe enemy movement. During the Franco-Prussian War of 1870–71, balloons were used to maintain communications between a besieged Paris and the outside world, as well as evacuating members of the French government from the city.

Eduard Schweizer, known as Captain Spelterini, was the first person to observe and photograph the Great Pyramids of Egypt from the air in 1890. Seven years later, Solomon Andrée and his two-man crew embarked on an arduous journey from Norway, hoping to drift across the North Pole. Their frozen bodies were found in 1930, a little more than two hundred miles from their starting point.

While most balloons in the Victorian era lacked propulsion systems, some engineers experimented with airships or dirigibles—power-driven, steerable balloons. French inventor Henri Giffard invented the first successful dirigible in 1852. American inventor Solomon Andrews obtained a patent for a lemon-shaped airship in 1864, and the next year formed the Aerial Navigation Company, the first American chartered airline. His airline had only carried a few passengers before a bank failure ruined the company. COUNT FERDINAND VON ZEPPELIN was more successful with the airship he completed in 1900, the first with a rigid frame.

Balmoral Castle Residence of the royal household. Located in the Scottish Highlands and purchased in 1852, it was enlarged and redecorated under the direction of Prince ALBERT. Royal excursions into the Highlands became part of Queen VICTORIA's 1868 book, *Leaves from the Journal of Our Life in the Scottish Highlands.*

Balzac, Honoré de (1799–1850) French novelist. Born at Tours, France. In 1816 he began studying law at Paris University but was soon convinced that he was destined to be a writer. By 1819 he had also convinced his father, who supplied him with a two-year allowance to support his writing. During this period, Balzac wrote a tragedy in verse, *Cromwell,* which prompted the advice from one reader that he should try anything in life except literature. Balzac, however, was undaunted and turned his attention toward fiction.

Balzac wrote at least a half-dozen novels and worked as a publisher and printer, but by 1828 he was in debt more than sixty thousand francs, and the rest of his life was spent in a constant struggle to appease his debtors.

Financially, Balzac was occasionally aided by his family and his mistress, Madame de Berny, who was twenty-two years his senior and the goddaughter of Louis XVI and Marie Antoinette. De Berny's death in 1836, the year in which Balzac dedicated *Le Lys dans la vallée* to her, caused him the deepest grief of his life.

The first novel to appear under Balzac's own name was *Le Dernier Chouan* (later retitled *Les Chouans*) in 1829, a historical novel depicting the royal insurrection of 1799. Starting in 1830, Balzac devoted himself to capturing in fiction the social history of his own time, in the vast cycle of novels and stories now known as *La Comédie humaine.* "French society was to be the historian," he wrote in 1842, "I was only to be its secretary."

Balzac's reputation quickly grew, and in February 1832, he received a letter from a secret admirer, Eveline Hanska, a Polish countess and wealthy landowner. She and Balzac continued to correspond for nearly sixteen years before marrying in March 1850, five months before Balzac's death. His letters to Hanska, published in four volumes, give a detailed account of his craft, his ambitions, and his indebtedness to Hanska.

In the three years between 1832 and 1835, Balzac produced more than twenty works, including *Séraphita,* a mystical work dedicated to Hanska. At about the same time, Balzac became interested in the occult and the writings of Emanuel Swedenborg, which influenced the writer's desire to capture and create the all-inclusive society found in *La Comédie humaine.*

Balzac wrote tirelessly, often spending more than a day at a time at his writing desk. He also revised constantly in an attempt to orchestrate perfectly the large number of characters he had created in his writing. The total number of named characters in the ninety-four titles of *La Comédie humaine* is estimated at nearly twenty-five hundred, with a further six hundred unnamed characters. Though he wrote in the early Victorian era, Balzac's narrative technique and his unflagging interest in re-creating the details of everyday life earned him his reputation as "the father of the modern novel." VICTOR HUGO provided the oration at his funeral.

Bank Charter Act of 1844 British law. The Bank Charter Act helped stabilize English currency and banking systems by checking the reckless issuing of notes by banks. The first half of the century saw a rapid proliferation of banks, many of which issued tender not backed by gold or bullion. This overexpansion of credit nearly led to a suspension of cash payments on notes when bad harvests of the late 1830s drained gold from England to buy foreign crops. These developments, plus the chilling example of the United States where every bank stopped cash payments in 1843, led to the passage of the Bank Charter Act.

The act separated the note issue department of the Bank of England from its other banking functions. All notes issued by the Bank above 14 million pounds had to be backed by gold or bullion. The issuing of banknotes by other banks was restricted, and new banks were prohibited from issuing any paper notes.

Bantu A group of languages spoken in equatorial and southern Africa, generally south of the Congo River. The term also refers to the many peoples speaking these languages, including MATABELE, Mbundu, Swahili, Xhosa (KAFFIR), and ZULU. Victorian explorers and colonists in the region met and often clashed with Bantu peoples.

Barbizon School Group of French landscape painters. Beginning in the early 1830s, the painters lived and worked in the tiny village of Barbizon, located in the middle of the forest of Fontainebleau. The Barbizon School epitomized the nineteenth-century Romantic attitude that man and nature could safely exist together free from modern urban life. THÉODORE ROUSSEAU, the most prominent member of the Barbizon School, even referred to the Fontainebleau forest as Arcadia, legendary home of pastoral bliss.

With Rousseau, other leading artists such as CAMILLE COROT, JEAN-FRANÇOIS MILLET, Jules Dupré, and Charles-François Daubigny were influenced by seventeenth-century Dutch landscapists and the English landscape painter John Constable. They opposed strict academic conventions and painted undramatic details of the countryside and of peasant life.

By the 1870s the Barbizon School's naturalistic attempts to record the truths of landscape influenced the goals of IMPRESSIONISM, which often repeated Barbizon motifs. The Barbizon School's view of portraying timeless nature and humble peasants spread rapidly throughout Europe and across the Atlantic, giving lesser-skilled commercial artists the opportunity to reproduce such harmonic landscape scenes in everything from calendar art to large-framed household oils.

Baring Prominent British family and banking house. Founded in London in 1763, the financial firm of John and Francis Baring & Co. still thrived during the Victorian era, as did the family that gave it its name. Alexander Baring, 1st Baron ASHBURTON, a negotiator of the WEBSTER-ASHBURTON TREATY, was the son of one of the company's founders, Sir Francis Baring (1704–1810). One of Sir Francis's grandsons, Sir Francis Thornhill Baring (1796–1866), served as M.P. (1826–65), chancellor of the Exchequer (1839–41), and First Lord of the Admiralty (1849–52) during Victoria's reign, and was named Baron Northbrook in 1866. Baron Northbrook's son Thomas George, 1st Earl of Northbrook (1826–1904), also served as an M.P. (1857–66), undersecretary of state for war (1861, 1868–72), governor-general of India (1872–76), and First Lord of the Admiralty (1880–85). Other Victorian era grandsons of Sir Francis Baring included Evelyn, 1st Earl of CROMER, *de facto* governor of Egypt; Charles Thomas (1807–1879), bishop of Durham; and Edward Charles, 1st Baron Revelstoke (1828–1897), who, as head of the family firm, guided it away from potential bankruptcy when Argentina defaulted on some bonds in 1890.

Barnum, P. T. [Phineas Taylor] (1810–1891) American showman. Born in Connecticut, he began his entertainment career in 1835 by exhibiting an elderly African-American woman whom he falsely claimed was George Washington's childhood nurse. In 1842 he established the American Museum in New York City, where he presented stage acts and sideshows displaying the "Bearded Lady" and other curiosities. As his overheated advertising and rabid hucksterism attracted huge crowds, his name became synonymous with the more florid forms of American entertainment.

In 1844 he organized a world tour featuring the dwarf Tom Thumb. He also arranged an American tour (1850–52) of the "Swedish Nightingale" JENNY LIND. Despite these successes he almost went bankrupt due to fires at his New York hall and his Connecticut mansion.

Barnum became best known for the circus he organized in 1871, which he billed as "the Greatest Show on Earth." Among its attractions was the famous elephant JUMBO, imported from Africa via Britain. Barnum merged his show with that of James Anthony Bailey (1847–1906) in 1881, a combination that dominated the circus field. After the death of both men, it was acquired in 1907 by the five Ringling Brothers, who had been in the circus business since 1884. Ringling Bros. and Barnum & Bailey Circus continues in operation to the present day. Barnum's dubious memoir, *Life,* was published in 1855 and revised many times. Another work, *The Humbugs of the World,* appeared in 1865.

Barry, Sir Charles (1795–1860) English architect. With AUGUSTUS PUGIN he designed and built the Houses of Parliament (WESTMINSTER PALACE) (1837–67) in GOTHIC REVIVAL style. He worked in many styles, including Greek revival, Scottish Baronial, and Elizabethan. With such edifices as the Travellers' Club (1829–32), the Reform Club (1837–41), and Bridgewater House (1845–50), he introduced the Renaissance Italianate style to Britain. His son Edward Middleton Barry (1830–1880) designed the Theatre Royal at the new COVENT GARDEN (1857) and the Charing Cross Hotel (1863–65), and completed his father's design for the Houses of Parliament.

Bartholdi, Frédéric Auguste See STATUE OF LIBERTY.

Barton, Clara [Clarissa Harlowe] (1821–1912) American humanitarian. Born in Oxford, Massachusetts, she was a schoolteacher and patent office clerk before turning her attention to soldiers wounded in the U.S. CIVIL WAR (1861–65). Known as the "Angel of the Battlefield," she established a medical supply service, served as a nurse, and led searches for the missing in action. During the FRANCO-PRUSSIAN WAR (1870–71), she served with the International RED CROSS behind German lines. She later campaigned to have the United States sign the first of the GENEVA CONVENTIONS and founded the American Red Cross in 1881, heading the organization until 1904.

baseball Sport. Contrary to popular legend, the sport of baseball did not spring fully formed from the mind of Abner Doubleday in Cooperstown, New York, in 1839. Like most games, baseball has a long lineage, with versions dating as far back as the fourteenth century. In 1834 Robin Carver published *The Book of Sports* in Boston, Massachusetts, in which he copied the rules for the English game of rounders but changed the name to "Base, or Goal Ball." Carver is considered the first person to codify the rules of the American sport.

The modern version of the game began in 1845 when a New York businessman, Alexander J. Cartwright, organized the Knickerbocker Base Ball Club of New York and altered the rules of play to make them safer for grown men. A base runner could no longer be struck with the ball but must be touched with the ball in order to be "out." Cartwright's team, the New York Knickerbockers, played the first game under his rules on June 19, 1846. They lost to the New York Nine at the Elysian Fields in Hoboken, New Jersey, by a score of 23–1. In those days the first team to score 21 runs won the game. The limit of nine innings to a game was adopted later.

Cartwright's brand of baseball spread rapidly throughout the northeastern United States. Those already familiar with the many variants of rounders found it easy to play. Its spread was also aided by Henry Chadwick, who wrote the first complete rule book in 1858. That year also saw the establishment of the first governing agency of the sport, the National Association of Base Ball Players (NABBP), which survived until the early 1870s.

By the outbreak of the Civil War baseball was already being hailed as the national game. During the war northern prisoners taught it to their Confederate captors. Millions of Americans played the game during the last half of the century through leagues formed by towns, churches, schools, fraternal organizations, and independent baseball clubs. In 1881 the Spalding sport equipment company stopped printing the rules in its annual guides because the game was so commonly known.

Al Reach of Philadelphia became the first professional baseball player in 1864, and five years later the Cincinnati Red Stockings became the first professional team, earning a net profit of $1.39 that year.

In the 1870s, following the demise of the NABBP, ten clubs formed the National Association of Professional Base-Ball Players, but contract jumping and gambling became so prevalent that this organization dissolved in 1876, supplanted by the NATIONAL LEAGUE OF PROFESSIONAL BASE BALL CLUBS. In 1882 the American Association was formed and engaged in an open rivalry with the National League. By 1891 the National League proved to be dominant, and the two leagues merged into a twelve-club organization. The Western League, formed in 1893, provided a meek rivalry. In 1901, however, the newly organized American League, offering higher salaries, lured more than one hundred players from the National League, including such stars as Napolean Lajoie and Cy Young.

By 1903 the battle for dominance between the National and American leagues had been resolved, giving each institution equal importance and ushering in the modern era of organized baseball. The first World Series was played that year; the American League's Boston Red Sox defeated the National League's Pittsburgh Pirates.

basketball Sport. The only major sport to originate wholly in the United States was invented in 1891 by Dr. James A. Naismith, a Canadian instructor at the International YMCA Training School in Springfield, Massachusetts. In an attempt to develop a game that could be played indoors during the winter months, Naismith, after trying unsuccessfully to modify lacrosse, rugby, and soccer, devised a noncontact sport that did not result in broken bones or broken windows. Dividing his eighteen students into two equal teams, Naismith briefed the players on his thirteen rules of the new game. In the first game, only one basket was scored and the ball was retrieved from the peach basket with the aid of a ladder.

Naismith and his class toured throughout the United States and Canada in order to demonstrate his new game, and by 1894 it had been played in France, China, and India. The same year it was played in London as part of the fiftieth anniversary celebration of the founding of the YMCA. The noncontact game quickly became popular with women, and the first intercollegiate game was played between Stanford and California in 1896. In January 16, 1896, the University of Chicago and the University of Iowa became the first teams to play with only five men on each side, and the change became a rule a year later. Players were first allowed to dribble the ball in 1900.

The sport was introduced as a demonstration sport in the Olympic games of 1904, held in St. Louis, Missouri. While some professional teams were in existence shortly after the invention of the game, the first professional organization, the National Basketball League, was not formed until 1937.

Basutoland British colony in southern AFRICA. Chief Moshesh formed the Basuto nation early in the nineteenth century. Threatened by incursions from the neighboring BOERS and British settlers in Cape Colony, Moshesh asked the British to protect his territory. They obliged, making Basutoland a native state under British protection in 1868 and a colony in 1884. Basutoland gained independence as Lesotho in 1966. The country is surrounded by the Republic of SOUTH AFRICA.

bathing suits Clothing. The use of a suit specifically for wading in public waters became popular in the mid-1800s when the benefits of swimming were extolled by the European medical community and the practice of outdoor bathing became widespread. Early suits for women were full-length wool dresses, worn with stockings, a complete set of undergarments, and shoes. Men's suits were similar, following street wear. By the 1880s women's bathing suits had evolved to a one-piece sack-like flannel gown. More revealing suits were not developed until the twentieth century.

Baudelaire, Charles Pierre (1821–1867) French poet. Born in Paris, he was left fatherless in 1827 and never forgave his mother for remarrying less than a year later.

After enrolling at the Ecole des Chartres, Baudelaire spent much of his time pursuing an extravagant social life, and it is during this time that he probably contracted syphilis. His stepfather was shocked at Baudelaire's decadent behavior, and after paying off his stepson's debts, he sent Baudelaire on a voyage to India. When the ship stopped near Madagascar for repairs, Baudelaire persuaded the captain to arrange for his passage back to France. After seven months, Baudelaire returned to Paris in February 1842. As much as he disliked the voyage, Baudelaire's poetry became filled with imagery influenced by his brief excursion.

Two months after his return, Baudelaire gained control of his inheritance, which he quickly spent in his desire to lead a luxuriant life. He also met a minor French actress of African descent, Jeanne Duval, who influenced his erotically charged "Black Venus" poems of *Les Fleurs du mal.*

While his relationship with Duval continued until 1860, Baudelaire became involved with another actress, Marie Daubron, in 1847; she is regarded as the inspiration for the "Green-Eyed Venus" cycle of poems. In 1851 he met his third mistress, Apollonie Sabatier, who inspired the cycle of the "White Venus" poems.

Dividing his time among three women and writing poetry for them, Baudelaire also managed to discover the works of EDGAR ALLAN POE, with whom he felt an immediate affinity. Baudelaire spent the years from 1852 to 1865 translating Poe's prose into French as well as writing critical essays on the writer.

Baudelaire's reputation as a translator and critic enabled him to publish eighteen of his own poems in 1855. Two years later *Les Fleurs du mal* was published by a friend who owned a printing press. Shortly afterward, Baudelaire and the publisher were prosecuted for obscenity and immorality. Baudelaire was fined three hundred francs (reduced to fifty), and six of his poems were banned. While praised by a few of his contemporaries, including Victor Hugo, Baudelaire was considered a scandalous pornographer by the general public.

A second edition of *Les Fleurs du mal* was published in 1861, excising the banned poems and including newer material, and a third edition was planned when the poet was stricken with paralysis resulting from his untreated syphilis. Baudelaire was placed in a convalescence center, where he died in obscurity. In May 1949 the ban on Baudelaire's poems was removed, and his sentence of 1857 was erased from the legal records.

Baum, L[yman] Frank (1856–1919) American writer. Born in Chittenango, New York, and eventually settling in Chicago, he worked as a journalist and playwright before winning success as a writer for children with *Father Goose* (1899). Interested in writing a fairy tale with a modern American setting, he published an even more successful book the following year, *The Wonderful Wizard of Oz* (1900), illustrated by William Wallace Denslow. The book tells of a Kansas farm girl, Dorothy Gale, who is whisked by a cyclone to the land of Oz, where she meets the Scarecrow, the Tin Woodman, and the Cowardly Lion. The novel led to a musical stage version with lyrics by Baum and to a movie. Baum wrote thirteen more books set in Oz, but none was as beloved as the first. Other authors continued the series after his death at his Hollywood home, named Ozcot.

Beaconsfield, Lord See DISRAELI, BENJAMIN, 1ST EARL OF BEACONSFIELD.

Beadle and Adams See DIME NOVEL.

Beardsley, Aubrey Vincent (1872–1898) English illustrator. Born in Brighton, he went to work in a London architect's office in 1888. Encouraged by the painter Sir EDWARD BURNE-JONES, he studied at the Westminster School of Art for a few months in 1891. A year later Beardsley was commissioned to provide 350 illustrations for J. M. Dent's edition of Sir Thomas Malory's *Le Morte d'Arthur*. An enthusiastic article on the illustrator's work in *The Studio* (1893) led to further commissions, including drawings for OSCAR WILDE's *Salome* (1894), for which the artist achieved international fame and notoriety for the grotesque and erotic nature of his work.

Aubrey Beardsley illustrates a scene in Sir Thomas Malory's Le Morte d'Arthur, *in the artist's characteristic curvilinear style. Courtesy of Max A. Polster Archive.*

Also in 1894, Beardsley was appointed art editor for a new quarterly, *THE YELLOW BOOK,* but was dismissed from the publication in 1895 in the wake of Wilde's arrest for homosexuality. Beardsley then became principal illustrator for another new magazine, *The Savoy,* and continued to illustrate other works, including Alexander Pope's *The Rape of the Lock* (1896), Aristophanes' *Lysistrata* (1896), and Ben Jonson's *Volpone* (1898). Influenced by AESTHETICISM, mentor Edward Burne-Jones, and Japanese woodblock prints, Beardsley's style was marked by innovative black-and-white patterning and long, curving lines. He was a major force in both the DECADENCE of the *fin de siècle* and the decorative style of ART NOUVEAU. Always prone to ill health, Beardsley died of tuberculosis at age twenty-five.

Bechuanaland African colony of Great Britain, now the independent Republic of Botswana. Located north of Cape Colony and east of the TRANSVAAL, both of which are now parts of SOUTH AFRICA, this arid landlocked region was the homeland of the Batawana, or Bechuana, tribes. Gold was discovered there in 1867, and the BOERS in the Transvaal tried to annex parts of it. To counter these incursions, the British made Bechuanaland a protectorate in 1885. It gained its independence as Botswana on September 30, 1966.

bed warmer A ceramic bottle filled with hot water or a brass or copper pan filled with hot coals. It was placed under the covers at the foot of a Victorian bed to provide warmth.

Bedchamber Crisis British political conflict. In 1839 when the Whig government led by Lord MELBOURNE fell, the head of the Tory Party, Sir ROBERT PEEL, set about forming a ministry. He insisted that Queen VICTORIA dismiss the Whig ladies of the bedchamber who held important appointments in the royal household. This two-day impasse became known as the Bedchamber Crisis. When negotiations between Peel and the Queen collapsed, he abandoned his efforts to form a government. The Queen asked Lord Melbourne, her close advisor, to return to power. Melbourne held together a weak majority in Parliament until 1841 when the Tories again held a majority. When Peel and the Queen faced each other again, she agreed to dismiss any ladies he wished but argued for retaining two of her favorite Whig attendants. Peel agreed, and a second crisis was averted.

Beddoes, Thomas Lovell (1803–1849) English writer and physician. Born in Clifton, Somerset, he studied at Pembroke College, Oxford, where he earned a bachelor's degree in 1825 and an M.A. degree in 1828. In 1821 he published *The Impovisatore,* three tales told in verse. Although he tried to recall and destroy the book, a few copies remained in public domain. A year later he published *The Bride's Tragedy,* a drama based on a murder committed by an undergraduate student.

After graduation, Beddoes traveled to Germany to study medicine and began work on *Death's Jest Book,* a tragedy in verse. He produced three different versions of the play, which was influenced by the poetry of Shelley and Elizabethan dramas. In 1848, Beddoes attempted suicide by slashing his leg; it became gangrenous and he eventually succumbed. His literary executor, T. F. Kelshall, then combined the three versions of *Death's Jest Book* into one cohesive play, which was published in 1850.

Beecher, Henry Ward (1813–1887) American orator and clergyman. He was born in Litchfield, Connecticut, son of Presbyterian minister LYMAN BEECHER and brother of author HARRIET BEECHER STOWE. He graduated from

Amherst College in 1834 and studied theology at a seminary in Cincinnati, Ohio, before becoming head of the Congregational Plymouth Church in Brooklyn, New York. His robust antics at the pulpit, inflated rhetoric, and spellbinding delivery quickly established him as one of America's most prominent clergy. People flocked to his sermons, and the vessels that ferried them to Brooklyn were called "Beecher boats." ABRAHAM LINCOLN once dubbed the man who made as much money as the president of the United States—$20,000 per year—the greatest man in America.

Beecher directed many of his passionate sermons against SLAVERY. He advised abolitionists to send rifles instead of Bibles to Kansas where advocates of slavery were fighting free soilers to determine if that territory would be admitted to the Union as a slave or free state. Crates of rifles labeled "Bibles" became known as "Beecher's Bibles" as his name became synonymous with the most militant brand of abolitionism. A speaking tour of England helped diminish British support of the Confederacy. After the CIVIL WAR he continued to fight for social reform and became a leading suffragist.

Beecher's fame and reputation were greatly harmed by accusations of adultery brought against him by a parishioner, Theodore Tilton, who named Beecher in a divorce suit in 1874. The church cleared him of any wrongdoing, but the civil trial ended in a hung jury. The lack of a clear verdict clouded his subsequent career.

In addition to many volumes of sermons, Beecher's published works include *The Life of Jesus, the Christ* (1871), *Yale Lectures on Preaching* (1872–74), and *Evolution and Religion* (1885). He also wrote the novel *Norwood; or Village Life in New England* (1867).

Beecher, Lyman (1775–1863) American minister and religious spokesman. Born in New Haven, Connecticut, Beecher became a Congregationalist minister and served three churches in New England and New York before being named president and professor of theology at Ohio's Lane Theological Seminary (1832–52). A forceful speaker, he established himself as a potent religious voice denouncing liquor, SLAVERY, dueling, and Unitarianism. His strict Calvinism led to his being charged by conservative factions with heresy, though he was later acquitted. *A Plea for the West,* his 1832 book, cautioned America about the effects of Roman Catholicism while it welcomed the growing frontier. He was the father of thirteen children, and his offspring include novelist HARRIET BEECHER STOWE and clergyman and writer HENRY WARD BEECHER. Author of the collection *Works* (1852) and *Autobiography* (1864).

Belgium Small kingdom in northwest Europe. It is bounded by France, Luxembourg, Germany, and the Netherlands. The population is divided between Flemish speakers in the north and French-speaking Walloons in the south. At the end of the Napoleonic Wars (1803–15), Belgium was incorporated into the Dutch-Belgian kingdom under a Dutch monarchy. The Catholic Belgian population resented being governed by a Protestant king, and tensions grew. Inspired by the revolution in France in 1830 that ousted French king Charles X and spurred by economic hardships, a nationalist assembly gathered in Brussels to demand reforms. After a series of proposals and counterproposals, war broke out. France intervened on behalf of Belgium and guaranteed its independence, though the war dragged on in a stalemate until 1839. Leopold I (1790–1865) of Saxe-Coburg-Saalfeld, uncle of England's

Queen Victoria, was selected as king in 1831. A national assembly drew up one of the most liberal constitutions in Europe.

Following the end of the war with the Netherlands, Belgium followed a cautious foreign policy, always seeking to have its neutrality in European affairs respected. INDUSTRIALIZATION, especially in the coal industry, began to take shape. Politically, the main conflict in Belgium's early years was between liberals and clerical conservatives who desired a more Catholic state. Belgium saw no outbreak of revolution in 1848, unlike most of Europe. In the 1860s, however, a Flemish nationalist movement began to form.

Leopold I was succeeded by his son Leopold II (1835–1909) in 1865. The new king favored the acquisition of African colonies for Belgium and in 1876 founded an association for exploration of the Congo River basin. In 1884, after sponsoring several exploratory journeys, Leopold had the Congo (modern Zaire) recognized as a sovereign state with himself as effective owner. The Congo Free State was largely run by non-Belgians and proved of little benefit to the Belgian economy. Despite Leopold's efforts to develop the ivory and rubber trades, the Congo was a money-losing venture. The Belgian government was forced to take over the colony in 1908 after Leopold was unable to pay his debts.

The Belgian economy grew rapidly in the later Victorian era, and working conditions gradually improved. In 1886, however, recession sparked a serious round of strikes and anarchist disturbances. Opposition parties rallied around the demand for universal male suffrage, which was granted in 1894. A Flemish separatist movement became a serious political factor in the 1890s. Still, in comparison to most European states of the period, Belgium enjoyed peace and stability throughout the Victorian era.

Bell, Alexander Graham (1847–1922) American inventor. Born in Edinburgh, Scotland, he was educated at home until the age of ten by his mother, a painter and musician, and by his father, a speech teacher. At the age of sixteen Bell became a student teacher in Elgin, and four years later worked as an assistant to his father, who originated the "visible speech" system for teaching the deaf.

Alexander Melville Bell and his son moved to Brantford, Ontario, Canada, in 1870, and a year later Alexander Graham Bell began teaching "visible speech" in Boston, Massachusetts. From 1873 to 1877 he was a professor of vocal physiology at Boston University, where he met Mabel Hubbard, a deaf student. The two were married on July 11, 1877.

Bell's interest in vocal physiology and telegraphy led to his conception of the telephone, which was granted a patent on March 7, 1876. Three days later Bell uttered the first intelligible sentence transmitted via the telephone: "Mr. Watson, come here; I want you." Nearly six hundred separate cases challenged Bell's patent, but the Supreme Court ultimately upheld his claim in an 1893 decision.

The Bell Telephone Company was organized in July 1877, and a month later Bell and his bride traveled to Europe to introduce the telephone there. In 1880 the French government awarded Bell the Volta Prize of 50,000 francs; Bell used the money to finance the Volta Laboratory, dedicated to research and investigation into the causes of congenital deafness. The Volta Laboratory also improved the tinfoil recordings made on THOMAS EDISON's phonograph and was awarded patents for the wax record and wax cylinder in 1886.

In 1888, Bell was a founding member of the National Geographic Society and served as its president from 1898 to 1903. He also had a keen interest in manned air travel and in 1907 founded the Aerial Experiment Association, which sponsored the first public flight of a heavier-than-air craft the following year.

Bell became a U.S. citizen in 1882 but spent much of his time in Nova Scotia, where he died.

Bellamy, Edward See SOCIALISM.

Benz, Karl Friedrich (1844–1929) German engineer and inventor. Karl Benz was born in Karlsruhe, Germany, to a locomotive engineer who died in 1846.

After studying at the Technical University, Benz established a small workshop in 1871 at Mannheim for the development and production of a gasoline engine. The Benz engines quickly gained an excellent reputation. By 1885, Benz had developed and patented the Patent Motor Car, a three-wheeled vehicle equipped with a "four-stroke" gasoline engine that enabled the car to travel up to speeds of ten miles per hour. Four cars were eventually produced and sold, only one of which still survives, in the Science Museum in London, England.

By 1900, Benz had developed the Comfortable car, of which four thousand were produced, making Benz the largest automobile manufacturer in Europe. Karl Benz retired from management of the company in 1903, and in 1926 the Benz Company merged with the Daimler Company to form Daimler-Benz AG, the maker of Mercedes-Benz automobiles.

beriberi Disease. Now known to be caused by a deficiency of Vitamin B1, or thiamine, the disorder, which is marked by nerve degeneration and muscular weakness, was first observed in Java in 1641; the name was based on the Sinhalese word *beri* for weakness. Not until the 1880s was the cause and treatment of beriberi determined. German bacteriologist Robert Koch incorrectly posited that it was caused by bacteria, but a Japanese navy study in 1884 indicated that it could be averted by proper diet, suggesting that the disease might have its roots in nutrition. Beginning in 1886, Dutch researcher Christiann Eijkman studied beriberi in Java, where it was still a major health problem; following studies with scientist Gerrit Grijns, it was determined in 1906 that the cause might be a missing nutrient in polished rice, a staple of the Java diet.

Berlin, Conference of (1884–85) International conference. The conference was held in Berlin, beginning December 1884, to determine the status of European colonies in AFRICA. Representatives attended from European nations, the United States, and Turkey. Resolutions were passed on such issues as free trade, SLAVERY, and terms for territorial claims. The gist of the meeting, however, was to legitimize the partitioning of Africa along existing colonial lines.

Berlin, Congress of (1878) International conference. All the major European powers convened to settle issues arising from the RUSSO-TURKISH WAR (1877–78). Alarmed by the Treaty of San Stefano, which seemed to give RUSSIA too much power in the BALKANS, leading diplomats concluded a series of agreements to maintain the balance of power in the region. The OTTOMAN EMPIRE kept Macedonia and Thrace; BULGARIA's independence, under Russian influence, was recognized; though its territory was reduced; Romanian independence was recognized; and AUSTRIA was allowed to adminster Bosnia. Great Britain gained Cyprus as a naval base. The Congress was dominated by OTTO VON BISMARCK, chancellor of GER-

MANY, and marked the new status of unified Germany as a major European power.

Berlin woolwork Type of *gros-point* (or cross-stitch) EMBROIDERY. Popular in the mid-nineteenth century and typically done with wool on canvas, the designs were often based on well-known paintings. Many depicted biblical or historical subjects. Victorian drawing rooms were full of Berlin woolwork—on mats, fire screens, and footstools. The name stems from the fact that earlier in the century the textiles and patterns used in it came chiefly from Berlin.

Berlioz, [Louis] Hector (1803–1869) French composer. Born in La Côte St. André, he was the son of a physician who taught him music, Latin, history, and geography, and hoped he would also study medicine. By the age of twelve, however, Berlioz had begun composing music for local chamber groups and seriously considering a career in music. In 1821, Berlioz was sent to study medicine in Paris, and while he studied intently for one year, he was then accepted as a student of Jean-François Lesueur, a famous opera composer. Berlioz fought bitterly with his father over the decision, and in 1826 he registered at the Conservatoire to continue his musical training.

Berlioz earned the prestigious Grand Prix de Rome in 1830, and the same year obtained a performance of his first great score, *Symphonie Fantastique.* FRANZ LISZT and ROBERT SCHUMANN were greatly influenced by Berlioz's unique use of harmony and orchestration, and quickly introduced his work in Germany.

From 1832 to 1848, Berlioz worked as a composer, conductor, and critic. After the premiere of *Harold en Italie* in 1834, the world-famous violinist Paganini declared Berlioz a genius and sent him 20,000 francs in appreciation. The money freed the composer from financial drudgery, and he composed *Roméo et Juliette* (1839), which he dedicated to Paganini.

After the failure of the opera *Benvenuto Cellini* in 1839, which severely damaged Berlioz's reputation in France, the composer spent his remaining years touring Europe. In 1849, however, he returned briefly to France to produce *Te Deum,* which was later performed at the opening of Carnegie Hall in New York City in 1891. Berlioz was still met with hostility in France but continued his success abroad, culminating in a series of well-received concerts in Russia in 1867.

Berlioz married the singer Marie Recio in 1854, after the death of his first wife, but she died suddenly in 1862. Berlioz's son, a sea captain, died of yellow fever at the age of thirty-three, two years before Berlioz's own death.

Bernadette of Lourdes, Saint See LOURDES.

Bernhardt, Sarah (1844–1923) French actress. "The Divine Sarah" was born Henriette Rosine Bernard in Paris, an illegitimate child whose parentage is poorly documented and the subject of some debate. After an education in a Roman Catholic convent, she studied at the Paris Conservatoire from 1858 to 1860 and made her stage debut on August 11, 1862, in the title role of Jean Racine's *Iphigénie,* but she was greeted with little interest.

Two years later Bernhardt gave birth to an illegitimate son and continued to perform. By 1869 her reputation was established with her appearance as Zanetto in François Coppeé's *Le Passant.* In 1872 she achieved further success in Victor Hugo's *Ruy Blas* and was acclaimed for her "golden voice."

Following a successful season in London in 1879, Bernhardt embarked on an independent career and the first of six tours to the United States. In 1882 she married Jacques Damala, a Greek actor, but the marriage ended after one year. In 1886 she performed in South America, and in 1891 she toured the world, including performances in Africa and Australia.

Performing in Rio de Janeiro in 1905, Bernhardt injured her right leg, which was eventually amputated in 1915. With the help of an artificial limb, she continued to perform. Bernhardt, who was hailed as the greatest French actress of all time, appeared on film twice, in 1911, starring in *La Reine Elizabeth* and *La Dame aux Camélias*. She died in Paris.

Besant, Annie Wood (1847–1933) English theosophist and reformer. Born Annie Wood, she married Anglican clergyman Frank Besant in 1867 but separated from him in 1872 over differences in beliefs. She rejected Christianity, joined the National Secular Society, and spent the rest of her life crusading for birth control, free thought, and women's rights. With journalist Charles Bradlaugh she republished Charles Knowlton's 1835 work "Fruits of Philosophy," which advocated contraception. In 1877 she and Bradlaugh were put on trial for publication of the work but were acquitted, effectively ending the ban on mailing public information on contraception. In 1889, Besant embraced the teachings of the THEOSOPHICAL SOCIETY and moved to India, which was to become her home for the rest of her life. In 1898 she founded the Central Hindu College, and in the early twentieth century she advocated for Indian home rule. Late in her life she adopted Indian mystical thinker Jidda Krishnamarti as her son and presented him to Britain and the United States as the new Messiah. Besant was also a member of the FABIAN SOCIETY.

Besant, Sir Walter (1836–1901) English novelist, essayist, and philanthropist. His popular novels included *The Golden Butterfly* (1876), written with James Rice; his nonfiction works *All Sorts and Conditions of Man* (1882) and *Children of Gloom* (1886) dealt with the hardship of poverty in London's East End. A generous philanthropist and friend of the working writer, Besant founded the Society of Authors in 1884. He advocated international copyright reform and more legal protection for writers. Among his other interests were the exploration of Palestine and the topography of London; the latter interest resulted in a ten-volume survey of the city published after his death (1902–12).

Knighted in 1895, Besant is best remembered today for his connection to other people. His sister-in-law was reformer and theosophist ANNIE WOOD BESANT. His remarks on the novel in his Royal Institution Lecture of 1884 provoked HENRY JAMES to write the celebrated response, "The Art of Fiction."

Bessemer process A steel purification operation. In the Bessemer process, pig iron—impure iron made in a blast furnace and set in blocks, or "pigs"—is decarbonized through the application of cold air. Developed in 1856 by British engineer Henry Bessemer (1813–1898), the Bessemer process consists of passing iron through a steel furnace, later known as a Bessemer converter, and forcing air through the metal. Impurities such as carbon, manganese, phosphorous, and silicon mix with oxygen, form oxides, and later become slag. The steel is guided through the upper end of the converter into molds. The process was of great importance in lowering the cost of steel production in the late nineteenth century.

Bhutan Mountainous kingdom in the southeastern Himalayas. It is bordered by Tibet (north and east) and INDIA (south, west, and east) in Asia. Ethnically related to Tibetans, the Bhutanese practice a form of Buddhism similar to that of Tibet. In January 1865 a border dispute between Bhutan and Assam, then part of British India, led to a British invasion of Bhutan, but the Bhutanese defeated the British at Dewangiri. Sir Henry Tombs then marched against the Bhutanese, who were forced later in 1865 to cede disputed southern mountain passes in return for an annual subsidy from Britain. In 1910, Bhutan agreed to allow Great Britain to run its foreign affairs; India has performed this role since 1949.

bicycle Two-wheeled conveyance. The bicycle was invented in 1839 by Kirkpatrick McMillan of Scotland and was first mass-produced by Pierre Michaux in France in 1867. The first ladies' bicycle, with a lowered crossbar, was introduced in 1885. In the Victorian era, bicycling gained popularity as a social, leisure-time pursuit and as a practice to improve health.

Bierce, Ambrose Gwinnett (1842–1914) American writer. Born in Meigs County, Ohio, he moved to Indiana as a child and joined the Ninth Indiana Infantry at the outbreak of the Civil War. Having served through some of the most difficult campaigns of the war, including Shiloh and Chickamauga, he made the grotesque absurdity of battle a dominant theme in his short stories. After the war he served as an attaché to General William B. Hazen on an inspection tour of the land and forts of the west, but discouraged by a lack of advancement, Bierce resigned his commission in 1866 and worked as a night watchman in San Francisco. He began con-

Cyclists enjoy London's Hyde Park during the late 1800's. Photo courtesy of Topham/Image Works.

tributing poems and articles to periodicals and by 1868 was editor of the *News Letter*.

The *Overland Monthly* published his first short story, "The Haunted Valley," in 1871; the same year he married Mary Ellen Day. During a honeymoon trip to England, Bierce joined the staff of the London periodical *Fun*, where he remained for four years. His misanthropic and caustic wit quickly earned him the sobriquet of "Bitter Bierce," and three compilations of his writing were published during his residency in England: *Nuggets and Dust Panned Out in California* (1872), *The Fiend's Delight* (1872), and *Cobwebs from an Empty Skull* (1874).

Upon his return to San Francisco around 1876, Bierce resumed his career as a journalist, and a year later he began a twenty-year association with William Randolph Hearst and the *San Francisco Examiner*, where he became the leading critic of the western states. Bierce's short stories, full of Gothic horror, black humor, and surprise endings, were first collected in 1891 in *Tales of Soldiers and Civilians*. While his fiction was largely ignored in his lifetime, Bierce preferred it to his journalism and spent the next decade editing his collected works. Nearly bankrupt and distraught over the deaths of his sons and wife, Bierce headed to Mexico in 1913 in hopes of finding Pancho Villa. He was never heard from again.

Big Ben Bell in the clock tower of London's Houses of Parliament. The bell housed in the floodlighted belfry was a tribute to the machine age in its size and efficiency. It measures 9 feet by 7½ feet, weighs 13.5 tons, and rings with a 400-pound hammer in "E". The clock dials are 22½ feet in diameter, and the minute hands are 14 feet long. First rung in 1859, the clock has never had an error greater than one second. Made by the WHITECHAPEL BELL FOUNDRY, the bell was named for Benjamin Hall, then commissioner of works, who was called "Big Ben" for his own rather tall, stout stature. The name also came to be used for the clock itself, which in its ornate detail remains a prominent example of GOTHIC REVIVAL architecture.

Billy the Kid [William H. Bonney] (1859–1881) American outlaw. Born in New York City but known for his exploits in the West, he was a thief, gambler, and murderer when still in his teens. In the late 1870s he began working as a cowboy in the New Mexico Territory for wealthy English-born rancher John H. Tunstall. Billy regarded Tunstall as a father, saying of him: "He was the only man that ever treated me like I was freeborn and white."

Tunstall was killed in 1878 in the Lincoln County War, a violent conflict between ranchers and mercantile interests for economic control of much of the New Mexico Territory. Billy the Kid made it his business to avenge the murder and carry on the ranchers' side of the war. Not long afterward, influential cattleman John Chisum made peace with his opponents, ending the war and ceding victory to Lincoln County's business interests. Billy fought on, however, refusing Governor LEW WALLACE's amnesty offer to all participants in the Lincoln County War. Organizing a gang of outlaws, Billy rustled cattle and killed numerous men. Convicted of the murder of a sheriff, he managed to escape from jail. He was finally killed at Fort Sumner at the age of twenty-one by Sheriff Pat Garrett.

Within weeks of Billy's death, a book about his exploits appeared. Many more followed, including one by his killer, Garrett. The legend of the young, reckless, cold-blooded, doomed outlaw has survived to the present day.

Bingham, George Caleb (1811–1879) American painter. He painted scenes from frontier life, portraits of wealthy Missouri citizens, and many political subjects. At first a cabinetmaker's apprentice, he became a student of law and of theology before turning to painting. In 1837 he studied for a short time at the Pennsylvania Academy of the Fine Arts. Bingham is best known for his GENRE PAINTINGS of life in the country or the towns and small cities of the Midwest. His journeys on the Mississippi and through the South resulted in such paintings as *The Jolly Flatboatmen* (1846) and *Daniel Boone Coming Through the Cumberland Gap* (1851). Like the work of the HUDSON RIVER SCHOOL, Bingham's *Fur Traders Descending the Missouri* (1845) is a contemplative statement on the relationship of man to the wilderness.

Bingham entered Missouri politics with his election to the legislature in 1848. His "election series" paintings were aimed directly at the mass market. Pictures such as *The Country Election* (1851–52) were full of narrative detail, faithfully representing their time and locale. From 1856 to 1859 Bingham traveled in Europe and studied in Düsseldorf. His paintings were very popular in his day, and engravings from them sold widely.

Bishop, Isabella Lucy Bird (1831–1904) English travel writer. Born in Yorkshire, Isabella Lucy Bird suffered from a spinal illness as a child and learned riding and swimming as part of her recuperation. After an operation in 1854, she spent several months convalescing in the United States, which she recounted in *The Englishwoman in America* (1856). She moved to Edinburgh, Scotland, in 1858 and continued her globe-trotting; by the end of her life she had circled the world three times. Much of her writing concentrated on Asia and the Far East, including *Unbeaten Tracks in Japan* (1880), *Journey in Persia and Kurdistan* (1891), and *Among the Tibetans* (1894).

In 1881 she married Dr. John Bishop, and after his death in 1886, she studied medicine and later traveled to India as a medical missionary. She founded two hospitals before returning home via a long journey on the Black Sea.

In 1892, Bishop became the first woman elected to the Royal Geographic Society, and two years later she embarked on her final journey. She traveled alone through Japan, Korea, China, and Tibet for three years and covered more than eight thousand miles. She helped start three more hospitals and photographed her experiences, collected in *Chinese Pictures* (1900). She died in Edinbugh while planning her next expedition.

Bismarck, Otto von (1815–1898) German politician. The so-called Iron Chancellor is commonly regarded as the architect of German unification under the leadership of PRUSSIA, one of the most important geopolitical events of the Victorian Age. Although opinions differ as to whether he followed a master plan or merely took advantage of favorable opportunities, his diplomatic skill and political perspicacity are universally acknowledged.

Bismarck was born on the family estate of Schönhausen in Brandenburg to a Prussian *Junker,* or noble, family. His early years were spent in Pomerania. He was educated in Berlin and studied law in Göttingen, entering the Prussian civil service in 1836. After a stint in the army, he retired from public life and devoted himself to improving his estates. In 1847 he married Johannna von Puttkamer, a member of the Pietist movement. That same year he served as a representative in a United Diet of Prussia and soon made a name for himself as a fervent and intelligent supporter of the reactionary party, against the liberal critics of the Prussian regime.

Following the collapse of the REVOLUTIONS OF 1848, Bismarck was given a position as Prussia's representative to the newly reconstituted GERMAN CONFEDERATION in Frankfurt. During this period his ambition to see Prussia become the head of a unified GERMANY became fixed. This desire was not shared by the government in Berlin, but Bismarck was allowed to remain in his position until a stroke rendered FREDERICK WILLIAM IV unable to govern. In 1859 the prince regent, the future WILLIAM I, had Bismarck removed from his post and made ambassador to Russia, where his pronouncements about German unification stirred up controversy. Bismarck soon became seriously ill with an infected leg and was forced to return to Prussia. In 1860, now in his mid-forties, he made an unsuccessful bid to become foreign minister, and his political career seemed finished.

In 1861, however, a constitutional crisis erupted in Prussia as the liberal assembly, the *Landtag,* refused to pass a military reform bill desired by the king. William I considered abdication, and Bismarck was pushed forward as the staunchest supporter of the monarchy. William appointed him prime minister in September 1862, beginning Bismarck's thirty-year career as leader of Prussia and Germany. Advocating a policy of "blood and iron" as a solution to German problems, Bismarck initially faced difficulties with the Landtag over military appropriations and his support of Russia's efforts to suppress the POLISH REBELLION of 1863. He gained credit for his handling of the war with Denmark in 1864, in which Austria and Prussia gained the right to dispose of the German territories of Schleswig and Holstein that had belonged to the Danish crown. By adroit diplomacy he managed to provoke Austria into war in 1866 over the question of the leadership of the German Confederation. The SEVEN WEEKS' WAR was a triumph for Prussia and Bismarck. Austria was excluded from the confederation, now reorganized under Prussian leadership as the North German Confederation. Bismarck was closer to his goal of German unification.

The final opportunity came as a result of another war. An attempt to place a Prussian prince on the Spanish throne panicked NAPOLEON III into issuing an ultimatum. Though the king seemed willing to let the matter drop, Bismarck manipulated the situation by releasing Napoleon's provocative telegram to the press and sending a dismissive reply. Public opinion in France and Germany swung sharply in favor of war. The FRANCO-PRUSSIAN WAR (1870–71) was another decisive victory for the Prussian army. At the close of the war, William I was declared emperor of Germany in Versailles, and Bismarck became the empire's first chancellor.

Following the establishment of the empire, Bismarck declared that Germany would devote itself to the cause of European stability and renounce all territorial ambitions, a policy to which he scrupulously adhered. Bismarck's main fear was that Germany would become surrounded by hostile powers. He therefore maintained a close alliance with Austria and sought to improve relations with Russia while preventing it from expanding too aggressively in the Balkans. The leading European statesman of the late nineteenth century, Bismarck even managed to produce a partial thaw in relations with France, despite French desire for revenge and the return of Alsace-Lorraine. He strongly urged that Germany refrain from the race to establish colonies in Africa and

Asia, though this advice was not heeded. Such was his worldwide fame that an American outpost in the North Dakota territory—now the state capital—was named Bismarck in his honor in 1873 in hopes of attracting German investment to that region's railway.

Domestically, the Iron Chancellor saw two main enemies to the new German state: SOCIALISM and Catholicism, the latter of which was strong in southern Germany and the Polish provinces. To head off socialist agitation, he banned socialist groups and supported a progressive program of welfare reforms, including unemployment insurance and subsidized pensions, though he resisted calls for regulation of working conditions. To fight the influence of Catholicism, Bismarck instituted the so-called Kulturkampf, or struggle for civilization, which included state approval of clerical appointments and a ban on certain Catholic organizations. He later abandoned the Kulturkampf when he saw that it created support for opposition parties.

Bismarck's later years were marked by worsening relations with France and Russia as well as a growing social democratic movement in Germany. The chancellor was also criticized for allowing Germany to fall behind in the competition for colonies. The death of his strongest supporter, William I, in 1888 left Bismarck vulnerable, especially since the new emperor, WILLIAM II, favored a more aggressive foreign and colonial policy, and more sweeping social legislation. After a series of confrontations, William had Bismarck removed from the chancellorship in 1890. Bismarck retired to his estates, where he was revered as a national hero; he devoted the remainder of his life to writing his memoirs.

Blackmore, Richard D. See *LORNA DOONE*.

Blackwell, Alice Stone See BLACKWELL, ELIZABETH.

Blackwell, Elizabeth (1821–1901) American physician. She was the first woman to become a fully accredited doctor in the United States and Great Britain. The daughter of a sugar refiner who, with his wife, was an advocate of social reform, Elizabeth emigrated with her family from Great Britain to the United States in 1832. The family was active in the antislavery movement, sheltering fugitive slaves in their home and conferring with abolitionist leader WILLIAM LLOYD GARRISON. After teaching school in Kentucky and struggling to be admitted to medical school, Elizabeth received her M.D. from Geneva College, New York, in 1849, then went to Europe for additional training (1849–51). She returned to the United States, where she practiced medicine from 1851 to 1869. Among her accomplishments was the founding of the New York Infirmary for Women and Children, which was supported by Lady Byron, widow of British poet, Lord Byron.

In 1869, Blackwell returned to her native Britain, where she had previously succeeded in placing her name on the medical register (1859) and where she practiced medicine until the end of her life. Her efforts paved the way for the opening of medicine to women generally, including ELIZABETH GARRETT ANDERSON, the second woman accredited to practice medicine in Britain (1869). By 1895, 264 women were registered as physicians in Britain.

For Blackwell, medicine was a tool in the struggle for social justice. In addition to crusading for women's rights, she strove to improve public hygiene and morality and to make medicine more available to the poor.

Blackwell's brother, Henry Brown Blackwell (1825–1909), was an editor and WOMAN SUFFRAGE advocate. His wife, Lucy Stone

(1818–1893), whom he married in 1855, was also a suffragist who organized the first national women's rights convention in Worcester, Massachusetts (1850), and the annual conventions that followed. She helped to form the American Woman Suffrage Association (1869) and to found *Woman's Journal* (1870), for which she served as coeditor with her husband from 1872 to 1893. Their daughter, Alice Stone Blackwell (1857–1950), an editor and poet, was also involved in the movement, helping her parents edit *Woman's Journal* and later serving as its chief editor (1893–1917).

Blackwell, Henry See BLACKWELL, ELIZABETH.

Blantyre City in Malawi, in southeast central Africa. Blantyre was founded in 1876 by Scottish missionaries who named it for the birthplace of their leader, explorer DAVID LIVINGSTONE. In the Victorian era it was a tiny settlement in the British colony of NYASALAND. It was dominated by an unusual church built in the years 1888 to 1897 by Scottish missionary David Clement Ruffelle Scott. With little knowledge of architecture, Scott constructed the church himself out of anthill clay; the finished work combined Byzantine, Gothic, and African influences.

Blavatsky, Madame [Helena Petrovna] (1831–1891) Russian-born SPIRITUALIST and occultist. She began developing a Theosophical movement in Russia in 1858, claiming to have studied for seven years in Tibet under Eastern teachers, a claim that is now disputed. In 1875 she cofounded the THEOSOPHICAL SOCIETY in New York and edited the *Theosophist Journal* from 1879 to 1888. Her works included *Iris Unveiled* (1877), *The Secret Doctrine* (1888), and *The Key to Theosophy* (1889). She continued to espouse her views and claim enlightenment by spiritual revelation despite being accused of fraud by both the Indian press and the London Society for Psychical Research. The poet WILLIAM BUTLER YEATS was influenced by her work.

blizzard of '88 Snowstorm that struck the northeastern United States from March 12 to March 14, 1888. Thoroughly unexpected after a mild winter and several days of warming, the blizzard dropped 20.9 inches of snow on New York, with snow drifts up to 20 feet high. Winds of forty-eight miles per hour were reported, with temperatures in the low teens. New York City, Washington, D.C., and other Atlantic cities were isolated from outside communication for days. At least five hundred deaths were reported on land and at sea, and two hundred ships were sunk or grounded. Among the casualties was former U.S. Senator from New York ROSCOE CONKLING, who died of pneumonia contracted during the storm.

blood transfusion Medical procedure. Although the transfer of blood into the vessels of human beings did not become a viable technique for replacing lost blood until the twentieth century, several nineteenth-century experiments laid the groundwork for the practice. These included transfusions performed successfully by British physician James Blundell as a treatment for postpartum hemorrhage. German physiologist Carl F. W. Ludwig (1816–1895) and the students at his Leipzig institute of physiology made blood transfusion more common. In 1867, Ludwig invented the stromuhr, a device for measuring the amount of blood passing through a vessel. He also invented the blood pump for sampling gases in the blood and introduced the method of keeping excised portions of an organism alive by injecting blood into them. Despite advances in blood transfusion, it was a risky, often fatal procedure and fell out of practice until the discovery of blood types by Austrian biologist Karl Landsteiner (1868–1943) in 1900, near the end of the Victorian Age. Landsteiner developed a system for classifying blood according to the presence or absence of specific antigens, substances that stimulate an immune response when injected into a person of incompatible blood group. His method of classifying blood as A, B, AB, or O allowed transfusions to become a safe part of medical practice and won Landsteiner the 1930 Nobel Prize in medicine and physiology.

Bloody Sunday (Trafalgar Square Riots) Uprising in England. The economic depression of the 1880s led to a series of mass demonstrations and street rioting in London by workers and their sympathizers. The most dramatic altercation occurred on Sunday, November 13, 1887, in Trafalgar Square, the site of many previous demonstrations. The Law and Liberty League called for the demonstration to protect the right of free assembly and free speech. Over one hundred thousand marchers from all parts of London descended on the square, among them WILLIAM MORRIS and GEORGE BERNARD SHAW. Some four thousand police and mounted soldiers, wielding clubs and bayonets, dispersed the demonstrators. One person died in the melee, and many others were injured. The rioting did not stop the street agitation; the following Sunday another person died at a demonstration in the Square.

blue books Blue-covered published results of British parliamentary investigations. Blue books delved into numerous aspects of national life, from working conditions to universities, often leading to reform legislation. In the 1840s blue books on the conditions of laborers inspired the authors of SOCIAL PROBLEM NOVELS.

Boas, Franz (1858–1942) American anthropologist. Born in Germany, he earned a doctorate in physics from the University of Kiel (1881) but turned to anthropology when he studied Eskimo culture during an expedition to Baffin Island in 1883–84. From 1886 to 1889, while at Clark University, he studied the Kwakiutl and other Native American peoples of British Columbia. From 1896 to 1905 he was curator of ethnology at the American Museum of Natural History, and in 1899 he became the first professor of anthropology at Columbia University, a position he held for thirty-seven years. Enormously influential, he became known as the father of American anthropology, partly through his training of twentieth-century scholars in the field, such as Ruth Benedict, Alfred L. Kroeber, and Margaret Mead. He emphasized a rigorous empirical approach based on careful collection and quantification of facts. His works include *The Mind of Primitive Man* (1911; revised 1938) and *Anthropology and Modern Life* (1928; revised 1932).

Boers Dutch settlers of southern Africa or their descendants. The word "Boer" is derived from the Dutch word for farmer or peasant. The Boers colonized the southern tip of Africa in the seventeenth century. The British annexed this territory in 1806. Many Boers migrated northward to the interior in the GREAT TREK (1835–40) to escape British rule. They established two independent republics, the Orange Free State and the South African Republic, also called the TRANSVAAL. The republics lost their independence in 1902 as a result of the BOER WAR.

Boer War (1899–1902) A war between GREAT BRITAIN and the allies of the BOERS, the TRANSVAAL and the Orange Free State. Also called the South African War, the outbreak of fighting resulted from four decades of territorial conflicts between Dutch settlers, commonly called Boers, and English colonists in the southern part of Africa. Great Britain took over the southern part of the continent in 1806 after some 150 years of Dutch rule. It established the Cape Colony and gradually acquired SWAZILAND, RHODESIA, and other lands. The original Dutch settlers resented these incursions, and in 1835 some five thousand began to migrate in the GREAT TREK north to the interior to escape British rule. They established two republics, the Orange Free State and the Transvaal.

The British government recognized the new states in 1854, but in 1877 Prime Minister BENJAMIN DISRAELI altered the policy and formally annexed the Transvaal. A revolt by the Boers led Prime Minister WILLIAM GLADSTONE to grant them control over their internal affairs but subjected their foreign policy to British control. The Pretoria Convention in 1881 formalized this arrangement, with the profoundly anti-British Transvaal president Paul Kruger (1825–1904) reluctantly accepting the agreement.

Territorial tensions increased in 1886 when vast lodes of gold were found near Johannesburg. Tens of thousands of British, Americans, and Germans flocked to the Transvaal. Laws were passed to protect the region from the UITLANDERS, or outsiders. A fourteen-year residency requirement for citizenship and voting was imposed, as were special taxes. The British government objected to these measures, but Kruger stood fast.

CECIL RHODES, the chairman of the British South African Company and prime minister of the Cape Colony, did more than protest. The Boers lay in the way of his plans for a CAPE-TO-CAIRO railroad and English dominance of all of eastern Africa. He plotted an uprising of the uitlanders for 1895 and provided them with guns and ammunition. He also instructed the company's private army, led by LEANDER STARR JAMESON, to assemble along the Transvaal border.

In December 1895, after the uprising was postponed several times, the impatient Jameson led his group of about five hundred men over the border. Jameson's raid, as it came to be known, ended in complete defeat of the freebooters, as Jameson's men were called. The incident worsened English-Boer tensions and also caused ill feelings between the British and German governments when WILLIAM II sent a congratulatory telegram to Kruger on the repulsion of the invaders.

In 1896 the Transvaal entered a military alliance with the Orange Free State and began buying arms from Germany. Kruger demanded close to £2 million to compensate for damages caused by Jameson's raid and also declared that the 1881 Pretoria Convention no longer gave Britain control over the Boer states' foreign policies. The British government responded by reinforcing troops along the Transvaal border. When Boer demands to pull back were ignored, Boer cavalry attacked on October 11, 1899. A string of Boer victories, most notably at Colenso in December where British troops suffered over one thousand casualties, shocked the army and the nation.

Reinforcements swelled the English army in southern Africa from about 25,000 troops to over 250,000, with General FREDERICK SLEIGH ROBERTS and Lord KITCHENER commanding the effort. The Boers retreated before the superior forces, and by the spring of 1900, Johannesburg and Pretoria had fallen. Kruger fled to Europe, never to return, and Britain formally annexed the Boer states.

Defeated on the battlefields, the Boers took to hit-and-run guerrilla warfare against the cumbersome British infantry and supply trains—the word "commando" comes from the Afrikaans word *kommando,* a detachment of Boer troops. Conventional military tactics proved useless against mobile troops who knew the countryside.

The army, now under Kitchener's sole command, erected thousands of blockhouses across the country joined together by barbed wire to impede the Boers. English troops swept each section in search-and-destroy missions, burning crops and destroying homes as they went. Residents, mostly women and children, were herded into twenty-four concentration camps where an estimated eighteen thousand to twenty-four thousand died from exposure, typhoid, and other diseases.

The Treaty of Vereeniging, signed in May 1902, finally ceased hostilities. The Boers acquiesced to British sovereignty, and Britain agreed to pay £3 million for property losses. More than 440,000 English and colonial troops had fought in the war, with a loss of over 20,000. More than 80,000 Boers had taken up arms, and 7,000 had died in addition to the concentration camp victims.

Bonheur, Rosa (1822–1899) French painter of animals. The daughter and artistic pupil of painter Raymond Bonheur, Bonheur exhibited her pictures in the Paris Salon beginning in 1841, to popular acclaim. Her subjects included lions, tigers, and horses. She is now best remembered for the vivid, dramatic painting *The Horse Fair* (1853; Metropolitan Museum of Art, New York). Bonheur was also a feminist who wore trousers, smoked cigarettes, and served as an inspiration to other women artists. In 1865 she became the first woman awarded the Cross of the French Legion of Honor, demonstrating, according to Empress Eugénie, that "genius has no sex."

Bonney, William H. See BILLY THE KID.

Boole, George (1815–1864) English mathematician and logician. Born in Lincoln, he was a schoolmaster before publishing *The Mathematical Analysis of Logic* (1847), in which he developed a mathematical analogy for logical arguments by using algebraic symbols and manipulation to represent logical operations. In so doing he founded what became known as Boolean algebra or symbolic logic, which proved to have important applications in investigating the foundations of mathematics and programming computers. He also published *An Investigation of the Laws of Thought* (1854) and wrote on differential equations and finite differences. He served as professor at Queen's College, Cork, Ireland, from 1849 until his death. He is known as the father of modern logic.

boot scraper Iron, wood, or brass Victorian household implement for removing mud and dirt from shoes. Usually decorated with rococo patterns and located in the entryway to a house, it had a flat metal edge to dislodge debris.

Booth, John Wilkes (1838–1865) U.S. actor and assassin. Born in Maryland to a famous acting family, Booth openly favored the South during the CIVIL WAR but continued to act in the North during the conflict. As the war neared its end, Booth planned to kidnap President ABRAHAM LINCOLN in a desperate attempt to thwart the final Union victory. When this scheme failed, Booth shot Lincoln during a performance of *Our American Cousin* at Ford's Theater in Washington, D.C., on April 14, 1865. Booth escaped from the theater, but Union troops tracked him down to a Virginia barn twelve days later. In the ensuing gun battle he either shot himself or was killed by the soldiers.

Booth, William (1829–1912) English religious leader. He and his wife and fellow evangelist Catherine Mumford Booth (1829–1890) founded a mission in Whitechapel, London, in 1865 that grew into the charitable and social reform movement known as the SALVATION ARMY (1878). A general of the army, he wrote *In Darkest England and the Way Out* (1890). His children, including Bramwell, Ballington, and Evangeline Cory, helped sustain and spread the organization worldwide.

bootjack Brass, iron, or wood implement with a U-shaped end. It eased removal of the high-top boots favored by Victorian gentlemen.

Borodin, Aleksandr Porfiryevich (1833–1887) Russian composer and chemist. Born in St. Petersburg, the illegitimate son of a prince, he displayed early in his life an impressive intellect and talent for music. Borodin learned German, French, and Italian as a child, wrote a polka for piano at age nine, and began composing chamber music when he was fourteen. From 1850 to 1856 he studied at St. Petersburg's Medico-Surgical Academy, where he became a professor of chemistry in 1864. Though he earned a reputation as one of the leading scientists in Europe, he continued his musical study, remarking, "Science is my work and music is my fun."

Borodin became a member of the group of composers known as THE FIVE, which also included NIKOLAY RIMSKY-KORSAKOV, MODEST MUSSORGSKY, César Cui, and Mili Balakirev. Balakirev conducted Borodin's first symphony, Symphony in E-flat Major, in 1869; it became an immediate success, with performances sponsored by the Countess de Mercy-Argenteau of Belgium. Borodin's interest in music remained a diversion, however, and he did not complete his Symphony in B Minor until 1875. His String Quartet No. 2 in D became the single most popular piece of Russian chamber music. His major work, the opera *Prince Igor,* was completed in 1890 by Rimsky-Korsakov and Alexander Glazunov three years after Borodin's death of a heart attack.

Boston Public Library Oldest tax-financed free public library in the world. It was founded in Boston, Massachusetts, in 1852. The present building was built in 1895, designed by McKim, Mead, and White. An addition was built in 1973, designed by Philip Johnson.

Botswana See BECHUANALAND.

Boucicault, Dion[ysius Lardner] (1820–1890) Irish playwright, theater manager, and actor. The author of nearly two hundred plays, Boucicault enjoyed success in England with early hits that included the five-act comedies *London Assurance* (1841) and *Old Heads and Young Hearts* (1844). He also wrote versions of French plays such as *The Corsican Brothers* (1852). He emigrated to the United States in 1853, where he wrote melodramas such as *The Poor of New York* (1857), *The Octoroon* (1859), the Irish crime drama *THE COLLEEN BAWN* (1860), and *The Shaughraun* (1874), in which he played the title role.

Boudin, Eugène-Louis (1824–1898) French painter. A precursor of the Impressionists, Boudin spent most of his life as an artist on the Normandy coast where he painted the shores of Le Havre, Trouville, and Honfleur. He became famous for his paintings of choppy seas, windy skies, and fashionable visitors. He painted outdoors rather than in the studio and introduced CLAUDE MONET to this method. In *Beach at Trouville* of 1863, Boudin rendered a path along the sea in flickering patches of light and color. His quick, broad brushstrokes give the painting a sense of immediacy and spontaneity. His style was later used in larger-scale attempts by Monet.

From the time of their first showing at the Salon of 1859, when Charles Baudelaire praised them, Boudin's sketchy beach paintings were well received by the public. He exhibited at the first IMPRESSIONIST exhibition in 1874. He was awarded a Salon medal in 1889 and the Legion of Honor in 1892. His style marks the transition from the classical landscapes of CAMILLE COROT to the breakthrough tendencies of Impressionism.

Boulanger, Georges-Ernest-Jean-Marie (1837–1891) French soldier and politician. A career officer, Boulanger served in the army of the SECOND EMPIRE (1852–70), most notably in the defense of Paris during the FRANCO-PRUSSIAN WAR (1870–71) and the suppression of the PARIS COMMUNE (1871). In the early years of the THIRD REPUBLIC (1870–1940), he made friends in high places; in 1880 he was promoted to general and in 1886–87 served as minister of war. Widely popular and known as the "Man on Horseback" for his mounted appearances before crowds in Paris, he gained support from those discontented with the government, longing for a dictatorial leader, and desiring military revenge against Germany. In 1888 he was forced to retire from the army for illegal political activities. In 1889 he ran for the Chamber of Deputies and was elected from Paris. Campaigning for the presidency that year, he raised fears of an imminent coup. The government responded by dissolving his main support organization, the League of Patriots, and trying him for treason. Boulanger fled to Belgium and was convicted *in absentia*. He continued his campaign in exile, but the Boulangists did poorly in the elections in October 1889. The movement lost popularity when Boulanger was discovered to have taken money from the royalists. Shortly afterward he committed suicide. Boulangism has been called France's first mass political movement.

Bournonville, Auguste (1805–1879) Danish dancer and choreographer. Born in Copenhagen, he was the son of the celebrated dancer Antoine Bournonville, under whom he studied before traveling to Paris to continue his training under Auguste Vestris and Pierre Gardel. In 1829, Bournonville returned to Copenhagen and became the leading dancer of the Royal Danish Ballet and director of its school. From 1836 to 1877 he was *maître de ballet*. He emphasized strong male roles and the use of mime, influences that have continued in Danish ballet; many of his works remain in the repertoire of the Royal Danish Ballet, including *Napoli* and a version of Filippo Taglioni's *La Sylphide*. He staged several of his works in Vienna in 1855–56, and from 1861 to 1864 directed the Swedish Royal Opera at Stockholm.

Boxer Rebellion (1898–1900) Uprising in CHINA. During the last half of the nineteenth century, the great powers carved up China into spheres of influence under which they controlled its commerce. In 1898 a secret society called the Boxers—the Chinese phrase for the group translates into "righteous, harmonious fists"—began attacking foreigners and Chinese Christians. The dowager empress of China, TZ'U-HSI, secretly inflamed the revolt in an effort to stop reform of the Chinese court, reorganization of the bureaucracy, modernization of the army, and other changes.

The rebellion culminated with the Boxers attacking Peking in 1900 and laying siege to the foreign section of the city. The major European powers, including Great Britain,

France, and Germany, along with Japan and the United States, sent an international force that defeated the uprising. China was forced to pay a huge indemnity and grant even more favorable trading rights to foreigners.

boxing Sport. One of the oldest and most universal of sports, boxing dates back to the beginnings of recorded history but saw significant changes during the Victorian Age. Though boxing had always been a bare-knuckled competition, English society gradually turned against the "ruffians of the ring," as some clergy called them. In an attempt to "humanize" the sport, John Graham Chambers, a member of the Amateur Athletic Club, in 1867 created a set of twelve rules that were sponsored by Sir JOHN SHOLTO DOUGLAS, 8TH MARQUIS OF QUEENSBERRY. Prescribing gloves, three-minute rounds, and a count of ten following a knockdown, the "Queensberry" rules provided the basis for the modern sport of boxing.

The last legal bare-knuckle championship bout occurred at Richburg, Mississippi, on July 8, 1889, between JOHN L. SULLIVAN and Jake Kilrain. Although illegal, bare-knuckle fights persisted in the United States until 1892. James L. Corbett became the first "Queensberry" heavyweight world champion when he defeated Sullivan in twenty-one rounds on September 7, 1892, in New Orleans. Under the new rules, boxing became more popular and more acceptable both legally and socially.

Boycott, Charles Cunningham (1832–1897) English land manager in Ireland. A retired English army officer, Boycott gained notoriety in 1880 when the Irish LAND LEAGUE demanded that he reduce rents. When he refused and tried to evict tenants, CHARLES STEWART PARNELL called on tenant farmers to shun completely anyone who refused to lower rents. Boycott was socially isolated and forced to hire laborers from outside the area to work his land. He left Ireland that same year and became a land agent in England. The agitation led to lower rents.

The word "boycott" came into general use after 1880 to mean an organized nonviolent attempt to coerce an opponent. The tactic, based mainly on a refusal to do business with the target, has been used in labor, civil rights, and anticolonial movements.

Bradlaugh, Charles (1833–1891) English politician. Born in London, Bradlaugh left school at age twelve and earned a living through various jobs before enlisting as a soldier in 1850. Three years later his mother paid to get him out of the service, and Bradlaugh worked as a lawyer's clerk.

He also started to gain a reputation as a free thought lecturer, and in 1860 he began editing the *National Reformer.* Bradlaugh brilliantly defended the paper in 1868 when it was prosecuted for alleged blasphemy and sedition. His refusal to take an oath on the Bible in court led to the Evidence Amendment Act of 1869.

In 1876–77, Bradlaugh was prosecuted for illegally publishing Charles Knowlton's *Fruits of Philosophy,* an American pamphlet on birth control; he was convicted and sentenced to a heavy fine and imprisonment, but the sentence was stayed due to a technicality.

Bradlaugh's interest in politics led to his election to Parliament in 1880, and he struggled for six years to gain formal recognition because, as an atheist, he refused to swear on the Bible to take his oath of office. Regarded as an honest and articulate politician, Bradlaugh gained a small measure of respect and popularity, and served in Parliament until his death.

Brady, Diamond Jim [James Buchanan] (1856–1917) American businessman and celebrity. Born in New York City, Brady built his fortune selling railway equipment and was named to high posts in several related firms. His name stems from not only his $2 million diamond jewelry collection but his larger-than-life habits of fine dining and entertainment. Urological maladies late in life led him to donate monies to Johns Hopkins Hospital where he was treated and where he founded the Brady Urological Institute in 1912. He died at age sixty in Atlantic City, New Jersey.

Brady, Mathew B. (1823–1896) American photographer. Born in Warren County, New York, Brady opened his first daguerreotype studio in New York City in 1844 and began to establish himself as a portrait photographer in 1845. Because photographic portraits were still the province of the well-known or well-to-do, Brady was able to amass portraits of a number of American luminaries, which he published in the collection *The Gallery of Illustrious Americans* (1850). A noted subject was Abraham Lincoln.

During the U.S. CIVIL WAR, Brady assembled a staff of over one dozen photographers to provide the first complete coverage of a war. The many hundreds of images they rendered not only offered a new and unsparing view of military conflict but helped to bring the photographic coverage of warfare into accepted practice. A number of Brady's staff members, including Timothy O'Sullivan and Alexander Gardner, became established photographers in their own right.

Brahms, Johannes (1833–1897) German composer and pianist. He was born in Hamburg, Germany, the son of Jakob Brahms, a double-bass player who encouraged him to study music. In 1843, Johannes was sent to study under Eduard Marxsen, who was so impressed with the boy's talents that he agreed to train him without pay. Between the ages of fourteen and sixteen, Brahms earned money to help his family by playing piano in the inns and taverns near the docks of Hamburg. In 1850 he met the violinist Eduard Reményi, who taught Brahms Hungarian national music, which became influential in the rest of Brahms's music. Reményi and Brahms embarked on a concert tour in 1853, and in Hanover they enlisted the services of another violinist, Joseph Joachim.

The trio arrived in Weimar, where they were welcomed by FRANZ LISZT, who was impressed by Brahms's compositions and wanted the composer to remain in Weimar and become part of the "neo-German" school of music, led by Liszt and RICHARD WAGNER. Although Brahms pursued an independent course, he was influenced to a degree by both composers.

Reményi remained in Weimar, but Brahms continued on his way until he arrived, with an introduction from Joachim, at the home of ROBERT SCHUMANN in Düsseldorf. Schumann was also impressed with Brahms's music and persuaded a Leipzig publisher to print the compositions.

Brahms became close friends with Schumann and his wife Clara, and after Schumann became mentally disturbed and was placed in an asylum in 1854, Brahms took care of the Schumann family.

From 1857 to 1859, Brahms moved between Detmold and Göttingen, teaching piano and conducting a choral society, before being appointed conductor of a women's choir in Hamburg.

After being passed over for conductor of the Hamburg Philharmonic Society, Brahms moved to Vienna. His reputation began to grow steadily, culminating in the success of the *Requiem,* performed in Bremen Cathedral in 1868. Brahms followed this success with his major works, including Symphony No. 1 in C Minor (1876), which shows the influence of Beethoven; Symphony No. 4 in E Minor (1885); and the Clarinet Quintet (1891).

On his way to Clara Schumann's funeral in May 1896, Brahms became ill. He was diagnosed with cancer and died in Vienna the following year.

brain fever Disease. Often contracted in Victorian novels, notably and fatally by Catherine Earnshaw in *WUTHERING HEIGHTS,* it is characterized by high fever and delirium. The ailment in its fictional form typically follows a severe emotional trauma, such as a broken heart. In reality the group of diseases collectively known as "brain fever" in Victorian times were caused by viruses or bacteria. Now known as encephalitis or inflammation of the brain, the diseases can produce symptoms similar to those encountered by fictional characters. These disorders can be fatal or lead to brain damage, and may be accompanied by meningitis, inflammation of the meninges, which are the membranes that envelop the brain and spinal cord.

Brentano, Franz (1838–1917) German philosopher and psychologist. He was the author of *Psychology from an Empirical Standpoint* (1874), in which he contributed to the founding of an independent science of psychology. Brentano's views on mental processes as acts worthy of study were highly influential. German philosopher Edmund Husserl and Austrian psychiatrist SIGMUND FREUD were among his students.

Breuer, Josef (1842–1925) Austrian physician. He was known for his successful treatment, beginning in 1880, of the hysterical patient he called Anna O. In what is often considered the founding case of psychoanalysis, Breuer developed the "cathartic method" for treating the patient's neuroses, inducing her to recall early traumas under hypnosis. He described his findings in *Studies in Hysteria* (1895), cowritten with SIGMUND FREUD.

Brewer's Dictionary of Phrase and Fable Reference book. The eclectic compendium of folklore, mythology, superstition, slang, and etymology was compiled by Ebeneezer Cobham Brewer (1810–1897) in 1870 and revised by the author in 1881 and 1895. Brewer called it a "treasury of literary bric-à-brac." It is still in print.

Bridges, Robert (1844–1930) English poet and critic. While at Corpus Christi College, Oxford, he met and became friends with GERARD MANLEY HOPKINS, whose poetry he admired and later championed.

Trained as a physician, Bridges gave up medical practice in 1882. His first volume of *Poems* (1873) was followed by a sonnet sequence *The Growth of Love* (1876), further collections of poems, and long poems including *Eros and Psyche* (1885) and *Demeter* (1905). Bridges's greatest success as a poet came after the Victorian era. His poetry is marked by its classical spirit and diction, with an emphasis on reason and subtle experimentation in metrics. He was appointed poet laureate in 1913.

A literary man of many interests, Bridges was a cofounder of the Society for Pure English, the editor of the *Yattendon Hymnal,* and the author of *A Practical Discourse on Hymn Singing.* His critical work included studies of John Keats and John Milton, and the popular wartime anthology *The Spirit of Man* (1916). Bridges also wrote plays on classical subjects and had several of his poems set to music.

Bridges is best remembered for promoting, editing, and publishing his late friend Hopkins's work in 1918.

Bright, John (1811–1889) English reformer and orator. The son of a Quaker cotton mill owner, he led his first major crusade against the CORN LAWS, helping to found the ANTI–CORN LAW LEAGUE in 1838. He and RICHARD COBDEN were the League's major public speakers until repeal of the law in 1846. By then Bright had been a member of Parliament for three years, where he led the Radicals, a group advocating reform. He became a leading critic of the CRIMEAN WAR and British IMPERIALISM, his oratory waxing so antagonistic that it cost him his seat in 1857. He also suffered a nervous breakdown at this time. Reelected from another district, he helped pass the REFORM BILL OF 1867, supported Irish land reform and the disestablishment of the Irish Church, and fought capital punishment. He also argued for less autocratic English rule of INDIA. WILLIAM GLADSTONE named him president of the Board of Trade in 1868, but he resigned in 1870 after another breakdown.

Despite his reform record, Bright, an adherent of the MANCHESTER school of economic thought, opposed trade unions and some of the FACTORY ACTS aimed at improving working conditions.

Britain See GREAT BRITAIN.

"Britannia, the Pride of the Ocean" Patriotic song. It appeared, with different titles and lyric variations for different countries, on opposite sides of the Atlantic. Entitled "Columbia, the Land of the Brave," the song first appeared in the United States in 1843 as a patriotic anthem; its date of debut in Britain is unclear. Composition credit is also unclear, claimed by both English singer David T. Shaw and English arranger Thomas à Becket.

British East India Company British company. Chartered by Queen Elizabeth I in 1600, the company concentrated on INDIA, establishing bases there at Surat in 1612 and Madras in 1640. In addition the company acquired the west coast port of Bombay in 1668 and founded Calcutta in the eastern region of Bengal about 1690. With trading privileges from India's Mogul emperor and broad powers from the British crown (including the right to coin money and wage war with non-Christian powers), the company flourished, making huge profits from the exports of cotton goods, tea, spices, silks, and saltpeter.

The decline of Mogul power in the eighteenth century led to war between the rival French and British East India companies (1751–60); Britain emerged as the victor under company agent Robert Clive, with the company running Bengal as a virtual client state. Concerned about the growing power and financial mismanagement of company officials, the British government began exercising greater control over the company in the 1770s. Warren Hastings, the first governor-general of British India, from 1774 to 1785, reformed the company's administration and extended its territories. Lord Charles Cornwallis, governor-general from 1786 to 1793, made the company more of an administrative entity than a commercial one. That transformation was completed by 1833 when the company's trade monopoly was all but abolished. Its remaining power of influencing administrative appointments was erased when the Indian Civil Service was instituted in 1853.

As British India grew in area and population, the East India Company became unable to cope with the demands of government and war. Its inadequacy was brought home in its handling of the INDIAN MUTINY of 1857, after which the East India Company was abolished (1858) and the British crown took over direct rule of India.

British Empire In 1897, at the time of Queen Victoria's DIAMOND JUBILEE, the British Empire encompassed roughly a quarter of the earth's territory and a quarter of its population. In numerical terms, it spanned about 11 million square miles and governed about 372 million people. In addition to the United Kingdom, which included GREAT BRITAIN and IRELAND, it consisted of the following lands:

Europe: Isle of Man, Channel Islands, Gibraltar, Malta.

Asia: INDIA (including modern India, Pakistan, Bangladesh, and Burma); CEYLON (Sri Lanka); Malay Federated States (now West Malaysia); Labuan, North Borneo (Sabah), and Sarawak (all now comprising East Malaysia); Brunei; Singapore; Papua New Guinea; Hong Kong; Aden (now part of YEMEN). Cyprus was nominally OTTOMAN but administered by Britain. See also SOUTHEAST ASIA.

Australia: AUSTRALIA (including New South Wales, Tasmania, Western Australia, South Australia, Victoria, and Queensland); NEW ZEALAND.

Africa: Ashanti (in West Africa); BASUTOLAND; BECHUANALAND; British East Africa; Cape Province; Gambia; Gold Coast; Natal; Nigeria; NYASALAND; RHODESIA; SIERRA LEONE; Somaliland; Uganda; ZANZIBAR. Authority over the TRANSVAAL was disputed with the BOERS. EGYPT was nominally Ottoman but occupied by the British. See also AFRICA.

Americas: CANADA; Newfoundland; British Honduras; British Guiana; Bermuda; British Virgin Islands; Jamaica; Leeward Islands; Windward Islands; Trinidad; Tobago; Turks and Caicos Islands; Falkland Islands. See also WEST INDIES.

Indian Ocean: MAURITIUS; SEYCHELLES; MALDIVES; other islands and groups.

Pacific Ocean: Gilbert, Ellice, Southern Solomon, Union groups; Fiji; Pitcairn; other islands and groups. See also OCEANIA.

Atlantic Ocean: Ascension; St. Helena; Tristan de Cunha.

British Museum National institution. Founded in 1753 in London with the acquisition of the massive books and natural history collection of Sir Hans Sloane and opened to the public in 1759, this landmark national institution underwent several changes during the Victorian era. By the mid–nineteenth century, more space was required to house important acquisitions such as the sculptures from the Parthenon known as the Elgin Marbles (1816) and George III's library (1823). To meet that need, a new building was designed by Sir Robert Smirke and finished in 1847. The domed reading room was completed in 1857, in accordance with the plans of Sir Anthony Panizzi (1797–1879), a museum staff member since 1831 and chief librarian from 1856 to 1867. Under Panizzi's leadership, the library of the British Museum evolved from a hard-to-use miscellany to a carefully catalogued, internationally renowned research center. Panizzi enforced the requirement that a copy of every book printed in the United Kingdom be deposited in the library.

The Natural History Museum was opened in South Kensington in 1883. In addition to the items mentioned above, the British Museum's collections include the Rosetta Stone, Assyrian sculptures of winged lions, a

Saxon ship from about A.D. 660, and the manuscripts of *Beowulf* and the Magna Carta.

British prime ministers The following served as prime minister of Great Britain during the reign of Queen VICTORIA (June 20, 1837 to January 22, 1901). For more information see chart below and individual entries.

Broca, Pierre-Paul (1824–1880) French surgeon and physical anthropologist. After earning his medical degree at the University of Paris in 1849, he chose to specialize in brain surgery. In 1861 he showed that the third convolution of the left frontal lobe of the brain, later called Broca's area, was associated with the control of articulate speech and that damage to the area resulted in aphasia, the loss of ability to speak. This discovery, the first definite connection between a portion of the brain and a specific human ability, inspired a rush of similar discoveries.

Broca's interest in the brain and skull led him to become an expert in physical anthropology, which at the time focused heavily on skull measurements. Broca invented new instruments for taking such measurements and founded the Société d'Anthropologie de Paris in 1858. When fossils of NEANDERTHAL MAN were discovered in Germany in 1856, Broca supported the theory that the bones were those of an early form of human rather than of a diseased individual. His impeccable credentials helped this view to prevail.

Brontë, Anne (1820–1849) English novelist. Younger sister of CHARLOTTE BRONTË (*q.v.* for

DATE	PRIME MINISTER	PARTY
1835–41	Viscount MELBOURNE	Whig
1841–46	Sir ROBERT PEEL	Tory
1846–52	Earl RUSSELL	Whig
1852	Earl of DERBY	Tory
1852–55	Earl of ABERDEEN	Coalition
1855–58	Viscount PALMERSTON	Liberal
1858–59	Earl of Derby	Conservative
1859–65	Viscount Palmerston	Liberal
1865–66	Earl Russell	Liberal
1866–68	Earl of Derby	Conservative
1868	BENJAMIN DISRAELI	Conservative
1868–74	WILLIAM E. GLADSTONE	Liberal
1874–80	Benjamin Disraeli	Conservative
1880–85	William E. Gladstone	Liberal
1885–86	Marquis of SALISBURY	Conservative
1886	William E. Gladstone	Liberal
1886–92	Marquis of Salisbury	Conservative
1892–94	William E. Gladstone	Liberal
1894–95	Earl of Rosebery	Liberal
1895–1902	Marquis of Salisbury	Conservative

family history) and EMILY BRONTË. She contributed poetry under the pseudonym Acton Bell to *Poems by Currer, Ellis, and Acton Bell* (1846), the sisters' first publication. Her lonely, melancholy experience as a governess at Thorp Green Hall near York was reflected in her novel *Agnes Grey* (1847). A second novel, *The Tenant of Wildfell Hall,* followed in 1848; its portrayal of a woman married to an alcoholic, drawing on the author's own experience caring for her alcoholic brother Branwell, sparked controversy but sold copies. She died of tuberculosis at the age of twenty-nine, a year after the deaths of Branwell and Emily.

Brontë, Charlotte (1816–1855) English novelist. Older sister of novelists EMILY [JANE] BRONTË and ANNE BRONTË and of Patrick Branwell Brontë (1817–1848), she was also the younger sister of Maria (1813–1825) and Elizabeth (1815–1825). Their parents were Cornishwoman Maria Branwell and the Reverend Patrick Brontë, an Anglican clergyman born in northern Ireland and educated in England. In 1820, soon after Anne was born, the Reverend Brontë became curate of Haworth, a Yorkshire village northwest of Thornton where most of the children, including Charlotte, Emily, and Anne, were born. The parsonage, surrounded by the stark beauty of the moors, remained home for the entire family for the rest of their lives. The children's lives were destined to be turbulent and short.

Maria, the mother, died in 1821 when the children were still small. Maria's sister Elizabeth Branwell took over the raising of the children, enforcing a stern Calvinist view of life, while a servant, Tabitha Aykroyd, exerted a counter-influence with her rich knowledge of folklore. Reverend Brontë's library of great Western works, the contemporary writings of Lord Byron and Sir Walter Scott, periodicals such as *Blackwood's Edinburgh Magazine,* and the fantastic tales of *The Arabian Nights' Entertainments* afforded other sources for the daughters' literary development. The children wrote adventure stories set in imaginary countries—Charlotte and Branwell in a land called Angria, Emily and Anne in Gondal.

As sheltered as was the world within the parsonage, so harsh was the world the children encountered outside. Beginning in 1824, Maria, Elizabeth, Charlotte, and Emily were all enrolled at the Clergy Daughters' School at Cowan Bridge. Their severe treatment there, fictionalized in the description of Lowood in Charlotte's novel *JANE EYRE,* led to the deaths in 1825 of Maria and Elizabeth, which left Charlotte the eldest daughter. Reverend Brontë removed his surviving daughters from the school; they received further education at Miss Wooler's School at Roe Head.

As they matured, the young women served as governesses, and Charlotte and Emily made plans, never realized, to open a school. Charlotte and Emily traveled to Brussels in 1842 to study foreign languages at a school run by M. and Mme. Constantin Heger; Charlotte returned to teach there from 1843 to 1844, but she conceived an unfulfilled passion for her employer that made the period an unhappy one, an experience reflected in *Jane Eyre.*

Back home at Haworth in 1844, Charlotte found more unhappiness. Her aunt Elizabeth had died, her father was going blind, and her brother Branwell, a failed portrait painter, was succumbing to opium and alcohol addiction. Writing poetry relieved the melancholy, and in 1845 she discovered that her sisters were also writing poems. Using pseudonyms that sounded vaguely masculine so as to avoid being belittled as women writers, Charlotte, Emily, and Anne jointly published a volume of poetry called *Poems by Currer, Ellis, and Acton Bell* (1846). The next year, urged on by Charlotte, the sisters each followed with a published novel. Charlotte's was *Jane Eyre,* Emily's *WUTHERING HEIGHTS,* and Anne's *Agnes Grey.* Of the three, only Charlotte's was a popular success, though it raised controversy for its Gothic violence and its portrayal of an independent-minded woman facing limited opportunities. Like Emily's *Wuthering Heights,* it remains a widely read and much studied Victorian classic.

In 1848 the sisters revealed their true identities to the public, and Charlotte followed with two more realistic novels. *Shirley* (1849), set at the time of the Luddite Riots (1811–12) honored her sisters in the characters of Shirley Keeldar and Caroline Helstone. *Villette* (1853), based on her experience in Brussels, is considered by many critics to be her masterpiece. In it she reworked material treated in her first novel, *The Professor,* which had been rejected by publishers when completed in 1846 but was published posthumously in 1857.

At the end of 1848, the Haworth parsonage was devastated by two deaths, that of Branwell in September and Emily in December. Anne died the following year. Charlotte was left alone to care for her increasingly needy father, though she managed to continue writing and to make the acquaintance of other literary figures. Among her acquaintances were WILLIAM MAKEPEACE THACKERAY, GEORGE HENRY LEWES, the Brontës' publisher George Smith, HARRIET MARTINEAU, and ELIZABETH GASKELL, who became her first biographer.

In 1854, in a match long opposed by her father, she married the Reverend Arthur Nicholls, his curate; all three of them lived together at the parsonage. The happy marriage ended the following year with Charlotte's death in March 1855, just weeks before her thirty-ninth birthday.

Brontë, Emily [Jane] (1818–1848) English novelist. Younger sister of CHARLOTTE BRONTË (*q.v.* for family history) and older sister of ANNE BRONTË, she shared with them a brief, reclusive, bookish life on the Yorkshire moors and contributed with them to *Poems by Currer, Ellis, and Acton Bell* (1846), their first publication. Continuing to use the pseudonym Ellis Bell, she published her only novel, *WUTHERING HEIGHTS,* in 1847. Though not a commercial success, the novel has since gained critical and popular acclaim for its narrative innovations, romantic power, and unusual blend of Gothic elements with regional detail and social commentary. Brontë's poems, influenced by Lord Byron and Sir Walter Scott, and steeped in the lore and landscape of her native region, have also gained an audience. Emily Brontë died of tuberculosis on December 19, 1848, three months after the death of her brother Branwell and less than a year before Anne. Introducing the 1850 second edition of *Wuthering Heights,* Charlotte wrote, "In Emily's nature the extremes of vigour and simplicity seemed to meet. Under an unsophisticated culture, inartificial tastes, and an unpretending outside, lay a secret power and fire that might have informed the brain and kindled the veins of a hero."

Brook Farm Utopian community. The communal farm was founded in 1841 in West Roxbury, Massachusetts, by transcendentalist George Ripley (1802–1880). Its residents and visitors included NATHANIEL HAWTHORNE and MARGARET FULLER. In 1844, it adopted the ideas of French social philosopher Charles Fourier (1772–1837). A fire in 1846 hastened Brook Farm's closing in 1847.

Brooklyn Bridge Suspended structure. Known in its day as the world's longest suspension bridge, the steel and wire link that measures 1,595½ feet, between Manhattan and Brooklyn over the East River, was opened to pedestrians on May 24, 1883. Known formally as the Great East River Bridge, it was designed by American engineer John Augustus Roebling (1806–1869), who died during the bridge's construction, and completed by son Washington Augustus Roebling (1837–1926) over the course of four years.

Broughton, Rhoda (1840–1920) English novelist. The daughter of a parson, she came from an old gentry lineage and was the niece of SHERIDAN LE FANU, who published her first novels in *Dublin University Magazine*. She was considered daring and somewhat improper for her wit and for the boldness and passion of her heroines. Beginning with her novels *Cometh Up as a Flower* and *Not Wisely but Too Well* (both 1867), she enjoyed popular success in the three-volume form until the 1890s when she turned to one-volume satirical novels such as *Mrs. Bligh* (1892) and *Dear Faustina* (1897).

Brown, Ford Madox (1821–1893) English painter. Born in France, he studied in Antwerp, Paris, and Rome before settling in London. DANTE GABRIEL ROSSETTI, who became Brown's pupil in 1848, introduced him to the PRE-RAPHAELITES, who had a profound effect on his work. Brown himself never actually joined the Pre-Raphaelites but, as a proponent of REALISM, agreed with their lofty goals to produce art that was morally empowering and truthful to observed facts.

Brown expressed his concerns about portraying real people in real living conditions in the large and ambitious painting entitled *Work,* completed in 1865 after more than a dozen years of labor. The urge to reform contemporary society attracted him to the thinking of WILLIAM MORRIS, with whom he became a partner in the manufacturing and decorating firm of Morris, Marshall, Faulkner and Company. Brown's painting *The Last of England* (1852–55) also reflects his concerns by the dramatization of conditions that drive a group of emigrants to leave England. Despite his social intent, Brown also acted as a precursor to IMPRESSIONISM in his attempts to render the brilliant summer sunlight he observed outdoors.

Brown, John (1800–1859) American abolitionist. Born in Connecticut and raised in rural Ohio, he was persuaded by a religious experience in 1850 to join the UNDERGROUND RAILROAD. In 1855 he joined the antislavery forces in the Kansas territory who were fighting proslavery settlers over whether the territory would be a free or slave state. By this time Brown, whose family had a long history of insanity, believed himself divinely appointed to end SLAVERY. During one military action Brown oversaw the murder of five southern sympathizers. The murders and his work on the underground railroad made him a national figure. He began envisioning a slave uprising, and in October 1859 he and twenty-one others captured the federal arsenal at Harpers Ferry, Virginia. Brown planned to establish a base for a slave insurrection, but the raid was quelled by marines led by Colonel ROBERT E. LEE. Ten of his followers, including two of his sons, died in the battle. Refusing to plead insanity at his trial, he was hanged for treason.

Browne, Hablot Knight (1815–1882) English illustrator. After an apprenticeship at Finden's, steel engravers, he concentrated on the freer methods of etching, wood engraving, drawing, and painting. In 1836 at the age of twenty he was chosen to illustrate *The Pickwick Papers* by CHARLES DICKENS. He became well known as "Phiz," a pseudonym chosen to go with Dickens's "Boz." In addition to his frequent work with Dickens, he illustrated periodicals and books by WILLIAM HARRISON AINSWORTH and others. His skillful characterizations and pleasing compositions made him a top illustrator until he suffered a stroke in 1867. After 1878 he was supported by an annuity from the Royal Academy.

Browning, Elizabeth Barrett (1806–1861) English poet. Raised on a country estate of Hope End near Malvern, the eldest of twelve children, she was educated by her governess while also taking part in her brother's lessons in Latin and Greek. After a nearly mortal illness at the age of fifteen, she turned to poetry, publishing her first volume, *The Battle of Marathon,* in 1820. She published several other volumes, including *The Seraphim and Other Poems* (1838), and suffered more bouts with illness and the deaths of two brothers before winning broader critical praise and an enthusiastic following with *Poems* (1844). Her admirers included ROBERT BROWNING, six years her junior, who initiated a correspondence with her that culminated in their meeting in 1843. To elude the opposition of her possessive father, the couple married secretly and moved to Italy in 1846. Their romantic union is celebrated in her sonnet sequence *Sonnets from the Portuguese* (1850), which includes the lyric that begins "How do I love thee? Let me count the ways" (Sonnet 43). After the publication of her long verse novel *Aurora Leigh* (1856), which dealt with the struggle of a female artist for literary independence, her reputation as the most important female poet in English was secure. Chronically ill, pale and ethereal in appearance, she died at Casa Guidi in Florence and was buried in the city's Protestant Cemetery.

Browning's chief achievement lay in her evocation of place, particularly her beloved Italy, and in her expansion of Victorian poem forms. Echoes of her work may be found in the later poems of ALFRED, Lord TENNYSON, the novels of GEORGE ELIOT, and in EMILY DICKINSON's verse. Her proto-feminist preoccupations influenced subsequent generations of female artists.

Browning, Robert (1812–1889) English poet. He and the poet ELIZABETH BARRETT BROWNING, after an ardent epistolary courtship, inaugurated one of the most celebrated marriages in English letters. Born in London, the son of a clerk in the Bank of England, Browning was largely educated at home, with the exception of a year studying Greek at University College, London. He took as an early model Percy Shelley, whose life briefly inspired Browning to become an atheist. Browning's first work was the anonymously published *Pauline: A Fragment of a Confession* (1833), which received scant critical notice but drew the attention of JOHN STUART MILL, who declared that the poet demonstrated a "more intense and morbid self-consciousness than I ever knew in any sane human being."

In the 1840s, Browning published his poems in the pamphlet series entitled *Bells and Pomegranates* (1841–46), which contained some of his best known work: the dramatic poem *Pippa Passes* and the dramatic monologues "Porphyria's Lover," "Johannes Agricola," "My Last Duchess," "Soliloquy of the Spanish Cloister," "The Bishop Orders His Tomb in St. Praxed's Church," and "How They Brought the Good News from Ghent to Aix."

Browning married Elizabeth Barrett secretly and moved with her to Italy in 1846, where the couple established their residence in Florence. Their son Robert Barrett was born in 1849. In 1850, Browning published the long poem *Christmas Eve and Easter Day*. His volume of verse, *Men and Women* (1855), garnered hostile notices but included such important poems as "Fra Lippo Lippi," "Childe Roland to the Dark Tower Came," "Bishop Blougram's Apology," and "Andrea Del Sarto." After his wife's death in 1861, Browning returned to England where he settled with his son, a painter.

Commercially unsuccessful for years, Browning finally achieved popularity with his long poem, *The Ring and the Book* (1868–69), published in serial form and based on a seventeenth-century Roman murder case. He published many works in his later years, including *Aristophanes' Apology* (1875), *The Inn Album* (1875), *Dramatic Idyls* (1875, 1880), a translation of Aeschylus' *Agamemnon* (1877), and *Asolando: Fancies and Facts* (1889). His late-won fame and critical reputation were reflected in the founding of the Browning Society in 1881. Browning died in Venice and was buried at Westminster Abbey.

Drawn to themes both prosaic and violent, Browning had a gift for lyric narrative as well as for love poetry of great sensuality. Having helped to free Victorian verse of its overly sophisticated polish, Browning alone among Victorian poets exercised considerable influence over such twentieth-century figures as T. S. Eliot and Ezra Pound.

Bruckner, [Joseph] Anton (1824–1896) Austrian organist, teacher, and composer of orchestral and vocal works. He taught and played the organ at St. Florian Abbey (1845–55) and was the organist at the cathedral in Linz (1855–68) before becoming a professor of harmony and counterpoint at the Vienna Conservatory in 1868. His symphonic works, strongly influenced by RICHARD WAGNER, were frequently revised as an outcome of his friend's criticisms, resulting in multiple versions of each piece. Bruckner wrote nine symphonies, a large body of sacred choral works, including a *Requiem,* a *Te Deum,* several Mass settings, and many motets.

Brunel, Isambard Kingdom (1806–1859) English engineer. Born in Portsmouth, England, he was the only son of Sir Marc Isambard Brunel (1769–1849), inventor of the tunneling shield (1818) and builder of the Thames tunnel (1825–43), the world's first underwater tunnel.

Brunel completed his education at the Collège Henri Quatre in Paris at the age of seventeen and joined his father on the construction of the Thames tunnel. He soon began building docks and bridges, and became chief engineer for the Great Western Railway in 1833. Besides building more than one thousand miles of railway, Brunel also designed the terminal stations at Paddington and Temple Meads, as well as the railway bridge at Chepstow (1852).

GREAT WESTERN (1837) was the first steamship designed to cross the Atlantic, and Brunel followed that success in 1843 with the construction of *GREAT BRITAIN,* the first large screw-driven vessel. *GREAT EASTERN* (1858) was not surpassed in size for nearly four decades, but a stroke in 1859 that led to Brunel's death prevented the engineer from seeing the ship's maiden voyage and its eventual fame when it helped place the first successful transatlantic cable.

Bryan, William Jennings (1860–1925) American lawyer and politician. He was an orator, defender of religious fundamentalism, and three-time presidential candidate. Born in Illinois, he served as congressman from Nebraska (1890–94) and was a leading advocate for the free coinage of silver as a way of relieving farmers' debts. His "Cross of Gold" speech at the 1896 DEMOCRATIC PARTY convention, in which he condemned Republicans and conservative Democrats for supporting the gold standard, brought him the presidential nomination. Bryan, who was also the standard-bearer of the Populist Party, lost to Republican WILLIAM MCKINLEY. He faced McKinley again in 1900 in an unsuccessful campaign marked by Bryan's opposition to the annexation of the Philippines, a spoil from the SPANISH-AMERICAN WAR, and IMPERIALISM in general. Bryan also lost to William Howard Taft in 1908.

Despite these losses, Bryan retained his power within the Democratic Party. He devoted his later years to defending prohibition and religious fundamentalism. In 1925 the "Great Commoner" helped prosecute John Scopes for breaking a Tennessee law against teaching EVOLUTION in the schools. The trial was highlighted by Bryan's duels with defense attorney CLARENCE DARROW over literal interpretations of the Bible. Exhausted from the trial, Bryan suffered a fatal heart attack a week after it ended.

Bryant, William Cullen (1794–1878) American poet, editor, and humanitarian. Born in Cummington, Massachusetts, he wrote his first books of poetry (*The Embargo,* 1808, *The Embargo and Other Poems,* 1809) while still a youth. After attending Williams College for a year, then becoming a lawyer working in Great Barrington, Massachusetts, he returned to the literary life, publishing "Thanatopsis" in *The North American Review* in 1817. A melding of European romantic and New England sensibilities, the poem established his talent. The collection *Poems* followed in 1821. In 1825 he moved to New York where he became editor and co-owner of the *New York Evening Post* and over the next five decades promoted liberal causes such as free speech, free trade, and the abolition of SLAVERY. In the mid-1850s he became active in the founding of the REPUBLICAN PARTY. Publishing widely throughout this time such poems as "A Forest Hymn" (1832) and "The Prairies" (1834), he contributed to the position of the Knickerbocker School as a force in American letters, and of the American writer in general. Collections include *The Fountain, and Other Poems* (1842) and *The White-Footed Doe* (1844). His final collection is *The Poetical Works of William Cullen Bryant* (1876). His blank verse translations of *The Iliad* (1870) and *The Odyssey* (1871–72) were critically well received. He died shortly after speaking at the opening of the Statue of Liberty.

Bryce, James, 1st Viscount (1838–1922) English barrister, politician, and historian. Bryce served as Regius Professor of Civil Law at Oxford from 1870 to 1893 and entered politics in 1880. After Queen VICTORIA's reign he served as chief secretary for Ireland (1905–6) and ambassador to Washington (1907–13). His works include *The Holy Roman Empire* (1864), *The American Commonwealth* (1880, rev. 1920), and *Studies in History and Jurisprudence* (1901). His *Impressions of South Africa* (1897) describes that country just prior to the BOER WAR.

Buchanan, James (1792–1868) Fifteenth president of the UNITED STATES (1857–61). Born near Mercersburg, Pennsylvania, he graduated from Dickinson College in 1809 and was admitted to the Pennsylvania bar in 1812. He served five terms in the House of Representatives (1821–31) and then was appointed minister to Russia (1832–33). Elected to the Senate in 1834, he served eleven years there before President JAMES POLK appointed him Secretary of State. While secretary he supported the annexation of Texas and the MEXICAN WAR. This pro-expansionist, pro-southern perspective was also displayed in his authorship of the secret Ostend Manifesto, which called for invading Cuba if Spain refused to sell it to the United States. The document was made public, enraging many northerners who opposed acquisition of territories that would later become slave states.

The Democrat was elected president in 1856. He lobbied for the proslavery constitution of the Kansas Territory, a decision that further divided Democrats over SLAVERY. As his term neared its end, seven southern states left the Union in reaction to the election of ABRAHAM LINCOLN, but Buchanan took no action to stop them. He retired to obscurity after Lincoln's inauguration.

Buckingham Palace Royal domicile. The London residence of British monarchs since 1837, beginning with Queen VICTORIA, was built in the City of Westminster in 1703 by the Duke of Buckingham and acquired for the royal family by King George III in 1761. The palace was remodeled by architect John Nash in 1825.

Buckland, William (1784–1856) English clergyman and geologist. A minister's son, he graduated from Corpus Christi College, Oxford, in 1804 and received holy orders in 1809. While a student he showed an interest in chemistry, mineralogy, and the new science of geology. His interest led to a scientific career that paralleled his ecclesiastical one in vigor and accomplishment. Appointed reader in mineralogy at Oxford in 1813, Buckland became the first to hold an endowed position in geology at Oxford just six years later. In 1818 he was elected to the Royal Society, and in 1824 became president of the Geological Society of London. He was dean of Westminster from 1845 to his death.

Far from seeing a conflict between religion and science, Buckland believed that geological findings supported Christian belief. In 1823, Buckland published *Reliquiae Diluvianae,* in which he posited the view that fossils attested to a "universal deluge" as described in the Bible. His *Geology and Mineralogy* (1836) was a widely read work that showed how God's "power, wisdom, and goodness" were "manifested in the Creation."

Buckland published scientific papers on a range of subjects: quartz, the structure of the Alps, the geology of Britain, the remains of Pleistocene mammals in England. In 1824 he wrote the original description of Megalosaurus, a Cretaceous DINOSAUR found in Stonesfield, England, and the first dinosaur to be described—Buckland believed it to be an extinct giant "lizard," the term "dinosaur" having not yet been invented. He was an early supporter of LOUIS AGASSIZ's idea that ice ages had taken place during the Pleistocene Epoch.

A much acclaimed man of science and religion, Buckland was also a genuine eccentric. In his house was a menagerie of animals, including guinea pigs, a jackal, and a young bear named Tiglath Pileser who sometimes rode on horseback with his master and enjoyed stealing sweets from the village grocer.

Buffalo Bill See CODY, WILLIAM FREDERICK.

Bulgaria Country in southeast Europe. It bordered on ROMANIA, SERBIA, and the OTTOMAN EMPIRE. At the beginning of the Victorian era, Bulgaria was part of the Ottoman Empire and was more heavily taxed and restricted than any other region in the BALKANS. In 1876 a revolt broke out. Irregular Ottoman troops began a brutal campaign of repression that was reported in the British press, prompting WILLIAM GLADSTONE to compose a popular anti-Turkish pamphlet on the "Bulgarian horrors."

Hoping to dominate the country, RUSSIA intervened in the RUSSO-TURKISH WAR (1877–78) and secured Bulgarian independence in 1878. Prince Alexander of Battenberg was chosen as king, and a liberal constitution was adopted. In 1885, Eastern Rumelia, a predominantly Bulgarian region to the south, rebelled against the Ottoman Empire and joined Bulgaria, despite Serbian attacks and Russian objectives. In 1886 a pro-Russian coup forced Alexander to abdicate, but the Bulgarians chose Ferdinand of Coburg as their new king and continued to resist Russian dominance.

After independence, Bulgarian education and infrastructure developed rapidly, but Bulgarian IRREDENTISM led the country into wars that ultimately proved costly.

Bulwer-Lytton, Edward George Earle, 1st Baron Lytton of Knebworth (1803–1873) English writer and statesman. Born in London as Edward Bulwer, he was the son of General William Bulwer and Elizabeth Barbara Lytton Bulwer. After studying at Trinity College in Cambridge, he married Rosina Doyle Wheeler, who was from an impoverished Irish family. The marriage went against his mother's wishes, and for his defiance, Bulwer lost the substantial allowance his mother had provided. Despite this, the couple lived extravagantly, and in order to maintain this way of life, Bulwer began writing. From 1827 to 1837 he published eleven novels, a survey of English culture, a history of Athens, and numerous articles, stories, essays, and poems. Bulwer also worked as editor of the *New Monthly* magazine from 1831 to 1833. His prodigious output placed a strain on the marriage, however, and the couple legally separated in 1836. His wife wrote an unflattering caricature of Bulwer in a novel published in 1839, *Cheveley,* before being declared insane.

Bulwer then produced three plays—*The Lady of Lyons* (1838), *Richelieu* (1839), and *Money* (1840)—that were popular successes. In 1851, the writer collaborated with CHARLES DICKENS in writing and producing performances for the stage.

Bulwer added the hyphenated "Lytton" to his name after inheriting his mother's estate at Knebworth, Hertfordshire in 1843. While he remained busy writing, Bulwer-Lytton also served in Parliament, from 1831 to 1841, and again from 1851 until 1866.

Bulwer-Lytton was a popular and innovative writer; his works include twelve volumes of poetry, translations, plays, and-more than twenty novels. *Paul Clifford* (1830) and *Eugene Aram* (1832) both depicted criminals in British society and influenced Dickens's novels on the same subject (see NEWGATE NOVEL). Bulwer-Lytton is also responsible for immortalizing the line "It was a dark and stormy night," which opens *Paul Clifford. Zanoni* (1842) and *A Strange Story* (1862) popularized the novel of the occult, and *The Coming Race* (1871) exemplified the utopian novel. Bulwer-Lytton's greatest success was *The Last Days of Pompeii* (1834), a historical fiction that vividly depicts the destruction of Pompeii in A.D. 79 by Mount Vesuvius.

Buntline, Ned (1823–1886) Pseudonym of American author Edward Zane Carroll Judson. Born in Stamford, New York, Buntline was an adventurer prone to drinking and fighting. He wrote more than four hundred action novels, many of them DIME NOVELS for the firm of Beadle and Adams, and he founded the sensational magazine *Ned Buntline's Own* in 1845. While traveling in the West, he became acquainted with scout WILLIAM F. CODY, whom Buntline turned into a dime novel hero under the name he reputedly coined, Buffalo Bill.

burlesque See VAUDEVILLE.

Burma See SOUTHEAST ASIA.

Burne-Jones, Sir Edward Coley (1833–1898) English painter. Born in Birmingham, he studied at Exeter College, Oxford, where he met WILLIAM MORRIS, with whom he shared an interest in medieval legends and the artistic theories of JOHN RUSKIN. In 1856, Burne-Jones met DANTE GABRIEL ROSSETTI, who had impressed him with his illustrations for William Allingham's *The Music Master and Other Poems*. Burne-Jones left Oxford without graduating and settled in London with Morris; together they studied under Rossetti. In 1857, Burne-Jones worked under Rossetti's guidance on a number of frescoes for the debating hall at Oxford.

Burne-Jones then accompanied Ruskin on a trip to Venice in 1862, where he was greatly impressed by the fifteenth-century Italian artists. He began exhibiting with the Royal Watercolor Society in 1864 but gradually abandoned the medium in favor of oils. Eight of his oil paintings were exhibited in 1877 at the opening of the Grosvenor Gallery in London.

Burne-Jones also had a reputation as a fine designer of stained glass, including the windows at Christ Church, Oxford, and the Cathedral of Birmingham. He also designed mosaic decorations for the American Church in Rome and illustrated a number of books, including the 1897 edition of the *Works of Geoffrey Chaucer*.

Burne-Jones received a baronetcy in 1894.

Burnett, Frances Eliza Hodgson (1849–1924) English-born American author. She and her family went to America in 1865 and settled near Knoxville, Tennessee. Burnett was the author of several plays and of novels such as *Haworth's* (1879) and *Through One Administration* (1883). She is best remembered, however, for her children's books, particularly *Little Lord Fauntleroy* (1886), which used her youngest son as a model. Her other memorable stories for children are *Sara Crewe* (1888), *Little Saint Elizabeth* (1890), and *The Secret Garden* (1911). In 1898 she divorced Dr. Swan M. Burnett and in 1900 married Dr. Stephen Townsend, retaining her former husband's name for professional use. Her other writings include *Louisiana* (1880), *A Lady of Quality* (1896), and her autobiography, *The One I Knew Best of All* (1893).

Burton, Sir Richard Francis (1821–1890) British diplomat, traveler, and Orientalist. Born at Torquay, he spent his childhood traveling through France and Italy. At Trinity College, Oxford, he studied Arabic but left without graduating after his eccentric behavior was found irksome—he once challenged a fellow student to a duel when the man made unkind comments about his mustache. Self-educated in an exceptionally thorough way—he was said to have mastered thirty-five languages as well as numerous dialects—Burton joined the Indian army in 1842. As a subaltern in the Bombay Native Infantry, he worked in London and then was sent to India, where he assisted in the survey of the western province of Sind. Often appearing in disguise and passing as a native, he wrote government reports and later published four books on India. From 1869 until 1871 he served as a consul at Damascus.

Burton's greatest fame, however, arose from his daring travel expeditions, beginning with his 1853 pilgrimage to the sacred city of Mecca, forbidden to non-Muslims. Burton entered the city disguised as a Pathan from northern India, a feat he accomplished by relying on his familiarity with Eastern customs. Spurred on by increasing fame in

Britain, the subsequent year Burton explored the Somali Desert in what proved to be an extremely arduous journey. In February 1858, sponsored by the British Foreign Office, he and JOHN SPEKE embarked on a search for the source of the Nile. They discovered Lake Tanganyika. Three years later Burton explored West Africa. Returning to the Foreign Office in 1861 as a consul, Burton was the translator of several books, the most famous of which were *The Kama Sutra* (1883) and *The Arabian Nights* (1885–88).

Burundi See GERMAN EAST AFRICA.

Bushmen European term for the San, the indigenous hunting-and-gathering people of southern AFRICA. They and the pastoral HOTTENTOTS, or Khoikhoi, another indigenous people speaking a similar Khoisan language, were decimated in clashes with the BOERS, the Dutch settlers of South Africa, beginning in the seventeenth century. Victorian British colonists in South Africa carried on the racist tradition against them. Some groups of Bushmen have continued to live as hunter-gatherers in the Kalahari Desert in recent times.

bustle Woman's undergarment designed to give bell-like fullness to the back of a skirt, the bustle was highly fashionable in the 1870s and afterward. It evolved from the CRINOLINE and was originally constructed of steel spring hoops. Later designs engineered it from a compressed pad of material.

An advertisement promotes the "evolution" of the bustle. Photo courtesy of Topham/Image Works.

Butler, Josephine Grey (1828–1906) Social reformer and advocate for women's rights. She was born to a politically powerful family that included her cousin, Charles Grey, prime minister from 1830 to 1834. In 1850 she married George Butler, an academic and clergyman who embraced the principles of Christian Socialism. Her career as a social reformer began in the 1860s when she moved to Liverpool because her husband had been appointed headmaster of Liverpool College. There she was shocked at the number of women who became prostitutes to avoid the degrading and exhausting labor at the local workhouses. She befriended prostitutes and scandalized her neighbors by inviting some of them into her home.

Butler's charity work inspired her to lead the fight against the Contagious Disease Acts in the 1860s. Aimed at controlling venereal disease among the armed forces, the laws subjected women to arbitrary arrest and degrading medical exams. Butler's lobbying and public agitation led to the repeal of the acts in 1886.

Butler was also a leading figure in the fight against child prostitution. Her struggles, aided by sensational press coverage of England's sexual slave trade, led to stiffer penalties for child abuse and a rise in the age of consent from twelve to sixteen.

Butler, Samuel (1835–1902) English writer. The son of a clergyman, he was born in Langar, Nottinghamshire, and educated at Shrewsbury School, where his grandfather, Bishop Samuel Butler, had served as headmaster. Upon his graduation from St. John's College, Cambridge, in 1858, with the urging of his father, Butler prepared for ordination but soon became convinced that he was not interested in following the family religious tradition. After a severe altercation with his father, Butler immigrated to New Zealand and bought a sheep run.

While in New Zealand, Butler read *THE ORIGIN OF SPECIES* by CHARLES DARWIN, which immediately influenced his thinking in a profound way. Butler wrote a number of articles for local newspapers based on Darwin's ideas; in 1864 he sold the sheep run at a substantial profit and returned to England.

Butler studied painting for a few years and exhibited occasionally at the Royal Academy until 1876. "Mr. Heatherley's Holiday" (1874) is now owned by the Tate Gallery in London. Butler also continued to write, and in 1872 published *EREWHON*—an anagram of *nowhere*—a satirical comment on contemporary England in the guise of an imagined land. The work was popular and proved to be the only writing from which Butler ever received a profit. His bitter commentary on religion further distanced him from his family. Butler turned his caustic pen on Darwin, producing a series of works in which he disagreed with Darwin's theory of natural selection. In works such as *Life and Habit* (1877), *Evolution, Old and New* (1879), and *Unconscious Memory* (1880), Butler proposed that hereditary characteristics were the result of unconscious memory of past habits, and while he meant his theories on the evolutionary process to be taken seriously, they were generally ignored by contemporary scientists.

Butler had better success with his literary criticism, including the satirical *The Authoress of the Odyssey* (1897) in which he argued that the epic poem was written by a woman because no man could be so ignorant of seafaring and so knowledgeable of household duties. Butler's acclaimed satirical masterpiece, the bitter autobiographical novel *The Way of All Flesh,* was written between 1873 and 1885 but was not published until 1903, after his death.

Butt, Isaac (1813–1879) Irish politician. He was the founder of the Irish Home Rule League and an early leader of the HOME RULE movement. Butt, a Protestant lawyer and accomplished scholar, was educated at Trinity College, Dublin. He originally opposed DANIEL O'CONNELL's efforts during the 1840s to establish an independent Irish Parliament to control Irish internal affairs. However, the British Parliament's inadequate relief efforts during the IRISH POTATO FAMINE of 1845 convinced him that only an Irish legislature could address the inequities of Irish landlord-tenant relations.

Butt defended leaders of the failed 1848 uprising against English rule, as he would later defend many FENIANS after the Fenian Rebellion of 1867. He was a member of Parliament from 1852 to 1865. In 1871 he was reelected to Parliament on a platform of separate parliaments to control the domestic affairs of

England, Ireland, and Scotland. He established the Irish Home Rule League in 1874. That year 59 members of the league were elected to Parliament out of a total of 103 members.

Electoral success did not ensure policy changes. On June 30 the House of Commons considered the first Home Rule motion, but only ten English members joined fifty-one Irish members in voting for the proposal. This parliamentary dead-end and Butt's lack of alternative strategies doomed his leadership.

His control of the Home Rule representatives eroded quickly with the election of CHARLES STEWART PARNELL to Parliament. Parnell and a small band of members began using dilatory tactics—filibustering, useless calls for votes—to slow down government business. Butt deplored this strategy and also objected to Parnell's talks with violent factions of the Irish nationalist movement. Despite his objections, Butt's power waned while Parnell's influence grew. Butt remained nominal head of the Home Rule members until his death in 1879, but by then Parnell was the actual leader of the movement.

Butt's scholarly accomplishments include *History of Italy* (1860).

Byron, Augusta Ada, Countess of Lovelace See LOVELACE, AUGUSTA ADA BYRON, COUNTESS OF.

cab A light two-wheeled carriage for hire. Introduced to England from France in the late 1820s, it largely displaced the four-wheeled hackney coach as a vehicle for hire. The name is an abbreviation of the French *cabriolet*. In the 1830s, the HANSOM CAB improved on the original cab design by placing the driver high up in the back while passengers sat in front with a clear view of the road ahead.

cable Communications equipment. The invention of the TELEGRAPH in the late 1830s led to the idea of telegraph cables strung underwater to connect distant lands. By 1848, Ernest Werner von Siemens of Germany had developed a suitable insulation for undersea cables. Two years later the first submarine telegraph cable was laid, connecting Dover and Calais. The cable failed, but a second cable was established in 1851 and remained in use for the next twenty-five years.

American businessman CYRUS WEST FIELD organized an attempt to establish a transatlantic cable in 1857. A year later the enterprise achieved success with a cable connecting Valentia, Ireland, to Heart's Content, Newfoundland. The cable remained in operation from August 5 to September 1, and during this time Queen Victoria sent a message to President James Buchanan. The cable failed, however, and Field went back to work organizing another attempt. Finally, in 1866, the first truly successful transatlantic cable, spanning 1,852 nautical miles, was in operation, and Queen Victoria was able to wire a message to President Andrew Johnson. By 1902 twelve cables crossed the Atlantic, and a few spanned the Pacific, including one stretching from Vancouver Island to Brisbane, Australia.

The success of submarine telegraph cables quickly led to the development of underwater TELEPHONE lines, the earliest of which was laid by the Danish government in 1902, though it covered only short distances. The first transatlantic telephone cable system was not established until 1956.

American inventor THOMAS EDISON demonstrated the utility of underground ELECTRIC POWER cables in 1880, which led to the establishment of the first commercial alternating current, AC, service in 1886 in Buffalo, New York. Though Edison favored the safer, lower-voltage DC, or direct current, system, Sebastian de Ferranti in England showed that high-voltage AC systems were more effective over large distances. By 1899, London had more than ninety miles of his paper-insulated cable in use.

Cadbury, George (1839–1922) English industrialist and reformer. He worked for his father's cocoa and chocolate firm, Cadbury Brothers, beginning in 1856 and managed it with his brother Richard from 1861 to 1899. He served as chairman from 1899 until his death. Alert to the needs of Victorian industrial workers, he promoted better housing, education, and welfare for employees. The workers' town he founded at Bournville was deeded in 1900 to the Bournville Village Trust.

cakewalk American dance. Its movements involved a series of intricate backward-prancing, tilting steps. It originated during the Civil War as a form of black entertainment in which a cake was awarded to the performer displaying the most complicated movements. Adapted for U.S. MINSTREL SHOWS by impresarios Harrigan and Hart, the cakewalk debuted in 1877 with the stage number "Walking for Dat Cake" and became a national craze.

Caldecott, Randolph (1846–1886) English illustrator and painter. He was educated at King Henry VIII's School at Chester and in 1872 went to London. In 1882 he became a member of the Royal Institute of Painters in Water Colors, exhibiting at the Royal Academy and at the Grosvenor Gallery. He is famous for his drawings of contemporary English country life and for his charming and

Randolph Caldecott's "A Frog He Would A-Wooing Go" demonstrates the illustrator's endearing and comical style. Photo courtesy of the Library of Congress, Rare Book and Special Collection Division.

humorous illustrations, including those for Washington Irving's *Old Christmas* and *Bracebridge Hall,* Blackburn's *Breton Folk,* and *Some of Aesop's Fables with Modern Instances.* His illustrations for a series of sixteen children's books, were among the first to make use of color wood engravings; they included *John Gilpin* and *The Grand Panjandrum Himself.* Since 1938, the Caldecott Award, named after the illustrator, has been given annually to the best illustrated children's book.

Calhoun, John (1782–1850) American politician and political thinker. Calhoun grew up on his father's plantation in South Carolina and attended Yale. He won a seat in the state legislature in 1808, and in 1810 he was elected to Congress, where he served until 1817.

In his younger days the future advocate of states' rights was a fervent nationalist. He supported higher tariffs, federal expenditures on roads, a larger army, and a national bank. He joined the other "War Hawks" in pushing the UNITED STATES into the War of 1812 against Great Britain. He was Secretary of War under President James Monroe, from 1817 to 1825. He was twice elected vice president, under JOHN QUINCY ADAMS from 1824 to 1829 and under Andrew Jackson from 1829 to 1832.

By the late 1820s Calhoun had changed his views on the issue of tariffs. These import taxes imposed duties on manufactured goods coming into the country in order to protect mostly northern manufacturers from foreign competition.

After bringing South Carolina to the brink of secession over the tariff issue, Calhoun resigned the vice presidency in December 1832 to accept a Senate seat from his state, a position he held until his death except for a year as Secretary of State (1844–45). As a senator he was the country's leading defender of states' rights and engaged DANIEL WEBSTER in debate about the nature of the union. He argued that SLAVERY was a positive good and claimed that slaves were better off than northern workers victimized by capitalism. He strongly supported the annexation of Texas and fought northern attempts to bar slavery from land acquired through the MEXICAN WAR.

Calhoun also proposed a dual presidency and Supreme Court for the north and south, with each region having an equal voice in developing, vetoing, and interpreting national laws. He hoped this theory of "concurrent majorities" would allay what he saw as the developing tyranny of a northern numerical majority. His major works on politics are *A Disquisition on Government* and *A Discourse on the Constitution and Government of the United States,* both published posthumously in 1851.

California Gold Rush Pursuit for minerals and riches. Gold had been mined in California as early as 1842; however, John Marshall's 1848 discovery of gold flakes at Sutter's Mill near San Francisco, soon after the U.S. acquisition of the territory following the MEXICAN WAR, touched off a huge rush of prospectors. California's population jumped from about fifteen thousand to over one hundred thousand by 1849, and San Francisco became a boom city. The prospectors, or "forty-niners," came from all over the world. Most of them came up empty and left or started other businesses. Disease and violence afflicted their hastily constructed miner camps. The boisterous settlements inspired BRET HARTE and MARK TWAIN, among others, to write about life during the rush.

Production peaked in 1852 with the extraction of more than $80 million worth of gold. By then California, which became a state in 1850, had a population of about 225,000. The rush was just about over by 1857, but limited amounts of gold continued to be mined after that.

calling card Identification for social purposes. Usually printed with one's name and carried in a silver case, the calling card was an important social marker for upper-class Victorians in Europe and America. When a lady visited an acquaintance, she routinely announced herself through a card that her servant delivered to the front door. The acquaintance could then choose to see the lady or return the call at a later time. In some cases—if the caller was a social climber straining to break into society, for example—the person called-upon might instruct her servant to say she was not at home. Calling-card etiquette had many fine points, including the expectation that calls would be made in the late afternoon, even though they were known as "morning calls." For those trying to rise in society, it was a mark of honor to display on one's mantelpiece the cards of distinguished guests.

The calling card was sometimes known by its French name, *carte de visite.* In the 1860s, cards known by this name sometimes featured photographic portraits of the caller, after French photographer André Adolphe-Eugène Disdéri discovered a method for making multiple-portait photographs on a single negative. These photographic *cartes de visite* became a fad, as the public avidly collected cards bearing photographs of famous people. See also FRANCIS FRITH.

cameo Jewelry. The cameo, a decorative brooch-sized sculpture, usually of semi-precious gems or shells, carved in relief and worn as women's jewelry, originated in Asia and was popular in ancient Greece and Rome. It experienced renewed popularity during the Victorian Age. Popular subjects for cameos included Greek and Roman scenes as well as current pastoral portraits, at times, of family members. Shell cameos are made by carving away parts of the shell's white exterior to expose its pink underside. The finest cameos then and now are cut finely enough to allow light to pass through.

Cameron, Julia Margaret (1815–1879) British photographer. Born in Calcutta, the daughter of a high official in the BRITISH EAST INDIA COMPANY, she married Charles Hay Cameron, who owned large tracts of land in Ceylon (now Sri Lanka). Upon his retirement they moved back to England where Julia Cameron befriended many artists and writers, including ALFRED, Lord TENNYSON. The friendship with Tennyson blossomed when the Camerons bought a cottage next to the poet's estate on the Isle of Wight in 1860.

The gift of a camera in 1863 initiated a burst of creative PHOTOGRAPHY by Cameron, prompting Bloomsbury artist Roger Fry to call her the finest artist of the Victorian era. Tennyson became one of her favorite subjects, and she trained her camera on many of his friends and colleagues. Her portraits captured the age's greatest figures: ANTHONY TROLLOPE, THOMAS CARLYLE, ROBERT BROWNING, HENRY WADSWORTH LONGFELLOW, CHARLES DARWIN, the actress ELLEN TERRY, and many others. She exhibited widely in Europe, and her plates adorned an edition of Tennyson's *Idylls of the King.* Her dark, brooding, and sometimes hazy photographs are thought to have influenced many artists of the period, including DANTE GABRIEL ROSSETTI.

In 1875 she and her husband returned to Ceylon to be near their sons, who were managing coffee plantations on their father's land. She continued to take pictures, but her most famous work was behind her. She died four years later.

Campbell, Mrs. Patrick (1865–1940) English actress. Born Beatrice Stella Tanner, she studied at the Guildhall School of Music before marrying Patrick Campbell in 1884. He left her with a son and daughter when he went off to seek fortune in South Africa, where he was killed during the Boer War. "Mrs. Pat," as she became known to her fans, made her stage debut in Liverpool in 1888. Talented, witty, and possessing a captivating beauty, she went on from her role as Paula in ARTHUR WING PINERO's *The Second Mrs. Tanqueray* (1893) to become one of the top actresses and drawing-room personalities of late Victorian and Edwardian times. She performed in plays by HENRIK IBSEN, Bjornson, MAURICE MAETERLINCK, and WILLIAM BUTLER YEATS; as a Shakespearean actress she played Juliet and Ophelia opposite male lead Forbes Robertson. In 1914 she played Eliza Doolittle in GEORGE BERNARD SHAW's *Pygmalion,* a role created for her, and she married George Cornwallis-West.

Canada Country comprising the northern portion of North America. The European population consists of French-speaking descendants of the original French colonists, English, Scots, and Irish as well as substantial eastern and southern European populations who began to arrive late in the Victorian era. The indigenous peoples, numerically much reduced after contact with Europeans, show a wide diversity of languages and cultures.

At the beginning of the Victorian era, Canada was governed directly by GREAT BRITAIN, as it had been since its acquisition from France in 1763 at the end of the Seven Years' War. It was divided into six provinces: Newfoundland, Nova Scotia, New Brunswick, Prince Edward Island (the Maritime provinces), Lower Canada (modern Quebec), and Upper Canada (modern Ontario). Most of western and northern Canada, still largely unexplored, was owned by the Hudson's Bay Company, a large fur-trading company. The provinces elected their own legislatures, but the crown-appointed governors had broad police and spending powers.

In 1837 rebellions broke out in Upper and Lower Canada. The rebels of Upper Canada were largely French Catholics who resented rule by a Protestant government. The Lower Canadians sought greater independence from Britain. Both rebellions were minor and easily put down. In response to the disturbances, Upper and Lower Canada were united in a single province—the United Province of Canada—in 1840. After 1848, British governors ceased to exercise their powers to intervene in the provincial legislatures, and Canadian provinces became nearly autonomous.

The 1850s were largely prosperous in Canada, as Irish immigrants fled there to escape the IRISH POTATO FAMINE, canals and railroads were built, and the country reaped the benefits of Britain's free trade policies. The United Province was split, however, by bitter ethnic disputes between French- and English-speaking Canadians. Other disputes about spending and railroad projects also seemed to require a central authority. In 1864 delegates met in Charlottetown, Prince Edward Island, to propose a plan for unifying all the provinces under one government. Though initially rejected by the Maritime Provinces, pressure from Britain eventually brought assent. In 1867, with the passing of the British North America Act, the dominion of Canada was declared. The United Province was divided into Ontario and Quebec. Canada gained a federal government and complete control of its internal affairs.

The first thirty years of dominion politics were dominated by the Conservative Party, which was led by JOHN A. MACDONALD until his death in 1891. The new government's first major act was the purchase of western Canada from the Hudson's Bay Company in 1869. Its first major crisis was the first Métis Rebellion on the Red River in 1870. The rebellion was resolved by entry of Manitoba into the dominion, with guarantees of rights for Native Americans and Métis (people of mixed Native American and European heritage). British Columbia entered the dominion in the same year. In the 1870s, Canada's Plains Indians, decimated by smallpox and faced with the extermination of the buffalo, were induced to give up their land claims. Settlers began moving onto the western prairies, which the Royal Canadian Mounted Police—the "Mounties"—was formed to patrol.

The Canadian government faced declining revenues and provincial dissatisfaction over the results of unification. In the 1880s the government resorted to high tariffs and industrial subsidies. The government also spent large sums on the Canadian Pacific Railway, completed in 1885. In the same year, the second and more serious Métis Rebellion broke out in Saskatchewan but was suppressed. The railroads eventually fostered the growth of a thriving wheat-growing economy in the west.

Canadian politics was also troubled by continuing ethnic conflict between French and English speakers. French Canadians resented the attempts to make English the sole language of government and fought for continued bilingual and Catholic instruction in state schools. In 1896 nearly thirty years of uninterrupted Conservative rule came to an end with the election of the Liberal Party candidate Wilfrid Laurier. Laurier followed the same economic policies as the Conservative government, continuing high tariffs and industrial subsidies, but he was more conciliatory toward French Canadians and allowed more provincial autonomy.

The last years of the Victorian era saw the beginnings of large-scale emigration from eastern and southern Europe. Although Canada remained closely tied to Great Britain, it began taking the first steps toward an independent foreign policy.

Canning, Charles John, Earl Canning (1812–1862) British statesman. The son of influential foreign secretary George Canning (1770–1827) entered Parliament in 1836, becoming undersecretary for foreign affairs under Sir ROBERT PEEL (1841–46). After serving as postmaster general (1853–55) he was named governor-general of INDIA in 1856 by Lord PALMERSTON's government.

Canning was soon faced with the shah of Persia's invasion of Herat, a British protectorate in AFGHANISTAN. In 1857 he organized a military expedition that forced the shah from Herat. The victory helped cement relations between England and Afghan ruler DOST MUHAMMAD.

In 1857 the INDIAN MUTINY, or the Sepoy Rebellion, broke out in northern India. Canning suppressed the revolt but afterward refused to accommodate popular British demands for vengeance against the rebels. He was made the first viceroy of INDIA (1858–62) after the British government ended the BRITISH EAST INDIA COMPANY's rule of the colony. He reorganized the army, arranged for famine relief, fostered the building of railways, and helped establish universities in Madras, Calcutta, and Bombay. He was made an earl in 1859. He resigned his post after his wife's death in 1862 and died the same year.

Canterbury, archbishop of Primate, or principal leader, in the Church of England, and archbishop of the ecclesiastical province of Canterbury. Appointed by the crown, he is also considered senior bishop, though not head, of the worldwide association of churches that comprises the Anglican communion. The post of archbishop of Canterbury was held in the Victorian era by the following individuals:

William Howley	1828–48
John Bird Sumner	1848–62
Charles Thomas Longley	1862–68
Archibald Campbell Tait	1868–82
Edward White Benson	1883–96
Frederick Temple	1896–1902

Cape Colony See SOUTH AFRICA.

Cape Frontier Wars See KAFFIR WARS.

Cape to Cairo A dream of empire envisioned in the 1880s and 1890s by British colonizer CECIL RHODES. Rhodes, who had made his fortune in the diamond fields of SOUTH AFRICA, hoped that an ALL-RED ROUTE—an uninterrupted line of British possessions connected, in this case, by one long railway—would run north from the Cape of Good Hope in South Africa through British-controlled BECHUANALAND and RHODESIA, on through Central Africa to the SUDAN and EGYPT, which was occupied by the British in 1882. The plan became unrealizable in 1885 when the Germans took over German East Africa, blocking the route.

capsule, medicine Ingestible container of a medicinal preparation. After being swallowed, the capsule (from the Latin *capsula*) dissolves and the medicine is released in the stomach. Its inventor is not known, but the medicine capsule was in use by the mid-nineteenth century. The first known use of the phrase occurred in 1875.

Cardigan, James Thomas Brudenell, 7th Earl of (1797–1868) British military officer. His disastrous charge against Russian artillery on October 25, 1854, during the CRIMEAN WAR was commemorated in ALFRED, Lord TENNYSON's poem "THE CHARGE OF THE LIGHT BRIGADE" (1855). He attained his military commissions by purchasing them, a practice that allowed rich men with little or no military expertise to lead troops in battle and that was not abolished until War Secretary Edward Cardwell did so in 1872. In 1835, Cardigan became lieutenant-colonel of the 11th Light Dragoons, the favorite unit of Prince ALBERT. Disliked by many of his fellow officers, he was criticized for showiness in dress and habits—the CARDIGAN SWEATER was named after him. He was also known for his rigid discipline and strict adherence to orders, qualities exemplified when he led his famous charge across a valley surrounded by Russian guns in response to mistaken orders. Cardigan was slightly wounded and returned home to popular acclaim and eventual criticism.

cardigan sweater Clothing. The front-buttoned, usually collarless sweater was named for James Thomas Brudenell, 7th Earl of CARDIGAN. He was known for his splendid attire, which included a knitted woolen vest worn for protection against the cold during the Crimean War. The vest became known as a cardigan, which later evolved into a sweater.

Carleton, William (1794–1869) Irish writer. Born to a poor farming family in County Tyrone, he contributed a series of articles to the *Christian Examiner* while he was a village tutor. They were collected into two series of *Traits and Stories of the Irish Peasantry,* 1830 and 1833. *Tales of Ireland* was published in 1834. His most noted novels are *Fardorougha, the Miser* (1839), a tale of a usurious farmer, and *Black Prophet* (1847), a gloomy story of the IRISH POTATO FAMINE. Other novels include *The Misfortunes of Barny Branagan* (1841), *Valentine McClutchy* (1845), and *The Evil Eye* (1860). His realistic depictions of rural Irish life touched a wide audience and were translated into Italian, French, and German.

Carlyle, Thomas (1795–1881) Scottish historian and essayist. Born in Ecclefechan, Scotland, Carlyle was the son of a mason and small farmer. His Calvinist family was very religious, and Carlyle originally intended to enter the ministry. In 1809 he entered Edinburgh University. Lonely, awkward, and poor, Carlyle began to doubt his vocation. He left the university in 1814 and worked as a tutor in schools until 1819 when he returned to Edinburgh and made a difficult living writing articles for Brewster's *Edinburgh Encyclopaedia.* He also began to study German, which would leave a lasting mark on his life and work. The years from 1818 through 1822 were particularly unhappy for him; in addition to a religious crisis, he suffered from the lack of a settled life and indigestion, which would plague him the rest of his life. He lost complete faith in the orthodox Christianity of his childhood, but it took years to formulate his alternative, a transcendental "Natural Supernaturalism."

In 1826 he married Jane Welsh; their affectionate and difficult marriage appears in his *Reminiscences* (1881) and in her letters, which he edited for publication. The Carlyles were childless, brilliant, and temperamental. Their London home, a Victorian example, is now a tourist attraction.

Carlyle began publishing translations and studies of German literature, including his *Life of Schiller* (1825), in the mid-1820s. He began to be known for his advocacy of German ROMANTICISM; however, due to financial worries from 1828 to 1834, the couple lived at Jane Carlyle's isolated farmhouse at Craigenputtock. There Carlyle wrote *Sartor Resartus* (1833–34), a peculiar and original work that is in part a disguised spiritual autobiography and in part philosophical treatise. It shows Carlyle's mature style—a blend of idiosyncratic, playful, and forceful speech, sometimes strained or raucous, always colorful. The book at first met with what Carlyle termed "universal disapprobation."

In 1834, Carlyle moved to London to research *The French Revolution* (1837), which established his popular and literary reputation. Carlyle emphasized the roots of the revolution in oppression of the poor, suggesting the need for reform in contemporary England. He frequently gave public lectures. In one series, published as *On Heroes, Hero-Worship, and the Heroic in History* (1841), he propounds the romantic and authoritarian idea that the hero articulates the true spirit of his age. *Past and Present* (1843) compared the Middle Ages favorably to contemporary England, especially regarding the conditions of the workingman; he published *Oliver Cromwell's Letters and Speeches* (1845), rescuing Cromwell from general disrepute, and the monumental, if sterile, biography, *The History of Friedrich II of Prussia, Called Frederick the Great* (1858–1865).

In the years after 1840, Carlyle was a leading intellectual figure in England, respected as a sage and an influence on the younger generation; his friends included JOHN STUART MILL, RALPH WALDO EMERSON, CHARLES DICKENS, ALFRED, Lord TENNYSON, GIUSEPPE MAZZINI, CHARLES KINGSLEY, ROBERT BROWNING, and JOHN RUSKIN. In 1865 he was elected lord rector of Edinburgh University. His wife died in 1866, and his last years were secluded, although he published several books on history and contemporary politics. His *Reminiscences* appeared posthumously. Other books of note include *Chartism* (1839), *Latter Day Pamphlets* (1850), and *The Life of Sterling* (1851). His influence had begun to decline in his own lifetime, and his work is read now more for its literary and historical value.

Carnegie, Andrew (1835–1919) Steel magnate and philanthropist. Born in Scotland, the son of a weaver, Carnegie emigrated to the United States with his family in 1848. He worked in a cotton factory near Pittsburgh and then as a telegraph operator. An official of the Pennsylvania Railroad hired him as a personal secretary, and Carnegie was named general superintendent of the railroad at the age of twenty-four. During the U.S. Civil War he organized the Union's military telegraphic system.

Afterward Carnegie developed seven iron and steel plants around Pittsburgh, including

Homestead Steel, the site of a violent strike in 1892. By 1900 the Carnegie Steel Company, run by Carnegie and his partner HENRY FRICK, was manufacturing about 25 percent of the country's steel and owned numerous iron mills, ore ships, and railroads. The U.S. Steel Company bought him out in 1901.

The retired Carnegie funded more than twenty-eight hundred public libraries, bankrolled the Carnegie-Mellon University in Pittsburgh, and established the Carnegie Corporation, which continued his charitable giving after his death. He published "The Gospel of Wealth" in 1900, arguing that the wealthy have a moral responsibility to serve the public. His *Autobiography* was published in 1902.

Carnot, Sadi (1837–1894) French politician. The scion of a famous revolutionary family, he was trained as an engineer. He entered politics as a moderate republican and in 1876, was elected to the Chamber of Deputies, where he gained a reputation for honesty and efficiency. As president of FRANCE from 1887 to 1894, Carnot vigorously opposed GEORGES BOULANGER's bid for the presidency, helping to persuade key politicians to withdraw their support for the general. He also contributed to the early stages of building a defensive alliance, or *entente,* with RUSSIA. Notable for an active style of administration, he made frequent trips outside of Paris. He was assassinated by an anarchist in 1894.

***Caroline* Affair** Series of incidents that increased tension between the UNITED STATES and GREAT BRITAIN from 1837 until 1842.

In late 1837 a rebellion against Great Britain was headed by WILLIAM LYON MACKENZIE, who enlisted the services of American volunteers in his effort to gain independence for Canada. In order to provide supplies to Mackenzie and his followers, the American steamboat *Caroline* was used to supply the Canadian rebels. On December 29, 1837, a British force of fifty men under Commander Andrew Drew of the Royal Navy crossed the Niagara River into New York and boarded the *Caroline,* killing Amos Durfee, an American citizen, and wounding others before setting the ship on fire, towing it into Canadian waters, and sinking the vessel.

President MARTIN VAN BUREN ordered troops to the American-Canadian border and issued a formal protest to the British prime minister. When the British government refused to apologize for the incident, border tensions increased, resulting in an attack on the British steamship *Sir Robert Peel* in the St. Lawrence River.

In November 1840, Alexander McLeod, a Canadian deputy sheriff, was arrested and charged with the murder of Amos Durfee. Britain refused to recognize the legality of the arrest and the ensuing trial; instead, the government demanded McLeod's release, arguing that even if McLeod had been part of the raid on the *Caroline,* he was acting under military orders to defend British territory.

As the trial dragged on, President JOHN TYLER issued a pronouncement decrying attacks along the border. In October 1841, McLeod was acquitted, and in 1842, while the U.S. Secretary of State DANIEL WEBSTER and Britain's Lord ASHBURTON were negotiating a treaty, Webster accepted Ashburton's contention that British forces had acted overzealously in self-defense. Webster accepted the statement as a formal apology and tactfully eased America's relations with Great Britain.

carriage Horse-drawn vehicle that carried people rather than cargo. Victorian examples were the brougham and the VICTORIA. COACHES and CABS were vehicles for carrying people, but unlike carriages, they did not connote use mainly by the upper classes.

Carroll, Lewis [Charles Lutwidge Dodgson] (1832–1898) English mathematician and writer. He was born at Daresbury, Cheshire, the eldest son and third child of a family of four boys and seven girls. Educated at home by his father, the Reverend Charles Dodgson, until the age of twelve, he then entered a grammar school where he displayed a remarkable talent for mathematics and logic. Carroll then studied at Christ Church, Oxford, where he graduated with honors in mathematics in 1854, and was ordained a deacon in 1861.

Due to a pronounced stammer, Carroll decided against parochial duties; however, he did remain at Christ Church as a mathematics lecturer. Carroll published a number of works on mathematics under his real name but gained his lasting fame under his pseudonym, first used in conjunction with the poem "Solitude," published in the magazine *The Train* in 1856.

Carroll's stammer is said to have disappeared in the company of children, and Carroll spent much of his time accompanying Alice Liddell and her sisters, the daughters of the dean of Christ Church, on picnics and other outings. In order to entertain the girls, Carroll invented elaborate, fantastic stories. Alice Liddell asked Carroll to write down his tales, which he later showed to Henry Kingsley and George MacDonald, who advised him to expand them for a wider audience. The stories were eventually published as *Alice's Adventures in Wonderland* (1865) and *Through the Looking-Glass* (1872). Combining dreams, logic, word games, parody, and nonsense, these remain among the most popular children's books in the English language.

Carroll was also known in his day for his PHOTOGRAPHY, not only for the portraits of Alice Liddell but also for his fine photographs of ALFRED, Lord TENNYSON, JOHN RUSKIN, DANTE GABRIEL ROSSETTI, and other celebrities of the Victorian Age.

Carroll died of influenza while visiting his sisters in Guildford, Surrey.

Carson, Kit [Christopher] (1809–1868) American frontiersman. Born in Kentucky, he spent his childhood in Missouri until age sixteen when he left for the West. From 1829 to 1842 he worked as a guide for groups of explorers. In 1842 he served as a guide for a group led by JOHN C. FRÉMONT in Oregon and California; during the MEXICAN WAR (1846–48), he worked as a messenger bearing news about California. A colonel for New Mexico volunteers during the CIVIL WAR, he led forces against Confederate attacks and in 1863 resettled a group of Navajo and Apache Indians on a reservation at Fort Sumner, New Mexico.

carte de visite See CALLING CARD.

Carver, George Washington (1864?–1943) Africa-American botanist. Born into SLAVERY in Missouri, he was raised by his former owner who urged him to further his education. Near the end of the Victorian era he earned a degree from Iowa State in agriculture and botany in 1894 and a master's in botany in 1896. BOOKER T. WASHINGTON invited Carver to join the Tuskegee Institute in Alabama in 1896, where he conducted agricultural research and taught for the rest of his life. Carver instructed local farmers on how to increase their soil's productivity and how to diversify their crops through planting soybeans, peanuts, and sweet potatoes. He developed hundreds of commercial uses for these alternative crops, helping southern farmers end their reliance on cotton. He also researched plant diseases and in 1935 began writing scientific papers for the U.S. Department of Agriculture. He is acknowledged as one of the most important agronomists of his time.

Casimir-Périer, Jean [Paul-Pierre] (1847–1907) French politician. A member of a powerful dynasty of industrialists and politicians, he served in several legislative positions, including prime minister (1893–94), before he became president of FRANCE (1894–95). As prime minister he oversaw the passage of widely unpopular anti-anarchist laws. During his brief presidency he was severely attacked by the left. He resigned after six months.

Cassatt, Mary [Stevenson] (1845–1926) American painter and printmaker. Born to a well-to-do family in Pittsburgh, Pennsylvania, Cassatt was raised in Philadelphia. After studying at the Philadelphia Academy of Fine Arts, she moved to Paris to pursue an artistic career. Following further study at the Louvre and in private studios, and a brief return to the United States during the Franco-Prussian War, Cassatt returned to Paris and in 1875 was profoundly taken by IMPRESSIONISM and especially by the pastels of EDGAR DEGAS. The elder artist wanted Cassatt to work and exhibit with the Impressionists. At that time, Cassatt's sister and parents moved to Paris to live with her. They became subjects of many of her vibrant oils and pastels of everyday life, particularly of mothers and children. In the late 1880s and early 1890s she worked extensively in printmaking, combining etching and drypoint in graceful creations that reflect an influence of Japanese art. In the Woman's Building at the Columbian Exhibition of 1893 she created a mural, *Modern Woman.* As she entered her fifties, Cassatt's eyesight failed, and in the final years of her life she was unable to work. She continued to shape artistic taste, however, by helping longtime American friends and patrons of the arts to assemble collections of Impressionist paintings and purchase Impressionist works.

caster Condiment holder. This small, usually silver, stand for the Victorian dinner table held bottles of condiments that were "cast" over the meal's foods.

cathode rays Streams of ELECTRONS. Visible as a fluorescent glow, cathodes are emitted at the cathode, or negative electrode, of an evacuated tube containing an electric current. Close observation of the phenomenon was made possible by the invention of the GEISSLER TUBE in 1855. In 1876, German physicist Eugen Goldstein (1850–1930) gave the radiation its name when he showed that it started at the cathode. Using a magnet to curve the path of the cathode rays, British physicist WILLIAM CROOKES demonstrated in 1880 that the rays consisted of streams of negatively charged particles; his results were confirmed by later experiments, notably those of French physicist Jean-Baptiste Perrin (1870–1942) in 1895 and British physicist Joseph John Thomson (1856–1940) in 1897. Thomson discovered that the cathode ray particles were electrons, the predicted fundamental units of electricity.

In the twentieth century, the cathode-ray tube—a vacuum tube in which a beam of electrons is projected toward a phosphorescent screen—became the fundamental technology behind the monitors used in televisions, oscilloscopes, and computers.

Cavour, Count Camillo di (1810–1861) Italian politician. Cavour was the main force behind the RISORGIMENTO movement of ITALY in the mid-nineteenth century. During the first half of the century, Italy remained fragmented into several kingdoms and duchies. AUSTRIA controlled Lombardy and Venetia in northern

Italy, while to the south a branch of the Bourbon royal family ruled the kingdom of Two Sicilies, which included half of the peninsula. Several other independent states occupied the rest of the boot. Only Sardinia in the northwest was ruled by a native Italian family.

Cavour hailed from a noble family in Sardinia. After resigning from the army, he entered politics and became a member of Parliament in the constitutional monarchy ruled by King VICTOR EMMANUEL II of the house of Savoy. He rose quickly to become the prime minister in 1852. Cavour instituted a program of public works, encouraged free trade, and abolished Church courts.

Cavour began the unification of Italy by sending Sardinian troops to the CRIMEAN WAR to secure a place at the peace negotiations. There he raised the question of Italian statehood and the Austrian presence in Italy. He arranged a secret agreement with NAPOLEON III and instigated a war with Austria in 1859. The French and Sardinian armies quickly defeated the Austrian troops at the battle of Magenta and Solferino. Rebellions against the other Italian states erupted throughout Italy.

Napoleon III, no friend of popular revolts and fearful of the Prussian reaction to his Sardinian alliance, promptly negotiated a treaty in 1859. Sardinia annexed Lombardy, but Austria retained Venetia. Cavour resigned, furious at the French peace terms, but returned to office in 1860. In the meantime, Tuscany, Modena, Parma, and Romagna fell to revolts and joined Sardinia. Cavour's statesmanship prevented foreign intervention on behalf of the moribund duchies. Cavour also staved off foreign support of the Pope whose papal States, with the exception of Rome, were made part of Sardinia.

A Sardinian army moved farther south, and the former king of Two Sicilies, now controlled by GIUSEPPE GARIBALDI, was peacefully annexed thanks to Cavour's negotiating abilities. The kingdom of Italy, under Victor Emmanuel II, was declared in 1861, two months before Cavour's death. Venetia was added in 1866 and Rome in 1870 to complete the unification.

Cawnpore City in Uttar Pradesh, northern India, now Kanpur. An unindustrialized village before capture by the British in 1801, the town was being developed into a center for trade and commerce. In 1857 the British presence was eliminated in a massacre during the INDIAN MUTINY, or Sepoy rebellion, when Indian rebels killed the inhabitants of the entire British settlement. In 1869 cotton mills were introduced to Cawnpore, and trade and manufacturing grew markedly. The town had a population of 1.9 million in 1991.

Cayley, Arthur (1821–1895) English mathematician. In 1843, while in his twenties, he began the development of *n*-dimensional analytic geometry (three or more dimensions). The author of more than nine hundred papers, he also developed algebraic matrices and the theory of invariants and contributed to theoretical dynamics and astronomy. He was a professor at Cambridge from 1863 until his death.

Cayley, Sir George (1773–1857) English scientist. Considered the founder of aerodynamics, he analyzed the conditions that would make flying machines possible, introducing the concepts of lift and drag, fixed wings, vertical tails with control surfaces, streamlined fuselages, and steering rudders. Although he envisioned the design of powered airplanes and their propulsion requirements, no engine powerful and light enough to do the job then existed. In 1853, however, he constructed the first successful man-carrying glider, piloted on its first flight by his coachman. Cayley also invented the caterpillar tractor.

cell theory Biological theory. The cell theory states that the cell is the fundamental structural and functional unit of living organisms. Although no one scientist can be credited with the discovery of the cellular structure of living matter, the theory that unified and made sense of previous observations was formulated at the beginning of the Victorian era by German botanist MATTHIAS JAKOB SCHLEIDEN and German biologist THEODOR SCHWANN. In 1838, Schleiden published his theory that all living plant tissue was constructed of cells; in 1839, Schwann made the same claim about animal tissue. Recognizing the basic similarity between their studies, the scientists argued that the cell was the basic structural unit of life and that all body activities are the result of cellular function. Their discoveries had a profound effect on the new specialties of physiology and histology, the microscopic study of living tissues. It would be years, however, before the theory was widely accepted and even longer before cell division was understood. Discoveries throughout the nineteenth century lent support to the cell theory, particularly those of German anatomist Rudolf Albert von Kölliker (1817–1905), who showed that eggs and sperm might be thought of as cells and that nerve fibers were outgrowths of cells.

Central America Region consisting of the isthmus between North and South America. The population is divided between a variety of indigenous groups and creoles, mixtures of Europeans and Native Americans. Prior to 1821 the entire region, with the exception of British Honduras (modern Belize), was owned by SPAIN. The successful revolution in MEXICO in 1821 led to a declaration of Central American union with Mexico, but shortly afterward, local revolutionaries declared the independence of the United Federation of Central America, comprising the modern countries of Guatemala, Honduras, Nicaragua, Costa Rica, and El Salvador. Panama became a province of Colombia. The federation lasted until 1840 when the various regions split off after political quarrels between liberals and conservatives.

Costa Rica enjoyed peace and stability for the remainder of the Victorian era. El Salvador suffered from political strife and came under military government. British control of British Honduras, colonized by English Jamaicans in the seventeenth century, was long contested by Spain and later by Guatemala. In 1981 it became the independent nation of Belize.

Guatemala, which had contained the capital of the federation, had a conservative government until 1873. Justo Rufino Barrios (1835–1885), president of Guatemala from 1873 until his death, instituted liberal reforms and tried to revive the federation but was killed while leading an invasion of El Salvador in 1885. Honduras also had a conservative government until 1876; a liberal constitution was adopted in 1880.

Nicaragua and Panama were objects of considerable foreign interest as possible sites for a canal linking the Atlantic and Pacific oceans. GREAT BRITAIN and the UNITED STATES vied for control of Nicaragua, with Britain expanding a pre-existing protectorate over the Mosquito Indians of the east coast, known as Mosquitia. In 1848, Britain declared its control of Greytown, the proposed eastern terminus for a canal. The resulting conflict with the United States culminated in 1854 when a U.S. warship bombarded and destroyed Greytown. Occupied with the Crimean War, the British government decided to overlook the matter and in 1859–60 ceded Mosquitia to Nicaragua.

In 1856, WILLIAM WALKER, an American adventurer, took over Nicaragua with a small army in an attempt to make it a slave-owning republic. After Walker's expulsion, Nicaragua was ruled by a conservative military government.

Panama became the site of an American-built railway in 1855 and of thirteen U.S. military interventions between 1850 and 1900. French engineer FERDINAND DE LESSEPS attempted without success to build a canal there in 1878–88. In 1903 the United States encouraged Panama to revolt and gain independence from Colombia, after which American military engineers promptly constructed the long-desired canal (1904–14).

Central American countries concentrated on agricultural exports. Industrialization was minimal even by the end of the Victorian era.

Ceylon Island off the southeast tip of India. It was first reached by Europeans in 1505. Its coastal regions underwent Portuguese and Dutch rule before being conquered by the British and made a crown colony in 1798. Military conquest of the interior kingdom of Kandy took place only in 1815. By the Victorian era, Ceylon was the site of flourishing coffee, tea, and rubber plantations. Prominent British landowners included the husband of photographer JULIA MARGARET CAMERON. The nation gained independence in 1948 and retained its traditional name, Sri Lanka, in 1972.

Cézanne, Paul (1839–1906) Born in Aix-en-Provence to a wealthy banking family, Cézanne studied in the same school as EMILE ZOLA, with whom he formed a close friendship. He studied law before devoting himself entirely to painting at the age of twenty-two. In 1861 he went to Paris to join Zola and applied for admission to the Ecole des Beaux-Arts. Cézanne admired the work of EUGÈNE DELACROIX and GUSTAVE COURBET, and his early drawings are informed by their presentation of forms. He was denied admission to the *école,* however, and when his paintings were rejected by the Salon, he exhibited them in the SALON DES REFUSÉS of 1863.

Cézanne began to absorb the influences of the sculptor Pierre Puget and EDOUARD MANET and to adapt Courbet's palette-knife technique for applying paint. In the 1870s he fell under the influence of IMPRESSIONISM. Working side by side with his friend CAMILLE PISSARRO at Auvers, he painted *The House of the Hanged Man* (1873–74), a classic example of his own Impressionist phase. Exhibited in the first Impressionist group show in 1874, it and Cézanne's other pictures were ferociously attacked by the critics. Stylistically, Cézanne's former heaviness gave way to a more controlled surface and a lighter palette with the increased use of primary colors.

Cézanne showed with the Impressionists again in 1877, then refused to take part in any more exhibitions and abandoned Paris altogether. He began to create a perspective expressed solely by color instead of vanishing points, as in his painting *L'Estaque and the Gulf of Marseilles* (1882–85). He continued to challenge the role of perspective in his *View of Gardanne* (1885–86), where a scene of houses rising on a slope is abstracted into a series of interlocking planes of color, an aspect of the style that came to be known as POST-IMPRESSIONISM.

After 1886, Cézanne painted numerous portraits, self-portraits, still-lifes, and figure studies, such as *The Card Players* (1890–92), where his subjects became interpreted in the more classical tradition of Nicolas Poussin. The climax of his figurative investigations was *The Great Bathers* (1898–1905), painted after a long series of compositions of bathers in landscape. He expressed volume and light in his own way through a system of overlapping pure color and tonal relations.

Cézanne successfully achieved a synthesis of reality and abstraction that firmly laid the foundation for Cubist painters in the twentieth century.

Chadwick, Sir Edwin (1800–1890) English reformer. Chief architect of the POOR LAW OF 1834, he served as secretary of the Poor Law Commission (1834–46). His reports on unacceptable sanitary conditions (see CHOLERA) helped bring about the passage of the Public Health Act (1848) and his assignment as commissioner for the first General Board of Health (1848–54). He also laid the groundwork for systems of government inspection by independent experts and wrote on education and civil service reform. A strong believer in central government administration of social services, he made many enemies but exercised lasting influence.

Chamberlain, Joseph (1836–1914) British politician. The son of a successful shoe manufacturer, he amassed a fortune in the hardware business but retired at the age of thirty-eight to devote himself to politics. As mayor of Birmingham (1873–76) he gained a national reputation by supporting improved housing for the poor, educational reforms, and other liberal causes. Elected to Parliament in 1876 as a member of the LIBERAL PARTY, he became WILLIAM GLADSTONE's right-hand man in the House of Commons where he continued to fight for better housing and other reforms. From 1880 to 1885 he was president of the Board of Trade.

Chamberlain split with Gladstone over the latter's support of HOME RULE for Ireland in 1886. He joined the Liberal Unionists in defeating the Home Rule bill and bringing down the government. He became leader of the Liberal Unionists in 1891 and swayed the ruling CONSERVATIVE PARTY into passing social reform legislation.

Chamberlain's dedication to domestic reform did not stop him from supporting colonial expansion. As colonial secretary from 1895 to 1902, he strongly supported the BOER WAR, and his anti-Boer stance led to wrongful allegations that he was involved in LEANDER STARR JAMESON's raid into the TRANSVAAL. After the war he championed a protectionist trade plan that would favor colonial products while raising high tariffs against other nations. He resigned in 1903 after Conservative Party leader ARTHUR BALFOUR rejected his idea. He spent the next three years campaigning for his scheme, an effort that split the Conservatives and led to their decisive defeat in the 1906 election. The popular Chamberlain retained his seat but suffered a paralyzing stroke in 1906. He was an invalid until his death.

Chambers, Robert (1802–1871) Scottish writer and publisher. Born in Peebles, he moved with his family to Edinburgh in 1813; Chambers's interest in the city led to his writing *Traditions of Edinburgh* (1825), which was greatly admired by his fellow citizen Sir Walter Scott. In 1832, Chambers joined his brother William in founding the W. & R. Chambers publishing company, which produced the successful *Chambers's Edinburgh Journal* and *Chambers's Encyclopaedia.*

Robert Chambers continued writing historical and literary works, the most significant of which was published anonymously: *Vestiges of the Natural History of Creation* (1843–46). Perceived as an attack on the conventional theory of creation, it caused great controversy but was praised by Charles Darwin. It was not until 1884, thirteen years after Chambers's death, that his authorship of the work was revealed.

Charcot, Jean-Martin (1825–1893) French neurologist. His account of the nature of hysteria was credited by SIGMUND FREUD as a critical step in the development of psychoanalysis. Charcot's clinic at Salpêtrière, Paris, was the best known center of its day for the treatment of nervous system disorders.

"Charge of the Light Brigade, The" English Poem. Written in 1855 by ALFRED, Lord TENNYSON, the poem commemorated the disastrous British cavalry charge against Russian forces on October 25, 1854, during the CRIMEAN WAR. The charge was led by James Thomas Brudenell, 7th Earl of CARDIGAN and lieutenant-colonel of the Eleventh Light Dragoons, during the BATTLE OF BALAKLAVA. Mistakenly believing that he had been ordered to capture guns at the far end of the valley of Balaklava, Cardigan led his troops across the valley, despite his knowledge that Russian artillery loomed on three sides and made the charge hopeless. The Russian fire was devastating: About half of the 673 men who began the charge were wounded or killed. The survivors included Cardigan, who, though slightly wounded, returned to Britain to a hero's welcome in 1855. Though Tennyson's poem acknowledged that "someone had blundered," it honored the courageous obedience of the light brigade:

Theirs not to make reply,
Theirs not to reason why,
Theirs but to do and die.
Into the valley of Death
Rode the six hundred.

Despite the popular praise, the "blunder" of Cardigan and the other officers soon attracted criticism, notably in Alexander William Kinglake's *The Invasion of the Crimea* (1863).

Chartism British political movement. The Chartist movement (1838–48) was among the earliest attempts by the working classes in Great Britain to wrest political concessions from the landed aristocracy and the emerging industrialists. The failure of the REFORM BILL OF 1832 to extend suffrage to most laborers and the enactment of the POOR LAW OF 1834 spurred a drive to demand political reforms. The movement took its name from the "People's Charter," a document drafted in 1838 that outlined the movement's demands. Foremost among them were the annual election of Parliament, the secret ballot, universal manhood suffrage, the end of property qualifications for members of Parliament, and "one man, one vote." One of the leaders of the movement and coauthor of the Charter was Francis Place, a former tailor who was active in the trade union movement.

A Chartist convention attended by representatives from labor unions and radical groups from across the country met in London in 1839. A rift developed between a "physical force" wing, which favored violence and a general strike, and a "moral force" faction, which argued for legal means of pressuring Parliament.

The convention organized a drive that gathered over 1 million signatures on a petition urging the House of Commons to adopt the Chartist platform. The members refused, and the violent wing of the movement stirred riots in some large cities, but these were suppressed. The petition was again submitted in 1842, this time with more than 3 million names collected from a population of about 19 million. The House of Commons overwhelmingly rejected it.

The movement died out by 1848, unable to sustain itself in the face of government repression or to overcome its own internal disagreements. Although it failed to win its immediate goals, it did help publicize workers' grievances, gave impetus to the trade union movement, and helped win passage of the Ten-Hour Act of 1847. All Chartist demands, except for the yearly election of Parliament, were slowly adopted during the eighty years following the drafting of the charter in 1838.

Chekhov, Anton Pavlovich (1860–1904) Russian writer. Born in Taganrog, he was the grandson of a serf who had bought the family's freedom in 1841 for 3,500 rubles. Chekhov's father owned a small grocery store before he fled from his debts in 1876.

In 1879, Chekhov obtained a scholarship from the Taganrog town council to study medicine at the Moscow university. While a student, Chekhov began writing and publishing stories, anecdotes, and jokes for humor magazines. By the time he earned his degree in 1884, he had a reputation as a fine writer. He thought of himself as a physician, however, until he received encouragement from the well-known novelist Dmitri Grigovovich in 1886. The same year Chekhov published *Motley Stories,* and his career as a writer began. His next volume of stories, *In the Twilight* (1888), was awarded the Pushkin Prize, and his first play, *Ivanov,* was staged around the same time.

By 1890, Chekhov had become influenced by the moral philosophy of LEO TOLSTOY, and as a result he traveled to the penal colony on the island of Sakhalin to study the appalling conditions of the convicts. He published his impressions in *The Island Sakhalin* (1894), declaring that every person in Russia should feel responsible for the prisoners' plight.

Chekhov then returned to his family near Moscow and began his tireless philanthropic activities, including providing free medical care for the peasants, conducting famine relief, and building local schools.

The Sea Gull premiered in St. Petersburg in 1896. The play was criticized so severely at the time that Chekhov vowed never again to write for the stage. Two years later, however, the Moscow Art Theatre formed and made the play a success; the company even adopted the gull as its emblem.

Chekhov had been stricken with tuberculosis in the late 1880s, and then in 1898 a severe hemorrhage of the lungs forced him to move to the milder climate of Yalta. He continued to work constantly—writing, practicing medicine, and meeting numerous authors, including Tolstoy and Maxim Gorky. Chekhov was so incensed by Gorky's exclusion from the Russian Academy for political reasons that he resigned his own membership in 1902.

More than six hundred short stories by Chekhov are known to exist, but he began to concentrate on writing for the stage at the turn of the century. His major plays, including *The Three Sisters* (1901) and *The Cherry Orchard* (1904), were written for the Moscow Art Theatre, which honored Chekhov by visiting him in Yalta in 1900 and performing his plays. The next year Chekhov married one of the company's actresses, Olga Knipper.

After completing *The Cherry Orchard,* Chekhov traveled to Moscow to attend its premiere, only to suffer a relapse. He was taken to a health resort in the Black Forest, where he died at the age of forty-four.

Chicago Fire Citywide disaster. One of the most famous calamities in American history, the twenty-nine-hour fire began on the night of October 8, 1871. It damaged about $200 million worth of property and left some ninety thousand people homeless. No evidence substantiates the legend that Mrs. O'Leary's cow started the blaze by kicking over a lantern in a barn, but the fire did begin in the barn of Patrick O'Leary located near the city's center. Wooden buildings and high winds combined to devastate about four square miles, including the business district. Relief workers set up camps in undamaged areas, and supplies arrived from around the world. Hardly any trace of the fire remained four years later as the city was rebuilt with steel and stone. The rebuilding effort served as a principal arena for the early development of SKYSCRAPERS.

Chicago School Group of American architects in the late nineteenth and early twentieth centuries. Based in Chicago, the school was closely connected with the evolution of the SKYSCRAPER from the CHICAGO FIRE of 1871 to the mid-1920s. The origins of true skyscraper construction began with William Le Baron Jenney's Home Insurance Building, designed and completed in Chicago between 1883 and 1885. Only ten stories high, it is considered a skycraper because its metal skeleton carried the weight of the external shell. The young architectural firm of Holabird and Roche continued the development of the skyscraper with their Tacoma Building, erected in Chicago in 1889. The more streamlined steel-skeleton construction was demonstrated in the twenty-story Masonic Temple Building, designed by the Chicago partnership of Burnham and Root in 1892. Many other architects were attracted to Chicago, including Dankmar Adler from Denmark and LOUIS SULLIVAN from Boston. In 1890 the firm of Adler and Sullivan contributed designs for the Wainwright Building in St. Louis to the field of skyscraper construction. Adler and Sullivan emphasized verticality and accentuated individual layers with ornamented bands. Louis Sullivan went on to create one of the first large-scale commercial buildings with his Carson Pirie Scott Department Store in Chicago, built in two stages, 1899–1901 and 1903–4.

China Vast east Asia country, site of one of the world's oldest civilizations. The population is mostly ethnic Chinese (*Han*), who speak various Chinese dialects and practice a mixture of Buddhism and traditional folk religion. In the arid western province lives a significant minority of nomadic peoples who speak Turkic languages and practice Islam.

China in the Victorian era was a troubled country, racked by internal strife and preyed on by the European powers. The country was ruled by the MANCHU DYNASTY (also known as Qing or Ch'ing), a nomadic people from Manchuria who succeeded the Ming Dynasty in 1644. The Manchu were generally conservative, preserving traditional Chinese structures but placing themselves in the highest positions. With a highly productive agricultural economy, the Chinese regarded themselves as self-sufficient, needing little or nothing from the outside world. The Manchu therefore pursued a policy of isolation, forbidding their subjects to trade abroad and limiting foreign merchants to a few selected ports, chiefly Canton. By the late eighteenth century, however, Manchu power was weakened by internal problems, including overexpanding population and government corruption and inefficiency, and by external pressure, as the European powers sought more favorable conditions of trade with the world's most populous country. British and American merchants began exporting officially banned, though widely used, opium on a large scale to China in order to avoid paying in cash for Chinese exports of tea and porcelain. Tension over the trade and Manchu attempts to curb it led to the OPIUM WARS (1839–42 and 1856–60). British and French forces easily defeated the technically inferior Chinese armies and forced China to lower its tariffs and to open several "treaty ports," protected enclaves whose foreign residents were immune to Chinese law. The result was a boom in foreign trade, and the profits went largely to Europe, causing further disruptions to the Chinese economy.

China's humiliation at the hands of the West was followed by an even more severe internal crisis. The Taiping Rebellion (1850–64), a millenarian movement directed against the Manchu and calling for moral regeneration, broke out in central China. At its height the Taiping movement controlled several provinces centering around Nanking (Nanjing). The Manchu managed to suppress the rebellion with Western help in 1864, including forces under the command of British soldier CHARLES GEORGE GORDON. But the rebellion was followed by large-scale peasant revolts and Muslim insurrections in the west.

The Western presence in China continued to expand in the decades following the Opium Wars. Western businessmen sought economic concessions and opportunities such as railroad projects. China became the scene of a substantial Christian missionary movement. Though the Westerners brought some benefits, their privileged position also caused tension and resentment. In response to the challenge posed by the West, the Manchu made some efforts to form a modern army and encourage industrial development, but were reluctant to make any governmental reforms that might threaten their power. Large areas of the country drifted out of their control or were turned over to virtually autonomous administrators, who became independent warlords.

In 1894–95, China was defeated by Japan in the SINO-JAPANESE WAR. An anti-Manchu, anti-Western movement called the Boxers, for their stress on martial arts as a mode of moral purification, took shape. The Manchu government managed to turn the Boxers against the Europeans, but the ensuing BOXER REBELLION (1900–1) was another disaster. The Manchu government was forced to pay a large indemnity and to make further concessions to the Europeans.

The Manchu dynasty was overthrown in 1911, shortly after the end of the Victorian era, by the Western-influenced republican movement led by physician Sun Yat-sen (1866–1925). Communist rule began in 1949.

chintz Multicolored cloth decorated with flowers and other motifs. Dating from the early eighteenth century, the English term originated as "chints," plural of the Hindi *chint,* and referred to painted calico cloth imported from India. They were very popular in Victorian Great Britain.

Chisholm Trail Cattle route. Named for American trader Jesse Chisholm (1806?–1868), who is said to have marked out the route when he drove his wagonload of buffalo hides through the Oklahoma Territory in 1866, the route began south of San Antonio, Texas, and ended in Abilene, Kansas, where railroad connections could be made; it was used into the 1880s. In 1871—the route's busiest year—five thousand cowboys drove seven hundred thousand cattle to market along this trail.

chit An IOU or voucher of money owed for food and drink. It derives from the Hindustani *citthi,* short note. The British picked up the term in India, where they complained that civil servants flooded their desks with chits. "Chit-COOLIES" became a derogatory term for Indian messengers.

chloroform Chemical. Discovered by American chemist Samuel Guthrie (1782–1848) in 1831, it was also called trichloromethane ($CHCl_3$). The colorless, sweet-smelling, volatile liquid was used as ANESTHESIA, along with ETHER, during the Victorian era. Chloroform fell out of favor because of the damage it could cause to the liver.

cholera Highly infectious disease. Caused by bacteria and transmitted by water contaminated with human waste, cholera is characterized by severe vomiting, diarrhea, and dehydration; if untreated, death results. Transmitted from India through Asia to Europe, it was the representative Western epidemic of the nineteenth century, associated with urban squalor and overcrowding, transmission across borders through increased trade and transportation, and eventual eradication through medical advances. Cholera was first recorded in Britain in 1831 and was the cause there of four major epidemics—in 1831–32, 1848–49, 1853–54, and 1866. Killing more than 140,000 in Britain alone and comparably high numbers across Europe and the United States, these epidemics were a major catalyst for widespread public health reform.

Before the discovery in 1883 by German bacteriologist ROBERT KOCH of the cause of cholera, the bacterium *Vibrio cholerae,* the disease was widely believed to be caused by various infractions of proper morality or ethics. Sanitary propagandists argued that weak religious and moral fiber was the cause of this "filth disease." Poverty-ridden urban dwellings with dirty, crowded conditions became targets of religious reformers, spiritualists, and conservative politicians. Many of Europe's poor believed that cholera was part of a plot by government officials, doctors, and the nobility to poison them. In Bristol, England, riots broke out, instigated by people who believed the medical profession was using the epidemic as a body-snatching opportunity for anatomical dissection.

In 1842, English lawyer EDWIN CHADWICK, author of the POOR LAW OF 1834, published his study of unsanitary conditions in Britain, *Report on the Sanitary Conditions of the Labouring Population of Great Britain.* Chadwick's report recommended the creation of a central public-health authority to direct local health boards, oversee sanitary regulations regarding "dwellings, nuisances, and offensive trades," and provide drainage, cleansing, paving, and potable water. The importance of a sanitary water supply became more obvious with physician JOHN SNOW's 1854 discovery that cholera was a waterborne disease. Studying a cholera outbreak near the intersection of Cambridge and Broad streets in London, Snow demonstrated that the spread of the disease was associated with water from a particular street pump; supplying clean water from a different source resulted in a dramatic drop in the infection rate. Subsequently, boards of health and other long-term public health policy initiatives were enacted. By the early twentieth century, cholera was largely under control in industrialized nations, although still a threat in regions of Asia and Africa plagued by poor sanitation.

Chopin, Frédéric (1810–1849) Polish composer. Born at Zelazowa Wola, Poland, he was the son of a Frenchman who had settled in Poland and of a Polish woman from an upper-class but impoverished family. Trained in piano from age six, he composed his first

POLONAISE at seven and within a year was performing in public. In 1830, a year after graduating from the Warsaw Conservatory, he left to tour western Europe and never returned to his homeland. After his first trip to London in 1837, Chopin became romantically linked to Aurore Dudevant, the writer better known as GEORGE SAND. In the autumn of 1838, Chopin and Sand traveled to Majorca, where they spent three months under terrible conditions and Chopin contracted tuberculosis. During the excursion, however, Chopin was able to complete his twenty-four Preludes.

Dividing his time between Paris and Sand's country house in France, Chopin continued to compose in what was his most productive period. Unlike other famous nineteenth-century musicians, Chopin was not a conductor or a renowned teacher, nor did he write symphonies or operas. Instead, he concentrated on music for the piano, thereby elevating the instrument to a new level of popularity and technical range. His works included polonaises, MAZURKAS that expressed a spirit of Polish nationalism, études, and piano concertos.

Chopin made no public appearances between 1842 and February 16, 1848, when he performed for the last time in Paris. He did perform frequently at parties, however. It was a common sight to see him and FRANZ LISZT sitting together at the piano while Sand, FELIX MENDELSSOHN, HECTOR BERLIOZ, EUGÈNE DELACROIX, and other notable figures of the day stood and watched.

The marriage of Sand's daughter Solange to August Clésinger, a sculptor of dubious reputation, caused an irrevocable split between Sand and Chopin in 1847. Sand wanted nothing to do with her daughter after the marriage, while Chopin sided with Solange. The revolution of February 1848 forced Chopin to leave France, and while a visit to England produced an enthusiastic response, including a private performance for Queen Victoria on May 15, 1848, Chopin returned to Paris in November. He died the following year, with Solange by his side.

Chopin, Katherine O'Flaherty (1851–1904) American writer. Born in St. Louis, Missouri, she married Oscar Chopin in 1870 and moved to New Orleans. Following her husband's death in 1882, she embarked on a writing career and published several atmospheric Louisiana-based stories later collected in the books *Bayou Folk* (1894), and *A Night in Acadie* (1897). Her novella *The Awakening* (1899), her best-known work, shocked contemporaries with its discussion of female sexuality and the search for identity. After being banned in Chopin's hometown, the book remained out of print until it was rediscovered in the mid-twentieth century and deemed a substantive literary and feminist contribution.

chow American slang term for food. It probably derived from Mandarin Chinese *Ch'ao,* meaning to cook or fry. "Chow" first appeared in the 1850s in California, where many Chinese immigrants were employed as laborers and cooks.

Christmas Carol, A English novella. The tale of redemption by CHARLES DICKENS was first published in 1843 as *A Christmas Carol in Prose.* The story contains some of the most enduring characters in English literature and helped forge the popular image of Victorian holiday celebrations.

The story centers on Ebenezer Scrooge, whose name has since become a generic term for miser. A series of ghostly visits from the spirits of Christmas Past, Present, and Future turn Scrooge away from his inhumanity and greed. The new Scrooge embraces his fellowman, most notably by befriending the family of his clerk, Bob Cratchit, especially Cratchit's lame son, Tiny Tim.

Christy, Edwin P. (1815–1862) American entertainer. Born in Philadelphia, this showman founded Christy's Minstrels around 1846, setting the pattern for the popular entertainment called minstrel shows in which white performers clowned and sang in blackface. The Christy Minstrels often performed the songs of STEPHEN FOSTER.

chromosome Threadlike structure in cell nuclei that carries genes, units of inheritance determining how an organism will develop. German anatomist Walther Flemming (1843–1905) first noted these structures, made of a material he called "chromatin," while studying cell division in 1882. The first to call them "chromosomes" was German anatomist Wilhelm von Waldeyer-Hartz (1836–1921) in 1888. The connection between chromosomes and the developing theory of GENETICS was not perceived until 1902 when American geneticist Walter S. Sutton hypothesized that chromosomes contained the genetic factors first identified by GREGOR MENDEL in 1865. In 1909, Dutch botanist Wilhelm L. Johannsen coined the term "genes" for the units of inheritance carried in long chains in the chromosomes.

The number of chromosomes in the cell of a particular species is constant, though the number varies between species. In a normal human cell there are twenty-three matched pairs of chromosomes. Chromosomes consist mainly of proteins and the compound DNA (deoxyribonucleic acid); it is the latter component that serves as genetic material, a discovery that was not made until the 1940s.

Church, Frederick (1826–1900) American painter. Called the "Michelangelo of landscape art," Church was born in Hartford, Connecticut. He studied under THOMAS COLE, the leading artist of the HUDSON RIVER SCHOOL. By the age of twenty Church was a leading painter whose landscapes commanded high prices and earned critical praise. His spectacular vistas, which were dominated by mist, smoke, and dramatic light, also won him great acclaim in Europe. He traveled extensively in South America and Europe, searching out exotic scenes for his canvas.

When he was fifty-one rheumatism laid waste to his right arm. He learned to paint with his left arm but soon lost control of this limb as well. For the last five years of his life he could not paint.

His *Niagara* (1857) was one of America's most popular landscape paintings and was sold for $12,500 in 1876. Other noted paintings include *Otopaxi* (1862), a view of Ecuadorian volcanoes, *Icebergs* (1863), *Heart of the Andes* (1859), *Jerusalem* (1871), and *Parthenon* (1891).

Church of England See CANTERBURY, ARCHBISHOP OF.

cinematograph *(cinématographe)* Film invention. The combined camera and projector that French cinema pioneers Louis and Auguste Lumière invented for their MOTION PICTURES was patented in 1895. The machine featured a clawlike device for advancing film. The first viable system for projecting films on a screen, it was an advance on the KINETOSCOPE by THOMAS EDISON.

Civil Service, British British administrative service system. It grew enormously in size and reputation during the Victorian era, from some 20,000 employees in the mid-nineteenth century to more than 275,000 by 1914. Legendary for its efficiency, the civil service was an indispensable arm of the empire. Yet the modern service had its roots in the failure of the EAST INDIA COMPANY to rule India efficiently. These problems led to reforms of the company's recruitment practices, including introduction of an examination system after 1833. In 1835 a parliamentary committee made further recommendations for change, and its work influenced the NORTHCOTE-TREVELYAN CIVIL SERVICE REPORT of 1854, which laid the groundwork for sweeping reform.

With the establishment of the Civil Service Commission in 1855, government positions were divided into two classes: routine clerical jobs and more intellectually demanding, policy-making positions. Examinations were instituted for some positions in 1855, and by 1900 the two original classes had been expanded to four to incorporate more specialized fields of knowledge. After 1870 all administrative positions were filled by examination, and most patronage was eliminated by the end of the century.

As the new system attracted recruits from the more prestigious universities, the service's upper ranks became dominated by the upper classes. The service developed a reputation for efficiency and honesty while parliamentary delegations of authority increased its power.

Civil Service, U.S. Administrative service system of the United States. Prior to the 1850s the selection of federal administrators was largely determined by party and personal loyalties with little reference to ability or experience. Congress first tried in 1853 to counteract this spoils system by requiring clerks to pass a basic literary exam.

Little else was done until 1871 when Congress gave President ULYSSES S. GRANT the power to establish a civil service agency to develop tests for federal service. After some congressmen realized, however, that the board would undermine their patronage, they balked at funding it. The assassination of President JAMES GARFIELD in 1881 by an unhappy office seeker spurred real reform. Garfield's successor, CHESTER ARTHUR, shocked his colleagues by rejecting his spoils-laden past and siding with civil service reformers. Public outrage at Garfield's murder and Democratic gains in the 1882 congressional elections prompted Congress to pass the PENDLETON CIVIL SERVICE ACT in 1883. The act established the Federal Civil Service Commission, which administered new regulations banning federal employees from paying kickbacks to their supervisors. It also set up a system of competitive examinations for some positions.

Civil War, U.S. (1861–65) American military conflict between northern states, the Union, and southern states, the CONFEDERACY. Political tensions between the free-labor states of the North and the slave states of the South had been worsening for decades when ABRAHAM LINCOLN was elected president in 1860. Compromise measures such as the COMPROMISE OF 1850 and the Kansas-Nebraska Act of 1854 could not heal the fundamental rift between the regions over the future of SLAVERY.

South Carolina seceded from the Union shortly after Lincoln's victory, despite his insistence that his opposition to slavery's extension into the western territories did not mean he would move against slavery in the South. Lame-duck president JAMES BUCHANAN did little to counter the secessionist movement before Lincoln's inauguration in March 1861. By that time six more states had seceded, and four more would join the Confederacy under its president JEFFERSON DAVIS. Hostilities began on April 12, 1861, when

South Carolina attacked FORT SUMTER in Charleston harbor.

The North had tremendous material advantages, including a population advantage of 21 million, in contrast to the South's 9 million, and vastly more developed industrial and transportation sectors. Confederate leaders had to forge a nation-state out of eleven states hostile to centralized government. Over one-third of the South's population were slaves whose loyalty could not be taken for granted. The South hoped to wage a short defensive war until they won recognition and support from France and Great Britain, countries dependent on southern cotton for their mills. This cotton strategy failed when the South, desperate to trade for arms, withheld its crop from Europe early in the conflict to speed recognition of the new government. Cotton supplies in Europe remained ample, and by the time the South reversed its policy, the northern naval blockade was starting to limit southern exports.

No major fighting occurred until late July when Confederate troops routed Union forces at the Battle of Bull Run, about twenty-five miles from Washington, D.C. The defeat and the danger to the capital shook the North's confidence and braced the South's resolve. The next major action took place in early 1862 when Union troops under the field command of ULYSSES S. GRANT took control of western Tennessee and the Mississippi River down to Vicksburg, Mississippi. When Union ships under David Farragut captured New Orleans, the North was close to splitting the Confederacy in two.

In the east, General GEORGE B. MCCLELLAN, appointed commander of the Army of the Potomac after the Bull Run disaster, mounted a campaign to capture Richmond, Virginia, the Confederate capital. McClellan's offensive developed so slowly that southern troops, despite being outnumbered, checked it at the Battle of Seven Pines in late May. ROBERT E. LEE took command of Confederate forces in Virginia after Joseph Johnston was wounded. Lee and McClellan fought a series of encounters called the Seven Days' Battles that ended the North's campaign against Richmond.

Northern military futility inspired Lee to take the offensive. He bested a Union Army under John Pope at the Second Battle of Bull Run and then marched north into Maryland in hopes of cutting the North's east-west transportation links. In September 1862 he met McClellan's army at the BATTLE OF ANTIETAM, one of the most savage battles of the war. Lee lost one-quarter of his army while the North suffered even worse casualties. Lee withdrew after the standstill, but the hesitant McClellan refused to pursue him, a decision that cost him his job. Lincoln took advantage of the North's relatively strong showing at Antietam to issue the EMANCIPATION PROCLAMATION on January 1, 1863. The proclamation's antislavery message won wide approval in Europe and further dampened the South's hopes of English and French recognition of the Confederacy.

McClellan's exit brought little improvement for the North as Ambrose Burnside's army was routed by Lee's outnumbered Army of Northern Virginia at Fredericksburg, Virginia, in December. The stalemate around the two capitals of Washington and Richmond continued into 1863, and in the west Grant captured Vicksburg, the last Confederate stronghold on the Mississippi River, in July. Four more months of heavy fighting in Tennessee secured a Union base for an invasion of the deep South.

Meanwhile, Lee again defeated the Army of the Potomac, this time at Chancellorsville, Virginia, in early May, despite being outnumbered two to one. However, one of the South's ablest commanders, Thomas "Stonewall" Jackson, was accidentally killed by a southern sentry during the battle. Lee again invaded the North but met a bloody defeat at the BATTLE OF GETTYSBURG in southern Pennsylvania in July. The disasters of Gettysburg and Vicksburg further weakened the South's already faint hopes of international recognition.

In 1864, Lincoln appointed Grant commander of all Union forces. Grant headquartered with the Army of the Potomac in the east, and in May pounded away at Lee's weakening army in the battles of Spotsylvania, WILDERNESS, and Cold Harbor. Grant could not engage Lee in a decisive battle, but his constant pressure continued to wear down the Confederate forces. In the west, Union forces under General WILLIAM T. SHERMAN captured Atlanta in September; from there Sherman launched his "march to the sea," destroying the South's last intact supply area and capturing Savannah in December.

Lincoln's reelection in 1864 on a strong war platform killed the last faint hopes of the Confederacy. Sherman wheeled north through the Carolinas to hook up with Grant, who captured Petersburg, an important railroad junction near Richmond, in early April. Lee tried to join the remaining Confederate forces in the south, but his army of only twenty-five thousand men was repulsed. He surrendered to Grant at APPOMATTOX COURT HOUSE on April 9, 1865, and Sherman accepted the surrender of the last large southern force two weeks later in North Carolina. Between the two surrenders, Lincoln was assassinated by JOHN WILKES BOOTH.

In addition to the devastation of its economy, the South suffered the loss of about 260,000 soldiers. The North lost more than 360,000 troops. In total, more Americans died in the Civil War than in any other military conflict before or since. The Civil War put to rest the concept of the United States as a loose confederation of sovereign states from which a state could secede. The legality of the Emancipation Proclamation was assured by the Thirteenth Amendment (1865), which abolished slavery in the United States. *De facto* subjugation of African Americans continued throughout the nineteenth century, despite temporary gains in civil rights made during the RECONSTRUCTION period (1865–77).

Clarendon, George William Frederick Villiers, 4th Earl of (1800–1870) English statesman. He served as customs commissioner in Paris and Dublin before being appointed ambassador to Spain, where he negotiated a treaty suppressing the slave trade in 1835. Back in England, he was made lord privy seal (1839–41) and president of the Board of Trade (1846–47). Appointed lord lieutenant of Ireland (1847–52), he promoted generally ineffective relief measures during the IRISH POTATO FAMINE and relied on coercion to forestall possible rebellion.

Clarendon was made Secretary of State for foreign affairs in 1853. He could not stop the outbreak of the CRIMEAN WAR in 1854, but he maintained the French-English alliance during the conflict and helped negotiate a peace agreement at the CONGRESS OF PARIS in 1856. He left office in 1858 but returned twice as foreign secretary (1865–66 and 1868–70). During the latter tenure he helped settle U.S. claims against England concerning the Confederate warship *ALABAMA*.

Clay, Henry (1777–1852) American politician. Clay was born in Virginia and moved to Kentucky in 1797. Elected to the House of Representatives in 1810, he was Speaker of the House almost continuously from 1811 to 1825. He supported the War of 1812 against Great Britain. In 1820 he helped hammer out the Missouri Compromise, which temporarily resolved the conflicts between the North and the South. As a senator he helped arrange the COMPROMISE OF 1850, the last peaceful settlement of sectional differences before the Civil War.

Clay ran unsuccessfully for president in 1824, 1832, and 1844. He was elected to the Senate three times (1830, 1836, and 1848). He is remembered for his "American System," a plan to stimulate the economy through high tariffs, public works, and a national banking system.

Cleveland, Grover (1837–1908) Twenty-second (1885–89) and twenty-fourth (1893–97) president of the UNITED STATES. Born in Caldwell, New Jersey, he practiced law in Buffalo, New York, where he was elected mayor in 1881. The Democrat's honest administration helped him win the 1882 gubernatorial election in a campaign against both TAMMANY HALL and corrupt Republicans. His reform politics carried him to the Democratic presidential nomination in 1884 and a defeat of Republican nominee James Blaine.

Cleveland supported the work of the Civil Service Commission, but he could not keep many of his reform promises and the system remained based on patronage. His opposition to higher tariffs and his support of the gold standard despite farmers' demands for liberal coinage of silver helped undermine his reelection bid in 1888. He won a plurality of the popular vote but not enough electoral votes to defeat BENJAMIN HARRISON.

Cleveland became the only president to serve two nonconsecutive terms when he defeated Harrison in 1892. A failing economy and his dispatch of troops to quell the PULLMAN STRIKE in 1894 cost him the 1896 nomination. He wrote *Presidential Problems* (1904) and *Fishing and Hunting Sketches* (1906).

clipper ship Sailing vessel. The term *clipper* was probably derived from the expression "going at a good clip" or a similar idiomatic phrase. The clipper ship, designed primarily for speed, was distinguished by its sharp hull, with a length five or six times its beam, and a heavy, lofty square rig, usually with three masts. While the first clipper is often cited as the five-hundred-ton *Ann McKim,* built by Baltimore merchant Isaac McKim in 1833, the great age of the clipper ships did not arrive until the repeal of the British navigation acts in 1849, which opened the China trade to American shippers and demanded fast ships to deliver cargo to San Francisco, California, and Melbourne, Australia, during their respective gold rushes. By 1860, as freight rates declined and steamships provided stiff competition, the great age of the clipper ship had ended. The most famous clipper ship, the British *CUTTY SARK,* was built in 1869. See also SHIPS.

Clough, Arthur Hugh (1819–1861) English poet. Born in Liverpool, the son of a cotton merchant, he spent his early childhood in South Carolina before returning to England in 1828, where he attended Rugby and became friends with MATTHEW ARNOLD, son of the school's headmaster THOMAS ARNOLD. Clough resided at Oxford University from 1837 to 1848: as a student until 1842 and then as a fellow and tutor of Oriel College. Religious doubts caused him to leave that position, however, and in his satiric, socially perceptive poetry he became a voice of mid-Victorian skepticism and spiritual malaise. Returning for a time to the United States, he became friends with such Massachusetts intellectuals as RALPH WALDO EMERSON and Ralph Eliot Norton. He returned to England and served as examiner in the Education Office from 1853 until his death in 1861. He published two volumes of poetry, the hexameter verse novel *The Bothie of Tober-na-Vuolich* (1848) and the collection *Ambervalia* (1849). His verse novel *Amours de Voyage* first appeared in *The Atlantic Monthly* in 1858. His uncompleted satire *Dipsychus* was published posthumously in 1865. Clough's poetic reputation languished for a long time, but it is now somewhat rehabilitated. He is memorialized in his friend Matthew Arnold's elegy "Thyrsis."

coach Enclosed four-wheeled vehicle for carrying people. Examples were stagecoaches, private coaches, and railroad coaches. Hackney coaches, coaches for hire, were largely displaced in the Victorian era by two-wheeled HANSOM CABS. See also CARRIAGE.

Cobden, Richard (1804–1865) English politician, anti-imperialist, and free trade advocate. The son of a poor farmer, he prospered as owner of a calico-printing mill, traveled extensively abroad, and began to promote free trade. He cofounded the ANTI–CORN LAW LEAGUE in 1838 and was its principal spokesperson and leader until repeal of the CORN LAWS in 1846. Cobden, JOHN BRIGHT, ROBERT PEEL, and JOHN RUSSELL were the primary architects of the repeal.

Cobden, who had been elected to Parliament in 1841, was also a leading opponent of British IMPERIALISM. He opposed the CRIMEAN WAR, criticized England's interventionist CHINA policy in the late 1850s, and resisted English military involvement over the Schleswig-Holstein question. He also supported English neutrality during the U.S. Civil War. His stand against foreign intervention cost him his seat in 1857, but he was reelected in 1859. He negotiated the Cobden Treaty in 1860, which reduced tariffs with France. The treaty included the "most favored nation clause," integrated into many later commercial treaties.

Domestically, Cobden opposed the FACTORY ACTS while deploring child labor. This opposition reflected the Manchester school of economic thought that contested government intervention in free enterprise. He espoused universal education, a reduction in the income tax, and cuts in military spending.

cocaine See NARCOTICS.

Cody, William Frederick [Buffalo Bill] (1846–1917) American frontiersman and showman. Born in Iowa, he rode as a youth for the PONY EXPRESS and was a Union frontier scout during the U.S. CIVIL WAR. He later hunted buffalo in Kansas to supply meat to railroad construction crews and served as a cavalry scout during the Sioux War of 1872–77. Cody's exploits and gift for self-promotion made him the subject of many DIME NOVELS, particularly those of NED BUNTLINE, who is said to have coined Cody's nickname, Buffalo Bill. Cody left the frontier for good in 1883 to capitalize on his fame. His famous "Wild West" show featured mock battles between Indians and cowboys, sharpshooters, rodeo acts, and other Western attractions. His poor investments negated the commercial success of his shows, however, and he relied on a small government pension during his last days.

Coercion Acts Series of British laws. Dating from 1765, the acts temporarily banned public meetings, suspended habeas corpus, curtailed civilian courts, and restricted other civil and political rights in selected parts of IRELAND. The frequent passing of the acts indicate the almost continual state of agitation or rebellion against English rule of Ireland. Some sixty-five Coercion Acts were passed or extended between 1800 and 1887 in response to agricultural violence and nationalist agitation. The most famous act of the Victorian era, passed in 1881, landed CHARLES STEWART PARNELL in jail for his leadership of the Irish LAND LEAGUE.

Cole, Thomas (1801–1848) English-born American landscape painter. One of the founders of the HUDSON RIVER SCHOOL, Cole left his native England for America in 1819, settling in New York in 1825 to study the physical and spiritual beauty of the landscape. Just as Americans were developing a taste for landscape painting, Cole began to paint Arcadian compositions such as *Expulsion from the Garden of Eden* and *View of the White Mountains,* both in 1828. Cole's paintings were driven by the desire to capture both the real and ideal essences of nature. After a two-year stay in Europe, Cole returned to the United States to create more overtly allegorical series paintings, such as *The Course of Empire* (1836) and *The Voyage of Life* (1840), stylistically derived from the landscapes of seventeenth-century French painter Claude Lorrain. However, his heroic subjects, infused with Romantic symbolism, were not well received by the public, who wanted typical American scenes.

Cole became best known for his ideal natural representations of specific sites along the Hudson River, including *The Oxbow* (1836) and *View of the Falls of Munda* (1847). His paintings of locales outside the Hudson River Valley retained the iconography of ROMANTICISM since they were invented reconstructions of settings. His interpretation of the real and imaginary through a careful examination and contemplation of the natural world had a great impact on other Hudson River painters, including Asher B. Durand and FREDERIC CHURCH.

Colenso, John William (1814–1883) British prelate. Appointed bishop of the new diocese of Natal, an annexed part of SOUTH AFRICA, in 1853, he became a champion of the ZULU natives, defending them against BOER oppression, compiling a grammar and dictionary of Zulu, and translating the Book of Common Prayer and the New Testament into Zulu. His broad-minded acceptance of polygamy among Zulu converts made him a controversial figure, as did his critical approach to the Bible, particularly in *The Pentateuch and Book of Joshua Critically Examined* (1862–79), in which he claimed that these books were historically inaccurate and were written during the post-Exile period. Deposed and excommunicated by the bishop of Cape Town in 1864, he was acquitted on appeal and confirmed in his position by the courts in 1866. The autonomous church of South Africa deposed him again in 1869.

Colette, [Sidonie-Gabrielle] (1873–1954) French writer. Born in Saint-Sauveur-en-Puisaye, she married thirty-four-year-old writer Henry Gauthier-Villars when she was twenty. The couple lived in Paris, where Colette began to write fictionalized reminiscences of her youth. The four "Claudine" books—*Claudine at School,* 1900; *Claudine in Paris,* 1901; *The Indulgent Husband,* 1902; *The Innocent Wife,* 1903—were published under her husband's pseudonym, "Willy." The couple divorced in 1906. After 1913 she published under the name that would make her one of the most famous French writers of her day. She produced more than fifty novels and short stories, including an affectionate portrait of her mother in *Sido* (1929), *Cheri* (1920), and *Gigi* (1945). In 1944 she became the first female member of the French Goncourt Academy. In 1953 she was named an officer in the Legion of Honor.

Colleen Bawn, The (1860) Irish melodrama. Written by Irish-born playwright DION BOUCICAULT, the play is based on the novel *The Collegians* (1829) by Gerald Griffin (1803–1840), which is based on a historical murder. A popular success, it was loved especially for its good-hearted, comic Irish vagabond Myles-na-Coppaleen. The play premiered at Laura Keene's Theatre in New York City. It concerns the attempted murder of poor *colleen bawn,* Anglo-Irish for "fair girl," Eily O'Connor, by her husband Hardress Cregan and her rescue by Myles.

Collins, Wilkie (1824–1889) English novelist. Born in London, he was the son of landscape painter William Collins. Self-educated and widely traveled, he became a friend of Charles Dickens and was a frequent contributor to his journal *Household Words.* Collins is best known for his highly literate detective novels, sometimes called "sensation fiction," which rely on intricate plots of great melodramatic skill. Among his most celebrated works are *The Moonstone* (1868), a work that concerns the search for a priceless Hindu diamond and was characterized by the poet T. S. Eliot as the greatest of modern detective novels. *The Woman in White* (1859) details the sudden appearance of a woman, escaped from an insane asylum, who harbors a terrible secret.

colonialism See IMPERIALISM and BRITISH EMPIRE.

Colt, Samuel (1814–1862) American gun manufacturer and inventor. Born in Hartford, Connecticut, the son of a textile manufacturer, he was fifteen when he began developing ideas for the revolver, a new concept in FIREARMS. He received an American patent in 1836, but his factory in Paterson, New Jersey, failed when the army refused to buy his revolver. The Texas Rangers used his weapons effectively, however, and the army changed its mind after Colt developed a heavier version with .44-caliber bullets. Colt set up a new factory in Hartford in 1848, which supplied Union soldiers during the CIVIL WAR and countless western settlers. His revolver became known as the "gun that helped win the West." Colt also invented a submarine battery for harbor defense and an underwater telegraph CABLE.

comic strip Printed cartoon narrative told in a series of pictures. Comic strips grew out of the cartoons, or humorous one-panel illustrations, made popular in late-nineteenth-century Europe by such artists as Rodolphe Topffer and J. J. Grandville. The first advance toward a serial form of cartoons was the 1896 debut of the American comic strip "The Yellow Kid" by Richard Outcault. His character was so popular that he was featured as a regular in the *New York World* and other newspapers. Words were displayed on the Kid's shirt, marking the first time words appeared inside the frame. *The Yellow Kid*'s popularity was due in part to new color-printing technologies and a growing newspaper-reading, urban audience.

Comic strips continued to develop with the "KATZENJAMMER KIDS," created by Rudolph Dirks in 1897. Dirks's strip started with one picture at a time and soon developed into a four-panel square describing continuous action and using balloons for dialogue. The enormous influence of comic strips on the public was demonstrated by Outcault's "Buster Brown" (1902) when Buster Brown fashions swept America at the turn of the century. By this time newspapers were featuring comics regularly, commonly in black and white during the week and in full color on Sunday.

communism See SOCIALISM and *THE COMMUNIST MANIFESTO.*

Communist Manifesto, The (1848) German political pamphlet. One of the many efforts by KARL MARX and FRIEDRICH ENGELS to communicate their idea of communism to the general public, the *Manifesto* is perhaps their most accessible and widely known work. It lays out the basic claims for communism as systematized by Marx and Engels. History was defined as a series of class struggles; the current phase was a struggle between bourgeois capitalists and the proletariat, the wage-earning working class. Communism, they asserted, was the only movement that fully embraced the interests of the proletariat. Furthermore, communism was destined to succeed because the capitalist system contained within it the seeds of its own destruction. Its dependence on a large alienated proletariat and ever-increasing production would inevitably lead to more frequent crises and finally to a proletarian uprising, just as the capitalists had overthrown the previous feudal system. The goal of communism was the dissolution of private property, which was considered an instrument of oppression. The *Manifesto* also contained warnings against the dangers posed by utopian socialists and feudal reactionaries to the true interests of the proletariat. Beginning with the words, "A specter is haunting Europe—the specter of Communism," the pamphlet closes with the words, "The proletariat has nothing to lose but its chains. It has a world to win. Workers of the world unite!"

Compromise of 1850 Series of U.S. legislative acts. The Compromise of 1850 temporarily settled the crisis over the extension of SLAVERY into the territories obtained by the United States as a result of the MEXICAN WAR. HENRY CLAY proposed the compromise when the California territory asked to join the Union as a free state and southern leaders threatened secession at the request. Clay proposed that California be a free state while residents of the New Mexico and Utah territories would decide later about slavery. The slave trade, though not slavery, would end in Washington, D.C., and federal and local governments would help hunt runaway slaves under a stricter Fugitive Slave Act. President ZACHARY TAYLOR opposed the arrangement, as did militant southerners led by JOHN C. CALHOUN. Supporters of the WILMOT PROVISO also vilified the compromise. Taylor died suddenly in July 1850, and his successor, MILLARD FILLMORE, supported Clay, as did Senate leaders DANIEL WEBSTER and STEPHEN DOUGLAS. After its enactment, diehards on both sides of the slavery issue denounced the compromise, but it helped delay the CIVIL WAR.

Comte, Auguste (1798–1857) French philosopher. Founder of the philosophical school of positivism, which regards observed phenomena as the basis of knowledge and exalts scientific inquiry. Comte is also one of the founders of sociology, a term he coined in 1838 for the systematic study of the unifying principles of society. Dedicated to republican ideals and social reform, he worked toward the goal of a more harmonious social order. Among his supporters was English philosopher JOHN STUART MILL, who helped secure him financial assistance. His works include *Cours de philosophie positive* (1830–42), *Ordre et progrès* (1848), and *Système de politique positive* (1851–54).

Coney Island American amusement center. Located in Brooklyn, New York, Coney Island opened as a seaside resort in the mid-nineteenth century. In addition to an Atlantic Ocean beachfront, it offered a two-mile boardwalk and nationally known amusement arcades that included Sea Lion Park (renamed Luna Park in 1903) and Steeplechase Park.

The latter became known as the first true amusement park in 1897 when promoter George Tilyou enclosed several unrelated rides and other attractions and charged an admission fee. Dance halls, band shells, circus acts, and a range of food stalls and eateries completed the experience.

Offering the illusion of extravagance for the cost of carfare, Coney Island and its many cohorts across the United States—Cleveland's Euclid Beach, Philadelphia's Willow Grove, among others—were popular among all social classes. Said the 1899 *Visitor's Guide to the City of New York,* Coney Island was "the great seaside playground for the people." It was the prime example of the amusements enjoyed by Victorian Americans in the newfound leisure time wrought by the Industrial Revolution.

Confederacy Common name of the Confederate States of America. The government that was formed by southern states leaving the Union after the election of ABRAHAM LINCOLN in 1860 was comprised of six states: South Carolina, Georgia, Florida, Alabama, Louisiana, and Mississippi. They established a temporary government at Montgomery, Alabama, in February 1861. Texas joined in March, followed by Virginia, North Carolina, Tennessee, and Arkansas in April, after the start of the CIVIL WAR. A convention adopted a constitution that resembled the U.S. constitution in many respects but recognized SLAVERY, abolished tariffs, and included states' rights clauses. JEFFERSON DAVIS was chosen president, and the capital moved to Richmond, Virginia, in July.

The Confederate attack on Fort Sumter and Lincoln's mobilization of troops ended any hopes of a peaceful secession. Early southern military victories raised optimism that the South could defend itself, but the Confederacy declared a disastrous embargo on cotton exports in a misguided effort to force diplomatic recognition from England and France. Both European countries recognized the Union naval blockade of the Confederate coast, isolating the South from its main potential trade partners. As the war dragged on, the North's superior numbers and manufacturing prowess began to translate into Union military victories. Conscription laws and other military measures failed as many state governments, founded on states' rights doctrines, refused to cooperate with Richmond. A ruinous inflation reduced the value of the Confederate dollar to below two cents by war's end. The Confederacy surrendered on April 9, 1865.

Conference of Berlin See BERLIN, CONFERENCE OF.

Congress of Berlin See BERLIN, CONGRESS OF.

Conkling, Roscoe (1829–1888) American political boss and senator. His father was a congressman from New York and U.S. judge. The junior Conkling was made Albany's district attorney at twenty-one. He served in the House of Representatives from 1859 to 1863 and again from 1865 to 1867. He was elected senator in 1867.

Conkling's support of President ULYSSES S. GRANT made him the chief dispenser of federal jobs in the state. Grant's successor, RUTHERFORD B. HAYES, challenged Conkling's control of the New York spoils system by removing future president CHESTER ARTHUR and future governor of New York Alonzo Cornell from their appointments to the New York Customs House. Conkling then led the "Stalwart" movement to nominate Grant for a third term in 1880, but the convention deadlocked and chose JAMES GARFIELD as a compromise candidate.

When Garfield made a Conkling adversary the customs collector of New York's port, Conkling resigned from the Senate in protest. He expected to be reelected, but the state legislature rejected him. He spent the rest of his days in private law practice in New York City. After getting caught in the famous BLIZZARD OF '88, he died of exposure.

Connolly, James (1870–1916) Irish labor organizer and nationalist leader. Connolly grew up in Edinburgh, Scotland, and joined the British army at fourteen to escape his family's poverty. Most of his seven years as a soldier were spent in IRELAND during the height of the LAND LEAGUE agitation.

Connolly returned to Scotland after leaving the service. He labored at odd jobs and worked for the Scottish Socialist Federation, then moved to Dublin in 1895 to organize for a socialist club. He helped form the Irish Socialist Republican Party in 1896. The party sought to create an Irish socialist republic, but it faltered and Connolly emigrated to the United States. He spent seven years there and helped organize the International Workers of the World, or "Wobblies."

Upon returning to Ireland in 1910, Connolly became an organizer in Belfast for the Irish Transport Workers Union. He helped organize a massive strike in 1913 and also developed the Irish Citizens Army, a small force trained to defend strikers from police violence. He joined the leaders of the Irish Republican Brotherhood (see FENIANS) in planning the Easter Rebellion of 1916 in Dublin and was executed by the British government in the rebellion's aftermath.

Conrad, Joseph [Józef Teodor Konrad Korzeniowski] (1857–1924) Polish-born British novelist. He was born in Berdichev, Poland, to aristocratic parents opposed to Russia's domination of Poland. In 1862, due to the political activities of his father Apollo, the family was sent into exile in northern Russia, where both parents fatally contracted tuberculosis. Orphaned in 1869, he left Poland in 1874 at sixteen to become a merchant seaman under the French flag. Four years later he sailed on a British ship for the first time and began to learn English, the language he would later employ in his fiction. He became a British subject and passed his master's examination in the British merchant marine in 1886. In 1894, after twenty years at sea, he left the merchant marine to become a writer in England, using the pen name Joseph Conrad. His first novel, *Almayer's Folly,* was published in 1895, and his second, *An Outcast of the Islands,* was published in 1896, the same year he married Jessie George.

Conrad's experiences at sea formed the basis for many of his works, including *The Nigger of the "Narcissus"* (1897) and *LORD JIM* (1900). With these novels Conrad embarked on a series of works that are among the greatest written in English, probing into the recesses of the human heart, reflecting on European imperialism in Africa, Asia, and Latin America, and experimenting with narrative levels, chronological structure, and style. Most of his works were written after Queen Victoria's reign, including *Heart of Darkness* (1902), generally considered his finest short novel, and *Nostromo* (1904), his greatest full-length novel. But his point of view was shaped in the Victorian world, which directly informs many of his works. *Heart of Darkness,* for example, is based on his actual voyage as captain of a steamer down the Congo River in 1890. A major modernist innovator, he was esteemed and befriended by such literary figures as John Galsworthy, Ford Madox Ford,

HENRY JAMES, and H. G. WELLS, though he did not achieve commercial success until *Chance* in 1913. His other works include *The Secret Agent* (1907), *The Secret Sharer* (1910), *Under Western Eyes* (1911), *Victory* (1915), *The Shadow-Line* (1917), *The Rover* (1923), and *Suspense* (1925). Nonfiction autobiographical works include *The Mirror of the Sea* (1906).

Conservative Party British political group. After the REFORM BILL OF 1832 enlarged the English electorate, some Tories began to form a new party to address the concerns of the emerging middle and business classes. The term "conservative" was first used by GEORGE CANNING in the mid-1820s, but the 1834 administration of ROBERT PEEL is considered the first Conservative Party government. Peel's Tamworth Manifesto and other declarations laid out the basic Conservative beliefs in aristocratic rule, a restricted franchise, law and order, a strong imperialist policy, and the sanctity of the Church of England.

Peel and the Conservatives ruled from 1841 to 1846, but his repeal of the CORN LAWS in 1846 split the party into an agricultural, protectionist wing led by BENJAMIN DISRAELI and a free trade wing called the Peelites. The rupture kept the Conservatives out of office from 1846 to 1874, except for three fleeting ministries. Disraeli reorganized the party and was prime minister from 1874 to 1880, basing his appeal on vigorous IMPERIALISM and a plan for domestic reform to woo an expanding electorate. Ousted in an 1880 rout by the LIBERAL PARTY, the Conservatives regained the prime ministry in 1886 after the Liberals split over Irish HOME RULE. Conservatives stayed in power until after Queen Victoria's death but lost power in 1906 when the plan by JOSEPH CHAMBERLAIN to reinstate higher tariffs ruptured the party.

contact lenses Corrective eyewear. The first practical contact lenses were introduced in 1877 by Swiss medical doctor A. E. Fick. Made of glass and covering the entire eyeball, the lenses were fairly uncomfortable but offered an alternative to eyeglasses for the self-conscious. Modern contact lenses, made of plastic, with high water content and covering only the cornea, were not developed until the mid-twentieth century.

Cook, Thomas (1808–1892) English tourist agent. He was the inventor of the guided group tour and founder of the first international travel agency. Cook left school at age ten, eventually becoming a Baptist missionary and an ardent advocate of temperance. In 1841 he negotiated with the Midland Counties Railway Company to run a special train between Leicester and Loughborough to bring participants to a temperance meeting. This journey led to a longstanding arrangement with the railroad and is believed to be the first advertised excursion train trip in England. Thereafter Cook organized other temperance tours in the British Isles until he was able to branch out and serve general travelers as well, setting up excursions and conducting grand tours of Europe. In 1865 he opened his London office and phased out guiding tours in favor of planning trips and selling tickets. The agency, taken over by his son after Cook's death in 1892, remains one of the world's largest travel service companies.

Cooke, Jay (1821–1905) American financier. Born in Ohio and relocated east as a teenager, he rose quickly through several Philadelphia banks and established his own firm, Jay Cooke & Company, in 1861. A year later Cooke marketed more than $500 million in government bonds to help finance the CIVIL WAR. Cooke sold the bonds not only to bankers but to average citizens in one of the first mass fund-raising campaigns in history. He repeated the performance in 1865 by raising another $830 million in bonds.

Cooke later tried to raise $100 million to build the Northern Pacific Railroad but could not sustain the financing. He was forced to close his New York branch in 1873, a move that helped start the Panic of 1873. Wiped out in the panic, Cooke rebuilt his fortune by 1880.

cookshop Precursor to the restaurant. Popular in nineteenth-century London, the cookshop was an establishment to which customers brought their own food to be cooked.

coolie Derogatory term for an unskilled laborer. Often associated with nineteenth-century Chinese immigrants to America, the term originated in British India. It derives from the Kuli tribe of the Indian province of Gujerat or possibly from the Urdu word "*kuli,*" which means "hireling." The first people to be called coolies were laborers from India hired under five-year contracts to work for low wages in British colonies after the British abolished slavery in the 1830s. Many of these laborers suffered through long ocean voyages in inhumane and life-threatening conditions; these transport vessels were called coolie ships.

Cooper, Peter (1791–1883) American inventor, industrialist, and philanthropist. Born in New York City, he invented the first American steam locomotive, *Tom Thumb,* for the Baltimore & Ohio Railroad in 1830. As a businessman, his investments included iron mines, foundries, telegraph lines, and shares of the transatlantic CABLE. He introduced the BESSEMER PROCESS into American steelmaking and invented such devices as a washing machine. As a philanthropist dedicated to his native city, he founded Cooper Union (1859), a free institution of higher learning, one of the first to focus on adult education in science, engineering, and art. He also supported New York City public schools and improved police and fire services. Near the end of his life he ran for president as the Greenback Party nominee (1876).

Copperheads Derogatory term for northern Democrats who opposed the U.S. CIVIL WAR. The name is derived from the copper pennies some of them wore as badges. Calling themselves "Peace Democrats," this group was strongest in the Midwest; their reasons for their stance included doubt that the war could restore the Union, opposition to the abolition of SLAVERY, sympathy for the South, and support for states' rights. The best known Copperhead leader was Clement Laird Vallandigham (1820–1871), an Ohio lawyer and politician who was banished from the Union for his views in 1863 but who returned in 1864 to persuade the Democratic Party to call the war a failure in the platform adopted at its national convention, at which GEORGE B. MCCLELLAN was nominated for president. Though often accused of disloyalty and of giving comfort to the enemy, the Copperheads enjoyed considerable support during the periods when the war was going poorly.

cordite Smokeless explosive. Invented by British chemists FREDERICK AUGUSTUS ABEL and JAMES DEWAR in 1889, cordite is a mixture of nitroglycerine, nitrocellulose, and petroleum jelly. The gelatinous material was squirted out and measured in cords, giving it its name.

Corn Laws Series of British regulations. The laws regulated the export and import of grains into Great Britain and other countries. In England a corn law passed in 1815 raised the protective tariff on grain imports. The law benefited the landed gentry that dominated

Parliament through the Tory Party, while raising the price of bread steeply for workers. Riots ensued when workers took to the streets to protest the tariff. Authorities suppressed the disturbances, and the laws remained in effect.

The political alliance among the Whigs and other liberal elements that had passed the REFORM BILL OF 1832 formed an ANTI-CORN LAW LEAGUE in 1838. Industrialists supported the league, which was led by RICHARD COBDEN, because the high prices resulting from the tariffs forced wages up. The Tory gentry, under the political leadership of BENJAMIN DISRAELI, fought to retain the laws. The league organized mass demonstrations and lecture tours while issuing educational pamphlets and books. The Protection Society tried to counter the league's campaign.

The famine in Ireland during the 1840s also put pressure on the Tory government of ROBERT PEEL to lower food prices. Peel repealed the laws temporarily in 1845. After a bitter struggle, Parliament voted in 1846 to phase out the laws over three years. Prices dropped somewhat, but Peel's government fell immediately after the repeal vote.

The corn law battle helped split the Tory Party into a conservative wing led by Disraeli and a liberal following headed by WILLIAM GLADSTONE. It was also another sign of the growing strength of the emerging factory owners and other segments of the middle class.

Cornelius, Peter von (1783–1867) German painter. He studied at Düsseldorf and in Rome where he joined the German Nazarene group and collaborated with other members in the decoration of Casa Bartholdy. In 1820 he was commissioned by Louis I of Bavaria to paint fresco decorations in the Glyptothek, Munich.

Cornelius revived the art of fresco painting. His masterpiece, *The Last Judgment* (1836–40), was one of his fresco decorations for the Ludwigskirche in Munich. At first Cornelius's fresco recalls Michelangelo's great composition in the Sistine Chapel, but stylistically it looks back to the fifteenth-century linearity and stiffness of Albrecht Dürer and Fra Angelico.

His favorite themes were religious or philosophical. In addition to his frescoes, Cornelius created notable illustrations for *Faust* and the *Nibelungenlied* and designs for the decoration of the royal mausoleum, done for Frederick William II of Prussia. Outside Germany, Cornelius had many admirers, including JEAN-AUGUSTE-DOMINIQUE INGRES and EUGÈNE DELACROIX, who respected his efforts to keep the ideal tradition of art free from the facts of modern nineteenth-century life.

Corot, [Jean-Baptiste-] Camille (1796–1875) French painter. Corot was trained in the classical tradition of French landscape inspired by Nicolas Poussin. After three visits to Italy, he executed classical landscapes that influenced followers of POST-IMPRESSIONISM, especially PAUL CÉZANNE, through rich panels of color. Popular success came to Corot during the 1850s when the emperor purchased one of his landscapes, *Souvenir de Marcoussis,* from the Salon of 1855. Though not actually a member, the style and appeal of his landscapes closely connected him with the BARBIZON SCHOOL. He is best known for his soft and silvery woodland scene *Souvenir de Mortefontaine* (1864), which became widely available through prints and engravings.

Like his landscapes, Corot's later portraits and figure studies formed a bridge between traditional and modern painting at the end of the nineteenth century. Corot's *Woman with the Pearl* (1868–70) is composed through a massing of volume to create a solid structure of form and color. Corot even allowed formal values to construct an abstraction of the human figure in his *Interrupted Reading* (1870).

Corot was an active man, serving on Salon juries, including the Salon jury of 1849, which awarded a medal to the unknown GUSTAVE COURBET. Corot traveled extensively and was greatly admired by contemporary painters.

corset A body-shaping undergarment for women with supports made of whalebone. The corset helped to effect an hourglass figure by compacting the flesh of the upper and middle parts of the body into the two-piece shaped undergarment and securing the fit by hooking the corset in the front and lacing it closed along the back. A consistent achievement of the minuscule Victorian waist—18 inches was the ideal—sometimes resulted in permanent back or spine deformities.

County Councils Act British electoral reform law. Despite the increase in the electorate brought about by the Reform Acts, English voters could not elect their local officials until the passing of the County Councils Act in 1888. The act reduced the power of the old justices of the peace who were appointed by powerful landowners to perform various government functions. Local elected councils gained control of public health, education, road maintenance, and other activities. Under the act, larger towns were treated as counties so they would not be dominated by their outlying rural areas.

Courbet, [Jean Désiré] Gustave (1819–1877) French Realist painter and controversial public figure. Born at Ornans and trained as a Neo-Baroque Romantic in the early 1840s, Courbet fell under the impact of the revolutionary spirit by 1848, declaring that the Romantic emphasis on feeling and imagination was an escape from the realities of the time.

The Stone Breakers (1849) was the first painting to fully embody REALISM by depicting two men working matter-of-factly without any pathos or sentiment. In 1850, Courbet's unidealized group portrait *Burial at Ornans* caused a sensation at the Salon, where it was seen as a cynical depiction of the clergy and an unflattering representation of the local peasants. By the time of the next Salon, in 1852, Courbet had achieved a reputation for attacking social and artistic standards through means of deliberate ugliness. Courbet's *Young Ladies of the Village* (1852) was not perceived as a charming pastoral outing but as a painting of three vulgar rural women in an awkward composition. At the Paris Exposition of 1855, Courbet failed to gain entry for his pictures. He therefore organized a private exhibition in a wooden shed, where he distributed a "manifesto of Realism" and showcased his most ambitious painting, *Interior of My Studio, a Real Allegory Summing Up Seven Years of My Life as an Artist* (1854–55).

Courbet continued to paint seascapes, landscapes, floral arrangements, animals, nudes, and a few large-scale genre paintings, all of which endured harsh criticism. Courbet withdrew from the 1867 Salon and once again held his own exhibition, an action that was followed by the founders of IMPRESSIONISM. By rejecting the ideals of both the neoclassical and the Romantic schools and by choosing subjects from the common life of the rural poor, Courbet's independent behavior and style prepared the way for other artists such as JEAN-FRANÇOIS MILLET and EDGAR DEGAS.

Covent Garden Retail and entertainment area of London. The site of the city's main fruit and vegetable market, it was also a haven for prostitutes and the location of the Theatre Royal. Founded in 1732, it had been a patent theater, one of two theaters—the other being DRURY LANE—with the exclusive legal right to stage legitimate plays in the city. After that monopoly was abolished in 1843, the theater concentrated on staging operas. After being destroyed by fires, the original building was replaced by a new one in 1809 and again in 1857. The latter building, designed by Edward Barry (1830–1880), son of architect Sir CHARLES BARRY, is now called the Royal Opera House and is the home of both the Royal Opera and the Royal Ballet.

Coxey's Army U.S. protest group. The army was made up of unemployed men who marched on the U.S. Capitol in 1894 in a "living petition" to advocate for measures to lessen unemployment following the Panic of 1893. Founded by Ohio populist leader Jacob Sechler Coxey (1854–1951), the group of about five hundred arrived for a May Day celebration, and although it was quickly disbanded by Capitol officials, it served as an example for future protest "armies."

Cracker Jack Candy-coated popcorn mixed with peanuts. It was developed by German-American immigrant brothers F. W. and Lewis Rueckheim at the 1893 Chicago World's Fair. Residents of Chicago for over two decades, the Rueckheims developed the product as an offshoot of their successful popcorn stand, intending to capitalize on the popularity of peanuts and popcorn as snacks. Legend holds that the name was a variation of the expression "Cracker, Jack!"—"Cracker" being a term for "excellent" and "Jack" a familiar moniker for an acquaintance. Prizes did not appear in Cracker Jack boxes until 1913; the sailor boy, Jack, and his dog, Bingo, first appeared on the wrapper in 1916.

Craik, Dinah Maria Mulock (1826–1887) English novelist. Craik published her first novel, *The Ogilvies,* in 1849 under her maiden name, Mulock. Her most popular work was *John Halifax, Gentleman* (1857), the tale of an orphan who rises from poverty to success; her favorite of her own novels was *A Life for a Life* (1859). In 1864 she married Scottish literary scholar George Lillie Craik (1798–1866). She also wrote poems, essays, and stories for children.

Crane, Stephen (1871–1900) American writer. Born in Newark, New Jersey, Crane was the son of a Methodist clergyman who died in 1880, leaving nine children. He briefly attended Lafayette College and Syracuse University but showed little interest in academic study. Instead Crane pursued what he called his "artistic education on the Bowery," exploring and meticulously observing the New York City slums. Crane worked intermittently as a freelance writer, although his accounts were more impressionistic than factual. In 1892 he borrowed money to have his novel *Maggie: A Girl of the Streets* published at his own expense under a pseudonym. While the author Hamlin Garland praised the book, its subject, the ruin of a slum girl, proved too grim for magazines.

Despite his bohemian life, Crane was very productive, and his masterpiece, *The Red Badge of Courage,* when serialized in late 1894 brought immediate acclaim. In 1895 he traveled as a correspondent for a newspaper syndicate through Mexico and the West, collecting background material for subsequent short stories, including "The Blue Hotel" and "The Bride Comes to Yellow Sky." His book of poems, *The Black Riders,* was criticized for its unconventional sensibility and free-verse form. Later that year *The Red Badge of Courage* was a best-seller. Other novels and short-story volumes briskly followed, including the reissue of *Maggie.*

The intense battle scenes in *The Red Badge of Courage* pegged Crane as a war correspondent. He went to Jacksonville, Florida, in 1896 to cover the Cuban revolution. There he met his future wife, Cora Taylor, proprietress of the Hotel de Dream. He left Jacksonville aboard the *Commodore,* which soon sank. His ordeal at sea is depicted in the short story "The Open Boat." Covering the Greco-Turkish War in 1897, Crane was joined by Cora. They lived in London briefly and became friends with novelist JOSEPH CONRAD before Crane went to Cuba to cover the SPANISH-AMERICAN WAR for JOSEPH PULITZER's *New York World.*

He returned to New York broken in health and notorious for the topics of his writing, his "disreputable" acquaintances, and his wan appearance. Disgusted, Crane returned to England on December 31, 1899. He lived until May 1900 at Brede Place in Sussex, England, a damp, partially restored manor. Constant hospitality offered to the likes of Conrad, H. G. WELLS, and HENRY JAMES strained the Cranes' limited finances and health. In April 1900, tuberculosis caused Crane two massive hemorrhages; he traveled to a sanitarium in Badenweiler, Germany, where he died later that year.

In his short life Crane published an astonishing amount, although of uneven quality. His works pioneered American literary REALISM. Crane's writing at best has a vivid, severe style and sincere, unusual observations; his sincerity is always tempered by his vision of an incomprehensible, possibly hostile universe and sharp criticism of man's moral lethargy.

Crane, Walter (1845–1915) English textile and wallpaper designer, painter, and illustrator of children's books. As a painter, Crane is a descendant of the PRE-RAPHAELITES and is associated with EDWARD BURNE-JONES. In 1862 his first painting, *The Lady of Shalot,* was accepted by the Royal Academy. Exhibiting frequently in London, he created such works as *Plato's Garden, Diana and the Shepherd,* and *Bridge of Life.* He is best known for his illustrations of the works of Edmund Spenser, Nathaniel Hawthorne's *Wonder Book,* and Grimm's *Fairy Tales. Baby's Opera* (1877), which is typical of his delicate style, was done for the publisher Edmund Evans who had commissioned him and KATE GREENAWAY for a series of children's books.

Crane was later linked with the ARTS AND CRAFTS MOVEMENT of WILLIAM MORRIS, producing textile designs, glass windows, tapestries, and house decoration. His interest in SOCIALISM was expressed in his cartoons for *Commonweal* and *Justice.* In 1888, Crane founded the Arts and Crafts Exhibition Society of London.

Crazy Horse (1849?–1877) Sioux Indian chief. Crazy Horse led his tribe's resistance against white settlers moving west. He first gained fame by defeating U.S. cavalry troops in a battle in 1866 and by leading raids against Union Pacific Railroad survey teams. He led the fight against encroachment into the sacred tribal areas of the Black Hills in what is now western South Dakota. In 1876 he defeated troops at Rosebud River and later joined with chiefs Sitting Bull and Gall to defeat GEORGE A. CUSTER at Little Big Horn. After many Sioux fled to Canada to escape army vengeance, Crazy Horse and his one thousand followers surrendered in January 1877 after a winter of near-starvation. Later that year he was arrested for leaving the reservation and was stabbed to death in army custody.

Creighton, Mandell (1843–1901) English prelate and historian. Appointed professor of ecclesiastical history at Cambridge in 1884, Mandell published the highly praised *A History of the Papacy During the Period of the Reformation* (1882–94). He also served as first editor of *English Historical Review* (1886–91). He was made bishop of Peterborough in 1891 and of London in 1897. Other works include *A History of Rome* (1875) and *Queen Elizabeth* (1896).

cribbage Card game. It involves two to four players, and the object is to achieve a pair, straight, fifteen, or thirty-one. Scoring is marked by placing pegs into the cribbage board, a wooden plank drilled with a requisite number of holes. Cribbage was very popular in Victorian times.

cricket Sport. The game originated in medieval England and was regarded in Victorian Britain as a unifying national symbol. It involves two opposing teams of eleven players; these include bowlers who attempt to knock down the bails, or crosspieces, of the other team's wicket and batsmen who defend the wicket with paddle-shaped bats. Cricket was seen as an integral, character-building part of the curriculum of public schools and universities, and was exported to the colonies. Many of Britain's former colonies, notably Australia, continue to play the game in international competition. In the 1860s county clubs emerged as the major form of professional cricket within Britain. The county championship, which continues to the present, was regularized after 1873. The Marylebone Cricket Club was of particular importance in the Victorian era for codifying cricket rules.

Crimean War (1853–56) Conflict fought in eastern Europe by RUSSIA against the OTTOMAN EMPIRE and its allies GREAT BRITAIN, FRANCE, and Sardinia. The only major war fought by Great Britain in Europe during the Victorian Age, it was actually one in a series of RUSSO-TURKISH WARS (1676 to 1878) in which Russia sought to expand at the expense of the decaying Ottoman Empire and against the opposition of the other great powers. It was seen by many in Britain as a tragic exercise in military bungling, which led to a wave of reform.

The Crimean War began in a dispute over control of Christian holy places in Palestine, then held by the Ottomans. In 1853, when the Ottoman Empire refused to allow Czar Nicholas I of Russia to establish a protectorate over Orthodox Christians within Ottoman borders, Russia sent troops to invade the Ottoman tributaries of Moldavia and Wallachia, known as the Danubian principalities, in eastern Europe. With support from France and Britain, the Ottoman Empire declared war on Russia on October 4 of that year. On November 30 the Russians sank an Ottoman flotilla at the Turkish port of Sinop on the Black Sea. In 1854, Britain and France demanded Russian withdrawal from the Danubian principalities, and when Russia failed to comply, they declared war. Sardinia (now part of Italy) declared war soon thereafter.

Russia abandoned Moldavia and Wallachia in 1854 when Austrian troops, along with Prussia, moved into the region; however, the British and French governments decided to pursue the war to Sevastopol (Sebastopol), the fortified base of the Russian fleet on the Black Sea coast of the Crimea (now part of Ukraine). In September 1854 an allied expeditionary force landed in the Crimea north of Sevastopol and advanced on the city. In the Battle of Alma River (September 20), the allies forced the Russians to withdraw to Sevastopol, where a yearlong siege was begun. At the BATTLE OF BALAKLAVA (October 25), a Russian attempt to lift the siege was turned back, with heavy casualties for the British in part as a result of the disastrous cavalry charge led by James Thomas Brudenell, 7th Earl of CARDIGAN, and commemorated in ALFRED, Lord TENNYSON's poem "THE CHARGE OF THE LIGHT BRIGADE." Another costly victory against the Russians took place at the Battle of Inkerman (November 5).

Worse than battle carnage were the effects of hunger and disease over the winter that followed. Inadequately supplied and facing severe shortages of food, clothing, and medicine, the British troops besieging Sevastopol died in droves from cholera and the cold. *London Times* war correspondent William Howard Russell (1820–1907) made sure that the public at home knew of the suffering, prompting an outcry that brought down Lord ABERDEEN's government in 1855 and made the name of Lord RAGLAN, commander of British forces, synonymous with incompetence. At the same time, public admiration soared for British nurse FLORENCE NIGHTINGALE, who organized medical efforts to relieve the misery in the Crimea. Raglan himself died of cholera in 1855.

After the winter came more fighting, with the fortified points of Malakov and Redan overlooking Sevastopol falling to the allies on September 8–9, 1855. The Russians evacuated Sevastopol on September 11. Russian czar Alexander II, who had succeeded to the throne on the death of his father Nicholas earlier that year, began to negotiate peace. The Treaty of Paris in 1856 formally ended the hostilities, with Russia's expansion temporarily stopped, the integrity of the Ottoman Empire and the Danubian principalities maintained, and principles related to the law of the seas recognized. As the czar began refortifying Sevastopol and rebuilding his fleet, however, the fruits of the war seemed trivial compared to the cost: More than twenty-one thousand British troops were lost, sixteen thousand of them from disease. Military and administrative reforms followed, leading to the establishment by the 1870s of a consolidated war department and to the abolition of the purchase system by which the wealthy could buy military commissions rather than earn them through merit.

crinoline Stiff, hoop-sized female undergarment designed to give shape to long skirts. Until the mid-nineteenth century a crinoline was a petticoat that achieved its stiffness by being lined with horsehair. In the 1850s crinolines were fashioned of steel hoops, using as many as thirty-five. One internationally famous design was the Crown crinoline, manufactured by W. S. and E. H. Thompson. By the 1860s the number of hoops in a crinoline was reduced to three or four as the preferred shape became a flat skirt front and half-crinoline in the back. Within a few years this shape evolved into the BUSTLE, which remained fashionable for decades.

Cro-Magnon man Prehistoric ancestor of modern humans. Evolving about forty thousand years ago and considered fully modern in anatomy and classified with modern humans as *Homo sapiens sapiens,* these people were first identified in 1868 by French paleontologist Edouard-Armand-Isidore-Hippolyte Lartet (1801–1871), who discovered four fossil skeletons in a cave called Cro-Magnon in France. The discovery made it clear that humanity was much older than literal interpreters of the Bible believed and, like the discovery of NEANDERTHAL MAN in 1856 and JAVA MAN in 1890, lent support to the theory of evolution by CHARLES DARWIN. Later discoveries of Cro-Magnon sites in such places as France, Germany, Czechoslovakia, and Spain (see ALTAMIRA CAVE PAINTINGS) gave insight into the Cro-Magnon culture, which lasted until about ten thousand years ago. The first humans to make paintings and sculptures, they hunted mammoths, engaged in trade, and invented sophisticated tools such as needles, fishhooks, and bows and arrows.

Cromer, Evelyn Baring, 1st Earl of (1841–1917) British administrator. The son of an M.P., Cromer received his first taste of colonial life as a soldier in the Ionian Islands, Malta, and Jamaica. He then took the post of private secretary to his cousin, Thomas George Baring, Lord Northbrook. From 1877 to 1880, Cromer held administrative positions in EGYPT, first as commissioner of the public debt and then as controller-general. In 1883, after General Garnet Wolseley had brought Egypt under British military occupation, Cromer took the job that was to become his life's work: British consul general in Egypt. From his seat in the British consulate, Cromer was the virtual ruler of Egypt until his retirement in 1907.

Officially, the KHEDIVE remained Egypt's ruler, but it was Cromer who held actual power. Known familiarly as "the Lord," he dedicated himself to developing Egypt's economy, reforming its administration and courts, and building public works. Under his management, massive irrigation projects were undertaken, railroads were improved, the Aswan Dam was built, and the Egyptian economy produced a surplus. Cromer's advice was instrumental in the reconquest of the SUDAN in 1898; after the reconquest, he oversaw the establishment of Anglo-Egyptian rule in the Sudan.

After twenty-four years as the untitled autocrat of Egypt, he returned to England in 1907. He wrote several works, most notably a memoir, *Modern Egypt* (1908).

Crookes, Sir William (1832–1919) English chemist and physicist. Born in London, he studied chemistry at the newly founded Royal College of Chemistry in 1848 and after graduating became an assistant in the meteorological department of the Radcliffe observatory. He then inherited a large fortune from his father, and from the time of his marriage to Ellen Humphrey in 1856, he devoted himself to his private laboratory in his house in Kensington Park gardens. His interest in PHOTOGRAPHY resulted in a position as editor of the *Journal* of the London Photographic Society in 1857. He also founded the scientific journal *Chemical News* in 1859.

In 1861, Crookes noticed a brilliant green line while investigating the residue left in the manufacture of sulfuric acid. After further investigation, he claimed the substance to be a new element and named it thallium, from the Greek for "green twig."

Crookes then began a study of the passage of an electric current through a gas and began constructing CATHODE-RAY tubes as early as 1879. The Crookes tube helped significantly in the discovery of X RAYS in 1895 and the ELECTRON in 1897.

Crookes was knighted in 1897 and was frequently consulted by the government on matters of scientific interest until his death in 1919.

Cross, Richard Assheton, 1st Viscount Cross (1823–1914) English lawyer and banker. One of the ablest home secretaries of the nineteenth century, he was a Conservative member of Parliament from 1857 to 1862 and again from 1868 to 1886. Despite his lack of cabinet experience, Prime Minister BENJAMIN DISRAELI made him home secretary in 1874, a position he held until 1880. The most important law passed under his stewardship was the Cross Act of 1875. It enabled municipalities to level slums and build rental housing for workers. Cross also helped pass a bill giving labor the right to picket peacefully, the Public Health Act regulating sanitation, and one of the FACTORY ACTS that regulated the employment of women and children in textile mills. Turned out of his cabinet post in the 1880 Conservative electoral defeat, Cross was again home secretary (1885–86) and secretary to India (1886–92). He was made viscount in 1886.

Cruikshank, George (1792–1878) English illustrator. Born in London, he learned the arts of etching and wood engraving from his father, painter Isaac Cruikshank. George Cruikshank began earning money from his drawings as early as 1804, but it was not until after his father's death six years later that he began creating the satirical illustrations that would make him famous.

Cruikshank's illustrations appeared in various political and humorous magazines and newspapers, and displayed an irreverence for all public figures, including Napoleon I, King George IV, as well as notable Tories, Whigs, Radicals, and members of the Church. George Cruikshank produced nearly five thousand etchings, lithographs, and wood engravings during his career, publishing many himself in collections such as *Cruikshankiana* (1835), *George Cruikshank's Omnibus* (1841), and *George Cruikshank's Table Book* (1845).

Cruikshank's illustrations also graced the pages of more than 860 books by other authors, including CHARLES DICKENS's *Oliver Twist* (1838) and *Sketches by Boz* (1836–37).

Crystal Palace Glass-and-iron enclosure designed by Sir Joseph Paxton to house the GREAT EXHIBITION OF 1851 in London. The glass walls and roofs of its central vault and wings were supported by a framework of iron and enclosed nearly one million square feet of floor area. Assembled from prefabricated elements, the Crystal Palace was a precursor to the steel and glass buildings of modern architecture. After the exhibition, the building was taken down and reassembled at Sydenham, South London. In 1936 it was destroyed by fire.

The Crystal Palace was designed by Sir Joseph Paxton for London's Great Exhibition in 1851. Courtesy of The New York Public Library.

Cuba See SPANISH-AMERICAN WAR.

Culture and Anarchy (1869) Volume of essays. By English writer MATTHEW ARNOLD, the essays originated as a series of lectures at Oxford. In what has become a classic of cultural criticism, Arnold contends that England is in a state of social, political, and cultural crisis. Writing against the background of the recent Reform Bill that expanded voting rights throughout England, Arnold argues that the solution lies in the culture, encapsulated in a belief in "perfection," whose aims are the cultivation of "sweetness and light" and "to render an intelligent being more intelligent." According to Arnold, the two greatest traditions of "Hebraism" ("strictness of conscience") and Hellenism ("spontaneity of consciousness") have ceased to complement each other given the former's dominance in English cultural life. The various classes—barbarians (the aristocracy), philistines (the middle class), and populace (the lower class)—are inadequate in achieving what culture alone can achieve, which is the development of the individual self in the interest of society.

Cunard Line British transatlantic shipping and packet firm. The Cunard Line saw its beginnings in 1838 with the development of the government-subsidized Royal Mail Steam Packet Company, formed by Nova Scotia native Samuel Cunard, along with Scottish businessmen George and James Burns and British businessman David McIver. Its first transatlantic voyage was that of the wooden steamship *Britannia* in 1839. By 1855, Cunard was using iron steamers and in 1862 achieved advanced efficiency and dominance by equipping ships with screw propellers instead of paddle wheels. The Cunard Line was also active in transporting Irish immigrants to the United States in the 1860s. See also SHIPS.

Curie, Marie Sklodowska and Pierre French scientists. Pierre Curie (1859–1906), a noted physicist who had already discovered the "Curie point"—the temperature at which ferromagnetic substances lose their magnetism—and Marie Sklodowska (1867–1934), a chemist from Poland, were married in Paris on July 25, 1895, and began an internationally famous scientific partnership.

In 1896, Antoine-Henri Becquerel discovered that uranium compounds emitted strong radiation. Marie Curie began to study Becquerel radiation, which she later named RADIOACTIVITY, and using laboratory instruments designed and built by her husband, investigated pitchblende, a mineral ore containing uranium. By the spring of 1898 her studies revealed that a highly radioactive element besides uranium was present in pitchblende. Pierre put aside his own research and joined the efforts of his wife. By the end of the year they announced the discovery of two elements they called polonium (after Poland) and radium.

Marie and Pierre Curie spent the next four years trying to obtain pure extracts of these elements, and by September 1902 they had isolated one-tenth of a gram of radium from several tons of pitchblende. Marie's analysis of the element became her doctoral dissertation. In 1903 she became the first woman awarded the Nobel Prize, an honor she shared with her husband and Becquerel.

In October 1904, Pierre was appointed professor of physics at the Sorbonne and Marie was named the superintendent of his laboratory. Pierre Curie was killed in 1906 after being run over by a dray. The Faculty Council appointed Marie Curie to her late husband's position, making her the first woman to teach at the Sorbonne. She continued her study of radioactivity, and in 1911 she became the first person ever to be awarded a second Nobel Prize. Her daughter Irène Joliot-Curie (1897–1956) also earned the Nobel Prize in chemistry, in 1935, one year after her mother's death.

currency, British The basic units of British currency in the nineteenth century were pounds, shillings, and pence. Twenty shillings equaled 1 pound, and 12 pence equaled 1 shilling. Hence, 240 pence equaled 1 pound. The symbol £ meant pound, *s.*, shilling, and *d.*, pence. There were also numerous coins in circulation with a variety of names—the guinea, the sovereign, the crown—that bore no logical relation to their value in shillings, pounds, or pence. Money was also exchanged in the form of paper currency called banknotes.

The following is a list of nineteenth-century coins with their established value. In modern Britain the pound sterling is now the basic

COIN	SLANG TERM	VALUE
guinea		21 shillings
sovereign	quid	20 shillings (1 pound)
half sovereign		10 shillings
crown	bull	5 shillings
half crown		2½ shillings
florin		2 shillings
shilling	bob, hog	12 pence
sixpence	tanner, bender	6 pence
groat		4 pence
threepence	thruppence	3 pence
twopence	tuppence	2 pence
penny	copper	1 pence
halfpenny	ha'pence	½ pence
farthing		¼ pence
half farthing		⅛ pence

unit and is made up of 100 new pence (abbreviated as *p*).

Currier & Ives American lithographers. Nathaniel Currier (1813–1888) issued his first prints in 1835; James Merritt Ives (1824–1895) joined him as a partner in 1857. Their many prints expressed popular sentiments and aesthetics and constitute a unique record of nineteenth-century America. Though associated with carriage rides in snow-covered country, they actually had a much wider range, bringing to life moments in American history, sea and ship scenes, American Indian tableaus, New York City in all its faces and seasons, hunting and fishing scenes, the Mississippi River, and days in the lives of railroaders and firemen. Reprinted many times, the images remain familiar to Americans, while the original prints are collectors' items.

Custer, George Armstrong (1839–1876) U.S. cavalry officer. Custer gained famed during the CIVIL WAR, distinguishing himself at the Battle of GETTYSBURG and other encounters. After the war he led successful campaigns against the Cheyenne and other Plains Indians. In 1874 he began a series of actions against the Sioux in the Black Hills of South Dakota and Wyoming. Two years later, on June 25–26, 1876, he and five companies of his Seventh Cavalry Division were annihilated by Sioux warriors led by SITTING BULL and CRAZY HORSE, in "Custer's Last Stand" at the Battle of Little Big Horn in Montana. *My Life on the Plains,* a memoir of his frontier career, was published in 1874.

Cutty Sark CLIPPER SHIP. Named for the witch in Robert Burns's poem "Tam O'Shanter," the black, three-masted, tea-trade ship had 32,000 square feet of canvas, 10 miles of rigging, and twenty-eight crewmen. It was launched in 1869. In its time it was the fastest ship in the water, faster even than steamships, traveling 363 miles in twenty-four hours. The ship is preserved in a permanent dry dock in Greenwich, England.

Daguerre, Louis-Jacques-Mandé (1789–1851) French painter and co-inventor of PHOTOGRAPHY. Daguerre first became famous in the 1820s and 1830s for his illusionistic stage sets and painted dioramas. He then began working with French chemist Joseph-Nicéphore Niépce (1765–1833), who in 1822 succeeded in making the first permanent photographic image. In 1839, Daguerre announced the development of the daguerreotype, a method for making a direct positive image on a silver-plated sheet of copper. Daguerreotypes became popular around the world but were eventually made obsolete by methods of printing any number of paper positives from an original negative. The first of these rival processes was the calotype, developed in 1841 by Daguerre's younger English contemporary WILLIAM HENRY FOX TALBOT.

daguerreotype See DAGUERRE, LOUIS-JACQUES-MANDÉ.

Daily Mail See *LONDON DAILY MAIL.*

Daily News See *LONDON DAILY NEWS.*

Daily Telegraph London newspaper. First published in 1855, after the Stamp Act was rescinded, it became the largest newspaper in the world during the middle of the Victorian Age. Its one-penny price and uncomplicated style helped to garner a wide readership. See also PERIODICALS.

Dalhousie, James Andrew Broun Ramsay, 10th Earl and 1st Marquis of (1812–1860) English governor-general of INDIA. Formerly president of the Board of Trade (1845–46), he became the chief administrator of British India in 1848. He expanded the empire, annexing Satara, Jaipur, Sambalpur, and Nagpur when the native leaders of those states died without heirs. He also presided over the annexations of the PUNJAB in 1849 following the Sikh Wars and of lower Burma in 1852.

Dalhousie was an aggressive agent for change in India, instituting administrative and social reforms, authoring India's first railroad, and constructing a Hindustan-Tibet road to link the British and Chinese empires. His attempts to modernize India and particularly his annexation of Oudh (1856) contributed to the resentment that erupted in the INDIAN MUTINY (1857). His policies also paved the way for the system of direct control of India by the British crown, begun under his successor, Charles John Canning, Earl Canning, in 1858.

Darrow, Clarence (1857–1938) American lawyer. Darrow was admitted to the Ohio bar in 1878. He moved to Chicago in 1888, where he became a successful corporate attorney and began a lifelong involvement with political reform efforts, especially penal reform. In 1894 he abandoned his practice to defend labor leader EUGENE V. DEBS against charges of violating a court injunction during the Pullman strike of that year. The successful and widely reported defense began Darrow's career as the most noted trial lawyer of the day. A vehement opponent of the death penalty, Darrow defended more than fifty accused murderers, none of whom was ever sentenced to death.

Darrow's fame peaked in the 1920s when he defended accused murderers Nathan Leopold and Richard Loeb, and then a Tennessee schoolteacher against charges of teaching EVOLUTION. His withering cross-examination of WILLIAM JENNINGS BRYAN, a guest prosecutor in the case, brought the conflicts between evolutionary theory and fundamentalist interpretations of the Bible into sharp perspective.

Darwin, Charles Robert (1809–1882) English naturalist. His theory of EVOLUTION by natural selection revolutionized the life sciences, stirred religious controversy, and profoundly altered humanity's view of itself. Born in Shrewsbury, the son of physician Robert Waring Darwin and Susannah Wedgwood, he was the grandson of potter Josiah Wedgwood and physician and poet Erasmus Darwin. Charles studied medicine at Edinburgh University and prepared for the ministry at Christ's College, Cambridge, but decided against either career as he became more interested in geology and natural history. Through his friend and Cambridge botany professor John Stevens Henslow, he secured an appointment as a naturalist on a five-year surveying expedition to South America's coasts, the Andean interior, and some Pacific islands. At the end of December 1831 he set sail with the expedition on the H.M.S. *Beagle.* The voyage from 1831 to 1836 proved to be the major turning point in his life, one that gave him the opportunity to study the flora, fauna, and geology of many lands. The distinctive life forms and fossils of the Galápagos Islands off the coast of Ecuador were of particular importance in providing inspiration and data for his

Charles Darwin dedicated the greater portion of his life to proving his controversial theory of evolution. Photo courtesy of Max A. Polster Archive.

growing interest in the origin of species. He described the voyage in *Journal of Researches into the Geology and Natural History of the Various Countries Visited by HMS Beagle* (1839).

Also of importance to Darwin's developing thought was his reading in 1838 of English economist Thomas Malthus's *Essay on Population* (1798). Reflecting on Malthus's argument that human population growth always tends to outstrip food supply, Darwin extended the principle to nature and realized that living things are perpetually engaged in a struggle for survival. Assuming that organisms naturally vary in small and random ways, he theorized that organisms better adapted to their environment are more likely to survive and reproduce, and therefore more likely to pass on their individual variations to their descendants. The variations are metaphorically "selected" by nature, and over long periods accumulate, bringing about the modification and creation of species. This theory of descent with modification accounted, in Darwin's view, for the diversity of extinct and present-day species, including humans.

The idea that species might evolve from more primitive ancestors was not in itself new. What was new was the mechanism—natural selection—proposed as an explanation for how evolution takes place. Because his theory contradicted prevailing beliefs in the literal truth of the Book of Genesis, Darwin realized that it would be extremely controversial. He decided to postpone publication until he gathered enough evidence to make a convincing claim; this took two decades. In the meantime, he gained a reputation as a geologist for such works as *Structure and Distribution of Coral Reefs* (1842). He served as secretary of the Geological Society from 1838 to 1841.

Encouraged by geologist Sir CHARLES LYELL, Darwin drafted two sketches of his developing theory of evolution in the 1840s and started work on a major book on the subject in 1856, but still declined to publish. Then English naturalist ALFRED RUSSEL WALLACE asked him to review a paper outlining essentially the same theory of evolution, independently developed. Realizing that time had run out, Darwin presented his findings jointly with Wallace to the Linnaean Society of London in 1858. In 1859, Darwin published a detailed, book-length exposition of his theory, *On the Origin of Species by Means of Natural Selection,* commonly known as *THE ORIGIN OF SPECIES*.

Carefully argued and supported by a mass of evidence, the theory encountered just the storm of controversy Darwin had feared. It was vilified in print, speech, and caricature by individuals inside and outside the scientific community. Though Darwin picked up prominent opponents, such as Bishop SAMUEL WILBERFORCE, he also found vocal allies, such as scientist T. H. HUXLEY. Newly discovered fossil evidence of transitional prehistoric forms, such as ARCHAEOPTERYX, was interpreted by some as supporting Darwin's theory, while others disagreed. Darwinian ideas found their way into arts and literature, such as the works of GEORGE BERNARD SHAW and H. G. WELLS. Some apparent allies of Darwin misinterpreted his work by applying it to the realm of human society, formulating doctrines that were called SOCIAL DARWINISM, though these were never sanctioned by the naturalist.

Darwin continued to gather evidence for his theory, publishing five more editions of *The Origin of Species* in his lifetime. In another work, *The Descent of Man and Selection in Relation to Sex* (1871), he extended his theory to his own species, arguing that humanity had evolved from an anthropoid animal ancestor; he also introduced the concept of sexual selection. Darwin treated other aspects of evolutionary theory in *The Variation of Animals and Plants Under Domestication* (1868) and *The Expression of the Emotions in Man and Animals* (1872). He also wrote a biography of his grandfather Erasmus Darwin (1879), whose ideas on evolution had anticipated some of his own, and several volumes on botany, including *The Power of Movement in Plants* (1880) and *Formation of Vegetable Mould Through the Action of Worms* (1881).

Darwin married a cousin, Emma Wedgwood, in 1839; they lived in Downe, Kent, from 1842. Four of his ten children were prominent scientists in their own right: mathematician and astronomer Sir George Howard (1845–1912); botanist Sir Francis (1848–1925), who was also his father's editor and biographer; engineer and economist Leonard (1850–1943); and civil engineer Sir Horace (1851–1928).

Chronically ill with fatigue and intestinal symptoms since his return from the *Beagle* voyage in 1836, Charles Darwin died in 1882 and was buried in Westminster Abbey. Not until the following century did his central ideas meet with widespread scientific acceptance. Synthesized with discoveries in GENETICS, a field founded by Darwin's contemporary GREGOR MENDEL, Darwinian evolution has become a unifying framework for research in the biological sciences. Though still misunderstood and rejected by many outside the scientific community, Darwin's ideas have become an inextricable part of modern consciousness.

Das Kapital Book on economics. Written by KARL MARX, the work appeared in three volumes (1867, 1885, 1894). The last two were edited by Marx's friend and collaborator FRIEDRICH ENGELS. *Das Kapital* contains the most complete rendition of Marx's economic theories, in particular his theory of "surplus value." According to Marx, the capitalist's sole source of profit springs from his ability to force the wage earner to work beyond the point of his or her own subsistence. Marx further asserted that investments in capital goods such as machinery do not produce true profits since their rapid diffusion soon blunts any individual capitalist's competitive edge. Hence, increasing mechanization should cause increasing downward pressure on wages, as capitalists try to wring ever more surplus value out of their workers to pay for the higher capital outlays. In the end, the system will collapse when capitalists can no longer offer even a living wage to their workers.

Marx employed vast amounts of data and numerous examples to prove his thesis. In hindsight, economists have observed that Marx neglected the importance of the trade union as a break on lowering wages and the importance of the "mental capital" of the entrepreneur.

Daughters of the American Revolution, National Society for the (DAR) U.S. patriotic association. Founded in 1890 for women with one or more ancestors who participated in the Revolutionary War, the group was officially chartered by the U.S. Congress in 1895. Historical preservation programs have always been among its civic activities.

Daumier, Honoré (1808–1879) French caricaturist, painter, and sculptor. His greatest success was with his lithographs, of which he produced about four thousand for Paris newspapers and magazines. Drawings, watercolors, oil paintings, and sculptures also survive. A Republican, he began his career with satirical caricatures of political figures, most notably LOUIS-PHILIPPE, whom he abhorred, and who reciprocated by imprisoning him for six months in 1832. Political satire was outlawed in 1835, and that phase of Daumier's career came to an end, though he returned to it during the REVOLUTIONS OF 1848. Daumier began to publish satirical caricatures of social life, particularly in the French periodical *Le Charivari.* Exuberantly drawn with broad, fluid, playful strokes, the pictures showed bourgeois Parisians going about their daily lives, and they embodied universal experience. Images of lawyers, judges, and courts satirized bureaucratic legalism; images of street performers and sideshow entertainers conveyed the precariousness of the artist's life; images of emigrants and fugitives expressed the pathos of displaced humanity.

Daumier had virtually no academic training, but his paintings were exhibited by the Salon several times and were admired by prominent artists, including EUGÈNE DELACROIX, CAMILLE COROT, and EDGAR DEGAS. Most of the paintings, such as *The Third-Class Carriage* (1863–65), depict contemporary social situations, but some are of Don Quixote and Sancho Panza. His sculptures, like his lithographs, are mostly caricatures formed with broad, telling lines. Nearly blind at the end of his life, Daumier lived his last years in a house at Valmondois-sur-Seine-et-Oise given to him by his friend Corot.

Davies, Emily See LANGHAM PLACE CIRCLE.

Davis, Jefferson (1808–1889) President of the Confederate States of America. Davis was born in Kentucky one year before the birth of ABRAHAM LINCOLN in the same state. He grew up in Mississippi and served in the army for seven years after graduating from West Point in 1828. After ten years as a Mississippi planter, Davis was elected to the House of Representatives in 1845. His heroics in the MEXICAN WAR (1846–48) made him a natural choice to complete an unexpired Senate term beginning in 1847. As a senator he proved a staunch defender of SLAVERY and advocate for its expansion into the western territories.

Davis ran for governor of Mississippi in 1851 but lost by fewer than one thousand votes. President FRANKLIN PIERCE made him Secretary of War (1853–57), a position Davis used to continue his call for American expansionism. He returned to the Senate in 1857 but resigned in 1861 after the election of Abraham Lincoln and the secession of Mississippi from the Union.

Davis hoped to be appointed commander of the new Confederate armies but was named president of the provisional Confederate government by a secession convention, a choice ratified by a general election in November 1861.

During the CIVIL WAR, Davis's leadership came under fire for his interference in military affairs, diplomatic failures to persuade Great Britain and France to recognize the CONFEDERACY, and his efforts to enforce conscription. He refused to accept the South's defeat even after ROBERT E. LEE surrendered his army in April 1865. That same month Davis fled from Richmond, Virginia, the rebel capital, but was apprehended by Union troops in Georgia on May 10, 1865. Accused of treason, he never stood trial and was released on bond after two years in a federal prison. He later wrote *The Rise and Fall of the Confederate Government* (1881). He never petitioned Washington for a pardon.

Davitt, Michael (1846–1906) Founder of the IRISH LAND LEAGUE. Davitt was born during the Irish famines of the 1840s and was five when his family was evicted from their land. At eleven he lost an arm in a factory mishap in England where his family had settled. He joined the FENIANS and became their chief gunrunner in northern England by the 1860s. He participated in the Fenian armed actions against English rule of Ireland in the late 1860s. He was arrested in 1870 and sentenced to fifteen years in prison for his alleged role in an assassination conspiracy.

Released before serving his full sentence, Davitt began to link the cause of Irish nationalism with land reform and Irish ownership of land. Independence would attract the Irish farmer only if land reform was part of the nationalist agenda. He helped organize successful protests against high rents in County Mayo in 1879 and formed the Land League of Mayo later that year. With CHARLES S. PARNELL he founded the National Land League in October 1879. The league's bold tactics, superior organization, and ample funding from the United States forced the English Parliament to pass laws that ultimately enabled farmers to buy land instead of renting it.

Davitt remained an important figure in the Irish nationalist movement after the league was banned by the English government. As a member of Parliament he fought for HOME RULE and helped heal the divisions in the IRISH PARTY caused by Parnell's political downfall and death. He also supported the British labor movement, independence for the BOERS, prison reform, and other liberal causes.

De Quincey, Thomas (1785–1859) English writer. Born in Manchester as Thomas Quincey, he was the fifth of eight children. He hardly knew his father, who died in 1792 from tuberculosis, a disease that also claimed several other members of the family. His mother added the "De" to the family name. After attending the Bath and Manchester grammar schools, he ran away to Wales and later to London, where he lived in poverty. He was befriended by a young prostitute, "Ann of Oxford Street," who remained in his thoughts and writings for the rest of his life.

Destitute, De Quincey returned home, and in 1803 he entered Worcester College, Oxford, where he first took opium to relieve physical ailments. While he studied diligently, De Quincey refused to take his oral examinations and left Oxford without a degree in 1807. That same year he met Samuel Taylor Coleridge, a fellow writer and opium user. They traveled to the Lake District together, and De Quincey was introduced to William Wordsworth and other writers. In 1839, De Quincey published his fond memories of this time in *Lake Reminiscences.*

By 1813, De Quincey had become addicted to laudanum, a form of opium. Three months after the birth of their first child, he married eighteen-year-old Margaret Simpson in 1817. In order to support his new family, De Quincey edited the *Westmoreland Gazette* for eighteen months, before writing and publishing *Confessions of an Opium-Eater* in *London Magazine* in 1821. Due to its popularity, *Confessions* was reprinted in book form a year later and became a great and immediate success.

De Quincey became a frequent contributor to periodicals, providing a number of essays on literature, ranging from the classics to his contemporaries. While his criticism is highly regarded, De Quincey could be quite severe; Carlyle described him as carrying "a laudanum bottle in his pocket, and the venom of a wasp in his heart." In February 1827, the funny, macabre essay "On Murder Considered as One of the Fine Arts" appeared in John Wilson's *Blackwood's Magazine.*

Constantly struggling with his opium addiction, De Quincey succumbed in 1837, after the death of his wife. He began ingesting huge amounts and was not able to gain control of his abuse until after his mother's death in 1846, but he never entirely quit using the drug.

From 1853, De Quincey spent his time editing *Selections Grave and Gay, from the Writings, Published and Unpublished, of Thomas De Quincey,* which appeared in 14 volumes between 1853 and 1860. De Quincey also revised and expanded *Confessions,* altering it from a warning of drug abuse to a more standard autobiography, with passages evoking almost an indebtedness to opium.

Debs, Eugene V. (1855–1926) American socialist. Born in Indiana, he began working for the railroads at fourteen. He became secretary of the Brotherhood of Locomotive Firemen in 1880 and was elected to the state legislature in 1885. He quickly abandoned the DEMOCRATIC PARTY when it failed to show an interest in labor law reform. As president of the American Railway Union, which he helped organize in 1892, he led the PULLMAN STRIKE of 1894. After being imprisoned for six months for conspiracy to obstruct the mail, he left prison a convert to SOCIALISM. Debs helped organize the Socialist Democratic Party in 1899 and ran for president on its ticket in 1900, 1904, 1908, 1912, and 1920. During that time he also helped organize the International Workers of the World (Wobblies). His opposition to World War I led to his imprisonment for sedition in 1918. Pardoned by President Warren Harding in 1921, he retired from active public life. Some of his books include *Unionism and Socialism, a Plea for Both* (1904), *Industrial Unionism* (1905), and *The Children of the Poor* (1911).

debtors' prison Institutions used to confine persons unwilling or unable to pay their debts. Debtors' prisons in England date back to the thirteenth century. Prisoners were kept until they could find the appropriate means to pay off any debt, no matter how small. An act of law in 1808, however, provided for the release of any person who had served more than one year for a debt of less than £20. The British government created Loan Societies in 1835 in order to allow the working class an opportunity to borrow up to £100 to keep out of debt. The Insolvent Debtors Act of 1844 abolished imprisonment for debts less than £20, and imprisonment for all debts was abolished in 1869.

The father of CHARLES DICKENS served time in the Marshalsea Prison in 1824, an experience recalled by the writer in several works, particularly *Little Dorrit* (1858), which described the small, crowded, and squalid conditions of prison life.

Debussy, [Achille-] Claude (1862–1918) French composer. Debussy was a representative of the extreme left-wing French school in finding new methods of expression in harmonic combinations. Defining musical IMPRESSIONISM, his piano works exploit the instrument's subtle coloristic possibilities and have been described as "pictures in sound." A student of Albert Lavignac, and Franck and Ernest Guiraud, Debussy studied at the Paris Conservatory from 1874 to 1884. He won the Prix de Rome in 1884 with his cantata *L'Enfant prodigue.* While in Rome he composed his cantata *La Damoiselle élue* (1888). Following his sojourn in Italy, Debussy spent his life composing in Paris, resulting in the *Prélude à l'après-midi d'un faune* (1892–94), an orchestral work inspired by the poem of Stephane Mallarmé. In addition to his *Nocturnes* (1893–99) and *La Mer* (1905), Debussy wrote such popular songs as *Clair de Lune* (1884) and *Pierrot* (1884), and the opera *Pelleas et Melisande* (1892–1902). In the remaining years of his life,

Debussy composed the ballet *Jeux* (1913) for Diaghilev's Ballets Russes.

decadence British literary and artistic movement. Decadence came to the fore in the 1890s, characterized by self-consciousness, artifice, overrefinement, perversity, morbidity, and sexuality. The term came from France where the movement was rooted in such literary precursors as THÉOPHILE GAUTIER and CHARLES BAUDELAIRE and associated with the SYMBOLISM poets, or *décadents,* such as ARTHUR RIMBAUD, PAUL VERLAINE, and STEPHANE MALLARMÉ. British decadence was also influenced by AESTHETICISM and its doctrine of ART FOR ART'S SAKE. Decadent British artists and writers included AUBREY BEARDSLEY, Ernest Dowson, ALGERNON SWINBURNE, ARTHUR SYMONS, and OSCAR WILDE. The movement found vehicles for expression in THE *YELLOW BOOK* and various other little magazines. The term "decadence" is also used to characterize the *FIN DE SIÈCLE* mood of the period.

Degas, [Hilaire-Germain-] Edgar (1834–1917) French painter, sculptor, and graphic artist. The son of a wealthy aristocrat, Degas at first studied law but went to the Ecole des Beaux-Arts in Paris in 1855. After a stay in Naples and Rome, Degas returned to Paris in 1861 where he painted portraits and compositions in a severely classical style reminiscent of JEAN-AUGUSTE-DOMINIQUE INGRES and Jacques-Louis David. Soon, however, Degas rejected traditional aesthetic rules, and although not following IMPRESSIONISM in practice, he allied himself with the Impressionist movement as a protest against academic theory. Degas explored the environment of nineteenth-century industrial man and began to paint townscapes, horse races, street scenes, and the working class. In order to capture the detailed behavior of his subjects, Degas experimented with PHOTOGRAPHY. He never painted on the spot but composed only after much observation and many studies.

A Woman with Chrysanthemums, completed in 1865, is an example of Degas's breakdown of traditional subject categories; its unbalanced composition is not a portrait or a still-life or a genre scene. Degas's paintings of the theater reveal his fragmented approach toward capturing a public spectacle. In *The Orchestra of the Paris Opera* (1868–69), Degas avoided a head-on view of the stage and chose to crop his subjects randomly from top to bottom.

The influence of Impressionism can be seen in Degas's work in pastel, including *Prima Ballerina* (1876). *The Rehearsal* (1878), a work shown with the fourth Impressionist exhibition of 1879, is one of many behind-the-scenes views of ballet dancers that allowed Degas the opportunity to study the motions of dancers' bodies in a single frozen moment. Degas strove for perfection in every possible way to gain a technical mastery over what he rendered. Besides the art of pastel and photography, Degas experimented with monotypes and etchings, and modeled in clay and wax. His sculptural studies were never intended for exhibition and were cast in bronze after his death.

Delacroix, [Ferdinand-Victor-] Eugène (1799–1863) French Romantic painter, lithographer, writer, and art critic. Delacroix helped define French ROMANTICISM through his exploration of exotic themes, his emphasis on violent subject matter and intense emotion, and his use of dramatic color and free brushstroke. Delacroix looked to the work of his contemporaries Théodore Géricault and Antoine-Jean Gros as well as to past masters Michelangelo, Nicolas Poussin, and Peter Paul Rubens as sources for his own compositions.

His painting *The Massacre at Chios* (1822–24) established him as the leading Neo-Baroque Romantic painter early in his career.

Delacroix's intense study of the nature and capabilities of color relationships came from his contact with English color painters John Constable and JOSEPH MALLORD WILLIAM TURNER. Delacroix saw color as the most important element to link the painter and the viewer. In 1832, a year after being awarded the Legion of Honor, Delacroix visited Morocco and Spain, a trip that proved to be crucial for the development of his work. Paintings such as *Women of Algiers* (1834) and *Odalisque* (1845–50) show Delacroix's originality in the use of complementary colors and simultaneous contrast for paintings of a sensual nature.

Toward the end of his career, Delacroix's concern for form and composition increased with the production of monumental mural and religious paintings. His steady loosening of contour and brushstroke is evident in the violently expressive *Lion Hunt* (1861), which became decisive in the formation of the movements known as REALISM and IMPRESSIONISM. He continued to have a significant influence on those who espoused POST-IMPRESSIONISM, particularly VINCENT VAN GOGH and PAUL CÉZANNE. He is best known for his paintings of the *Death of Sardanapalus* (1827) and *Liberty Leading the People* (1830).

Democratic Party U.S. political group. The oldest continuous political party in the world, the modern Democratic Party emerged from the Democratic-Republican Party headed by Thomas Jefferson in the early nineteenth century. That party split bitterly over the presidential election of 1824 in which the House of Representatives chose JOHN QUINCY ADAMS over Andrew Jackson, who had won a plurality of the popular vote. The Jackson wing won the next presidential election in 1828 and in 1832 held the first national nominating convention of the Democratic Party. Jackson won again in 1832, basing his success on the emergence of universal white male suffrage, the organizational abilities of MARTIN VAN BUREN, and Jackson's own frontier, common-man appeal.

The party managed to win four of the six presidential elections between 1836 and 1856 despite growing tensions among Democrats over the expansion of SLAVERY into the western territories. Party frictions exploded at the national convention in 1860 where a northern faction nominated STEPHEN DOUGLAS and a southern wing chose John Breckenridge. This split helped REPUBLICAN PARTY candidate ABRAHAM LINCOLN win the White House.

The southern cause retained enough Democratic sympathizers to allow the Republicans to associate the party with rebellion during and after the CIVIL WAR. The Democrats won the presidency only twice between 1864 and 1908, with GROVER CLEVELAND winning nonconsecutive terms in 1884 and 1892. They did maintain a near political monopoly in the southern states after 1876 and nationally managed to gain control of one or both houses of Congress at various times during the last three decades of the century. Party strength lay in the South, in the West where farmers and miners favored the cheap money ideas of Democratic candidate WILLIAM JENNINGS BRYAN, and in the cities of the East where Democratic organizations controlled the votes of the swelling numbers of immigrants. But the very diverse coalition proved too unwieldy to form a strong national party.

Democrats and Republicans hardly differed on major issues until 1896 when Bryan ran on a platform of anti-imperialism, increased regulation of businesses and trusts, and increased coinage of silver to increase the money supply. Bryan suffered a huge defeat against WILLIAM MCKINLEY. It was not until a Republican Party split in 1912 that the party put a candidate back on Pennsylvania Avenue—Woodrow Wilson.

department store Retail establishment. An offshoot of the dry goods store, the widely stocked emporium was born during the Victorian era in response to the buying needs of a growing, sophisticated urban populace. Providing high-quality customer service, it also acted as a source of entertainment. In Britain the department store had its genesis in the Bazaar in MANCHESTER, which united several traders under one roof. The country's first true department store was Whiteley's of London, opened in 1863. Known as the "Universal Provider" for its wealth of merchandise, it was developed by British merchant William Whiteley (1831–1907). HARROD'S originated in London in 1849 as a food emporium run by Henry Charles Harrod. His son, Charles Digby Harrod, transformed it in the 1860s into a department store that would become the world's largest.

In the United States, an early example of the department store was the Marble Dry Goods Palace, opened in New York City by Irish merchant Alexander Turney Stewart (1803–1876) in 1848. His "Cast Iron" Palace, which opened in New York City in 1862, was considered a fully realized department store; it became a favored stop for women for decades to come.

Over the next few years, department stores dotted the cities of most of the major industrialized nations. In 1865, French entrepreneur Aristide Boucicaut opened his Bon Marché. In the same year Marshall Field's opened in Chicago, built by the American businessman for whom it is named. One of the most innovative department store pioneers was John Wanamaker (1838–1922), whose Wanamaker's store opened in Philadelphia in 1876. His three-acre store, encompassing two-thirds of a city block, was, in Wanamaker's words, the "largest space in the world devoted to retail selling on a single floor." In 1896 he would open a Wanamaker's on the site of Stewart's cast-iron palace.

With the growing use of the SKYSCRAPER in architectural design, department stores came to be designed as multifloor structures. One of the most prolific designers of department stores was Chicago architect Daniel Burnham, who designed for Wanamaker and Carson Pirie Scott, among others, at the turn of the century.

In addition to providing more shopping space with ever higher buildings, department stores constantly searched for novel ways to attract customers. Improvements in plate glass windows in the 1890s made window shopping a common pastime. Special events in the store, such as the debut of the first commercial ELEVATOR—from the company founded by ELISHA GRAVES OTIS—in the E. G. Haughwout Store in New York City in 1857, also drew customers.

Derby, Edward George Geoffrey Smith Stanley, 14th Earl of (1799–1869) Politician, orator, and three-time prime minister of GREAT BRITAIN (1852, 1858–59, and 1866). Elected to Parliament in 1820 as a Whig, he became George Canning's undersecretary of the colonies in 1827. He was chief secretary to Ireland (1830–33) and supported the REFORM BILL OF 1832. Appointed head of the colonial office in 1833, he helped convince

Parliament to abolish SLAVERY. In 1838 he left the Whigs to join the CONSERVATIVE PARTY. Named colonial secretary to Prime Minister ROBERT PEEL (1841–45), he resigned in opposition to Peel's repeal of the CORN LAWS, siding with BENJAMIN DISRAELI and other Conservative protectionists. His ministries are most noted for the passage of the REFORM BILL OF 1867, the end of the administration of India by the BRITISH EAST INDIA COMPANY, and the heavy influence of Disraeli in running the government and the party.

Dewar, Sir James (1842–1923) Scottish chemist. In 1889, with English chemist FREDERICK AUGUSTUS ABEL, he invented CORDITE, a smokeless explosive that when used cut down on the clouds of obscuring smoke prevalent in nineteenth-century battlefields. Experimenting with the production of low temperatures, he invented the Dewar flask (1892), a double-walled container with a vacuum between the walls. It was the forerunner of the modern thermos bottle. He was also the first to liquefy (1898) and solidify (1899) hydrogen. He was a professor at Cambridge (1875–1923) and the Royal Institution, London (1877–1923).

Dewey, Melvil (1851–1931) American library pioneer. Born in New York State, he attended Amherst College and became acting librarian at Amherst in 1874. In that post he responded to the Victorian information explosion by developing a system of classifying knowledge into ten major areas, with these areas divided into narrower fields signified by decimal points. While librarian of Columbia College (1883–88), he established the first training school for librarians. As head of the New York State Library at Albany (1889–1906), he established a prestigious library school. He also helped found the New York State Library Association, the American Library Association, and *Library Journal,* and was involved in the spelling reform movement and promotion of the metric system.

Diamond Jubilee Festival held throughout the British Empire on June 22, 1897, celebrating the sixtieth anniversary of the accession to the throne of Queen VICTORIA. From Buckingham Palace, Victoria, then seventy-eight years old, telegraphed a jubilee message to her subjects around the world: "From my heart I thank my beloved people. May God bless them." Contingents of colonial officials and native troops arrived in London from every part of the empire, including Canada, Tasmania, India, New South Wales, North Borneo, Jamaica, Malaysia, and Africa's Gold Coast. Festivities on the eve of the jubilee included an Imperial Fete in Regents' Park, an Imperial Ballet at Majesty's Theatre, and a performance by Australian soprano NELLIE MELBA at the Opera. On the day itself, a military procession of fifty thousand troops from every imperial possession marched in two separate columns through London's streets, converging at St. Paul's Cathedral for a thanksgiving service. Representatives of the Pope and the emperor of China attended, as did Indian rajahs wearing diamonds. Queen Victoria herself wore a regal bonnet decorated with ostrich feathers. In a special "Golden Issue" printed in gold ink, the *Daily Mail* called the procession such a testimony to the "greatness of the British race that there was not an Imperialist in the crowd who did not gain a new view of the glory of the British Empire."

Smaller thanksgiving services were held across the empire. Statues were unveiled; grand balls were held; troops were inspected; selected convicts were set free. In places such as Somalia and Aden, free food was given to the poor; in Hong Kong, the Hallelujah Chorus was performed. Foreign countries sent congratulations to the Queen.

The Diamond Jubilee marked the peak of Britain's imperial position in the years before two world wars brought it down. Unable to conceive of an alternative possibility, *The New York Times* editorialized on this occasion: "We are a part, and a great part, of the Greater Britain which seems so plainly destined to dominate this planet."

Dickens, Charles [John Huffam] (1812–1870) English writer, editor, and social reformer. The most popular author of the early to mid-Victorian era, he is generally recognized as one of the world's great writers. Born at Portsea, Portsmouth, he grew up in genteel poverty as the second of eight children of John Dickens, a clerk in the Naval Pay Office who lived chronically beyond his means. Moving his family often, to London, Chatham, and back to London, John was incarcerated for debt in Marshalsea DEBTORS' PRISON for several months in 1824. At the age of twelve, Charles was forced to leave school, live by himself in London, and work at labeling bottles in a blacking, or shoe-dye, factory. The memory of his loneliness and shame during this period never left him. In later years he disclosed the experience only to his closest friend, John Forster (1812–76), who reported it after the novelist's death in his popular biography, *Life of Dickens* (1871–74). The experience, however, is reflected throughout Dickens's work in his portrayal of orphans and in his pervasive sympathy for the poor.

After studying at Wellington House Academy, Dickens worked as a solicitor's clerk, then taught himself shorthand and became a court stenographer and reporter of parliamentary debates. The years 1829 to 1833 were marked by his fruitless passion for a banker's daughter, Maria Beadnell, whose family disapproved of their union. About this time Dickens also came to know London intimately as a result of his long, rambling walks through its streets and squares, a knowledge that would greatly enrich his writing.

Charles Dickens, novelist best known for such works as A Christmas Carol, Oliver Twist, *and* David Copperfield, *is often acknowledged as one of the world's greatest writers. Photo courtesy of Topham/Image Works.*

Using the pen name Boz, Dickens turned to writing sketches of London life for periodicals. His first story, "A Dinner at Poplar Walk," was published in December 1833 in *The Monthly Magazine*. These pieces, some fictional, some journalistic, were collected in *Sketches by Boz* (1836) and were the beginning of his public fame. Even more successful was his first novel, *The Posthumous Papers of the Pickwick Club,* better known as *The Pickwick Papers* (1836–37). These humorous sketches were published originally in monthly serial form, a venue that Dickens adopted for his subsequent novels and that was taken up by other Victorian writers. Enormously popular, it launched his career as a novelist with an international following.

His early period continued with *Oliver Twist* (1837–39), *Nicholas Nickleby* (1838–39), *The Old Curiosity Shop* (1840–41), and *Barnaby Rudge* (1841). These novels were marked by vivid characterization and description of place, a sharp, humorous, idiosyncratic style, and an abundance of strong feeling, sometimes veering into sentiment and melodrama. Dickens had an ability to capture every aspect of English society and showed special sympathy for outcasts and people of the lower classes, particularly suffering children. He was active in charitable causes and a strong advocate for social reform in many areas, including child labor, education, criminal law, and housing. He also favored the abolition of SLAVERY and international copyright protection.

In 1842 he embarked on a speaking tour of the United States. Sharply critical of American society, he published his biting observations in *American Notes* (1842) and the novel *Martin Chuzzlewit* (1843–44), incurring the resentment of Americans. During this decade he also lived in Italy (1844–45), recounting his experiences there in *Pictures from Italy* (1845), and traveled to Switzerland and Paris (1846).

Also during this period he wrote the novella *A CHRISTMAS CAROL* (1843), undoubtedly his best known work. Introducing the archetypal miser Ebenezer Scrooge, it is perhaps the author's purest statement of one of his central themes: the death and resurrection of the heart. Its numerous later incarnations in films, stage productions, public readings, retellings, and parodies have done more than any other work to perpetuate the image of mid-Victorian England in the popular imagination. *A Christmas Carol* was collected with his other Christmas-related tales of the 1840s—*The Chimes, The Cricket on the Hearth, The Battle of Life,* and *The Haunted Man*—in the anthology *Christmas Books* (1852).

The publication of *Dombey and Son* (1846–48) marked a shift toward the mature period of Dickens's art when his novels demonstrated more careful planning of complex plots, greater seriousness of theme, increasing psychological introspection, and assured control of imagery. *Dombey and Son* concerns Mr. Dombey's inability to appreciate his daughter Florence as a result of his overpowering ambition to have a son succeed him in his business. Dickens's next novel, *David Copperfield* (1849–50), was his most autobiographical work and his personal favorite. His next three novels focused on a particular aspect of social and political injustice: *Bleak House* (1852–53) on court delays; *Hard Times* (1854) on UTILITARIANISM and industrial oppressiveness; *Little Dorrit* (1855–57) on bureaucracy and imprisonment for debt.

A Tale of Two Cities (1859), set during the French Revolution, was his second of two historical novels; *Barnaby Rudge* was the other. *GREAT EXPECTATIONS* (1860–61) portrays the conflict between social ambition and reality and is considered by many his finest full-length novel. *Our Mutual Friend* (1864–65), his last completed novel, is perhaps his most pessimistic in its portrayal of England's materialistic culture. His last novel, *The Mystery of Edwin Drood,* remained unfinished at his death.

Throughout his career, Dickens's novels were illustrated by an assortment of graphic artists, most notably GEORGE CRUIKSHANK, illustrator of the author's first book, *Sketches by Boz,* and HABLOT KNIGHT BROWNE ("Phiz"). Dickens was the first editor of *Bentley's Miscellany* (1837–39) and founded the radical newspaper *The Daily News* in 1846, along with other PERIODICALS in which many of his own works were first serialized. These included *Master Humphrey's Clock,* founded in 1840, the weekly journal *Household Words* (1850), and *All the Year Round* (1859). He also wrote *A Child's History of England* (1851–53), short stories, comic plays, and copious letters.

From 1836, Dickens was married to Catherine Hogarth, daughter of his friend and early editor George Hogarth. Though the marriage produced ten children, it was evidently not a happy one, and the couple separated in 1858, with Dickens moving to his new home in Gad's Hill, Kent. In his later years he pursued a relationship with actress Ellen Ternan.

Famed for his energy and restlessness, Dickens managed and acted in amateur theatrics and was popular as a public reader of his works beginning in 1858. This new career, which included a reading tour in the United States in 1867–68, his second visit there, was lucrative but exhausting, and contributed to his growing ill health. He died one day after suffering a stroke; crowds paid final respects for weeks at his grave in Poet's Corner, Westminster Abbey. It has been argued that Dickens's death marked the end of the high Victorian period and the beginning of the transition to the modern age.

Many of his phrases have entered the language, such as the opening words of *A Tale of Two Cities:* "It was the best of times, it was the worst of times." Many of his characters—including Fagin, Scrooge, Uriah Heep, and Miss Havisham—have become part of the culture. Though Dickens has often been criticized for sentimentality and caricature, his works remain among the lasting achievements of the English language.

Dickinson, Emily (1830–1886) American poet. Born in Amherst, Massachusetts, she was the second of three children in a well-established New England family that had long held high administrative positions at Amherst College. Her father, lawyer Edward Dickinson, was treasurer at Amherst, a one-term congressman, and a firm Calvinist. After attending Amherst Academy and spending one year at Mount Holyoke Female Seminary, she came to reject established Protestant denominations and immersed herself in TRANSCENDENTALISM.

Dickinson wrote numerous poems in the 1850s, but it was not until 1862 and afterward that she wrote with the intensity and originality that came to mark her finest poetry. It is speculated that a root of her poetic development was an unhappy romantic attachment, possibly to Philadelphia clergyman Charles Wadsworth or *Springfield Daily Republican* newspaper editor Samuel Bowles. Following her schooling and particularly during the 1860s, she developed a reclusive way of life, never venturing from her house or grounds, dressing solely in white. Yet she retained strong family attachments, corresponded with friends and select business acquaintances, and enjoyed a late romantic friendship with Judge Otis P. Lord.

Her well-chronicled aversion to publishing her poetry is likely to have arisen from her early correspondence with critic Thomas Wentworth Higginson, to whom she wrote for advice in 1862. He suggested that her intense and syntactically and rhythmically odd works were not suitable for popular audiences. Believing her work would not be understood, she published only sporadically; throughout her life between two and seven of her poems were published. After she died of Bright's disease, the first concerted attempts at publishing her work were undertaken by Higginson and Dickinson's friend Mabel L. Todd. The two editors largely conventionalized Dickinson's rhymes, meter, and grammar. Unprofessional editing of her poems continued by various editors in a number of editions until 1955 when a complete, unbowdlerized edition, *The Poems of Emily Dickinson,* was published.

diesel engine See INTERNAL COMBUSTION ENGINE.

dime novel Paperback story of crime or adventure. These sensational narratives were often set in the frontier West or in historical periods such as the American Revolution or the Civil War. Costing ten cents, they were first published by the firm of Beadle and Adams, founded in New York City in 1858 by Erastus F. and Irwin P. Beadle and Robert Adams. Under the slogan "a dollar book for a dime," the firm issued its first dime novel in 1860. Enormously popular up to the 1890s, the books were written quickly for mass consumption under the editorship of Orville J. Victor. Dime novelists included Edward S. Ellis, author of *Seth Jones, or The Captive of the Frontier* (1860); Edward L. Wheeler, creator of the Deadwood Dick series; and NED BUNTLINE, writer of the Buffalo Bill series.

dinosaur Prehistoric reptile. Comprising the orders *Saurischia* and *Ornithischia,* dinosaurs lived 225 million to 65 million years ago during the Mesozoic era. Most were terrestrial and some gigantic; some were carnivorous and others herbivorous. Fossil bones of dinosaurs may have been found as early as 1787 in New Jersey but were not identified as such. In 1824, British geologist WILLIAM BUCKLAND was the first to describe the fossil remains found in Stonesfield, England, that he believed were those of a giant extinct lizard, *Megalosaurus*—now considered the first known dinosaur. The following year, *Iguanodon* became the second known dinosaur when English physician Gideon Mantell identified it on the basis of fossil teeth discovered by his wife Mary Ann. In the following years several more dinosaur genera were discovered, including *Hylaeosaurus, Plateosaurus,* and *Cladeidon.* Not until 1841 did English anatomist and paleontologist Sir Richard Owen (1804–1892) coin the term *Dinosauria* (from the Greek, meaning "terrible lizard") for the group of extinct reptiles represented by these specimens.

In an age when science was constantly yielding wonders, dinosaurs captured the imagination of the Victorians. Life-size models of dinosaurs, constructed by sculptor Waterhouse Hawkins under Owen's supervision, were exhibited for the first time at the CRYSTAL PALACE in Sydenham, England, in 1854. *Megalosaurus* was featured in the opening lines of CHARLES DICKENS's novel *Bleak House* (1852–53).

With the publication of *THE ORIGIN OF SPECIES* by CHARLES DARWIN in 1859, dinosaurs added to the evidence of the mutability of species. Throughout the Victorian era, more dinosaur genera were found around the world, in Belgium, South Africa, the United States, Canada, and Argentina. In 1887, British paleontologist Harry Govier Seeley divided dinosaurs into two orders based primarily on the structure of the pelvic girdle: *Ornithischia* ("bird-hipped") and *Saurischia* ("lizard-hipped"). He also grouped dinosaurs in one complex with crocodiles, birds, and the extinct reptiles known as thecodonts.

Some of the most famous dinosaur genera were discovered in the United States by American paleontologists Othniel Charles Marsh and Edward Drinker Cope, whose bitter, lifelong rivalry led them to compete for who could discover the greatest number of new kinds of dinosaurs. Among their finds in the 1870s and 1880s were *Allosaurus, Apatosaurus* (also called *Brontosaurus*), *Stegosaurus,* and *Triceratops.*

dirigible See BALLOON.

Disraeli, Benjamin, 1st Earl of Beaconsfield (1804–1881) English statesman and novelist. Born in London, he was the eldest son and second child of Isaac D'Israeli and Maria Basevi. After a dispute with the Sephardic synagogue of Bevis Marks, Isaac D'Israeli baptized his children as Anglican Christians in 1817, an event that would later help his son's political career since Jews were excluded from Parliament until 1858.

At the age of seventeen, Disraeli began work as a lawyer's clerk but quickly tired of his duties and embarked on a series of disastrous financial dealings. In 1824 he encumbered a huge debt from shares in South American mines and the failure of a daily newspaper, the *Representative.* Disraeli's inability to pay his share of the capital for the paper resulted in animosity with the publisher, John Murray, as well as with J. G. Lockhart, J. W. Croker, and other people of the Tory literary-political world. Disraeli responded with the anonymous publication of the five-volume novel *Vivian Grey* (1826–27), in which he described the story of the newspaper fiasco in thinly veiled fashion.

The strain of these events placed Disraeli on the brink of an emotional collapse, and in 1830 he embarked on a sixteen-month tour of the Mediterranean that took him as far as Egypt and Palestine.

Upon his return to England, Disraeli was determined to enter politics, and after three losses as an independent candidate, he aligned himself with the Tory-Conservative Party. His extravagant behavior, financial debts, and well-known relationship with Henrietta Sykes, wife of Sir Francis Sykes, earned the young politician a dubious reputation.

In 1837, Disraeli was elected as a CONSERVATIVE PARTY member of Parliament, a title he would claim until 1880. His first speech before the House of Commons was shouted down. Disraeli prophetically shouted, "I will sit down now, but the time will come when you will hear me."

While adapting himself to political life, Disraeli continued to publish novels. In 1839 he married Mary Anne Wyndham Lewis, the widow of a colleague. During the 1840s, Disraeli emerged as the leader of a Conservative faction called YOUNG ENGLAND, which opposed the free trade policies and utilitarian rationalism of party leader ROBERT PEEL, advocating instead a nostalgic return to aristocratic paternalism. His political views were expressed in his trilogy of novels, *Coningsby* (1844), *Sybil* (1845), and *Tancred* (1847). In 1845, during a heated debate in which Disraeli delivered several brilliant speeches opposing the repeal of the CORN LAWS, he earned a claim to the leadership of the opposition and helped to bring down Peel's government in 1846.

Disraeli served as chancellor of the Exchequer in the governments of 1852, 1858–59, and 1866–67. His position as leader of the Conservative Party was cemented with his deft handling of the REFORM BILL OF 1867. In February 1868 he succeeded DERBY as prime minister and declared, "I have climbed to the top of the greasy pole." Facing a LIBERAL majority, however, Disraeli resigned without waiting for a meeting of Parliament.

Disraeli's wife died of cancer in December 1872, and despite her devotion to him, she passed her fortune on to her cousins. Disraeli began a romantic friendship with two sisters, Lady Chesterfield and Lady Bradford, to whom the politician divulged the secrets of his life and work in a voluminous series of letters.

From 1874 to 1880, Disraeli served as prime minister, but this time the Conservative Party was in command of the House of Commons. In August 1876 he accepted the title of Earl of Beaconsfield, taken from the name of a character in his first novel. His administration was marked by a vigorous imperialist foreign policy. Russian victories in the RUSSO-TURKISH WAR of 1877–78 renewed fears for the safety of GREAT BRITAIN's passage to India, and the prime minister was determined not to allow Russia to dictate a victor's peace. The threat of British intervention resulted in a treaty in which Disraeli obtained nearly all the concessions he desired. He returned to London from the Congress of BERLIN (1878) in triumph, declaring that he had brought back "peace with honor." Disraeli also gained British control of the SUEZ CANAL (1875) and prosecuted the second of the ANGLO-AFGHAN WARS (1878–80) and the ZULU WAR (1879).

On the domestic front, Disraeli favored social reforms to promote harmonious relations between the upper and lower classes. Much of his government's reform legislation was initiated by his home secretary RICHARD CROSS and other cabinet members. In his ongoing struggle with his principal adversary, Liberal Party leader WILLIAM GLADSTONE, Disraeli earned the friendship and support of Queen VICTORIA, who detested Gladstone nearly as much as she admired Disraeli. Always attentive and tactful with Queen Victoria, Disraeli had her named Empress of India in 1876.

The Queen then offered him a dukedom, but he refused, only to watch his political fortunes wane; in the general election of 1880 the Conservatives were easily defeated. Disraeli agreed to retain party leadership, but his failing health led to his death in 1881. Queen Victoria personally placed a wreath on his coffin in tribute.

Disraeli's other works include the novels *Lothair* (1870) and *Endymion* (1880), and the nonfiction works *Vindication of the British Constitution* (1835) and *Lord George Bentinck: A Political Biography* (1852).

Dix, Dorothea Lynde (1802–1887) American social reformer. Dix's advocacy for the mentally ill was instrumental in the establishment of the first hospitals for treatment of INSANITY in North America and Europe. Born in Hampden, Maine, she worked as a schoolteacher in Boston before making a detailed study of the unsanitary, inhumane living conditions of the insane in Massachusetts. Her report to the state legislature in 1842 of unclothed, unwashed patients living among criminals prompted a revamping of the Worcester asylum and began a crusade that would result in the building of more than thirty new facilities. She also served as superintendent of female nurses during the U.S. CIVIL WAR.

Dr. Jekyll and Mr. Hyde See STRANGE CASE OF DR. JEKYLL AND MR. HYDE, THE.

Dodgson, Charles Lutwidge See CARROLL, LEWIS.

doll Human figurine usually designed as a child's toy. Since ancient times in virtually all cultures, dolls have been used both as icons and as playthings. By the nineteenth-century, dollmaking had become an art form, dolls were considered collectors' items, and doll clothes symbolized contemporary fashion.

In Victorian times, dolls were made from a wide range of materials including wood, composition (a mixture of pulped wood), porcelain, bisque, celluloid, wax, rubber, and cloth. Germany, France, and England emerged as the leading manufacturers of dolls in the world, and the Great Exhibition of 1851 at the Crystal Palace in London established the reputation of many of these doll makers. The German designers, particularly Cuno and Otto Dressel, and Stephan Schilling, were noted for dolls with fine porcelain or bisque heads; the French designers Gaultier, Pierre Jumeau, and Bru, Jne. et Cie, were known for dolls with mechanical capabilities such as the ability to speak and close their eyes. The English artists gained fame through portraiture, particularly Madame Augusta Montana who created dolls that resembled Queen Victoria's children. By contrast, American doll makers had not reached the sophistication of the European artisans, and American dolls were made of rustic materials such as wood, pegs, clothespins, and rags.

Victorian dolls, often astonishingly beautiful, reflected the elaborate, overdone quality characteristic of nineteenth-century style. The dolls were exquisitely made and clothed in silks, satins, and lace. Though intended for children, they symbolized the adult values and pretenses of the age. Only at the end of the nineteenth century did the concept of the "baby doll" for children emerge.

Don Pacifico affair See PALMERSTON.

Donner party American disaster. A group of American settlers left the Midwest in April 1846 on their way to California. When they reached Wyoming, eighty-seven of them decided to follow George Donner on a little-used route south of the Great Salt Lake. Many of the party's animals died, and their food supply dwindled. They reached the foot of the Sierra Nevada mountains on October 31 but found the pass clogged with snow. They built shelters, but new snows trapped them there without food. As people began to die of starvation and exposure, fifteen of the party set across the Sierras in mid-December to find relief. It took them two months to cross the mountains and send back rescue parties, and during that time both they and the main party resorted to cannibalism to survive. Thirty-nine died, while most of the settlers who traveled the customary route from Wyoming made it safely to California.

Doppler effect The apparent change in the observed frequency of a wave as a result of the relative motion between the source of the wave and the observer. Victorians became well acquainted with this phenomenon when standing by railroad tracks: They noticed that the warning whistle of a locomotive became higher in pitch as the train approached, then dropped in pitch as the locomotive passed by and receded. Austrian physicist Christian Johann Doppler (1803–1853) was the first to explain that as a locomotive approaches, more sound waves per second reach the ear, resulting in a higher frequency, or higher pitch. As the source recedes, fewer sound waves per second reach the ear, resulting in the opposite effect.

In 1848, French physicist Armand-Hippolyte-Louis Fizeau observed that this effect would apply not only to sound but to any wave phenomenon, including light—sometimes called the Doppler-Fizeau effect. The dark lines in the spectrum of an approaching source of light would shift toward the higher-frequency violet end of the spectrum, but the lines would shift toward the lower-frequency red end for a receding source of light. The "red shift" became an important tool of astronomy, allowing astronomers to gauge, for example, how quickly galaxies are receding by analyzing the displacement of their spectral lines toward the red end. The Doppler-Fizeau effect is also used in radar to determine the velocity of objects by analyzing the difference in frequency between transmitted radio signals and reflected radio signals.

Doré, Paul-Gustave (1832–1883) French illustrator, engraver, painter, and sculptor. From 1848 to 1851 he drew cartoons for the weekly magazine *Journal pour Rire.* He also published books of his ink drawings. At first Doré did his own engraving on wood, but as his success grew, his later work was done in collaboration with numerous engravers.

Although he wanted to be a great painter, Doré's fame came from his illustrations in famous books. His work relied on his keen sense of humor and fantasy. He produced more than ninety illustrated books. He illustrated *Works of Rabelais* (1854), *Droll Stories of Balzac* (1855), Dante's *Inferno* (1861), Cervantes's *Don Quixote* (1863), the Bible (1865–66), Alfred, Lord TENNYSON's poems *Elaine* and *Vivien* (1866–68) and many others. Many of his drawings were based on myth and legend, while his paintings often treated religious or historical themes, as in *Rebel Angels Cast Down* (1866) and *The Neophyte* (1868). In 1861, Doré was decorated with the Legion of Honor.

Dost Muhammad (1793–1863) Emir of AFGHANISTAN, 1826–63. A member of the seminomadic people known as Pathans, he founded a dynasty that attempted to secure control of all Afghanistan, a task completed by his grandson ABDUR RAHMAN KHAN (who reigned from 1880 to 1901). Dost Muhammad was deposed by Britain during the First ANGLO-AFGHAN WAR (1838–42) but was restored at the end. He succeeded in preventing either Britain or Russia from dominating Afghanistan.

Dostoyevsky, Fyodor Mikhaylovich (1821–1881) Russian writer. Master of the psychological novel, he is generally considered one of the greatest writers in history. Born in Moscow, he attended the St. Petersburg School of Military Engineering but was more interested in reading foreign literature. From 1841 to 1844 he served in the army, resigning to devote himself entirely to writing. He began his literary career as a novelist with *Poor Folk,* finished in 1845 and published the following year. The work was praised by the influential critic Vissarion Belinsky and brought Dostoyevsky recognition as a major force in Russian literature. Between 1846 and 1849, Dostoyevsky wrote twelve short pieces of fiction that foreshadowed his later novels.

In 1849 he was arrested for political activities as a member of the Fourierist Petrashevski circle. Originally condemned to death by firing squad, Dostoyevsky was sentenced to four years at hard labor in Siberia, with four years of service in the army thereafter. These years of suffering, hardship, and close acquaintance with the lower classes were partly responsible for the deep compassion for humanity that appears in his novels. His many readings of the New Testament—the only book permitted to him while in prison—nourished the religious faith that informs his later work.

In 1859, Dostoyevsky was permitted to return to St. Petersburg where he resumed his literary career. With his brother Michael, he founded the magazine *Time,* which was a success even though it was suppressed by the government in 1863. The magazine gave him the opportunity to serialize several of his novels, notably *The Insulted and Injured* (1861–62) and *The House of the Dead* (1862). He and Michael revived their magazine under the name *Epoch* in 1864, the same year his novel *Notes from the Underground* appeared.

During the years of financial hardship, from 1864 to 1866, the first of Dostoyevsky's great novels took shape. *Crime and Punishment* (1866) centers on the impoverished student Raskolnikov's murder of an old woman pawnbroker and her sister, and the torments of guilt that later force him to confess. Combining psychological acuity, philosophical subtlety, moral and spiritual power, and vivid characterization, the novel is a classic of world literature.

In a period of about ten years, Dostoyevsky wrote the rest of his major novels, including *The Idiot* (1869), *The Possessed* (1872), *A Raw Youth* (1875) and *The Brothers Karamazov* (1879–80). He also edited a weekly, *The Citizen,* from 1873 to 1874, and published the series of articles and sketches entitled *A Diary of a Writer* (1873, 1876–77, 1880–81). His novels have been translated into many languages.

Doughty, Charles Montagu (1843–1926) English traveler and writer. Best known for *TRAVELS IN ARABIA DESERTA* (1888). Doughty was born at Theberton Hall, Suffolk, and educated at Cambridge; He began his travels in North Africa and the Middle East in 1870. In 1875 he settled in Damascus, Syria, where he learned Arabic. He made the pilgrimage to Mecca in Arabia in 1876. Doughty's volumes of poetry include *The Dawn in Britain* (1906–7) and *Mansoul, or, The Riddle of the World* (1920).

Douglas, Stephen (1813–1861) American politician. Born in Vermont, he moved to Illinois at age twenty. Admitted to the bar, he quickly rose in the ranks of the DEMOCRATIC PARTY to become a member of the state legislature, judge on the state Supreme Court, U.S. congressman (1843–47), and senator (1847–61). As chairman of the Senate Committee on Territories, he tried to reconcile conflicts between northerners who opposed the extension of SLAVERY into the territories and southerners who demanded it. He and HENRY CLAY hammered out the COMPROMISE OF 1850, and Douglas incorporated the principle of "popular sovereignty" into the Kansas-Nebraska Act, which allowed residents of those territories to settle the slavery question for themselves. Douglas's search for a middle ground alienated many in both sections of the country, however, and he failed to win the Democratic Party's presidential nomination in 1852 and 1856. In the 1858 Illinois Senate campaign, he defeated Republican opponent ABRAHAM LINCOLN in a contest highlighted by the Lincoln-Douglas debates. As Democratic candidate for president in 1860, he lost to Lincoln after the southern wing of the party bolted to nominate its own pro-slavery ticket. After Lincoln's election, Douglas worked to keep southern states in the Union and then toured the country after the CIVIL WAR began to drum up enthusiasm for the Union cause. He died of typhoid fever contracted on tour.

Douglass, Frederick (1817?–1895) American abolitionist. The son of a white father and African-American mother, Douglass was born into SLAVERY in Maryland. He taught himself to read and write before he escaped in 1838. Settling in Massachusetts where he adopted his name, he worked as a laborer and was hired as a lecturer and agent of the Massachusetts Anti-Slavery Society after addressing an anti-slavery convention. By the 1840s he had become famous for his oratory and his passionate commitment to abolitionism. In 1845 he published *Narrative of the Life of Frederick Douglass,* an account of his slave years. Its publication raised the possibility that he might be recaptured, and he fled to England where he continued to speak out against slavery. Returning to the United States in 1847, he bought his freedom and settled in Rochester, New York, where he published *North Star,* a weekly for African Americans, until 1864. He also supported the women's suffrage movement. During the CIVIL WAR he urged African Americans to fight the CONFEDERACY and organized two regiments. After the war he fought for civil rights and held various federal positions, including minister to Haiti from 1889 to 1891. Douglass wrote two other autobiographies, *My Bondage and My Freedom* (1855) and *Life and Times of Frederick Douglass* (1881).

Dowager Empress See TZ'U-HSI, EMPRESS.

dowry Funds or property given by a bride's family to a husband at marriage. Because a dowry could represent sizable sums and could influence the wealth of a household, it was an important element of the Victorian British courtship process. All wealth brought by the bride to the marriage became the property of the husband; by law, women were for the most part forbidden to own land or money.

Dowson, Ernest See RHYMERS' CLUB.

Doyle, Sir Arthur Conan (1859–1930) English writer and creator of SHERLOCK HOLMES. Born in Edinburgh, Scotland, he studied at the Jesuit colleges of Stonyhurst, Lancashire, and Feldkirchin, Austria, and received his M.D. from Edinburgh University in 1885. He began his medical practice in Southsea, England, specializing in ophthalmology, but when his practice floundered, he began to write. In 1887 he published *A Study in Scarlet* in *Beeton's Christmas Annual,* introducing the characters of Sherlock Holmes (originally named Sherringford Holmes) and Dr. John Watson. After the publication of *The Sign of Four* in 1890, Doyle abandoned his medical practice and concentrated on writing, producing sixty stories about the exploits of his fictional detective.

In 1893, Doyle grew weary of the Holmes character and devised his death, but after a huge public outcry, Holmes returned in *The Hound of the Baskervilles* (1902). Doyle also spent his time working at a field hospital in Bloemfontein and wrote a history of the BOER WAR in an attempt to defend British policy. For his efforts he was knighted in 1902.

Despite creating a character who seemed to epitomize rationality and discernment, Doyle was a committed believer in spiritualism, and in 1917 he began a crusade to convince others of the ability to contact the inhabitants of an afterlife. Doyle met considerable resistance, especially from his friend Harry Houdini who spent a great deal of time exposing frauds and fakers. Nevertheless, Doyle continued his efforts, and in 1926 published the two-volume *History of Spiritualism.*

Dracula (1897) Horror novel. Written by Irish writer BRAM STOKER, *Dracula* is the most celebrated of all vampire stories. It is rivaled only by *Frankenstein* as the world's best known horror narrative. Through a series of diaries, journals, newspaper extracts, and letters, the novel opens with the London solicitor Jonathan Harker's account of his journey to Transylvania, where he falls prey to Count Dracula and several female vampires at the count's castle. The Count journeys to England, arriving after having assumed the form of a bat aboard a ship whose crew and passengers have perished under mysterious circumstances. The narrative shifts to the story of Harker's fiancée, Mina Murray; her friend, the coquettish Lucy Westerna; Dr. John Seward; and Van Helsing, a Dutch doctor who leads the others in hunting the Count. Lucy is the first to fall victim to Dracula when he bites her neck. She thereby joins the "undead," vampires who have neither a human existence nor a genuine death. Only when a stake is driven through Lucy's heart can she die in peace. When Dracula turns his attention to Mina, he is driven back to Transylvania where he is vanquished.

Often forceful and compellingly told, the novel is ambitious in its formal design. It has often been adapted for stage and screen. In addition to its effectiveness as a terrifying vampire tale, *Dracula* has been variously interpreted as a tale of the perils of romantic ardor, a metaphor for the uncontrollable effects of disease, and a myth about the avaricious aristocratic class.

draughts British game of checkers. It was popular during the Victorian era.

drawing room Formal area in a residence. Used in Victorian times for the formal entertaining of afternoon and evening dinner guests before and after the meal was served, but not all residences contained a drawing room.

Dred Scott decision U.S. Supreme Court decision in 1857 which ruled that Congress had no constitutional right to ban SLAVERY from the western territories. The slave Dred Scott (1795?–1858) was taken by his master from Missouri, a slave state, to live in the Wisconsin territory, now Minnesota. After his master died, ownership of Scott reverted to his owner's widow, an opponent of slavery who agreed to be sued by Scott for his freedom on the grounds that living in a free territory had ended his servitude. The Missouri Supreme Court rejected his suit, but another suit reached the Supreme Court in 1856.

Scott lost his suit again, but Chief Justice Roger Taney's ruling had implications that went far beyond the matter of the case. He ruled that no African American, slave or free, had the right to sue. Further, a slave owner had the right to take slaves into free territories because the Fifth Amendment stipulated that no one can be stripped of his property without due process of law. This invalidated the Missouri Compromise and rendered unconstitutional all other attempts by Congress to bar slavery from the territories. The decision enraged antislavery forces in the North, split the DEMOCRATIC PARTY, and worsened the sectional tensions that led to the CIVIL WAR. Scott was freed a few days after the decision and lived in St. Louis until his death the following year.

Dreiser, Theodore (1871–1945) American novelist. A leading writer of American NATURALISM, he was raised in poverty in Indiana and grew up to espouse a grim, deterministic view of life. His first novel, *Sister Carrie,* was published in 1900, but the publisher's concerns about its alleged immorality kept it from being widely distributed until 1912. The novel describes the harsh life of Midwestern country girl Carrie Meeber as she faces urban unemployment and squalor and becomes the mistress of two different men. Dreiser's unhappiness at the fate of this first novel led him to stop writing for a decade, during which time he worked as an editor for Butterick Publications, publishers of women's magazines. The commercial success of his next novel, *Jessie Gerhardt* (1911), at last launched Dreiser on a prolific literary career. Of his later novels, among the most respected are the three books of the "Cowperwood" trilogy

(*The Financier,* 1912; *The Titan,* 1914; and *The Stoic,* 1947) and *An American Tragedy* (1925.)

Dreyfus, Alfred (1859–1935) French army officer. Dreyfus, of Jewish ancestry, was convicted of treason on false evidence. The controversy over the Dreyfus affair grew into a major crisis of the THIRD REPUBLIC (1870–1940). In 1894, Dreyfus, at the time an obscure captain, was serving on the army's general staff when it was discovered that military secrets had been leaked to the German embassy. A hasty investigation determined that Dreyfus was the culprit, and he was summarily tried, convicted, and imprisoned on Devil's Island from 1895 to 1899. Meanwhile, Dreyfus's wife and son managed to create some interest in reopening the case. In 1896 a new army intelligence chief uncovered overwhelming evidence that another officer, Ferdinand Esterhazy, was the guilty party. But a powerful faction within the army resisted efforts to reopen the case. Esterhazy was cleared in a new trial in 1898. It was not then publicly known that forged documents had been added to the files to implicate Dreyfus and clear Esterhazy.

Following Esterhazy's acquittal, EMILE ZOLA wrote his famous article *"J'accuse,"* bitterly criticizing the handling of the case. This touched off anti-Semitic attacks across France. The Dreyfus affair became a flashpoint of conflict and violence between socialists and republicans on one side and ultranationalists and anti-Semites on the other. Public opinion was sharply divided not only over Dreyfus's guilt or innocence but also on whether clearing him would cause too much damage to the army and country. Finally, in 1899, Dreyfus was returned from Devil's Island and retried. He was again convicted "with extenuating circumstances" and quickly pardoned. In 1906 the forgeries and Esterhazy's guilt were finally revealed. Dreyfus was reinstated and served in the army during World War I, winning the Legion of Honor.

dribbler British toy train of the nineteenth century. Driven by steam and usually made of solid brass, it was called a dribbler, or piddler, for the trail of water it left behind on the floor. Toy trains gained an international following as RAILROADS became a ubiquitous symbol of progress.

Drury Lane, Theatre Royal London building for theatrical performances. Since 1662 it had been a patent theater, one of two theaters—the other being COVENT GARDEN—with the exclusive legal right to arrange performances of legitimate plays in the City of Westminster. An Act of Parliament in 1843 abolished that monopoly, but Drury Lane carried on, becoming famous not for its legitimate drama but for spectacle and pantomime. Housed in a big building—erected in 1812 and with a capacity of 2,283—it is still in business, staging mostly musicals.

Du Bois, W. E. B. [William Edward Burghart] (1868–1963) African-American writer, educator, and social activist. Born in Great Barrington, Massachusetts, he worked as a Massachusetts correspondent for several New York newspapers as early as age fifteen. He received a B.A. from Fisk University in Nashville, Tennessee, in 1888 and entered Harvard that same year as a junior. After graduating from Harvard in 1890, he studied history and economics at the University of Berlin. After returning to the United States, he taught at Wilberforce University, the University of Pennsylvania, and Atlanta University.

Du Bois led the opposition against the other great black American leader of the time, BOOKER T. WASHINGTON. Washington's acceptance of segregation and his gradualist approach to black progress led Du Bois to form the Niagara Movement, a group of black intellectuals who believed in complete and prompt equality for blacks. In 1909 he helped form the National Association for the Advancement of Colored People (NAACP). The following year he founded *The Crisis,* the most influential black periodical of the time, which he edited until 1934.

DuBois's politics became increasingly radical. He joined the Communist Party of the United States in 1961, the same year he moved to Ghana. He died there two years later after renouncing his U.S. citizenship.

Du Bois wrote extensively on many subjects. His most famous historical works include *The Souls of Black Folk* (1903), a wide-ranging collection of essays on sharecroppers, the Freedman's Bureau, and Booker T. Washington. He also wrote *Black Reconstruction* (1935), *The Autobiography of W. E. B. Du Bois* (1968), and several novels.

Du Maurier, George Louis Palmella Busson (1834–1896) English illustrator and novelist. Born in Paris to a French father of noble lineage and an English mother, he studied art in Paris and later at Antwerp, where he lost the sight in his left eye and abandoned painting in favor of drawing. In 1860 he moved to London and quickly established himself as an illustrator, providing drawings to the satirical magazine *PUNCH,* where he became a regular contributor in 1864. Du Maurier also provided illustrations to books by WILLIAM MAKEPEACE THACKERAY and HENRY JAMES until his failing eyesight led to his decision to begin a career writing his own novels.

Peter Ibbetson, a fictionalized account of the author's childhood, was published in 1891. Its popularity led to two other novels, *Trilby* (1894) and *The Martian* (1896). *Trilby,* the story of an artist's model who falls under the hypnotic control of the sinister Svengali, remains Du Maurier's most popular work. It was produced on the stage in 1895, and three film versions were eventually made.

Dumas, Alexandre [known as Dumas *père*] (1802–1870) French novelist and playwright. Author of about three hundred volumes, though many were written in collaboration. He began his career as a melodramatic playwright influenced by Shakespeare but became best known for his swashbuckling romantic novels, influenced by Walter Scott. *The Three Musketeers* (1844), his most enduring work, is set in seventeenth-century France and is loosely based on the memoirs of the historical figure Charles d'Artagnan. The title characters, Athos, Porthos, and Aramis, have never ceased to entertain readers. Two sequels followed, *Twenty Years After* (1845) and the story "The Man in the Iron Mask" in *The Viscount of Bragelonne* (1848–50). Other novels, such as *The Count of Monte Cristo* (1844–45), set in Napoleonic times, and *The Black Tulip* (1895), set in seventeenth-century Holland, are also enduring parts of popular literature. Critics have taken Dumas to task for his melodrama, wild coincidences, and absence of psychological depth but praised him for his vividness and energy. His early plays, including *Henri III and His Court* (1829), were important contributions to French ROMANTICISM. Dumas's life was as colorful as his adventure sagas; his many travels included participation in GIUSEPPE GARIBALDI's Sicily campaign of 1860. His illegitimate son ALEXANDRE DUMAS, known as *Dumas fils,* was also a novelist and playwright.

Dumas, Alexandre [known as Dumas *fils*] (1824–1895) French playwright. The illegitimate son of novelist ALEXANDRE DUMAS, he wrote some novels but became best known for his plays. He is regarded as the founder of the problem play, which explores contemporary issues in a naturalistic style. His most acclaimed work is *La Dame aux camélias,* published as a novel in 1848 and as a play in 1852, and known in English as *Camille.* Telling the story of Marguerite Gauthier, or Camille, a fashionable Parisian courtesan who sacrifices happiness for love, it was the source for the opera *La Traviata* (1853) by GIUSEPPE VERDI. Other popular works included *Le Demi-Monde* (1855), *La Question d'argent* (1857), *Un Père prodigue* (1859), and *L'Ami des femmes* (1864).

Dunant, Jean-Henri (1828–1910) Swiss humanitarian. Born in Geneva, Switzerland, he became active in the World Evangelical Alliance and ministered to the wounded at the Battle of Solferino in 1859. He wrote about his experiences in *Un Souvenir de Solferino* in 1862 and devoted himself to the formation of an international organization for the prevention and alleviation of suffering in war and peace.

Dunant's efforts were responsible in part for the GENEVA CONVENTION of 1864, which attempted to avert war through international negotiations. Dunant conceived the RED CROSS, which became famous during the Franco-Prussian War of 1870–71.

Neglected business affairs resulted in bankruptcy in 1867, and Dunant lived in poverty and obscurity, working ceaselessly for humanitarian goals, until 1895 when a journalist found him in Heiden, Switzerland. Dunant was subsequently awarded the first Nobel Peace Prize in 1901.

Durham, John George Lambton, 1st Earl of Durham (1792–1840) English statesman. Born in London, he was educated at Eton and entered the army in 1809. Three years later he eloped with the daughter of Lord Cholmondeley; she died in 1815. In 1813 he was elected to the House of Commons as a Whig, and three years later, following his marriage to Louisa Elizabeth, the eldest daughter of Lord Grey, Durham was admitted into the higher ranks of the Whig Party, where he earned the sobriquet "Radical Jack."

After serving in Lord Grey's cabinet for three years, he resigned in 1833, ostensibly for reasons of failing health; it has been suggested, however, that the resignation was a result of his disagreement with the government's policy in Ireland. He then served as ambassador to Russia until January 1838 when he accepted the post of governor-general and lord high commissioner in Canada.

In an attempt to solve the problems and quell the spirit of revolt in British North America, he was granted almost dictatorial powers. On June 28, 1838, the day of Queen Victoria's coronation, he issued a proclamation of amnesty to the leaders of rebellion. Louis Joseph Papineau and fifteen others were excepted from the amnesty and were exiled from Canada.

After an extensive dispute with the British government over his actions, he resigned in November 1838. In January 1839 he presented his *Report on the Affairs of British North America* to Parliament, in which he defended his policy and outlined his principles, advocating "responsible government." This report eventually became the blueprint for promoting self-government throughout the colonies of the British Empire.

Durkheim, Émile (1858–1917) French sociologist. Influenced by the views of French thinker AUGUST COMTE, he helped to found modern sociology by bringing to bear the kind of methodological rigor characteristic of the natural sciences. Empirical data and statistical analysis were central to his work, as was his theory of a collective social mind and a social order bound by common values. His works include *The Rules of Sociological Method* (1895), *Suicide* (1897), and *The Elementary Forms of Religious Life* (1915).

Duse, Eleanora (1859–1924) Italian actress. Duse's early life was full of hardship, especially the death of her mother when she was fourteen. That same year, 1872, she played Juliet with great success in Verona. In 1878 she gained recognition in Emile Augier's *Les Fourchambault.* The important manager Cesare Rossi engaged Duse for his company, and her repertoire soon included *Divorcons, Fedora, La Locandiera,* and *Theodora.*

Duse toured South America in 1885, and in 1892 she astonished Vienna with her performance in *La Dame aux Camelias.* She repeated the performance in 1893 for her New York debut, which was considered a rare dramatic event. In 1895, while playing in London, she participated in a historic contest with SARAH BERNHARDT. Both actresses played Sudermann's *Magda* and invited the critics to make their choice. GEORGE BERNARD SHAW declared Duse far superior.

In 1899, Duse began her romantic and artistic association with Italian playwright Gabriele D'Annunzio, having acted in his plays *La Citta morta* and *La Giocanda.* In 1902 she went to America with the dramas. She retired prior to World War I, but in 1921 she returned to the stage after a twelve-year absence.

Duse's acting was characterized by extreme simplicity and lack of theatrical artifice. She is considered by many to have been the greatest tragic actress of the modern theater. Perhaps her most important contribution was her playing of HENRIK IBSEN heroines throughout Europe and America.

Dutch East Indies See INDONESIA.

dyes Coloring matter. Made since antiquity from natural materials such as roots, bark, and berries, clothing dyes were first made synthetically in the nineteenth century. The first synthetic dye was MAUVE, concocted from coal tar in 1856 by English chemist William Henry Perkin (1838–1907), then still in his teens. Other synthetic dyes followed, including violet hues made from rosaniline and blue shades from potassium. Perkin, who with B. F. Duppa was the first to synthesize an amino acid (glycine, in 1858), also founded the commercial synthetic dye industry.

dynamite Explosive made from nitroglycerine and inert, absorbent filler. The explosive chemical nitroglycerine was discovered by Italian chemist Ascanio Sobrero in 1847. Although it was soon put to use in such tasks as blasting roads and digging canals, it was unstable and dangerous. In 1866, Swedish inventor ALFRED NOBEL, who had lost a brother in a nitroglycerine explosion, developed a more stable mixture of nitroglycerine and kieselguhr (diatomaceous earth) that could be pressed into cylindrical form and detonated from a distance. He called it dynamite, from the Greek for "power," and it became an important tool of construction, earthmoving, and war. Modern dynamite uses other fillers, such as wood pulp, and have sodium or ammonium nitrate added.

Eakins, Thomas (1844–1916) American painter and photographer. Trained as a painter in Paris in 1866 and influenced by EDOUARD MANET, Jean-Léon Gérôme, and seventeenth-century Spanish artists such as Diego Velázquez, Eakins became one of the major American practitioners of REALISM. He returned to Philadelphia in 1870 to record the sporting events on the Schuylkill River. Eakins's vision was not as casual and relaxed as those found in IMPRESSIONISM but more detached, with a scientific intensity. This can be seen in Eakins's early masterpiece *The Biglen Brothers Turning the Stake* (1873), where even the play of light was studied as a mathematical problem in perspective.

Photography proved to be another device for Eakins to seek the recording of visual truth on which his art was founded. As a photographer, Eakins continued the experiments by EADWEARD MUYBRIDGE in the photography of motion, using a single camera to produce a series of images on a single plate. Eakins's fascination with the truth of art and the truth of science is best seen in his famous painting *The Gross Clinic* (1875), which reflects the interest in anatomy he developed as a student at Jefferson Medical College in Philadelphia. Considered offensive, the depiction of a surgical operation in progress was not included with the other works of art at the Philadelphia Centennial Exhibition of 1876 but was shown separately at the U.S. Army Post Hospital. The subject interested Eakins enough for him to paint *The Agnew Clinic* (1889) showing a breast-cancer operation. Both paintings have precedents in Rembrandt's *Anatomy Lesson* and mid-nineteenth-century French paintings of surgical demonstrations.

As a teacher at the Pennsylvania Academy, Eakins revolutionized the teaching of art in the United States, insisting on drawing from live nude models and anatomical studies. Conservative critics routinely denounced as degrading the forceful realism of Eakins's nudes in such paintings as *Crucifixion* (1880) and *The Swimming Hole* (1883).

Earp, Wyatt Berry Stapp (1848–1929) American lawman. He was born on a farm near Monmouth, Illinois. By his late twenties he had worked as a stagecoach driver, wagoner, and hunter before becoming the deputy marshal of Wichita, Kansas, in 1875. When his term of office expired a year later, he accepted the job as city marshal in Dodge City, but after reading about rich silver strikes in the Arizona Territory, he left for Tombstone along with his brothers Jim and Warren, as well as his friend John H. "Doc" Holliday. His other brothers, Virgil and Morgan, joined him along the way to Arizona.

After failing to strike it rich in the outlaw-filled town of Tombstone, Wyatt Earp quickly accepted the job of deputy sheriff and appointed Virgil chief of police and Morgan and Warren as constables. The Earps had as many enemies as friends in town, and in October 1881 the Earps and Doc Holliday faced Ike Clanton and four other men in a showdown at the O.K. Corral. The actual gunfight lasted less than one minute, during which time three members of the Clanton gang were killed and Virgil and Morgan Earp were wounded. The citizens of Tombstone were almost equally divided between regarding Earp and his men as heroes or as villains.

About 1883, Wyatt Earp left Arizona, shortly after avenging the murder of Morgan, and settled in California. In 1898 he joined the gold rush to Alaska, and once again missing the mother lode, he opened the Dexter Saloon in Nome. He returned to California, finally settling in Los Angeles, where he spent the rest of his life cultivating his own legend.

Eastlake, Sir Charles Lock (1793–1865) English painter, art historian, and administrator. In 1808, Eastlake studied under Benjamin Robert Haydon before becoming a student in the Royal Academy Schools. He painted his famous *Napoleon on Board the Bellerophon* in 1815 from sketches he made when he witnessed Napoleon standing at the gangway of the ship. After successfully selling this work, Eastlake lived in Rome from 1816 to 1830 where he painted picturesque scenes of the Roman Campagna. He first exhibited at the Royal Academy in 1823 where he was elected an associate in 1827. He practiced religious, historical, and GENRE PAINTING. His works, including *Pilgrims in Sight of Rome* (1828), were very popular in England.

Charles Lock Eastlake, British writer on art, architecture, and furniture design, influenced the revival of Gothic and Jacobean furniture in both England and America.

Eastlake turned increasingly to administration and achieved a remarkable record as a public servant. Upon his return to London in 1830, he was elected a Royal Academician. In 1840 he became secretary to the Royal Commission for the decoration of the palace of Westminster and for the promotion of the fine arts. In 1842 he was made librarian of the Royal Academy, and in the following year he became keeper of the National Gallery, until 1847.

Eastlake was elected president of the Royal Academy in 1850 and received the customary honor of knighthood. He later became the Director of the National Gallery from 1855 until his death. During this time he was instrumental in acquiring an important collection of early Italian paintings.

Eastlake's literary work was all connected with art, including a translation of Franz Kugler's *Italian Schools of Painting* (1842), as well as his own *Materials for a History of Oil Painting* (1847) and *Contributions to the Literature of the Fine Arts* (1848). His emphasis in his books was on the decorative possibilities of the materials themselves and even on the spirit of the Gothic, which was being copied by many architects and designers at the time.

Eastlake, Charles Lock (1836–1906) English designer and artist. Like his uncle, Sir CHARLES LOCK EASTLAKE, he was keeper of the National Gallery from 1878 to 1898 and published several works on art and decoration. The best known of his writings was *Hints on Household Taste* (1868) in which he advocated quality of materials and workmanship. His support for the Gothic and Jacobean revivals in architecture and furniture design proved highly influential in England, especially during the ARTS AND CRAFTS MOVEMENT, and even more so in America. Eastlake criticized so-called American Eastlake furniture, however, finding its production and design completely alien to his own style. He also wrote *A History of the Gothic Revival* (1871), which became the pioneering work on the subject and the standard until the early twentieth century.

Eastman, George See PHOTOGRAPHY.

ecology The study of the interrelationships of organisms and their natural environment. Given its name by German biologist and philosopher Ernst von Haeckel (1834–1919) in 1866, the field of study developed in the twentieth century into a discipline with important scientific, political, and social consequences.

Eddy, Mary Baker (1821–1910) American founder of Christian Science. Born in Bow, New Hampshire, and educated at home, she was married three times. From childhood onward her health was precarious. In 1862 she became a patient of a mental healer, Phineas P. Quimby, who had a great influence over her; she later rejected his methods.

In 1866, while reading in the Bible of one of Jesus' healings (Matthew 9:1–8), she recovered from critical injuries received in a fall. This experience was the basis of her discovery of Christian Science. She began attracting followers and published her system of beliefs in *Science and Health with Key to the Scriptures* (1875), which she revised repeatedly in order to clarify its teachings. This book, along with the Bible, is still the central text in Christian Science. Her followers grew steadily. In 1876 the Christian Science Association was formed, and in 1879 the Church of Christ, Scientist was chartered, a merging of the various associations. In 1883 she founded the *Journal of Christian Science,* a monthly magazine, and in 1888 began the first Christian Science reading room.

She established the Christian Science publishing society in 1892, and in 1908 the *Christian Science Monitor,* an influential daily newspaper. Among her many books are *Unity of Good* (1891); the autobiography *Retrospection and Introspection* (1891); *Church Manual,* also known as *Manual of the Mother Church, the First Church of Christ, Scientist, in Boston, Massachusetts* (1895–1910); and *Miscellaneous Writings* (1896).

In her last years, despite her retirement, she worked to establish a church that would survive her death. Her basic teachings preached Christianity through Bible study, what she termed "Principle and rule of spiritual Science and metaphysical healing—in a word, Christian Science."

Edison, Thomas Alva (1847–1931) American inventor. His creations came to represent the advances of the industrial age, and his personality became a symbol of American ingenuity. Born in Ohio, Edison was the son of a once prosperous shingle manufacturer who moved his family to Michigan when his business faltered. After three months of formal schooling, Edison became a railroad newspaper boy at the age of twelve. Educated at home by his mother, Edison read voraciously about chemistry and set up a home laboratory. At this time Edison began to go deaf, probably the result of a childhood bout with scarlet fever.

From 1862 to 1869, Edison was a traveling telegraph operator and began developing telegraph-related devices. He registered his first patent in 1869 for a vote recorder. He arrived in New York City in 1869, destitute from bankrolling inventions that did not catch on. In 1870 he received $40,000 for improvements to the stock ticker and started a business and laboratory that he moved to Menlo Park, New Jersey, in 1876. It was to be the site of some of the most prodigious wizardry of the nineteenth century. Within a decade, Edison invented the PHONOGRAPH (1877), the first practical electric lamp (1879), and the telephone transmitter (1877). He also generated the ideas that later made talking MOTION PICTURES possible.

During 1881 and 1882 he developed the first central electric power station—Pearl Street Station in New York City—which formed the basis for the modern electric light and power industry.

The "Wizard of Menlo Park" lived up to his contention that genius is "1 percent inspiration and 99 percent perspiration." By 1931 he had tallied more than thirteen hundred patents, and his labs prefigured the practices of later research facilities, employing team approaches to working on a problem. His last breath was claimed to have been captured and contained by fellow American entrepreneur Henry Ford; it is now on display at the Henry Ford Museum in Dearborn, Michigan.

Education Acts Series of British laws. The acts established state-supported schools and ultimately made attendance compulsory. As of 1869 only one-half of elementary-school-age children attended classes in the religious, or "voluntary," schools. The contentious issue of teaching religion in state-financed schools had hindered the establishment of a system of education available to all children regardless of ability to pay. The Education Act of 1870, the brainchild of WILLIAM EDWARD FORSTER, enabled local governments to set up elected school boards that could establish schools. The schools were supported by local and national taxes as well as fees that were waived for poor families. State aid to voluntary schools, run mostly by the Church of England, was increased and religious instruction unchanged. Religious education in the new board schools, which in

America would be called public schools, was optional for students and nonsectarian.

The Education Act of 1876 enabled school boards to compel attendance in elementary schools. In 1880 education was made compulsory up to the age of ten, and in 1891 all fees were ended. The Education Act of 1902 abolished local school boards and made the county and borough councils responsible for public and voluntary schools. Religious instruction became optional for students in voluntary schools. This act also authorized the establishment of academic secondary schools and vocational-technical schools.

Edward VII [Albert Edward] (1841–1910) King of the United Kingdom of GREAT BRITAIN and Ireland from 1901. As the second child and eldest son of Queen VICTORIA and Prince ALBERT, he was named Prince of Wales while still an infant. He attended Oxford and Cambridge, but his real loves were sports (especially racing, hunting, and yachting) and conviviality. His dalliance with an actress in 1861 scandalized his parents and was said to contribute to Albert's early death. During his mother's reclusive widowhood, Edward often represented the monarchy at public events, though he was largely kept out of matters of government until late in Victoria's reign. In 1863 he married Princess Alexandra, eldest daughter of the future King Christian IX of Denmark, but his eye continued to rove, notably onto actress LILLIE LANGTRY. Acceding to the throne upon his mother's death in 1901, he was a popular and gracious king who helped forge alliances with France and Russia and supported renewal of British military strength. Upon his death, his son George Frederick succeeded him as George V.

Egg, Augustus Leopold (1816–1863) British painter. Egg's work consisted of historical and literary scenes as well as GENRE PAINTINGS, everyday scenes that often had a moral message. His series of three pictures *Past and Present* (1858) depicts the harmful consequences of adultery. He was a friend of novelist WILKIE COLLINS and acted in CHARLES DICKENS's amateur theater company.

Egypt Nation in the northeast corner of AFRICA. It is bounded by the Mediterranean Sea on the north, the Red Sea on the east, Libya to the west, and the Sudan to the south. The Sinai Peninsula, separated from the rest of Egypt by the Red Sea, borders Israel on the east.

At the beginning of the nineteenth century, Egypt remained part of the weakening OTTOMAN EMPIRE that had conquered it in 1517. Revolts against the Ottomans in 1805 led to the appointment of MUHAMMAD ALI as the new viceroy.

Nominally under the Ottoman sultan, Ali's army quickly established Egypt's autonomy. Between 1811 and 1840, Egypt conquered much of the northern SUDAN, central Arabia, and Ottoman Syria. Only European intervention in 1840 prevented Egypt from toppling the entire Ottoman Empire. Ali died in 1849, but his power had waned by then and the Ottomans began to reassert their authority.

Ali's sons reversed some of the Western administrative reforms established in the 1830s, but Egypt became dependent on France and Great Britain to maintain its autonomy against the sultan. The British were allowed to build a railway from Cairo to Alexandria (1851–56) that improved communication with India. In 1854 the French won a concession to build the SUEZ CANAL, which opened in 1869.

Ali's grandson Ismail ruled Egypt from 1863 to 1879. A boom in cotton exports caused by the loss of American cotton during the U.S. Civil War enabled him to finance military expeditions led by CHARLES GORDON and other Europeans that conquered the remoter areas of the Sudan and the coast of Somalia. He also modernized the administration of the government. Ismail bribed the sultan to grant him special concessions, which included the approval of his dynastic arrangements and bestowing on him the title of KHEDIVE, which distinguished him from other national rulers in the empire.

Ismail's ambitions, coupled with the end of the cotton boom, finally bankrupted the country. Britain and France forced Ismail's abdication in 1879 in favor of his son Tewfik who was dependent on his European sponsors. His close relationship with them fed an anticolonial nationalist movement that led to riots in Alexandria. British troops quelled the disturbances, and Egypt became a protectorate of the crown over the protests of France. Evelyn Baring, 1st Earl of CROMER, the British consul from 1883 to 1907, led the reorganization of the economy and ensured interest payments to foreign bondholders. But he could not prevent the fall of KHARTOUM in the Sudan to rebels under the MAHDI.

Tewfik died in 1892. His son, Abbas Hilmi II, tried to cultivate a moderate nationalism among the middle classes but continued to rely on Britain for protection against foreign invasion. Under his rule, Lord KITCHENER retook the Sudan in 1898.

The British protectorate ended in 1922 when Egypt became an independent state.

Eiffel Tower French architectural landmark. French engineer Alexandre-Gustave Eiffel (1832–1923) designed the Eiffel Tower for the Paris Centennial Exposition of 1889. Erected in the Champ-de-Mars, the tower is 984 feet high, and its iron framework, four columns that form one shaft, stands on four masonry piers. Three platforms at different heights are reached by stairs and elevators. After the 1889 fair closed, Eiffel supervised changes to accommodate a meteorological station in 1890, a military telegraph station in 1903, and a laboratory for studying aerodynamics in 1909. The Eiffel Tower was the tallest structure in the world until 1930. The tower's designer is also known for his iron bridge over the Garonne River (1858), the railway bridge over the Douro River (1877), and the framework for the STATUE OF LIBERTY (1885–86).

Constructed for the 1889 World's Fair in Paris, the Eiffel Tower was the tallest building in the world until 1930. It continues to serve as one of the city's main tourist attractions. Courtesy of Max A. Polster Archive.

electric power Current generated by the conversion of energy from a given source, usually falling water or steam from the burning of fossil fuels. The electric generator was invented independently by English physicist MICHAEL FARADAY and American physicist Joseph Henry in 1831; Henry also invented the electric motor. Steam from the burning of coal continued to be the preferred power source for the Victorian world, however, even after public electric power stations were installed in London and New York City in 1882. For long-distance power transmission, the invention of alternating current (AC) by Croatian engineer Nikola Tesla in 1883 was a distinct improvement over the direct current (DC) used previously. The first practical AC power station was installed in Germany in the mid-1890s. Electrification in the twentieth century was accelerated because of the popularity of electric lighting, which was invented by American THOMAS ALVA EDISON in 1879 and was soon found preferable to Victorian gas lighting. See also CABLE.

electron Negatively charged subatomic particle. Irish physicist George Johnstone Stoney (1826–1911) coined the term in 1891 for the fundamental particles that he theorized were the carriers of electric charge. In 1897, British physicist Joseph John Thomson (1856–1940) showed that CATHODE RAYS, known to science since 1876, were Stoney's predicted electrons; Thomson is therefore credited as the discoverer of the electron. He also discovered the ratio of the electron's charge to its mass, though it remained for twentieth-century researchers to calculate exact values for the charge and mass and to show that the electron was an intrinsic part of the atom.

elements Of the ninety-two chemical elements that occur naturally on earth, thirty were discovered during the Victorian era. The pace of discovery was sped by new methods of isolating elements—such as electrolysis, first used for this purpose in 1807 by British chemist Humphry Davy to isolate potassium, and spectral analysis, used to discover cesium in 1860. Since at least the seventeenth century, elements had been defined as substances that could not be decomposed by chemical means. But the nineteenth century saw new ways of understanding the uniqueness of elements, particularly the notion that elements differed in their atomic weight—an idea first advanced by British chemist John Dalton in 1803. Of great importance in encouraging discovery was the PERIODIC TABLE OF ELEMENTS, the classification system devised by DMITRY MENDELEYEV in 1869, which predicted the existence of elements not yet discovered.

After 1901, only a few naturally occurring elements were left to be discovered. The development of nuclear technology led however, to the manufacture of sixteen synthetic elements—unstable, radioactive elements that occur only in minute quantities in nature or not at all.

For a list of the elements discovered in the Victorian era, see page 152.

elevator Conveyance. The first modern safety elevator was developed in 1852 by U.S. mechanic and inventor ELISHA GRAVES OTIS. Although this device for moving people and items from level to level had existed since the early 1800s, it lacked a safety feature to keep from falling if the carrying mechanism broke. In Otis's model of 1852, a series of spring-operated cams attached to the elevator cage kept the cage in place even if the cable holding the elevator were removed. Early elevators were steam-powered. The first electric-powered model was installed in the United States in 1889.

DATE	ELEMENT	DISCOVERER	COUNTRY
1839	lanthanum	Carl Gustaf Mosander	Sweden
1843	erbium	Carl Gustaf Mosander	Sweden
	terbium	Carl Gustaf Mosander	Sweden
1844	ruthenium	Karl K. Klaus	Russia
1860	cesium	Robert Bunsen and Gustav R. Kirchhoff	Germany
	rubidium	Gustav R. Kirchhoff	Germany
1861	thallium	Sir WILLIAM CROOKES	Britain
1863	indium	Ferdinand Reich	Germany
		Theodor Richter	
1868	helium	Pierre-J.-C. Janssen	France
		JOSEPH N. LOCKYER	Britain
1875	gallium	Paul-Emile Lecoq de Boisbaudran	France
1878	holmium	Jacques L. Soret	France
		Marc Delafontaine	
	ytterbium	Jean-Charles de Marignac	Switzerland
1879	samarium	Paul-Emile Lecoq de Boisbaudran	France
	scandium	Lars Fredrik Nilson	Sweden
	thulium	Per Teodor Cleve	Sweden
1885	neodymium	Carl von Welsbach	Austria
	praseodymium	Carl von Welsbach	Austria
1886	dysprosium	Paul-Emile Lecoq de Boisbaudran	France
	fluorine	Henri Moissan	France
	germanium	Clemens Alexander Winkler	Germany
	gadolinium	Jean-Charles de Marignac	Switzerland
1894	argon	Baron RAYLEIGH and William Ramsay	Britain
1896	europium	Eugène-Anatole Demarçay	France
1898	krypton	William Ramsay and Morris W. Travers	Britain
	neon	William Ramsay and Morris W. Travers	Britain
	xenon	William Ramsay and Morris W. Travers	Britain
1898	radium	PIERRE CURIE and MARIE SKLODOWSKA CURIE	France
	polonium	Pierre Curie and Marie Sklodowska Curie	France
1899	actinium	André-Louis Debierne	France
1900	radon	Friedrich Ernst Dorn	Germany

Eliot, Charles William (1834–1926) American educator. Born in Boston, he graduated from Harvard University in 1853. The next year he became a mathematics tutor there, until 1858 when he became an assistant professor of mathematics and chemistry.

In 1863, Eliot began a two-year study in Europe, and upon his return became professor of chemistry at the Massachusetts Institute of Technology. Eliot's interest in education led to his publication of "The New Education: Its Organization" in 1869 in *The Atlantic Monthly*. His insight into contemporary pedagogy led to his appointment as president of Harvard in October 1869, where he remained for the next forty years.

As president, Eliot helped Harvard evolve from a small college into one of the world's foremost universities. In his last year there he acted as editor of the *Harvard Classics,* a fifty-volume set of the world's great literature, which quickly became the canon at most institutions. After his retirement in 1909, Eliot traveled the world working for international peace, labor reform, and a continued improvement in education. He died in Northeast Harbor, Maine.

This illustration is from George Eliot's first novel Adam Bede. *She later wrote such highly regarded works as* Middlemarch, Silas Marner, *and* Daniel Deronda.

Eliot, George [Mary Ann or Marian Evans] (1819–1880) English writer. One of the most popular and esteemed English novelists and essayists of the Victorian Age, Eliot was appreciated in her time and afterward for the intelligence and moral realism of her works. Born and educated in Warwickshire, she became the caretaker for her father at age sixteen when her mother died, until his death in 1849. While living with her father in Warwickshire and later in Coventry, she tutored herself in the liberal arts, theology, and foreign languages, and joined with a group of iconoclastic thinkers, including Charles Bray and Charles Hennell. The group's humanist ideals reflected and informed her own views, particularly her spiritual beliefs, which were manifested when she refused in January 1842 to accompany her father to his evangelical Protestant services. The divergence of their beliefs would remain a source of conflict until his death.

In the early 1850s, Eliot moved to London and through her friend John Chapman became the assistant editor of the *Westminster Review.* In 1854 she translated Ludwig Feuerbach's *Essence of Christianity,* which reflected much of her thinking. That year she also began what would be a twenty-four-year common-law marriage to critic and novelist GEORGE HENRY LEWES, which ended only with his death in 1878.

With his encouragement, she began writing stories. Her first published narratives appeared in 1857 in *Blackwood's Edinburgh Magazine:* "The Sad Fortunes of the Reverend Amos Barton," "Mr. Gilfil's Love-Story," and "Janet's Repentance." They appeared together in *Scenes of Clerical Life,* published in 1858 to great public success. She followed it with the novels ADAM BEDE (1859), *The Mill on the Floss* (1860), and *Silas Marner* (1861), all novels that indicate the consequences of society's limitations and moral choice. Following a trip to Florence, she completed the 1863 novel *Romola,* her only offering set during the Renaissance. The 1866 work *Felix Holt the Radical* prefigured some of the literary concerns that later critics considered her strongest commentary on Victorian society, MIDDLEMARCH: A STUDY OF PROVINCIAL LIFE (1871–72). Its characters—the intelligent, compassionate Dorothea Brooke and the well-meaning but pompous Mr. Casaubon—have since become prototypical representatives of the Victorian Age. *Middlemarch* was followed by *Daniel Deronda* (1874–76), her last novel.

Eliot also wrote letters, poetry, and essays. Among her best known poems is "The Spanish Gypsy" (1868); among her best known nonfiction is the essay collection *The Impressions of Theophrastus Such* (1879), her final work.

In 1880, two years after Lewes's death, Eliot married John Walter Cross, twenty years her junior. Despite the age difference, it was apparently a happy marriage, offering a coda to a life more unbridled in thought and deed than those of her characters, who usually grappled with the limits of society. For her own age and afterward, her work scrutinized the Victorian way of life.

Ellis, [Henry] Havelock (1859–1939) English physician and psychologist. Ellis pioneered the study of human sexual behavior in his seven-volume *Studies in the Psychology of Sex* (1897–1928). The book was banned for obscenity in England and available in the United States only to medical professionals until 1935. An advocate of women's rights and sex education, Ellis was influential in opening up public discussion of sexual problems. Among other things, he discussed the ubiquity of masturbation and the role of psychological factors in sexual dysfunction. Ellis also edited seventeenth-century British drama.

Ellis, Sarah Stickney (1799–1882) English writer. In fictional works such as the story collection *Pictures of Private Life* (1833–37) and the novel *The Brewer's Family* (1863), she laced her realistic portraits of domestic life with moral admonishment. Her advice book *The Women of England* (1838), which spawned several sequels, argued that women should devote themselves to domestic duty, concealing their own feelings and talents while accepting the male claim to superiority.

Emancipation Proclamation U.S. official announcement. Issued by President ABRAHAM LINCOLN, it decreed that slaves held in areas under the control of the CONFEDERACY would be free effective January 1, 1863. A preliminary decree was issued on September 22, 1862, and the final one on January 1.

Lincoln had been under pressure since the start of the CIVIL WAR to abolish SLAVERY. Abolitionists and some REPUBLICAN PARTY congressmen pressured him on moral grounds, while many of his generals saw the military value of the 3 million slaves in the Confederacy.

Lincoln hesitated, afraid that Kentucky, Missouri, and the other slave-holding states still in the Union might secede if the slaves were freed. He also pondered the reaction of northern whites; they might fight to save the Union but balk at enlisting in a war of liberation.

The President tried to persuade the loyal slave states to accept a program of gradual, compensated emancipation. Despite approval of the proposal by Congress, these border states refused to budge. As 1862 dragged on with no progress in quelling the rebellion, Lincoln reluctantly issued his proclamation.

The proclamation itself did not end slavery. It excluded the loyal slave states in order to keep them in the Union. It also excluded the areas of Virginia and Louisiana under the control of Union forces. The decree referred only to slaves in areas governed by the Confederacy, places where it could not be enforced.

Lincoln's balancing act worked. Abolitionists and the more radical Republicans were mostly satisfied with the proclamation as a first step toward liberation and as a sign of Lincoln's ultimate intentions. The border states remained loyal, and support for the war among northern whites did not decline. It also helped stiffen public opinion in Great Britain in favor of the Union. Some three hundred thousand ex-slaves would join the Union army as more and more Confederate territory came under northern control.

While the immediate effect of the Emancipation Proclamation was limited, it made the end of slavery inevitable. The ratification of the Thirteenth Amendment in 1865 abolished slavery throughout the United States.

embroidery Ornamentation of textiles with decorative needlework. The Victorian Age saw several innovations in this ancient art, notably the introduction of machine embroidery. The first embroidery machine was exhibited by M. Hellman of Mulhouse, France, at the French Industrial Exhibition of 1854. It was patented in England and led to several improved models. Victorians liked to decorate their homes with embroidered pictures, particularly copies of well-known paintings; the style known as BERLIN WOOLWORK was very popular, decorating such household objects as footstools and fire screens. Many amateur embroiderers were inspired by the colored-wool pictures of Mary Linwood (1755–1854). Beginning in the 1850s, WILLIAM MORRIS tried to restore artistic standards to embroidery and revive the art of TAPESTRY; The founding of the Royal School of Art Needlework in 1872 led to the founding of a number of embroidery schools and work societies in Europe and America.

Emerson, Ralph Waldo (1803–1882) Essayist, philosopher, and poet. This foremost exponent of American TRANSCENDENTALISM was born in Boston, the son of Unitarian minister William Emerson, and was educated at the Boston Latin School and Harvard. After a brief teaching stint, he studied divinity at Harvard and became a minister. He served at several churches, including the Second Unitarian Church in Boston, until the 1831 death of his wife Ellen Louisa Tucker. The tragedy led him to reexamine his beliefs and eventually leave pastoral service. In 1832 he traveled to Europe where he encountered, among others, William Wordsworth and THOMAS CARLYLE, who was to become an influential and lifelong friend.

After he returned to the United States in 1833, he settled in Concord, Massachusetts, and married Lydia Jackson. Informed by European thought, he came to develop his transcendentalist philosophy of nature and spirituality. Working as a lecturer, he became the center of the transcendentalist movement in New England, leader of a literary group that included HENRY DAVID THOREAU, MARGARET FULLER, and BRONSON ALCOTT. He was also an early champion of WALT WHITMAN. Like other transcendentalist thinkers, he studied mystical philosophy.

A successful lecturer, he began to publish his highly influential essays in 1836. *Nature,* his first book, outlined his conception of the unity of life as manifested in the relation of the natural and spiritual worlds. His 1837 speech to the Phi Beta Kappa Society at Harvard, "The American Scholar," inspired American thinkers by proclaiming for the first time their distinctive duties to the world: to "take up . . . all the ability of the time, all the contributions of the past, all the hopes of the future. . . . It is for you to know all; it is for you to dare all." His 1838 speech at Harvard, "The Divinity School Address," caused a decades-long break in his relations with the school by suggesting that established church thinking was less important than each person's intuitive experience of spirituality.

Throughout the next two decades, Emerson's fame and influence continued to grow. While cofounding (in 1840) and editing (1842–44) the transcendentalist journal *The Dial,* he published several essay collections, including *Essays,* First and Second Series (1841, 1844), and *Representative Men* (1850). In these works he broadens his discussion of philosophy, nature, religion, and the responsibility of the individual and the artist. In "Self-Reliance" (1841), he describes the struggle between the individual and society but proclaims the necessity of the individual to prevail because "nothing can bring you peace but the triumph of your principles." In "The Poet" (1843), he praises the American artist as one who "represents beauty" but admonishes him to embrace his country as "a poem in our eyes; its ample geography dazzles the imagination, and it will not wait long for meters." "The Over-Soul" details his pantheistic conception of the world, in which there is no positive evil but only an absence of good.

As the years passed, Emerson's views of nature and fate grew darker. One influence on his views may have been the tensions leading to the Civil War. He was active in the antislavery movement, speaking for JOHN BROWN and against the Fugitive Slave Act. Another influential event was the death in 1842 of his five-year-old son Waldo.

As a poet, Emerson was widely read in his day, though he saw his limitations, calling himself "a bard least of bards . . . [who speaks] interruptedly words and half stanzas which have the like scope and aim." Among his better known poems are "Threnody" (1846, written for his son Waldo), "Hamatreya" (1846), and "Days" (1857).

Emin Pasha [Eduard Schnitzer] (1840–1892) German explorer of Africa. Trained as a physician, Schnitzer was a medical officer in the SUDAN in 1876–78. In 1880 he succeeded CHARLES GEORGE GORDON as governor of the Equatoria, or the Egyptian Sudan. The revolt of the MAHDI in 1881 forced Egypt out of the Sudan and stranded the German doctor, known by the honorific title Emin Pasha, in the Upper Sudan. British-American adventurer HENRY STANLEY led an expedition to rescue him, searching the African interior from 1887 to 1889 and suffering a loss of five thousand lives until he found him.

After this episode, Germany sent Schnitzer on an expansionist mission into Central Africa. He was killed in 1892 in an altercation with slave traders near Stanley Falls on the Congo River.

Engels, Friedrich (1820–1895) German economist and social philosopher. Engels is known chiefly for his long collaboration with fellow German KARL MARX, whom he supported and whose works he edited. He was born in Barmen, Prussia, the son of a wealthy textile manufacturer. He joined the family firm in 1838 but by 1842 was converted to the cause of bettering the worker's lot through communism. While employed at his father's office in Manchester, he secretly worked for radical trade union organizations. In 1845 he published *The Condition of the Working Class in England,* a meticulous portrait of the harsh life led by workers in Manchester. By that time he had left his father's firm and met Marx, with whom he formed a lifelong partnership after moving to Paris in 1844. In 1848 the two published *The Communist Manifesto,* which outlined a program of revolutionary socialism. When revolution broke out in Germany that year (see REVOLUTIONS OF 1848), Engels and Marx returned to their homeland and founded a socialist newspaper.

When the German revolutions were crushed, Engels rejoined his father's firm (1850), again working in Manchester, and helped support Marx, now living in London. Engels married Elizabeth Burns in 1864. In 1869, following the death of his father, Engels sold his share of the business and moved to London. He acted as secretary for the First Workers' International and edited Marx's work. Following Marx's death in 1883, he continued this work, publishing the last two volumes of Marx's *DAS KAPITAL.* He also published works of his own, including *Private Property and the State* (1884) and *Socialism, Utopian and Scientific* (1891).

Ensor, James Sydney, Baron (1860–1949) Belgian painter and etcher. Ensor's grotesque, nightmarish work in the late nineteenth century prepared the way for surrealism in the 1920s. His paintings included provocative treatments of Christian themes, notably *Entry of Christ into Brussels* and *The Temptation of St. Anthony.*

entropy Measure for the disorder of a closed system. Coined by German physicist Rudolf Clausius, the term technically means the ratio of a system's heat content to its absolute temperature. It indicates the degree to which energy is available for doing useful work—more entropy means less energy available. The second law of THERMODYNAMICS, formulated by Clausius in 1850, states that the entropy of a closed system increases with time or, at best, remains constant. As a consequence, the universe as a whole tends toward maximum entropy. In the works of many Victorian writers and artists, including HENRY ADAMS, H. G. WELLS, and ALGERNON CHARLES SWINBURNE, entropy became an image for irreversible social decline.

Erewhon (1872) Satirical novel by SAMUEL BUTLER. The novel centers around a visit by the narrator Higgs to a fictitious place called Erewhon, an anagram of "nowhere." The customs and institutions of that country allow Butler to satirize contemporary British attitudes toward crime, religion, science, child-rearing, and more. A sequel followed, *Erewhon Revisited* (1901).

Esperanto Artificial language. It was designed in 1887 by Polish philologist Ludwik Lejzer Zamenhof (1859–1917). The name, meaning "hope," symbolized Zamenhof's aspiration that the language would facilitate international communication, understanding, and peace. The vocabulary and grammar are based on Latin, Greek, the Romance languages, and the Germanic languages; the spelling is phonetic. Esperanto never succeeded as Zamenhof intended, and few people speak it today.

Essays and Reviews (1860) British collection of theological essays edited by Henry Bristow Wilson. The scholarly contributors were C. W. Goodwin, Benjamin Jowett, Mark Pattison, Robert S. Baden-Powell, Frederick Temple, who was archbishop of

Canterbury from 1896 to 1902, and Rowland Williams. The contributors advocated a liberal Christianity informed by modern science and modern biblical scholarship. *Essays and Reviews* immediately stirred opposition, with offended Christians calling the authors the "Seven Against Christ." A meeting of bishops in 1861 condemned the book, as did the synod of the Church of England in 1864.

ether The etical substance formerly believed to be the medium for transmission of waves of light *or* the chemical compound. Drawing on concepts first developed by the ancient Greeks, ether was believed to be invisible, stationary, and present throughout space. It was an accepted part of nineteenth-century physics until the MICHELSON-MORLEY EXPERIMENT (1887) raised doubts as to its existence. Albert Einstein's theory of relativity (1905, 1915) eliminated the need for the concept of ether.

The chemical compound ether—ethoxyethane or diethyl ether—was introduced as an ANESTHETIC by American surgeon Crawford W. Long in an operation in Georgia for the removal of a neck tumor in 1842. It and other forms of anesthesia, particularly CHLOROFORM, were used increasingly by surgeons throughout the nineteenth century.

eugenics See GALTON, Sir FRANCIS.

Eugénie (1826–1920) Empress of FRANCE. Eugénie Marie de Montijo de Guzmán was born in Granada, Spain, the daughter of the Count of Montijo and Maria Manuela Kirkpatrick, an American of Scottish origin.

As a young woman, Eugénie attended the royal balls given by Louis Napoleon, and while he was attracted to her, Eugénie made it clear that she would be a consort but not a mistress. After prospects for another marriage dissipated, and five weeks after the proclamation of the second empire in France, Louis Napoleon, now NAPOLEON III, proposed marriage to her. They were married in the Cathedral of Notre Dame in 1853. Their son, Prince Louis Napoleon, was born in 1856.

Eugénie had a strong interest in the policies of her husband and even acted as regent during three of his absences. Upon the collapse of the empire in September 1870, the family fled to England. Widowed in 1873, Eugénie became friends with Queen VICTORIA. While fighting for the British in the ZULU WAR of 1879, Eugénie's son Louis Napoleon was killed. She made a pilgrimage to the battlefield a year later.

From then on, Eugénie spent most of her time at Farnborough, where she erected a tomb for her husband and son, and at Cap Martin on the Riviera. She died in Madrid.

evolution Theory that all existing biological species descended, with gradual modification, from primitive ancestors of different form. Varieties of this explanation for the diversity of life have been suggested since antiquity, but French naturalist Jean Lamarck, in 1801, was the first to state a modern scientific version. However, his belief that acquired characteristics are the engine of evolutionary change is no longer held. In 1858, English naturalists CHARLES DARWIN and ALFRED RUSSEL WALLACE independently proposed the alternative theory of natural selection. This theory holds that organisms naturally vary and that those better adapted to their environment are more likely to survive and reproduce, and are therefore more likely to pass on their individual variations. As systematically expounded by Darwin in *THE ORIGIN OF SPECIES* (1859), the theory aroused a storm of controversy, threatening existing religious beliefs and inspiring philosophers—for example, those who espoused SOCIAL DARWINISM. In the twentieth century Darwinian thought has been synthesized with discoveries in GENETICS, a field founded by nineteenth-century Austrian monk GREGOR MENDEL, and in this form has become the indispensable theoretical framework for research in the life sciences.

Eyre, Edward John (1815–1901) English explorer and colonial administrator. Born in Yorkshire, he emigrated at seventeen to Australia where he became a sheep farmer and magistrate, earning a reputation as "protector of the Aborigine." He explored the interior, discovering a lake that was then named for him, marking out a livestock route from New South Wales to South Australia, and making an intrepid journey in 1841 across the waterless desert from Adelaide to King George Sound. In 1845 he published *Discoveries in Central Australia,* then served as a colonial administrator in New Zealand and St. Vincent before going to Jamaica in the WEST INDIES to serve as acting governor (1861–64) and governor (1864–66). In October 1865 he brutally suppressed a revolt of the black people of Morant Bay, executing more than four hundred, flogging hundreds more, and burning hundreds of homes. The ensuing public debate over Eyre's actions—known as the Governor Eyre Controversy—brought to the fore conflicting Victorian attitudes about the use of martial law to control colonial subjects. Condemnation of Eyre came from such prominent individuals as JOHN STUART MILL, T. H. HUXLEY, and HERBERT SPENCER, while his supporters included ALFRED, Lord TENNYSON, JOHN RUSKIN, and THOMAS CARLYLE, who called Eyre's accusers "nigger-philanthropists." Eyre was recalled from office, though legal charges against him were dropped. He ended his life in seclusion.

Fabian Society Founded in 1884, this loosely knit British group comprised socialists who advocated logically conceived, evenly paced social reform, as opposed to immediate revolutionary action. Led by SIDNEY and BEATRICE WEBB, who together helped to found the London School of Economics in 1895, this organization included GEORGE BERNARD SHAW, H. G. WELLS, and Leonard Woolf. More politically engaged than the roughly contemporaneous members of Bloomsbury, the group from its inception supported women's rights—women made up more than a quarter of its total membership in the society's early stages—as well as all forms of political, economic, and social justice. The Fabian Society was known for its endorsement of high-minded, intelligent debate on controversial public issues. In such landmark works as *The History of Trade Unionism* (1894), the Webbs established labor history as a separate area of intellectual study. In *The Intelligent Woman's Guide to Socialism and Capitalism* (1928), Shaw added a wittily acerbic note to Fabian concerns.

Factory Acts Series of British laws. The Factory Acts started in 1833 and aimed at improving working conditions in factories, particularly for women and children. Acts passed in 1802 and 1819 lacked enforcement mechanisms, and few factory owners heeded them. The EARL OF SHAFTESBURY, then Lord Ashley, a Tory aristocrat known as "the children's friend," introduced a bill directed at textile factories. The Factory Act of 1833 prohibited the hiring of children under age nine, set a work limit of nine hours for children under thirteen and twelve hours for children from thirteen to eighteen, and provided for inspectors to enforce the law.

The Factory Act of 1844 limited women to twelve hours of work each day and imposed a limit on children of 6½ hours. It also mandated safety measures. The Factory Act of 1847 cut the working day to ten hours for women and children between thirteen and eighteen. Acts in 1867 and 1878 further improved working and sanitary conditions.

fainting couch Sofa-length lounging chair with a tilted, cushioned back. Also known as a chaise longue or lounge.

Faraday, Michael (1791–1867) English scientist. Faraday made many of his scientific discoveries, including the laws of electrical induction and the laws of electrochemistry, in the early 1800s. His tireless work ethic led to a breakdown in 1839, and Faraday did not continue his work until 1845 when he began to investigate the nature of magnetism. A series of experiments involving heavy optical glasses he had produced led to the discovery of the effect of magnetism on polarized light, called the Faraday Effect. Faraday had many speculations about magnetism, but his mind began to fail and he retired in 1858 to a house in Hampton Court, presented to him by Queen Victoria. Faraday's speculations later developed into the classical field theory and Einstein's theory of relativity. Faraday was also responsible for the introduction of a number of scientific terms, including *electrode, ion, electrolyte,* and *electrolysis.*

Farragut, David Glasgow (1801–1870) American naval officer. He was born near Knoxville, Tennessee, to a father who was a sea captain and a veteran of the Revolutionary War. Farragut's mother died when he was seven years old, and at age nine he entered the navy with the help of Commander David Porter, whose dying father had been cared for by the Farragut family. David Farragut was made a midshipman and later served in the War of 1812 on the *Essex* under Porter's command.

Farragut commanded his own ship, the *Saratoga,* and was made captain in 1855. When the CIVIL WAR started in 1861, Secretary of the Navy Gideon Welles doubted Farragut's loyalty to the Union because of his southern heritage and did not assign him to duty until January 1862. Farragut was then given orders to capture New Orleans.

Commanding seventeen ships, Farragut led his fleet south of New Orleans, destroying the *Manassas* on April 24 and attacking the fort of New Orleans, which surrendered the next day. Farragut was immediately promoted to rear admiral, and by the end of 1862 he had control of the entire Gulf of Mexico except for Mobile, Alabama.

On August 5, 1864, Farragut attacked forts Morgan and Gaines, which guarded the entrance to Mobile Bay. As the admiral led his eighteen ships through the bay, the *Tecumseh* hit a mine—called "torpedoes" at the time—and sank. As confusion threatened the advance on Mobile, Farragut shouted his famous order: "Damn the torpedoes, full speed ahead!" The mines that were hit failed to detonate, and the fleet passed safely and secured a victory. Farragut was promoted to vice admiral in December 1864 and to admiral, a rank created especially for him, in 1866.

Upon Farragut's death, his body was transported from New Hampshire to New York City where President Grant, Cabinet members, military officers, and ten thousand soldiers escorted it to Woodlawn Cemetery. A statue of Farragut, sculpted by Augustus Saint-Gaudens in 1881, now stands in Madison Square, New York City.

fashion, men's Enjoying a much simpler style of dress than women during the Victorian era (see WOMEN'S FASHION), the appropriately dressed Victorian man had a generally somber collection of clothing, with a few nods to vibrant color. A knee-length frock coat, preferably in black, was suitable day wear. Waistcoats, or vests, might be colorful, particularly in the 1850s when it was popular to imitate Prince ALBERT and his plaid waistcoat. By the 1870s, with the dominance of the three-piece matching ditto suit, the waistcoat lost favor. Brightly colored silk cravats were also popular for a time. A linen shirt—the finer the material, the more socially rarefied the wearer—a cane, and facial whiskers completed the look of the mid-nineteenth-century post–Crimean War British male. Clothing was custom-sewn by tailors or made at home until the development of standard anthropometric sizing in the 1860s after the American Civil War.

By the end of the century, in the United States in particular, the frock and ditto suit were evolving into the business suit. Its matching pants and arm-length jacket, with its starched collar and tie, were the blueprint for men's business clothing for the twentieth century. American formalwear was changing as well. Introduced in 1886 in Tuxedo, New York, the arm-length black dress coat known as the tuxedo would replace the tailcoat and become standard formal attire. In addition, work clothing was revolutionized in 1850 by the invention of "bibless overalls" or "blue jeans" developed by American entrepreneur Levi Strauss. The canvas, later denim, pants were developed for participants in the California Gold Rush. See also CARDIGAN SWEATER.

fashion, women's Women's fashion in the Victorian Age reflected important trends in society, including the introduction of mass-produced ready-to-wear clothes, the voice of Paris as the arbiter of fashion taste, general economic trends, the changing ideal of the female body, and the place of women in society.

Improving economic conditions in Britain after the 1840s gave rise to a more generous, billowy look. Not only were dresses made from more delicate fabrics in brighter colors, their natural bell shape became more pronounced. Achieving the circular look of the skirt was the job of the bell-shaped steel spring form known as the cage CRINOLINE. Its hoops allowed for proper shape and sway, and though sometimes dangerous on stairways and a hindrance to sitting, it was simpler to wear than its predecessor, the horsehair-stuffed petticoat. The full hoop skirt remained popular into the 1860s when the half-crinoline, and eventually the BUSTLE, became popular. Attached under the back of a skirt, the bustle remained popular until the 1870s and then experienced a brief renaissance in the 1880s.

Contrasting with the wide bell skirt was the slim waist, which was achieved by the use of a CORSET. Often made of whalebone, it was laced up a woman's back to cinch the waist, midriff, and abdomen to the desired waspish look. Such sculpting—a preferred waist measurement was 20 inches—at times resulted in lifelong internal injuries. Gloves and a hat, rather than a cap or bonnet, were appropriate accessories.

While impractical and derided by the upper classes, machine production and DEPARTMENT STORES made heretofore exclusive styles increasingly available to middle- and working-class women. During the U.S. Civil War, standard sizing for men was developed; within decades the same followed for women. By the end of the century, while CHARLES F. WORTH was designing for Empress Eugénie and other royalty in Paris, inexpensive machine-made copies of his works were appearing at emporiums in cities across the United States and

Great Britain. The democratization of fashion had begun.

The later decades of the century saw other changes in fashion wrought by the industrial age. They included more vividly colored fabrics, thanks to experimentation with DYES, notably by William Perkin who in 1856 discovered the first synthetic dye, MAUVE. Modern machinery also allowed for more ornamentation on clothing, such as machine-made LACE and EMBROIDERY. Perhaps in part to distinguish themselves from other social groups, the upper classes in the late Victorian Age applied more hand-wrought ornamentation to their clothes in the form of lacework and jewel encrustation, among other elaborations.

At the close of the century, female clerical workers made their mark on fashion by popularizing the shirtwaist. Practical, feminine, and inexpensive, starting at less than one dollar, it became an office uniform. Though not a fully liberating piece of clothing, it signaled a move toward simplicity and durability in women's clothing—something American social activist Amelia Bloomer had attempted in 1851 when she introduced the trouserlike garment known as the bloomer.

Fashoda Crisis (1898) Confrontation between FRANCE and GREAT BRITAIN in AFRICA. Geopolitical rivalry led to the incident at Fashoda, a small fort in the SUDAN. The British had occupied Egypt since 1882 and had stationed English and Egyptian troops in the Sudan until the fall of KHARTOUM in 1885. By the early 1890s they had also taken control of Kenya and Uganda. If Britain could establish its authority over the Sudan and the Upper Nile, it could realize its imperial dream of controlling eastern Africa along a north-south axis from the Cape Colony to Cairo (see CAPE TO CAIRO).

The French government had its own designs on the continent. It dominated northwest Africa and had established settlements in Somaliland in east Africa. If the French controlled the Upper Nile, they would dominate a huge swath of territory running along an east-west axis from the Atlantic to the Indian oceans. A showdown between the imperial powers seemed inevitable.

In 1895 the British, under the leadership of General HORATIO KITCHENER, began building a railway and special gunboats for a move south along the Nile. In September 1898 a joint army of twenty-six thousand English and Egyptian troops defeated an army of local Muslims at Omdurman. Two days later they marched into Khartoum, and from there a detachment of troops set out for Fashoda, a fort once used by Egyptian troops to suppress the slave trade. Kitchener's expedition was made urgent by British knowledge of French troops moving toward the Upper Nile from the west.

This very small force of eleven French officers and 150 Senegalese troops had embarked from Lake Chad in the summer of 1896. Under the command of Jean-Baptiste Marchand, the soldiers covered thirty-five hundred miles in two years. Marchand raised the French flag over Fashoda in July and claimed the Upper Nile for his country. Kitchener arrived at Fashoda two weeks later and demanded that the French leave the fort.

Hopelessly outnumbered and totally isolated, Marchand refused to leave without orders from Paris. The British government refused to drop its claims to the area and threatened war if France pursued its territorial ambitions. The deadlock dragged on until December. Russia, France's ally, claimed its treaty obligations did not apply to this African adventure and declined to support France in case of a war. Diplomatically isolated and fearful of the British navy, France backed down and ordered Marchand out of Fashoda. France then formally recognized British claims to the Upper Nile while Great Britain agreed to respect French interests in western Africa.

Faure, François-Félix (1841–1899) Politician. President of FRANCE from 1895 to 1899, Faure in his term of office saw colonial conquests in Madagascar and the Congo and a confrontation with Britain in the FASHODA CRISIS. His administration concluded a mutual defense treaty with Russia. Faure resisted attempts to reopen the Dreyfus case. He died in office.

Fawcett, Dame Millicent Garrett (1847–1929) British leader of the WOMAN SUFFRAGE movement. As a child, she was influenced by the efforts of her sister ELIZABETH GARRETT ANDERSON to become a physician. In 1867 she married Cambridge economist and liberal member of parliament Henry Fawcett (1833–1884), who encouraged her to struggle for woman's rights. In 1871 she helped to found Newnham College for women at Cambridge. She later served as president of the National Union of Women's Suffrage Societies (1897–1919). Her numerous books include *Political Economy for Beginners* (1870) and *The Women's Victory—and After* (1920).

Fawcett, Henry See ANDERSON, ELIZABETH GARRETT.

fedora Popular soft-brimmed felt hat. It was named for a character in the 1882 play *Fedora* by French dramatist Victorien Sardou, starring Sarah Bernhardt. Originally a favorite, with adornments, of females, it came to be accepted wear for both sexes.

fender See FIREPLACE TOOLS.

Fenians A clandestine Irish and American revolutionary group. They were also known as the Irish Republican Brotherhood, or IRB, and were dedicated to HOME RULE and the violent overthrow of the English rule of IRELAND. The general term *Fenians* referred to a legal Fenian Brotherhood founded in 1858 in America by John O'Mahoney who had fled Ireland after the failed Irish uprising in 1848. The name "Fenian" came from the Irish *Fianna,* an elite corps of Irish warriors from the third century A.D. James Stephens, another exile from 1848 who worked in cooperation with O'Mahoney, founded a secret, illegal society in 1858 in Dublin whose members also became known as Fenians through their association with the American group. By the late 1860s they would be more commonly known as the Irish Republican Brotherhood.

Stephens tried unsuccessfully in 1859 to interest the French government in supporting a rebellion. He returned to Ireland in 1860 and began recruiting a secret army. O'Mahoney remained in America to raise money, arms, and soldiers for the coming revolt. Secret drilling in the Irish countryside and stockpiling of weapons continued during the 1860s. Stephens claimed to have two hundred thousand men under the Fenian oath, including twelve thousand members of the British garrison in Ireland.

Such large preparations did not escape the notice of the British government. A series of raids in 1865 and 1866, coupled with the suspension of habeas corpus in February 1866, forced the Fenian leaders to postpone their plans. Stephens himself was captured but escaped to America.

Meanwhile, across the Atlantic three thousand armed Fenians of the American branch crossed the Niagara River into Canada on the night of May 31, 1866. This bizarre attempt to establish a beachhead for Irish independence was quickly beaten back by Canadian and United States troops.

Despite the setbacks, the Fenians in Ireland launched their long-awaited uprising in March 1867. They planned to attack police stations, cut telegraph wires, and destroy rail lines throughout the country. They planned to declare an independent Irish republic, and then aid would pour in from Irish people around the world.

The attacks, poorly led and undermanned, failed miserably. By the end of March the rebellion was crushed and many Fenian leaders were in jail. The Irish people had failed to support the insurrection.

Though they were military failures, the Fenians still contributed to the cause of Irish nationalism. Fenian violence, especially some violent prison escapes and bombings in England, riveted the English public's attention on the Irish disaffection. It helped push Prime Minister WILLIAM GLADSTONE to pass the IRISH LAND ACT OF 1870 and made the Irish question one of his main concerns. The continuing threat of violence also gave the IRISH PARTY in Parliament a valuable card to play in its negotiations.

In 1873 the Irish Republican Brotherhood reconstituted itself but could claim fewer than twenty thousand members by 1877. By the end of the century it was nearly moribund. Much of its influence was based on the pipeline of contributions from America that funded parliamentary campaigns. Some members joined the parliamentary movement headed by CHARLES STEWART PARNELL, while others enlisted in the LAND LEAGUE. Some members, like the men who joined the Invincibles and participated in the PHOENIX PARK MURDERS, never gave up the idea of physical force. The organization's last hurrah occurred during World War I when some of its remaining members helped plan and carry out the Easter Rebellion in Dublin in 1916.

Fenton, Roger (1819–1869) English photographer. Trained in law and art, he photographed views of Moscow and portraits of Queen Victoria's family in the early 1850s before gaining lasting fame for his photographs of the Crimean War from March to June 1855. Although limited by lengthy exposure times for portraits and landscapes, his work marked the first extensive photographic coverage of a war.

Ferris wheel Electrically-powered upright steel amusement ride. It was invented by American engineer Washington Gale Ferris and was introduced in 1893 at the Chicago World's Fair. The first Ferris wheel was 250 feet wide and had thirty-six cars for riders. The ride soon became a drawing card for public parks and amusement areas, such as Vienna's Prater Park and New York's Coney Island.

Feydeau, Georges (1862–1921) French playwright. Born in Paris, he was the son of writer Ernest Feydeau, who was friends with many literary figures of the day, including GUSTAVE FLAUBERT and CHARLES P. BAUDELAIRE. Georges Feydeau was educated at home by a private tutor and began writing plays as an escape from his homework. His first produced play, *Out the Window* (1881), was written when he was eighteen. Seven years later Feydeau achieved his first success with *Ladies' Tailor,* but his subsequent plays received little acclaim until 1892 when *The Gentleman's in Pursuit!* and *Champignol in Spite of Himself* opened within three weeks of each other. Each production was quite popular and ran for more than one thousand performances.

Feydeau had found fame and fortune, but he lived extravagantly and invested foolishly, amassing large debts. In 1903 he was forced to sell his large collection of Impressionist paintings to appease some of his debtors. After writing nearly forty plays, Feydeau died from a cerebral hemorrhage in 1921.

Feydeau is best remembered for his farces, which are filled with outlandish events staged at a frantic pace. While his plays remain popular in France, they are rarely performed for English-speaking audiences.

Field, Cyrus West (1819–1892) American financier. After retiring from his paper business with a small fortune in 1853, he promoted the laying of the first transatlantic CABLE, organizing companies in the United States and England and raising funds for the venture. When the first cable failed after three weeks of use in 1858, Field raised funds for a new, more permanent one, which was laid in 1866. In later years he helped develop the Wabash Railroad and was owner and president of the New York Elevated Railroad Company (1877–80). He also promoted the building of a transpacific cable.

Fillmore, Millard (1800–1874) Thirteenth president of the UNITED STATES (1850–53). Fillmore was born in New York State and was a successful Buffalo attorney before he was elected to the state legislature in 1828 and to the U.S. Congress four times (1832–40). He joined the Whig Party by 1834 and in 1848 was elected vice-president as the running mate of ZACHARY TAYLOR. Fillmore became president in 1850 after Taylor's death. He strongly supported the COMPROMISE OF 1850, which attempted to reconcile differences between northern and southern states; however, his support of the Fugitive Slave Act of 1850, which was part of this compromise, cost him northern support. His efforts alienated both sides of the SLAVERY issue, and he lost the nomination in 1852. He ran for president in 1856 as the candidate of the anti-Catholic American (Know Nothing) Party but carried only one state. He returned to private life after this defeat.

fin de siècle Historical period and artistic sensibility. This late-Victorian tendency, termed for French "end of century," encompasses such diverse qualities as stylish artifice, DECADENCE, AESTHETICISM, unconventional sexual taste, and apocalyptic thinking. Often understood as an importation of French decadence to English shores, *fin de siècle* temperament historically had a strong homosexual undercurrent, particularly in the work of its leading figure in England, OSCAR WILDE, and was in part a reaction to a strain of Victorian high-mindedness as articulated by MATTHEW ARNOLD. Typical preoccupations of *fin de siècle* literary works are the figure of the New Woman, the femme fatale, and the dandy. Artists associated with the *fin de siècle* period are, in addition to Wilde, AUBREY BEARDSLEY, CHARLES BAUDELAIRE, PAUL VERLAINE, ROBERT LOUIS STEVENSON, and, to an extent, GEORGE BERNARD SHAW.

Shaw's play *Mrs. Warren's Profession* (1893) addressed typical *fin de siècle* anxieties in its focus on the independent female, the daughter of a madam, who seems to herald a new era of empowered females. The journal *The Yellow Book* (1894–97) published writing by many of the figures affiliated with the movement, while a key text of *fin de siècle* interest was the French writer J. K. Huysman's *A Rebours (Against Nature)* (1884), whose hero Des Esseintes lives a monastic life as an effete, art-collecting voluptuary.

An influential book was Wilde's novel *The Picture of Dorian Gray* (1891). At once an embodiment of *fin de siècle* sensibility and a cautionary allegory against its dangers, it narrated the tale of a beautiful young man's decline into narcissism, corruption, and murder. Wilde's *Salome* (1894), a poetic drama that premiered in Paris after being banned from the English stage, concerned the biblical Salome's horrifying desire to kiss the head of a decapitated John the Baptist. Beardsley's illustrations for the play were a licentious, stylized benchmark of *fin de siècle* artistry.

fire screen Protective fireplace covering. The decorative wooden frame and textile screen were designed to shield inhabitants of a room from the glare of a fire. Screen designs, frequently created by Victorian household members, were often highly intricate painted, woven, or needlepointed works of art. See also FIREPLACE TOOLS.

firearms Weapons. They increased considerably in power, range, accuracy, and ease of use in the Victorian Age, with many of the innovations coming from the United States. In the field of heavy weapons, breech-loading, rifled, and shell-firing artillery became dominant by the late nineteenth century, replacing the smooth-bore, muzzle-loaded, round-shot guns that had prevailed for centuries. MACHINE GUNS, weapons that fire small-arms ammunition rapidly and continuously, began to be developed in the nineteenth century, presaging the greater carnage of twentieth-century warfare and urban violence. The GATLING GUN, developed by American Richard Gatling in 1862, and the Maxim gun, developed by American Sir Hiram Maxim in 1883, were two important steps in the machine gun's development. American SAMUEL COLT introduced the first modern revolver around 1835, reducing the frequency of reloading for small arms. Breech-loading rifles, such as the needle-gun and the SHARPS RIFLE invented by American Christian Sharps in 1848, became standard issue after 1870, while magazine-loading rifles, bolt action, and smokeless powder were introduced by the 1880s. See also JEZAIL.

fireplace tools Implements used to tend the household fire, fireplace, and hearth. In Victorian times, fireplace tools were elaborately designed and were meant to be as ornamental as they were utilitarian. Fireplace tools included the fender, an iron or brass guard that surrounded the hearth in order to protect the hearth rug; the fender curb, a shallow variety of fender; the fender stool, also called the seat curb or the club fender, a low stool incorporated into the fender as a padded seat; the fire back, a cast-iron plate at the back of an open fireplace; the fire guard, a high screen of vertical metal bars or wire mesh used to prevent coals from flying out of a fire; fire irons, implements used for tending a fire, particularly tongs, poker, and shovel, which were often designed in sets to match the fender; the andirons, also called fire dogs or andogs, a pair of iron bars that stood independently on a hearth to support the logs; and the FIRE SCREEN, also called the pole screen or the banner screen, which consisted of a panel of wood decorated with paint, wicker, or needlework that was attached to a pole supported by a tripod or was mounted on legs. Some fire screens were fixed while others could slide or had swinging leaves.

Fisher, John Arbuthnot, 1st Baron Fisher of Kilverstone (1841–1920) British naval officer. Despite his high cheekbones and "Mandarin" features, there was no substance to the rumor that his mother was a Sinhalese princess. Born in Ceylon, he was the son of a British coffee planter. While still in his early teens, he entered the Royal Navy (1854); by the 1880s he had served in the Mediterranean, the West Indies, China, and Egypt. Known popularly as "Jacky," he was dedicated to technological and structural reform of the navy, a position that won him both disciples and detractors. He became admiral of the fleet in 1905 and was the First Sea Lord in the Admiralty (1904–10). The reforms he instituted in the latter capacity helped prepare the British for World War I. These included the 1906 introduction of the Dreadnought, a more powerful class of battleship, and the conversion of the fleet from coal to oil, which led the British to acquire Middle East oil interests. Fisher served as the First Sea Lord again in 1914–15, during World War I, before resigning due to policy disagreements.

Fisk, James (1834–1872) American speculator and robber baron. After beginning his career as a circus hand and peddler, he made a fortune during the CIVIL WAR by selling confiscated southern cotton and Confederate bonds in Great Britain. He, Daniel Drew, and JAY GOULD took the Erie Railroad from CORNELIUS VANDERBILT in 1868 by selling him counterfeit stock; Fisk and Gould later ruined the railroad through stock manipulations that made them millions. They were less successful in cornering the gold market and set off the Black Friday panic of 1869. Fisk was murdered by Edward Stokes, a former partner and Fisk's rival for the affections of the famous actress Josie Mansfield.

FitzGerald, Edward (1809–1883) English writer. Fitzgerald is most famous for his poem *THE RUBÁIYÁT OF OMAR KHAYYÁM*, a loose verse adaptation of the work of an eleventh-century Persian mathematician and poet. He was born into a wealthy family and entered Trinity College, Cambridge, where he befriended ALFRED, Lord TENNYSON, WILLIAM MAKEPEACE THACKERAY, and Edward Cowell. The latter, a student of the Eastern civilizations, introduced FitzGerald to Persian literature.

FitzGerald published his first book in 1849, a biography of Quaker poet Bernard Barton. In 1851 he issued *Euphranor, a Dialogue on Youth,* which recalled his Cambridge days. He was also the author of *Polonius* (1852), a collection of aphorisms.

In 1859, FitzGerald anonymously published the *Rubáiyát,* which is the Persian word for *quatrain.* At first a failure, the little book soon caused a sensation among DANTE GABRIEL ROSSETTI, Sir RICHARD BURTON, and other artists and writers. FitzGerald revised the book for subsequent editions in 1868, 1872, and 1879. The work was to become one of the best known poems in the English language.

FitzGerald also loosely translated works by Aeschylus, Sophocles, and the Spanish playwright Calderon. For the most part he led a very quiet life, living off his family's wealth on an estate in remote East Anglia. He maintained a lifelong friendship with Tennyson, who dedicated his last poem to Fitzgerald's memory. His letters to his friends, including THOMAS CARLYLE, are also considered literary achievements.

FitzGerald, George Francis See LORENTZ, HENDRIK ANTOON.

Five, The Nineteenth-century Russian composers also known as "The Mighty Handful." Coined by sympathetic critic Vladimir Stasov (1824–1906), the term refers to the nationalistic composers Mily Alekseyevich Balakirev (1837–1910), ALEKSANDR PORFIRYEVICH BORODIN (1833–1887), César Antonovich Cui (1835–1918), MODEST PETROVICH MUSSORGSKY (1839–1881), and NIKOLAY ANDREYEVICH RIMSKY-KORSAKOV (1844–1908). Drawing on Russian history, literature, and folklore, their music was considered distinctively Russian, in contrast to more "westernized" composers such as PYOTR ILICH TCHAIKOVSKY (1840–1893).

five-and-ten-cents store Retail establishment where all items are priced at no more than ten cents. Woolworth stores, originated in New York and Pennsylvania by FRANK WINFIELD WOOLWORTH in 1879, became popular across the United States. By the 1890s the concept behind the five-and-ten-cents store—that of offering a wide range of low-priced merchandise—spread to country stores, many of which had a "five-and-ten-cent" counter. Such goods were often provided by wholesale jobbers, such as the Boston-based Butler Brothers. They were also known as dime stores and five-and-dimes.

Flatland: A Romance of Many Dimensions (1884) Mathematical fantasy. Written by English clergyman and headmaster EDWIN A. ABBOTT, *Flatland* was first published under the pseudonym "A. Square" with illustrations by the author. The satirical fantasy describes the journeys of mathematician A. Square in the two-dimensional country of Flatland. The narrator also ventures into Spaceland (three dimensions), Lineland (one dimension), and Pointland (no dimensions). The novel instructs the reader in geometrical concepts while satirizing the hierarchical society of the Victorian Age.

Flaubert, Gustave (1821–1880) French writer. While a student at the *lycée* in Rouen, Flaubert showed an early interest in literature. His first published work, *Song of Death,* appeared in the review *Le Colibri* in 1837 when he was sixteen. Flaubert went to Paris in 1841 to study law before returning to Croisset in 1846 to devote all of his time to writing.

Often regarded as the master of literary REALISM, Flaubert sought to make literature a pure art. His aim was to write faultless prose. Because of his concern for form and precise detail, he often struggled in a search for the exact phrasing of what he wanted to say.

He took four years and seven months to write *Madame Bovary,* which first appeared in 1856 as a magazine serial in *La Revue de Paris.* Flaubert was subsequently brought to trial for publishing a morally offensive work. He was acquitted in 1857, the same year the novel came out in book form. He also published parts of *La Tentation de Saint Antoine* in *L'Artiste,* though the work was not completed until 1874.

In 1858 he visited the site of ancient Carthage and in 1862 published *Salammbo.* This was followed in 1869 by *L'Education sentimentale, roman d'un jeune homme,* and in 1877 by *Trois contes,* containing "Un Coeur simple," "La Legende de Saint-Julien-l'Hospitalier," and "Herodias."

During his later years Flaubert spent the winter in Paris, where he held literary gatherings. One of his guests was the writer GUY DE MAUPASSANT, whom he tutored for ten years. His influence over his friends, among them EMILE ZOLA and Alphonse Daudet, was great, especially his naturalistic approach to the novel depicting true psychological portraits.

Flaubert's plays, *Le Candidat* and *Le Chateau des coeurs,* were published in *La Vie moderne* (1885) after his death. His other posthumous publications include the satirical novel *Bouvard et Pecuchet, Lettres à George Sand,* and reminiscences of Brittany in *Le Gaulois.*

flowers General term for plants cultivated specifically for their fragrance or colorful blossoms. The Victorian sensibility hastened the end of the formal gardens of the eighteenth century, and brought in a garden style with a tousled, rangy look and a decidedly Romantic aspect. Nowhere in the world were flowers cultivated more passionately than in England, but to a great extent the rest of Europe and the United States also loved flowers and gardening.

Victorian flower gardens were based on perennials such as daisies, clematis, day lilies, iris, foxglove, helianthus, columbine, coreopsis, sweet alyssum, asters, peonies, trillium, primroses, poppies, and bellflowers. Bulbs were also planted for tulips, hyacinths, narcissus, and sweet William. Vivid annuals were also popular, including fucshias, geraniums, pansies, marigolds, zinnias, and cornflowers. Flowering herbs such as lavender and heather; flowering trees such as dogwood and magnolia; and flowering shrubs such as hydrangea and azaleas were also prized. Finally, roses, always a favorite, were cultivated with renewed vigor.

Flowers served as important visual images in the decoration of Victorian furniture, wallpaper, and fabric. Fresh flowers were used throughout the house. Dried flowers became popular in wreaths, potpourri, small nosegays, and Victorian posies known as "tussie-mussies."

fob Small pocket sewn into a pair of pants or vest at the waist to hold a pocket watch. It also refers to the chain used to hold a pocket watch.

food, processed As industrialization gave rise to mass production and improved methods of transportation, the means for commercially prepared foods was born. While it was not until 1911 that American engineer Clarence Birdseye (1886–1956) discovered the process for fast-freezing food, the nineteenth century saw the entrenchment of other ways of processing food, including condensing, canning, and the long-term boxing of dry foods. These are a few examples:

- In 1856, after observing the need for safely preserved milk for children during a 1851 transatlantic voyage, American inventor Gail Borden patented a method for condensing milk to be vacuum-sealed in cans. Sugar is used to aid preservation; a sugarless alternative was invented in 1885. In 1866, Swiss entrepreneur Henri Nestle developed a canned baby's formula made with canned milk and farina.
- Canned condensed milk was widely used by troops during combat, notably in the U.S. Civil War. The war also spawned other canned goods, such as Van Camp's Pork and Beans, which was developed by American grocer and metalworker Gilbert Van Camp in 1861. Eight years later, in New Jersey, vegetables were canned for the first time by Americans Abram Anderson and Joseph Campbell, marking the birth of the Campbell Soup Company. With the discovery of the process for making concentrated "condensed" soup in 1894, the Campbell Company became the major producer of soups in the country. Still, it was dwarfed by processed food giant H. J. Heinz and Company of Pittsburgh. Beginning in 1869 with commercially prepared horseradish, it produced more than two hundred different foods by the end of the century, including baked beans, pickles, relishes, fruit butters, and ketchup.
- In the United States, the quest for healthy living led to the development of the first dry cereals, as American progressives CHARLES WILLIAM POST and J. H. and WILL KEITH KELLOGG both introduced dry cereals as healthful breakfast alternatives to eggs, breakfast meats, and other fatty morning foods. Throughout the 1890s the

two families introduced a number of cereals, including Kellogg's Granose wheat flakes (1895), Post's wheat-and-barley Grape Nuts (1897), and Kellogg's Sanitas corn flakes (1898).

- Among other popular processed food items was deviled meat, developed by American William Underwood and granted the country's first food patent in 1870. The chocolate bar was made possible by the processing of cocoa by the CADBURY brothers of Britain; they began the process in 1842 and continued with refinements that included the development of completely unadulterated cocoa powder in 1866. The American Hershey Company introduced the first Hershey bar in 1894.

football A direct descendent of SOCCER and RUGBY, American football was played as an intramural sport in colleges in the early nineteenth century. The rough nature of the game caused its banishment on a number of campuses, including Yale and Harvard, around 1860. Interest in the game continued to grow, however, and the first intercollegiate game, closely resembling soccer, was played on November 6, 1869, between Rutgers and Princeton. Each team consisted of twenty-five players, and the game was decided by the first team to score six goals.

Harvard lifted its ban in 1871, and their game, which resembled rugby in that a player could carry the ball, was soon called the "Boston game." Due to the difference in rules, Harvard was excluded from intercollegiate competition until Yale agreed to play the Boston game in 1875; a year later the university officially adopted the Harvard rules.

The Intercollegiate Football Association was organized in 1876, at which time the rugby rules were adopted, but a game was now decided by a majority of "touchdowns." The same year also brought the arrival of Walter C. Camp, a Yale freshman who became known as the father of American football.

Camp insisted on teams of eleven players per side, and this rule was finally adopted in 1880, which also saw the emergence of the scrimmage line and the quarterback. The problem with the American game was that teams were not obligated to surrender possession of the ball, which often resulted in boring games ending in scoreless ties. In 1882, Camp introduced the system of downs and a rule that required a team to gain five yards in three downs or surrender the ball. This rule resulted in white lines on the field at intervals of five yards and introduced the term "gridiron" into sport lexicon.

The first professional football game was played on August 31, 1895, in Latrobe, Pennsylvania, but football remained a predominantly collegiate sport until after World War II.

Foreign Legion See FRENCH FOREIGN LEGION.

Forster, William Edward (1818–1886) English politician and reformer. Born in Dorsetshire, he was steeped in reformism through his Quaker upbringing. A successful businessman in woolens, he entered politics in 1861 as an "advanced Liberal" in the House of Commons. Forster's long campaign for universal education began to bear fruit with the passage of the EDUCATION ACT of 1870, which established a national system of elementary education in England. After the temporary retirement of WILLIAM GLADSTONE in 1875, Forster almost took over the leadership of the LIBERAL PARTY but deferred to another candidate. Gladstone made the reluctant Forster chief secretary for Ireland in 1880. Forster's support of Irish land reform did not prevent him from sternly repressing agrarian violence to the point where he earned the nickname "Buckshot Forster." Several attempts were made on his life, and four days after his resignation as chief secretary for Ireland in 1882, his successor was brutally murdered in Dublin in the PHOENIX PARK MURDERS. Forster's offer to resume his post was turned down. He later firmly opposed HOME RULE for Ireland. He was a brother-in-law of poet and critic MATTHEW ARNOLD. Forster held his seat in Parliament until his death in 1886.

Fort Sumter Union fort in the harbor of Charleston, South Carolina; site of the first battle of the U.S. CIVIL WAR. After seceding from the Union in December 1860, South Carolina demanded Fort Sumter's surrender, and a siege ensued. When President ABRAHAM LINCOLN took office in March 1861, he informed the South Carolina government that he was dispatching a naval force to relieve the garrison. Eager to settle the issue before the arrival of the relief force, state troops opened fire on the fort on April 12. Thirty-four hours later the garrison surrendered. The fort was recaptured by the Union in April 1865 and later made into a national monument.

Fortnightly Review, The Monthly magazine known for its attention to current affairs and stellar writing. It was first published in 1865 by Edward Chapman and William Hall. Its editors included critic and adventurer Frank Harris, who brought to the magazine such liberal contributors as GEORGE BERNARD SHAW and SIDNEY WEBB, who in turn recruited leading late Victorian writers. Over the years, critic WALTER PATER was also a contributor, as was positivist Frederic Harrison.

Foster, Stephen (1826–1864) American songwriter. Although a northerner from Pennsylvania, Foster is best known for his songs of the South and plantation slaves. Many of his songs are sentimental reminiscences of family and home.

At the age of fifteen, Foster composed a waltz for four flutes. Largely self-taught, his songwriting began in the late 1840s. Some of his ballads were published in 1848, including "Uncle Ned" and "Oh! Susanna."

When his first compositions met with success, Foster was commissioned to write songs for EDWIN P. CHRISTY and the Christy Minstrels. He made an arrangement to give them exclusive first-performance rights to any song he produced. One of his best known songs, "Old Folks at Home," or "Swanee River," appeared in 1851 under Edwin P. Christy's name and continued under the Christy name until 1879.

In 1857, Foster sold all rights to future songs to his publishers for $1,900. Profits went mostly to the publishers and performers. In 1860 he moved to New York City. He died homeless in Bellevue Hospital four years later.

Foster left about two hundred songs, including many ballads, minstrel songs, and hymns. For most of them he wrote both words and music. Among the most popular are "Camptown Races" (1850), "My Old Kentucky Home" (1853), the state song of Kentucky, and "Jeannie with the Light Brown Hair" (1854).

France Western European country. It borders Spain, Italy, Switzerland, Germany, Luxembourg, and Belgium. In the Victorian era, France underwent several political upheavals and steady but slow economic growth. At the end of the period it remained a major power, but it had been surpassed by Germany.

Following his final defeat at Waterloo (1815), Napoleon Bonaparte's empire was dismantled, and the Bourbon monarchy that had ruled France before the revolution was restored. Two brothers of Louis XVI reigned in succession: Louis XVIII (1815–24) and Charles X (1824–30). Though the restoration maintained some important features of the Napoleonic era, such as the reformed Civil Code and the principle of equality before the law, the government was increasingly repressive. Finally, in July 1830, Charles X tried to dissolve the Assembly, which was elected by a small portion of the population, and a popular insurrection broke out in Paris. Charles fled, and the wealthy bourgeoisie, fearing radical revolution, backed his cousin, the Duke of Orléans. He took the throne as LOUIS-PHILIPPE, initiating the July Monarchy (1830–48).

Louis-Philippe ruled as a constitutional monarch. Suffrage was extended to about 250,000 propertied men out of a population of 30 million, and the government was essentially under the control of the wealthy bourgeoisie. The July Monarchy saw the first significant industrialization in France, in the textile industry. France also reasserted itself as a colonial power, beginning a long campaign to subdue ALGERIA (1830) and intervening in favor of Egypt against the Ottoman Empire (1839). Internal tensions persisted, however. Republicans and Bonapartists called for wider suffrage and a change of government. Socialist agitation among the growing working class added to the regime's worries.

Serious food shortages beginning in 1846 threw the country into depression while political unrest continued. Full-scale rebellion erupted in Paris in February 1848. Louis Philippe abdicated, and the SECOND REPUBLIC (1848–52) was declared. Universal male suffrage and other political reforms followed, but bitter struggles pitting conservatives against socialists and other radicals broke out. Louis Napoleon, nephew of Napoleon I, was elected president in November 1848. In 1851 he seized power; in December 1852 he had himself crowned Emperor NAPOLEON III.

The SECOND EMPIRE (1852–70) saw further growth and industrialization. The French railroad network was greatly expanded. The living conditions of the average worker generally improved. Paris regained its status as the European center for fashion, culture, and the arts. Napoleon III also scored some foreign policy successes early in his reign, in the CRIMEAN WAR (1853–56) and the intervention on behalf of Sardinia against Austria–Hungary (1859), which helped secure the unification of Italy.

Napoleon also faced a costly ongoing war in Algeria and suffered a major reverse in his Mexican campaign (1861–66). Most important, he misjudged the rising power of Prussia and allowed himself to be drawn into war in 1870. The FRANCO-PRUSSIAN WAR (1870–71) resulted in his ignominious defeat and capture.

The THIRD REPUBLIC (1870–1940) was declared in the midst of the war. France was defeated and lost Alsace-Lorraine to the newly united Germany. At the end of the war, a revolutionary commune was formed in Paris. It was suppressed by rearmed troops and volunteers from the provinces.

The Third Republic was only gradually established on a permanent political basis. It was marked by constant electoral shifts and struggles between conservative and liberal parties. At the same time, major educational reforms were accomplished, and France continued to expand its colonies in Africa and SOUTHEAST ASIA. The possibility of armed insurrection receded as many groups, especially socialists, joined the political process. Although the ALFRED DREYFUS affair (1894–1906) split the nation over issues of patriotism and religion, desire to avenge the French defeat at Germany's hands in the Franco-Prussian War was a powerful unifying force. Throughout the Third Republic, France made great efforts to prepare for a rematch with Germany, leading to World War I.

Franco-Prussian War (1870–71) Armed conflict between FRANCE under NAPOLEON III and PRUSSIA under OTTO VON BISMARCK. The conflict resulted from Bismarck's policy of unifying independent German states under Prussia, already the strongest military power in central Europe by virtue of its defeat of Austria in the SEVEN WEEKS' WAR of 1866.

The immediate cause of the Franco-Prussian War was the negotiations between Prussia and Spain to put a member of the Prussian royal family on the throne of Spain. When France protested, Prussia withdrew the nomination but refused to guarantee that the candidacy would not be pursued in the future. France declared war in July 1870.

The Prussian army crushed the French forces in a little over six weeks. The Battle of Sedan in eastern France was the decisive engagement. After Napoleon III's surrender at Sedan and the collapse of France's Second Empire, a revolution broke out in Paris. The new government resisted a Prussian siege until January 1871.

The Peace of Frankfurt ceded the province of Alsace and part of Lorraine to Prussia. France also agreed to pay an enormous indemnity. France was further humiliated when WILLIAM I of Prussia was crowned German emperor at Versailles, marking the beginning of modern Germany.

Frankland, Sir Edward (1825–1899) English chemist. In 1852 he published his theory of what came to be called valence or valency, from Latin for "power," the capacity of an atom of a particular element to combine with fixed numbers of other atoms. This discovery became the foundation of the PERIODIC TABLE OF ELEMENTS and of modern structural chemistry. Frankland was also known for assisting astronomer Sir JOSEPH NORMAN LOCKYER in his studies of the sun.

Franklin, Sir John (1786–1847) English explorer. As a seaman, Franklin distinguished himself in battle at Trafalgar (1805) and New Orleans (1814–15). He led exploratory expeditions in northern Canada and the Arctic in 1818, 1819–22, and 1825–27, and was knighted in 1829. After serving as governor of Van Diemen's Land (now Tasmania) from 1836 to 1843, he launched his last Canadian expedition, in search of the NORTHWEST PASSAGE, in 1845. His ships, *Erebus* and *Terror,* were lost, with all 129 men presumed dead. More than forty expeditions were sent looking for him; in 1859, one of these confirmed that Franklin had died and had discovered the Northwest Passage.

Franz Joseph (1831–1916) Hapsburg emperor of AUSTRIA from 1848 to 1916. During his long reign, the empire suffered loss of territory, revolution, and repression, followed by a period of relative stability and openness. Born in the imperial palace near Vienna, the nephew of Ferdinand I (who reigned from 1835 to 1848), Franz Joseph received a military education and served in the fight against the Italian REVOLUTIONS OF 1848. On the death of Ferdinand, who was childless, Franz Joseph was crowned emperor, just after the Austrian army had suppressed the students' and workers' revolt in Vienna. In response to this and other rebellions in the empire, Franz Joseph governed as an absolute monarch in his first decade. But the loss of northern Italy in a war with Piedmont-

Sardinia and France in 1859 convinced the emperor of the need for change and liberalization, though the growing rivalry with Prussia delayed the reform program.

Following Austria's defeat in the SEVEN WEEKS' WAR (1866), Franz Joseph authorized a complete reform program. Hungary was given a measure of autonomy, other nationalities were declared equal to Germans, and Germanization programs were largely dropped. The reforms gave the empire a degree of stability for most of his later reign. Franz Joseph cherished dreams of revenge against PRUSSIA for the humiliation of 1866 but was realistic enough to see that the unified GERMANY could be Austria's most valuable ally. In 1874 he joined WILLIAM I and Alexander II of Russia in the THREE EMPERORS LEAGUE and later concluded the Dual Alliance with Germany (1879), which lasted until the breakup of the Austrian Empire in 1918.

Franz Joseph was noted for cultivating personal friendships with other monarchs as a means of diplomacy, a style that became increasingly ineffective as alliances and secret negotiations became rife in the late Victorian era. Still, he has been given partial credit for Austria's surprising decades of stability. His principal mistake was in becoming too deeply embroiled in the BALKANS, resulting in tension with Russian and Serbia that ultimately sparked World War I.

Frazer, Sir James George (1854–1941) English anthropologist and scholar. Born in Glasgow, Scotland, James Frazer was educated at Glasgow University and entered Trinity College, Cambridge, in 1874, where he became a fellow in 1879. His association with W. Robertson Smith at Cambridge led to his study of comparative religion and the publication of *The Golden Bough* in 1890.

Frazer's monumental work posits a "psychic unity," a similarity of psychic development, for all people. Frazer rarely left Cambridge, however, and the information on which *The Golden Bough* was based was taken from questionnaires he had sent to missionaries around the world. While Frazer's theories have long since proven to be seriously flawed, the text still remains a useful comprehensive encyclopedia of multicultural religious beliefs and practices.

Frazer was awarded a civil list pension at £2,000 a year in 1905 and was knighted in 1914. He continued to publish scholarly works, including *Folk-Lore in the Old Testament* (1918) and *The Gorgon's Head* (1927), and remained at Cambridge for the rest of his life.

Frederick III (1831–1888) King of PRUSSIA and emperor of GERMANY for three months (March to June 1888). Son of WILLIAM I, he served in the Prussian army in the SEVEN WEEKS' WAR against Austria and the FRANCO-PRUSSIAN WAR. He was married to Princess Victoria of England, daughter of Queen Victoria. Known to have liberal, pro-British sympathies, he was a frequent critic of OTTO VON BISMARCK and militarist interests in the government. He was already seriously ill with throat cancer when he took the throne, and he died shortly afterward. He was succeeded by his son WILLIAM II, who reigned from 1888 to 1918.

Frederick William III (1770–1840) King of PRUSSIA from 1797 to 1840. He ruled Prussia throughout the Napoleonic wars, presiding over its defeats and ultimately the victorious alliance with Great Britain, Russia, and Austria that vanquished Napoleon in 1815. In domestic matters, he was highly conservative, resisting attempts to liberalize the government and issue a constitution. He cooperated with

Austria in efforts to stamp out liberal and nationalist organizations throughout the GERMAN CONFEDERATION.

Frederick William IV (1795–1861) King of PRUSSIA from 1840 to 1861. His reign was marked by political crisis and reaction as well as rapid industrial growth in Prussia. Like his father, FREDERICK WILLIAM III, the king was suspicious of liberal nationalists who called for a constitution and a unified German nation. When the REVOLUTIONS OF 1848 broke out and the Frankfurt Parliament assembled and invited him to be "citizen-king" of a united GERMANY, Frederick William temporized. He promised a constitution and a representative assembly, and forbade the army from intervening. He declared a "union of Prussia and Germany," then waited while the Frankfurt Parliament began to fall apart. In 1849 he refused the Parliament's offer of a crown and intervened to quell a new round of uprisings.

Following the revolutions, Frederick William attempted to assert Prussian supremacy in the GERMAN CONFEDERATION but was blocked by Austria. At the same time, industrial growth was rapid, particularly in textiles, railroads, and iron. Liberalism and German nationalism revived in Prussia and elsewhere in Germany, but Frederick William continued his repressive measures. In 1858 he suffered an incapacitating stroke, and his brother, the future WILLIAM I, took over as regent.

Frémont, John Charles (1813–1890) American explorer and politician. Born in Georgia, he began his trailblazing career as an officer in the army's topographical engineers in the 1830s. In 1842 he organized the first of his three major explorations of the West, mapping the famous Oregon Trail on his first trip and exploring the Sierra Nevadas and California on the next two (1843–44, 1845). His reports and maps on the Oregon Trail and the South Pass in the Rockies helped open up the West to settlement and earned him popular acclaim as the nation's "Pathfinder." On his second expedition to California (1846), Frémont encouraged a revolt against Mexico. When two American officers claimed command of the territory, Frémont supported the ultimate loser in the dispute and was court-martialed. He led two additional expeditions in 1848 and 1853 and was briefly U.S. senator from California (1850–51). His great popularity and vigorous antislavery views led the newly formed REPUBLICAN PARTY to nominate him as its first presidential candidate in 1856, an election he lost to Democrat JAMES BUCHANAN.

When the CIVIL WAR began, Frémont was made commander of the Western Department. He placed Missouri under martial law and freed slaves belonging to southern sympathizers. When he refused to countermand his orders, President ABRAHAM LINCOLN fired him, and he played no further major role in the war. After the conflict, Frémont was bankrupted by failed investments in western railroads. His wife, Jessie Ann Benton Frémont (1824–1902), who had helped him write his reports from the West, supported them by writing books recounting her experiences. The socially prominent daughter of Senator Thomas Hart Benton (1782–1858), she would later help her husband with his memoirs, which remained unfinished at his death. Frémont was appointed governor of the Arizona Territory (1878–81). His wife's appeals to Congress won Frémont an army pension shortly before he died.

French Foreign Legion Military force. Commissioned by French King LOUIS PHILIPPE in 1831, the *Légion Etrangère* was originally designed for service to the French colonies. Stationed in the French colony of ALGERIA until the country gained independence in

1962, the Legion has long carried an air of mystery about its recruits, who may hail from any country and who, upon becoming members, swear allegiance to the Legion but not to France.

Freud, Sigmund (1856–1939) Austrian neurologist and founder of psychoanalysis. Born in Freiberg, Moravia (now Pribor, Czech Republic), he was the son of Jewish merchant Jakob Freud and his second wife. In his early childhood the family moved to Leipzig, Germany, and then to Vienna, where Freud stayed for most of his life, receiving his M.D. from the University of Vienna in 1881. He specialized in neurology, studying in Paris under neurologist JEAN-MARTIN CHARCOT (1885–86), but turned from the study of the brain to that of the mind when he learned of the experiments by JOSEF BREUER in treating hysteria, notably in the case of Anna O. Freud adopted Breuer's hypothesis that repressed memories of early trauma were responsible for neurotic symptoms, which could be cured by bringing the memories out of the unconscious mind and into conscious recognition. This is called the "cathartic method." At first Freud used Breuer's technique of having patients recall symptoms while under hypnosis, but soon he shifted to free association, in which unconscious memories and feelings emerge while patients talk freely under the therapist's guidance. Freud and Breuer published their findings in *Studies in Hysteria* (1895), generally regarded as the founding work of psychoanalysis. Soon, however, Breuer split from his colleague over Freud's view that repression of childhood sexuality was the principal cause of neurosis.

Following his break with Breuer and the death of Freud's father in 1896, Freud analyzed himself, using his dreams as a guide to understanding his unconscious mind. The result of his psychoanalysis of himself and his patients was *The Interpretation of Dreams,* the first major exposition of his theories. Published in late 1899 but dated 1900, it presented his concept of the Oedipus complex—the child's attraction to the parent of the opposite sex and hostility toward the parent of the same sex—and his view that a dream is a fulfillment of a wish. So important did Freud view the latter discovery that, in a letter to his friend Wilhelm Fliess, he suggested it be memorialized in a plaque in the house where his self-analysis

Sigmund Freud, creator of psychoanalytic theory, was the first to recognize the power of the unconscious. Photo courtesy of National Library of Medicine, Bethesda, Maryland.

revealed it to him: IN THIS HOUSE, ON JULY 24TH, 1895, THE SECRET OF DREAMS WAS REVEALED TO DR. SIGM. FREUD.

Despite Freud's own confidence in his theories, they were largely ignored or attacked by his Victorian contemporaries, who were disturbed by his focus on sexuality as the key to the workings of the human mind. His research and therapeutic successes attracted followers, however, some of whom, in 1908, formed a society that would become the International Congress of Psychoanalysis. Founding members included Alfred Adler and Carl Jung, who later broke away to found their own schools of psychoanalysis.

By the time of Freud's death in 1939, his ideas were widely known and accepted, though controversy over them has never ceased. Still, many of Freud's key concepts have entered the mainstream of twentieth-century thought, including the existence of the unconscious mind, the significance of dreams, the organization of the mind into id, ego, and superego, the value of talk therapy, and the role of sexual repression in causing at least some kinds of mental disorder. Influenced greatly by his analysis of literature and art, Freud in turn contributed inspiration to artists, writers, and critical theorists.

Freud's post-Victorian works include *Totem and Taboo* (1913), *Introduction to Psychoanalysis* (1917), *The Ego and the Id* (1923), *The Future of an Illusion* (1927), *Civilization and Its Discontents* (1930), and *Moses and Monotheism* (1939). His life endangered by the Nazi occupation of Austria, he fled Vienna in 1938 and settled in England. After nearly two decades of struggling with cancer, he died there the following year.

Frick, Henry Clay (1849–1919) American industrialist. Frick is known for his role in fostering the Homestead Strike and later for helping to form the United States Steel Corporation. Born in West Overton, Pennsylvania, he entered the coal mining business in 1871 by forming Frick & Company to run coke ovens in the Connellsville coal district. His success in controlling nearly 70 percent of the area's coal capacity attracted the attention of ANDREW CARNEGIE, who invested heavily in Frick's company. In turn, Frick was central in the organization of the Carnegie Steel Corporation, and as chairman (1889–90) and later managing head, he expanded the company's land and railroad holdings. Fiercely opposed to unions, he refused a contract to the workers, which led to the bloody Homestead Strike in 1892. The union walkout at the Carnegie plant in Homestead, Pennsylvania, lasted for nearly five months and resulted in many deaths on both sides, many of workers at the hands of the guards employed by ALLAN PINKERTON ordered by Frick to break the strike. Frick recovered from a knife and gun injury at the hands of Polish-American anarchist Alexander Berkman. After the unions were quelled and twelve-hour days were commonplace, he continued his involvement with Carnegie, eventually serving as director of the United States Steel Corporation. Upon his death, Frick's New York mansion and artwork were donated to the city, which established it as a museum bearing his name.

Frith, Francis (1822–1898) English photographer. Frith pioneered the production and sale of popular stock photography. An accomplished photographer by the mid-nineteenth century, Frith established his reputation in the newly burgeoning fields of travel and topographical photography with his photos of the Holy Land and Europe. Yet it was with the creation of the mass-market photography business, F. Frith and Company, that he reached his widest audience. Through his vast library of inexpensively produced European and British photos, he made it possible for all social classes to own photographs. The availability of stock photos paralleled the sale of the *carte de visite,* or an inexpensive portrait printed on a CALLING CARD, and pointed to the development of photography as a popular art. Frith's photography collections include *Palestine, Egypt, and Ethiopia* (1862).

Frith, William Powell (1819–1909) English painter. Frith specialized in GENRE PAINTING crowded scenes of contemporary life, such as *Life at the Seaside (Ramsgate Sands)* (1854), which was purchased by Queen Victoria, *Derby Day* (1858), and *The Railway Station* (1862).

Froude, James Anthony (1818–1894) English historian. The son of a clergyman, he was educated at Oriel College, Oxford. His elder brother was Richard Hurrell Froude (1803–1836), an early leader in the OXFORD MOVEMENT and a friend of JOHN HENRY NEWMAN. Dismayed by Newman's conversion to Roman Catholicism in 1845, James Froude suffered religious doubts, expressed in the autobiographical novel *The Nemesis of Faith* (1849). He defended the founding of the Church of England in *The History of England from the Fall of Wolsey to the Defeat of the Spanish Armada* (1856–70); a later supplement was *The Divorce of Catherine of Aragon* (1891). He opposed Irish self-rule in *The English in Ireland in the Eighteenth Century* (1872–74). Despite an eloquent prose style, Froude was criticized for his polemical interpretations. Friend, disciple, and literary executor of THOMAS CARLYLE, he published a four-volume biography on that writer (1882–84). The influence of Carlyle's doctrine of hero worship is evident in Froude's biographical studies of great men, including *Becket* (1878), *Caesar* (1879), *Bunyan* (1880), and *Lord Beaconsfield* (1890); see DISRAELI, BENJAMIN. A supporter of strong ties between Britain and its colonies, Froude traveled to South Africa in 1874–75 on a government mission to examine the possibilities for confederation. In 1892 he was named Regius Professor of Modern History at Oxford.

Fuller, Loie [Marie Louise] (1862–1928) American dancer. Born in Fullersburg, Illinois, she emigrated to Europe, making her continental debut in Paris in 1892. Self-taught and relentlessly innovative, she integrated theatrical techniques and modernist influences into dance, winning the admiration of contemporary writers and artists such as HENRI DE TOULOUSE-LAUTREC and AUGUSTE RODIN. Her serpentine dance, performed with a troupe of Japanese dancers, became an image of cyclical change in the poem "Nineteen Hundred and Nineteen" (1919) by WILLIAM BUTLER YEATS. She was noted for her creative use of light variations and flowing skirts. She influenced such twentieth-century dancers and choreographers as American Isadora Duncan (1878–1927).

Fuller, [Sarah] Margaret (1810–1850) American writer, teacher, and intellectual. Fuller was one of the earliest female American writers, editors, and thinkers, and a leading nineteenth-century literary critic. Born in Cambridgeport, Massachusetts, she was enrolled by her father, a lawyer, in a disciplined course of study that included learning Latin and Greek as a young child. Her intellectual prowess and erudition led to a teaching position in the 1830s in a progressive school established by BRONSON ALCOTT and later to the formation of a school of her own. Through her association with intellectuals in the Harvard-Cambridge area during her school years and her meeting with RALPH

WALDO EMERSON and HENRY DAVID THOREAU in the 1830s, she established herself as a leading proponent of TRANSCENDENTALISM, translating *Eckermann's Conversations with Goethe* in 1839. By invitation from Emerson, she edited the influential journal *The Dial* from 1840 to 1842; she also began conducting her "Conversations" on intellectual and literary topics (1839–44). She became literary critic and the first female journalist of the *New York Tribune,* and in 1845 she published the important women's study *Woman in the Nineteenth Century,* in which she posited that America might be a country where women could transcend social oppression. Sent to Europe in 1846 to cover international unrest, she became the first female foreign correspondent. During her time in Italy, she met Count Giovanni Angelo Ossoli who was a decade her senior; she gave birth to his son in 1848 and married him in 1849. A supporter of the revolutionary movement of GIUSEPPE MAZZINI in Italy, she embarked on a history of the subject. It was left unfinished, however, when she and her family were killed in a shipwreck off the coast of New York's Fire Island in 1850. A commanding and unorthodox woman, she was highly respected but often inadequately understood, even by peers. She was the probable inspiration for the character of Zenobia in *The Blithedale Romance* (1852) by NATHANIEL HAWTHORNE. Her books included *Summer on the Lakes* (1844), a travel work, and *Papers on Literature and Art* (1846).

Fuller, Melville Weston (1833–1910) American jurist. He was the eighth chief justice of the U.S. Supreme Court (1888–1910). Born in Augusta, Maine, and educated at Harvard Law School (1854–55), he was notable as the first chief justice to have academic training in law, though he did not receive a degree. He succeeded MORRISON R. WAITE in the post of chief justice. The landmark PLESSY V. FERGUSON decision of 1896, upholding racial segregation, was handed down during his tenure.

furniture Victorian furniture design was astonishingly varied not only because many styles were popular during the Queen's long reign but manufacturers often combined elements of diverse styles in a single piece (see VICTORIAN STYLE). The most important designs included Elizabethan Revival, an adaptation of sixteenth- and seventeenth-century spool designs; Louis XVI Revival, a French-inspired form; Renaissance Revival, a solid, massive style characterized by rectangular panels, molded medallions, and floral carvings; Rococo Revival, an adaptation of eighteenth-century French court furniture of Louis XIV or Louis IV; Turkish, a pseudo-Oriental style of overstuffed furniture upholstered in velvet and brocade; and GOTHIC REVIVAL, a style inspired by medieval architecture. Particularly in America, two eccentric styles also emerged: Rustic, which featured chairs and tables made of unturned tree branches or the horns of cattle or game, and Patent furniture, which consisted of contrived designs such as folding chairs made by the George Hunzinger Company of New York City, and the large oak Wooton desk that unfolded into a complete working cabinet.

In general, Victorian furniture was massive, ornate, and awkward, lacking in comfort and good proportion. Dark, heavy woods such as rosewood, oak, and ebony were commonly used, and pieces of furniture were often highly decorated with inlaid marble or carving. Strides were made in furniture manufacturing in the mid-1870s. While possibly stronger, it lacked the finesse of the eighteenth-century artisans but made such things as matched bedroom and dining room "suites" and odd little pieces such as whatnot shelves affordable to the middle class.

Despite the imitative quality of most Victorian design, some unique and elegant creations emerged. In 1842, Michael Thonet, an Austrian cabinetmaker, invented a bentwood rocking chair using steamed strips of beech. The style became so popular that firms such as J. & J. Kohn of Austria and the Sheboygan Chair Company of Wisconsin made thousands of copies. WILLIAM MORRIS also was responsible for reviving good standards of craftsmanship and design.

fustian Coarse cotton fabrics, often dark in color, such as corduroy and velveteen. The term originates from Fostat, a suburb of Cairo, from where the material—then made of cotton and flax—was first imported to Europe in the Middle Ages. By the mid-seventeenth century it was being manufactured in England and was a commonly used material in Victorian times.

Gadsden Purchase Treaty between the United States and Mexico. After the MEXICAN WAR, Mexico surrendered a large section of western territory to the United States, but the status of the area in what is now southern New Mexico and southern Arizona remained in question. Proponents of a southern transcontinental railroad route urged the government to buy this land. In 1853, President FRANKLIN PIERCE appointed James Gadsden minister to Mexico with instructions to secure the land. Gadsden negotiated a $15 million deal for 45 million, square miles, but Congress approved only $10 million for 30 million square miles. The Civil War delayed the construction of a rail line through the area until 1884 when the Southern Pacific Railroad completed a line.

Gage, Phineas P. (c.1823–1861) American railroad foreman. Gage was famous for a freak accident that spurred research in the workings of the brain. While using an iron rod to tamp down blasting powder, Gage set off a premature explosion that blew the rod into the left side of his face, out the top of his skull, and onto the ground some distance away. Though the rod destroyed his left eye and part of his brain, Gage was able to talk and walk only moments after the accident and recovered from the wound within weeks. Yet there was a conspicuous difference. Once an upright, hardworking man, Gage became a social misfit, given to lying, swearing, and untrustworthy behavior. Unable to hold down a job, he wandered as far as Chile and finally died in San Francisco in his mother's home in 1861.

His physician, John Harlow, intrigued by the implications of the accident for the developing science of neurology, exhumed Gage's skull and the tamping rod, which had been buried with him. Harlow argued that the accident pointed to the existence of a region of the brain dedicated to making moral decisions, but other Victorian scientists denied the possibility. The case has continued to attract the attention of brain researchers.

Galton, Sir Francis (1822–1911) English anthropologist. Cousin of CHARLES DARWIN and grandson of physician and poet Erasmus Darwin, Galton studied medicine until he became independently wealthy on his father's death. He then turned to numerous other scientific pursuits, focusing particularly on human heredity. In *Hereditary Genius: An Inquiry into Its Laws and Consequences* (1869) and *Inquiries into the Human Faculty and Its Development* (1883), he argued that heredity was more important than environment in determining mental abilities. He founded and coined the term "eugenics" for the movement to improve the human species through selective breeding—discouraging the reproduction of people with undesirable traits, encouraging the reproduction of those with superior traits. Though ultimately discredited as unscientific and inhumane, Galton's ideas had a wide influence in Europe and the United States in the early twentieth century.

A more lasting accomplishment was Galton's development of a method of classifying fingerprints and using them for identification. He also contributed to the fields of meteorology, where he coined the term "anticyclone," and biostatistics. He entered the Royal Society in 1856 and was knighted in 1909. An autobiography, *Memories of My Life,* appeared in 1908.

gamma rays High-frequency electromagnetic radiation emitted by atomic nuclei during radioactive decay. Gamma rays were first detected in 1900 by French physicist Paul Ulrich Villard (1860–1934) while studying uranium radiation. They were named for the third letter of the Greek alphabet, following the pattern set in naming ALPHA AND BETA RAYS, which differ from gamma rays in that they are particles rather than electromagnetic radiation.

gardens The Victorian tendency to encompass art, science, and nature in one view was embodied in the gardens of the day. Elaborately designed in carpets, ribbons, and curious shapes, they were formed and fortified by exotic plants from warm climates for most of the century, following the Victorian fascination with science. Indeed, many gardens resembled a museum of plants more than places to stroll, with pretty and precious greenhouses provided for the foreign plants to live in and an almost complete absence of FLOWERS, in order to make room for more and more green exotics. Toward the end of the century, however, and the beginning of the next, gardens once again became an extension of the living area of the house, with benches, gazebos, and winding pathways set everywhere for reading, courting, and playing and storytelling for children. And luxurious flowers and elaborate statues—sometimes in the form of mythological figures such as Zeus that actually wept tears gathered from a nearby fountain when a particular stone was stepped on, for instance—marked a return to romanticism in the garden. Public gardens were planned and planted in America with a fervor for horticulture and urban planning, with landscape architects such as FREDERICK LAW OLMSTED giving cities their first green gathering places.

Garfield, James Abram (1831–1881) Twentieth president of the UNITED STATES (1881). Born near Orange, Ohio, he graduated from Williams College before returning to Ohio where he was elected to the state senate in 1859. During the Civil War he was promoted to major general in the Union Army. He was elected to Congress in 1863 as a REPUBLICAN and served for eighteen years, rarely straying from the party line on RECONSTRUCTION, the tariff, and other issues. He was elected to the Senate in 1880. The Republican nominating convention became deadlocked that year, however, and Garfield emerged as a compromise candidate. He defeated Democratic candidate Winfield Scott Hancock.

During his short term Garfield successfully resisted the patronage demands of ROSCOE CONKLING, New York senator and political boss. Garfield also supported an investigation into the corrupt Post Office Department, a major source of federal patronage. Garfield was shot in the back on July 2, 1881, by Charles Guiteau, a disappointed office seeker. He died eighty days later and was succeeded as president by CHESTER A. ARTHUR.

Garibaldi, Giuseppe (1807–1882) Italian nationalist and military leader. Garibaldi is best known for his role in the RISORGIMENTO, or period that led to unification of ITALY, but he and his group also fought for nationalist causes throughout Europe and the Americas. Especially after his conquest of southern Italy, Garibaldi became a romantic symbol of nationalist aspirations. Born in Nice to a merchant family, he made several trading voyages in the Mediterranean in his youth. In 1833 he joined GIUSEPPE MAZZINI's Young Italy movement, a society devoted to the creation of a unified Italian republic. In 1834 he was involved in an unsuccessful uprising against the kingdom of Piedmont-Sardinia. He fled to Rio de Janeiro, Brazil, where there was an Italian expatriate community.

In South America he soon became involved in a rebellion in southern Brazil and then in a war between Uruguay and Argentina. During these conflicts with a group of Italians and other Europeans, he formed the nucleus of his nationalist legion, the Red Shirts. He also married Anita Ribeiro da Silva in 1842. She accompanied him on nearly all his campaigns and bore him two sons and a daughter.

When the REVOLUTIONS OF 1848 broke out in Italy against Austrian rule, Garibaldi and a small force left South America to join the fight. The kingdom of Piedmont rejected Garibaldi and his men, but the revolutionary government of Milan made him a general. Austrian victories forced him to flee from northern Italy to Rome, from which Pope Pius IX had departed, allowing the establishment of a Roman republic. The Red Shirts helped defend Rome against attacks by Austrians and Neapolitans in support of the pope, but a large French force sent by Louis Napoleon, later Napoleon III, proved too strong and recaptured Rome for the pope in 1849. Garibaldi fled Rome, disbanded the Red Shirts, and left Italy. His wife died during the retreat.

Giuseppe Garibaldi, a fervent nationalist, was a military leader in the unification of Italy during the 1800s. Photo courtesy of Deutsche Fotolhek Dresden.

Garibaldi moved to New York where he worked as a manual laborer and then a merchant captain. In 1857 he moved to Caprera, a small island off Sardinia which he had purchased with an inheritance. He gave up his commitment to an Italian republic and declared his support for the establishment of an Italian kingdom led by Piedmont-Sardinia.

In 1859 war broke out between Austria and Piedmont, which was supported by France. Garibaldi took a commission in the Piedmontese army and attracted volunteers from all across Italy and Europe. His unit fought with distinction, but the war ended after Piedmont had acquired only Lombardy from Austria. In 1860, Sicily revolted against the Bourbon monarchy, and Garibaldi gathered a force of one thousand Red Shirts and invaded, without Piedmontese approval. The Red Shirts quickly gained local support and easily defeated the Neapolitan forces on the island. They then landed on the mainland and after a more difficult campaign defeated the Neapolitans again. The Piedmontese army intervened to finish the war and to prevent Garibaldi's troops from marching on Rome. Garibaldi met VICTOR EMMANUEL II, presented him with the conquered territories, and retired to Caprera. The kingdom of Italy was proclaimed in 1861.

Garibaldi became increasingly radical and anticlerical in the following years, and his followers became involved in nationalist struggles in Poland, Greece, and the Balkans. Many *Garibaldini* also fought for the North in the U.S. Civil War, and Garibaldi himself was offered a command in the Union Army. In 1862 and 1867 he attempted unsuccessfully to invade Rome, and in 1866 he served in the SEVEN WEEKS' WAR against Austria, a conflict resulting in Italy's annexation of Venice. With the fall of Napoleon III and the establishment of the THIRD REPUBLIC, Garibaldi offered his services to France in the last stages of the FRANCO-PRUSSIAN WAR (1870–71). His small army fought well but had little effect on the outcome.

Following France's defeat, Garibaldi returned to Italy. He served as a deputy from Rome in the Italian Parliament but spent most of his remaining years in retirement on Caprera, writing historical novels and his memoirs.

Garrison, William Lloyd (1805–1879) American abolitionist. Garrison was born in Newburyport, Massachusetts. He coedited the antislavery newspaper *The Genius of Universal Emancipation* (1829–30) in Baltimore where he was jailed for libel. He moved to Boston in 1831 and founded *The Liberator,* an antislavery newspaper that endured for thirty-four years. He helped found the New England Anti-Slavery Society and the American Anti-Slavery Society.

Garrison accepted no compromise with SLAVERY. He called for the free states to leave the Union rather than live under a Constitution that he called "a covenant with death and an agreement with the Devil" because it countenanced human bondage. He dramatically accentuated this point in 1854 when he publicly burned the Constitution to protest the Kansas-Nebraska Act, which rescinded the provisions of the Missouri Compromise and permitted territories "popular sovereignty" on slavery. His extremism helped split the abolitionist movement, but it also exposed the horror of slavery.

Garrison was also interested in women's rights and the temperance movement. He left public life after the Civil War. His works include *Thoughts on African Colonization* (1832) and *Selections* (1852)

Gaskell, Elizabeth Cleghorn Stevenson (1810–1865) English writer. Born Elizabeth

Stevenson in Chelsea, England, she spent her childhood in Knutsford under the guardianship of her aunt. In 1832 she married Unitarian minister William Gaskell. Her work with him over the next several years in the industrial north of England provided intimate acquaintance with British social inequities and informed her first novel, *Mary Barton* (1848). While this book focused on social unrest among the working poor of MANCHESTER, later works touched on other social problems: *Ruth* (1853) concerned attitudes toward sexual mores; *North and South* (1855), the conflict between mill owners and laborers. Her later novels, including *Sylvia's Lovers* (1863), *Cousin Phillis* (1865), and especially *Wives and Daughters* (published posthumously in 1866), revealed a refinement of form and characterization. Adept in a variety of literary forms, Gaskell also wrote a biography of her friend CHARLOTTE BRONTË, *The Life of Charlotte Brontë* (1857), and beginning in the 1850s was a regular contributor to CHARLES DICKENS's periodical *Household Words,* where her examination of country life, *Cranford* (1855), was serialized from 1851 to 1853. Respected by such contemporary thinkers as Dickens, THOMAS CARLYLE, and BENJAMIN DISRAELI, she was one of her age's leading novelists and arbiters of compassion.

Gatling gun FIREARM. Invented by American Richard Jordan Gatling (1818–1903) in 1861, the Gatling gun was the forerunner of the modern machine gun. It had six revolving barrels capable of firing three hundred rounds in a minute. The weapon saw limited service in the U.S. CIVIL WAR and at Charasia (1879) in the second of the ANGLO-AFGHAN WARS, but machine guns did not achieve their full potential until World War I.

Gaudi y Cornet, Antonio (1852–1926) Spanish architect. Gaudi's work at first paralleled the styles of ART NOUVEAU and his early architecture tended to follow the currents of Spain's GOTHIC REVIVAL, with an emphasis on imaginative use of materials and ironwork. His first major commission was to complete the Church of the Sagrada Familia in Barcelona, already designed as a neo-Gothic structure by architect Francisco de Villar. Gaudi worked on the church from 1883 until his death in 1926, leaving it unfinished. Gaudi retained Gothic elements in his own design of the interior while exaggerating the church's exterior ornamentation with naturalistic figuration and abstract decoration.

Gaudi exhibited parabolic arches that were to become one of his trademarks in the facade of the Güell Palace in 1885. The arched entrances were filled with complex ironwork grilles. In his design for the College of Santa Teresa de Jesus in Barcelona, begun in 1889, the parabolic curve appears as a narrow plaster arch in the arcades of the ground floor, creating an overwhelming effect of structural articulation.

Toward the end of the nineteenth century, Gaudi abandoned the vertical and began to incline or curve his columns and arches. His designs became more sculptural, as seen in his creations for Barcelona's Güell Park in 1900. Gaudi covered his curving walls and benches, grottoes, porticoes, and arcades with brilliant mosaics of broken pottery and glass. In the early twentieth century, Gaudi dramatically transformed the exterior and interior of his buildings, as seen in the Casa Batlló and Casa Milá apartment houses begun in 1905. The facades are treated as a fantasy of curving projections while the airy interiors provide a sense of flowing movement and light. Gaudi's daring engineering experiments and independent, original use of form encouraged twentieth-century architects to create organic structures within natural environments.

Gauguin, [Eugène-Henri-]Paul (1848–1903) French painter, sculptor, and graphic artist. Gauguin was the central figure of the movement in POST-IMPRESSIONISM called SYMBOLISM or Synthetism. His work, informed by the search for religious experience, had a strong formative influence on twentieth-century art. He was born in Paris but was brought up with his mother's family in Peru. A successful stockbroker, he painted in his spare time and submitted eight paintings to the Exhibition of IMPRESSIONISM of 1881, including *Study of the Nude* (1880). Gauguin was included with the Impressionists up until their last group exhibition in 1886.

After an attempt to support his family through his art in Denmark, he left them in 1887 and sailed to Central America and the Caribbean where he worked on the construction of the Panama Canal. He spent six months in Martinique and captured the bright colors and lush foliage of the exotic scenery in *Martinique Landscape* (1887).

Gauguin returned to western France to live among the peasants of Brittany in 1888 and began working with painter Emile Bernard. Both artists painted in a style that they hoped might convey a concealed world of ideas and emotion. They even coined the word, "Synthetism" to describe in conceptual terms their efforts to depict a generalized, synthetic world of deeper meaning. They developed a simplified, non-naturalistic manner of painting with an emphasis on decorative line and the use of flat, bright color.

Gauguin's approach to the religious convictions of the Breton peasants was not as a participant but as an observer and interpreter of human feeling. In 1888 he painted *The Vision After the Sermon (Jacob Wrestling with the Angel)* as an abstract depiction of the country peasants' simple faith. Among his other unorthodox religious paintings is *Yellow Christ* (1889), in which the crucifix is crudely painted in simplified colors and contours.

In 1891 Gauguin went to Tahiti, where he became one of the first European artists to find visual models in the arts of "primitive" peoples. He spent the rest of his life in the South Seas, except for an unsuccessful attempt to sell his paintings in France in 1893. His tribute to the universality of religion and myth, *Ia Orana Maria* (1891)—a translation into the Maori language of the words "Ave Maria"—depicts a Tahitian Angel of the Annunciation pointing out to two bare-breasted native women the naked infant Jesus seated on the shoulder of Mary.

Deciding to take his own life in 1897, Gauguin intended to leave a last will and testament in the form of a canvas over twelve feet wide entitled *Where Do We Come From? What Are We? Where Are We Going?* His efforts to kill himself with arsenic failed, and the painting was sent to Paris in 1898 for viewing at Ambroise Vollard's gallery. Gauguin died in poverty at Atuana, Marquesas Islands, leaving behind many paintings, carvings, woodcuts, watercolors, lithographs, ceramics, and several journals, including *Noa-Noa* and *Avant et apres.*

Gautier, Théophile (1811–1872) French poet, novelist, and critic. An advocate of *l'art pour l'art* (ART FOR ART'S SAKE), Gautier's poetry emphasized purity and perfection of form and influenced the Parnassian school of French poetry. His early works, such as the narrative poem *Albertus* (1832), dealt with the macabre and fantastic, but he is best known for later, finely crafted works such as the poem *Emaux at camées* (*Enamels and Cameos,* 1852). His novels and stories include *Made-*

moiselle de Maupin (1835), *La Jettatura* (1856), and *Le Capitaine Fracasse* (1861–63).

gazebo Small decorative building for a garden, usually open on all sides. A favorite of Victorian gardens, the gazebo first appeared in *New Designs for Chinese Temples* (1752) by British architects William and John Halfpenny.

Geissler tube Vacuum container more thoroughly evacuated than any previous such device. It was developed in 1855 by German inventor Johann Heinrich Geissler (1815–1879). It became useful in the study of fluorescence, the glow of electric discharges passing through a low-pressure gas. Building on Geissler's work, WILLIAM CROOKES in 1875 invented a still superior vacuum tube, the Crookes tube, which became important in the study of atomic structure (see CATHODE RAYS) and in the development of the cathode-ray tube used in television sets and computer monitors.

genetics Study of heredity and variation. The founder of the field is Austrian monk and botanist GREGOR MENDEL, who published his laws of heredity—Mendel's laws of inheritance—in 1866, stating in essence that an inherited trait is determined by the combination of two hereditary factors, now called genes, one from each of the parental reproductive cells, now called gametes. Mendel also identified what happens when there are two forms, or alleles, of a gene, one dominant and one recessive. Mendel's work remained unknown until 1900 when three botanists—Dutchman Hugo Marie De Vries, German Karl Erich Correns, and Austrian Erich von Seysenegg—who had independently worked out the same laws of heredity were searching the literature for possible antecedents. The three men credited Mendel as the discoverer of the laws, though it was their rediscovery that initiated future work in the field. De Vries also introduced the concept of mutations, changes in the genetic material that result in visible bodily changes.

In 1902, American geneticist Walter S. Sutton suggested that CHROMOSOMES, cell structures discovered in the 1880s, contained the genetic factors predicted by Mendel. This insight led to discoveries concerning the chromosomal material called DNA and the molecular basis for inheritance. Mendel's work was also synthesized with that of another Victorian-era scientist, English naturalist CHARLES DARWIN, originator of the theory of EVOLUTION.

Geneva conventions Series of international agreements signed in Geneva, Switzerland, to provide for humane treatment in wartime of the wounded, prisoners of war, and civilians. It was the brainchild of Swiss philanthropist JEAN-HENRI DUNANT, who brought about an international conference on the issue in Geneva in 1863. In August 1864 representatives of sixteen countries signed the first Geneva convention, vowing to treat sick and wounded soldiers humanely, respect civilian neutrality, and allow the passage of medical personnel bearing the neutral emblem of the RED CROSS. Conventions in 1899, 1906, 1929, and 1949 extended the areas of agreement to maritime warfare and prisoners of war, further protected civilian neutrality, and codified the laws of war.

genre painting Paintings depicting scenes from daily life. It is associated with several places and eras, notably the seventeenth-century Netherlands and Victorian Britain. In the latter period, the paintings often told a story and carried a moral message. The most popular paintings were made into inexpensive engraved prints purchased by a middle class hungry for art. Painters of genre paintings included THOMAS WEBSTER, WILLIAM HOLMAN

HUNT, WILLIAM POWELL FRITH, AUGUSTUS LEOPOLD EGG, and FREDERICK WALKER. Many of the paintings depicted domesticity and childhood, but others, particularly in the 1870s and later, depicted the ravages of poverty.

George, Henry (1839–1897) American social reformer, economist, and writer. George was born in Philadelphia, the son of a deeply religious, middle-class Democrat with a position in the city's Customs House. He left school at fourteen and after working at various odd jobs shipped aboard a merchant ship for a fourteen-month voyage. During a trip to Calcutta he witnessed the extreme differences of poverty and wealth that were to inform his thinking.

Back in the United States, George decided to make his fortune in the gold fields of the far West. He arrived in San Francisco in May 1858, but two attempts at prospecting failed. He worked as a typesetter in a San Francisco printing firm and turned to journalism to support himself. He started the *Daily Evening Journal;* after its failure, he bought a printing plant that also foundered. By 1865, after struggling through the California depression caused by the Civil War, he was able to earn a living through his writing.

George's struggles with poverty and his analysis of California politics and land issues helped form his most important economic and political idea, the theory of the single tax. George developed this theory in a series of pamphlets and in *Progress and Poverty* (1879), a book read by millions. In it he argued that since society at large created the value of land, society should reap its benefits instead of private landowners who did nothing to earn their wealth. Rents and other income from land enrich only a few while millions of others become impoverished. A single tax on landowners would abolish the need for other public levies, make both labor and capital more productive, and end poverty altogether.

This theory, also espoused in his lectures and in his weekly paper *The Standard* (1886–92), won him international acclaim. His single tax movement influenced the fiscal laws of Great Britain, Canada, Germany, and other countries while drawing attention to the unequal distribution of wealth in the United States. In 1886 trade unions in New York City formed the United Labor Party and nominated George for mayor. He finished second in the three-way race, beating out the Republican nominee THEODORE ROOSEVELT but losing to Democrat Abram Hewitt. He ran again in 1897 at the request of reform Democrats but died of a stroke before election day.

germ theory of disease Scientific theory that certain diseases are caused by microorganisms invading the body. First proposed by French biochemist LOUIS PASTEUR in 1862 as a result of his studies on fermentation, the formulation and acceptance of this theory during the Victorian era was one of the most important advances in the history of medicine. It provided a framework for discovering the causes of, and preventing or curing, numerous diseases. It also provided the underlying basis for ANTISEPTIC agents and techniques, which dramatically lowered death rates from surgery. The germ theory was accepted only slowly, however, encountering opposition worldwide from many scientists and physicians, among them the founder of cellular pathology, RUDOLF VIRCHOW. One objection was the belief that the role of germs in disease was secondary, an idea stemming from the assumption that microscopic organisms could not destroy larger ones. Many scientists held to the belief that contagious diseases were caused by such agents as miasma, or bad air. Nonetheless, Pasteur and others, including ROBERT KOCH, accumulated evidence for the germ theory, most strikingly through their success in developing vaccines. By the end of the nineteenth century the theory was widely accepted.

German Confederation Union of German-speaking states formed in 1815, in the aftermath of the Napoleonic Wars. The confederation consisted of thirty-five monarchies and four free cities, and the main powers were PRUSSIA and AUSTRIA. It was designed to create a modicum of stability in Germany while preventing German unification, which could threaten the balance of power in Europe. It was governed by a Diet in Frankfurt, representatives to which were chosen by the heads of state and tended to be conservative. Austria, the dominant power and the one most anxious to prevent unification, held the presidency of the Diet on a permanent basis. The confederation primarily acted as a collective security arrangement against outside aggression and as a means of settling disputes between the various German states.

In 1833 the confederation established the *Zollverein,* or customs union, which largely abolished tariffs between most of the German states and greatly increased trade. Most states within the confederation saw the growth of liberal and nationalist movements. These culminated in the REVOLUTIONS OF 1848 and the establishment of the Frankfurt Parliament (1848–49), which tried to transform the confederation into a unified German state under one constitution. The failure of the Parliament was followed by a reconstitution of the confederation in its original form. Following Prussia's victory over Austria in the SEVEN WEEKS' WAR (1866), the German Confederation was dissolved. It was replaced by the North German Confederation, which excluded southern German states such as Bavaria and Austria, and was dominated by Prussia. The North German Confederation was itself replaced by a unified German empire in 1871.

German East Africa German colony on the east coast of AFRICA, now the independent nations of Tanzania, Rwanda, and Burundi. The largest part of it was Tanganyika (now part of Tanzania), a region of plateau and mountains stretching hundreds of miles from the lakes of Victoria, Tanganyika, and Nyasa in the west to the Indian Ocean on the east. One of the oldest sites in human history, Tanganyika is the location of Olduvai Gorge, where fossil remains dating from about 1.8 million years ago have been found of the extinct hominids *Australopithecus robustus* and *Homo habilis.* Alexandrian traders knew of Tanganyika's existence in the fourth century A.D., and Arabic traders reached it in the ninth century. BANTU-speaking peoples also settled here; among their languages was the ancestor of the Swahili tongue.

By the thirteenth century, the Tanganyikan coast was the site of flourishing Islamic communities built on the trade in ivory, slaves, gold, and other commodities. The Portuguese reached the coast about 1500 and took control of much of the coast for about two hundred years when, at the end of the seventeenth century Arab traders from Oman took control of the region. In the first part of the nineteenth century, that control expanded due to the aggressive drive of Imam Seyyid Said, the sultan of Muscat in Oman from 1806 to 1856. He moved his capital to ZANZIBAR, an island off the coast of Tanganyika, and made it the commercial nexus of the East African coast. New trade routes for slaves and ivory were opened up not only by the Zanzibar Arabs but by the Nyamwezi people of West-Central Tanganyika, who were also famous for their strength and endurance as carriers.

British influence weakened the control of the Zanzibar Arabs over East African commerce. In the 1880s, Germany took an interest in Tanganyika as a playing card in the complex game of colonial politics with Great Britain and France. In 1885, Tanganyika became the colony of German East Africa. Annexed in 1890 were Burundi and Rwanda, two small mountainous regions bordering Tanganyika in the northwest.

German East Africa lasted until World War I when it was occupied and divided by the victorious powers. Belgium took control of Rwanda and Burundi as the mandate of Rwanda-Urundi in 1919. In 1946 this became a United Nations trust territory and in 1962 the independent nations of Burundi and Rwanda. Tanganyika became a British mandate in 1919 and won independence in 1961. In 1964, Tanganiyka merged with Zanzibar (independent from 1963) to form Tanzania.

Germany Political unit. Now a federal republic, Germany started the Victorian era as a confederation of independent states and ended it as a unified empire. During the Victorian era Germany bordered Russia, AUSTRIA, Switzerland, France, Luxembourg, Belgium, the Netherlands, and Denmark. The population spoke a variety of regional dialects and was divided principally between Lutherans and Roman Catholics. Significant minorities in the Victorian Age included Poles in the east and Jews in urban areas.

At the beginning of Queen Victoria's reign, Germany was fragmented into dozens of independent states, the most powerful of which was PRUSSIA in the northeast. Most of the states were grouped into the Austria-dominated GERMAN CONFEDERATION, whose Parliament met in Frankfurt and regulated disputes between states and set a common foreign policy. Many German states were also linked by the *Zollverein,* a customs union that had abolished tolls and tariffs between the signatory states, greatly encouraging trade.

Though the idea of German unification had been discussed for a long time, the governments of the German states were by and large conservative and suspicious of changing the status quo. In general, nationalist movements were suppressed since they were frequently associated with republican agitation. In 1848 economic distress sparked uprisings across Europe, known as the REVOLUTIONS OF 1848. Rebellions in Germany overthrew several small state governments. A group of liberal nationalists formed the Frankfurt Parliament, calling for a unified Germany under a constitutional monarchy. The Parliament offered the crown to FREDERICK WILLIAM IV, king of Prussia, but he ultimately rejected it. Suffering from disunity and a lack of means of enforcement, the Parliament soon collapsed. In the following months Prussian and Austrian forces cooperated in suppressing the revolutionary movements across Germany and reestablished the German Confederation on its original terms.

The 1850s was a time of dramatic economic growth and industrialization, combined with political repression. In the 1860s, Prussia, under the direction of OTTO VON BISMARCK, set out to unite the German states under its monarchy. A series of disputes arose between Austria and Prussia. In 1866 the SEVEN WEEKS' WAR resulted in an overwhelming Prussian victory. The confederation was dissolved, Austria lost its say in German affairs, and the small states were joined with Prussia in a close confederation. The final act of German unification also occurred through an act of war. Bismarck maneuvered NAPOLEON III of France into a declaration of war. The German states all aligned with Prussia. The FRANCO-PRUSSIAN WAR (1870–71) was another lopsided Prussian victory. As the war was ending, WILLIAM I was crowned emperor of Germany at Versailles.

In the years following political unification, the government moved rapidly to create institutions such as a postal service, a national bank, and a unified legal code. Economic growth continued, enabling Germany to support a growing military. The empire was given a two-chambered legislature, with the lower chamber, the *Reichstag,* elected by universal male suffrage. Bismarck, as imperial chancellor, was able to keep firm control of the legislature during his entire career.

Rapid industrialization and poor working conditions fueled a growing socialist movement in Germany. The government response was a ban on some socialist organizations and writings followed by social welfare provisions such as subsidized pensions and insurance. The legislature also introduced tariffs to protect German industry. Working conditions remained poor, however, and socialists continued to gain strength. Many left Germany for North America, seeking a better life.

In foreign policy, Germany's status as a great power was immediately recognized in Europe. Anxious to avoid having Germany become surrounded by enemies, Bismarck worked to establish a complex set of alliances that would preserve Germany's position. Alexander II of Russia and FRANZ JOSEPH of Austria joined William in the THREE EMPERORS LEAGUE in 1873. In 1879, Austria entered into the Dual Alliance with Germany, which lasted until World War I. Even relations with France underwent a thaw in the 1880s, despite French resentment of the seizure of Alsace-Lorrain in the Franco-Prussian War. Over Bismarck's protests, Germany began acquiring colonies in Africa and the Pacific.

The stability of Bismarck's domestic and foreign arrangements began to decay after he fell from power in 1890. The new emperor, WILLIAM II (reigned from 1888 to 1918), launched an ambitious program of workplace regulation. More ominously, he allowed Bismarck's alliance system to erode significantly until only Austria remained as Germany's sure ally. He instituted a strong naval building program, which Great Britain saw as a threat. He also pressed several colonial confrontations and aroused British indignation when, in the so-called Kruger telegram (1896), he expressed support for the defeat of the TRANSVAAL in the British raid under the command of LEANDER STARR JAMESON. The buildup of the army was accelerated, giving rise to increasing fears of German aggression.

Despite these warning signs of tendencies that would lead to World War I, the last years of the Victorian era were peaceful and prosperous for most Germans.

Geronimo [Goyathlay, "One Who Yawns"] (1829–1909) American Apache chief. After the murder of his family by Mexicans during his youth, he joined a band of Apaches known as Chiricahuas that launched raids on both sides of the Mexican–United States border. Nicknamed Geronimo, which is Spanish for Jerome, he became leader of the band, and his widely reported raids prompted a national outcry for his capture. In 1876 he was forced onto a reservation in Arizona but escaped to Mexico. He was recaptured several times but each time fled to continue his attacks. His final surrender came in 1886 after a yearlong pursuit by some five thousand American troops. Deported to Florida, he was later moved to Oklahoma where he became a successful farmer and a national celebrity who marched in the inaugural procession of THEODORE ROOSEVELT. He dictated his autobiography in 1906 and the last great Apache chief died of pneumonia.

Gettysburg, Battle of (July 1–3, 1863) U.S. CIVIL WAR conflict. The battle was fought west of Gettysburg in southern Pennsylvania. General ROBERT E. LEE invaded the North with seventy-five thousand Confederate troops. He was met by ninety thousand Union troops led by General George Meade. The battle swayed back and forth, culminating on July 3 with the disastrous charge on the Union center by Confederate general George Edward Pickett (1825–1875). The following day Lee retreated, and Meade was later criticized for not pursuing the retreating southern army. Lee suffered twenty-five thousand casualties, a devastating number for the sparsely populated CONFEDERACY. The Union side suffered about twenty-three thousand casualties. This pivotal battle marked the last southern invasion of the North and the start of the South's military decline. On November 19, 1863, President ABRAHAM LINCOLN delivered his famous Gettysburg Address at the battle site to commemorate a national cemetery.

Gibson, Charles Dana (1867–1944) American illustrator. Born in Roxbury, Massachusetts, he was apprenticed to Augustus Saint-Gaudens and was working actively as a magazine illustrator when, in 1877, he created the first drawing of the Gibson girl for illustrator John Mitchell's *Life* magazine. The poised, self-assured Gibson girl set an ideal for American womanhood for several decades to follow. In 1890 Gibson signed an agreement to work exclusively for *Life* and *Colliers* for four years. His books include *The Education of Mr. Pipp* (1890), based on another Gibson character. He was also known for his oil paintings.

Charles Dana Gibson's "Gibson Girl" provided a model for fashionable American women.

Gilbert and Sullivan English writing and composing team of popular comic operas. Born in London, William Schwenck Gilbert (1836–1911) was first a government clerk, then a lawyer, and finally a dramatist. While studying law at Kings College, he wrote verses that were eventually collected in two books, *Bab Ballads* and *More Bab Ballads*. One of his first dramatic works to be produced was

Dulcamara (1866). Also born in London, Arthur Seymour Sullivan (1842–1900) was a soloist with the Chapel Royal choristers. He won the Mendelssohn scholarship in 1856 and studied at both the Royal Academy of Music in London and the Leipzig Conservatory in Germany. He wrote a large body of work, mostly sacred songs and oratorios. "Onward! Christian Soldiers" is his best-known hymn.

Gilbert and Sullivan met in 1870 and within a year their first opera *Thespis* was performed to unfavorable reviews. They did not team up again until 1875 when they created the judicial comedy *Trial by Jury* for English impresario Richard D'Oyly Carte (1844–1901). Within three years he formed the D'Oyly Carte Company to produce the first truly successful Gilbert and Sullivan operas, *H.M.S. Pinafore* (1878) and *The Pirates of Penzance* (1879). Between 1871 and 1896 the duo created words and music for thirteen operas.

After 1881 the Gilbert and Sullivan operas were produced in London at the Savoy Theatre, which was built especially for their popular productions and was the first public building in England to be lighted by electricity. Gilbert and Sullivan's large following was known as the "Savoyards" in honor of the theater. The Savoy operas, considered the best of their musical collaboration, include *Patience* (1881), *Iolanthe* (1882), *The Mikado* (1885), and *The Yeoman of the Guard* (1888).

Gilbert's lyrics were highly satirical. His caricatures of government so angered Queen VICTORIA that she refused to knight him. Instead, she knighted Sullivan in 1883. Gilbert was knighted by Edward in 1907.

Gilded Age Name given to the twenty-five-year period following the U.S. Civil War. The period was marked by tremendous industrial expansion, political and financial scandals, and the amassing of fantastic wealth by a few individuals, often through unscrupulous business practices. The term was taken from *The Gilded Age: A Tale of Today,* a novel by MARK TWAIN and C. D. Warner published in 1874. The scandals and speculative schemes of the age included the bilking of the Union Pacific Railroad by the Credit Mobilier construction company and the "Whiskey Ring," a conspiracy by liquor distillers and government officials that defrauded the national government of millions of dollars. Officials in state and city governments also bellied up to the "great barbecue," another name for the Gilded Age, the most notorious feaster being WILLIAM MARCY TWEED of New York City.

Gilman, Charlotte Anna Perkins (1860–1935) American feminist, humanist, and author. Born in Hartford, Connecticut, she became known as a social critic with the publication of *Women and Economics: The Economic Relation between Men and Women as a Factor in Social Evolution* (1898). In it she discusses the rise of social and economic domination by men since the agricultural age and the possibilities for a new society built on the female qualities of nurturing and regeneration. She believed such changes could come only when women saw the need to fight for their autonomy. Best known of her fiction is the short story of one woman's madness, "The Yellow Wallpaper" (1892). A highly influential theorist in her day, she lost influence in the twentieth century until the advent of the women's movement. Her twentieth-century works include *The Home* (1903), *The Man-Made World* (1911), and *Herland,* a utopian novel serialized in her magazine *Forerunner* but not published in volume form until 1979.

Gissing, George Robert (1857–1903) English writer. Born in Yorkshire, he was admitted to Owens College on a scholarship but was expelled and imprisoned in 1876 for stealing in an attempt to help a prostitute.

After a brief trip to the United States, where he taught school in Waltham, Massachusetts, and wrote fiction for Chicago newspapers, Gissing returned to England in 1879 and married the prostitute he had tried to reform. The marriage quickly ended in disaster, but Gissing tried to support the woman until her death in 1888.

Gissing's first novel, *Workers in the Dawn,* was published in 1880, and the writer continued to produce his social realist fiction at a rate of about one novel each year, but he failed to earn much money from any of them. His 1891 novel *New Grub Street,* is generally considered his best work; it addresses the problems of poverty and commercialism connected with Victorian literary life. Gissing was also known for his nonfiction, including a critical study of CHARLES DICKENS published in 1898 and *Private Papers of Henry Ryecroft,* a collection of short essays published after his death.

Gissing remarried in 1891 but left his wife and two sons six years later and married Gabrielle Fleury, the French translator of *New Grub Street.* He remained in France until his death.

Gladstone, William [Ewart] (1809–1898) English politician. Four times the prime minister of GREAT BRITAIN, Gladstone was a dominant figure in English politics during the Victorian era. He was born in Liverpool to a Scottish father who had made his fortune in the slave trade. After attending Eton and Oxford, he was encouraged by his father, a Tory member of Parliament, to run for office. He was first elected as a Tory in 1833.

Gladstone held several cabinet posts under ROBERT PEEL and other prime ministers. He was undersecretary of war and colonies (1834–35), vice-president (1841), and president (1843) of the Board of Trade, and Colonial Secretary (1845–46). His most notable Cabinet post was chancellor of the Exchequer (1852–55 and 1859–66).

During the 1840s and 1850s the old Tory and Whig parties began to decline as more Englishmen secured suffrage. Both parties gave way to the LIBERAL PARTY and the CONSERVATIVE PARTY. Gladstone, who had come to question England's treatment of IRELAND, joined the Liberals in 1859 and became its leader in 1866. Under his stewardship the Liberal Party stood for free trade, religious freedom, anti-imperialism, expanded suffrage, and more conciliatory policies toward Ireland. Gladstone's major adversary was Conservative Party leader BENJAMIN DISRAELI, who was more highly favored by Queen VICTORIA but served as prime minister only briefly, in 1868 and again in 1874–80, while Gladstone served in that office four times: 1868–74, 1880–85, 1886, and 1892–94.

The Liberals won a majority of Parliament seats in 1868, and Gladstone began his first

William Gladstone, who served as England's prime minister for four terms, fought to extend religious and political rights for Ireland.

term as prime minister. His disestablishment of the Church of Ireland in 1869 freed Irish Catholics from supporting a religion contrary to their beliefs. The IRISH LAND ACT OF 1870 gave Irish tenants some rights in their relations with landowners. Gladstone also oversaw the introduction of the secret ballot and ended the sale of military commissions.

Gladstone lost the election of 1874 and retired from public life. Motivated by Disraeli's prosecution of the ANGLO-AFGHAN WARS, he returned to politics in 1879. He won a parliamentary seat and was elected prime minister in 1880. The 1879 election was the first of his MIDLOTHIAN CAMPAIGNS. The campaigns were a new way of electioneering in England and were marked by huge rallies addressed by a national figure. During the campaign Gladstone denounced the Anglo-Afghan Wars and opposed any alliance with the Ottoman Empire, which had killed thousands of its Bulgarian subjects in the 1870s. His second ministry featured two parliamentary reform bills that gave virtually every Englishman the right to vote.

His third ministry was highlighted by the introduction of the first HOME RULE bill in 1886. The bill would have given Ireland control of some of its domestic affairs. The House of Commons rejected it. Controversy over the bill brought down the Liberal government and precipitated the decline of the Liberal Party, as many members bolted to the Conservative Party rather than support Irish autonomy. Gladstone's last tenure as prime minister also foundered on the defeat of Home Rule legislation.

Despite a life dominated by politics, Gladstone found time for other pursuits. He took a special interest in the welfare of London's prostitutes. He often cornered them on the street and lectured them on the moral and physical dangers of their profession. In the 1840s he and his friends established the House of St. Barnabas as a haven for prostitutes. This concern took an unusual turn when he formed the habit of flagellating himself after talks with prostitutes.

Devoutly religious, Gladstone is said to have attended church at least once a day. His love for Homer led him to translate the *Iliad* and write *Studies on Homer and the Homeric Age* (1858).

Godey's Ladies Book See HALE, SARAH JOSEPHA BUELL.

Gogol, Nikolay Vasilyevich (1809–1852) Russian writer. Born in the Ukraine, he grew up on his family's small estate. His father spent much of his free time writing sketches, plays, and poems about Ukrainian life. After finishing school in 1828, Nikolay Gogol moved to St. Petersburg to seek his literary fame. The next year he published *Hans Kuechelgarten,* a long narrative poem that was ridiculed unsparingly by the critics. Gogol immediately bought as many copies of the book as he could find, burned them, and left the country.

Intending to emigrate to the United States, Gogol traveled as far as Sweden before deciding to return to St. Petersburg. In 1831 he published a collection of stories under the pseudonym of Rudy Panko. The same year he met ALEXANDER PUSHKIN, who influenced the writer's choice of subject matter for his stories.

In 1834, Gogol was appointed a professor of history at the University of St. Petersburg. He was an inadequate lecturer, however, and resigned in 1835, pronouncing, "Ignorant I mounted my professor's chair and ignorant I descended." He then turned his attention to literature completely and by year's end had published two volumes of stories, *Mirgorod* and *Arabesques.*

After severe criticism of his play *Revizor* (*The Inspector-General*), which was first performed on April 19, 1836, Gogol traveled to Palestine and then to Rome, where he remained for twelve years. He spent nearly eight years writing the first part of *Dead Souls,* his satiric masterpiece on the corruption, inequality, and stagnation of Russian society. Fyodor DOSTOYEVSKY described the characters in Gogol's novel as "the most profound creations of the Russian genius."

In 1845, Gogol began work on the second part of *Dead Souls,* but in a fit of desperation he burned the manuscript. He then published *Selected Passages from Correspondence with My Friends* (1847), a collection of articles based on letters he had written. The work was also harshly criticized, even by Gogol's friends, but Gogol, rather than fleeing the country, was inspired to return to work on the continuation of *Dead Souls.*

After a trip to Jerusalem in 1848, where Gogol had hoped for a religious epiphany but failed to experience one, he became involved with Matthew Konstantinovski, a fanatical priest who convinced the writer that his literature was sinful. Gogol, fearing that he was eternally damned, burned his second draft of his manuscript, began fasting, and died in 1852.

Gompers, Samuel (1850–1924) English-born American labor leader. Born in London, he went to New York City in 1863. He worked as a cigar maker and at age twenty-four became head of the industry local (1874–81). In his organizing tactics he rejected radical politics and ideological arguments in favor of achieving practical, short-term goals such as higher wages, shorter hours, and better working conditions. In 1881 he helped found the Federation of Organized Trades and Labor Unions, which was reorganized in 1886 as the American Federation of Labor (AFL). Gompers was elected president of the AFL and helped make it the first association of trade unions in the United States. He led drives to organize skilled craftsmen such as plumbers and electricians but mostly ignored unskilled laborers. During World War I he served on several government boards and ensured labor loyalty to the war effort. Although he kept his distance from unskilled workers, his rejection of socialism and revolutionary appeals helped win acceptance for the labor movement, thereby indirectly assisting the organizing efforts of lesser-skilled workers. His autobiography, *Seventy Years of Life and Labor,* was published in 1925.

Gonne, Maud (1866–1953) Irish political activist. Born in Surrey, England, to English parents, she moved with her father to Dublin when he was assigned to the British garrison. In the 1890s she worked for famine relief in the western counties and became a prominent voice for Irish independence. A supporter of the LAND LEAGUE and of JAMES CONNOLLY, she led protests against the DIAMOND JUBILEE visit by Queen VICTORIA to Ireland. Because women were barred from most revolutionary groups, Gonne organized a women's group in 1900, called Inghinidhe na hEireann (Daughters of Erin), which was allied with Sinn Fein. She was also an actress, painter, linguist, and one of the most famous beauties of late Victorian times. She was immortalized in several poems and plays by poet WILLIAM BUTLER YEATS, whose passionate love for her "beauty like a tightened bow" was never completely returned. She was briefly married (1903–5) to Irish revolutionary Major John MacBride, who was executed for his part in the Easter 1916 Rebellion. In later years she worked for the rights of political prisoners. An autobiography, *A Servant of the Queen,* appeared in 1938.

Goodrich, Benjamin Franklin (1841–1888) American businessman and rubber maker. A physician by trade, Goodrich became a businessman after his medical service during the Civil War, concentrating his efforts on developing uses for rubber. The development of the VULCANIZATION process in 1839 greatly increased the potential applications for rubber, particularly in transportation and medical and household uses. One of his early inventions was the rubber fire hose, which was more durable than the leather hoses previously used in firefighting. The hose became a best-selling item for Goodrich's business, the B. F. Goodrich Company, which was founded in 1872. In 1898 the company introduced varieties of multi-ply "clincher" rubber tires, another popular product.

Goodyear, Charles (1800–1860) American inventor. Born in New Haven, Connecticut, Goodyear was working in the hardware business in Philadelphia when he began experimenting with alternative processes for "curing" rubber, which became unusable in extreme temperatures—brittle when cold, sticky when hot. In 1839 while experimenting in his kitchen, Goodyear accidentally overheated a mixture of rubber, sulfur, and white lead that produced the supple, elastic substance he was looking for. Because he had exhausted his savings in experimentation, he was unable to perfect the curing or VULCANIZATION process and did not obtain a patent until 1844. By that time a British scientist, Thomas Hancock, had studied Goodyear's work and obtained a British patent. Other competitors profited from Goodyear's discovery, but he remained poor; he was in and out of debtors' prisons and was $200,000 in debt at his death. In 1898, four decades after his death, the Goodyear Tire and Rubber Company was founded in Akron, Ohio. Other than the name, it had no link to Charles Goodyear or his family.

Gordon, Charles George (1833–1885) English soldier and administrator. Gordon, the son of a military officer, distinguished himself during the CRIMEAN WAR at Sebastopol. In 1860 he fought in CHINA in the "Arrow War," or Second OPIUM WAR, taking part in the burning of Peking's Summer Palace. His "Ever Victorious Army" played an important role in crushing the Taiping Rebellion in 1863 and 1864. His exploits earned him the nickname "Chinese" Gordon.

In 1873 the khedive of Egypt commissioned him to establish control over the SUDAN and fight the slave trade. He was appointed governor of the Sudan in 1877, but bad health caused him to resign in 1880. He then served in India, China, and South Africa.

Gordon returned to the Sudan in 1884 to evacuate Egyptian troops from KHARTOUM, which was besieged by the MAHDI, the Sudanese rebel leader. In January 1885, Khartoum was overrun, and Gordon was killed just days before a relief column arrived. The popular Gordon's death horrified Britain and helped bring down the government of WILLIAM GLADSTONE.

Gothic Revival Architectural movement. The revival took its inspiration from the medieval building aesthetic known as Gothic. Interest in the Gothic style had been growing in Britain since the late eighteenth century, following a long period when architects inspired by classical models derided the medieval style as barbaric. Early neo-Gothic structures, such as the Strawberry Hill home of eighteenth-century English author Horace Walpole, were exaggerated and picturesque, designed to titillate with a creepy sense of superstition and ruin. But theorists of the Victorian Gothic Revival, such as AUGUSTUS PUGIN and JOHN RUSKIN, emphasized the structural clarity, coherence, and functionalism of the Gothic style, together with its organic expression of moral and spiritual values. The neo-Gothic style of WESTMINSTER PALACE, seat of the Houses of Parliament, was designed by CHARLES BARRY and AUGUSTUS PUGIN (1837–67). Numerous secular buildings, churches, and country houses were also designed in this style: Manchester Town Hall (1868–77) by Alfred Waterhouse; New Law Courts in London (1874–82) by George Edmund Street; and St. Pancras Station in London (1868–74) by GEORGE GILBERT SCOTT. The style was also popular in the United States, employed notably by JAMES RENWICK in St. Patrick's Cathedral, New York City (1858–79). Despite its influence, neo-Gothic was but one of the many revivals that characterized VICTORIAN STYLE. Slow and expensive to carry out, Gothic designs declined as the SKYSCRAPER and other new forms took advantage of modern materials and speedier construction methods. Gothic Revival can be seen as one aspect of Victorian MEDIEVALISM, a broadly expressed interest in the culture and ethos of the Middle Ages.

Gould, Jay (1836–1892) American speculator and railroad magnate. Born in Roxbury, New York, he worked as a store clerk and surveyor's assistant before acquiring a tannery. By the 1860s he was a Wall Street broker who specialized in buying railroads. In 1865 he and JAMES FISK bamboozled CORNELIUS VANDERBILT into buying phony Erie Railroad stock and became the company's majority owners. Gould continued to buy railroads, and by the time of his death was said to own 10 percent of the mileage in the United States. He also controlled the WESTERN UNION telegraph company. He and Fisk tried to corner the gold market in 1869, a maneuver that bankrupted many other speculators but swelled Gould's coffers. He was widely detested because of his unscrupulous financial schemes, and he admitted to being "the most hated man in America."

graft American term for dishonest earnings, usually those of politicians. Its first recorded use in this sense was in 1859; it may have come from the British slang word "graft," meaning "any kind of work, especially illicit work." See TAMMANY HALL.

Grant, Ulysses Simpson (1822–1885) Eighteenth president of the UNITED STATES. Born in Ohio, Grant graduated from West Point in 1843 with a mediocre record. Captain Grant served with distinction in the MEXICAN WAR but resigned his commission in 1854, perhaps due to heavy drinking. He struggled unsuccessfully to support himself and his family through farming until 1860 when his family hired him as a clerk at its dry goods store in Illinois.

The U.S. CIVIL WAR lifted Grant from obscurity. Commissioned a colonel, then brigadier general, of a volunteer regiment shortly after the outbreak of war, Grant fought his first battle at Belmont, Missouri, in 1861. In 1862 his victories at forts Henry and Donelson in Tennessee won him national recognition and a promotion to major general. After his next great victory, the capture of Vicksburg in 1863, he was given command of the armies in the western theater. His string of triumphs continued, and he was made commander of all Union forces in 1864. He then faced Confederate general ROBERT E. LEE in a series of battles in Virginia that led to Lee's surrender in April 1865.

After the war, Grant was Secretary of War under President ANDREW JOHNSON, but he alienated Johnson by making alliances with REPUBLICANS who wished to pursue harsher RECONSTRUCTION policies against the South. He won the Republican nomination for president in 1868 and defeated Democrat Horatio Seymour in a landslide.

Grant's eight-year presidency was marred by scandal and corruption. The scandals never touched him personally, but he seemed incapable of appointing honest and capable high officials. He failed to win the Republican presidential nomination in 1876 and again in 1880. Financial hardship struck again in 1884 when the brokerage firm he helped establish went bankrupt due to his partner's dishonesty.

Deeply in debt and suffering from terminal throat cancer, Grant spent the next two years writing his memoirs. Despite the agony of his illness, he finished the two-volume *Personal Memoirs* two days before he died. An instant commercial and critical success, it remains one of the great works of military history.

Gray's Anatomy (1858) Text on the human body by English anatomist Henry Gray (1825?–1861). Famous for its completeness, clarity, and innovative illustrations by Henry Van Dyke Carter, it has remained a basic resource for physicians and medical students. Its original title was *Anatomy, Descriptive and Surgical.*

Great Britain Island off the northwest coast of Europe comprising England, Scotland, and Wales. In the Victorian Age, it was the dominant partner in the United Kingdom of Great Britain and IRELAND. The reign of Queen VICTORIA, from 1837 to 1901, marked the climax of centuries of political and economic expansion for this small island nation. This was Britain's heyday, the moment when London seemed the capital of the world. During Victoria's reign, Britain was the center of a world empire, the greatest naval and shipping power, the bearer of vast political influence, the world leader in manufacturing and commerce. From its scientists, inventors, and engineers came a host of discoveries and innovations. Its architecture, decorative style, and fashion were imitated from America to New Zealand. Its writers, artists, and scholars brought forth an abundance of works, many surviving their time. Its distinctive values, obsessions, habits, and contradictions influenced mores and manners throughout the world.

At the time of Victoria's accession on June 20, 1837, Great Britain was undergoing dramatic economic, social, and political change. The British economy had been transformed by INDUSTRIALIZATION in the eighteenth and early nineteenth centuries. Using machinery with STEAM POWER, the textile industry had soared, attracting capitalists and drawing in masses of laborers. The workers lived in newly burgeoning towns—MANCHESTER, Birmingham, Glasgow—that sprouted around the mills of the north, in Lancashire, Lanarkshire, Monmouthshire. Iron and coal were in high demand, as RAILROADS sped transportation of raw materials and finished product.

With the economic changes came demographic changes that made some aspects of Britain's parliamentary system obsolete. Over the course of the nineteenth century, the British population grew by more than 200 percent, from 11 million in 1801 to 16 million in 1831 and 37 million in 1901. The population growth was lopsided, with the industrial north vastly outstripping the agricultural south. As a result, by century's end, Britain's population had shifted from being predominantly rural to being predominantly urban and industrial. Until 1832, however, elected representation in the House of Commons—one of the two divisions of Parliament, the other being the House of Lords—failed to reflect these changes. The new industrial towns were excluded, while "rotten boroughs"—thinly populated rural districts dominated by hereditary landowners—were overrepresented. The REFORM BILL OF 1832, which increased the electorate by about 50 percent and transferred some representation to the industrial cities, began the process of parliamentary reform that would continue throughout the age.

Class structure was also changing. The new industrial wealth had already brought about the formation of new middle classes—bankers, businessmen, lawyers, engineers, clerks—that grew in numbers and political power throughout the Victorian Age. The more prosperous members of these classes sought to live as "gentlefolk," imitating and seeking the approval of the gentry or landed aristocracy, perhaps even being admitted through marriage or the awarding of titles for public service. But the interests of nobility and middle classes remained distinct. At the same time, the new lower class of industrial workers—termed the proletariat by KARL MARX and the populace by MATTHEW ARNOLD—increasingly demanded that its voice be heard as well.

Its voice was heard in CHARTISM, a movement in 1838–48, by working people rooted in the period of economic distress with which the Victorian Age began. Unsatisfied with the Reform Bill of 1832, the Chartists called for political reforms that included universal male suffrage, abolition of property qualifications for members of Parliament, and a secret ballot. Diverse in its aims, Chartism included people who sought to redistribute land, abolish the harsh POOR LAW OF 1834, and promote trade unions and cooperatives. Though the movement generally took a constitutional rather than a revolutionary approach, some Chartists advocated violent means, and the movement aroused fear and denunciation from many in the upper classes. Though Chartism ended in apparent failure in 1848, many of its demands eventually were enacted into law.

Contemporary with Chartism was the middle-class ANTI–CORN LAW LEAGUE, organized in 1839 to demand repeal of the CORN LAWS. By imposing duties on imported "corn"—the British term for grain or wheat—these laws protected the agricultural income of Britain's landed aristocracy but kept the price of food high. A symbol of the faith of the commercial middle classes in free trade, the Anti–Corn Law League was helped by economic depression, worker unrest, and the IRISH POTATO FAMINE that began in 1845. With the prime ministry of ROBERT PEEL, free trade gained the day. Peel's government reduced or abolished hundreds of duties, repealed the restrictive Navigation Acts (1849, 1854), and in 1846 repealed the CORN LAWS.

Free trade proved instrumental to the nearly three decades of economic boom that followed. In record quantities, Britain produced and exported iron, coal, textiles, heavy machinery, and manufactured goods. The country was unified by railroads, TELEGRAPH lines, bridges, tunnels, and cheap and efficient POSTAL SERVICES, while British SHIPS provided ready access to distant markets. The credit and insurance of British financial houses and the expertise of British engineers were sought throughout the world. The middle classes grew as new fortunes were made. Having weathered a period when other European nations were undergoing the REVOLUTIONS OF 1848, prosperous mid-Victorians expressed their optimism and self-confidence in the GREAT EXHIBITION OF 1851, celebrating the growth of industry and technology.

During this period, British political parties underwent a realignment that did not end until the late 1860s. While the former Tory Party reemerged as the CONSERVATIVE PARTY and the former Whig party as the LIBERAL PARTY, no single party was able to guarantee extended control over the House of Commons. The task of forming coalition cabinets fell frequently to Queen Victoria and ALBERT, her husband and primary advisor who died in 1861. After the REFORM BILL OF 1867 doubled the electorate and redistributed parliamentary seats, however, a strong two-party system emerged. For nearly two decades the government was led by one of two men: Conservative leader BENJAMIN DISRAELI (1868, 1874–80) or Liberal leader WILLIAM GLADSTONE (1868–74, 1880–85). Gladstone returned to govern in 1886 and 1892–94, while the Conservative MARQUIS OF SALISBURY served for most of the remaining years of Victoria's reign (1885–86, 1886–92, 1895–1902). (See also BRITISH PRIME MINISTERS.)

Disraeli and Gladstone instituted reforms that extended political participation and improved social conditions. Ballots became secret in 1872, while the REFORM BILL OF 1884 and that of 1885 ushered in almost universal male suffrage and continued to redistribute seats to the larger towns. The army, CIVIL SERVICE, and judiciary underwent needed reform. Social legislation was enacted to improve public health and sanitation; regulate factories, housing, and pure food; institute a national system of primary education (see EDUCATION ACTS); and strengthen the position of labor unions, such as the Trades Union Congress instituted in 1868. Together with falling food prices after 1873, such legislation did much to improve the lot of the working classes and ensure the stability of Victorian society.

In foreign affairs, Victorian Britain, for the most part, kept peace with the other European powers and the growing United States. Under Lord PALMERSTON, who dominated foreign policy from the 1830s to the early 1860s, and later under the professional handling of the expanded Foreign and Colonial offices, Britain used skillful diplomacy and economic and military leverage to maintain a balance of power in Europe. Its only major European military involvement was the CRIMEAN WAR (1853–56) when Britain and France joined forces to check Russian expansion at the expense of a weakened Ottoman Empire. There were frequent near-clashes, such as the Don Pacifico Affair with Greece in 1850 (see PALMERSTON) and the Oregon dispute with the United States in 1845, which led to the OREGON TREATY. But for the most part Britain stayed at peace with other Western powers, hence the term "Pax Britannica." At the same time it wielded enormous influence in such diplomatic forums as the Congress of BERLIN (1878) in which Britain gained possession of Cyprus and helped block Russian expansion in the Ottoman Empire.

During the Victorian Age, Britain greatly expanded and consolidated its own empire. British IMPERIALISM, like that of other European powers, was motivated by many factors: the hunger for raw materials and markets; the vital interest in supplying merchant ships and protecting them with naval bases; humanitarian goals such as the abolition of SLAVERY, accomplished in the British Empire in 1833; the missionary goal of spreading Christianity; an attitude, epitomized by "The White Man's Burden," a poem by RUDYARD KIPLING, that held Western civilization, particularly in its British form, to be superior and of benefit to colonial natives (see WHITE MAN'S BURDEN); the pride and prestige that came from seeing British red painted on so many parts of the world map (see JINGOISM, ALL-RED ROUTE, CAPE TO CAIRO). Under Queen Victoria, the British Empire, already hundreds of years old and incorporating such lands as INDIA, CANADA, AUSTRALIA, and the Cape Colony (see SOUTH AFRICA), grew even larger and more profitable. In AFRICA, the new additions included RHODESIA, UGANDA, Kenya, and Nigeria; in Asia, HONG KONG, THE PUNJAB, Burma, Malaya (see SOUTHEAST ASIA), and Aden (see YEMEN); in OCEANIA, NEW ZEALAND, Papua New Guinea, Fiji, and Pitcairn Island. Britain also gained *de facto* rule of EGYPT and the SUDAN, increased its influence over CHINA and AFGHANISTAN, and exercised varying degrees of suzerainty over the TRANSVAAL.

The benefits of empire came at a high cost in blood and treasure. Despite the term "Pax Britannica," the Victorian Age was a time of almost continuous colonial warfare. In any given year Britain's military forces were fighting somewhere, in some corner of the globe: suppressing revolts, retaliating for attacks, conquering territory, asserting trade rights, competing for authority with a rival imperial power. The larger conflicts included the OPIUM WARS with China (1839–42, 1856–60), the INDIAN MUTINY or Sepoy Rebellion (1857–59), the Sikh Wars in the Punjab (1845–46, 1848–49), the ANGLO-AFGHAN WARS (1838–42, 1878–80), the Sudanese Wars (1881–85, 1896–99), and the BOER WAR (1899–1902). But there were hundreds of smaller conflicts and actions: the Maori Wars in New Zealand (1860–72), the Anglo-Persian War over Persian encroachment on Afghanistan (1856–57), the Abyssinian War over Ethiopian imprisonment of British diplomats (1867–68), the suppression of revolt in Jamaica (1865), action against pirates in Borneo (1845) and Malay (1863), suppression of numerous insurrections in India, and numerous clashes with indigenous Africans, including the ZULU WAR (1879).

No one system of administration prevailed in all of Britain's colonies. Some were protectorates, some crown colonies, some chartered to private companies. Colonies with large white settlements, such as Australia and New Zealand, were gradually given a large degree of self-government. In Canada, for example, the British North America Act of 1867 established a self-governing dominion. In colonies that were mostly nonwhite, government was generally autocratic, masterminded at a distance by the Colonial Office in London. Forms of administration could change rapidly. India began the Victorian era under the rule of the BRITISH EAST INDIA COMPANY, but the Indian Mutiny (1857–59) persuaded Britain to transfer it to direct crown rule.

Agitation to be free of Britain's rule was nowhere stronger than within the United Kingdom itself, in Ireland. By the 1870s and 1880s, under the leadership of ISAAC BUTT and CHARLES STEWART PARNELL, a movement for Irish HOME RULE gained force. Though supported by Gladstone, who instituted such reforms as the disestablishment of the Irish church, Home Rule bills failed to pass in 1886 and 1893, leaving Irish nationalism unsatisfied.

The conflict over Home Rule was one source of the darker mood that prevailed in late Victorian times. The GREAT DEPRESSION of 1873–96, a period marked by lower prices, profits, and interest rates, hurt business and the middle classes, though it paradoxically boosted living standards for the working classes, who enjoyed a lower cost of living. Britain's international preeminence as a military and industrial power was threatened by the emergence of a unified Germany in 1871 and the rapid expansion and industrialization of the United States. Faith in free trade grew weaker as moderate protective measures were instituted. Doubts about the empire were fed by military defeats such as that of General CHARLES GORDON at KHARTOUM in 1885 and the initial reverses in the Boer War in 1899. Still, Britain remained powerful and prosperous even at the century's end.

Victorian artists and writers made numerous contributions to the world's cultural heritage. The novel was the era's most characteristic form of expression, handled with richness and power by, among others, CHARLES DICKENS, WILLIAM MAKEPEACE THACKERAY, EMILY BRONTË, CHARLOTTE BRONTË, GEORGE ELIOT, ELIZABETH GASKELL, ANTHONY TROLLOPE, and THOMAS HARDY. Poets included ALFRED, Lord TENNYSON, ROBERT BROWNING, ELIZABETH BARRETT BROWNING, and GERARD MANLEY HOPKINS; nonfiction prose stylists JOHN RUSKIN, THOMAS CARLYLE, JOHN HENRY NEWMAN, MATTHEW ARNOLD, THOMAS BABINGTON MACAULAY, and WALTER PATER. Irish voices included GEORGE BERNARD SHAW, OSCAR WILDE, and WILLIAM BUTLER YEATS. Painters included J. M. W. TURNER, DANTE GABRIEL ROSSETTI, WILLIAM HOLMAN HUNT, JOHN EVERETT MILLAIS, and EDWARD BURNE-JONES; architects and designers CHARLES BARRY, AUGUSTUS PUGIN, and WILLIAM MORRIS; illustrators GEORGE CRUIKSHANK and AUBREY BEARDSLEY.

Victorian scientists included CHARLES DARWIN, JAMES CLERK MAXWELL, WILLIAM THOMSON LORD KELVIN, Sir CHARLES LYELL, MICHAEL FARADAY, RODERICK I. MURCHISON, JOHN SNOW, and JOSEPH LISTER. Victorian explorers included DAVID LIVINGSTONE, Sir HENRY STANLEY, and Sir RICHARD FRANCIS BURTON. Victorian philosophers included JOHN STUART MILL and HERBERT SPENCER.

Many Victorians took their moral attitudes seriously, while others viewed them with a jaundiced eye. The Victorians believed in strength of character and earnestness of purpose, but such attitudes were wickedly lampooned by aesthetes such as Oscar Wilde, notably in his play *The Importance of Being Earnest* (1895). They were notoriously prim about sexual matters, yet many were patrons of the flourishing PROSTITUTION and PORNOGRAPHY industries. They believed in rigid separation of gender roles, but a flourishing feminist movement pointed out the oppressive aspects of those roles. Christianity was esteemed and practiced in a variety of forms: the OXFORD MOVEMENT of the 1830s, the Evangelicalism of the SALVATION ARMY, the quiet devotion of many Church of England members. But religious doubt was widespread, with traditional faith threatened by such works as Charles Darwin's *THE ORIGIN OF SPECIES* (1859) and ESSAYS AND REVIEWS (1860), and atheism, agnosticism, and unconventional beliefs such as SPIRITUALISM openly espoused.

Queen Victoria died on January 22, 1901, and was succeeded by her son EDWARD VII. The climax of Great Britain's power was over, although the signs were not yet apparent to all. Not until Britain withstood two world wars, surrendered industrial and military preeminence to the United States, and divested itself of most of its empire was its new and humbler status clear. Yet its moment of glory in the Victorian Age still reverberates culturally and politically and persists in the world's imagination.

Great Britain Steamship. Launched in 1843 and designed by English engineer ISAMBARD KINGDOM BRUNEL, the huge vessel combined an iron hull with screw propulsion, a design that paved the way for still larger and more powerful steamships. It was an advance on Brunel's earlier wooden paddle steamer, the *Great Western* (1837); it was vastly surpassed in size by his later GREAT EASTERN (1858). See also SHIPS.

Great Depression Sustained economic slump. Not to be confused with the Great Depression of the 1930s, the "Great Depression" of the nineteenth century was a worldwide period of deflation that ran from 1873 to 1896, despite overall economic growth. Lowering prices, interest rates, and profits, the depression actually improved living standards for the British working classes by making food and other necessities cheaper. For the middle classes, however, who were less concerned with necessities and more with the expenses of maintaining middle-class social status, lower profits and interest income proved highly uncomfortable.

Great Eastern Steamship. Launched in 1858 and designed by British engineer ISAMBARD KINGDOM BRUNEL, it was originally called *Leviathan*. It was the largest of the SHIPS of its day. At 700 feet in length, it was more than five times the size of Brunel's previous design, the GREAT BRITAIN (1843). Though incorporating sails and screw and paddle-wheel propulsion, the enormous ship was underpowered and was not commercially successful. It did inspire, however, the development of future ocean liners with more efficient engines and was used to lay the first permanent transatlantic CABLE in 1865–66. It is not to be confused with the first of Brunel's three steamship designs, the GREAT WESTERN (1837), a paddle steamer.

Great Exhibition of 1851 The common name of the "Great Exhibition of the Works of Industry of All Nations." It was also popularly known as the CRYSTAL PALACE Exhibition after the monumental structure that housed it in Hyde Park, London. The Society of Arts, headed by Prince ALBERT who helped plan the event, organized this first international exhibition. Some one hundred thousand displays of industrial progress and mechanical ingenuity, along with works of art, filled the 1.75 miles of galleries. Six million people visited the show, which opened in May and closed in October. Fittingly, this celebration of the prosperity and material progress of the Victorian era returned a profit of £186,000, which served to endow the VICTORIA AND ALBERT MUSEUM.

Great Expectations English novel. Written by CHARLES DICKENS in 1860–61, it is considered by some his greatest work. The novel is narrated by its principal character, Phillip Pirrip, called "Pip," who recounts the melodramatic fortunes of his upbringing by his volatile sister and her husband, the kindly blacksmith Joe Gargery. Introduced to the beautiful Estella at the house of the embittered Miss Havisham, who is morbidly obssessed with her abandonment by her fiancé on her wedding night, Pip strives to become a gentleman in order to win Estella's heart. Aided by a mysterious benefactor, he cruelly abandons Joe and travels to London, where he is shocked to learn that his benefactor is Abel Magwitch, an ex-convict whom Pip had helped as a boy in the novel's opening scenes. Pip also learns that Estella is unhappily married to his old adversary Bentley Drummle. In the original ending, Pip and Estella remain apart, but Dickens substituted a happy conclusion, in which the two characters are united.

Great Game Nineteenth-century contest for power between the British and Russian empires in central Asia. The Great Game involved diplomacy, warfare, and espionage. The term was coined by British officer Arthur Conolly and made famous by RUDYARD KIPLING in his 1901 novel *Kim.*

Great Trek Series of eastward and northward migrations carried out by BOERS, or Afrikaners, in Cape Colony (now part of SOUTH AFRICA) from 1835 to the 1840s. The Boers, descendants of Dutch settlers, resented the takeover of Cape Colony by the British in 1806. They particularly disliked the abolition of slavery in 1833 and what seemed to them the excessively liberal influence of missionaries and humanitarians in dealing with black Africans. Migration also resulted from less political motives, notably exhaustion of land needed for herding and farming. About fourteen thousand people, including Boers and black Africans, moved out of Cape Colony in wagon trains and established three republics in the African interior: the TRANSVAAL (South African Republic), the Orange Free State, and Natal. All eventually became part of modern South Africa. The Great Trek helped to forge a national consciousness for the Boers; the conflict between the British and the Boers came to a head in the BOER WAR (1899–1902).

Great Western Wooden paddle wheel steamer. Launched in 1837 and designed by British engineer ISAMBARD KINGDOM BRUNEL, it was the first of his three steamship designs. The others were *GREAT BRITAIN* (1843) and *GREAT EASTERN* (1858). The largest of its day, it was the first regularly scheduled steamship. (Also see SHIPS.)

Great Western Railway Railroad from London to Bristol. Opened in 1838 and designed by ISAMBARD KINGDOM BRUNEL, it was later extended into Devon and Cornwall. The fastest railway of its time, it incorporated the latest engineering and was much admired by the public. Its stations included Paddington, Bath, and Bristol Temple Meads; its bridges included Maidenhead and Wharncliffe. Its rails were 7 feet apart, wider than the 4-feet 8.5-inch gauge used by George and Robert Stephenson and allowing for more spacious rolling stock. The Great Western Railway is depicted in J. M. W. TURNER'S famous painting *Rain, Steam, and Speed* (1844).

Greece Country in the extreme southeast of Europe. Greece consists of the mountainous extension of the Balkan peninsula and adjacent islands in the Aegean and Ionian seas. The present-day population is largely Greek-speaking and Eastern Orthodox Christian, though it was less homogenous in the Victorian era. Prior to 1832, Greece was part of the OTTOMAN EMPIRE. Outside Greece, a large Greek-speaking population played an important part in the government and commerce of the empire in the Balkans and the cities of Asia Minor. The Greek Orthodox Church enjoyed a privileged position in the empire and effectively ruled large areas of the Balkans.

Dissatisfaction with the corruption of the local Ottoman Turkish government and the infusion of Western ideas of nationalism led to revolts beginning in 1821. The long Greek war for independence was notable for the enthusiastic support of Romantics such as English poet Lord Byron, who died in Greece in 1824, and for chronic internal dissension. The intervention of England, France, and Russia finally assured Greek independence in 1832. Prince Otto of Wittelsbach, son of King Ludwig of Bavaria, was chosen by the intervening powers to be king. The new kingdom of Greece consisted of about half the territory of modern Greece and a quarter of the extant Greek-speaking population.

The early years of the kingdom saw continuous fighting among various factions. After several years of autocratic rule, Otto finally issued a long-promised constitution in 1843 after a revolt was squelched by the army. He avidly embraced the cause of Greek IRREDENTISM, proclaiming the *Megali Idea* ("Great Idea") that Greece should include all Greek areas within its boundaries. With this in mind, he covertly sided with Russia in the CRIMEAN WAR, supporting the infiltration of guerrilla bands into northern Greece in an unsucessful bid to annex it. He continued to rule virtually at will through extensive manipulation of the electoral process. Disgust with his policies and his failure to secure any new territory led to a coup in 1862.

Again the great powers intervened and picked George of Holstein to be king. He took power in 1863, and Britain ceded the Ionian Islands to Greece in 1864. Earlier, Great Britain had clashed with Greece in the Don Pacifico affair (1850) in which British foreign secretary Lord PALMERSTON ordered the seizure of Greek ships in the harbor of Piraeus in pursuit of the unheeded property claims of British subject David Pacifico. The intervention raised protests from France and Russia, and led Queen VICTORIA to require Palmerston to consult with her in advance about his future actions.

George ruled as a constitutional monarch with extensive power, but the political system was reformed to ensure the power of the majority party even when not preferred by the king. Under George, Greece gained Thessaly by Turkish cession in 1881. The 1870s and 1880s were a time of moderate growth and industrialization. A rivalry developed among Greece, Serbia, and Bulgaria for control of Macedonia and other remaining Ottoman possessions.

In the 1890s Greece suffered from a debt crisis and economic depression. Tens of thousands of Greeks immigrated, mostly to the United States. In 1897, Greece was easily defeated by the Ottoman Empire in a war over Crete, which still belonged to the Turks. The *Megali Idea* was not abandoned until the disastrous Greco-Turkish War (1920–23) ended in a wholesale exchange of minority populations, ending the presence of Greeks in Turkey.

Greeley, Horace (1811–1872) American journalist and politician. Greeley grew up in New Hampshire, the son of a poor farmer, and began his journalism career in 1826 at the age of fifteen when he joined a Vermont newspaper. He left Vermont after the paper closed and moved to New York City in 1831. There he worked as a newspaper compositor and started a printing business. In 1834 he established the *New Yorker*, a penny newspaper that he ran until 1841. He contributed articles to the *Daily Whig*, a paper of the Whig Party, and at the urging of the state's Whig leaders he started the *New York Tribune* in 1841 as an inexpensive pro-Whig newspaper. A national edition, the *Weekly Tribune*, was established the same year.

Under his thirty-year editorship the *Tribune* became one of the most popular and influential papers in the nation. It minimized sensationalist crime reporting and devoted more space to political and literary matters than its rivals. This approach was successful, and by 1906 the national edition had a circulation of two hundred thousand.

The paper made Greeley a force in New York state politics and gave him a national audience for his provocative editorials on the issues of the day. At various times he supported the temperance movement, women's rights, free public education, and the labor movement. The famous phrase attributed to him, "Go west, young man, go west," which actually originated in an article by John Babsone Soule reprinted by Greeley, indicated his support for distributing free western lands to homesteaders.

Greeley aligned himself with the country's antislavery forces. He opposed the MEXICAN WAR and eloquently denounced the Kansas-Nebraska Act, which allowed settlers in northern territories to approve the extension of slavery into lands historically closed to it. He abandoned the moribund Whig Party and helped form the REPUBLICAN PARTY in 1854. Greeley backed ABRAHAM LINCOLN in the 1860 election but at first opposed going to war to keep the seceding states in the Union. He later vigorously supported the war. His support of Lincoln's 1864 campaign was qualified because the president had refused to free the slaves in the border states that had remained in the Union. After the war he supported suffrage for blacks while at the same time helping to bail JEFFERSON DAVIS out of prison.

Greeley's spirited editorials attacked the corrupt administration of the first presidency of ULYSSES GRANT (1869–72). The head of the *Tribune* ran for president against Grant in 1872. He was backed by reform elements of the Republican Party under the banner of the Liberal Republican Party. He also won the nomination of a DEMOCRATIC PARTY he had formerly excoriated for its pro-southern sympathies and its association with the corruption of TAMMANY HALL. Greeley's reputation as a crank and the Democrats' tepid support translated into a Grant landslide. The vicious campaign, coupled with the death of his wife, left Greeley insane. He died shortly after the election.

Greeley wrote *The American Conflict,* a two-volume history of the CIVIL WAR and the abolitionist movement (1864–66). He also published *Recollections of a Busy Life* (1868).

Greenaway, Kate (1846–1901) English illustrator and watercolor painter. A close friend of JOHN RUSKIN, Greenaway is famous for her fanciful, humorous, delicately colored illustrations for children's books. Her characters were oddly costumed in the Empire style of France, which soon became known as the "Kate Greenaway style." As a result, she influenced the design of contemporary children's clothes.

Among the books for which she provided text as well as illustrations are *Under the Window* (1879), *A Day in a Child's Life* (1881), and *The Language of Flowers* (1885).

greenhouse Glass-enclosed structure in which plants that require controlled temperature and humidity are propagated, cultivated, and maintained. A greenhouse can be an independent structure or attached to another building, such

In her drawing from Under the Window, *Kate Greenaway's illustrations set the trend for clothing design throughout Europe. Photo courtesy of the Library of Congress, Rare Book and Special Collections Division.*

as a conservatory. During Victorian times the greenhouse became exceptionally popular. From the moment prefabricated glass and iron structures were perfected in the mid-nineteenth century, symbolized by the Crystal Palace of 1851, which was erected in Hyde Park around existing trees, public botanical gardens burgeoned, and no grand house was built without a greenhouse.

greenhouse effect Warming effect due to atmospheric gases that tend to trap heat on the earth. Irish physicist John Tyndall discovered the effect in 1863 when he noted that gases such as carbon dioxide and water vapor are transparent to visible light coming from the sun but opaque to INFRARED RADIATION, the form into which sunlight is converted as it strikes the earth's surface. Like the glass walls of a greenhouse, these gases tend to keep the planet warm. Industrial processes that rapidly accelerated in the nineteenth century—notably the burning of coal, wood, and oil—released large quantities of carbon dioxide that may already be leading to the worldwide climatic change known as global warming. Many scientists believe this unintended result of INDUSTRIALIZATION, if not addressed, will have devastating consequences for civilization and ecology.

Gregg shorthand Method of abbreviated writing for use in transcribing words as they are spoken. It was devised in 1888 by Irish inventor John Robert Gregg (1867–1948). Other systems of shorthand were in use, but Gregg shorthand superseded them and came to dominate the field of stenography.

Gregory, Lady [Isabella] Augusta [Persse] (1852–1932) Irish playwright. Following the death of her husband Sir William Gregory in 1892, she became active in the Irish literary renaissance. With her friend WILLIAM BUTLER YEATS, she was instrumental in founding the Irish Literary Theatre in 1899, a precursor to the Abbey Theatre, founded in 1904. She later wrote several one-act plays, including *Spreading the News* (1904) and *The Rising of the Moon* (1906). In his poems Yeats celebrated her noble personality and, in "The Wild Swans at Coole," her estate at Coole Park, a favorite retreat of his.

Gregory XVI, Pope (1765–1846) Head of the Roman Catholic Church, 1831–46. Born Bartolomeo Alberto Cappellari, in the first year of his PAPACY he suppressed a revolution in the Papal States (1831–32) and contended with a period of French occupation (1832–

38). His opposition to religious liberalism was continued on a larger scale by his successor, POPE PIUS IX.

Grévy, François-Paul-Jules (1807–1891) French politician. Grévy served briefly as a local official in the SECOND REPUBLIC (1848–52) but devoted most of his career to law until he entered the Chamber of Deputies in 1868. After the establishment of the THIRD REPUBLIC (1870–1940), he strove to protect it from what he considered dangerous populist tendencies. In 1879 he was elected president of FRANCE, following the resignation of MARIE E. P. M. DE MACMAHON. In his eight years as president, Grévy oversaw colonial expeditions in Tunisia and Indochina. He also presided over the revitalization of the public school system. A corruption scandal involving his closest advisor caused him to resign in 1887.

Grimm, Jacob Ludwig Carl (1785–1863) and **Grimm, Wilhelm Carl** (1786–1859) German philologists and folklorists. The founders of systematic Germanic philology, the two brothers helped establish the field of comparative philology. But they are best known for the collection of tales known as *Grimm's Fairy Tales* (1812–15), which they compiled mostly from oral sources. Originally titled *Kinder-und Hausmärchen,* or *Tales for Young and Old,* the stories were called fairy tales in England despite their lack of fairies. They became popular reading for children around the world, often in bowdlerized form. The most popular tales include "The Frog King," "Rapunzel," and "Hansel and Gretel." In philological circles, Jacob is remembered for "Grimm's law," a principle governing consonant shifts in Indo-European languages, formulated in 1822. The brothers, mainly Jacob, also wrote a German grammar, begun in 1819, and a German dictionary, begun in 1852.

Grove, George (1820–1900) English writer and editor. Born in London, he began his career as a civil engineer, and after working on a number of construction projects, was appointed secretary of the Society of Arts in 1850.

He became secretary of the CRYSTAL PALACE in 1852 and served for almost forty years, writing the program notes for the palace's concerts. With no musical training, Grove's analysis and commentary provided a model that was greatly admired and influential.

In 1867 Grove and the English composer Arthur Seymour Sullivan (see GILBERT AND SULLIVAN) traveled to Vienna and discovered "lost" parts of Schubert's *Rosamunde.* A year later Grove began editing the *Macmillan Magazine,* where he remained for fifteen years, and began to edit *Grove's Dictionary of Music and Musicians,* which quickly became a standard reference work.

When the Royal College of Music was established in 1882, Grove was appointed its first director, a position he maintained for eleven years. He was knighted in 1883.

gruel Mealy, insubstantial corn or oat mixture. It was often served as a primary form of sustenance in the nineteenth-century WORKHOUSE. Distributed in niggardly amounts, it prompted the plea by the title character in *Oliver Twist,* the 1837–39 novel by CHARLES DICKENS: "Please, sir, I want some more."

Guadalupe Hidalgo, Treaty of Agreement that ended the MEXICAN WAR. Signed in the Mexican town of Guadalupe Hidalgo on February 2, 1848, the treaty was negotiated by U.S. peace commissioner Nicholas Trist against the orders of President JAMES K. POLK that he return home. The treaty was nevertheless ratified by the U.S. Senate on March 10 since it gave the Americans everything for which they had gone to war. MEXICO surrendered its claim to Texas and accepted the boundary at the Rio Grande. In what is known as the Mexican Cession, Mexico ceded the lands that are today California, Nevada, and Utah, along with parts of New Mexico, Arizona, Wyoming, and Colorado. In return, the United States paid Mexico $15 million and assessed $3 million in unpaid claims of American citizens against Mexico. The treaty also granted citizenship rights, including protection of property, to Mexicans who chose to remain in the ceded regions, although Mexicans who did remain found those rights frequently violated by Americans hungry for their land.

Guizot, François-Pierre-Guillaume (1787–1874) French historian and statesman. Born in Nîmes, France, he faced early upheaval when his family was forced to leave France in 1794 after his father was guillotined during the Terror. Following six years in Geneva, Guizot returned to France and later studied law in Paris, where he worked as a tutor for a Swiss Protestant minister. He also spent time with writers who opposed Napoleon. In 1807 he met Pauline de Meulan, a thirty-four-year-old writer, and worked with her for almost four years as a reporter for *Le Publiciste.* The couple married in 1812.

Guizot's writing led to his appointment as professor of history at the Sorbonne in 1812. After the fall of Napoleon in 1814, Guizot held a number of positions in the government, and by 1819 he was an active Doctrinaire, supporting limited monarchy and opposed to both the extreme royalists, or Ultras, and the revolutionists. The Ultras successfully worked for Guizot's dismissal, and in 1820 he returned to the university and continued his work as a historian and journalist.

In January 1830, Guizot reentered politics when he was elected to the Chamber of Deputies. He advocated peaceful change but accepted the revolution that brought LOUIS-PHILIPPE to power. Philippe later named Guizot minister of the interior. From 1832 to 1839 he served as minister of education, passing laws on primary education, establishing teacher-training facilities, and founding the Société d'Histoire de France.

In February 1840, Guizot accepted the post of ambassador to London but was quickly named minister of foreign affairs. He became one of the most influential members of Louis-Philippe's reign, but his conservative policies and indifference to public opinion made him unpopular.

Reforms were demanded after the economic crisis of 1847, and when Louis Philippe ignored the calls for his dismissal, a revolution erupted in 1848. Guizot and the emperor were driven into exile in England, but Guizot returned a year later and peacefully resumed his work as a historian, abstaining from politics.

guncotton Cottony cellulose-based polymer. Also known as nitrocellulose, it has been treated with sulfuric and nitric acids and is used as a component in explosives. It was discovered by German chemist Christian Friedrich Schönbein (1799–1868) in 1845.

gutta-percha Brittle plastic. Also known as thermoplastic. Made by a process developed in the 1850s, it was used for many items, including buttons and canes. The most widely known was the gutta-percha-handled cane that South Carolina congressman Preston Brooks used to beat Senator Charles Sumner in 1856 in the U.S. Senate when the latter voted to admit Kansas as a free state.

Haggard, Sir Henry Rider (1856–1925) English novelist. The son of a Norfolk squire, he failed his army entrance examination and instead joined the colonial service in SOUTH AFRICA (1875–79, 1880–81). A participant in the annexation of the TRANSVAAL (1877), he was as dedicated to the ideals of IMPERIALISM as his friend RUDYARD KIPLING. Upon returning in 1881 to his native England, he studied law for a short time but then turned to the study of agriculture and the writing of novels. An author of major agricultural works such as *Rural England* (1902), he served on several royal commissions and was appointed to the Colonial Office in 1905. He was made a knight in 1912 and a Knight of the British Empire in 1919. His greatest fame came, however, as the author of highly popular novels of romantic adventure, including *King Solomon's Mines* (1885), *She* (1887), *Allan Quatermain* (1887), *Ayesha* (1905), and *Marie* (1912). Often set in Africa, these tales were built on daring adventurers, exotic locales, and idealized portraits of African natives. With ROBERT LOUIS STEVENSON he helped establish the romance as a distinct subgenre of fiction. An autobiography, *The Days of My Life,* appeared posthumously in 1926.

Hague Conferences (1899, 1907) International peace meetings held in the Netherlands. The first conference was requested by Czar Nicholas II, who wanted to limit "the progressive development of existing armaments" in order to secure a lasting peace. Twenty-six nations of Europe, Asia, and America met from May 18 to July 29, 1899, but were unable to agree on any programs for limitation. Three declarations were adopted, however, banning the discharge of projectiles from balloons, the use of asphyxiating gas, and the use of expanding bullets. The representatives also agreed to the formation of a permanent Court of Arbitration in an attempt to find a peaceful settlement of international disputes.

Nicholas II, with encouragement from President THEODORE ROOSEVELT, also called the second conference, held from June 15 to October 18, 1907. Forty-four governments were represented, and again an agreement on disarmament failed. Future conferences were planned, beginning in 1915, but the outbreak of World War I intervened.

hair receiver Object for dressing table used to collect hair from brush and comb. The receiver was usually oval or circular in shape, with an open top in which to deposit hair. The hair, considered valuable, could be used by the well-to-do for wall hangings and sold or "harvested" by the poor for wigs.

Hale, Sarah Josepha Buell (1788–1879) American editor, writer, and social activist. Following the death of her husband, noted lawyer David Hale, she supported her family of five children through writing. Two of her many notable works were the early antislavery novel *North-wood, or, Life North and South* (1827) and the children's verse "Mary Had a Little Lamb" (1830). In 1828 she became editor of the women's PERIODICAL, *The Ladies' Magazine,* which in 1837 became *Godey's Lady's Book,* following the sale of the magazine to Louis Godey. Under Hale's strong editorship, *Godey's* became an influential periodical that published important writers and upheld the nineteenth-century feminine ideal of moral strength. Her quest to make Thanksgiving, in her words, "a national and fixed Union festival" began in 1846 and continued for the next two decades with magazine issues devoted to the holiday and a letter-writing campaign to government officials. Her efforts bore fruit on October 3, 1863, when President Abraham Lincoln proclaimed an annual day of national thanksgiving to be held on the last Thursday of November.

hangings, public See NEWGATE PRISON.

Hanna, Mark (1837–1904) American politician and businessman. Born in Ohio, he amassed a fortune in coal, iron, shipping, and other enterprises. By 1890 he had become the boss of the Ohio REPUBLICAN PARTY and backed unsuccessful gubernatorial campaigns of WILLIAM MCKINLEY in 1891 and 1893. He masterminded the rest of McKinley's political career, supervising his bid for the Republican presidential nomination in 1896 and his winning campaign for president that year. He became a U.S. senator in 1897, and many expected him to fight THEODORE ROOSEVELT for the 1904 Republican presidential nomination; however, he died several months before the convention.

Hanslick, Eduard (1825–1904) Austrian critic and musical aesthetician. He championed ROBERT SCHUMANN and JOHANNES BRAHMS, and opposed the "New Music" of FRANZ LIZST and RICHARD WAGNER. Wagner retaliated by lampooning him as Beckmesser in *The Mastersingers of Nuremberg* (1868). Hanslick's works include *The Beautiful in Music* (1854).

hansom cab Two-wheeled, horse-drawn vehicle for hire. It was introduced in England in the late 1830s. The driver sat perched high up in the back while the passengers sat in front, enjoying an unobstructed view. See also CAB.

Harare See SALISBURY and RHODESIA.

Hardie, [James] Keir (1856–1915) British labor leader and politician. Born in Scotland, he entered the coal mines as a child, working as a miner from 1866 to 1878. He organized a miners' union, became secretary of the Scottish Miners' Federation in 1886, and published labor-related newspapers. In 1892, running for office as an independent, he became the first labor representative to be elected to the British Parliament (1892–95, 1900–15). He helped found the Independent Labour Party in 1893 and the Labour Representation Committee in 1900, which, under his leadership, became the Labour Party in 1906.

hardtack Hard flour-and-water biscuits. Eaten by nineteenth-century sailors at sea and American pioneers. The simple concoction could be made and stored more easily than traditional biscuits and breads.

Hardy, Thomas (1840–1928) English novelist and poet. The son of a mason, he was born in Higher Bockhampton near Dorchester, which became the model for the fictional town of Wessex, the setting for many of his works. During his youth, Hardy became familiar with local folklore as well as with the severe harshness of village life.

Trained as an architect, he began to practice in 1867 but was more interested in writing. His poetry failed to find a publisher, as did his first novel, *The Poor Man and the Lady.* He found publishers for the novels *Desperate Remedies* (1871) and *Under the Greenwood Tree* (1872), both of which appeared anonymously. The first novel published under his name was *A Pair of Blue Eyes* (1873), but his first great success was *Far from the Madding Crowd* (1874), which produced enough revenue to allow him to marry Emma Gifford. This work was followed by such critical triumphs as *The Return of the Native* (1878), *The Mayor of Casterbridge* (1886), and *Tess of the D'Urbervilles* (1891), the story of a beautiful "pure woman" spoiled by cruel circumstances. *Jude the Obscure* (1895), a novel partly inspired by Hardy's alienation from British institutions and the problems of his married life, proved so controversial that it helped persuade Hardy to abandon fiction. He returned to his original love, poetry, and published several volumes, beginning with *Wessex Poems* (1898). His lyric poems included such classics as "The Ruined Maid," "The Darkling Thrush," "She Hears the Storm," and "Hap." His verse drama *The Dynasts* (1903, 1906, 1908) concerned the Napoleonic wars.

Thomas Hardy, novelist, is best known as the author of such works as The Mayor of Casterbridge *and* Jude the Obscure. *Photo courtesy of Topham/Image Works.*

Hardy ended his long life as a much-heralded elder statesman of English letters.

In a career that spanned both the Victorian and modern eras, Hardy achieved greatness as the author of fictional works of extraordinary tragic force and natural detail. Several were successfully translated into film. His poetry remains some of the finest in the language.

Harper's magazines Publications in the Victorian era by the firm of Harper and Brothers in New York. *Harper's Monthly Magazine* was founded in 1850 under the editorship of Henry J. Raymond. By 1860 its circulation was two hundred thousand. At first it emphasized British fiction by such authors as CHARLES DICKENS,

THOMAS HARDY, and WILLIAM MAKEPEACE THACKERAY, but it came to showcase American authors as well, including WILLIAM DEAN HOWELLS, SARAH ORNE JEWETT, and Hamlin Garland. By 1900 it was known as *Harper's New Monthly Magazine,* and it included less fiction and more articles on political and social issues. It is now known simply as *Harper's.*

Harper and Brothers also produced *Harper's Weekly,* which specialized in news and travel features along with fiction, and *Harper's Bazaar,* which emphasized fashion and was directed primarily toward women. See also PERIODICALS.

Harris, Joel Chandler (1848–1908) American writer. Born in Georgia and raised on plantations, he became famous for his comic adaptations of African-American folklore, narrated in southern black dialect by former slave Uncle Remus. Harris's folkloric works include *Uncle Remus: His Songs and Sayings* (1881), *The Tar Baby* (1904), and *Uncle Remus and Br'er Rabbit* (1906). His other works include *Mingo and Other Sketches in Black and White* (1884) and the autobiographical *On the Plantation* (1892).

Harrison, Benjamin (1833–1901) Twenty-third president of the UNITED STATES. (1889–93). The grandson of the ninth president, WILLIAM HENRY HARRISON, Benjamin Harrison was born in Ohio, and established a successful law practice in Indiana. He joined the REPUBLICAN PARTY in 1856, and during the Civil War he achieved the rank of brigadier general in the Union Army. He lost a bid for the governor's seat in Indiana in 1876 but in 1880 was elected to the Senate, where he supported high tariffs and substantial pensions for Union veterans.

He defeated Democratic incumbent GROVER CLEVELAND in the 1888 presidential election, losing the popular vote but winning the electoral vote. The Republican campaign was marked by vote buying and huge campaign contributions from the mining and manufacturing sectors. Harrison was forced to pay off many political debts during his term. Government purchases of silver aided the mining industry; high tariffs helped manufacturers; increased benefits assisted veterans; and Republican job seekers prospered as civil service reform languished. His most important foreign policy initiative was the founding of the International Bureau of American Republics to promote hemispheric cooperation. It was renamed the Pan-American Union in 1910.

Cleveland defeated Harrison in the 1892 election. Afterward, Harrison returned to Indianapolis to practice law.

Harrison, William Henry (1773–1841) Ninth president of the UNITED STATES (1841). Harrison was born in Virginia, the son of a rich plantation owner. He joined the army in 1791 and served with distinction against Indian tribes in Ohio. He was governor of the Indian Territory from 1800 to 1812 and commanded troops against the Indian chief Tecumseh, most famously at the Battle of Tippecanoe in 1811. During the War of 1812 he secured the frontier against Indian attacks by defeating Tecumseh for a final time.

Harrison was a congressman from Ohio from 1816 to 1819 and a senator from 1825 to 1828, supporting the Whig policies of HENRY CLAY. He lost the 1836 election to Democrat MARTIN VAN BUREN but defeated Van Buren in 1840 in a campaign marked by the slogan "Tippecanoe and Tyler, too," and a successful attempt to depict the Virginia aristocrat as a rough-hewn backwoodsman. The first Whig president spent only one month in office before succumbing to pneumonia. JOHN

TYLER succeeded him as president. Harrison's grandson, BENJAMIN HARRISON, became the twenty-third president.

Harrod's World's largest DEPARTMENT STORE. Harrod's had its beginnings as a mid-nineteenth-century London grocery. In 1849 it was taken over by Henry Charles Harrod, who maintained it as a food emporium until 1861 when his son Charles Digby Harrod assumed directorship of the property and transformed it into a department store, a modern form of merchandising that captured Continental and American fancy by the end of the century. In December 1884 a new Harrod's opened in London, in part to replace the one damaged by fire in 1883; it experienced twice the commercial volume of the former site. In 1889, Harrod sold his interest in the firm, already a shopping institution.

Harte, Bret [Francis Brett] (1836–1902) American editor, short-story writer, and humorist. Harte's colorful tales of California helped to mark it as a literary center in the nineteenth century. Born in Albany, New York, he was largely self-educated and a writer since his youth, publishing his first poem in 1847. After moving with his sister to San Francisco, he wrote for various local periodicals, eventually editing *The Overland Monthly,* which published two of his best known stories, "The Luck of Roaring Camp" (1868) and "The Outcasts of Poker Flat" (1869). These and other stories of local color and Dickensian melodrama were published in *The Luck of Roaring Camp and Other Stories* (1870). After a stint as writer for *Atlantic Monthly* in Boston ended in artistic disappointment and termination, he worked on various pieces of writing, including a play with MARK TWAIN, *Ah Sin* (1877), and advertising verse for Sapolio soap. From 1878 he spent his remaining years as United States consul in Germany and Scotland, and later as an expatriate *bon vivant* in London. A prolific writer, some of his other story collections include *A Protégé of Jack Hamlin's* (1894) and *Poetical Works of Bret Harte* (1896).

Hawthorne, Nathaniel (1804–1864) American novelist and short-story writer. Hawthorne was an artistic explorer of the Puritan mind and its persistence in the American psyche. Born Nathaniel Hathorne in Salem, Massachusetts, to an established New England family that included a judge in the Salem witchcraft trials, he lost his father at a young age and went with his two sisters and widowed mother to live with her family, the Mannings. Surrounded by adults, he pursued reading and intellectual studies in solitude. After graduating from Bowdoin College, where he made the acquaintance of poet HENRY WADSWORTH LONGFELLOW, he returned to the Manning estate in 1825 and pursued his writing for the next twelve years. During that time he published anonymously or under a pen name a number of fiction and nonfiction works in worthy periodicals that included *New-England Magazine* and *The Knickerbocker Magazine.* He also self-published the romance *Fanshawe* (1828). Not until the publication of the short-story collection *Twice-Told Tales* (1838) did Hawthorne attach his name to a work and become known to a wider audience.

In 1839, to provide an income not possible through writing, Hawthorne took a job as a surveyor at the Boston Customs House. That and his later position as a surveyor at the Salem Customs House (1846–49) informed the opening section, "The Custom-House," of his first major novel, *The Scarlet Letter* (1850). Another experience, his several months in 1841 at the utopian community BROOK FARM, spurred his 1852 novel *The Blithedale Romance.*

In 1842 he married Sophia Peabody, sister of the influential bookstore owner and educator Elizabeth Palmer Peabody, and for three years lived in Concord, Massachusetts, on property owned by philosopher RALPH WALDO EMERSON. Here Hawthorne came to know several writers who espoused TRANSCENDENTALISM, most notably Emerson and HENRY DAVID THOREAU. *Mosses from an Old Manse,* referring to the name of the property where he lived, was published in 1846. It contained several definitive works, including "The Birthmark," "Rappacini's Daughter," and "Young Goodman Brown," each exploring the darkness of human emotions.

That year, again facing the inability to support his family through writing, he accepted the post at the Salem Customs House. His three years there resulted in limited literary output. When a change in administrations lost him his position, however, he redoubled his writing efforts, publishing a short story collection and three novels, *The House of the Seven Gables* (1851), *The Blithedale Romance* (1852), and *The Scarlet Letter* (1850), the seventeenth-century tale of sin, guilt, and redemption as seen through the lives of adulteress Hester Prynne, her lover, the Reverend Arthur Dimmesdale, and Prynne's husband, Roger Chillingworth.

Few in Hawthorne's time understood the author as well as fellow author HERMAN MELVILLE. Their acquaintance was captured by Melville in the essay "Hawthorne and His Mosses." Though separated in age by fifteen years, the younger Melville immediately understood the "great power of blackness" that permeated all of Hawthorne's writing. Their lasting literary friendship affected each writer's future work, particularly Melville's *Moby-Dick,* which was dedicated to Hawthorne.

After the election of Bowdoin friend FRANKLIN PIERCE as U.S. president, Hawthorne was appointed consul to England. Following a four-year stay, he and his family moved to Liverpool, where he completed *The Marble Faun* (1860). His last major work, this study of American expatriates remains a prototypical Hawthorne exploration of sin and guilt. In 1863 he published his last book, a collection of sketches, *Our Old Home* (1863).

After being stricken by a brain disorder, Hawthorne died in Plymouth, New Hampshire. He is buried with other literary contemporaries at Sleepy Hollow Cemetery in Massachusetts. Despite his contention to Longfellow that "I have made a captive of myself . . . and now I cannot find the key to let myself out," Hawthorne experienced enough of American life to inform several of his novels and, more important, to become one of the first to speak knowingly about its inner psychological darkness.

Hayes, Rutherford Birchard (1822–1893) Nineteenth president of the UNITED STATES (1877–81). Hayes was born in Delaware, Ohio. A graduate of Kenyon College, he established a prosperous law practice in Cincinnati and helped found the Ohio REPUBLICAN PARTY in 1856. Wounded five times during the Civil War, Hayes was elected to Congress in 1864, where he supported the RECONSTRUCTION measures of radical Republicans. He resigned from Congress to run for governor of Ohio, an office he held from 1867 to 1871 and from 1875 to 1877.

Hayes's integrity as governor led to the presidential nomination in 1876. His opponent, Samuel Tilden, won a plurality of the popular vote but was one vote shy of a majority in the electoral college. The electoral votes of four states were in dispute and a bipartisan commission was formed to settle the impasse. Southern DEMOCRATS and Republicans struck a deal, known as the Compromise of 1876, that made Hayes president in return for withdrawing the remaining federal troops from the South. This withdrawal helped Democrats regain control of the South at the expense of the civil rights of the emancipated slaves. Hayes retired after one term and spent his remaining years advocating prison reform and assistance for former slaves.

Haymarket Square Riot Police and labor encounter in Chicago, Illinois, on May 4, 1886. The riot became a symbol of anti-labor violence and JINGOISM. On May 3, 1886, to protest the hiring of nonunion workers during a strike for the eight-hour day at the McCormick Reaper Company, union workers staged a demonstration. Police shooting into the crowd killed four people. Anarchists claiming police brutality called a rally at Haymarket Square the following day. During the rally, a bomb was released in the phalanx of police, causing rioting and the deaths of eleven people. While the source of the bomb remained unidentified, a highly prejudiced trial saw the conviction of eight anarchists, all but one German immigrants, as accessories to murder. In 1893 the three living prisoners—four others were hanged, one committed suicide—were pardoned by Illinois governor JOHN PETER ALTGELD, but antiforeigner sentiment remained high.

Hearst, William Randolph (1863–1951) American publisher and newspaper tycoon. Born in San Francisco, California, he was the son of mining magnate George Hearst, who gave him the *San Francisco Examiner* in 1887. The younger Hearst increased the paper's circulation through the same kind of sensationalist reporting already associated with JOSEPH PULITZER, a style that would become known as "yellow journalism." In 1895 Hearst bought the *New York Morning Journal* and challenged Pulitzer's *New York World* with price cutting and raids on its staff. Hearst helped ease U.S. entry into the SPANISH-AMERICAN WAR with his paper's often exaggerated accounts of Spanish atrocities against Cuban rebels. Hearst had political ambitions but lost New York mayoralty races in 1905 and 1909, and a gubernatorial bid in 1906. He served in the U.S. Congress from 1903 to 1907 but failed to get the presidential nomination of the DEMOCRATIC PARTY. He continued to build his newspaper empire; when he died he owned eighteen papers in twelve cities, nine magazines, and a news and photo service. He ended his last years as a near recluse at his grandiose estate in San Simeon, California. See also PERIODICALS.

helium Element. The first element discovered in an extraterrestrial source, helium was identified by French astronomer Pierre-Jules-César Janssen (1824–1907) and English astronomer Sir JOSEPH NORMAN LOCKYER in 1868, as a result of spectroscopic analysis of sunlight during a total eclipse that year. The same element, identified by its spectral lines, was discovered on earth in uranium ore by English chemist William Ramsay in 1895. By 1898 it was recognized as one of a family of INERT (NOBLE) GASES and has turned out to be unusual in many ways. Colorless, odorless, gaseous, and nonmetallic, the element has no known compounds, has the lowest boiling point of any substance, and can be frozen solid only under pressure. Because of its lightness and noncombustibility, it is useful with the BALLOON and airship; it is also used in low-temperature physics, arc welding, and gas discharge lasers. The ALPHA RAYS discovered in 1897 were later found to be helium nuclei resulting in the

RADIOACTIVITY of uranium atoms, a fact that retrospectively accounted for helium's presence in uranium ore. Helium's presence in the sun's atmosphere was later found to be the result of the thermonuclear fusion of hydrogen.

Helmholtz, Hermann von See THERMODYNAMICS.

heredity, laws of See GENETICS and GREGOR MENDEL.

Hertz, Heinrich Rudolph See RADIO WAVES.

Herzl, Theodor (1860–1904) Founder of ZIONISM. He was born in Budapest to a middle-class Jewish family. In order to escape the anti-Semitism of the Hungarian capital and to give them better educational opportunities, the family moved to Vienna in 1878, where Herzl attended the university. In 1891 he received an assignment as the literary correspondent to Paris for a Vienna newspaper. He was shocked by the anti-Semitism displayed in the cultural capital of Europe, especially during the ALFRED DREYFUS affair. Although he had previously believed that anti-Semitism would disappear if Jews assimilated into Gentile society, he now became convinced of the need for a Jewish homeland. In 1896 he published the pamphlet "The Jewish State" and in the following year organized the first Zionist Congress in Basle. His cause was not initially popular, but Herzl succeeded in keeping the question of a Jewish state open. Near the end of his life he was criticized by Zionists holding out for a Jewish state in Palestine when he seriously considered Great Britain's offer of land in Uganda. Significant Jewish migration to Palestine did not begin until after his death. Ultimately, Zionism became a viable option when the Nazi attempt to exterminate the Jews of Europe confirmed the fragility of assimilation.

"Hiawatha, The Song of" (1855) See SONG OF HIAWATHA, THE

Hickok, Wild Bill [James Butler] (1837–1876) American gunfighter and marshal. Born in Illinois, he drove a stagecoach in Kansas before serving as a scout and spy for the Union in the U.S. CIVIL WAR. After the war he was appointed marshal in various towns, most notably Abilene, Kansas, one of the frontier's roughest spots. His prowess with a gun made him a legend, and he toured with WILLIAM "BUFFALO BILL" CODY's Wild West Show. He was murdered in Deadwood in the Dakota Territory by Jack McCall, who shot him in the back of the head during a poker game.

Hill, Rowland See POSTAL SERVICES.

Hissarlik See TROY and SCHLIEMANN HEINRICH.

Holmes, Oliver Wendell (1809–1894) American author and physician. Born in Cambridge, Massachusetts, he received his M.D. from Harvard in 1836 and was a professor of anatomy at Dartmouth (1838–40) and Harvard Medical School (1847–82). He wrote *The Contagiousness of Puerperal Fever* (1842), anticipating the findings of IGNAZ SEMMELWEIS, and coined the terms anesthetic and ANESTHESIA. But he is better known as a man of letters who established his reputation while still in his twenties with the patriotic poem "Old Ironsides" (1830), which rallied popular support for rescuing the frigate U.S.S. *Constitution* from being scrapped. Later poems included "The Chambered Nautilus" and "The Deacon's Masterpiece." As an essayist he produced the series of sketches called "The Autocrat of the Breakfast-Table," which originally appeared in the *Atlantic Monthly,* beginning with its founding issue. Collected in book form in 1858, the witty and original series, modeled on eighteenth-century predecessors Joseph Addison and Sir Richard Steele, combined fictional conversation, monologue-essay, and verse.

The essays continued in the series "The Professor at the Breakfast-Table" (in book form, 1860) and "The Poet at the Breakfast-Table" (in book form, 1872). He also wrote biographies, including one of his literary colleague RALPH WALDO EMERSON, and novels, including *Elsie Venner* (1861), a work that critiques Calvinist theology while telling a semi-fantastic story with psychological depth. A great conversationalist, Holmes was much sought as a speaker and dinner guest. He was the father of jurist Oliver Wendell Holmes (1841–1935), who became a well-known and respected Supreme Court justice (1902–32).

Holmes, Sherlock Fictional character. The brilliant, urbane fictional detective who appears in a total of four novels and fifty-six short stories by British writer Sir ARTHUR CONAN DOYLE, making him arguably the most popular fictional crime-solver of all time. In tales that strongly evoke the atmosphere of Victorian and Edwardian London, the ingenious Holmes, with his signature deerstalker cap and meerschaum pipe, solves a series of daunting problems and mysteries, the answers to which are always provided at the narrative's end. With his impeccable logic and vast knowledge of science, the amateur Holmes is vastly more effective than the slower-witted SCOTLAND YARD police detectives. Highly influential, the Holmes narratives were indebted to the detective-fiction form pioneered by American writer EDGAR ALLAN POE.

A drawing of Sherlock Holmes by Frederic Door Steele captures the sleuth in contemplation. Private Collection.

With his loyal colleague Dr. Watson, who narrated the adventures, Holmes made his first appearance in the novel *A Study in Scarlet,* published in *Beeton's Christmas Annual* of 1887. After the American publisher Lippincott commissioned a second volume, Holmes and Watson appeared in *The Sign of the Four* (1890), but wide-scale success came when Doyle's tales began appearing in *The Strand Magazine* in July 1891. They were collected in *The Adventures of Sherlock Holmes* (1892) and *The Memoirs of Sherlock Holmes* (1894), in which the final story, "The Final Problem," details the archvillain Moriarty's murder of Holmes. A public uproar required that Doyle revive his hero, first in *The Hound of the Baskervilles* (1902), which claimed to narrate an early case of Holmes, and then in "The Adventure of the Empty House," a story at the beginning of *The Return of Sherlock Holmes* (1905). Here it was revealed that Holmes had survived his earlier attack, a recuperation that led to a further novel, *The Valley of Fear* (1915), and two collections, *His Last Bow* and *The Case-Book of Sherlock Holmes* (1927).

Home Rule Irish political movement. In 1800, Great Britain's Act of Union dissolved the Irish Parliament and forced Irish representatives to sit in the British Parliament. The Home Rule movement sought to regain Irish control of internal affairs by reestablishing the Irish Parliament. ISAAC BUTT founded the Irish Home Rule League, but the most famous leader of the movement was CHARLES STEWART PARNELL, a member of Parliament whose political genius and iron will controlled the Home Rule Party's parliamentary votes during the 1880s. Parnell, armed with this formidable bloc of votes, exploited conflicts between the LIBERAL PARTY and CONSERVATIVE PARTY. He was also aided by English fears of growing agrarian unrest and political violence in IRELAND.

In 1886, WILLIAM GLADSTONE, leader of the Liberal Party, came out in support of Home Rule. The Liberals introduced a series of Home Rule bills between 1886 and 1912 that mandated varying degrees of Irish control over domestic affairs. The Conservative Party and the House of Lords defeated each bill because they feared loss of English land holdings in Ireland and Catholic domination over predominantly Protestant Northern Ireland.

Parnell lost control of the Home Rule Party in 1890, and the more radical Irish leaders became disenchanted with the parliamentary approach. A Home Rule bill was finally passed in 1914 with the proviso that Northern Ireland be excluded from its provisions. It was to take effect after World War I but was made academic by the Easter Rebellion of 1916 in Dublin, which triggered a successful movement for complete independence from Great Britain.

Homer, Winslow (1836–1910) American painter. A landscape, marine, and genre painter, Homer was also a pictorial journalist and illustrator. He worked in Boston as a lithographer before being sent to the battlefront as a war correspondent for *Harper's Weekly* in 1861. Homer's Civil War pictures and studies of black American life after the war won him international popularity. He achieved recognition as a painter with his first oil painting, *Prisoners from the Front* (1866).

In 1876, Homer abandoned illustration to devote himself to painting. He found his inspiration primarily in the American scene and painted pictures of everyday life, such as in *Crack the Whip* (1872). Through 1880 his subjects were broadly treated rural genre scenes such as *Gloucester Farm* (1874).

Homer went to England in 1881 and stayed there for a year to work in watercolor. Upon his return to America, he left his rural pastorals and settled in Prout's Neck, Maine, to paint violently realistic scenes of the sea. *The Life Line* (1884) is one of many paintings showing wrecks or rescues at sea.

Both his oils and watercolors are characterized by their directness, realism, objectivity, and vivid color. Homer excelled as a watercolorist, however, and his dramatic paintings earned him widespread popularity. After 1884, Homer lived the life of a recluse. He made frequent trips to the West Indies and adopted a more Impressionistic watercolor technique to capture a variety of tropical beach scenes. See also GENRE PAINTING, HARPER'S MAGAZINES, IMPRESSIONISM, and REALISM.

Homestead Act U.S. Law. Passed in 1862, it allotted 160 acres of western land to settlers who paid a small fee and occupied the land for five years. Labor groups and some political parties, including the Free Soil Party and the REPUBLICAN PARTY, had been demanding free distribution of government land for years. This policy was opposed by southern slave owners who feared that settlers would fight the extension of SLAVERY into the West. Eastern businessmen, fearing the westward migration of cheap labor, also fought the law.

This combination defeated the bill in Congress in 1852 and 1859. Congress passed a bill in 1860, but President JAMES BUCHANAN vetoed it. The secession of the southern states and the election of ABRAHAM LINCOLN ensured passage of the bill.

Despite its provisions, the act never peopled the interior with small farmers. Many tenant farmers and seaboard workers could not afford to travel west or buy supplies needed to start a farm. The default rate for those who established residence was very high, due partly to the dry conditions of the high plains.

Speculators, cattlemen, and the railroad acquired vast tracts of land by hiring people to file claims that the land grabbers bought later for $1.25 an acre. They also purchased the land of failed homesteaders. The inefficient and sometimes corrupt administration of the law also swelled their land holdings. By the end of the century more than 80 million acres had been distributed, but many immigrants and others who traveled west in hopes of finding free or cheap land were greeted by inflated prices, mortgages, and long-term tenancy.

Homestead Strike See FRICK, HENRY CLAY.

Hong Kong British crown colony in southeastern China. It is comprised of Hong Kong island and, on the mainland, the Kowloon peninsula and the New Territories. The British occupied Hong Kong during the first of the OPIUM WARS (1839–42); China ceded it to Britain in 1842. The peninsula was ceded in 1860. The New Territories were leased in 1898 for ninety-nine years. A free port, the colony flourished throughout the Victorian Age as a hub for east-west trade. Its capital, Victoria, is on Hong Kong island. Return of the colony to China is scheduled for 1997 when the lease on the New Territories ends.

Hood, Thomas (1799–1845) English poet, prose writer, editor, and engraver. Known first as an engraver, he joined the editorial staff of *London Magazine* in 1821 and became acquainted with William Hazlitt, Charles Lamb, and William Wordsworth. He went on to write comic and satiric poems, including *Odes and Addresses to Great People* (1825), with brother-in-law J. H. Reynolds, and humanitarian poems on social concerns, including "The Song of the Shirt" (1843) and "The Bridge of Sighs" (1844). His comic poetry was marked by a talent for puns and an interest in the macabre and grotesque. As an editor he worked on *The Athenaeum* and *New Monthly Magazine,* along with his own periodicals, including *Hood's Own Magazine* (begun in 1838) and *Comic Miscellany* (begun in 1844).

Hooker, Joseph (1814–1879) American Union Army general. Born in Hadley, Massachusetts, he graduated from West Point in 1837. He served during the Seminole War in Florida and during the MEXICAN WAR, where he was promoted to the rank of captain and then lieutenant colonel. He resigned from the army in 1853 and moved to California, where he worked as a farmer until 1858 when he accepted the appointment as superintendent of military roads in Oregon.

At the outbreak of the CIVIL WAR in 1861, Hooker was appointed a brigadier general of volunteers. His troops fought gallantly to defend Washington, D.C., and Hooker was promoted to major general. With the sobriquet "Fighting Joe," Hooker took part in the second Battle of Bull Run (Manassas) and the Battle of ANTIETAM, where he engaged the Confederate Army in a massive attack, resulting in heavy casualties on both sides. Hooker was also wounded at Antietam.

After the Union defeat at Fredericksburg in December 1862, President ABRAHAM LINCOLN selected Hooker to lead the Army of the Potomac. Hooker's role as commander was brief, however. In May he led the 138,000 Union troops into combat with the troops of General ROBERT E. LEE near Chancellorsville, Virginia. The 62,500 Confederates refused to retreat, however, and launched a counterattack. Hooker hesitated in his command and quickly turned a Union victory into certain defeat.

General Hooker was quickly relieved of his command, but he continued to serve, leading a victory in the Battle Above the Clouds at Lookout Mountain, Tennessee, on November 24, 1863. He also served as corps commander in the Atlanta campaign, but when General WILLIAM T. SHERMAN gave General O. O. Howard the command of the Army of the Tennessee over Hooker, who was in line for the promotion, Hooker asked to be relieved of field duty, saying, "Justice and self-respect alike require my removal from an army in which rank and service are ignored." He retired from the army in 1868.

hoop skirt Floor-length attire with attached supports that allowed it to maintain its circular shape. There was also an undergarment worn under a non-hoop skirt to effect the circular shape; it was known as a cage CRINOLINE. The bell-shaped skirt became popular during the mid-nineteenth century; it was replaced after several years by the BUSTLE.

Hopkins, Gerard Manley (1844–1889) English poet. Born in Stratford, Essex, and raised as an Anglican, Hopkins distinguished himself early as a student and poet at Highgate School. He entered Oxford in 1863 and came under the influence of the aesthetic teachings of WALTER PATER and JOHN RUSKIN; however, he was also exposed to the OXFORD MOVEMENT during this time. His growing asceticism led him to approach JOHN HENRY NEWMAN, himself a convert to Roman Catholicism, about accepting the faith of Rome and became a Catholic in 1866. He left Oxford with high honors in 1867 and spent a term as a layman in Newman's Oratory School. In 1868 he joined the Society of Jesus and began studying for the priesthood at a novitiate near London. He burned most of his poetry upon entering the order and was prepared to surrender it forever.

In 1875, after seven years of poetic abstinence, his rector suggested he write a poem about the recent shipwreck death of five nuns who had been expelled from Germany under OTTO VON BISMARCK's anti-Catholic Falk laws. "The Wreck of the Deutschland," characterized by Hopkins's unconventional style and detailing the plight of the doomed nuns, was rejected by the Jesuit magazine. Hopkins continued to write until his death.

Ordained in 1877, Hopkins served as parish priest and lecturer in various places until 1884 when he was appointed professor of Greek literature at Dublin's University College. He died five years later of typhoid fever at the age of forty-five. Except for a few early poems, none of his verse was published until 1918 when his close friend and fellow poet ROBERT BRIDGES prepared a first edition of his work.

Hopkins's poetry differed radically from the rhythms and structures of more conventional Victorian verse. His most famous departure was his invention of "sprung rhythm" in which the poem is read by counting accents or stresses in the line without counting the unaccented syllables. He named it sprung rhythm because it allows for one stress to be followed immediately by another with no syllable in between. This stacatto effect gives the lines a driven, surging, or "sprung" feeling. It contrasts with other rhyme schemes, such as iambic pentameter, that allow the reader to pause after accented syllables.

Hopkins used sprung rhythm because it was "the nearest to the rhythm of prose, that is the native and natural rhythm of speech, the least forced, the most rhetorical and emphatic of all possible rhythms."

Hopkins used other poetic devices to charge his poems with emotional intensity. Liberal use of alliteration and ejaculations, neologisms, newly minted compound words, unusual syntax, and startling and sometimes obscure imagery give his poetry a feeling more modern than Victorian. It is probable that he influenced James Joyce, Dylan Thomas, e. e. cummings, and poets of the 1930s such as W. H. Auden and Stephen Spender.

Hopkins's poetry was also marked by its deep spirituality and its view of nature as a reflection of God's power and glory. Among his most famous poems are "The Windhover," "God's Grandeur," "Spring and Fall: To a Young Child," "As Kingfishers Catch Fire," and "Pied Beauty."

Hottentot European term for the Khoikhoi, a nomadic, pastoral people of Namibia and SOUTH AFRICA. They speak a Khoisan language similar to that of the hunter-gatherer BUSHMEN, or San. Both Hottentots and Bushmen were greatly reduced in numbers in violent conflict with the Dutch settlers of South Africa, the BOERS, beginning in the seventeenth century. The British colonists who entered the region in Victorian times carried on the tradition of conflict.

Houses of Parliament See WESTMINSTER PALACE.

Housman, Alfred Edward (1859–1936) English poet and classical scholar. He grew up in Worcestershire and left St. John's College, Oxford, in 1881 after failing a final exam, a failure occasioned more by his contempt for the reading list than lack of scholarly abilities. He spent the next ten years as a clerk in a patent office in London. During this time he wrote scholarly articles of such worth that he became a professor of Latin at University College in London in 1892 and then at Cambridge starting in 1911. He published editions of Juvenal in 1905, Lucan in 1926, and a five-volume edition of Manilius between 1903 and 1930.

Housman's popularity as a poet rests mainly on *A Shropshire Lad,* published in 1896. These rueful poems are set in the English countryside and are written in a very simple style. They deal with unrequited love, early death, suicide, fleeting youth, and nature's pitiless responses to human hopes. The often despairing content and tone of his poetry is sometimes attributed to his unrequited love for Moses Jackson, a college friend. The early death of his mother also affected him deeply.

Last Poems was published in 1922 and contained material written about the same time as the poems in *The Shropshire Lad. More Poems* was released posthumously in 1936. His most famous poems include "To an Athlete Dying Young," "When I Was One and Twenty," "Terence This Is Stupid Stuff," and "With Rue My Heart Is Laden."

Howe, Elias See SEWING MACHINE.

Howe, Julia Ward (1819–1910) American poet. Her poem "The Battle Hymn of the Republic" (1862) became an anthem of the U.S. CIVIL WAR. Born in New York City, she settled in Boston and married leading humanitarian Samuel Gridley Howe, with whom she edited the newspaper *Commonwealth* and promoted abolition and WOMAN SUFFRAGE. She continued their work after his death, lecturing and writing extensively. Her works include poetry collections, a biography of MARGARET FULLER (1882), and *Modern Society* (1881). President of several leading women's organizations, including the American Women's Suffrage Association, she was also the first female elected to the American Academy of Arts and Letters.

Howells, William Dean (1837–1920) American novelist, critic, journalist, and editor. Howells was called in his day the "Dean of American Letters" and was acknowledged as a foremost promoter of REALISM in fiction. Born in Ohio, he was trained in his father's profession of typesetting and parlayed that skill and knowledge of PERIODICALS into several printing and writing positions on local periodicals. In 1860 he further established himself as a writer when he coauthored with John J. Piatt *Poems of Two Friends* and a campaign biography of Abraham Lincoln. The latter work gained for him a consulship in Venice, and this experience yielded two books, *Venetian Life* (1866) and *Italian Journeys* (1867). For years a staff member and frequent contributor to U.S. periodicals, he was named editor in chief of the *Atlantic Monthly* in 1871, a position he held until 1881. Some of the writers he encouraged for the magazine were MARK TWAIN and HENRY JAMES. Following his tenure as editor, he became a columnist for *Harper's Monthly,* contributing the "Editor's Study" column from 1886 to 1892 and the "Easy Chair" column from 1900 to 1920.

Influenced by GEORGE ELIOT, who was immersed in the quotidian, and by LEO TOLSTOY, who believed in art as a social tool, he developed his own theory of realism, calling it "nothing more or less than the truthful treatment of material." He devoted much of the last decades of his life to writing socially conscious, realistic works. Of his dozens of novels, two of his best known include *The Rise of Silas Lapham* (1885), about the deleterious effects of a materialistic life, and *A Hazard of New Fortunes* (1890), about American business, labor policies, and police violence. He was also active in other genres and forms, however, such as story collections (*The Coast of Bohemia,* 1893), romances (*April Hopes,* 1888), historical fiction (*The Leatherwood God,* 1916), and article collections (*My Mark Twain,* 1910). Late in his life he was named president of the American Academy of Arts and Letters. Praised in his day for his unrelenting examinations of social issues, Howells lost critical favor in the early twentieth century for, among other reasons, his sentimentality and lack of attention to sexual conflicts. Later critical reappraisal has secured his historical importance in American letters.

Hudson River School American artistic movement. This group of mid-nineteenth-century landscape painters helped define American ROMANTICISM and worked mainly, but not exclusively, in the region of the Catskill Mountains and the Hudson River. They shared a grandiose view of natural American scenery, which they painted in closely observed detail. The grand, idyllic paintings of the American landscape by THOMAS COLE in the 1830s prepared younger artists such as Asher B. Durand and John F. Kensett to continue the tradition of recording brilliant nature scenes. These artists chose to work beyond the clichéd and static landscape compositions of earlier years. They created paintings as objective studies of nature in a unique *luminist* style. Luminism, popular among landscape artists throughout the

1840s, was a poetic rather than an analytic approach to solving the problem of rendering light and atmosphere.

By the 1850s, Hudson River artists Albert Bierstadt and FREDERICK CHURCH underscored the American landscape's grandeur in epic-sized canvases painted with a glowing, all-encompassing light. Their goal was to astound and awe the viewer with the power of nature. Though accused of overidealizing their subjects, their work was immensely popular. As painters, they shared an interest in light and matter-of-fact recording that united them with the natural and objective investigations of all Hudson River artists.

Hughes, Thomas See TOM BROWN'S SCHOOL DAYS.

Hugo, Victor [-Marie] (1802–1885) French poet and novelist. Having begun writing at the age of fourteen, Hugo published his first book of poems, *Odes et poésies diverses,* in 1822. Many of the poems were inspired by his new bride, Adele Foucher, and the collection garnered recognition from King Louis XVIII, who awarded the poet an annuity of 1,200 francs. The following year Hugo published his first novel, *Han d'Islande;* his first play, *Cromwell,* appeared in 1827.

By 1826, Hugo was considered the leader of ROMANTICISM in French literature and hailed as the "prince of poets." Perhaps his most famous novel, *The Hunchback of Notre Dame (Notre-Dame de Paris),* was published in 1831. The same year he published *Les Feuilles d'automne,* considered his most beautiful collection of verse. These poems are filled with sadness and melancholy, a reflection of the fact that his wife had begun an affair with the poet's friend, man of letters Charles Sainte-Beuve. Hugo, in turn, fell in love with Juliette Drouet, who lived as a kept woman, in squalid conditions, always near Hugo and his family, for the next fifty years.

After the REVOLUTIONS OF 1848, Hugo was elected to the National Assembly, but after the coup d'état of 1851, he was forced to flee the country. Hugo and his family lived in Brussels for a year and then moved to the Channel Islands, where he wrote a satirical attack on NAPOLEON III entitled *Les Chatiments* (1853). While in exile, Hugo's family deserted him; his daughter Adele ran off in pursuit of a married English soldier, and his wife returned to Brussels, where she died in 1868. Only Juliette remained by his side. During this time he worked on the novel *Les Misérables,* which was published in 1862.

After the downfall of Napoleon III in 1870, Hugo triumphantly returned to France, where he was again elected to the National Assembly but soon resigned in protest against the conservative majority. After his death, the body of the man considered France's greatest poet lay in state under the Arc de Triomphe before being provided a national funeral.

Humperdinck, Engelbert (1854–1921) German composer. A friend of composer RICHARD WAGNER, he assisted Wagner at Bayreuth in 1880–81. The most famous of Humperdinck's six operas is *Hänsel und Gretel* (1893), which in its folk-based music and subject matter bears the influence of Wagner. He also wrote choral works, songs, and other compositions, and taught in Barcelona, Berlin, and Frankfurt.

Hunt, [James Henry] Leigh (1784–1859) English journalist, critic, and poet. Hunt was an early and constant champion of many writers, including John Keats and Percy Bysshe Shelley. In 1808 he became editor of the liberal periodical the *Examiner,* which he established with his brother John.

From 1819 to 1821 Hunt published the *Indicator* and then accepted an invitation from Shelley to move to Italy and edit the *Liberal.* After returning to England in 1825, Hunt wrote *Lord Byron and His Contemporaries* (1828), which many readers perceived as a breach of confidence because Hunt divulged intimate details about his literary friends. *Poetical Works,* a collection of Hunt's poetry, was published in 1832 and he continued to edit and write for periodicals, including the *Tatler* and *Leigh Hunt's London Journal.* His best-known poems include the lyrics "Abou Ben Adhem" (1834) and "Jenny Kissed Me" (1844). Other works include *Men, Women, and Books* (1847) and the play *A Legend of Florence* (1840), which was popular in its day.

Hunt was awarded a royal pension in 1847 and published his autobiography in 1850.

Hunt, William Holman (1827–1910) English artist. Born in London, he began taking painting lessons at the age of twelve. In 1843 he began studying in the British Museum, and the following year he was accepted into the Royal Academy where he met JOHN EVERETT MILLAIS and DANTE GABRIEL ROSSETTI.

Hunt's first painting for the Royal Academy—*Hark!*—was exhibited in 1846, and by the time he exhibited *Rienzi* in 1849, the initials *P.R.B.* had been added after his signature. The "Pre-Raphaelite Brotherhood," included Hunt, Millais, and Rossetti, and their 1850 exhibition was severely criticized by many leading figures of the day, including CHARLES DICKENS. JOHN RUSKIN, however, defended the group's attempts to depict fictional and historical figures in a realistic fashion.

Hunt increasingly turned toward religious subjects, and his 1854 painting of *The Light of the World,* an allegorical painting of Christ knocking at a door with a lantern in one hand, was publicly praised by Ruskin and brought Hunt his first public success.

In an attempt to add realistic accuracy to his religious paintings, Hunt traveled to Syria and Palestine, and after his return in July 1855, he exhibited *The Scapegoat* and *The Finding of the Saviour in the Temple,* which was sold for a record 5,500 guineas.

Even after Millais and Rossetti defected from the PRE-RAPHAELITES, Hunt continued to uphold their commitment to detail and realism. He published an account of the movement, *Pre-Raphaelitism and the Pre-Raphaelite Brotherhood,* in 1905.

Huxley, Thomas Henry (1825–1895) English biologist. The seventh of eight children, Thomas Huxley was born in Ealing. Although he received only two years of formal education as a child, he was awarded a scholarship to Charing Cross Hospital Medical School in 1842. He graduated in 1845 and the same year published a scientific paper describing a part of the hair follicle that became known as "Huxley's layer."

After passing the Royal College of Surgeons examination in 1846, Huxley was appointed an assistant surgeon in the Royal Navy. He spent his time aboard ship collecting and studying marine life; his detailed research papers were sent back to England, where shortly after his return in 1850 he was elected a Fellow of the Royal Society. Huxley's scientific work became the basis for all future classifications of a number of classes of sea life, including jellyfish and their relatives, and squids and their relatives. The publication of *The Origin of Species* by CHARLES DARWIN in 1859 became a call to arms for Huxley as he constantly trumpeted his friend's brilliant and controversial ideas. Huxley's debate with

Bishop Samuel Wilberforce about Darwin's theories at the Oxford meeting of the British Association for the Advancement of Science in 1860 securely pitted evolution against theology, and Huxley's effective defense reportedly caused women to faint in the aisles.

While Darwin had tactfully avoided applying his theories to the human species, Huxley boldly declared that humans had evolved from other animals in the 1863 publication *Man's Place in Nature.* Huxley also concluded that there was no evidence for racial superiority and published several papers on the subject during the 1860s.

"That there is no evidence of the existence of such a being as the God of the theologians is true enough," Huxley wrote. In 1869, in an attempt to define his philosophy of life, he coined the term "agnostic." From 1870, Huxley was drawn away from his scientific study as demands upon his time increased. He served on numerous commissions, was president of the Royal Society from 1883 to 1885, and was a member of the first London School Board.

Huxley's interest in education led to his involvement with many institutions, including Eton College, the University of London, and the Royal College of Science, and in 1876 he traveled to Baltimore to speak at the opening of Johns Hopkins University. In 1890 he moved from London to Eastbourne, where he died.

Ibsen, Henrik Johan (1828–1906) Norwegian playwright and poet. Ibsen was the father of modern realistic drama. His work provides a harsh critique of the conventional society of his day and reflects his remarkable psychological insight into character. Most of his major plays are realistic, though in the latter part of his career he turned increasingly to symbolism.

Born in Skien, Norway, he left home at fifteen to become an apothecary's apprentice. He soon turned to theater, working as a stage manager and artistic director while writing his first plays. He initially experimented with various styles, producing historical, nationalistic, and romantic plays. He moved to Rome in 1864 and lived in Italy and Germany for the next twenty-seven years, flourishing artistically much more than he had in his native land. He returned to Norway in 1891, settling in Christiania (now Oslo) for the rest of his life.

His first significant plays were the verse dramas *Brand* (1866) and *Peer Gynt* (1867). They were followed by *Emperor and Galilean* (1873), a two-part prose drama. Beginning in the late 1870s, his greatest works, all prose drama, began to appear. *The Pillars of Society* (1877) was followed by *A Doll's House* (1879), *Ghosts* (1891), and *An Enemy of the People* (1882). These four plays, which continue to be revived frequently, explore the parochialism, hypocrisy, and corruption of the small-town world in which Ibsen grew up.

His subsequent plays—THE WILD DUCK (1884), *Rosmersholm* (1886), and *The Lady from the Sea* (1888)—became more and more symbolic. *Hedda Gabler* (1890) has turned out to be one of his most popular and enduring dramas. His late plays—*The Master Builder* (1892), *Little Eyolf* (1894), and *John Gabriel Borkman* (1896)—are more psychological in theme. *When We Dead Awaken* (1899), his final play—or, as he called it, his "dramatic epilogue"—is an autobiographical work analyzing the role of the artist.

ice ages See AGASSIZ, LOUIS.

ice hockey Sport. While the exact origin of ice hockey is obscure, it is generally believed that the first organized game was played in

Kingston, Ontario, Canada, in 1855 by British soldiers stationed there. Some legends contend, however, that the game was devised at Windsor Castle in 1853 when royal family members attempted to play a form of field hockey on a frozen lake. It is suggested that Queen Victoria watched and offered encouragement and spiced rum to the participants.

Montreal is usually cited as the birthplace of hockey. Students at McGill University proposed a set of rules in 1875 and formed a league. In 1885 the Amateur Hockey Association (AHA) was formed and comprised teams from Montreal, Quebec, and Ottawa. By the winter of 1894 the game had entered the northern states of America, and the first official league game on record in the United States was played in New York City on December 15, 1896.

In 1893, Frederick Arthur, Lord Stanley of Preston, donated a $48.67 trophy to the AHA champions, the Montreal Amateur Athletic Association team, with directions that it be a challenge trophy. From 1894 until 1909 two trustees oversaw the trophy. In 1910, however, the four-team National Hockey Association (NHA), which had formed the previous year, convinced the trustees that professional hockey was stronger than amateur hockey and gained control of the Stanley Cup. The NHA was renamed the National Hockey League in 1917.

icebox Food storage device. First patented in 1803, the icebox, or refrigerator, was a wooden cabinet lined with tin or zinc and containing ice to keep food cool. For most of the Victorian era, iceboxes were principally for commercial use; the high cost of ice made home refrigeration a luxury. Ice harvesting companies cut their product from northern lakes and ponds in winter and stored it in insulated icehouses year round. In 1834 American inventor Jacob Perkins patented the first mechanical refrigeration system, based on the principle that evaporation of a liquid reduces the temperature of the objects around it. Though the mechanical refrigerator would not become a domestic staple until the twentieth century, the technology was a boon to the nineteenth-century ice industry, allowing it to produce ice artificially. This lowered the cost of ice for home delivery, and helped bring about the widespread domestic use of iceboxes by the 1890s.

Iddesleigh, Earl of See NORTHCOTE, Sir STAFFORD.

Immaculate Conception Religious doctrine. The Roman Catholic teaching states that Mary, the mother of Jesus, was preserved from the effects of original sin from the moment of her conception. Though proposed and debated since at least the Middle Ages, it was not defined as dogma until Pope Pius IX did so in 1854. See PAPACY.

imperialism Expansion of governing power or influence over other nations or societies. For nineteenth-century Western powers, imperialism was a way of life. FRANCE, for example, acquired Indochina (see SOUTHEAST ASIA); GREAT BRITAIN expanded from its existing possessions in INDIA into the PUNJAB and Burma; the UNITED STATES acquired the PHILIPPINES from SPAIN; and all of Europe scrambled for control of AFRICA at the end of the century. Imperialism frequently took the form of colonialism, with the dominant society exploiting the less powerful one economically while declining to grant self-government or genuine political participation to the colony's inhabitants; for example, this was the British practice in India. In other cases, imperialism resulted in the granting of self-government, as Britain did with CANADA and AUSTRALIA, or took the form of coercive influence in weaker nations' affairs, as the British did in CHINA. The factors motivating imperialism included the desire for raw materials, markets, and trade routes; competition with other imperial powers; humanitarian and missionary goals; belief in the superiority of one's culture; and the appetite for national pride and prestige. See also BRITISH EMPIRE.

Impressionism Artistic movement. The Impressionists used contemporary color theory to achieve a more exact representation of nature's colors and tones. The majority of Impressionists applied paint in small, quick brush strokes and believed in painting outdoors in order to capture a fleeting image of color and light.

The 1860s were formative years in which artists explored working in the open air, using a lighter palette, and studying the colors of the landscape. Some of these artists, who included EDOUARD MANET and PAUL CÉZANNE, first exhibited their works in 1862 in Paris at the *SALON DES REFUSES,* but the official exhibition of Impressionist works did not occur for over a decade. In fact, the name "Impressionism" was not coined until 1874, following a derogatory comment by the critic Louis Leroy after seeing the Claude Monet painting *Impression Sunrise.* Soon the term "Impressionists" was used as a label for the whole group of artists who exhibited outside of the Salon's conservative agenda as the "Society of Painters, Etchers, and Engravers."

The first official Impressionist exhibition opened to the public in the vacant studio of the photographer Nadar on April 15, 1874, and included work by Monet, PIERRE-AUGUSTE RENOIR, ALFRED SISLEY, CAMILLE PISSARRO, PAUL CÉZANNE, EDGAR DEGAS, EUGÈNE BOUDIN, and BERTHE MORISOT. These Impressionist painters were absorbed by the natural play of light and aimed to capture the visual impression made by a scene rather than duplicate it in calculated, minute detail.

The Impressionists were divided as to who should exhibit. Degas wanted to show work by other artists such as Manet, although his influential paintings were never exhibited with the group. In the 1880s, Impressionism became less of a common style as subject matter became more varied and general. Sisley continued to paint landscapes while Renoir became a portraitist and Pissarro came under the influence of the POINTILLISM of GEORGES SEURAT.

The last Impressionist exhibition was held in 1886. By the 1890s, Impressionism had become widely accepted as an independent artistic style throughout most of Europe. It even had an impact on music. CLAUDE DEBUSSY wrote Impressionist compositions that were designed to create vague impressions and moods through rich and varied harmonies.

In Memoriam (1850) Long poem by ALFRED, Lord TENNYSON. Composed in memory of his friend Arthur Hallam (1811–1833), the elegy is considered one of the greatest in English. While expressing Tennyson's personal grief, it also gives voice to the characteristic Victorian conflict between faith and doubt. The highly popular poem gave comfort to Queen VICTORIA after her husband Prince ALBERT'S death.

India South central Asian nation. It is bordered at the present time by Pakistan and the Arabian Sea to the west; China, Bhutan, and Nepal to the north; Bangladesh, Burma, and the Bay of Bengal to the east; and the Indian Ocean to the south. During the nineteenth century the Indian subcontinent, mostly Hindu but with a sizable Muslim minority,

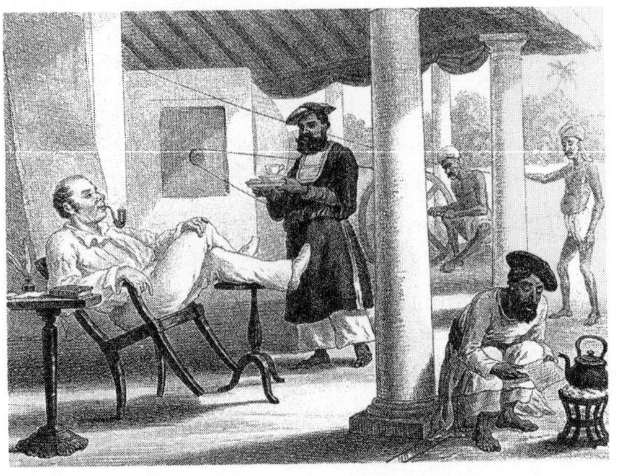

An 1860 drawing by G. F. Atkinson illustrates a scene from a British outpost in India. Private Collection.

was a hodgepodge of independent states brought under British control.

By the late Victorian Age, India was considered the jewel of the BRITISH EMPIRE, the symbol of Britain's imperial splendor, wealth, and might. Yet at the beginning of Victoria's reign, it was only a distant possession administered by the BRITISH EAST INDIA COMPANY, which had established its first outpost there at Surat in 1613. By 1805 the British East India Company controlled the regions of Madras and Bengal while subordinating other principalities to their rule, often by exploiting existing regional antagonisms. Wars against AFGHANISTAN (see ANGLO-AFGHAN WARS), Sind, the PUNJAB, and Burma (see SOUTHEAST ASIA) from the 1820s to the 1850s expanded the company's control. By 1857 almost the entire subcontinent was in British hands.

The British subjection brought vast changes to the economy of the area. India grew as a supplier of raw materials when its tea, coffee, and coal mining industries developed. The colony became a valued market for English machine-produced cotton goods, while a ban on Indian textile imports to Britain all but destroyed the Indian handicraft industry. The economy was also changed by the introduction of RAILROADS, STEAM POWER, and the TELEGRAPH and other Western inventions.

Social change accompanied English colonization. Exorbitant land taxes reduced many small landholders to tenant farmers. The English tried to suppress traditional practices that they found repugnant, including SUTTEE—the burning of widows—and infanticide.

Indian resistance took many forms, most notably the unsuccessful but bloody INDIAN MUTINY (Sepoy Rebellion) of 1857–58. The uprising began among Bengali soldiers, SEPOYS, angered by Britain's annexation of their homeland, Oudh, in 1856 and by rumors that British military authorities were forcing them to violate Hindu and Muslim laws against the use of beef fat and pork fat. The mutiny became a general Indian uprising that prompted the crown to abolish the British East India Company and rule India directly through a viceroy. Rule was centralized in this office, and its policies were administered by the largest imperial bureaucracy in the world (see CIVIL SERVICE, BRITISH). The liberalizing tendencies of some previous India hands, such as JOHN STUART MILL and THOMAS BABINGTON MACAULAY, who had hoped to teach Indians to participate in Western civilization, were forgotten in a wave of conservatism. The new Anglo-Indian officials believed that law and order were needed to restrain a people they viewed as anarchic and intellectually inferior.

Both before and after the Indian Mutiny, paternalistic British officials ruled autocratically, making a good living in well-appointed encampments divorced from the natives. Often they returned home to England after several years with substantial savings and pensions paid for by Indian taxpayers. They also brought stories of their adventures that fed the growing public interest in the far-off colony. The opening of the SUEZ CANAL in 1869 eased the passage to India, reducing travel time from Britain, which was about four months in the 1830s, to about seventeen days by century's end. Traveling in luxury aboard SHIPS run by the Peninsular and Oriental and other lines, aristocratic and middle-class Britons made their way to India to do business and make or increase fortunes. Britain's power and majesty over the subcontinent was symbolized in 1876 when Queen VICTORIA was made empress of India.

Economic changes accelerated in the second half of the century. Commercial agricultural production for export outstripped subsistence farming, aided by the tremendous growth in railroads. Tea, jute, coal, coffee, and indigo were developed as export commodities, while the British government maintained control of the immensely profitable sale of opium by India to China (see OPIUM WARS).

In the area of foreign policy, Russia's annexation of lands close to Afghanistan's northern borders prompted the start of the Second Afghan War (1878–80). The Anglo-Russian agreement of 1887 settled Afghanistan's borders. Viceroy Lord Curzon tried to stabilize the Afghan-Indian border, an area of constant tribal rebellions, by establishing the North-West Frontier Province, but British troops were often called out to fight local uprisings. In 1886, Upper Burma, with an area larger than Britain, was incorporated into India.

Indian opposition to English rule developed throughout the century. Its most important manifestation was the Indian National Congress founded in 1885. Dominated by middle-class and professional Hindus, many of them educated in the British universities in India, the congress demanded the curtailment of the viceroy's powers and other reforms. Muslim nationalists founded the Muslim League in 1906. Nationalist agitation, including mass nonviolent resistance led by Mohandas (Mahatma) Gandhi (1869–1948), lasted until 1947 when the British granted independence to their most prized possession, which was divided into Muslim Pakistan and an overwhelmingly Hindu India.

Indian Mutiny (Sepoy Mutiny, Sepoy Rebellion) (1857–58) In 1857, SEPOYS the native soldiers in the Bengal army, one of the three armies in British India, rebelled against British rule in what was one of the largest mutinies in history. Various policies, both long and short term, ignited the uprising. The BRITISH EAST INDIA COMPANY had expanded its political domain by dethroning local leaders and transferring property to Indians more sympathetic to British rule. In 1853 the company announced that the Mogul dynasty would end with the death of the current emperor, a decision that angered Bengalese troops. The annexation of the Muslim kingdom of Oudh in 1856 also embittered sepoys from that region. In addition, the British had fomented religious unrest by suppressing some religious rituals, including SUTTEE, or widow burning.

Policies within the army also worsened relations between sepoys and their British leaders. The British East India Company, which controlled the army, had reduced sepoy allowances. An 1856 order subjected them to military duty outside India. The number of ethnic British troops in the Indian army had been reduced by transfers to the Crimean and Chinese theaters, so that by the time of the rebellion, five-sixths of the army were sepoys.

One of the largest mutinies ever recorded, the Indian rebellion of 1857 set Sepoys against the British colonists. Courtesy of the National Army Museum, London.

Against this background, new cartridges for the Enfield rifle arrived in India in 1857. Rumors spread among the sepoys that the cartridges were greased with fat from pigs and cows. It was also rumored that they would have to rip off one end of the cartridge with their teeth to free the gunpowder. This horrified the Hindus who held the cow sacred and the Muslims who were forbidden to eat pig flesh. The facts were different: Vegetable fat could be used to grease the cartridge, and soldiers could open them with their hands.

The mutiny began when eighty-five sepoys refused to use the cartridges. Their religious commitment brought them a court martial and with it a sentence of ten years of road labor in chains. In response, the Indian troops rebelled on May 10, 1857, in Meerut near Delhi. They quickly captured Delhi, killing many European soldiers and civilians. The revolt spread throughout the upper Ganges River valley with tens of thousands of Indian civilians joining the soldiers to proclaim the last Mogul emperor the ruler of all India.

A series of pitched battles and sieges followed, highlighted by the sepoy siege of Lucknow. Sir Colin Campbell, who had been appointed commander in chief with orders to end the mutiny, lifted the siege in November. Fortunately for the British, the Indian troops in the rest of India remained loyal. The sepoys in the north and the thousands who joined them proved no match for the disciplined British and Indian troops. By June 1858 the mutiny was over, and its suppression was marked by many atrocities on both sides.

The rebellion shocked Victorian England. The East India Company was dismantled in 1858, and the English government took direct control of India. Land annexations ended, and independent states were left intact as protectorates. The British also discovered the virtue of religious tolerance and the wisdom of maintaining more British troops in Indian regiments.

Indian Wars General name given to decades of conflict between Native Americans in North America and the UNITED STATES military. By the beginning of Queen Victoria's reign, Native Americans in the Northeast and around the Great Lakes had been defeated and/or resettled farther west. In the Florida Territory the Seminoles waged a fierce but losing struggle (1835–42) that left two thousand American soldiers and settlers dead.

Native Americans in the Northwest offered little organized resistance to European settlement until 1847 when a brief war erupted. The Modoc tribe lost another struggle in Oregon in 1872. In 1877, Chief JOSEPH of the Nez Percé tribe led the most sustained resistance to American troops, but real resistance had ended by the 1880s.

In the Southwest troops subdued a revolt by the Pueblos in New Mexico in 1847. Between 1862 and 1871, the Apaches almost regained control of what is now Arizona but were ultimately defeated. Warriors continued to raid on both sides of the United States–Mexico border until their most successful chief, GERONIMO, surrendered in 1886.

The most famous Indian struggles occurred in what is now South Dakota and Wyoming. The Sioux and Cheyenne tribes resisted white settlement of the area until the 1870s. Railroad construction and the discovery of gold attracted new settlers, but the tribes refused to resettle. Chiefs SITTING BULL and CRAZY HORSE defeated the troops of GEORGE CUSTER at the Battle of the Little Big Horn in 1876 but were eventually defeated. The last major event of the wars occurred at the Battle of WOUNDED KNEE in South Dakota in 1890 when a band of Sioux refused to surrender their arms and troops killed more than two hundred men, women, and children.

Indonesia Republic comprising more than three thousand islands in the Malay archipelago off the mainland of SOUTHEAST ASIA. Indonesia includes Java, Sumatra, Bali, Madura, most of Borneo, Celebes (Sulawesi), Timor, the Moluccas, and Irian Jaya (West New Guinea). In the Victorian era, the predominantly Muslim region was known as the Dutch East Indies. The Dutch had dominated it since 1595, although parts of the region were colonized by other European powers. Eastern Timor, for example, was Portuguese until annexed by modern Indonesia in 1975, while Brunei and East Malaysia, both parts of the island Borneo, were under British control. The Dutch East Indies gained worldwide attention with the volcanic eruption of KRAKATOA in 1883; it was also notable to Victorian scientists for the discovery of fossils of the early human ancestor JAVA MAN in 1891 and of a dietary cure for BERIBERI in 1896. Indonesia gained its independence in 1949.

industrialization Generic term for the economic and social processes by which a society shifts from an agricultural basis to a manufacturing basis dependent on modern machinery. It began in the mid-eighteenth century in Britain with the industrial revolution brought about by STEAM POWER used in machinery for making textiles. In Britain the revolution was essentially over by the early years of the Victorian era, with a flourishing factory system in place, a large urban population at work, and a powerful capitalist class thriving. For the other Western powers, however, the industrial revolution was just beginning. France underwent it after 1830, Germany after 1850, and the United States after 1865. Meanwhile, Great Britain continued to grow as a manufacturing power. By the end of the Victorian era, industrialization had become a fact of life throughout much of the Western world. Elsewhere—Russia, China, Japan, and what is now called the developing world—it would become a fact of life in the twentieth century.

inert (noble) gases Colorless, odorless, shapeless elements with valence 0 and very low chemical activity. English physicist John William Strutt, Lord RAYLEIGH, and English chemist William Ramsay discovered the first known member of the group, argon, in 1894. HELIUM, discovered in 1868 in the sun's atmosphere by French astronomer Pierre-Jules-César Janssen and English astronomer Sir JOSEPH NORMAN LOCKYER, was identified as another member of the family by Ramsay in 1895, who found it occurring on earth. Ramsay and his colleague Morris William Travers went on to discover neon, krypton, and xenon in 1898, while the sixth and last member of this group, radon, was discovered by German chemist Friedrich Ernst Dorn in 1900. Because these elements seemed incapable of forming compounds, they were called "inert gases." However, after experiments beginning in 1962 showed that some of them could be induced to form compounds, the term "noble gases" became preferred. They are also sometimes called the rare gases.

infrared radiation Electromagnetic emission with wavelengths longer than those of visible light but shorter than radio waves; the wavelength range is 0.7 micrometers to 1.0 millimeter. German-born English astronomer William Herschel discovered it in 1800 when he found that the temperature measured by a thermometer rose in the area beyond the red end of a sunlight spectrum, though no light was visible. In 1850, Italian physicist Macedonio Melloni constructed a device called a thermopile that allowed him to study the heating effects of infrared rays. He showed that infrared waves had the same structure as light waves but were longer. This showed that the electromagnetic spectrum extended beyond visible light. In time, the spectrum was also understood to contain RADIO WAVES, ultraviolet waves, X RAYS, and GAMMA RAYS.

Ingemann, Bernhard Severin (1789–1862) Danish poet and novelist. He was a schoolteacher in Sorø. His popular historical novels set in medieval Denmark helped awaken the sense of a Danish national literature. His novels include *Valdemar Seier* (*Waldemar, Surnamed Seir, or the Victorious,* 1826) and *Kong Erik og de Fredløse* (*King Eric and the Outlaws,* 1833). His *Morning and Evening Songs* (*Morgen og aftensange,* 1839), a collection of poems expressing a naive worldview, contains some of the most highly regarded Danish lyric poetry.

Ingres, Jean-Auguste-Dominique (1780–1867) French painter. A pupil of neoclassical master Jacques-Louis David, Ingres continued the Davidian classical tradition throughout most of his career and remained an opponent to the new, modern trends of ROMANTICISM and REALISM. A successful portraitist, Ingres was considered the last great artist in the field of portraiture before the growth of photography. His pencil drawing and painting of Louis Bertin (1832) reveal a psychological insight and physical accuracy that would be lost among later neo-Baroque Romantics.

By the beginning of the Victorian era, Ingres was established as a champion of neoclassicism with such paintings as *La Grande Baigneuse* (1808) and *La Grande Odalisque* (1819) as well as the controversial portrait of *Napoleon I on the Imperial Throne* that had been exhibited in the Salon of 1806. Commissions such as *The Apotheosis of Homer,* which he created for a ceiling at the Louvre, pointed to his position in the traditional artistic community.

Ingres's compositions offer a clear, precise space and tend to be dominated by icy local colors. He painted his figures with a cool detachment while emphasizing their frozen solidity and voluptuousness. Later works such as the sumptuous *Turkish Bath* (1863) emphasize such voluptuousness.

To younger artists, Ingres's perfection of craftsmanship embodied the spirit of Renaissance classicism, especially that of Raphael. EDGAR DEGAS in particular would later reinterpret Ingres's classical draftsmanship.

insanity A mental condition that renders the afflicted unable to function in society. In Britain during the Victorian era, the causes and diagnosis of insanity were the center of an ongoing medical debate and a matter of great public interest. Insanity was also a target of legal reform and a staple of literature. There was no consensus on the causes of insanity. Physical factors were believed to play a role, including advanced old age, poor circulation, head injuries, and sunstroke. It was also postulated that insanity might be caused by immoral behavior, such as masturbation, debauchery, and overindulgence of any kind. The reproductive system of females was believed to make them more susceptible to insanity than males.

Numerous varieties of insanity were identified. These included melancholia, a severe depression; mania, a raving lunacy; hysteria, an emotional disorder associated with women; hypochondria, a depression related to imaginary physical ailments; and moral insanity, a loss of self-control and ability to act in a socially acceptable fashion.

Interest in the insane led to a number of legislative developments in England, including the Lunatics Asylum Act of 1845, which established a permanent central commission on lunacy and required the building of county asylums. Asylum conditions improved in many places, with humane treatment emphasized by reformers. Harsh restraints such as straitjackets, leg locks, and wrist locks continued to be common, along with such medical treatments as drugging with opium, leeching, and purging. But more humane treatments were also introduced, including moral management, which sought to establish a homelike environment for the moral reform of patients, and hydrotherapy, or the "water cure," which treated patients with baths and drinking water. By the end of the century the medical profession was developing two distinct approaches to the treatment of insanity: the neurological approach, which sought to treat the brain, and the psychoanalytic approach of SIGMUND FREUD, which sought to treat the mind.

As much as it was a medical and legislative matter, insanity was a subject for representation in the arts. Of particular interest were women gone mad, portrayed often in poetry, prose, and painting. Examples included CHARLOTTE BRONTË's Mrs. Rochester in JANE EYRE, ALFRED, Lord TENNYSON's Lady of Shalott, and Victorian stage incarnations of Shakespeare's Ophelia in *Hamlet*.

internal combustion engine Mechanical device. The internal combustion engine converts heat into power by burning fuel in chambers within the engine, instead of in an external furnace, as in a steam engine (see STEAM POWER). Belgian-born French inventor Jean-Joseph-Etienne Lenoir (1822–1900) built the first internal combustion engine in 1860, but it was inefficient. In 1876, German engineer Nikolaus August Otto (1832–1891) built a more efficient gas-powered four-stroke cycle engine that became the basis for the modern AUTOMOBILE engine. In it, a piston inside a cylinder makes four strokes: (1) it moves outward, drawing in a mixture of air and fuel through an intake valve; (2) it moves inward, compressing the mixture, which is ignited by an electric spark near the top of the stroke; (3) the resulting explosion drives the piston outward, supplying power that does the work; (4) the piston moves inward again, forcing the waste gases out through an exhaust valve. The cycle is then repeated. With the invention of the carburetor, a device that produces a mixture of vaporized fuel and air, invented by René Panhard and Emile Lavassor of France in 1891, and the development of the OIL (*petroleum*) industry, it became possible by the end of the nineteenth century to use liquid gasoline as a fuel.

An alternative to the Otto engine was the diesel engine, invented by German engineer

Rudolf Diesel (1858–1913) about 1896. In this type of engine, the fuel-air mixture is ignited not by an electric spark but by the heat developed through high compression. Since the compression is greater than in an Otto engine, the diesel engine is larger and heavier, but it eliminates the need for an electrical system and can use cheaper and less flammable fuels. It is widely used in trucks, buses, locomotives, and ships, as well as electric generators and oil pumps.

Ireland Western European island nation in the Atlantic Ocean. It is separated from GREAT BRITAIN by the North Channel, Irish Sea, and St. George's Channel. During the Victorian era, Ireland, overwhelmingly Roman Catholic, remained under the rule of Protestant Great Britain. Irish attempts to end the eight centuries of British rule shaped the country's politics throughout the period.

At the beginning of the nineteenth century, Ireland was impoverished and politically disorganized. Irish Catholics were legally prevented from leasing or buying land until the late eighteenth century. The so-called Penal Laws also forced Catholic landowners to bequeath their property equally among their sons rather than keep estates intact. The land was further divided by landlords looking to increase their rent rolls. The continuing subdivision of the land and the lack of tenant protections against eviction or arbitrary rent hikes helped keep the Irish economy at subsistence levels and spawned chronic agricultural violence. Absentee landlordism and English laws restricting the export of Irish goods, particularly wool, also crippled the economy.

The last shred of Irish political independence ended in 1800 when the Act of Union abolished the Irish Parliament and forced Irish members to sit in the English Parliament. The first great resistance to English rule in the nineteenth century was led by DANIEL O'CONNELL who headed a successful movement to end the ban on Catholic representatives in Parliament. He himself was elected to Parliament in 1828 and then used his political organization to wage a battle to repeal the Union and restore the Irish Parliament. The sight of hundreds of thousands of Irishmen dressed in "Repealer coats" and marching in military formation at huge demonstrations terrified the English. In 1843 the British government banned a huge planned meeting, and O'Connell canceled the demonstration, a decision that crippled his leadership.

O'Connell's failures led many younger men to embrace violent rebellion as the only way to win independence. The group known as YOUNG IRELAND, led first by poet and writer Thomas Davis and then by John Mitchel, tried to resurrect past glories of Celtic warriors and began to address the issue of land reform. Their efforts were crippled by the beginning of the IRISH POTATO FAMINE in 1845, which by 1851 had killed one million people and drove more than one million to immigrate, most to the United States from where they supported subsequent independence efforts. Inadequate English relief efforts and the continuation of evictions during the famine—over 100,000 in 1849—further embittered the Irish against English rule. Young Ireland mounted a weak rebellion in 1848 that was easily suppressed. Most of its leaders fled the country or were transported.

Post-famine Ireland remained relatively quiescent for a decade. The Irish members in Parliament tried to organize themselves into a unified voting bloc to win Irish control over Ireland's internal affairs, or HOME RULE, but failed to wring significant concessions from the English LIBERAL PARTY or the CONSERVATIVE PARTY. Local tenant organizations sprang up throughout the country, but no progress was made toward radically altering the land system. A new militant group, the Irish Republican Brotherhood, also known as FENIANS, emerged in the late 1850s under the leadership of James Stephens, but their rebellion in 1867 failed dismally.

The most significant event in Irish politics during the Victorian era was the emergence of CHARLES STEWART PARNELL as leader of a revived IRISH PARTY in Parliament. Parnell ousted ISAAC BUTT, founder of the Home Rule movement, from the party's leadership and whipped the Irish members into a disciplined voting bloc. Parnell allied the party with Irish National LAND LEAGUE of MICHAEL DAVITT, an organization that channeled agrarian unrest into a disciplined, sometimes violent, campaign to win fair rents and lease security for tenants. Poor harvests in the late 1870s fueled tenant attacks against landlords and troops. Parnell used the threat of tenant violence and his bloc of votes in Parliament to demand land reform and to push for passage of a Home Rule bill. The Liberal government of WILLIAM GLADSTONE passed a land reform bill in 1881 but failed to force a Home Rule bill through Parliament.

Parnell's attempt to retain control of the party after being named correspondent in the notorious divorce suit of KATHARINE "KITTY" O'SHEA split the party. Parnell died in 1891, and the Irish Party remained divided for over a decade before its reunification under JOHN REDMOND. The Party would never recapture its former influence, and Home Rule—vehemently opposed by Irish Protestants in the north and by the Conservative Party in England—would never be realized. In the twentieth century parliamentary strategies would be eclipsed by violent uprisings and guerrilla warfare aimed at winning complete national independence. Agitation for land reform—now led by the United Irish League—continued both its violent and parliamentary paths, winning passage of a 1903 land law that enabled many tenants to buy land.

The failure of parliamentary politics helped revive an interest in Irish culture, literature, and history. Douglas Hyde founded the Gaelic League in 1893 to promote the use of the Irish language and to popularize Irish folk culture. Playwrights John Millington Synge and Lady AUGUSTA GREGORY and poet WILLIAM BUTLER YEATS were other prominent figures in the movement.

Irish Land Act of 1870 British legislation. The first in a series of land acts, the 1870 law was passed by the British Parliament to address inequities of landlord-tenant relations in Ireland. English landlords, many of them absentee owners, could charge exorbitant rents, evict tenants on short notice and for little cause, and refuse to compensate tenants for improvements they made to the land. The result was an impoverished peasantry whose lot was made more desperate by the famines of the 1840s.

The Irish Land Act of 1870, supported by Prime Minister WILLIAM GLADSTONE, offered some relief by limiting powers of eviction and by providing for compensation for land improvements. It did little to regulate rents, however, and it did not stop evictions for failure to pay rent. It did establish the precedent of tenant rights and paved the way for more effective land acts.

Irish Party General term for Irish politicians during the Victorian era. The term refers more to a common set of interests and goals among the Irish members of the English Parliament than it does to a traditional party organization such as the English LIBERAL PARTY and the CONSERVATIVE PARTY of the time. The Irish members united themselves around various causes in the nineteenth century including Catholic emancipation, the repeal of the union between Ireland and England, and HOME RULE. Their unity was undermined, however, by shifting issues and the tendency of key members to be bought off with governmental appointments.

ISAAC BUTT organized the Irish members around the Home Rule issue, and the group was commonly known at the Home Rule Party in the 1860s and 1870s. He was succeeded by CHARLES STEWART PARNELL who organized the Irish members into a disciplined voting bloc that was the balance of power between the Liberals and Conservatives in the 1880s. Parnell's disgrace in a divorce case and death in 1891 divided the party until 1900 when JOHN REDMOND reunited it in a quest for Home Rule. The party was ultimately replaced by the modern parties that developed in independent Ireland after 1920.

Irish potato famine A series of crop failures (1845–48) caused by a fungus that attacked Ireland's staple food. Between 750,000 and 1 million people died of starvation and disease between 1846 and 1851. By 1855, 1 million Irish had emigrated, most of them to the United States. This emigration continued throughout the century; Ireland's population decreased from 8 million in 1840 to 4.5 million by 1900.

British relief response was slow, but by 1848 some 2 million people were being fed. The slow reaction and the continuation of evictions for nonpayment of rent throughout the famine further embittered the Irish against British rule. The famine led to the repeal of the CORN LAWS and gave impetus to land reform movements later in the century.

Irish Republican Brotherhood See FENIANS.

iron, clothes Household device. It was first developed in Greece during the fourth century. Clothes irons underwent several improvements during the 1800s, all of which reflected the aesthetic preferences and technological advances of the age. Sadirons—"sad" meaning "heavy"—were the hand-sized iron slabs that were heated and reheated during the process of ironing; they became highly decorative or were made from semiprecious metals, as was the trivet used for resting the iron safely. In 1882, with the advent of electricity, the first electric iron was introduced. But inefficient design, combined with the low numbers of families who had electricity in their homes, kept the electric iron from becoming popular until the twentieth century.

irredentism Nationalist policy demanding the recovery of territories and populations thought of as belonging to the parent state. The term originated in the years after Italian unification in 1861 when superpatriots called for the liberation of *Italia irredenta* ("unredeemed Italy"), referring to areas held by Austria-Hungary and France. Irrendentism played an important role in the politics of FRANCE and ITALY and the BALKANS in the Victorian Age.

Irving, Sir Henry [born John Henry Brodribb] (1838–1905) English actor and impresario. Founder and manager of the celebrated LYCEUM THEATRE, Irving became equally well known for his daring creativity with the theater and his spellbinding performances as tortured souls in such roles as Mephistopheles in *Faust* and as Macbeth, his favorite role. Two years before the founding of the Lyceum, in 1876, he met then-Dublin newspaper theater reviewer BRAM STOKER. Almost immediately the two formed what Stoker called "a friendship as profound, as close, as lasting as can be between two men," lasting thirty years. So affected was Stoker by the forceful, commanding Irving that the actor acted at least as a partial influence in his creation of *Dracula*. Another influential association in his life was with British actress ELLEN TERRY, who was defined as an actress by their many joint appearances on the Lyceum stage.

Italo-Ethiopian Wars Series of conflicts between ITALY and Ethiopia. In the war of 1887–89, Italy operated with the support of the British, who wanted a friendly power in the region to counter the Muslim Mahdists (see MAHDI) who ruled neighboring Sudan. With Britain's assistance, the Italians established a base at Massawa (Mitsiwa) on the Ethiopean coast in Eritrea in 1885 and were attempting to penetrate deeper into the interior. Ethiopian emperor Yohannes (John) IV offered resistance, defeating Italian forces in the Battle of Dogali on January 26, 1887. In the brief conflict, Yohannes was killed not by Italians but by invading Mahdists at the Battle of Metemma (Gallabat) on March 12, 1889. An Ethiopian chieftain who was an ally of Italy took the throne as Emperor Menelik II and negotiated peace later that year in the Treaty of Uccialli (May 2, 1889). The result was Ethiopia's becoming an Italian protectorate, which was disputed by Menelik but accepted by the British.

In the war of 1895–96, Ethiopian emperor Menelik, unsatisfied with Italy's territorial claims, declared war when Italy occupied the district of Tigre. After a major Ethiopian victory at the Battle of Aduwa on March 1, 1896, Italy recognized Ethiopia's independence in the Treaty of Addis Ababa on October 26, 1896. Italy retained a colony on the Eritrean coast.

Italy again invaded Ethiopia under Benito Mussolini in the 1930s.

Italy Southern European country consisting of the Italian peninsula and the large islands of Sicily and Sardinia. The population is ethnically homogenous, though it speaks a wide variety of regional dialects and is predominantly Roman Catholic.

Italy began the Victorian era politically divided. Its eventual unification through its RISORGIMENTO movement was one of the central political events of the time and was widely seen as a triumph of nationalism. Northern Italy was divided between the kingdom of Piedmont-Sardinia, the only native Italian dynasty, and Austria, which ruled most of Lombardy and Tuscany through client states. The Roman Catholic PAPACY controlled a group of small states comprising a belt of territory across central Italy. Southern Italy and Sicily made up the kingdom of Naples, also called the kingdom of the Two Sicilies, which was ruled by a Bourbon dynasty.

Napoleon I's rule of Italy (1797–1815) had a decisive effect on Italian nationalism. Although the French emperor never unified the entire peninsula into one political unit, he did give Italians the experience of participating in relatively liberal governments. Following Napoleon's defeat, conservative, legitimist governments were reinstalled, causing resentment and encouraging rebellions throughout the 1820s and 1830s. Opposition to the current regimes was split among monarchists, republicans, and papists.

The REVOLUTIONS OF 1848 touched Italy, breaking out in Lombardy and Venice against the Austrians. Charles Albert of Piedmont-Sardinia issued a new code of law and sent troops into Lombardy. Initially, Naples and the Pope supported Piedmont but withdrew their forces as revolts broke out at home. The Piedmontese forces were defeated by the Austrians, while the Neapolitan government was able to suppress the revolts against it. Meanwhile, the Pope fled Rome, and a Roman Republic was declared, headed by GIUSEPPE MAZZINI and defended by the troops of GIUSEPPE GARIBALDI. French intervention put an end to the republic after a few months (1849).

In the following decade, Piedmont-Sardinia followed a program of liberalization and gradually won over most Italian nationalists to the monarchist cause. In 1859, under the direction of Count Camillo di CAVOUR, they concluded an alliance with NAPOLEON III and provoked Austria into war. French and Piedmontese troops defeated Austria in a bloody campaign, and Piedmont acquired Lombardy.

The following year Garibaldi, who had fought in the Lombard campaign, launched an invasion of Sicily in support of a rebellion there, without Piedmontese approval. Quickly gathering local support, Garibaldi defeated the Neapolitans in Sicily, then crossed over to the mainland and was again victorious. Uncertain of Garibaldi's intentions, the Piedmontese government intervened and finished the conquest of Naples. In a famous meeting, Garibaldi presented VICTOR EMMANUEL II with the conquered territories. The kingdom of Italy was declared in 1861, although Rome and the Papal States remained under papal control, while Venice was still Austrian.

The Piedmontese faced a major insurgency in the south that was not pacified until 1866. The status of Rome was also a source of friction during the next decade. Napoleon III sent troops to prevent the Italians from taking Rome. Italy sided with Prussia against Austria in the SEVEN WEEKS' WAR (1866) and received Venice as its reward. Finally, in 1870, Napoleon was forced to withdraw his troops from Rome due to the outbreak of the FRANCO-PRUSSIAN WAR. The Italian army conducted the MARCH ON ROME, which was declared the Italian capital.

The newly unified kingdom faced many difficulties. The papacy remained hostile. Resistance to the Piedmontese-dominated government continued in the south. There was a shortage of experienced administrators. The nobility, who formed the upper chamber of the legislature, resentful of their loss of privileges, did not support the king. The lower chamber had no stable parties, and governments formed out of unstable coalitions frequently collapsed. Bribery and corruption became endemic in Italian politics. Many of the nationalists who had worked for the liberation of Italy became disillusioned by the new regime's failings.

Economic growth and industrialization were slow in Italy, and a wide economic gap opened between the better developed north and the poorer south. Large numbers of Italians emigrated to North America.

Italian foreign policy pulled the country in conflicting directions. Italy concluded the Triple Alliance with Germany and Austria in 1882, but later concluded secret defensive pacts with France. Irredentists clamored for the liberation of Italian populations in the Tyrol and the Adriatic coast. Italy joined in the scramble for African colonies, taking Eritrea and Somalia. An attempt to conquer Abyssinia (modern Ethiopia) ended in disaster at the battle of Adowah (1896). Italy ended the Victorian era in the midst of uncertainty.

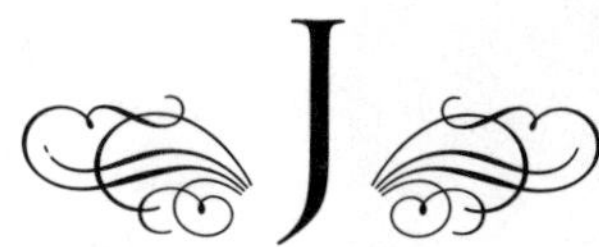

J'accuse See DREYFUS, ALFRED, and ZOLA, EMILE.

Jack the Ripper British murderer. Name given to the murderer of at least five, perhaps seven, women between August and November 1888 in London's East End neighborhood. The victims attributed to Jack were prostitutes or virtually prostitutes. The murderer cut their throats, sexually mutilated them, and in some cases dismembered them. Jack's skill with his tools led many to guess that he was a doctor, perhaps a surgeon. The nickname arose when police received teasing notes about the murders from someone calling himself Jack the Ripper.

Terror gripped London during his grisly career. SCOTLAND YARD saturated the area with police, and vigilantes roamed the streets. Despite these efforts the Ripper was never arrested and Police Commissioner Sir Charles Warren was forced to resign.

After the fifth murder the police ended their investigation, leading to speculation that they received information about the murderer that has never been disclosed. Theories continue to be expressed about Jack's identity.

James, Henry (1843–1916) American fiction writer and critic. James was acknowledged in his day and afterward as a major force in establishing the breadth of American literary expression and in bridging a link between nineteenth- and twentieth-century literary sensibilities. Born in New York City, he was the son of a wealthy intellectual vagabond, theologian Henry James, Sr., and Mary Walsh James, who moved the family—which included brother WILLIAM JAMES—to England, France, Germany, Switzerland, and New England before James was twenty. The experience introduced him to the culture and complexities of established European society in contrast to a young America, a contrast that would permeate his works.

Two years after his year at Harvard Law School, in 1862, James published his first short story and book review. With the encouragement of WILLIAM DEAN HOWELLS, future editor

Henry James, author of the novels Daisy Miller, The Bostonians, *and* Portrait of a Lady, *represented a prominent literary link between the nineteenth and twentieth centuries. Portrait by John Singer Sargent, courtesy of the National Portrait Gallery, London.*

of *The Atlantic,* he published widely. A lengthy trip to Europe in 1869 deepened his literary work by engendering questions about European and American culture. A second trip in 1872–74 resulted in James's initial work on his first substantive novel, *Roderick Hudson* (1876). In 1875 he moved to Paris and associated with literary figures GUSTAVE FLAUBERT, GUY DE MAUPASSANT, EMILE ZOLA, and IVAN TURGENEV, who was to influence him greatly. He also completed the novel *The American* (1877).

Finding Paris uncongenial, James settled in London in 1876 and established himself with literary figures, including ROBERT BROWNING, GEORGE ELIOT, and ALFRED, Lord TENNYSON. Among his many works during the rest of the fruitful decade were *The Europeans* (1878) and the popular, controversial short novel *Daisy Miller* (1878), about an innocent young American woman colored by the complexities of European society.

The next decade began with James's study of New York City mores, *Washington Square* (1880), followed by his masterwork *Portrait of a Lady* (1881). In decades to come the book's main character, Isabel Archer, would become a literary archetype of American innocence, and Madame Merle a symbol of continental deception. Other important novels of the decade include *The Bostonians* (1886), *The Princess Casamassima* (1886), and *The Aspern Papers* (1888).

The 1890s began with the publication of *The Tragic Muse* (1890), which concerns the pursuit of art in a world driven by money. Its commercial failure, coupled with that of his other recent works, led him to the theater, but his play *Guy Domville* (1895) was also a disappointment.

For the rest of his life he concentrated on novels and stories, written with more intricacy of style and structure. By the close of the Victorian Age his prodigious output included the novels *The Spoils of Poynton* (1897), *What Maisie Knew* (1897), *In the Cage* (1898), and *The Awkward Age* (1899). His shorter works included the tale of horror that was perhaps his most critically analyzed story, "The Turn of the Screw" (1898).

The twentieth century was marked by several major novels, including *The Sacred Fount* (1901), *The Wings of the Dove* (1902), *The Golden Bowl* (1904), and *The Ambassadors* (1903), believed by James to be "the best, all 'round, of my productions." His acquaintance with American writer EDITH WHARTON, which would affect the art of both writers, began in 1903. The final years of his life saw the publication of two insightful travel works: *The American Scene* (1907) and *Italian Hours* (1909);

two volumes of autobiography, *A Small Boy and Others* (1913) and *Notes of a Son and Brother* (1914); and the American publication of his works (1907–9), for which he provided revisions and wrote new prefaces. Seven months before his death, James became a British citizen. His unfinished novels include *The Ivory Tower* and *The Sense of the Past.* His third autobiographical work, *The Middle Years,* was published posthumously in 1917. His legacy to modern writers such as Wharton, Virginia Woolf, and James Joyce is immense. It lay partly in his powers to convey the contemporary obsessions of psychological complexity and ambiguity. In the words of JOSEPH CONRAD, he was "the historian of fine consciences."

James, Jesse [Woodson] (1847–1882) American outlaw. James was born in Missouri, where he joined Confederate forces in waging guerrilla warfare against Union troops during the U.S. CIVIL WAR. From 1866 to 1881 he and his brother Frank were joined by the YOUNGER BROTHERS and others in a criminal spree of bank robberies, train holdups, and murder. Jesse was killed in St. Joseph, Missouri, by fellow gang member Bob Ford for reward money. Frank was tried twice for various crimes but never convicted and became a successful farmer. Despite their ruthlessness and self-serving criminal careers, the James brothers inspired many Robin Hood–like legends and filled the pages of DIME NOVELS.

James, William (1842–1910) American philosopher. Elder brother of the novelist HENRY JAMES, William James was born in New York and studied medicine at Harvard in 1869. Afterward his interest shifted to psychology, whereupon he opened a laboratory at Harvard, one of the first of its kind in the world. His *Principles of Psychology,* the result of twelve years of work and a pioneering study of the mechanisms of psychological process, was published in 1890. His position as professor of natural religion at Edinburgh University from 1901 until 1902 brought him international attention when his two lectures there were published as *The Varieties of Religious Experience* (1902). His most intellectually enduring work, however, was *Pragmatism* (1907), which argued in a lucidly accessible style that an idea has meaning only in relation to the consequences in meaning and action. To James, the moral rightness of a man's conduct should be judged in terms of its practical value to him and not by a preestablished standard, a principle he described as "empirical radicalism." The focus of intense philosophical controversy, James responded to his critics in *The Meaning of Truth* (1909) and continued to write and lecture widely. During his lifetime he was perhaps the most renowned philosopher in the United States.

Jameson, Sir Leander Starr (1853–1917) British colonial administrator in SOUTH AFRICA. A friend of colonizer CECIL RHODES, he led the unauthorized Jameson Raid into the TRANSVAAL in December 1895. The botched attempt to unseat the government of the BOERS resulted in his surrender in January 1896 and brief imprisonment in England. Returning to South Africa, he became prime minister of Cape Colony (1904–8).

Jane Eyre (1847) English novel. Published under the pseudonym "Currer Bell," this novel by English novelist CHARLOTTE BRONTË became an immediate international best-seller, establishing its author as a major literary figure.

Narrated by a penniless orphan named Jane Eyre, this fictional autobiography begins as Jane has been left in the care of cruel Aunt Reed, who shows favoritism to Jane's unkind cousins. After banishment to the solitary confinement of the Red Room, Jane is taken to Lowood Asylum, a charitable institution run by a hard-hearted headmaster and a kindly but weak mistress of the school, Maria Temple. Jane finds friendship with the sickly, penitent Helen Burns. After Helen's death from consumption and several years as a teacher herself, Jane leaves Lowood to become a governess for Adele Varens, the ward of Edward Rochester of Thornfield Hall.

As Jane becomes drawn to her dark, moody overseer, and he to her independence of spirit and sharp wit, Rochester asks Jane to marry him. Their wedding plans are interrupted by the unexpected arrival of Richard Mason, who reveals that Rochester is already wedded to Mason's sister Bertha, a madwoman who has been confined to the attic of Thornfield Hall. Jane abruptly leaves Thornfield, and after wandering destitute, she is taken in by a clergyman, the austerely handsome St. John Rivers, and his two sisters. After Rivers proposes to Jane and requests that she accompany him to India, Jane hears a voice that seems to be that of Rochester imploring her to return to Thornfield Hall. She returns to find that Thornfield has been destroyed in a fire set by Bertha Mason, who has died in the flames. Finding Rochester half-blind and injured, Jane is at last reunited with her beloved, and they marry.

Because of the passionate temper of its prose and the spirited energy of its independent heroine, *Jane Eyre* proved controversial on its publication when some reviewers denounced it as un-Christian. Yet it has proven an enduring work of Victorian fiction, inspiring such twentieth-century novels as Daphne du Maurier's *Rebecca* and Jean Rhys's *Wide Sargasso Sea.*

Japan East Asian country consisting of four main islands off the northeast coast of the Eurasian land mass. Japan's terrain is generally mountainous with a few coastal plains. The climate is temperate to subtropical.

In the early Victorian era, Japan was ruled by the Tokugawa family. Since the early seventeenth century, this dynasty had held the office of *shogun,* originally a military command, and governed the country from Edo (modern Tokyo). The emperor, who resided in Kyoto, served as a unifying symbol but had no real power. The Tokugawa shoguns ruled through *samurai,* warriors, who lived in castle towns and held land grants in a system similar to European feudalism. Society was organized in a hierarchy, according to Confucian principles. Individual social status was fixed at birth, and the behavior of the various classes was strictly regulated by the government.

The Tokugawa Shogunate tried to maintain a policy of isolation from the outside world. The only trading post permitted was a small Dutch and Chinese settlement at Nagasaki. Foreigners were not allowed to enter Japan, nor could Japanese leave. Christianity was illegal.

In the early nineteenth century the Tokugawa government faced increasing pressure from impoverished samurai who could not maintain their life-style and merchants who wanted greater opportunities. The peasants, faced with increasing difficulty in paying their taxes and feeding themselves, frequently rebelled. At the same time, the treatment of CHINA during the OPIUM WARS showed how vulnerable Japan was to the Western powers.

In 1853 an American fleet under Commodore MATTHEW C. PERRY arrived in Japan and demanded that the Shogunate enter into diplomatic relations with the Western powers. Faced with superior weaponry, Japan acceded and within a few years had concluded trade agreements that kept import tariffs low and allowed foreigners immunity to Japanese law. The subsequent rapid influx of Western goods and outflow of cash disrupted the economy and the tax system, leading to greater discontent. The treaties were seen as humiliating. Opponents to the Tokugawa government adopted the slogan, "Reverence the emperor and expel the barbarians."

In 1863–64, the *daimyo,* or lord, of the Choshu clan, in an attempt to expel the foreigners, led the firing on American, French, and Dutch ships in the Straits of Shimonoseki. In response, these nations and Great Britain sent a fleet that destroyed the enemy batteries. After this Shimonoseki War, the daimyos turned their anger against the Tokugawa Shogunate, forcing the shogun to resign and declaring the emperor the supreme head of state. This event is called the Meiji Restoration (1867–68) for the reign name of the emperor, Mutsuhito (1852–1912; reigned from 1867), who was only a boy at his accession.

Japanese society was rapidly transformed over the next decades. Feudalism was abolished, along with many social regulations, and the privileges of samurai were ended. Western literature, philosophy, and technology were introduced. The tax system was rationalized. A system of compulsory public education was established with a nationalistic program. A national police force was formed. A Western-style conscript army with modern weaponry was raised. These changes were met with considerable resistance, particularly from peasants who expected lower taxes and samurai who resented their loss of status, but by and large they were accepted. The most significant insurrection by the samurai, the SATSUMA REVOLT (1877), was defeated by an army of peasants and other civilians.

Japan adopted a parliamentary-based constitutional monarchy in 1890 and eventually instituted universal male suffrage (1925). Military and industrial interests tended to dominate the government.

Using its new strength, Japan embarked on an aggressive foreign policy. It acquired the Ryuku Islands in 1874 and with China became "co-protector" of Korea in 1885. In 1894 the unequal treaties with the Western powers were renegotiated on more favorable terms. In the same year a dispute over Korea led to war with China. The first SINO-JAPANESE WAR (1894–95) was a resounding success for Japan's new army. China surrendered its rights over Korea, ceded Formosa (Taiwan) to Japan, and paid a large indemnity. Japan acquired the right to establish treaty ports and factories in China. Japan also tried to seize the Liaodong Peninsula but was prevented from doing so by the diplomatic intervention of Germany, France, and Russia (the Triple Intervention).

The pride generated by this first foreign victory and the anger over European intervention gave militarist elements in the government overwhelming support, and Japan's foreign policy remained expansionistic until the end of World War II. A military treaty with Great Britain and the defeat of Russia in the Russo-Japanese War (1904–5) marked Japan's arrival as the first great modern power in Asia.

Java man Early human fossil type. Discovered in 1890 by Dutch paleontologist Marie Eugène Dubois at Kedung Brebus, Java, in the Dutch East Indies, the remains included a primitive skull with heavy brow ridges and a brain size no more than three-fifths that of modern humans. But there was also a humanlike thighbone indicating an erect posture. The discovery strengthened the argument that humans had evolved from other organisms. Although Dubois named the creature *Pithecanthropus erectus* (erect ape-man), later discoveries in China,

Europe, and Africa showed that Java man was a specimen of *Homo erectus,* an ancestor of *Homo sapiens* that originated in Africa about 1.5 million years ago. *Homo erectus* was the first hominid species to use fire and to move out of Africa into Europe and Asia. See also CRO-MAGNON MAN and NEANDERTHAL MAN.

Jell-O Registered trademark for fruit-flavored gelatin desserts. Based on the gelatin dessert created by Peter Cooper in 1845, Jell-O was developed and named in the late 1890s by Mr. and Mrs. Pearl B. Wait of LeRoy, New York. Meant to be an early example of packaged foods, it was first put into mass production in 1897. Not until the early 1900s did Jell-O become popular, when the business was sold to distributor Francis Woodward of the Genessee Pure Food Company, forerunner to General Foods.

jet Coal that can be polished to a high black luster and used in jewelry and other ornamentation. In the nineteenth century it was widely used in jewelry worn by women during the mandatory grieving period following the loss of a family member.

Jewett, [Theodora] Sarah Orne (1849–1909) American writer. Jewett is best known for her grasp of the natural life and inner character of the people in her native Maine. Born in South Berwick, Maine, she was primarily an autodidact, gaining her education in her family library and on visits to patients around Maine with her physician father. Her acquaintance with the work of HARRIET BEECHER STOWE on New England led her to try to capture the desolation she observed in Maine. She established herself as a force in the genre of local-color writing with her first short story collection, *Deephaven* (1877). More acclaimed were her second collection, *A White Heron and Other Stories* (1886), and her novel about the solitary lives in a Maine town, *The Country of Pointed Firs* (1896).

Jex-Blake, Sophia Louisa (1840–1912) English physician. Born in Hastings, England, Jex-Blake gained her medical apprenticeship under ELIZABETH BLACKWELL and Lucy Sewall in the United States, and due to a need to return home after the death of her father, she attempted to complete her medical studies at the University of Edinburgh. Once at school, students, teachers, and university officials effected barriers to study by females; in 1872, after the University Court offered a certificate of proficiency but not a chance to graduate, they brought the case to the courts. Four years later, thanks in large part to their efforts, the Russell Gurney Enabling Act was passed granting medical testing groups the right to test women. But Jex-Blake did not gain certification for the practice of medicine in Great Britain until 1877, from the Irish College of Physicians. Meanwhile, in 1874 she founded the London School of Medicine for Women. In 1885 she founded the Edinburgh Women's Hospital, and in 1886, the Edinburgh School of Medicine for Women. She is also the author of several books, including *Medical Women,* a memoir.

jezail Long-barreled rifle used by Afghan warriors in the first of the ANGLO-AFGHAN WARS (1838–42). It had a longer range and was more accurate than the smooth-bore muskets of the British. See FIREARMS.

jingoism Bellicose or excessive patriotism. Jingoism was a sentiment often ascribed to ardent supporters of the BRITISH EMPIRE. The term, deriving ultimately from the seventeenth-century slang expression "By jingo," a euphemism for "By Jesus," originated in an 1878 British music hall song "The Great MacDermott." The song, composed during the RUSSO-TURKISH

WAR of 1877–78, urged the British to defend Constantinople against the Russians:

We don't want to fight,
But by jingo if we do,
We've got the ships,
We've got the men,
We've got the money too!

jodhpurs Clothing. Jodhpurs were pants for horseback riding worn in the district of Jodhpur in northwest India and introduced to Britain in the nineteenth century.

Johnson, Andrew (1808–1875) Seventeenth president of the UNITED STATES (1865–69). Johnson was born in North Carolina and moved to Tennessee where he worked as a tailor. After entering local politics he served ten years in the House of Representatives (1843–53) and four years as governor of Tennessee (1853–57). The Democrat became a senator in 1857, and when Tennessee seceded in 1861, he was the only southern Senator to remain loyal to the Union. He was military governor of Tennessee from 1862 to 1864, and in 1864 was the vice presidential running mate with ABRAHAM LINCOLN on the National Union Party slate.

Johnson became president after Lincoln's assassination in April 1865. He tried to follow Lincoln's blueprint for RECONSTRUCTION, but Congress overrode his vetoes of stricter Reconstruction measures. In 1867, Johnson defied the Tenure of Office Act, which prohibited the president from firing Cabinet members without Senate approval, a law later deemed unconstitutional by the Supreme Court. The House impeached him in 1868, but the Senate fell one vote short of removing him from office. He retired to Tennessee after his term expired. Elected senator six years later, he died after only a few months in office.

Johnstown Flood Natural disaster. The May 31, 1889, break in the Conemaugh River dam was the deadliest flood in American history, causing the deaths of more than twenty-two hundred people in the western Pennsylvania town of Johnstown nearly fifteen miles away. Tons of water coursed through the town at a rate of fifty miles per hour. The record devastation was recounted in periodicals, music, artworks, and legend for decades after the Victorian era.

Jones, Owen (1809–1874) English architect and designer. After studying architecture and art in England, in part at the Royal Academy, he traveled through the Middle East and Spain, an experience that influenced his development of a Moorish style in mosaic and tile design. As joint architect of the GREAT EXHIBITION OF 1851, he oversaw its interior color scheme but was critical of the design of most of the exhibits. He summarized his views on design in the influential book *The Grammar of Ornament* (1856). He argued that decoration should follow function, favored abstract ornamentation, and advocated the use of new industrial materials, including iron and glass. He served as architect for St. James Hall (1858) and as director of decorations for the CRYSTAL PALACE in Sydenham (1852).

Joseph, Chief (1840?–1904) American Indian leader of the Nez Percé tribe. Chief Joseph was a symbol of Native American resistance to the UNITED STATES. Born in Oregon, he became tribal chief in 1871 and from the beginning fought his tribe's relocation, refusing to recognize U.S. claims to its lands. Facing removal he agreed to depart peacefully to a reservation in Idaho in 1877, but fighting broke out between U.S. troops and Nez Percé warriors. Joseph then led six hundred of his tribe north toward Canada in an attempt to join SITTING BULL's tribe of Sioux Indians. The tribe trekked some sixteen hundred miles in three months and fought more than thirteen battles with the army in brilliant rearguard maneuvering. The army finally captured Joseph and his people in Montana, thirty miles from Canada. In his statement of surrender, he said, "Hear me, my chiefs, I am tired; my heart is sick and sad. From where the sun now stands, I will fight no more forever." Some four hundred Nez Percé were returned to Idaho; Chief Joseph was sent to a reservation in Washington, where he died.

Joule, James Prescott (1818–1889) English physicist. In 1840 he formulated Joule's law, which described the rate at which heat is produced by an electric current. In 1843 he determined the mechanical equivalence of heat, establishing that a given quantity of mechanical energy is converted into a fixed amount of heat. He also contributed to the development of the first law of THERMODYNAMICS, the law of conservation of energy. In 1852 he collaborated with British physicist William Thomson, Lord KELVIN, a supporter of his work, in discovering the Joule-Thomson effect: the drop in temperature that occurs when a gas expands into a vacuum. The joule, a unit of work or energy defined as 10 million ergs, is named for him.

Jumbo (d. 1885) African elephant. He was captured as a calf in Africa in 1861 and displayed first at the Paris zoo, the Jardin des Plantes. In 1865 he went to the London zoo, where he delighted British fans. Eleven feet tall and weighing over fourteen thousand pounds, Jumbo was the biggest elephant ever seen by the Victorians—bigger than the more familiar Indian elephants, with bigger ears and a rounded forehead. For years he was gentle enough to carry children on his back, but eventually he developed violent fits of temper, possibly due to dental problems. In 1882 the London zoo sold the elephant to American circus owner P. T. BARNUM. British fans protested the sale vehemently, but too late. On Easter Sunday, April 9, 1882, Jumbo arrived in the United States and made his first appearance at New York's Madison Square Garden.

Jumbo traveled the United States and Canada with Barnum's "Greatest Show on Earth" for three years, until he was killed by a locomotive in a railroad accident in Ontario, Canada. During these three years he became known to millions; his image and name were used to advertise products from Castoria baby medicine to Sterling baking powder. His skeleton is preserved at the American Museum of Natural History, New York, and his name has passed into the English language as a synonym for "big."

Jungle Book, The (1894, 1895) Series of stories by RUDYARD KIPLING. The first collection was published in 1894; *The Second Jungle Book* followed in 1895. The fifteen stories are now published under the title *The Jungle Books.* Most of the stories relate the adventures of Mowgli, a boy raised by wolves in the Indian jungle. Mowgli's intelligence and bravery enable him to become master of the jungle. In the end he returns to human society. Another famous story in the collection is "Rikki-Tikki-Tavi," the tale of a mongoose who saves a child from a cobra.

Jupiter Fifth planet from the sun. Jupiter has been known since antiquity. In 1610, Italian astronomer Galileo Galilei (1564–1642) discovered the four largest of its moons, Callisto, Ganymede, Io, and Europa. In 1892, American astronomer EDWARD EMERSON BARNARD discovered a fifth satellite, smaller and closer to Jupiter than the other four. After being tentatively called Barnard's satellite and Jupiter V, it was given the name Amalthea at the suggestion of French astronomer Camille Flammarion. This was the name of the goat-nymph in Roman mythology who served as wet nurse to the infant Jupiter.

Amalthea was the last satellite to be discovered without photographic means, and no further Jovian moons were discovered until 1904. As a result of telescopic studies and space probe visits in the twentieth century, Jupiter is now known to have at least sixteen satellites.

Kabul to Kandahar British military operation. The famous march was undertaken in August 1880 by British general FREDERICK SLEIGH ROBERTS to relieve British troops near Kandahar during the second of the ANGLO-AFGHAN WARS. The march was commemorated in a medal struck after the war.

Kaffir (Kafir) Derogatory term. Originally an Arabic term applied by Muslims to unbelievers, Kaffir became a derogatory term used by the British to refer to the BANTU-speaking indigenous peoples of southern Africa. It also refers specifically to the Xhosa tribes of what is now Transkei, SOUTH AFRICA. The Xhosa traditionally practiced agriculture, animal husbandry, and metal-working. In a series of armed conflicts called the KAFFIR WARS, the Xhosa suffered drastic loss of land and political power.

"Kafir," usually with one *f,* also refers to the Nuri people of the Hindu Kush in northern Pakistan and Afghanistan. Though many were converted to Islam by force late in the Victorian era, some still practice their traditional polytheistic, shamanistic religion.

Kaffir Wars Series of armed encounters between European invaders and the indigenous peoples of SOUTH AFRICA, particularly the Xhosa, known to Europeans as KAFFIRS. The first Kaffir Wars were fought by Dutch settlers, or BOERS, in the eighteenth century. Upon acquiring Cape Colony in 1815, the British inherited the struggle. British soldiers fought three Kaffir Wars against the Xhosa during Queen Victoria's reign: in 1846–47, 1850–53, and 1877–78. Sir Harry Smith, governor and commander in chief of Cape Colony, was known for his exploits against the Xhosa in the 1846–47 war in which the British conquered and annexed Kaffraria, or Kaffirland, in the region east of Cape Colony. The Xhosa renewed their attack against the British in the two later wars, but to no avail. The Xhosa now live in the Transkei region of South Africa's southeast coast.

Kalevala, The Finnish national epic. *The Kalevala* was compiled from folk songs and oral tradition by Finnish philologist Elias Lonnrott (1802–1884). The first edition of twelve thousand verses was published in 1835; the second edition in 1849 was nearly twice as long. The poem had an unrhymed trochaic meter, as did a German translation that was imitated by American poet HENRY WADSWORTH LONGFELLOW in "THE SONG OF HIAWATHA" (1855).

Kanpur See CAWNPORE.

"Katzenjammer Kids" Comic strip. This early example of a comic strip, launched in 1897 in the *New York Journal,* became hugely popular. In response to anti-German sentiment during World War I, it was renamed "The Captain and the Kids."

Keble, John (1792–1866) English poet and clergyman. His collection of devotional verse *The Christian Year* (1827) remained popular throughout the nineteenth century and earned him a professorship of poetry at Oxford (1831–41). His sermon "National Apostasy" (1833) was considered by JOHN HENRY NEWMAN the beginning of the OXFORD MOVEMENT. With Newman and others he wrote several "Tracts for the Times," affirming the movement's High Church principles. From 1835 to his death he served as vicar of Hursley, near Winchester. Other works of poetry included an English *Psalter* (1839) and *Lyra Innocentium* (1846). Keble College, Oxford, was founded in his honor in 1869.

Kekule von Stradonitz, Friedrich August (1829–1896) German organic chemist and professor at Bonn. In 1861, with help from Scottish chemist Archibald Scott Couper, he devised the system of structural formulas for representing how the atoms of a carbon molecule are arranged in space. He also discovered in 1865 that the benzene molecule is a ring, in which six hydrogen atoms bond to a hexagonal ring of six carbon atoms, the "Kekule structure." The insight into the structure, which had eluded chemists since MICHAEL FARADAY discovered benzene in 1825, came to Kekule while he dozed on a bus and dreamed of a chain of carbon atoms coiling on itself like a snake.

Kellogg, Will Keith (1860–1951) American businessman. Born in Battle Creek, Michigan, Kellogg worked with his brothers Dr. John H. Kellogg and James H. Kellogg to develop and promote the idea of increased healthfulness through the consumption of cold breakfast cereals. In 1895, Will Keith and John H. developed the first breakfast flakes, the wheat-based Granose. Their Sanitas cornflakes were unsuccessfully introduced in 1898; an improved version, with a longer shelf life, entered the market in 1902. Later renamed Kellogg's Cornflakes, they eventually became the most popular cereal in the United States. In 1906, Will K. and John H. set up the Battle Creek Toasted Corn Flake Company and marketed their cereal products, primarily cornflakes, with massive advertising. Dr. John H.'s Battle Creek Sanitarium was the site of many experiments on health food and healthful living, and the center for many of the Kellogg family discoveries.

Kelmscott Press Book printing facility. The Kelmscott Press was the high-quality but short-lived facility developed by Pre-Raphaelite artists WILLIAM MORRIS and Sir EDWARD BURNE-JONES in London in 1891. Following years of rebellion against manufacturing shoddiness, marked by their involvement in the ARTS AND CRAFTS MOVEMENT in which they reintroduced hand-turned textiles and home furnishings, Morris and Jones turned their interests to book production. Using handmade paper and Morris's personally designed typefaces, several titles were printed, including the multi-year project, the *Kelmscott Chaucer* (1896). The Kelmscott Press was dissolved in 1898, shortly after Morris's death.

Kelvin, William Thomson, 1st Baron (1824–1907) British mathematician and physicist. Born in Belfast, Ireland, Thomson was the son of a mathematician. A child prodigy who entered the University of Glasgow before age twelve, he wrote his first paper on mathematics while in his teens. He graduated from Cambridge in 1845 as second in his class in mathematics. For more than fifty years, beginning at age twenty-two, he was professor of natural history at the University of Glasgow (1846–99).

In addition to his many mathematical papers, Thomson became renowned for his work in the natural sciences. He first gained notice in 1846 when he calculated the age of the earth as between 20 million and 400 million years, based on the premise that the earth had originally been the temperature of the sun and had been cooling steadily ever since. This view—supported on independent grounds by German physicist Hermann Ludwig von Helmholtz—conflicted with that of geologists who believed the earth much older. The controversy was not resolved until after the discovery of RADIOACTIVITY showed that the earth contained an independent source of heat. The earth is now believed to be 4.6 billion years old.

Although his view on this issue was eventually proven wrong, Thomson was correct in his early support for the existence of a law of conservation of energy (see THERMODYNAMICS), advanced by British physicist JAMES PRESCOTT JOULE and formulated precisely by Helmholtz (1847). Thomson's most important contribution to science was in this field of thermodynamics, the study of the interrelation of energy, heat, and work. In 1848 he proposed that there is an absolute temperature—absolute zero—below which no further energy loss is possible and that this temperature should be the starting point of an absolute scale of temperature. Absolute zero was later defined as −273.15 degrees centigrade, and the scale, which proved essential to thermodynamics, was called the Kelvin scale in his honor.

In 1852, Thomson collaborated with Joule on the Joule-Thomson effect: the drop in temperature that occurs when a gas expands into a vacuum. This discovery made it possible to liquefy the permanent gases, such as oxygen and nitrogen, and to reach very low temperatures useful in science and industry.

Thomson was also a renowned inventor. His work on electricity and his improvements of cables and galvanometers made possible the TELEGRAPH cable across the Atlantic Ocean. His nautical inventions included improvements in the mariner's compass, tide predictors, and sounding gauges.

Thomson received many honors for his achievements. He was made a fellow of the Royal Society (1851) and later served as its president (1890–1894). He was knighted in 1866, and in 1892 was made Baron Kelvin of Largs. In 1902 he was given the Order of Merit and made Privy Councillor.

In his last years, Thomson spoke out vigorously against the new discoveries about radioactivity made by PIERRE AND MARIE CURIE and Ernest Rutherford. Unable to accept that an atom could disintegrate, he argued that radium and polonium were not elements but molecular compounds. He died before further experiments proved him wrong.

Kelvin scale Instrument for measuring temperature proposed in 1848 by British physicist William Thomson, later Lord KELVIN. Also known as the absolute temperature scale, its zero mark is at absolute zero—the point below which further energy loss is theoretically unattainable. Its degrees are equal to those on the centigrade scale. Kelvin considered absolute zero to be −273 degrees centigrade; scientists now consider it −273.15 degrees centigrade (−459.67 degrees Fahrenheit). The scale became an essential part of THERMODYNAMICS, the study of the interrelation of energy, heat, and work.

Kensington Palace House in western London acquired in 1689 by William and Mary. Since the late eighteenth century, it has been the residence of members of the royal family other than the reigning monarch. Queen VICTORIA was sleeping here in 1837 when news came that her uncle King William IV had died and she was now the queen. In Kensington Gardens, outside the palace, is the ALBERT MEMORIAL, a monument completed in 1872 to Victoria's husband Prince ALBERT.

Kenya Republic on the east coast of central AFRICA. It is bounded by the Sudan and Ethiopia on the north, Somalia and the Indian Ocean on the east, Tanzania on the south, and Uganda on the west. Located on the equator, it is one of the oldest places of human habitation, inhabited by our hominid ancestors as early as two million years ago.

Indigenous people introduced farming and herding to what is now Kenya by 1000 B.C. Arab traders established city-states on the coast by the eighth century A.D. After a period of Portuguese domination of the coast beginning in the sixteenth century, the Arabs regained control in 1729. In 1886, as the British and Germans made their partition of east Africa, most of what is now Kenya was delivered to British rule. Indian colonists arrived, the town of Nairobi was founded in 1899, and a railroad was built into the interior; European colonists followed in 1903. In 1905, Nairobi became the capital of the British protectorate of Kenya, which was declared a crown colony in 1920. Kenya gained independence on December 12, 1963. Nairobi is still the capital.

khaki Yellowish or greenish brown cotton or wool fabric. Introduced by Lieutenant Harry Burnett of the Queen's Own Corps of Guides to camouflage soldiers in dusty surroundings, khaki was first worn by Burnett's soldiers in India in 1847. The word comes from the Hindi for "dust-colored." It became the official fabric of the army uniforms of Britain and eventually many other countries.

Khartoum Capital city of the SUDAN. Khartoum is located south of where the Blue Nile and the White Nile meet in the northeast quarter of the country. It was established as an Egyptian army base in 1821. On January 26, 1885, it was the scene of a famous event in British imperial history when native forces commanded by the MAHDI overran the city after a ten-month siege. The legendary English soldier and then governor-general of the Sudan, CHARLES GEORGE GORDON, died in the fighting. The fall of Khartoum shocked England and helped bring down the government of WILLIAM GLADSTONE. Recaptured in 1898 by Lord HORATIO HERBERT KITCHENER, Khartoum was the capital of the Anglo-Egyptian government until 1956 when it became the capital of independent Sudan.

khedive Title taken by the successors to MUHAMMAD ALI, the Macedonian Turk who ruled Egypt from 1805 to 1848. The first in the dynasty to be called "khedive" was Isma'il PASHA (reigned 1863 to 1879). The khedives governed virtually as independent rulers under the nominal suzerainty of the Ottoman sultan of Turkey and, after 1882, as figurehead rulers under British occupation. The last khedive, ABBAS II, was deposed by the British in 1914.

Khoikhoi See HOTTENTOT.

Khyber Pass Thirty-mile mountain road that links Afghanistan with Pakistan. Invading armies, traders, and migrants have used the route for centuries. The pass was the scene of bitter battles between the British army and native tribes during the ANGLO-AFGHAN WARS (1839–42 and 1878–80). Control of the pass was vital to Great Britain's efforts to keep Russia from invading central Asia.

Kierkegaard, Søren Aabye (1813–1855) Danish theologian and philosopher. Kierkegaard was the prolific author of works that are credited with initiating existentialist trends in modern philosophy. With an accent on concrete examples and strong belief in individual free choice, his works endorse a philosophy of risk and commitment viewed as essential to a fully engaged life. Rejecting what he considered Hegel's flawed assumptions concerning universal categories, he explored freedom as an inescapable, often terrifying but ultimately essential aspect of existence in such works as *Either-Or* (1843), *Fear and Trembling* (1843), and *Philosophical Fragments* (1844). His views on the structure of faith and personal encounter with God proved highly influential for later Protestant theologians.

Kimberley City in SOUTH AFRICA. In 1867 it was the site of the discovery of diamonds, in what was then the Orange Free State, an independent republic governed by the Afrikaners (BOERS). Between 1871 and 1888, English empire builder CECIL RHODES made his fortune in Kimberley and eventually established it as the headquarters of his British South Africa Company (founded 1889).

Kinetoscope A film projection machine developed by THOMAS ALVA EDISON and W. K. L. Dickson. Introduced in New York in 1894, it projected images recorded by the kinetograph. See also MOTION PICTURES.

The Khyber Pass, which links Afghanistan to Pakistan, served as a main battleground during the Anglo-Afghan Wars.

King, Clarence (1842–1901) American geologist. Born in Newport, Rhode Island, at age twenty-five he organized and directed a geological survey along the route of the transcontinental railroad, mapping the area and evaluating potential resources along the fortieth parallel. At King's insistence the survey also included photographic and artistic documentation of the West. Upon completion he served as the first director of the U.S. Geological Survey (1879–81). King also developed a reputation as a man of action, which grew from his lively published accounts of his adventures. In 1872, King proved that a rumored Colorado diamond field was a clever hoax, thus saving investors millions of dollars. After 1881, King worked as a mining consultant and geologist and published both popular and scientific articles.

Kingsley, Charles (1819–1875) English novelist, scholar, and clergyman. Kingsley promoted reform of societal iniquities through Christian Socialism. Son of a vicar in Devon, he graduated from Cambridge, was ordained in the Church of England, and served for more than fifteen years in local parishes before being appointed chaplain for Queen Victoria. Throughout the 1860s he was a professor of modern history at Cambridge. In 1869 he became canon of Chester; in 1873, canon of Westminster. During his service as clergyman and academic he explored through his writings the hardships of workers and the need for labor reform. Two notable works on labor are the novels *Alton Locke* (1850) and *Yeast* (1851), about urban and rural laborers, respectively. His best known works, however, are relatively unrelated to his social causes: *Westward Ho!* (1855) and *Hereward the Wake* (1865) are historical novels; *The Water-Babies* (1863) is a children's tale about seashore life. The controversy surrounding a review he wrote for *Macmillan's Magazine* is said to have provided the impetus for Cardinal JOHN HENRY NEWMAN to write *APOLOGIA PRO VITA SUA*.

Kipling, Rudyard (1865–1936) English writer. Kipling is esteemed for the variety of his work and for artistically capturing the British Empire at its height. He was born in Bombay, India, into a notable family: His father, Lockwood Kipling, was an illustrator and the future director of the Lahore Museum; his maternal uncle was painter Sir EDWARD BURNE-JONES. After attending the United Services College, he returned home and began to write stories and poems for *The Civil and Military Gazette*. These and other early works were later published in the collections *Departmental Ditties* (1886) and *Soldiers Three* (1892).

In 1889, following the publication of *Wee Willie Winkie* and *The Phantom Rickshaw* in 1888, Kipling resettled in England. His subsequent story collections, *Life's Handicap* (1891) and *Many Inventions* (1893), a book of poems, *Barrack-Room Ballads and Other Verses* (1892), and to a lesser extent his novel, *The Light That Failed* (1891), established him as a major British literary spokesman. In 1892 he married Caroline Balestier, sister of writer Wolcott Balestier, with whom Kipling had collaborated that year on the novel *The Naulahka*.

Shortly thereafter Kipling and his wife moved to the United States, settling for the next four years in Vermont. The locale proved fruitful: Two of his most beloved works, THE JUNGLE BOOK (1894) and *The Second Jungle Book* (1895), were published during his stay. These collections of stories and poems center on the experiences of Mowgli, who leaves the human world to live in the jungle and who upon his return to his people discovers the animal world more orderly and fulfilling. Both a commentary on society and a series of tales of jungle life, the Jungle books further broadened his popularity.

But it was in England that he wrote his most appreciated work: *Kim*. Published in 1901, the picaresque novel explored the conflicts between the life of the mind and the pursuit of action through the life of orphan Kimball "Kim" O'Hara, who finds adventure in the worlds of British espionage and spiritual journey, the latter with a Tibetan lama on a quest for freedom from the Wheel of Life. The mix of high adventure and inner conflict spoke to a British society in transition at the beginning of a new century.

Yet it was a poem, "THE WHITE MAN'S BURDEN" (1899), that most succinctly captured Kipling's view of the role of imperialist nations in the world. Though written to the American public to advise proper behavior following the SPANISH-AMERICAN WAR, its discussion of the moral obligation of imperialist nations toward their colonies applies to all nineteenth-century nations of empire.

Kipling's artistic growth was marred by the death of his eldest daughter during a Kipling family return to the United States in 1899. His son John was born in 1897.

Kipling produced a number of notable works during the early twentieth century, including the children's works *The Just So Stories* (1902) and *Puck of Pook's Hill* (1906). In his later story collections, notably *Traffics and Discoveries* (1904) and *A Diversity of Creatures* (1917), he came to comment on the human price of sustaining an empire as vast as Britain's. For such breadth in 1907 he was awarded the first Nobel Prize in literature given to an English author. His unfinished autobiography, *Something of Myself* (1937), was published after his death.

Kitchener, Horatio Herbert (1850–1916), 1st Earl Kitchener of Khartoum. British field marshal and administrator. Kitchener is widely recognized as one of Britain's greatest imperial generals. After graduating from the Royal Military Academy, he served in the Middle East from 1874 on. In 1883 he was assigned to the Egyptian army, then under British control. In 1884 he led an unsuccessful attempt to lift the siege of KHARTOUM. As governor-general of the eastern SUDAN (1886–88) he helped defeat the last of the Mahdist (see MAHDI) invasions of Egypt.

As commander in chief of the Egyptian army, Kitchener recaptured Khartoum in 1898 after crushing Sudanese forces at the battle of Omdurman. His success at checking French territorial claims in the Sudan during the FASHODA CRISIS helped prevent war between France and Britain.

In 1900 he took command of British forces fighting the BOER WAR (1899–1902). His policies of burning Boer homes and forcing civilians into concentration camps to counter the Boers' guerrilla tactics were widely criticized.

After the war he was made commander in chief of the British Indian army. He was general consul in Egypt from 1909 until the beginning of World War I. As Secretary of State for War he organized a huge expansion of the army. He died when a ship carrying him to Russia hit a German mine.

Klimt, Gustav (1862–1918) Austrian painter. Klimt was born in Vienna, and in 1883, after studying decorative arts, he opened a studio specializing in mural painting. In 1897 he founded the VIENNA SECESSION, a group of artists who rejected the prevalent realistic style of the time. Klimt's paintings were characterized by his use of bright colors and ornate details arranged in a mosaiclike pattern, and he quickly became the leading ART NOUVEAU painter in Austria. His work was often symbolic, including the allegorical murals painted for the University of Vienna: *Philosophy* (1900), *Medicine* (1901), and *Jurisprudence* (1903). He died in Vienna.

knee jerk Involuntary forward kick produced when a light blow on the patellar ligament of the knee causes a reflex contraction of the quadriceps muscle of the thigh. Also called the "patellar reflex," it was discovered by English neurologist Sir Michael Foster, who first called it a "knee jerk" in his *Text-Book of Physiology* (1878). The term soon became slang for any reaction that is automatic or unthinking, as in "knee-jerk conservative or liberal."

Knights of Labor See LABOR MOVEMENT.

Know-Nothing movement American political group. Taking shape in the American northeast in the 1840s in reaction to increased immigration, the movement championed "native" American culture and opposed "foreign" influences. Members believed that Catholics and foreign-born Americans should be kept out of public office. Characterized by secret orders, whose members answered questions about their activities with a claim to "know nothing," the movement sought to influence the major political parties and in 1855 produced its own, openly active "American party." Members were split over the issue of slavery, and the party fell apart after its candidate, MILLARD FILLMORE, was defeated in the 1856 presidential election.

Koch, Robert (1843–1910) German physician. Acknowledged as the founder of modern medical bacteriology, Koch made his first major discovery in bacteriology in 1876 when he proved that the infectious disease anthrax developed in animals only when viable anthrax bacillus spores were placed in the animal's bloodstream. This marked the first time that the causative agent of an infectious disease was unquestionably established. By showing that a microorganism was the cause of a specific illness, Koch lent important support to the GERM THEORY OF DISEASE proposed by LOUIS PASTEUR. In the process he also developed modern methods for obtaining microorganisms, culturing them, and destroying them.

Later in the century, Koch discovered the causes of other diseases. In 1882 he discovered the tubercule bacillus that causes TUBERCULOSIS; he also developed tuberculin, an extract of the bacillus still used today in diagnosing the disease. In 1883, while traveling in India, he identified *Vibrio cholerae,* the bacillus that causes CHOLERA. He also became known for his studies of insect-borne diseases, including malaria. In 1905 he was awarded the Nobel Prize in medicine and physiology.

kraal Afrikaner (BOER) word for a village raised by indigenous peoples in southern Africa. Adopted by nineteenth-century British colonists in the region, the word derives from the Portuguese word for cattle pen and also refers to an enclosure for livestock.

Krafft-Ebing, Richard von [Freiherr] (1840–1902) German neuropsychologist. Renowned for his studies in sexual psychopathology, most notably *Psycopathia Sexualis* (1886), a collection of sexual deviation case histories, Krafft-Ebing was known throughout Europe for his investigations into the legal and genetic aspects of criminal and deviant sexual behavior and often served as a court consultant. His investigations into mental illness, criminology, and forensic psychopathology advanced psychology as a clinical science.

Krakatoa (Krakatau) Volcano in western Indonesia (the Dutch East Indies in Victorian times). The volcano forms an island in the Sunda Strait, between Sumatra and Java. On August 26–28, 1883, it erupted violently, destroying two-thirds of the island and raising tsunamis (tidal waves) that devastated nearby coastal areas. It is estimated that thirty-six thousand people were killed. Extraordinarily high waves were experienced as far away as Cape Horn, Africa; debris reached as far as Madagascar off the African coast, and skies were darkened over large areas.

Kroeber, Alfred Louis (1876–1960) American anthropologist. Born in Hoboken, New Jersey, Alfred Kroeber later attended Columbia University, where he received a master's degree in English in 1897 and then began studying under FRANZ BOAS, who had recently established the anthropology department. After the Arctic explorer Robert E. Peary escorted a group of Eskimos to New York, Kroeber published his recordings of Eskimo tales in 1898 and 1899.

He earned his Ph.D. in 1901 with a dissertation on the symbolism of the Arapaho tribe of Montana. Later the same year Kroeber founded the anthropology department at the University of California at Berkeley, where he remained until his retirement in 1946. Kroeber continued to work in the field, studying the more than one hundred tribes in California, which resulted in the publication of the *Handbook of the Indians of California* in 1925. Kroeber also authored *Anthropology* (1923), the first textbook in the field. Kroeber held a number of distinguished positions throughout his career, including president and founder of the American Anthropological Association in 1917.

Kropotkin, Peter (1842–1921) Russian anarchist. Born in Moscow to a noble Russian family, he was trained as an imperial page and served as an aide to Czar Alexander II. From 1861 to 1867 he was an officer in Siberia, conducting geologic surveys and writing internationally respected articles on geography and geology. At the end of his tour of duty he refused an appointment as secretary of the Russian Geological Society and instead threw himself into social activism.

He joined an anarchist group in 1872 and was arrested for sedition in 1874. Two years later he made a dramatic escape and fled to Switzerland. At the request of the Russian government, he was expelled from Switzerland in 1881, following the assassination of Alexander II. He settled in Paris but was imprisoned for seditious activities in 1883. On his release in 1886, he moved to England where he lived for the next thirty years, writing and refining his anarchistic philosophy.

In contrast to the prevailing notions of SOCIAL DARWINISM, Kropotkin argued that cooperation rather than competition between individuals was the fundamental law of nature. Modern capitalistic society had distorted man's essentially cooperative, communal tendencies and must be abolished. Kropotkin imagined a world where people lived in small communities, each working at a variety of tasks and taking only what he or she required from the common property, a means of distribution Kropotkin called the "principle of need." He wrote numerous works elaborating his theories, the most famous of which is *Mutual Aid* (1902).

Kropotkin advocated a program of violent, highly visible political acts that he hoped would awaken the latent rebelliousness of the oppressed classes. He also called for a program of mental, physical, and moral education for children to prepare the next generation to form anarchistic communes.

Kropotkin was the founder and inspiration of the international anarchist movement. The overthrow of the Romanovs in 1917 allowed Kropotkin to return to Russia.

Kruger, Paul See TRANSVAAL and SOUTH AFRICA.

Ku Klux Klan Secret American organization. Founded by young white men in Pulaski, Tennessee, in 1866, the Ku Klux Klan was initially a social fraternity but soon developed into a terrorist vehicle for reestablishing political and social domination of whites over blacks freed as a result of the U.S. CIVIL WAR. Klan members were defined by their hooded white garb and other arcane practices, as well as by their violent tactics. As the group grew in number, it used intimidation, lynchings, and other forms of brutality to rescind RECONSTRUCTION-era political advances made by blacks and return southern states to prewar Democratic rule. The group's name was based on the Greek word *Kuklos,* or circle; its most prominent leader was former Confederate general Nathan Bedford Forrest. Federal intervention all but wiped out the Klan by the early 1870s, but the group reemerged as an even stronger force in the first half of the twentieth century.

labor movement Economic, political, and social movement. As nineteenth-century INDUSTRIALIZATION proceeded, various organizations aimed at reforming and regulating the factory system in the interest of workers arose in Britain, the United States, and the European continent. In the years immediately following the REFORM BILL OF 1832, several unions were founded, most of them short-lived. As a rule they represented skilled workers in single trades. Among these unions were the Operative Builders Union (1832–34) and the Grand National Consolidated Trades Union (1832), founded by philanthropist ROBERT OWEN, an early proponent of the eight-hour day. Mining and textile unions appeared widely from the 1840s to 1860s, notably the Miners Association of Great Britain (1842–48), the Amalgamated Association of Operative Cotton Spinners (1853), and the Amalgamated Society of Engineers.

Of groups representing a number of unions and a number of issues, the most powerful was the Trades Union Congress, an umbrella organization founded in Manchester in 1868 and reorganized in 1871. Among its accomplishments was the establishment of a link with the LIBERAL PARTY, then under the leadership of WILLIAM GLADSTONE.

As the century drew to a close, growing numbers of unskilled British workers came to be represented by alliances known as general unions, which offered open admission, regardless of profession. They and other new unions, including the Matchmakers Union of ANNIE BESANT, were often influenced by the ideals of SOCIALISM and its related philosophy of syndicalism, which advocated the establishment of one central union. Seeking stronger government representation, labor leader KEIR HARDIE became a member of Parliament (1892–95, 1900–15) and in 1900 founded the organization that became the Labour Party.

For the first decades of the Victorian era, the American labor movement was divided into skilled trade unions such as the International Typographical Union (1852) and reform organizations such as the National Labor Union

(1866) and the widely popular Knights of Labor (1869), which advocated redress of the injustices of industrial capitalism as well as specific labor grievances. Among the causes championed by the Knights of Labor were the eight-hour workday and cessation of child labor.

The Knights of Labor flourished until the 1880s when the supremacy of industrial capitalism became evident and the chances for and interest in social reform dimmed. In response to what now appeared an unfocused approach to labor representation, American labor leader SAMUEL GOMPERS founded the American Federation of Labor (AFL). A "pure and simple" union, it acknowledged the power of capitalism and concentrated instead on improving the worker's lot within the system, through such practices as collective bargaining. A socialist himself, Gompers believed that his approach would best grant workers the tools needed for "industrial emancipation."

The end of the century in American labor saw two responses to the "bread and butter" unionism of the AFL. New unions that represented growing numbers of minority workers including women, blacks, and recent immigrants, were developing to counter all-white unions. In addition, the union as an instrument of social reform was reborn. A radical unionism, focusing on the need for social revolution through socialism, stirred. Among its leaders in the early twentieth century were William D. Haywood of the International Workers of the World (I.W.W.), or "Wobblies," and EUGENE V. DEBS, a founder of the American socialist party.

lace Delicate fabric woven in an open weblike pattern of threads, usually of linen, cotton, silk, or wool. Since its development in Venice and Brussels in the 1500s, lace was traditionally made by hand using needlepoint or tatting—knotting threads with a shuttle. However, the invention of the bobbin net machine in the mid-nineteenth century allowed for lace to be manufactured in mass quantities. A substitute lace was also popular in the nineteenth century, made from machine-generated net that was hand-embroidered. Given the quantity and homogeneity of machine-made lace, the ornamentation lost some of its social exclusivity during the Victorian Age. As lace became democratized, other forms of decoration gained popularity, such as beading, encrustation of jewels, elaborately dyed fabrics, and feathers. Handmade lace still denoted class worth, but its practice declined to near nonexistence in the twentieth century.

Land League Irish agrarian and political reform movement. Centuries of English rule in IRELAND left Irish tenant farmers with no protection against high rents, sudden evictions, and other landlord abuses. The system impoverished the Irish peasantry and left them with almost no opportunity to own the land they tended.

The National Land League of Ireland was established in 1879 by MICHAEL DAVITT, with CHARLES STEWART PARNELL as its president. The league was formed against a backdrop of continuing agrarian violence by farmers against landlords, their agents, and other farmers willing to occupy lands left empty by eviction. The violence was heightened by failures of the potato crop, which had raised fears of a repeat of the famine of the 1840s. The league focused on the land question, but its leadership saw the league as another weapon in the struggle for Irish control of its domestic affairs.

The league set about organizing tenants to fight for reduced rents, protection from eviction, and the establishment of affordable purchase agreements that would allow tenants to buy their own land over time. This last goal was technically possible in 1879, but the required down payment was prohibitive.

The Land League, financed by Irish Americans and led by ex-FENIANS, quickly mobilized the countryside. Demonstrations were mounted to obtain rent reductions and prevent evictions. Violent night visits terrorized peasants willing to pay high rents or take over land from evicted farmers. The term "boycott" originated with the social and commercial ostracism of Captain CHARLES BOYCOTT, a notorious land agent. A powerful force, the league supplanted the jurisdiction of the regular courts and government administration in some parts of Ireland.

League agitation led to the passing of one of the COERCION ACTS in January 1881 and the arrest of important league members. It also led to the Land Act of 1881, which created land courts to determine fair rents and allowed the government to buy land that tenants could purchase at reasonable installments.

Parnell, however, who was also the leader of the IRISH PARTY in Parliament, withheld his support for the law until test cases could be made in the new courts concerning rent hikes. English prime minister WILLIAM GLADSTONE had him and other league leaders arrested. The prisoners issued a "No Rent Manifesto," and on October 20, 1881, the league was banned.

It was never resurrected. Parnell formed a new organization, the Irish National League, which called for rent strikes against extortionate owners, but it, too, was suppressed.

The Land League's legacy to generations of farmers proved substantial. The new land courts kept rents at relatively reasonable levels; more important, the terms under which tenants could purchase land became more favorable over the years. By 1921 some 400,000 of the 470,000 parcels of land in Ireland were owned by former tenants under long-term purchase agreements.

Landor, Walter Savage (1775–1864) English writer. Born in Warwick, he was the eldest son of a wealthy physician. He was educated at Rugby School and at Trinity College, and while he distinguished himself in writing Latin verse, he was dismissed from both institutions due to disagreements with the school authorities.

After a bitter argument with his father, Landor spent three years traveling before returning to England in 1804. He inherited a large fortune after his father's death a year later and used some of it in 1808 to support the Spanish army's fight against Napoleon.

Landor married Julia Thullier, nearly twenty years his junior, in 1811 and settled in Llanthony, but differences with local authorities forced him to leave his estate in 1814, and he moved his family to Florence.

In 1824 he published the first two volumes of *Imaginary Conversations,* a collection of imagined dialogues between famous historical figures. Landor constantly added to his collection, and by the end of his life he had produced about 150 dialogues.

In 1838, Landor left his wife and three children and returned to England. Between 1839 and 1840 he completed a dramatic trilogy—*Andrea of Hungary, Giovanna of Naples,* and *Fra Rupert.* Although his plays are considered of minor quality, many of his contemporaries, including ROBERT BROWNING and CHARLES DICKENS, professed their admiration and indebtedness to his sense of drama.

Landor collected his writings in two volumes in 1846 and included a new set of poems, called "Hellenics." A libel suit forced him to leave England in 1858, and he returned to Florence where Browning offered him financial assistance.

Landseer, Sir Edwin Henry (1802–1873) English artist. Born in London, Landseer learned drawing at an early age from his father, John Landseer, an engraver and writer. At the age of thirteen, Edwin Landseer exhibited *Portrait of a Mule* and *Portrait of a Pointer Bitch and Puppy* at the Royal Academy, where he became a student the following year.

Landseer continued to exhibit frequently, and his renderings of anthropomorphized animals became enormously popular. Elected to the Royal Academy in 1831, Landseer was invited to paint Queen Victoria's portrait in 1839 and was also hired to teach etching to members of the royal family.

Knighted in 1850, Landseer earned a gold medal at the Paris Exposition in 1855. Regarded as one of the finest nineteenth-century animal painters, due to *The Monarch of the Glen* (1850), *Stag at Bay* (1846), and other works, Landseer also distinguished himself as a sculptor, creating the four bronze lions at the base of the Nelson monument in Trafalgar Square, which were unveiled in 1867.

Lang, Andrew (1844–1912) Scottish writer. Andrew Lang was born in Selkirk, Scotland. Educated at Glasgow University and Balliol College, Oxford, he was elected a fellow of Meron College in 1868.

In 1875 he moved to London and began his literary career, writing critical essays for the *Daily News* and other newspapers. He also published a volume of poetry, *Ballads and Lyrics of Old France* (1879), before collaborating with SAMUEL HENRY BUTLER on a translation of the *Odyssey* in 1879 and with Walter Leaf and Ernest Myers on a translation of the *Iliad* in 1883.

Lang then began publishing a twelve-volume collection of international fairy tales, beginning with *The Blue Fairy Book* (1889) and titling each subsequent volume with another color; he completed the series in 1910 with *The Lilac Fairy Book.* He also published original stories for children, including *The Gold of Fairmilee* (1883) and *Prince Prigio* (1889).

Lang's interest in anthropology and history led to the publication of a number of nonfiction works, including *Myth, Ritual and Religion* (1887), and the four-volume *History of Scotland from the Roman Occupation to the Suppression of the Last Jacobite Rising* (1900–1907). Lang's final work, *History of English Literature,* was published two days after his death.

Langham Place Circle Political activist group. Meeting in the 1850s and 1860s, the Langham Place Circle helped to found the woman's rights movement in Britain. Led by BESSIE PARKES, Barbara Bodichon (1827–1891), and Emily Davies (1831–1921), the group initiated the campaign for WOMAN SUFFRAGE and called for legal, employment, and education reform. The club was named after its meeting place at 19 Langham Circle, which also contained offices and reading rooms. Their publications included the *English Woman's Journal* (1858–64) and the *Alexandra Magazine* (1864–65). Members also founded such organizations as the Society for the Promotion of the Employment of Women (1859). One member, Emily Faithfull (1835–1895), founded the Victoria Press (1860) to give women employment opportunities in the printing trade. The press became the printer for the *English Woman's Journal* and for a new periodical founded by Faithfull, *Victoria Magazine* (1863–80). Although the circle had dissolved by 1870, many of its members and those inspired by them continued to work for woman's rights throughout the century.

Langtry, Lillie [Emilie Charlotte Le Breton] (1853–1929) British actress. Renowned for her beauty, she was known as the "Jersey Lily." The only daughter of William Courbet Le Breton, dean of Jersey, she made her stage debut in London in 1881 and afterward played a variety of roles, most notably that of Rosalind in *As You Like It.* Unhappily married from 1874 to Edward Langtry, the magnetic beauty came into the orbits of several notable men of the day. Her involvement with them was varied: She was admired by JAMES MCNEILL WHISTLER and Judge Roy Bean, painted by JOHN MILLAIS, who named her Jersey Lilly, in 1876–77, bore a daughter, Jeanne-Marie, to Prince Louis of Battenberg in 1881, and in 1877 was the first publicly known mistress of EDWARD, Prince of Wales. Late in her life she married Hugh de Bathe.

laudanum Drug. Laudanum, a mixture of alcohol and opium, was prescribed by physicians and used as a home remedy to treat a variety of ailments in nineteenth-century Britain. Highly addictive, it was sold without restriction until the Pharmacy Act of 1868 regulated its use. By the end of the century the drug, like NARCOTICS in general, was widely considered a social evil.

law of octaves See PERIODIC TABLE OF ELEMENTS.

Lazarus, Emma (1849–1887) American poet and translator. Lazarus is best known for her paean to freedom and refuge, "The New Colossus," which is imprinted on the pedestal of the STATUE OF LIBERTY. Born in New York City, she incorporated many aspects of Jewish life in her later works, which included the poetry collection *Songs of a Semite* (1882) and the medieval Hebrew drama *The Dance of Death.* In the 1880s she also supported Russian Jews terrorized by government-directed pogroms.

Le Fanu, [Joseph] Sheridan (1814–1873) Irish writer. Born to a Dublin family of French Huguenot descent, he was educated at Trinity College in Dublin, where he studied law. In 1839 he abandoned his practice and pursued a career as a journalist. Between 1845 and 1873, Le Fanu published fourteen novels, including *The House by the Churchyard* (1863) and his best known work, *Uncle Silas* (1864), a brooding tale of a girl victimized by her criminal uncle. From 1861 to 1869, Le Fanu owned and edited the *Dublin University Magazine,* in which he also published his short stories, almost all of which dealt with supernatural themes. A collection of his stories, *In a Glass Darkly,* was published in 1872 and contains "Carmilla," a vampire tale often considered, alongside *DRACULA* by BRAM STOKER, the best of that genre.

After his wife's death in 1858, Le Fanu became a recluse and was often referred to as the "Invisible Prince of Merrion Square."

Lear, Edward (1812–1888) English writer and artist. Born in London into a family of twenty children, he was educated at home and began to earn a living in his mid-teens when he was asked to draw illustrations for the Zoological Gardens and later the Earl of Derby. The limericks and other amusing poems he recited to the Earl's family became part of his 1846 collection, *A Book of Nonsense.* The enlarged 1861 version was a success and was followed by four other entertaining works: *A Book of Nonsense and More Nonsense* (1862), *Nonsense Songs, Stories, Botany, and Alphabets* (1871), *More Nonsense Songs, Pictures, Rhymes, Botany, Etc.* (1872), and *Laughable Lyrics, a Fresh Book of Nonsense Poems* (1877). The 1871 *Nonsense Songs* included what would become one of his best-known ditties, "The Owl and the Pussycat." Also a popular landscape painter, he taught painting to Queen VICTORIA and compiled travel books with sketches of Mediterranean countries he visited: *Illustrated Excursions in Italy* (1846) and *A Tour in Sicily* (1847), among others.

Leaves of Grass (1855) First collection of poems published by American poet WALT WHITMAN. Originally appearing in a small unsigned edition, the poems were untitled. As Whitman revised and expanded the collection, it came to include many of what are now his best known works, including "Out of the Cradle Endlessly Rocking," "When Lilacs Last in the Dooryard Bloom'd," and the opening poem of the first edition, "Song of Myself." Published to a mixed reception in the United States, the collection first gained critical attention in England and ultimately became central to the formation of an American voice in writing. This voice was characterized in part by the preface to the 1855 edition, in which Whitman asserts that "the United States themselves are essentially the greatest poem. . . . The genius of the United States is not best or most in its executives or legislatures, nor in its ambassadors or authors or colleges or churches or parlors, nor even in its newspapers or inventors . . . but always most in the common people."

Lee, Robert Edward (1807–1870) American soldier. He was the commander of the army of the CONFEDERACY in the U.S. CIVIL WAR. Lee was born at the family estate in Westmoreland County, Virginia. After graduating second in his class from the U.S. Military Academy at West Point in 1829, Lee was commissioned a lieutenant of engineers and worked for the next fifteen years improving the channel of the Mississippi. In 1831 he married Mary Ann Randolph Custis, whose father was a grandson of Martha Washington.

In 1844, Lee was ordered to the Mexican border, where he distinguished himself in the ensuing campaign. He was wounded in the attack on Chapultepec in 1847, an attack that also included twenty-five-year-old ULYSSES S. GRANT. General Winfield Scott praised Lee as "the very best soldier" he had seen in the field.

In 1852, Lee was appointed superintendent of the U.S. Military Academy, where his cadets included the artist James McNeill Whistler and "Jeb" Stuart. Three years later, with the help of Secretary of War JEFFERSON DAVIS, he became a colonel in the newly formed Second Cavalry and served in Texas before the death of his father-in-law in 1857. Lee returned to Arlington to settle the family estate, move into the Custis House—now part of Arlington Cemetery—and provide care for his ill wife, who had become an invalid from arthritis. Lee was still on leave in 1859 when orders took him to Harpers Ferry, Virginia, where he and a group of marines captured JOHN BROWN.

In April 1861, General Scott offered Lee command of all the federal forces at the outbreak of the Civil War. While opposing slavery and disapproving of "disunion, strife, and civil war," Lee's loyalties remained with his beloved state of Virginia. When Virginia seceded, Lee followed and became commander of all military and naval forces in that state.

By June 1861, Lee had been appointed a full general in the Confederate army, with orders to organize the poorly trained rebel soldiers in western Virginia into an efficient fighting force. Although many of Lee's subordinates ignored his orders, making the campaign a failure, Jefferson Davis was so impressed with Lee's methods that in March 1862 he named Lee chief military advisor.

Lee quickly became known as an exceptional military strategist. Always heavily outnumbered, he frequently defied common sense and military wisdom by dividing his smaller forces and attacking the enemy with a flanking movement used to divert attention from an attack on the front. Lee continually confounded the Union troops with his well-orchestrated feints, diversions, and attacks, defeating them at Fredericksburg and Chancellorsville before suffering heavy losses at the Battle of GETTYSBURG.

With the appointment of Grant as commander of the Union army in October 1863, Lee faced a determined and exceptional soldier, who also possessed a much larger, better equipped fighting force. After costly fighting in the Battle of the Wilderness, where the two generals engaged in combat for the first time, Lee realized that his army was no longer capable of attacking, and he concentrated on defending the South. Grant doggedly pursued the Confederate army, however, driving it back to Richmond where he began a nine-month siege on the city.

With "no food, no horses, no reinforcements," Lee abandoned Richmond and tried to join forces with General Joseph E. Johnston's troops in North Carolina. The Union troops followed, however, and stopped Lee in his path. After engaging in losing battles in early April, Lee agreed to surrender on April 9, 1865, at APPOMATTOX COURT HOUSE.

Twenty days later, President ANDREW JOHNSON issued a proclamation of amnesty, but Lee and other ranking Confederate officers were excluded. In June a federal court indicted Lee on charges of treason, but no subsequent action was taken. Although Lee publicly swore allegiance to the Union, his citizenship was not returned until 1975.

Named president of Washington College (now Washington and Lee University) in Lexington, Virginia, in 1865, Lee's main goals after the war were the education of the youth of the South and the restoration of the cultural and intellectual ties between the North and the South.

Leo XIII, Pope (1810–1903) Head of the Roman Catholic Church, 1878–1903. Born Gioacchino Vincenzo Pecci, he was less conservative than his predecessor, PIUS IX. He strove to reconcile the Roman Catholic Church with the modern world. Although he was unable to persuade Italy to restore his temporal power over any portion of the former Papal States (see PAPACY), he improved relations with other governments, including Great Britain, Russia, and Japan. He negotiated an end to the *Kulturkampf,* the conflict with German chancellor OTTO VON BISMARCK over control of the German church that had begun in 1871. He relaxed the Victorian era tension between religion and science by taking a more open view of scientific progress, while defending the Church's intellectual heritage in *Aeterni Patris* (1879), the encyclical that made the system of thirteenth-century thinker St. Thomas Aquinas the official philosophy of the Church. He also opened the Vatican archives to all scholars and argued that Catholics could and should live as responsible citizens within modern states. In his most important encyclical, *Rerum Novarum* (1891), he outlined the social ideals of the Church, speaking out against both the social abuses of industrial capitalism and the weaknesses of Marxism, upholding the principle of collective bargaining, and explaining the mutual obligations of employers and workers.

Leonowens, Anna Harriette [Crawford] (1834–1914) Welsh educator and writer. Born in Carnarvonshire, Wales, Leonowens was the widow of Major Thomas Lewis Leonowens when she was asked to become the governess to the children of Siam's King

Mongkut (Rama IV), who favored westernizing influences (see SOUTHEAST ASIA). For years she lived with the household in Bangkok; upon her departure she wrote *The English Governess at the Siamese Court* (1870) and *The Romance of the Harem* (1872). More than seventy years later, the book *Anna and the King of Siam* (1944) was written by Margaret Landon. It served as the basis for the Broadway musical *The King and I* by Richard Rodgers and Oscar Hammerstein.

Lesotho See BASUTOLAND.

Lesseps, Ferdinand-Marie, Vicomte de (1805–1894) French diplomat and engineer. After many years in the consular service, he conceived the idea of the SUEZ CANAL and supervised its construction (1859–69). In later years he headed a company that attempted to build a Panama Canal (1881–88), but the venture went bankrupt and he was convicted for misappropriating funds, though the decision was reversed. The United States successfully completed the Panama Canal in 1904–14.

Leverrier, Urbain-Jean-Joseph (1811–1877) French astronomer and mathematician. Born in Saint-Lô, Leverrier was the son of a local government official. In June 1846 he became the first to publish calculations predicting the existence of an unknown planet, based on irregularities in the orbit of Uranus. Englishman JOHN COUCH ADAMS had reached the same conclusion the previous year but had not published the results. Leverrier convinced astronomers at the Berlin Observatory to train their telescope on the predicted region of the sky, leading to the discovery of NEPTUNE on September 23, 1846.

In 1845, Leverrier also discovered an unexplained advance of Mercury's perihelion—or nearest approach to the sun—which he suggested might result from an undiscovered planet nearer to the sun than Mercury. This planet, known as Vulcan, was never discovered, and the discrepancy in Mercury's orbit was not explained until Einstein's general theory of relativity (1915).

Lewes, George Henry (1817–1878) English writer. Born in London, the versatile writer was variously a journalist, editor, critic, biographer, dramatist, novelist, essayist, philosopher, and scientist. With Thornton Leigh Hunt he edited and wrote for *The Leader* (1850–54); he later helped to found and served as the first editor of *Fortnightly Review*. Liberal in his opinions, he supported REALISM in fiction, a position expounded in his famous review of *JANE EYRE* (1847) by CHARLOTTE BRONTË. He practiced his realist ideas in his two novels *Ranthorpe* (1845) and *Rose, Blanche, and Violet* (1848). He wrote plays and books on the theater; of his biographies, *The Life and Works of Goethe* (1855) is considered his best. As a philosopher he wrote the multivolume work *Problems of Life and Mind* (1874–79). He turned to scientific subjects in such works as *Seaside Studies* (1858) and *Studies of Animal Life* (1862).

Lewes is best remembered today for living with GEORGE ELIOT from 1854 until his death. Lewes's wife Agnes Jervis was involved in a long-term extramarital relationship of her own, with Lewes's colleague Thornton Hunt. Lewes encouraged Eliot in her writing, and Eliot in turn contributed to his work, most notably supplying prose translations for his study of Goethe.

Liberal Party English political organization. The Liberal Party developed in the mid-nineteenth century at the expense of the Whigs. Members of the middle class, newly enfranchised by the REFORM BILL OF 1832, joined some Whigs, Radicals, and anti-protectionist members of the CONSERVATIVE

PARTY to form the basis of a new party. It never developed a rigid ideology, and its members fought over IMPERIALISM and domestic legislation. The party embraced the general principles of laissez-faire economics, religious freedom and individual rights, free trade, and the idea of progress.

Lord JOHN RUSSELL is credited with coining the term "liberal" in the late 1830s, and some regard his 1846 administration as the first Liberal government. It was not until the 1868 administration of WILLIAM GLADSTONE and another enlargement of the electorate resulting from the REFORM BILL OF 1867 that the Liberals became an organized parliamentary force. Gladstone dominated the party, which was in power for more than twelve years between 1868 and 1894.

The Liberals were damaged in 1886 when a large number of businessmen, most notably JOSEPH CHAMBERLAIN, deserted the party for the Conservatives over Gladstone's support of Irish HOME RULE. In opposition, the Liberals courted the labor and Irish vote, and managed to regain power (1892–94) under Gladstone and again under Sir Henry Campbell-Bannerman (1905–8). Liberals ruled or shared power from 1905 to 1922, but they declined greatly between the world wars as the Labor Party grew in strength.

libraries See BOSTON PUBLIC LIBRARY and MUDIE'S LIBRARY.

Lincoln, Abraham (1809–1865) Sixteenth president of the UNITED STATES. Perhaps the most revered politician in American history, Lincoln was born in Kentucky, the son of Thomas Lincoln and Nancy Hanks. His early years were marked by poverty as his family moved from failed farm to failed farm before settling in Illinois in 1830. Lincoln himself moved to New Salem, Illinois, the next year. There he spent six years working as a rail-splitter, postmaster, general store manager, and at other odd jobs while reading voraciously to compensate for his almost complete lack of formal schooling.

His popularity among the townspeople led to his election to the state legislature in 1834 for the first of four terms where he became a leading local figure of the Whig Party. During this time he also served as the captain of a militia company during the Black Hawk War but saw no fighting.

In 1836, Lincoln began to practice law and soon moved to Springfield, the Illinois state

In this 1862 photo by famed photographer Mathew Brady, President Abraham Lincoln poses with Major Allan Pinkerton and General John McClelland at Antietam during the height of the Civil War. Photo courtesy of the Library of Congress.

capital. He wed the socially prominent MARY TODD LINCOLN in 1842. His continuing interest in politics led to a term in the House of Representatives (1847–49). His otherwise obscure congressional career was highlighted by his opposition to the MEXICAN WAR, which he saw as an attempt by the DEMOCRATIC PARTY to extend slavery beyond the southern states.

When he failed to get a desired government position from the ZACHARY TAYLOR administration, despite his support of Taylor over HENRY CLAY for the 1848 Whig presidential nomination, Lincoln withdrew from active political life. He returned to politics in 1854, the year that the Kansas-Nebraska Act allowed settlers to vote on bringing slavery into northern territories historically closed to slavery under the Missouri Compromise of 1820. He vehemently opposed the extension of slavery and mounted a Senate campaign, which he abandoned in favor of a Democrat who opposed the Kansas legislation. It was to be his last campaign as a Whig. He joined the newly formed REPUBLICAN PARTY in 1856 and fought strenuously for its 1856 presidential candidate JOHN C. FRÉMONT, gaining power as a Republican leader in the western states.

By the end of 1858 when he ran unsuccessfully for the Senate against incumbent STEPHEN DOUGLAS in a campaign highlighted by the Lincoln-Douglas debates, Lincoln had become one of the nation's strongest voices against the spread of slavery beyond the borders of the southern states. His famous acceptance speech of the Republican nomination for the Senate articulates plainly his basic view on slavery: "A house divided against itself cannot stand. I believe that this government cannot endure permanently half-slave and half-free."

Although he considered slavery morally wrong, Lincoln based his Senate campaign on the northern white laborer's dread of competing with slave labor. As such, the spread of slavery would be a detriment to the Republican Party's key constituents—white laborers and farmers. As he put it in his masterfully simple prose: "It [the Union] will become all one thing or all the other."

The lost Senate campaign lifted him to national prominence and carried him to the Republican presidential nomination in 1860. The slavery controversy split the Democratic Party into a northern faction led by Stephen Douglas and a southern one headed by John Breckenridge. A third party, the Constitutional Union, also joined the fray. Lincoln won only 40 percent of the fragmented popular vote but amassed an overwhelming majority of the electoral vote to become president.

By the time Lincoln took office in March 1861, seven southern states had left the Union rather than accept the electoral outcome. Four more joined them to form the Confederate States of America. Lincoln was reluctant to initiate hostilities against the CONFEDERACY but did not shrink from trying to provision Fort Sumter, a besieged Union fort in Charleston, South Carolina, harbor. Southern forces fired on the fort on April 12, 1861. The CIVIL WAR had begun.

As the war dragged on through 1862, Lincoln came under attack by defeatists on one hand who urged him to negotiate a compromise and hard-line members of his party on the other who called for more vigorous prosecution of the war, including emancipation of the slaves as a military tactic and moral imperative. Lincoln navigated these waters by issuing the EMANCIPATION PROCLAMATION in 1863, which freed slaves only in areas controlled by the South. This appeased the slave states that had remained in the Union while signaling to the antislavery Republicans his ultimate intentions. Throughout the war he stressed that the conflict was about saving the Union and not ending slavery, although the latter could help accomplish the main goal of the war.

The Union's military fortunes grew brighter in 1863 with the capture of Vicksburg, Mississippi, by forces led by General ULYSSES S. GRANT and a Union victory at GETTYSBURG, Pennsylvania, which ended the last southern invasion of northern territory. In November 1863, Lincoln gave one of the modern world's great speeches at that battle site, the Gettysburg Address.

Lincoln chose General Grant to lead all Union forces in 1864. In a series of offenses in Virginia, Union forces inflicted great casualties on Confederate armies while suffering even larger losses themselves. Still, no immediate end to the fighting seemed in sight. Lincoln faced a reelection campaign against Democrat GEORGE MCCLELLAN, a general he had dismissed for lack of fighting spirit. Growing war weariness and the economic drain of the war imperiled his reelection, but Union success in the autumn of 1864—especially General WILLIAM T. SHERMAN's taking of Atlanta—secured his second term.

With the end of the war in sight, Lincoln began preparing to restore the Union and for what he called in his second inaugural address "a just and lasting peace." His plan for RECONSTRUCTION, promulgated in late 1863, included restoring southerners to full citizenship rights if they swore allegiance to the United States and readmitting southern representatives to Congress if their reconstructed state governments accepted emancipation.

It was not to be. In April 1865, five days after Confederate general ROBERT E. LEE surrendered his army, Lincoln was shot by JOHN WILKES BOOTH during a play at Ford's Theatre in Washington, D.C. He died the next morning.

Lincoln's semi-mythical historical stature as well as his actual importance in American history have obscured his status as one of the nation's great writers. His letters, speeches, and state papers have been collected many times. *The Collected Works* (1953) comprise nine volumes.

Lincoln, Mary Todd (1818–1882) Wife of President ABRAHAM LINCOLN. Mary Todd came from a distinguished Kentucky family. She met her future husband in 1839 while living in Springfield, Illinois, and they married in 1842. Her ambitions for her husband helped Lincoln gain the presidency.

She was accused of southern sympathies during the U.S. CIVIL WAR because of her Kentucky origins and because of a relative who wore Confederate gray. Lincoln was even forced to defend her allegiance to the Union before a congressional committee.

Her unfortunate family life caused her great stress and led to periods of mental imbalance. The death of her son William in 1862 was a great blow, followed three years later by her husband's assassination while she was at his side. Her condition worsened after 1871 when another son, Tad, died. Robert Todd Lincoln had her committed for months to an asylum, but the judgment of insanity was overturned. She died at her sister's home in Springfield. An unfair and unsympathetic portrayal by Lincoln's friend and biographer William Herndon tarnished her historical reputation.

Lincoln County War See BILLY THE KID.

Lind, Jenny [Johanna Maria] (1820–1887) Swedish soprano. Known as the "Swedish nightingale" for her delicate coloratura voice, Lind was established as a leading operatic soprano in Europe before joining American impresario P. T. BARNUM and embarking on her two-year tour of the United States in 1850. So wildly successful was the tour that she continued performing in concert until 1870.

Lipton, Sir Thomas Johnstone (1850–1931) British merchant. Founder and purveyor of Lipton Ltd., he was born in Glasgow, Scotland, and worked in a U.S. grocery during his teens to learn the nation's merchandising techniques. He amplified these when he used embossed marching pigs to advertise his first Glasgow shop in 1876. After achieving success with several shops throughout the United Kingdom, he entered the tea market in 1890, offering "the Finest Tea the World Can Produce" at discount prices for his shops. Not until 1909 did he begin packaging tea in the United States; three years after his death his mustached face appeared on Lipton tea packages. An avid yachtsman, he attempted five times to win the America's Cup, beginning in 1899 and ending in 1930. See also PROCESSED FOODS.

Lister, Joseph, 1st Baron Lister of Lyme Regis (1827–1912) English surgeon. Born in Essex, he was the second son of Joseph Jackson Lister, a Quaker wine merchant interested in optics who later became important in the development of the microscope. The younger Lister studied medicine at University College in London and in 1852 graduated and obtained a fellowship in the Royal College of Surgeons. In 1861 he was appointed surgeon of the Glasgow Royal Infirmary in Scotland. There he headed a new surgery unit created to decrease the incidence of "hospital fever" and "hospital gangrene," which were associated with high mortality rates following surgery and were believed to be caused by bad air.

After unsuccessful attempts to clean the air with a solution of carbolic acid (phenol), Lister studied the GERM THEORY OF DISEASE by French biochemist LOUIS PASTEUR and in 1865 began applying the solution directly to wounds, instruments, and dressings. By 1877 he had shown that this practice reduced surgical mortality by more than 50 percent. Lister's work in ANTISEPSIS revolutionized surgery and led to his being created a baron in 1897 by a former patient, Queen Victoria. Such was his fame as the founder of antiseptic surgery that in 1880 American physician Joseph Lawrence named an antibacterial mouthwash in his honor: Listerine.

Liszt, Franz (1811–1886) Hungarian pianist, conductor, and teacher. Instructed on the piano by his father, Liszt gave a concert at the age of nine at Sopron and Pozsony, and at Prince Nicolas Esterhazy's palace. Liszt then went to Vienna where he studied with two well-known teachers, Karl Czerny and Antonio Salieri. His first public concerts took place in Vienna in 1822, and in Paris and London in 1824. Triumphant concert tours dominated Liszt's life until September 1847 when he made his last appearance as a pianist.

In 1848, Lizst assumed a full-time position as musical director to the duke of Weimar, which became the center of German avant-garde in music, known as the "New German School." He supported the music of RICHARD WAGNER and revived the works of other contemporary composers. During his most productive period he composed twelve of his symphonic poems, the *Faust* and *Dante* symphonies, the piano sonata, two piano concertos, and *Totentanz* for piano and orchestra. He also revised versions of the *Paganini Etudes* and the *Transcendental Etudes* for piano.

At the age of fifty, Liszt retired to Rome and composed two oratorios and a number of smaller works. After visiting Weimar regularly, the Hungarian government named him president of the Academy of Music at Budapest in 1870. His last works were harmonially very advanced, anticipating musical forms of the twentieth century.

Little Big Horn See CUSTER, GEORGE ARMSTRONG.

Livingstone, David (1813–1873) Scottish missionary and explorer. Having worked in a cotton mill from age ten, he taught himself Latin and studied medicine and Greek before being ordained as a missionary by the London Missionary Society (1840). While serving as a medical missionary in BECHUANALAND, southern Africa (1841–52), he organized exploratory expeditions and discovered Lake Ngami and the ZAMBEZI RIVER. On another vast expedition across southern Africa, he discovered VICTORIA FALLS (1855) and then returned to Britain, where he published the best-seller *Missionary Researches and Travels in South Africa* (1957). In 1858 he was appointed a consul for Africa's east coast and undertook more expeditions; on one he discovered LAKE NYASA (1859). After a brief stay in England, he launched another African expedition in 1866, this time to central Africa to search for the sources of the Zambezi, Congo, and Nile rivers. The journey was plagued by disease and food shortages, and for a time Livingstone was out of contact and feared dead. English-born journalist HENRY MORTON STANLEY, sent by the *New York Herald,* found him in 1871 and allegedly greeted him with the phrase, "Dr. Livingstone, I presume?" Although ill, Livingstone refused to return to England, and he died two years later in what is now ZAMBIA, having failed to find the source of the Nile. His body was returned to England and buried in Westminster Abbey. Acclaimed as a hero for his courage as an explorer, his missionary zeal, and his opposition to the slave trade, he had helped to build British interest in Africa and prepare the way for further colonization.

Lloyd, Marie [Matilda Alice Victoria Wood] (1870–1922) English music hall entertainer. Born in Hoxton, she made her stage debut at fifteen in 1885. By the following year she was playing in the most popular music halls of London's West End and had taken on her stage name. Known for her suggestive wink and her rapport with audiences, she gained a somewhat exaggerated reputation for lewdness. Her trademark songs included "The Boy in the Gallery" and "Twiggy Vous." Known to her working-class fans as "Our Marie," she died after collapsing on stage at age fifty-two.

Lockwood, Belva Ann Bennett (1830–1917) American lawyer and feminist. Born in Royalton, New York, she was admitted to the bar in 1873 and practiced in Washington, D.C., where in 1879 she became the first woman to argue a case before the Supreme Court. A supporter of WOMAN SUFFRAGE and woman's rights, she argued for passage of an "equal pay for equal work" law for federal employees in 1872. Lockwood was nominated by the National Equal Rights Party for president of the United States in 1884 and 1888. She was the first woman to be nominated for the presidency.

Lockyer, Sir Joseph Norman (1836–1920) English astronomer. With French astronomer Pierre-Jules-César Janssen (1824–1907), he codiscovered HELIUM in 1868 by analyzing the spectra of solar prominences during the total eclipse visible in India that year. Also in 1868 he discovered and named the sun's chromosphere and invented a way to observe solar prominences in daylight. Lockyer was known for his studies of sunspots and was one of the first to make spectroscopic analyses of celestial light sources. From 1890 to 1913 he was director of the Solar Physics Laboratory. He was the founder and first editor (1896–1919) of the highly influential scientific journal *Nature.*

Lodge, Oliver Joseph See RADIO WAVES.

Log Cabin Syrup Commercial food product. Log Cabin Syrup is a maple sugar and cane syrup mix developed by Minnesota grocer P. J. Towle. Intended as an alternative to nineteenth-century corn syrup and molasses-based syrups, Towle's maple syrup entered the American market in 1887. It was packaged in house-shaped tin containers and named in honor of Towle's boyhood hero, Abraham Lincoln. It continued to be packed in tin cabins until World War II when metal was needed for the war effort. See also PROCESSED FOODS.

London Capital of the United Kingdom. One of the world's oldest and most historic cities, London at the dawn of the Victorian era was the center of Britain's vast overseas empire, although the city itself consisted of only its ancient center, called "The City," together with the boroughs of Westminster and Mayfair. Between 1810 and 1900, industrialization expanded London's physical size almost eightfold, incorporating neighborhoods such as Chelsea, Battersea, Belgravia, Brompton, Kensington, Hampstead, and Southwark into the city proper. Concurrently, the population rose from about 850,000 citizens in 1810 to almost 5 million by the turn of the century.

The architecture of nineteenth-century London represented a hodgepodge of styles, particularly GOTHIC REVIVAL, Elizabethan, and Jacobean (see VICTORIAN STYLE). Paradoxically, despite the Victorians' grandiose notions of art, most of the structures served the practical needs generated by the city's rapid growth. Among them were railroad terminals: particularly Euston, Victoria, Charing Cross, PADDINGTON, and Waterloo stations; bridges: Blackfriars, ALBERT; museums: VICTORIA AND ALBERT, Natural History; theaters: Royal ALBERT HALL; public buildings: Public Record Office; parks: KENSINGTON Gardens; colleges: Royal College of Music; stores: HARROD'S; churches: Brompton Oratory; and row upon row of connected private houses, from exclusive Kensington to middle-class Islington to poverty-stricken Paddington.

Although much nineteenth-century architecture was elaborate and heavy, Victorian

Gustave Doré's drawing of Daily Life in Victorian England *depicts the energy and chaos generated in London by the Industrial Revolution. Private collection.*

design occasionally erupted in an exquisite edifice such as the Natural History Museum designed by Alfred Waterhouse in 1881 and employing a revolutionary technique of using arches to conceal an iron-and-steel framework, or the Italianate Westminster Cathedral designed by J. F. Bentley in 1903. The most famous Victorian structures, the Houses of Parliament, WESTMINSTER PALACE, designed by Sir Charles Barry and constructed during the mid-1800s to replace the old palace buildings that had burned in 1834, are arguably the most refined and lovely of Victorian edifices. The palace's fine clock tower, known as BIG BEN, has become a symbol of London.

Victorian London was not a particularly pleasant place to live. Soft coal was burned for heat, making the air black and sooty. A growing urban population brought the spread of disease and poverty. Serious cholera epidemics occurred in 1832 and 1849, and large pockets of slums arose, particularly in the East End and surrounding the newly structured railroad stations. In 1858 the already noxious River Thames became so foul that Parliament was forced to go into recess, resulting in an incident known as the Big Stink. Engineer Joseph Bazalgette's sewage system (1875), which involved banking both sides of the Thames, eased the problem only slightly.

Still, many of the Victorian world's greatest statesmen, philosophers, writers, poets, and artists at one point or another called London home. Among them were KARL MARX, JOHN STUART MILL, RICHARD WAGNER, THOMAS CARLYLE, HENRY JAMES, CHARLES DICKENS, OSCAR WILDE, ARTHUR CONAN DOYLE, GEORGE BERNARD SHAW, ROBERT PEEL, BENJAMIN DISRAELI, WILLIAM GLADSTONE, JENNY LIND, ELLEN TERRY, WILLIAM MORRIS, DANTE GABRIEL ROSSETTI, JAMES MCNEILL WHISTLER, J. M. W. TURNER, JOHN SINGER SARGENT, and Queen VICTORIA herself.

London, Jack [John Griffith] (1876–1916) American writer. Born in San Francisco, California, he was the illegitimate son of Flora Wellman and William Henry Chaney, an itinerant astrologer. When the boy was eight months old, his mother married John London, and the boy was given his stepfather's last name.

Raised in poverty, London began working at a canning factory at age fourteen; he was paid a dime an hour and worked ten- to eighteen-hour shifts. To earn better money, he borrowed funds to buy his own boat, which he used to rob privately owned oyster beds. By age fifteen, London was known around the harbor as the "Prince of the Oyster Pirates."

London spent much of his time along the waterfront in taverns and as a teenager began what would become a lifelong struggle with alcohol. *John Barleycorn* (1913) recounts London's life and struggle, and while intending to be a strong warning against the consumption of alcohol, the autobiography belies a romanticism about drink and intoxication.

London also worked at a variety of other jobs as a young man, including newsboy, janitor, shipmate on vessels sailing to Japan and Siberia, before joining the Alaska gold rush in 1897. He returned within a year, however, sick with scurvy.

In 1893, shortly after he had been awarded a newspaper prize for a story on a typhoon off the coast of Japan, London traveled across America and was arrested in Niagara Falls for vagrancy. After a month in jail he returned to Oakland and finished high school. He then entered the University of California but left after one semester due to his inability to pay his tuition.

Starting in December 1898, London began contributing stories to the *Overland Monthly.* Using his experiences in Alaska as his subject matter, London's tales of adventure became popular, and in January 1900 the *Atlantic Monthly* published "An Odyssey of the North." The same year he married Elizabeth Maddern and published his first collection of stories, *The Son of the Wolf,* which immediately gained a wide audience.

London's first novel, *A Daughter of the Snows* (1902), was not a success, but he quickly followed with *The Call of the Wild,* the now classic story of Buck, a family pet who must learn to survive in the Alaskan wilderness.

In January 1904, London was sent by the *San Francisco Examiner* to cover the war between Japan and Russia; when he returned six months later, his wife sued for divorce. The day after their divorce became final, he married Charmian Kittredge.

London published nearly fifty books in his brief career, and aside from his popular novels, he wrote a number of socialist works, influenced by KARL MARX and FRIEDRICH NIETZSCHE. *War of the Classes* (1905) depicts London's view on the class struggle, and *The Iron Heel* (1907) predicts a time when America will resort to brutal totalitarian rule in order to preserve capitalism and the separation of rich and poor.

Always more interested in his socialist writings than other works, he professed, "I never would put pen to paper—except to write a socialist essay to tell the bourgeois world how much I despise it." But London's fortune was made from his adventure tales, and he spent it all on extravagances, including Wolf House, which took four years to build, cost more than $100,000 at the time, and burned in 1913 before London was able to move into it. London committed suicide with a fatal dose of morphine.

London Bridge Structure that spanned the Thames River. Of at least three permanent structures known as London Bridge, the 1831 construction was the only one used during the Victorian era. Designed by John Rennie, the masonry overpass boasted five arches and replaced the twelfth-century Old London Bridge, the final timber bridge built to cross the 800- to 1,500-foot-wide Thames. The timber bridge was designed by Peter of Colechurch. A six-lane concrete London Bridge replaced the nineteenth-century model in 1972. In the Victorian Age, as at other times, hundreds of acres of bustling docks lined the area near the bridge.

London Daily Mail Newspaper. Founded in 1896 as "the penny newspaper for one halfpenny," the newspaper over the next decades would become known for coining popular phrases, sponsoring travel contests, and introducing the COMIC STRIP to Britain. Its publisher was C. W. Hamsworth.

London Daily News Newspaper. The first inexpensive newspaper in London was founded in 1846, and its first editor was CHARLES DICKENS. His book *Pictures from Italy* was serialized from January to March 1846 in the paper as *Travelling Letters Written on the Road.*

London dock strike (1889) Labor dispute. The strike that involved more than sixty thousand unskilled dockworkers and paralyzed Thames River shipping began on August 14, 1889. Initially organized by Ben Tillet, who had been organizing dockers and warehousemen for some time, he was joined in leadership by John Burns, a skilled worker who was a member of the Amalgamated Society of Engineers. This cooperation between unskilled and skilled workers was new to trade unionism. Until the strike, the trade union movement was dominated by skilled workers who had little to do with manual laborers and other unskilled workers.

The strikers' wage demand for the "docker's tanner," or six pence, generated broad public sympathy. Mass demonstrations by sympathizers, along with financial support, forced the companies to capitulate. Roman Catholic cardinal HENRY EDWARD MANNING, who had supported the strike, was instrumental in settling it. The strike helped other segments of unskilled workers—including gas workers and general laborers—to organize themselves, a movement called the "new unionism." Many of its leaders laid the foundations for the Labour Party. See also LABOR MOVEMENT.

Longfellow, Henry Wadsworth (1807–1882) American poet. Born in Portland, Maine, into a well-to-do Puritan family, he heeded his father's wishes and in the 1820s pursued a career as a professor of foreign languages rather than devote himself solely to writing. While his academic position as a Harvard professor allowed him to develop into an important translator and conveyor of European culture to the United States, it was his accessible and affecting poetry championing the American ethos that made him America's most popular international celebrity.

Longfellow's early works, including "The Wreck of the Hesperus" (1841), "The Village Blacksmith" (1842), and "Evangeline: A Tale of Acadie" (1847) established him as the country's "Chief Singer," according to American jurist and author OLIVER WENDELL HOLMES. By the time of later publications such as "THE SONG OF HIAWATHA" (1855) and "The Courtship of Miles Standish" (1858), his works were selling several thousand copies each on publication. His popularity in the United States could be matched by few other artists, except writers such as HARRIET BEECHER STOWE, whose literary treatment of topical concerns in works like *UNCLE TOM'S CABIN* struck a similar vein of national interest. During his lifetime his works were translated into several languages. He later became the only non-British author to gain a place at the Poet's Corner in Westminster Abbey.

In addition to his lyrical poems and ballads, Longfellow was an accomplished writer of sonnets, including "Nature" (1878), written some years after the death of his second wife Fanny, and the "Divina Commedia" cycle (1867), published at the same time as his translations of Dante. His fiction included *Hyperion* (1839) and *Kavanagh* (1849); other thoughtful poems ranged from "A Psalm of Life" (1839) to "The Jewish Cemetery at Newport" (1858).

As revered as he was during his lifetime, Longfellow came to be as equally dismissed after his death. His works, so reflective of nineteenth-century American and European thinking, came to be considered marginal. Subsequent generations are beginning to modify this view and assess Longfellow's work in terms of its lyricism and grasp of literary forms as well as its historical importance, considered immense by contemporary WALT WHITMAN. "I should have to think long," he said in *The Critic,* "if I were asked to name the man who had done more, and in more valuable directions, for America."

Lord Jim (1900) Novel. Written by Polish-born British novelist JOSEPH CONRAD, it was the only one of his masterworks published during Queen Victoria's reign. Combining the exotic colonial locales of late-nineteenth century romance with the moral concerns of high fiction, the novel tells the story of a wandering outcast named Jim. As third officer on an unseaworthy steamer, the *Patna,* Jim deserts the ship along with his fellow officers, all believing the ship will sink with its load of eight hundred sleeping Muslim pilgrims. The *Patna,* however, is towed by a French steamer to Jidda. Publicly condemned for dereliction of duty, Jim is befriended by Marlow, who recognizes Jim's unwavering belief in honor despite his own failure to be honorable. After some time of wandering, holding jobs only until he is recognized, Jim finds sanctuary in a small trading post, Patusan. The natives honor him with the title *Tuan Jim* ("Lord Jim"). This idyll is invaded by a group of ruffians led by the ironically named Gentleman Brown, who after being granted safe passage to depart by Jim repays him by murdering Jim's best friend, Dain Waris, son of the chief Doramin. Jim nobly accepts tribal justice. Doramin kills him with a single shot, thus morally redeeming him.

Not only is Jim a puzzling, flawed hero, but the story has a unique framework, jumping around in time, and is told partly by an omniscient narrator, by Marlow, and through a letter by Marlow. Like many of the modernist writers who began working in the last years of the Victorian era, Conrad experiments here with narrative technique, devising a method that has been likened to the peeling of an onion, where the reader unravels layers of complex meaning.

Lorentz, Hendrik Antoon (1853–1928) Dutch physicist. With Irish physicist George Francis FitzGerald (1851–1901), he postulated a tentative explanation, known as the Lorentz-FitzGerald contraction, for the negative results of the MICHELSON-MORLEY EXPERIMENT. Formulated in the 1890s, the explanation stated that a body's length contracts as its velocity increases, though this contraction is negligible except at velocities close to that of light. Lorentz also argued that a body's mass increased at such speeds, a prediction borne out experimentally when physicists measured the mass of high-velocity ELECTRONS in 1900. Lorentz formulated the Lorentz transformations, a set of equations for correlating the space and time coordinates of a moving system with that of a known reference point. Lorentz's and FitzGerald's discoveries laid the groundwork for German physicist Albert Einstein's theory of relativity (1905, 1916), which in turn confirmed and explained those discoveries.

In addition, Lorentz developed a theory that light was produced by oscillating charged atomic particles, later given the name electrons, and in 1896 was codiscoverer with PIETER ZEEMAN of the ZEEMAN EFFECT, for which the two men shared the 1902 Nobel Prize in physics. Lorentz's colleague FitzGerald was also known for his contributions to the electromagnetic theory of radiation.

Lorna Doone: A Romance of Exmoor (1869) Novel. The most successful work by English writer Richard Doddridge Blackmore (1825–1900) is set in seventeenth-century Devonshire at the time of the unsuccessful rebellion of the Protestant duke of Monmouth against the Catholic king of Britain, James II. It tells the story of the vengeance of young John Ridd against the outlaw clan of Doone who killed his father, and of Ridd's love for Lorna Doone, daughter of his father's murderer.

Loubet, Emile-François (1838–1929) Politician and president of FRANCE (1899–1906). His term of office saw the creation of the Triple Entente of Britain, Russia, and France, the alliance that defeated the central powers in World War I. At Loubet's urging, the ALFRED DREYFUS affair was settled in 1906 when Dreyfus was cleared of espionage charges.

Louis Napoleon See NAPOLEON III.

Louis-Philippe (1773–1850) King of FRANCE. Born at the Palais Royal in Paris, he was the eldest son of Louis-Philippe-Joseph de Bourbon-Orléans. At the beginning of the French Revolution he joined the Jacobin Club but broke with the revolutionary movement in 1793 when his father voted for the execution of Louis XVI. Louis-Philippe defected to Austria and remained in exile for twenty-one years. His father was arrested and executed in November 1793.

In February 1797, Louis-Philippe sailed to the United States and settled in Philadelphia, Pennsylvania, until Napoleon Bonaparte's rise to power two years later. Louis-Philippe returned to Europe and in 1809 married Maria Amelia, daughter of Ferdinand IV of Naples.

During the July Revolution of 1830, directed against his cousin Charles X, the throne was declared vacant, and on August 9, Louis-Philippe was proclaimed "king of the French by the grace of God and the will of the people."

As king, Louis-Philippe sought the political middle ground. In foreign affairs he tried to avoid conflict and create closer ties with Great Britain; in the domestic arena he tried to create a secure governmental majority and eliminate revolutionary sentiment. He was not an entirely popular ruler, facing eleven assassination plots during his reign.

The King's close advisor and confidant was FRANÇOIS GUIZOT, and together they maintained the peace and majority until 1847 when an economic collapse and increased revolutionary fervor endangered the king's control. Amid the REVOLUTIONS OF 1848, the King and Queen escaped to England, where Queen VICTORIA provided a safe and comfortable home. He died in England.

Lourdes Pilgrimage site. Lourdes is located in southwestern France in the foothills of the Pyrenees. From February 11 through July 16, 1858, fourteen-year-old Bernadette Soubirous (1844–1879) had eighteen visions of the Virgin Mary in the Massabielle grotto. In 1862 the visions were pronounced authentic by the Pope. Miraculous cures have been associated with the underground spring in the grotto, which was revealed to Bernadette, although chemically the water is identical to Lourdes drinking water. Lourdes has become a major pilgrimage center for millions of pilgrims from every nation, including many ill or disabled. In 1958 a huge underground church was built to accommodate the ever-increasing number of pilgrims who visit the site.

Lovelace, Augusta Ada Byron, Countess of (1815–1852) English mathematician. She was the daughter of the English poet George Gordon, Lord Byron (1788–1824), and Annabella (Anne Isabella) Milbanke, who took Ada and left Byron after little more than a year of their unhappy marriage. Ada cultivated an interest in mathematics and science, receiving instruction from logician and mathematician Augustus DeMorgan (1806–1871) and scientist MARY SOMERVILLE. In 1833 she learned about the "difference engine," a calculating machine invented by CHARLES BABBAGE. On meeting him, they embarked on a lifelong friendship and collaboration. In 1843 she published the *Sketch of the Analytical Engine,* a translation of a French treatise on Babbage's proposed ANALYTICAL ENGINE, the unfinished forerunner of the modern digital computer. Her commentary on the treatise expanded it to three times its original size. Although the words were hers, the mathematical substance appears to have originated with Babbage, including sketches for programs by which calculations could be performed.

In 1835, Ada married William, Eighth Lord King, who became Earl of Lovelace in 1838 and with whom she had three children. He supported her intellectual pursuits, which led her to attempt unsuccessfully to become a pupil of scientist MICHAEL FARADAY. With friend John Crosse (1810–1880) she became involved in betting on horse races, which left her deeply in debt. She died of cervical cancer at age thirty-six.

Lowell, James Russell (1819–1891) American poet, editor, and critic. Admired as a humanist and a stalwart of American ROMANTICISM, Lowell was born in Cambridge, Massachusetts, and attended Harvard College and Harvard Law School, practicing law briefly before turning to writing. He married poet and abolitionist Maria White in 1844.

After contributing to serious periodicals such as *The Dial* and publishing two collections of poetry (*A Year's Life* in 1841 and *Poems* in 1842), he gained wide attention with the satiric verse collection *The Biglow Papers* (1848). Its attacks on the MEXICAN WAR and the Confederate position in the U.S. CIVIL WAR, written in Yankee dialect, conveyed both his literary talents and his humanist, antislavery beliefs. The same year he published two more of his best known works: the poem "The Vision of Sir Launfel" and the poetic satire of American writers, *A Fable for Critics.* In 1855 he accepted HENRY WADSWORTH LONGFELLOW's position as professor of French and Spanish at Harvard, and he remained active as a journalist, cofounding with OLIVER WENDELL HOLMES *The Atlantic Monthly* in 1857 and acting as its first editor until 1861. In 1864 he joined with CHARLES ELIOT NORTON to edit *The North American Review.* Among his political writings were the *Second Series* of *The Biglow Papers* (1867), written for the *Atlantic* to criticize England's activity in the U.S. Civil War. He served as ambassador to Spain from 1876 to 1880 and to Great Britain from 1880 to 1885. His later works include the poetry collection *The Cathedral* (1870) and the essay collections *Among My Books* (1870, *Second Series,* 1876), and *My Study Window* (1871).

Lumière, Louis (1864–1948) and **Auguste** (1862–1954) French film pioneers, inventors, and directors. Considered among the founders of MOTION PICTURES, the Lumière brothers developed the cinématographe (or CINEMATOGRAPH), a combination camera and projector patented on February 13, 1895. It incorporated the ideas of Etienne-Jules Marey, EADWEARD MUYBRIDGE, and THOMAS EDISON. Whereas Edison's KINETOSCOPE allowed viewers to see films peepshow-style, the Lumières' invention projected films on a screen.

On March 22, 1895, the Lumière brothers projected their first film, *La Sortie des usines Lumière,* showing workers leaving their factory, to members of the Société d'Encouragement pour l'Industrie Nationale. They showed their films for the first time to a paying public at the Grand Café on the Boulevard des Capucines in Paris on December 28, 1895. The program included a number of other brief film clips, including *L'Arrivée d'un train en Gare de la Ciotat* and *L'Arroseur arrose,* the world's first piece of comedic film fiction.

The Lumière films were typically straightforward records of real life and current events. They can be seen as predecessors of the newsreel and documentary film styles.

Louis Lumière directed and shot his first films himself but soon turned the job over to a group of trained photographers, building a catalogue of newsworthy footage and short subjects. By 1898 the Lumière catalogue listed more than one thousand titles, mostly news footage from all over the world as well as such dramatizations as *Faust* and *The Life and Passion of Jesus Christ*.

After the Paris Exposition of 1900, Louis Lumière abandoned film production and turned his energies to the invention and manufacture of photographic equipment and processes.

Luxembourg Small western European country. It is bounded by Belgium, France, and Germany, and the terrain is hilly and wooded. The population is largely German-speaking. The present country consists of the eastern third of a medieval principality called the Grand Duchy of Luxembourg, which had been the hereditary possession of William I, king of the Netherlands. During the Belgian war of independence against the Netherlands (1830–39), Luxembourg was occupied by Belgian forces. In the peace settlement, the western, French-speaking, portion was joined to Belgium. The remainder, modern Luxembourg, was made part of the German Confederation and continued under the personal rule of William and his successors. In 1866, William III created a major international incident when he offered to sell Luxembourg to NAPOLEON III. Prussia protested vigorously, and the proposal was dropped. Instead, Luxembourg was declared neutral, and all its fortifications were dismantled.

Lyceum Theatre Performing hall in London. Originally known as the English Opera House, the Lyceum Theatre was relaunched in the 1870s by Shakespearean actor Sir HENRY IRVING and was managed for a time by author BRAM STOKER. Its productions spanned the range of drama from Shakespeare to mediocre melodramas. It was demolished in 1904.

Lyell, Sir Charles (1797–1875) Scottish geologist. He was educated at Oxford, where the lectures of William Buckland turned his interests toward geology. At his father's behest he studied law, but in 1819 he was elected to the Geological Society and in 1824 made a geological tour of Scotland with Buckland.

Lyell was elected a Fellow of the Royal Society in 1826, and two years later he abandoned his law practice to devote himself to geology. Between 1830 and 1833 he produced the landmark three-volume text *Principles of Geology* in which he adopted the uniformitarian theory of eighteenth-century Scottish geologist James Hutton. Lyell argued that geologic changes occurred gradually over a vast time frame from causes that could be seen presently in operation, not from extraordinary worldwide cataclysms such as earthquakes or floods, the theory known as catastrophism. By persuading his colleagues to adopt uniformitarianism, this work became the basis of modern geology. It also influenced the development of CHARLES DARWIN's theory of EVOLUTION, which Lyell supported. On the basis of shell fossils, Lyell also identified three distinct epochs within the Tertiary period: Eocene, dawn of recent; Miocene, less recent; and Pliocene, more recent.

In 1834, Lyell was elected president of the Geological Society. He traveled to North America to lecture in Boston in 1841 and to study Nova Scotian geology in 1842 and 1852, where he discovered the earliest known land shell. He was knighted in 1848.

In the early 1850s his eyesight began to fail him, hindering his scientific work. He was created a baronet in 1864; at his death he was buried in Westminster Abbey. His will provided for the creation of the Lyell Medal, to be awarded annually by the council of the Geological Society.

M

Macaulay, Thomas Babington, 1st Baron Macaulay (1800–1859) English historian, writer, and statesman. A man of many talents, Thomas Macaulay was uniquely influential in the realms of politics, history, and letters. He was born into a prominent family of devout evangelicals. He displayed the influences of his childhood throughout his public life by advocating vehemently for the abolition of slavery and other social reforms.

Early in his academic career at Trinity College, Oxford, Macaulay distinguished himself as an imaginative and powerful writer. At the age of twenty-four he earned wide popularity for his first published essay, on Milton, which appeared in the *Edinburgh Review.* The following year he was called to the bar, and by 1830 he had been elected to the House of Commons. In Parliament his gift for powerful oratory and strong sentiments regarding racial and religious tolerance found their forum. In 1834, due largely to his family's financial problems, he accepted a seat on the Supreme Council of British INDIA, where he spent the next four years. He worked to establish a British-style educational system in India that would be implemented in English. He believed such a system would allow Indians to assimilate into Western culture, which he considered essential to their participation in world trade. He also drafted a new penal code that effectively equalized the British and the Indians under the law.

Soon after his return from India, Macaulay began to devote his energies to writing. He published a book of poetry, *The Lays of Ancient Rome,* in 1842. He followed this with a collection of essays (1843) and a collection of his speeches in Parliament (1854). His most famous work was an examination of English history, the five-volume *History of England From the Accession of King James II* (1848–61), which was unfinished at his death. It was revered for its highly readable dramatic style but criticized by scholars for factual inaccuracies and a bias in favor of Whig politics.

McClellan, George Brinton (1826–1885) American soldier and politician. Born in

Philadelphia, he graduated from West Point in 1846, fought in the MEXICAN WAR, and left the army in 1857. He was made a major general after the outbreak of the U.S. CIVIL WAR in 1861 and then commander of all Union forces after his successful campaign in western Virginia and after the North's disastrous defeat at the first battle of Bull Run. He reorganized the army but upset President ABRAHAM LINCOLN with his reluctance to attack smaller Confederate forces. In March 1862, Lincoln relieved him of overall command so he could lead the Army of the Potomac against Richmond, the Confederate capital. The campaign failed, and he withdrew after the Seven Days' Battle in June.

After that, McClellan's forces played a subordinate role to a newly formed army under General John Pope. Pope's defeat at the second battle of Bull Run led Lincoln to reappoint McClellan commander of the main Union force. Lincoln dismissed him after he allowed General ROBERT E. LEE's outnumbered troops to withdraw after the Battle of ANTIETAM in November 1862. He was the presidential candidate of the DEMOCRATIC PARTY against Lincoln in 1864 and later governor of New Jersey (1878–81).

McClure, Sir Robert John Le Mesurier See NORTHWEST PASSAGE.

McClure's Magazine American PERIODICAL. Founded in 1893 by Irish-born journalist and entrepreneur Samuel Sidney McClure, it became known for its fiction, poetry, and political writing by some of the era's greatest writers, including RUDYARD KIPLING and Booth Tarkington. Beginning in 1903 it also distinguished itself through its muckraking journalism, reported by the writers who would define the term—IDA TARBELL, Lincoln Steffens, and Ray Stannard Baker.

MacDonald, Sir John Alexander (1815–1891) Canadian politician. Known as the founding father of CANADA, MacDonald was of central importance in Canadian politics during the turbulent years of its confederation, or birth as a nation. Born in Glasgow, Scotland, he emigrated to Canada at the age of five. At fifteen he began studying law and by twenty-nine had been elected a member of the Canadian Parliament. Throughout his forty-seven nonconsecutive years in public office, spanning 1834 to 1891, he was characterized by his volatile temper and heavy drinking as well as his generosity and sense of humor. Politically he was known for his moderate conservatism and ability to form coalitions.

The most important of these coalitions was with the French Canadian politician George Etienne Cartier. Together they united disputatious British and French Canadian factions, forming the Coalition of 1854, which paved the way for the Liberal-Conservative Party. In 1864, MacDonald was one of a group of statesmen attending the Charlottetown Conference to draft the constitution of the dominion of Canada. He was among the first to envision a Canadian nation stretching from sea to sea and worked tirelessly to bring this dream to fruition. In 1867 the British North America Act was passed in British Parliament, and the dominion of Canada was born. MacDonald became its first prime minister.

Six years later he was forced to resign because of his implication in the Pacific Scandal in which he and his allies were accused of accepting large campaign contributions in return for the contract for the construction of the Pacific Railway. MacDonald denied any wrongdoing, was reelected prime minister in 1878, and served until his death. During his last years in public life he helped strengthen the Canadian nation with his protectionist laws, his distrust of the United States, his loyalty to Great Britain, and his encouragement of western homesteading.

Mach, Ernst (1838–1916) Austrian philosopher and physicist. Ernst Mach was one of the greatest thinkers of his day and developed theories that are now accepted as basic principles of science and scientific inquiry. Born in Moravia, Austria, he was primarily educated at home until at the age of seventeen he began at the University of Vienna. He studied there from 1855 until 1860 when he was awarded a doctorate in physics. He spent most of his life in academe, teaching at the University of Vienna (1860–64, 1895–1901), the University of Graz (1864–67), and the Charles University in Prague (1867–92). He believed that no idea was valid unless empirically proved, that is, obtained through sensory experience such as observation. This view caused Mach to reject many previously accepted "facts"—such as Newton's model of absolute space and time, and an undetectable, massless ETHER—and to become fascinated with sensory processing. He conducted studies on the physiology of sensation and on the sensory experience of movement and acceleration. Among his most famous theories and discoveries are Mach's Principle, which states that bodies at rest remain at rest and bodies in motion remain in motion; the Mach Number, which is the ratio of the speed of an object to the speed of sound; and Mach Bands, which are bands of light and dark seen by the human eye near areas of sharp contrast. He significantly influenced Albert Einstein, although the two men disagreed on many central issues of science.

He survived a stroke in 1901 and retired from research, but was appointed to the Austrian Parliament where he served for several years.

machine gun Firearms. The machine gun is capable of shooting small-arms ammunition rapidly and continuously. During the Victorian era, several advances were made in technology that changed war significantly. During the U.S. Civil War era, Richard Gatling developed his famous GATLING GUN (1862), a gun improved by a hand-crank. In 1883, American inventor Sir Hiram Maxim further refined this technology in the Maxim gun. By World War I the expansion of machine-gun technology put them into wide use.

MacKenzie, Alexander (1822–1892) Canadian politician. Like Conservative Canadian leader Sir JOHN A. MACDONALD, Alexander Mackenzie was born in Scotland, emigrated to CANADA, and rose to political power. MacKenzie left formal education at the age of fourteen to learn the trade of stone masonry. He worked as a builder in Sarnia, a town in what is now southern Ontario. He became interested in reform and began editing a local liberal newspaper, *The Lambton Shield.* Through his work he became a friend and political ally of MacDonald's major political foe, George Brown, who was then editor of Toronto's liberal paper *The Globe.*

After the dominion of Canada was created in 1867, MacKenzie was elected to the House of Commons and soon became the leader of the liberal faction. In 1873 when Prime Minister MacDonald was ousted during the Pacific Scandal, MacKenzie was elected to replace him, becoming the first liberal prime minister of Canada; however, economic depression, controversy over trade with the United States, and difficulties completing the Pacific Railway precipitated MacKenzie's rejection after one term. He had defeated MacDonald five years earlier but lost to his old adversary in 1878. MacKenzie continued to serve in Parliament until his death.

MacKenzie, William Lyon (1795–1861) Canadian politician and journalist. Born in Scotland, he emigrated to what is now Ontario, CANADA, at age twenty-five, where he attempted unsuccessfully to establish himself as a merchant. He was drawn into politics by the widespread dissatisfaction with the system of government he discovered in his new country. A movement for greater democracy was under way, and MacKenzie allied himself with those who wanted reform. He founded a reactionary antigovernment newspaper called the *Colonial Advocate.* He was elected to Parliament and served intermittently from 1828 to 1836, during which time he was expelled twice—partly for his volatile anti-Tory writings—and reelected both times. Finally, his expulsion was secured by his foes when they temporarily disenfranchised his county, York. In 1834, during a break in his service in Parliament, he was elected the first mayor of Toronto.

Largely due to his acquaintance with another reform leader, Louis J. Papineau, MacKenzie led a wild revolt against the government in which he hoped to free his region from British rule. The Rebellion of 1837 was quickly suppressed, and MacKenzie fled to the United States, where he lived for several years, becoming a U.S. citizen in 1843. He returned to Canada and in 1851 was reelected to the legislature, where he served as a force against both Reformers and Tories until his death.

McKinley, William (1843–1901) Twenty-fifth president of the UNITED STATES (1897–1901). Born in Niles, Ohio, he rose from private to major in the U.S. CIVIL WAR and was a REPUBLICAN congressman (1876–82, 1884–90) who strongly defended high tariffs. He lost his seat in 1890 because of the tariff issue and was elected governor of Ohio (1892–96). The backing of Cleveland industrialist MARK HANNA helped him win the 1896 Republican presidential nomination and defeat WILLIAM JENNINGS BRYAN in the election. Domestically, McKinley supported high tariffs and put the country on the gold standard, through which every dollar could be converted to gold.

Despite anti-imperialist campaign promises, McKinley presided over the emergence of the United States as a colonial power through its victory in the SPANISH-AMERICAN WAR. He also ensured the United States equal trading rights with other countries in CHINA through the Open-Door policy and sent American troops to help crush the BOXER REBELLION. The annexation of Hawaii and several Samoan islands occurred during his administration.

McKinley again defeated Bryan to win reelection in 1900. He was shot by anarchist Leo Czolgosz on September 6, 1901, and died eight days later. THEODORE ROOSEVELT succeeded him as president.

MacMahon, Marie E. P. M de (1808–1893) French soldier and politician. As an officer in the army MacMahon had a distinguished career, serving in Algeria, the CRIMEAN WAR (1853–56), and the Italian War (1859). As a marshal in the FRANCO-PRUSSIAN WAR (1870–71), he was wounded at Sédan and emerged from the disastrous war with his reputation largely intact. He commanded the troops that suppressed the Paris Commune in 1871. In 1873, he was elected president of FRANCE, with the hope that he would step aside in favor of a Bourbon restoration. But MacMahon refused to engineer a royalist coup, though he did try to resist the republican left. He was forced to resign in 1879 when the republicans gained a majority in both houses of Parliament.

Macmillan's Monthly magazine. First published in 1859 after the rescinding of TAXES ON KNOWLEDGE, *Macmillan's* aimed at offering high-quality writing and production at a lower cost than established PERIODICALS such as *Blackwood's Edinburgh Magazine.* During its forty-six-year run, it became known for book serialization, featuring many novels from its publisher, Macmillan, and thoughtful articles on issues of the day.

Madagascar Country off the southeastern coast of AFRICA. It is comprised of one large and several smaller islands. Physically, the people of Madagascar represent a unique combination of traits from Asia and Africa, with Asian characteristics dominant. The Malagasy language is a closer relative to the Polynesian languages than to those of Africa. Prior to European contact, several large indigenous groups vied for power. During the Victorian era, a group from central Madagascar called the Merina was in control.

In the early 1800s the Merina king, Radama I, formed an alliance with the British who occupied MAURITIUS and cultivated ties with the French, with whom slaves had been traded in the past. At his invitation some British and French settled in Madagascar and quickly established Christianity and the use of the Latin alphabet in lieu of the Arabic alphabet.

Radama I died young and was succeeded by his widow, Queen Ranavolona I, who reversed her husband's policies on contact with Europeans and expelled many of the European settlers. Her goal was to isolate Madagascar from outside influences, and during her lifetime she was successful. After her death in 1861, however, the French returned to Madagascar and began to struggle to colonize it. The Merina forces grappled with the French until 1896 when Madagascar fell.

Madagascar remained under French domination until 1958. After several violent struggles, the autonomous Malagasy Republic was created.

Maeterlinck, Maurice (1862–1949) Belgian playwright, poet, and essayist. Winner in 1911 of the Nobel Prize for literature, Maurice Maeterlinck is regarded as a visionary in the world of drama. Born in Ghent, Maeterlinck studied law and was admitted to the bar at the age of twenty-four. He soon abandoned that profession, however, and began a career in letters, beginning with poems and essays published in Belgian magazines. In 1889 he published his first dramatic work, *La Princess Maleine,* which was well received and used as the basis for an opera by CLAUDE DEBUSSY. His reputation was built on a series of plays characterized by their vague, ethereal style and their focus on abstract realities, such as those in dreams or that lie beyond death. His usage of severe set design and fantastic symbolic images made possible the modern Theater of the Absurd. The most famous and popular of his plays is *L'Oiseau Bleu* (*The Blue Bird;* 1909).

Maeterlinck was also interested in natural science and in philosophy. He wrote several essays on the mystical aspects of natural life, as in *La Vie des abeilles* (*The Life of Bees;* 1901), as well as investigations of other insects and plant life. After 1890 he lived mostly in France, although he and his wife Renée Dahon escaped to the United States during World War II. He died in France.

Maha Bodhi Society A society to promote the study of Buddhism. Founded in Ceylon (now Sri Lanka) in 1891, the Maha Bodhi Society was named for the reason it was established: the restoration of the site of Buddha's enlightenment, the Mahabodhi temple in India.

Mahan, Alfred Thayer (1840–1914) American naval officer and historian. A great admirer of the British fleet, he felt that a strong navy was the key to power in the world. His writings, particularly *The Influence of Sea Power upon History, 1660–1783* (1890) and *The Influence of Sea Power upon the French Revolution and the Empire, 1793–1812* (2 volumes, 1892) became fundamental resources for naval strategists and officers in all the major navies of the world. His work led to significant changes in the American navy, particularly the use of battleships to surprise the enemy on the high seas.

Mahdi [Mohammad Ahmad] (1844–1885) Muslim military and religious leader of the SUDAN. The son of a boat builder, he was one of several religious reformers throughout Islamic history who claimed to be the "Mahdi," "the redeemer" or "one who is guided." He led a successful revolt against Egyptian and British rule of the Sudan in the early 1880s, stirring up religious fervor and capitalizing on resentment against British suppression of the immense Sudanese slave trade. He defeated a large Egyptian army at Shoykan in 1883 and captured KHARTOUM in 1885, killing the English commander CHARLES GEORGE GORDON. He died a few months after Khartoum fell. Mahdist rule ended in 1898 with Lord HORATIO KITCHENER's victory at Omdurman.

Mahler, Gustav (1860–1911) Austrian composer and conductor. Born in Bohemia, Mahler studied at the Vienna Conservatory where he was influenced by the music of Austrian composer ANTON BRUCKNER. Although he aimed to work solely as a composer, he turned to a conducting career and worked at a series of small opera houses throughout Germany. While in Kassel, he composed the song cycle *Lieder Eines Fahrenden* (1883–85). Mahler conducted for a year at the Deutsches Landestheater in Prague and for two years at the Neues Stadttheater in Leipzig. In Leipzig, he completed Weber's comic opera *Die drei Pintos* (1888).

The pinnacle of Mahler's career was his ten years at the Vienna Court Opera (1897–1907). In addition to conducting, he composed nine symphonies, which aroused controversy over their unconventional methods and structure, and several songs with orchestra including the song cycles *Kindertotenlieder* [*Songs on the Death of Children*] (1901–4) and *Das Lied von der Erde* [*Song of the Earth*] (1908).

Strongly informed by Anton Bruckner, RICHARD WAGNER, and Ludwig Beethoven, Mahler's works display an exceptional command of vocal and instrumental writing that bridged nineteenth-century romanticism and twentieth-century eclecticism and influenced many composers at the turn of the century. Among his most important pieces are a set of *Humoresken* for orchestra and a cantata, *Das klagende Lied.* Mahler's final years were spent in New York conducting at the Metropolitan Opera.

Maillol, Aristide (1861–1944) French sculptor. Maillol began his artistic career as a painter of SYMBOLISM in the early 1880s, falling under the influence of PAUL GAUGUIN and Emile Bernard. In the 1890s he worked as a tapestry designer with the French anti-Impressionist artists known as the Nabis.

Due to poor eyesight, Maillol turned to sculpture near the end of the nineteenth century, creating wood carvings before moving to clay modeling. His early works of terra-cotta statuettes provided the basis for his later sculpture, most of which was cast in bronze.

Maillol was at first influenced by AUGUSTE RODIN in the mid-1890s but turned away from his expressive and somewhat erotic Romantic treatment of the nude to focus on a more classic, massive simplicity. Figures such as *The Mediterranean* (1901), *Night* (1902), and *Action in Chains* (1906) show Maillol's respect for mass and form as opposed to the fluid surfaces of Rodin.

Maillol's entire work is centered around the single female nude either standing, sitting, or relaxing. His treatment of the human figure strengthened with a trip to Greece in 1906. Maillol's statues at the beginning of the twentieth-century are best remembered as self-sufficient figures that recall the quiet strength of early archaic Greek sculpture.

***Maison Worth* (House of Worth)** Clothing salon. The first salon of high fashion that carried designer creations, *Maison Worth* was opened in 1858 on the rue de la Paix in Paris by British clothing maker CHARLES FREDERICK WORTH (1825–1895). Offering his own designs, he and his salon came to epitomize fine taste across the Continent and established Paris as its fashion center. Among his clients were the courts of Austria and France.

Malawi See NYASALAND.

Maldives Island group in the north Indian Ocean, southwest of Sri Lanka. Populated mainly by Muslims of mixed Indian, Sinhalese, and Arab heritage, the islands became a British protectorate and military base in 1887 while retaining internal self-government. The islands gained independence in 1965; the sultanate that had ruled since the fourteenth century was replaced by a republic in 1968.

Mallarmé, Stephane (1842–1898) French poet. One of the leading theorists of SYMBOLISM, he exemplified his views in such poems as *Herodias* (1869), *The Swan* (1885), and *The Afternoon of a Faun* (1876), which inspired CLAUDE DEBUSSY to compose the tone poem *Prelude to the Afternoon of a Faun* (1894). Mallarmé's poetry is typically built around a single symbol or idea and is characterized by obscure, evocative language and untraditional syntax.

Manchester City in northwestern England. Although settled since Celtic and Roman times, Manchester grew dramatically as a result of INDUSTRIALIZATION in the late eighteenth and early nineteenth centuries. The center of the nation's textile industry, it swelled with factories and boomed in population, becoming a symbol for the rising industrial north and the tense relationship between capitalists and laborers. The REFORM BILL OF 1832 gave Manchester parliamentary representation, but social problems of poverty and crime continued, making it the nexus for protest and reform movements such as CHARTISM and Owenite SOCIALISM (see ROBERT OWEN). In the 1840s and 1850s the city was associated with the Manchester school of economics, led by RICHARD COBDEN and JOHN BRIGHT, founders of the ANTI–CORN LAW LEAGUE. The Manchester school advocated free trade and minimal state interference in the economy. At the other end of the economic spectrum, German cofounder of communism FRIEDRICH ENGELS was inspired to write *The Condition of the Working Class in England in 1844* (1845) based on his experiences as a factory manager in Manchester.

Population growth slowed in the late nineteenth century as many of Manchester's textile factories moved to surrounding towns. Other enterprises moved into place, including chemical and engineering concerns. In 1894 the thirty-five-mile-long Manchester Ship Canal was completed, a waterway linking the city to the sea.

Manchu Dynasty Last imperial dynasty of CHINA. (It was also called the Qing Dynasty.) Prior to 1644 the Manchus were a non-Chinese seminomadic people living under a Chinese protectorate. The weakness and disorder under the last Ming emperors allowed the Manchus to rebel and take Peking (modern Beijing) in 1644, eventually conquering the entire empire.

The Manchus were never more than a small minority in China and tended to be socially conservative. By law, Manchus were guaranteed administrative and military posts and government pensions. But the Manchu emperors preserved the Ming system of imperial bureaucracy, the Confucian social order, and Chinese isolation. Within a few generations the Manchus had adopted Chinese language and culture almost completely.

The first half of their rule was a period of prosperity and expansion for China, but beginning in the late eighteenth century, population growth, economic dislocation, and outside pressure destabilized the empire and encouraged anti-Manchu movements. China was opened to unfavorable forms of trade and exploitation by the Europeans following the OPIUM WARS (1839–42 and 1856–60). The Manchu government had to contend with the T'ai Ping Rebellion (1848–64) and other revolts. The government attempted some military and industrial reforms but was hampered by revenue shortfalls and its own conservatism in administrative matters. Large areas of the country became virtually independent. Dowager Empress TZ'U-HSI secretly encouraged the BOXER REBELLION (1898–1900), an uprising against foreign influence that was crushed by an international force and left the Manchu government in an even weaker position. A republican and nationalist movement took shape, fueled by resentment of the Manchus and the Europeans, and the government was unable to field an effective army to resist it. In January 1912 the imperial house issued an edict resigning the throne and recognizing the newly formed Chinese republic.

Manet, Edouard (1832–1883) French painter. Manet's controversial paintings helped define modern aesthetics at the end of the nineteenth century. Not only did they reflect the world around him but they demonstrated a break from academic traditions. They were full of historical references as well as formal exercises in flattened pattern and color.

Manet studied at the Ecole des Beaux-Arts under Thomas Couture from 1850 to 1856 and was awarded an honorable mention at the 1861 Salon for his *Spanish Guitar Player* (1860). From the beginning of his career Manet had followed the advice of CHARLES BAUDELAIRE and GUSTAVE COURBET to paint modern life. Manet therefore chose to record the parks, cafés, and racetracks he observed as accurate representations of modern thinking.

Manet's *Le Déjeuner sur l'herbe* (1863) was rejected by the Salon of 1863 and created a major scandal when it was exhibited in the *SALON DES REFUSES*. Although the subject was based on respectable academic examples, the main public objection was that reality was not disguised. The nakedness of a contemporary female figure was seen as offensive if not placed in a mythical or classical setting.

Manet was little concerned with actual subject matter but instead concentrated on asserting his paintings as two-dimensional surfaces composed of limited depth, sketchy contours, and vivid patches of color. His canvases represented a bold artistic step, both technically and conceptually, toward the modern doctrine of ART FOR ART'S SAKE.

Manet's *Olympia,* painted in 1863 and exhibited in the Salon of 1865, created an even greater uproar than *Déjeuner.* The painting of a contemporary prostitute is a provocative parody of Titian's Renaissance masterpiece *Venus of Urbino* as well as a display of modern sexuality. Stylistically, *Olympia* was also controversial; the entire composition is flooded with a strong frontal light, providing simple tonal contrasts and flattening form and space.

Manet visited Spain in 1865 and fell under the influence of Diego Velázquez's paintings. *The Fifer* (1866) and *Le Déjeuner a l'Atelier* (1868) reveal Manet's attraction to Velazquez's cool silver and green palette and nondescript gray background.

Manet painted the portrait of EMILE ZOLA in 1868. Zola had defended Manet's *Le Déjeuner sur l'herbe* and *Olympia* as masterpieces and championed Manet's right to follow his own artistic instincts in defiance of academic rules.

During the 1870s at Argenteuil, Manet turned his attention to painting outdoors where he could apply his quick brushstrokes in full color under natural light. He came under the influence of IMPRESSIONISM and was often linked with them by his contemporaries but in fact never exhibited with them, choosing instead to paint highly composed studio pictures such as *In the Conservatory* (1879).

Manet's last major painting, *A Bar at the Folies-Bergère* (1881–82), was exhibited at the Salon of 1882, one year before his death. Manet received the Legion of Honor in 1882, and a large memorial exhibition was held at the Ecole des Beaux-Arts in 1884.

manifest destiny American credo. Manifest destiny is the belief, prevalent in the 1840s, that the United States was clearly intended by God to expand westward across the continent. Coined by American editor John L. O'Sullivan in 1845, the phrase was much used by Democratic followers of President JAMES K. POLK to justify American annexation of Texas and conquest of Mexican territories. The MEXICAN WAR (1846–48), in which much of the American West and Southwest were won from Mexico, was seen as a triumph of manifest destiny. Some extended the concept further, placing no limits to the potential for American expansion.

Mann, Horace (1796–1859) American educator and reformer. Born in Franklin, Massachusetts, he graduated from Brown University in 1819 and served in the Massachusetts House of Representatives from 1827 to 1833 and state Senate from 1834 to 1837. There he helped to institute the first state board of education in the United States and became its first secretary in 1837. In 1838 he established the first publicly supported normal school or teacher's college, in Lexington, Massachusetts. He crusaded for public high schools and better paid public school teachers, believing that good education is fundamental to a democracy. From 1848 to 1852 he served in the U.S. House of Representatives; from 1852 until his death he was president of Antioch College, where he worked to raise academic standards and successfully implement coeducation.

Manning, Henry Edward (1808–1892) English prelate. Ordained an Anglican priest in 1832, he became associated with the OXFORD MOVEMENT and its opposition to state dominance of the church. In 1851 he followed the example of JOHN HENRY NEWMAN and was received into the Roman Catholic communion. Ordained a Roman Catholic priest, he was made archbishop of Westminster in 1865 and cardinal in 1875. His career was marked by dedication to the poor, particularly through the expansion of Catholic primary education. He was also an outspoken advocate for social reform legislation and the rights of laborers. A strong supporter of the LONDON DOCK STRIKE of 1889, he helped negotiate its resolution. He supported the dogma of PAPAL INFALLIBILITY, an issue on which he differed from fellow convert Newman. Manning founded the society of Oblates of St. Charles (1857). His published works include *The Unity of the Church* (1842), *The Grounds of Faith* (1852), and *The Eternal Priesthood* (1883).

Maori Wars See NEW ZEALAND.

March on Rome (1870) Last act of Italian unification. Prior to the march, the Pope still ruled Rome and the Patrimony of St. Peter, a small surrounding region. A French garrison protected the PAPACY, but it was withdrawn when the FRANCO-PRUSSIAN WAR (1870–71) broke out. An Italian army marched on Rome and entered the city on September 20, encountering only token resistance. The VATICAN COUNCIL then in progress was forced to suspend its operations, while POPE PIUS IX withdrew to the Vatican. Rome became the capital of the kingdom of ITALY.

Marconi, Guglielmo See RADIO WAVES.

Mars Fourth planet from the sun. Mars was the object of much study during its close approach to the earth in 1877. At that conjunction when the red planet was about 35 million miles distant, American astronomer Asaph Hall (1829–1907) discovered its two small satellites, which he named Phobos (fear) and Deimos (terror) for the two sons of the Greek god Ares. That same year Italian astronomer GIOVANNI SCHIAPARELLI mapped the surface of Mars and reported the discovery of dark, narrow markings that he called *canali,* or channels, because he believed they were bodies of water. Mistranslated into English as "canals," the discovery led to the notion that Mars was the home of an advanced civilization which had built a global network of canals. The misconception was fostered by the apocryphal discoveries of American astronomer Percival Lowell (1855–1916) who from 1894 claimed to be able to map the canals in detail. English novelist H. G. WELLS exploited the science fiction possibilities of these claims in *The War of the Worlds* (1894).

Marshall, Alfred (1842–1924) English economist. Marshall laid the foundation of the neoclassical school of economics while a professor at Cambridge University (1885–1908). His areas of research included cost, value, and distribution, and he developed a concept of marginal utility. His *Principles of Economics* (1890) became a standard textbook, dominating the field until the ascendancy of his student John Maynard Keynes (1883–1946) in the 1930s.

Martineau, Harriet (1802–1876) English writer. Deaf since childhood, Martineau began writing religious works but became known for lengthy educational works—*Illustrations of Political Economy* (1832–34), *Illustrations of Taxation* (1843), and *Forest and Game Law Tables* (1845)—that combined stories and theoretical précis to explain complex political and economic ideas. Though known for her popularizing of the themes of thinkers such as Thomas Malthus, AUGUSTE COMTE, and JOHN STUART MILL, she is also noted for her travel books and her critiques of America as well as for her *Autobiography* (1877).

Marx, Karl (1818–1883) German political philosopher and historian. Marx's theories of

German political philosopher Karl Marx is considered to be the founder and foremost theorist of modern socialism and communism.

revolutionary SOCIALISM and world historical development became the basis of the greatest challenge to liberal capitalism and the guiding ideology of the communist world in the twentieth century.

Marx's personal life was relatively uneventful in contrast to the revolutionary upheavals he foretold. He was born in Trier, then part of Prussia. He studied law in Bonn and Berlin, then philosophy, modern languages, and classics, receiving his doctorate in classics from the University of Jena in 1841. Failing to gain a university position, he trained for business and began writing critical articles for the *Rheinische Zeitung,* a liberal journal published in Cologne. In 1842 he became the editor of the *Zeitung*. He resigned in 1843 when the Prussian government began strict censoring of its content.

In the same year he cofounded a new journal, the *Deutsch-Französiche Jahrbucher*. Also in 1843 he married Jenny von Westphalen and moved to Paris to avoid further censorship. In Paris he studied political economy and began a lifelong collaboration with FRIEDRICH ENGELS, whose ideas were evolving along similar lines. Engels contributed some new ideas to Marx's thought, but his main role was that of an editor and supporter.

The nationalist REVOLUTIONS OF 1848 offered Marx and Engels another opportunity to take an active part in German politics. They returned to Cologne and coedited the *Neue Rheinische Zeitung,* advocating the total overthrow of the capitalist system. In 1848 they also published their landmark work *THE COMMUNIST MANIFESTO.* The collapse of the revolutionary movements in 1849 forced them to flee to England, where Engels had earlier worked in the import business. Marx lived in London for the remainder of his life, largely supported by Engels. Marx was occasionally involved in the running of international socialist organizations, but his main occupation in these years was writing books, pamphlets, and articles, and developing his theory of political economy and history. His most important work was the monumental three-volume *DAS KAPITAL* (1867–94), completed by Engels after his death.

The main influence on Marx's ideas was Hegel, whose idealist philosophy dominated the German universities of the time. Hegel held that history was a dynamic process in which an overriding historical spirit or idea realized itself in the events and institutions of the time through a process of conflict and concordance he called the *dialectic.* Marx retained Hegel's notion of conflict but reversed his priorities, claiming that material conditions were the driving force of history and determined the institutions and ideas that governed particular eras.

Marx saw history as a series of confrontations between economic classes, which he defined in relation to the "means of production." Each of the three ages of the world so far had a characteristic dominant mode of production: slavery, serfdom, or capitalism. Marx believed that in each age there was only one truly productive class, the subordinate one, and that the superior class—the slave owners, the seigneurs, or the capitalists—was essentially parasitic, gaining its living by siphoning off the "surplus value" created by the laboring class. In Marx's vision each mode of production eventually destroyed itself, giving rise to the next phase. This process would culminate in the last stage of history in which the proletariat—the wage-earning class—would seize the means of production for itself and put an end to exploitation forever, creating a worldwide socialist society.

Marx was anxious to distinguish his concept of socialism from utopian schemes, which he saw as too limited or even counterproductive. His work was also notable for the scientific precision he attempted to bring to the analysis of the economic forces of history. Marx was also a brilliant stylist and produced mordantly witty studies of current events such as the rise of Louis Napoleon (NAPOLEON III) and the PARIS COMMUNE.

Although they have been characterized as historical determinists, Marx and Engels believed that the overthrow of capitalism by the proletariat would be achieved with the help of disaffected intellectuals produced by the capitalist system, such as themselves. Thus the work of historical analysis and the propagation of the communist message was a vital individual contribution to the cause of world revolution.

With Engels, Marx helped to found the International Workingmen's Association in London in 1864, but Marx's philosophical dispute with Russian anarchist Mikhail Bakunin (1814–1876) led to the dissolution of the organization.

Marx saw heavily industrialized countries such as Britain, the United States, and Germany as places where socialist revolution would first occur. In fact, partly as a response to the perceived threat of Marxism, these countries led the way in welfare and labor reform. Ironically, Russia, one of the least industrialized countries of Europe, became the site of the first successful Marxist revolution in the midst of the chaos of World War I.

Mashona (Shona) African tribe. The indigenous BANTU-speaking people of ZIMBABWE and MOZAMBIQUE in southern Africa, now known as the Shona, were known to the British as the Mashona. In the 1830s the MATABELE (or Ndebele) conquered the Mashona; in the 1890s the Matabele and Shona joined in trying to drive out the British in CECIL RHODES's colony of RHODESIA (now modern Zimbabwe). The final Shona uprising of the Victorian era was defeated in 1897. Resistance to white rule was reignited in the twentieth century, and in 1980 the descendants of the Ndebele and Shona won independence for a majority-ruled Zimbabwe.

Matabele (Ndebele) African tribe. The BANTU-speaking people now living in the TRANSVAAL region of South Africa and in Zimbabwe, known as RHODESIA in Victorian times are now called the Ndebele, but the British knew them as the Matabele. They were followers of Chief Mzilikazi who broke away from the ZULU tribe and established their own state of Matabeleland, in modern Zimbabwe, in 1838. In the 1890s, they did battle repeatedly with the British settlers in CECIL RHODES's colony of Rhodesia. Their chief, Lobengula, who held sway over both the

Matabele and the MASHONA (or Shona), attempted unsuccessfully to drive the British out in the First Matabele War (1893). The British were also victorious in the Second Matabele War (1895–96) and crushed an uprising by the Mashona in 1897.

In 1980 years of pressure from the Ndebele and Shona majority forced the white-run government of Zimbabwe to yield power to the majority. The Ndebele and Shona languages are still spoken widely, though English is the official language, and many Ndebele and Shona still practice their traditional religions.

Matisse, Henri [Emile-Benoit] (1869–1954) French painter and sculptor. Born in Le Cateau, France, Matisse was the son of a druggist and grain seller. Showing little interest in art as a youth, he studied law in Paris in 1887 and returned to northern France to work as a law clerk. While recovering from appendicitis, the twenty-year-old began drawing and painting. By October 1892 he was back in Paris, this time to study painting under Gustave Moreau.

Matisse's first public exhibition was held in 1896 at the Salon of the Société Nationale des Beaux-Arts. He sold several paintings and was appointed a permanent member of the salon.

This initial success was short-lived. His impressionist painting *The Dinner Table* sparked a controversy, and his status at the salon suffered. Moreau and an important patron died, further isolating Matisse.

During this time Matisse continued to work in the impressionist vein and experimented briefly with the pointilist technique of GEORGES SEURAT. PAUL CÉZANNE also became an influence, as did André Derain, a young painter with whom Matisse spent the summer of 1905 at a fishing village near Spain. There the two painters experimented with daring hues and with "color for color's sake," in the words of Derain. This style was later called Fauvism.

By 1909 Matisse had a steady clientele. His approach to painting changed over the years: He adapted a more constrained palette after his fauvist outburst but returned to brighter colors in his later years. Throughout his career his paintings of still lives, domestic scenes, dancing figures, and harem women were marked by clean, strongly drawn lines and vivid colors. His more famous works include the very large paintings *Dance* (1910) and *Music* (1910), as well as *Pink Nude* (1935), and *Large Red Interior* (1948).

Maupassant, [Henri-René-Albert] Guy de (1850–1893) French writer. He was born near Deippe, the child of Laure Le Poittevin, a sister of a friend of GUSTAVE FLAUBERT. In 1870, Maupassant enlisted in the army and fought in the FRANCO-PRUSSIAN WAR. After his discharge he worked in a minor position in the navy. Hating his job and meager salary, he spent much of his time writing and waiting for weekends, which he spent with Flaubert. Flaubert enjoyed his role as mentor and critic, and forbade his young prodigy to publish anything until his style had formed. Flaubert also encouraged Maupassant to write poetry, which was collected in *Des Vers,* published in 1880.

The same year Maupassant published his first short story, "Boule de suif" (Ball of Fat), which appeared in a collection about the Franco-Prussian conflict. The story received immediate acclaim, which provided Flaubert great satisfaction before his death a month after the story's publication.

During the next decade Maupassant wrote more than three hundred short stories, six novels, and over two hundred articles and essays. Maupassant is best remembered for his short fiction, characterized by an almost unsurpassed craftsmanship.

As early as 1884, Maupassant was troubled by headaches and hallucinations, possibly caused by syphilis. His mental disorders reached a breaking point in January 1892 when he tried to commit suicide by slashing his throat. He was confined to an asylum in Paris where he died.

Maurice, [John] Frederick Denison (1805–1872) English theologian and author. Maurice is best known as a founder of Christian Socialism (see SOCIALISM). He attended Cambridge and Oxford, and was ordained in 1834, the same year he published *Eustace Conway,* his only novel. *The Kingdom of Christ* (1838) helped establish his reputation as a theologian. He taught history and English literature at Cambridge (1840–46) and was professor of divinity at King's College. There he joined other liberal Anglicans, including Thomas Hughes, the author of *TOM BROWN'S SCHOOL DAYS,* and CHARLES KINGSLEY, to found the Christian Socialist movement. The movement advocated the alleviation of the social abuses of capitalism through legislative reform and the founding of workingmen's associations and cooperatives. Maurice was dismissed in 1853 because he did not believe in the eternity of hell, but he retained his chaplaincy at Lincoln's Inn, an academy of law located in London.

Maurice also helped establish Working Men's College in 1854 and Queen's College for Women in 1848 while assisting workers to form cooperative associations. He became professor of moral philosophy at Cambridge in 1866 and three years later published his famous *Social Morality,* which detailed his Christian socialist beliefs, in 1869. His other important works include *Theological Essays* (1853), *The Doctrine of Sacrifice* (1854), *What Is Revelation?* (1859), and *Moral and Metaphysical Philosophy* (1850–62).

Mauritius Island nation in the Indian Ocean, east of MADAGASCAR off the east African coast. The mountainous, subtropical, cyclone-prone island was uninhabited until the Dutch settled it in 1638, naming it for Prince Maurice of Nassau. At that time it was the home of the dodo, but the Dutch exterminated the flightless bird by the time the French took over in 1715. Renaming it Ile de France, the French brought in slaves to work the sugar plantations. The British captured it in 1810 and restored its Dutch name. After slavery was abolished in the British Empire in 1833, indentured laborers from India were brought in. Almost 450,000 Indians arrived on Mauritius between 1837 and 1907. Chinese traders also settled on the island, forming a minority population that survives today.

Mauritius became independent within the British Commonwealth in 1968.

Maury, Matthew Fontaine (1806–1873) American oceanographer. A naval officer, he was posted to the depot of charts and instruments after being disabled in an accident. While serving in this position he developed charts of the Atlantic Ocean's winds and currents, notably the Gulf Stream, reducing nautical travel time on a number of routes. In 1855 he published the first textbook of oceanography, *Physical Geography of the Sea.* He also discovered TELEGRAPH PLATEAU, a land form on the floor of the Atlantic Ocean, and was the moving force behind a landmark international conference on oceanography in Brussels in 1853. Maury Hall at the Naval Academy in Annapolis, Maryland, is named in his honor.

mauve Medium violet or purple color made possible by the 1856 invention of the first synthetic DYE. In an unsuccessful attempt to synthesize quinine in 1856, British chemistry student William Henry Perkin (1838–1907) created a substance that, with the addition of alcohol, colored a solution an attractive purplish color. Perkin learned to manufacture it as a DYE and named the color.

Maxwell, James Clerk (1831–1879) Scottish physicist. His unifying equations on electricity and magnetism represented one of the greatest advances in theoretical physics of the nineteenth century. Born in Edinburgh, Maxwell was educated at the University of Edinburgh and at Cambridge University, where he graduated with high honors. His essay on the structure of Saturn's rings earned the Adams Prize at Cambridge in 1857. He was a professor in physics from 1860 to 1865 at King's College, London, but resigned in order to return to the family estate.

Maxwell's first major contribution to the study of electricity came in 1855 when he developed a mathematical basis for MICHAEL FARADAY's concept of a magnetic field consisting of lines of force. In *A Treatise on Electricity and Magnetism* (1873), he showed that electricity and magnetism were aspects of a single electromagnetic force; he suggested that light itself was a form of electromagnetic radiation; and he developed a set of equations, called Maxwell's equations, to describe electromagnetic phenomena. German physicist Heinrich Hertz verified Maxwell's equations in 1888 when he used them to discover RADIO WAVES, a previously unknown part of the electromagnetic spectrum.

Maxwell also contributed to the kinetic theory of gases, which explains the properties of gases in terms of the motion of constituent molecules. In this field, sharing credit with Austrian physicist Ludwig Boltzmann (1844–1906), he developed the Maxwell-Boltzmann distribution law. Maxwell's research in color perception in 1861 led to the conclusion that all colors in nature can be derived from the three primary colors, which provided the basis for color photography.

Maxwell was elected the first professor of experimental physics at Cambridge in 1871, and three years later he established the Cavendish Laboratory, a major scientific laboratory. He was the author of four books and more than one hundred papers.

May Day Holiday on the first day of May. Originally a spring fertility celebration in India and Egypt, May Day was adapted by the Roman Empire and medieval England. In the late 1800s it became a radical labor holiday. In some instances, particularly in the United States, it became the occasion for one-day strikes for better wages and working conditions. In 1889 the labor organization the Second Socialist International proclaimed May Day a labor holiday. In some countries May Day is known as International Workers' Day and is a national holiday.

mazurka Polish folk dance. Performed in three-quarter time, the mazurka is danced by couples in multiples of four. Its basic steps allow for much improvisation, and its tempos range from moderately slow to very fast. In the nineteenth century it became a stylized instrumental dance form. FRÉDÉRIC CHOPIN wrote fifty-two mazurkas for the piano. Mikhail Ivanovich Glinka (1804–57), MODEST P. MUSSORGSKY, and PYOTR ILICH TCHAIKOVSKY also wrote mazurkas.

Mazzini, Giuseppe (1805–1872) Italian nationalist agitator. The son of a doctor and university professor, Mazzini attended the University of Genoa and began writing articles in support of Italian independence from Austria. In 1827 he joined the Carbonari, a secret nationalist organization. He was imprisoned briefly by Piedmontese authorities and then exiled to France. An inept Carbonari revolt in the Papal States in 1831 convinced Mazzini to form his own group, called Young Italy, the most radical faction formed during the period of Italian unification known as the RISORGIMENTO.

Through Young Italy, Mazzini began actively plotting the overthrow of the Piedmontese monarchy. The plots were exposed, and several Young Italians were executed. In 1834, Mazzini launched an abortive invasion from Switzerland. In 1836 he was expelled from Switzerland and moved to England.

While in England, Mazzini continued to work for Italian unification. He also developed a system of theology compatible with liberal nationalism. As the REVOLUTIONS OF 1848 broke out in ITALY, he returned and served briefly under GIUSEPPE GARIBALDI in Lombardy. He went to Rome, which had expelled the pope in 1849, and was elected a triumvir of the Roman republic. He headed the government in its few months of existence before French intervention put an end to it, then fled the country again.

After this defeat, many Italian nationalists reconciled themselves to a unified monarchy led by Piedmont, but Mazzini held out for an Italian republic. When Italy was unified under VICTOR EMMANUEL II, Mazzini returned, but in 1870 he was arrested and briefly imprisoned for agreeing to lead a Sicilian revolt against the new monarchy. He was quickly pardoned and devoted his last years to the cause of workers' rights.

medievalism Interest in the culture and ethos of the Middle Ages. Medievalism was expressed widely in Victorian arts and letters and in the architectural movement called GOTHIC REVIVAL. Critics and thinkers such as JOHN RUSKIN, HENRY ADAMS, THOMAS CARLYLE, AUGUSTUS PUGIN, and WILLIAM MORRIS idealized the Middle Ages as a time when the moral, spiritual, aesthetic, social, and economic aspects of life formed a more organic whole. Poets such as ALFRED, Lord TENNYSON in *Idylls of the King* (1859–85) reworked material from medieval sources. Artists known as PRE-RAPHAELITES emphasized medieval subjects and models.

Melba, Dame Nellie [Helen Porter Mitchell] (1861–1931) Australian singer. Helen Porter Mitchell was born in Richmond, near Melbourne. She began singing at the age of six but did not commence serious training until after her marriage to Charles Nesbitt Armstrong in 1882.

In 1886 she appeared in London before continuing her study in Paris the following year. She then took the stage name of Nellie Melba, derived from Melbourne, and made her operatic debut as Gilda in Verdi's *Rigoletto* in Brussels in 1887. A year later she appeared at COVENT GARDEN in London, where she performed regularly for the next forty years and established herself as the leading soprano of her day. She made her New York City debut in 1893 at the Metropolitan Opera.

She was created a dame of the British Empire in 1918, and in 1926 she returned to Australia where she became president of the Melbourne Conservatory. The light dessert PEACH MELBA was named in her honor, as was MELBA TOAST.

melba toast Food product. Thin white toast was created in the 1890s by French chef Auguste Escoffier and hotelier César Ritz for Ritz's wife Marie. The food gained its name from Australian opera singer NELLIE MELBA, to whom Escoffier served it during an illness.

Melbourne, William Lamb, 2nd Viscount (1779–1848) English statesman. Born in London, he entered the House of Commons as a Whig in 1806 and served as chief secretary for Ireland in the governments of George Canning and the Duke of Wellington (1827–28). He became a member of the House of Lords after his father's death in 1828.

His Whig loyalties did not stop him from holding conservative views. He only grudgingly supported the REFORM BILL OF 1832 during his tenure (1830–34) as Prime Minister Charles Grey's home secretary. In that office he also energetically suppressed agrarian unrest. In 1834 he approved the swift transportation of the famous "Tolpuddle martyrs," six workers who had tried to organize for better wages. A public outcry from all segments of society caused Melbourne to remit the sentences.

He was twice prime minister (1834, 1835–41), and when Queen VICTORIA took the throne, Melbourne became one of her most trusted confidants. The Queen's affection for him helped embroil her in the BEDCHAMBER CRISIS in 1839. Melbourne's governments were hampered by weak majorities and unstable political alliances. As prime minister he resisted further extension of the suffrage and fought against repeal of the CORN LAWS. His governments are known for the reform of the Canadian government, military involvement in Afghanistan and China, and the introduction of the penny postage.

Melbourne's private life was dogged by scandal. His wife's open affair with Lord Byron led to a separation in 1825, and he was later named correspondent in two unsuccessful divorce suits.

Méliès, Georges (1861–1938) French film director and producer. Méliès is considered the pioneer of fiction and fantasy filmmaking. After completing his military service as a corporal with the French infantry, Méliès enrolled at the Ecole des Beaux-Arts. In 1884 he went to London where he continued his art studies and became fascinated by the exhibition of stage magic by conjurers. Returning to Paris, Méliès became a conjurer and illusionist himself before purchasing a theater in 1888 as a stage for his magic and illusion show.

After witnessing the LUMIÈRE CINEMATOGRAPH exhibition by Louis and Auguste at the Grand Cafe in Paris, Méliès himself turned to filmmaking. He at first imitated the Lumière films through recordings of everyday events. Becoming more skilled as a camera operator, he explored the more optical-mechanical characteristics of motion pictures and soon created the trick and fantasy film.

By the end of 1896, Méliès had produced seventy-eight short films and had converted his theater exclusively to the showing of motion pictures. In 1897 he built Europe's first film studio at Montreuil and began making films indoors with the aid of artificial lighting.

In 1899 he filmed a twenty-scene presentation of *Cinderella,* followed by a twelve-scene *Jeanne d'Arc* in 1900. Méliès's best known film, *Le Voyage dans la Lune* (1902), is characteristic of his experiments in the realm of cinematic fantasy. Méliès's films enjoyed great popularity on both sides of the Atlantic and were widely distributed and illegally copied throughout the United States.

Mellon, Andrew William (1855–1937) American financier. Born in Pittsburgh, Pennsylvania he and his brother Richard assumed control of their father's bank after his retirement in 1886. In 1889, Mellon formed the Union Trust Company of Pittsburgh, which later became one of the largest banks in the country. He also invested large sums in the Gulf Oil Company, the Aluminum Company of America, and other basic industries; by 1920 he was one of the wealthiest men in America.

In 1921, Mellon resigned as president of the Mellon National Bank to join President Herbert Hoover's Cabinet as Secretary of the Treasury, a position he held until 1931. He led the fight for lower income taxes and was instrumental in lowering the national debt. He was ambassador to Great Britain from 1931 to 1932.

Melville, Herman (1819–1891) American fiction writer. Born in New York City, he had to quit school to work following his father's death in 1832. Drawn to the sea at an early age, he worked on his first ship as a cabin boy in 1839 and followed with a spate of ship voyages. Desertion from the whaler *Acushnet* at the Marquesas Islands in 1841–42 landed him among cannibals at Nuku Hiva, and he also had a months-long stay on the American frigate *United States* (1843–44). These experiences formed the basis for his first, highly successful novel *Typee* (1846) and in various ways informed those that followed: *Omoo* (1847), *Mardi* (1849), *Redburn* (1849), and *White Jacket* (1850). The only commercial failure among these was the ambitious though not fully realized *Mardi;* the others, written fluidly and aimed squarely at nineteenth-century tastes, were financially successful.

With his newfound financial security, Melville moved with his wife and family from New York to Pittsfield, Massachusetts, where he bought a farm and wrote what was to be another whaling book, *Moby-Dick* (1851). During that time he began what would become one of the most mutually influential friendships in American literary history, with novelist NATHANIEL HAWTHORNE. Strongly affected by Hawthorne, who was fifteen years his senior and already a towering figure in American literature, Melville read widely and expanded *Moby-Dick* in imagery, depth, and diction. He dedicated the book to his friend: "In token of my admiration for his genius this book is inscribed to Nathaniel Hawthorne."

Although, as Melville told Hawthorne, *Moby-Dick* was "a wicked book," he was disconcerted at its meager sales and the lack of critical understanding for the work. The meaning of Ahab's quest for the white whale, the complex structure, the Shakespearean and biblical resonances, and the implied commentary on American culture went largely unnoticed by critics. Attempting anew to regain some of his early popularity, he aimed his next book, *Pierre,* at a popular readership, but its dark psychology and eccentric style, along with its discussion of incest, made it even less popular than *Moby-Dick.*

Unsettled by the reception of these two books, he turned to short-story writing and over the next several years produced numerous works for magazines, including "Bartleby the Scrivener" (1853) about the rejection of a meaningless modern life in the character of the Wall Street copyist who "prefers not to." In 1855 he also wrote "Benito Cereno," the short story of mutiny and race, and the Revolutionary War novel *Israel Potter,* which was serialized in *Putnam's.* Other late works include the collection of magazine stories *The Piazza Tales* (1856) and the satiric, eccentric, and poorly received novel *The Confidence Man* (1857).

Melville then turned to writing poetry, some of it collected in *Battle-Pieces and Aspects of the War* (1866). After a partial sale in 1856, Melville sold the remaining portion of his farm in 1863 and returned to New York. Three years later he gained an appointment as a deputy customs inspector, a job he would hold for nearly twenty years. In addition to writing poetry, which included the collection *John Marr and Other Sailors* (1888), Melville began but did not complete the short novel *Billy Budd.* The archetypal work of innocence and evil was not published until 1924, around the time that the nineteenth-century assessment of him as a popular writer was being overturned. He now stands as a foremost American writer, acclaimed for his dark, epic views, particularly in *Moby-Dick.* Melville was married to Elizabeth Knapp Shaw, daughter of Massachusetts chief justice Lemuel Shaw, and was the father of four children.

memsahib Term of address. It was used by Indians in British India for a European woman of high status. *Sahib* ("sir," "master") is the Hindi term of address for a European man of high status, and *mem* is derived from the English "ma'am."

Mendel, Gregor Johann (1822–1884) Austrian monk and botanist. Born in Heinzdorf, Austria (now Hyncice, Czechoslovakia), to peasant parents, he received his early education under the guidance of Pastor Schreiber, who had caused a scandal when he included natural science in the curriculum. Schreiber persuaded the family to send Mendel for further schooling, and after two years of study at the Philosophical Institute at Olmutz, Czechoslovakia, Mendel entered the Augustinian monastery at Brünn, Austria (now Brno, Czechoslovakia), where he was ordained a priest in 1847.

From 1851 to 1853, Mendel studied mathematics, zoology, botany, and microscopy at the University of Vienna, but he failed to pass the examination for teacher certification. Nevertheless, he worked as a substitute teacher for the next fourteen years at the Brünn Modern School.

In the mid-1850s, Mendel began to plant hybridization experiments in the monastery gardens. Using distinct varieties of peas that differed in some simple character such as size or shape, Mendel discovered that crossbreeding the varieties yielded simple and repeatable ratios of the characteristics in the offspring. His conclusions took the form of two laws of inheritance—the law of segregation and the law of independent assortment—stating in essence that an inherited characteristic is determined by the combination of two "factors," one from each of the parental reproductive cells. Mendel's "factors" are now called alleles, or alternative forms of a gene, one of which may be dominant and the other recessive.

Mendel presented his findings at a meeting of the Natural Sciences Society of Brünn in the spring of 1865. His essay on the subject was published the following year but was generally ignored. He was elected the abbot of his monastery in 1868 and died in 1884. The value of his studies was not acknowledged until 1900 when Dutch botanist Hugo Marie de Vries and two colleagues independently performed similar experiments and derived the same conclusions as Mendel. Subsequent investigations established Gregor Mendel as the discoverer of Mendel's laws of inheritance and father of the new science of GENETICS.

Mendeleyev, Dmitry Ivanovich (1834–1907) Russian chemist. He was born in Tobolsk, Siberia, the son of a literature teacher. He graduated from the Main Pedagogical Institute in St. Petersburg in 1855 and went on to work at the Odessa lyceum (1855–56) and the University of Heidelberg

(1859–60). While in Heidelberg he worked with German chemist Robert Bunsen. In 1860 he attended the first international conference of chemists at Karlsruhe, Germany, where he heard Italian chemist Stanislao Cannizzaro urge his fellow scientists to reconsider the matter of atomic weights.

Mendeleyev returned to Russia and eventually became a professor of chemistry at the University of St. Petersburg (1867–90). Finding himself dissatisfied with the textbooks available to students, he embarked on the writing of *Principles of Chemistry* (1868–71). This landmark work was to undergo several revised editions in Russian, French, German, and English. In the course of writing it, Mendeleyev discovered the periodic law of elements, stating that the properties of ELEMENTS are a periodic function of their atomic weight. On the basis of this law he developed the PERIODIC TABLE, a chart that made sense of the morass of unconnected facts hitherto determined about the elements. Chemists at first doubted the validity of the table, but after three elements predicted in detail by Mendeleyev—gallium, scandium, and germanium—were discovered, the table gained wide acceptance and Mendeleyev became a scientific celebrity.

Mendeleyev was also fascinated by technological and industrial applications of science. He advised the Russian government on petroleum production, directed the bureau of weights and measures, and helped found the Russian Chemical Society in 1868. He also studied liquefaction of gases, the chemistry of coal, the expansion of liquids, and many other subjects.

Mendelssohn[-Bartholdy], [Jakob Ludwig] Felix (1809–1847) German composer. The grandson of eighteenth-century German-Jewish philosopher Moses Mendelssohn, he converted in childhood from Judaism to Christianity. A prodigy, he composed as a child and gave his first public piano performance in 1818. In 1829 he initiated the revival of interest in eighteenth-century German composer Johann Sebastian Bach by conducting a performance in Berlin of Bach's *St. Matthew Passion*. Making his first of ten visits to England in 1829, he was popular there and throughout Europe as both a conductor and pianist. He helped to make Leipzig, Germany, an important musical center with his conducting of the Leipzig Gewandhaus Orchestra and his cofounding of the Leipzig Conservatory (1843).

As a composer, he is admired for his craftmanship, emotional restraint, and melodic style. He wrote five symphonies: the *C Minor* (1824), *Reformation* (1830), *Italian* (1833), *Scottish* (1842), and the symphony cantata *Lobgesang* (1840). His other works include the overtures *A Midsummer Night's Dream* (1826) and *The Hebrides* (1830–32), the oratorios *St. Paul* (1836) and *Elijah* (1846), a violin concerto (1844), and two piano concertos (1831, 1837).

mercerization Method for treating textiles. Mercerization was invented by British calico printer John Mercer (1791–1866) in 1850. Now commonly used, the process shrinks and strengthens yarns and fabrics, facilitates dyeing, and adds a silky luster. It involves treating the fabric under tension with a caustic soda solution and acid. Mercer's process, which he called "sodaization," did not become widely used until technical improvements near the end of the century made it more workable.

Meredith, George (1828–1909) English writer. He was born in Portsmouth, Hampshire; his mother died when he was five, and his father abandoned him five years later, emigrating to South Africa with the housekeeper in order to escape financial debts. In 1849 he married Mary Ellen Nicholls, the widowed daughter of novelist Thomas Love Peacock. "The marriage was a blunder," Meredith later proclaimed, and in 1858 his wife went to Capri in order to live with artist Henry Wallis, leaving a child in Meredith's care.

At a personal cost of £60, Meredith published *Poems* in 1851, and while the collection contained one of his most popular poems, "Love in the Valley," the volume was a failure. Meredith followed with two prose fantasies, *The Shaving of Shagpat* (1855) and *Farina* (1857), which were even less well received.

In 1860, Meredith became a reader for the publishing firm of Chapman & Hall, where he remained for thirty-five years. He was distressed by the mediocre quality of the manuscripts he read and became committed to improving his own writing. While working for the publishing firm, he encouraged THOMAS HARDY and GEORGE GISSING. He also rejected manuscripts by GEORGE BERNARD SHAW and *EREWHON* by SAMUEL BUTLER.

Shortly after the death of his estranged wife in 1864, Meredith married Marie Vulliamy. He struggled to gain critical recognition until 1879 when he published *The Egoist,* a social comedy and subtle analysis of human nature. In 1885 he published his most popular novel, *Diana of the Crossways,* which depicted a strong, intelligent woman trying to survive alone in a male-dominated society. He also continued to write poetry, publishing *Poems and Lyrics of the Joy of Earth* (1883) and *Ballads and Poems of Tragic Life* in 1887, after the death of his wife.

In 1892, Meredith succeeded ALFRED Lord TENNYSON as president of the Royal Society of Authors, and in 1905 he was awarded the Order of Merit. Meredith died after suffering for nearly a decade with paralysis.

Metternich, Klemens von (1773–1859) Austrian diplomat and politician. Throughout his long career, Metternich unswervingly followed a conservative political line and was one of the key figures in maintaining Europe's political stability in the post-Napoleonic period. Metternich was born in Vienna of an aristocratic family. He studied in Vienna and Paris, entered the Austrian foreign service in 1801, and served as ambassador to France from 1806 to 1809. He was one of the most influential figures at the Congress of Vienna (1814–15), which settled the political shape of Europe after Napoleon's defeat.

Metternich's influence remained undiminished after the congress, and he was one of a group of ministers who effectively ruled the Austrian Empire during the reign of the mentally incompetent Ferdinand I (1835–48). Metternich consistently acted to suppress liberal and nationalistic movements within the empire and the GERMAN CONFEDERATION, of which AUSTRIA was the strongest member.

When revolution broke out in Vienna (see REVOLUTIONS OF 1848), Metternich was a target of popular anger. The emperor refused to send the army into the streets and gave in to demands for a constitution. Metternich was forced to resign and went into exile in England. His fall marked the end of an era of reactionary, legitimist politics in Europe.

Mexican War (1846–48) Armed conflict between the UNITED STATES and MEXICO. It was the first in which American troops captured a foreign capital. The precipitating cause of the war was the U.S. annexation of Texas in December 1845. Although Texas, formerly part of Mexico, had militarily won its independence in 1836, Mexico did not recognize that status. Another cause of the war was the determination of U.S. President JAMES K. POLK to acquire the Mexican territories of California, for its Pacific Ocean ports, and New Mexico, as a land route to California. In addition, the United States wanted Mexico to settle long-standing financial claims, and the two countries disagreed over the southern border of Texas, which the United States considered the Rio Grande. After the failure of a U.S. diplomatic mission led by John Slidell, Polk ordered General ZACHARY TAYLOR to advance to the Rio Grande in March 1846. This provoked Mexico into launching an attack on April 25, producing sixteen American casualties, enough for Polk to demand and obtain a declaration of war on May 13.

Taylor meanwhile had won the battles of Palo Alto (May 8) and Resaca de la Palma (May 9); he went into Mexico to capture Matamoros (May 18) and Monterrey (September 20–24) and drive off the enemy at Buena Vista (February 1847). A second theater of operations was opened in what is now the American Southwest. Colonel Stephen W. Kearny captured Santa Fe, New Mexico (August 1846), and advanced to California where Captain JOHN C. FRÉMONT had already led a revolt of American settlers in Sonoma, declaring California an independent republic (July 4, 1846), and it was then turned over to U.S. forces. By August the California ports of Monterey, San Francisco, and Los Angeles had been captured by U.S. naval forces, who succeeded in suppressing a Mexican revolt later that year.

A third front was opened in the heart of Mexico by General Winfield Scott, who launched an amphibious landing near Veracruz, which his troops bombarded and captured in March 1847. Following the ancient invasion route of the Spanish conquistadors, they marched westward toward the capital of Mexico City, defeating Mexican president and commander in chief Santa Anna at Cerro Gordo (April), Contreras (August), and Molino del Rey (September). On September 12 they captured the military school Chapultepec, despite fierce opposition from the young cadets remembered in Mexican history as *LOS NIÑOS HÉROES*. Two days later, American troops accepted the surrender of Mexico City. In the Treaty of GUADALUPE HIDALGO, signed on February 2, 1848, Mexico gave up its claim to Texas, accepted the Rio Grande boundary, and ceded to the United States nearly 2 million square miles of land. Known as the Mexican Cession, it included all of present-day California, Nevada, and Utah, along with most of Arizona and New Mexico. In return, the United States paid Mexico $15 million and assumed the $3 million in unpaid claims of U.S. citizens against Mexico.

Approximately 13,000 Americans died in the Mexican War: 1,733 in battle, most of the rest from disease. The war vastly increased the territory of the United States, opening the way for settlement, which soon began in earnest with the CALIFORNIA GOLD RUSH of 1849. However, controversy over whether the new territories would be slave or free led directly to the U.S. CIVIL WAR.

The Mexican War, the first to be thoroughly reported by newspaper correspondents, was generally popular in the United States. War spirit was fed by the notion of MANIFEST DESTINY and the high profile of WILLIAM PRESCOTT's book, *History of the Conquest of Mexico*. Abolitionists and others opposed the war, among them Illinois congressman ABRAHAM LINCOLN and New England philosopher HENRY DAVID THOREAU.

Mexico Southernmost country in North America. Occupied since antiquity by such civilizations as the Olmec, Zapotec, Maya, and Toltec, the region was ruled by the Aztecs when Spaniard Hernán Cortés conquered it in 1519–21. The territory became the Spanish viceroyalty of New Spain, which grew to include much of the present-day American West and Southwest before gaining independence as Mexico in 1821.

Throughout the remainder of the nineteenth century, Mexico was the site of numerous revolts, coups, and rapid changes in government. In the early Victorian era, the country was dominated by Antonio López de Santa Anna (1794–1876), a general who ruled as a dictator for most of 1824 to 1855, with intermittent periods of exile. Santa Anna's defeat by Texan rebels in 1836 led to independence for Texas and its annexation by the United States in 1845; his defeat by the United States in the MEXICAN WAR (1846–48) forced Mexico to cede California, Nevada, Utah, and parts of several other states, including Arizona and New Mexico. The GADSDEN PURCHASE in 1853 completed Santa Anna's ceding of land to the United States.

A period of liberal reform followed (1854–76), during which the dominant statesman was the Native American Benito Juárez (1806–1872), who led the revolution that overthrew Santa Anna for the last time in 1855. In his terms as president (1857–65, 1867–72), Juárez instituted social and political reforms and disestablished the Roman Catholic Church. This period was interrupted by the establishment of a short-lived French empire (1864–67), ruled by Austrian archduke Maximilian.

The dominant Mexican statesman of the late nineteenth century was Porfirio Díaz (1830– 1915), who ruled as dictator for most of the period from 1876 to 1911. By encouraging foreign investment, Díaz did much to develop Mexico's economy and infrastructure, including railroads, telegraph and telephone lines, and modern mining and oil-drilling operations. The benefits went almost entirely to foreigners, however, and to Mexico's small wealthy class, at the expense of the poor. By 1900, American companies such as U.S. Steel and Standard Oil controlled about 75 percent of Mexico's mineral wealth, while American and British investors each owned about half of Mexico's oil-bearing lands. Díaz was overthrown in 1911, at the start of the Mexican Revolution, which resulted in the establishment of a new constitution in 1917.

Michelson, Albert Abraham (1852–1931) German-born American physicist. He invented the modern interferometer and made highly accurate estimates of the speed of light. He also defined the international meter in terms of the wavelength of the red line of the spectrum of cadmium and invented such instruments as the range finder and the chevron diffraction grating. His most famous accomplishment, however, was the negative result of the MICHELSON-MORLEY EXPERIMENT, undertaken with Edward Morley in 1887, in which the scientists failed to detect earth's motion through the hypothetical ether. The result supplied evidence for Einstein's theory of relativity. In 1907, Michelson became the first American to win the Nobel Prize for physics.

Michelson-Morley experiment (1887) Scientific test. The Michelson-Morley experiment contributed to refuting the existence of the luminiferous ETHER, the hypothetical substance believed to be the medium for transmission of light waves. German-born American physicist ALBERT ABRAHAM MICHELSON first attempted to measure the speed of the earth's motion through the stationary, invisible ether in 1881. He used an interferometer, a device of his own invention, to measure the difference, if any, between light rays striking the observer from directions ninety degrees apart. Contemporary theory predicted that the motion of the earth through the ether would affect the speed of light as observed on earth: There should be a shift in light speed depending on whether the light rays traveled with the earth's motion, against it, or perpendicular to it. But when Michelson tried to measure that shift, he was unable to detect any difference at all.

In 1887, Michelson teamed with American chemist Edward William Morley (1838–1923) to attempt the experiment again, this time with refined procedures and instruments. Again the experiment failed to detect any motion with respect to the ether. The results perplexed physicists, but ether continued to seem an indispensable concept until German physicist Albert Einstein proposed the theory of relativity in 1905. Einstein made clear that there is no ether, no absolute frame of reference from which to judge earth's motion; the speed of light is constant regardless of the observer's motion. Though Einstein apparently did not know of the Michelson-Morley experiment before 1905, it supported his theory and remains the most famous "negative result" in scientific history.

Middle East See OTTOMAN EMPIRE.

Middlemarch (1871–72) English novel. Subtitled "A Study of Provincial Life," George Eliot's novel was originally published in serial form. Its affluent, high-minded heroine Dorothea Brooke, called a latter-day St. Teresa, becomes trapped in a marriage to the emotionally sterile scholar Casaubon, who labors unfruitfully on his mammoth *Key to All Mythologies.* Upon his death Dorothea marries Casaubon's cousin, the idealistic young reformer Ladislaw. Paralleling Dorothea's search for enlightened purpose are several intricately interwoven subsidiary plots involving the progressive physician Tertius Lydgate, whose own idealism is stymied by his marriage to the socially ambitious, frivolous spendthrift Rosamond Vincy; the relationship between Rosamond's profligate brother Fred and the good-hearted Mary, daughter of the honest estate manager Caleb Garth; and the doomed business affairs of the banker Bulstrode, whose nefarious past returns to haunt and finally destroy him.

In this richly detailed novel presenting informed discussion of social, political, and theological issues of the day, Eliot masterfully explores the failure of ideals as individuals ignore the "web of society" to which they belong.

Midlothian campaigns Political events. In November 1879, WILLIAM GLADSTONE, the "grand old man" of the LIBERAL PARTY, gave up his parliamentary seat from Greenwich to run against the CONSERVATIVE PARTY candidate in Midlothian, a county in southeastern Scotland. This by-election campaign became famous for Gladstone's rousing speeches to vast, enthusiastic audiences. The mass demonstrations, organized with the help of Lord ROSEBERY, who had attended a Democratic Party convention in the United States, were unprecedented in English electoral history.

Gladstone won the election and launched another energetic Midlothian campaign in the general election in the spring of 1880. His passionate oratory in front of huge crowds helped defeat the Conservative Party nationally, making Gladstone prime minister until 1885.

Mill, Harriet Hardy Taylor (1807–1858) British liberal social thinker. She was a member of the Unitarian circle at South Place Chapel and early supporter of WOMAN SUFFRAGE. Her second husband was political philosopher JOHN STUART MILL, who claimed that Taylor was the dominant intellectual influence of his life. Her influential essay in the *Westminster Review,* "The Enfranchisement of Women" (1858), trenchantly suggested that women should be allowed to enter the "free play of competition" in order to realize their naturally given abilities.

Mill, John Stuart (1806–1873) English philosopher, political economist, and reformer. The leading British philosopher of his day, he was the son of philosopher James Mill (1773–1836) who espoused UTILITARIANISM. James educated the boy at home in a rigorous program of instruction that began with the study of Greek at age three. John Stuart Mill gave up law studies in 1823 to become a clerk in India House, and from 1836 to 1856 he presided over the BRITISH EAST INDIA COMPANY's relations with the Indian states. During this time Mill contributed articles on politics, literature, economics, and other topics to many liberal newspapers and magazines. He also participated in the London Debating Society and other discussion groups.

Mill became famous for the works on logic and economics published during his India House tenure. *A System of Logic* (1843) set forth rules for the scientific process of induction and emphasized empiricism as the ultimate source of knowledge. In 1848 his two-volume *Principles of Political Economy* questioned the sanctity of private property and criticized capitalism for the wretched living conditions of much of the working class.

Mill was named chief of the examiner's office in the India House in 1856, a position he held until the British East India Company's demise in 1858. He retired after that and spent most of his time in France near Avignon. He published books on politics and ethics, some of which had been written with his wife HARRIET TAYLOR MILL, who died almost immediately after his retirement. *On Liberty* (1859) is a classic argument for personal freedom and an examination of the limits of governmental power. *Utilitarianism* (1863) examines the philosophical system developed by his father and Jeremy Bentham (1748–1832).

Mill's own views were more eclectic than his father's, influenced not only by the "greatest happiness principle" of utilitarianism but by the social and political views of other thinkers, including his wife and French philosopher AUGUSTE COMTE, whom Mill championed in *Auguste Comte and Positivism* (1865). Learned and logical, Mill stressed the connection between theory and practice, implementing his liberal humanitarian views through vigorous political action.

Mill was elected to Parliament in 1865, and helped win passage of the REFORM BILL OF 1867, fought for Irish land reform, and supported WOMAN SUFFRAGE. Defeated for reelection in 1868, he again retired to France where he continued to write on philosophical and ethical issues. He helped found one of the first suffragist societies and also helped establish the Land Tenure Reform Association, which called for cooperative agricultural production and a heavy tax on "unearned" income from land. His famous *Autobiography* appeared in 1874, one year after his death.

Millais, Sir John Everett (1829–1896) English painter. At the age of eleven Millais began studying at the Royal Academy. Less than a decade later, in 1848, he cofounded along with WILLIAM HOLMAN HUNT and DANTE GABRIEL ROSSETTI the Pre-Raphaelites, who sought to regain an artistic directness epitomized in Italian art before the high Renaissance and in the hyperrealism of fifteenth-century Flemish painters such as Hans Memling and Jan Van Eyck.

Millais's early work shows a painstaking rendering of detail and careful draftsmanship. His double portrait of *Mr. James Wyatt and His Granddaughter Mary* (1849) is full of intricate material detail while at the same time it displays a sympathetic portrayal of two people in their setting.

Millais's masterpiece, *Christ in the House of His Parents* (*The Carpenter's Shop*) (1850), caused a scandal by its realistic treatment of the Holy Family. The extreme naturalism that Millais adopted was an effort to represent the scene without any sentimental feeling. The painting was also Millais's attempt to resurrect through the Pre-Raphaelite doctrine the naive realism and complex symbolism of late medieval painting.

JOHN RUSKIN was a close friend and champion of Millais's work. Millais's friendship with Ruskin ended in 1855, however, when he married Ruskin's former wife. By this time Millais had distanced himself from Ruskin's ideas and those of the Pre-Raphaelite Brotherhood.

He excelled in painting biblical and medieval subjects and was a popular portrait painter. Millais soon became the most noted academic painter of his day, and in 1896 he became president of the Royal Academy.

Millet, Jean-François (1814–1875) French painter. With GUSTAVE COURBET, Millet became one of the leading exponents of French REALISM.

Born to a poor farming family, Millet received an award from the municipality of Cherbourg in 1837 to study in Paris under Paul Delaroche. He moved to Paris in 1845 before settling in Barbizon in 1848 where he created his most significant works.

Influenced by Flemish painting and the French classicism of Nicolas Poussin, Millet created a style that blended the hard facets of Realism with his own personal impressions from nature. He painted epic canvases that explored the facts of rural peasant life. Two of his best known paintings, *The Gleaners* (1857) and *The Angelus* (1858–59), express his sympathy for the peasants' simplicity and devotion to the land.

Dramatically exhibited in the Paris Salons, Millet's large-scale paintings implied that the peasant class should be taken seriously. As a Realist, Millet transformed his scenes of heartbreaking poverty and labor into images of epic nobility.

minstrel show See CHRISTY, EDWIN P., and VAUDEVILLE.

Mistral, Frédéric (1830–1914) French poet. Born in southern France, Mistral devoted his life to the study of the Provençal culture and language, which had once been the speech of his native region and used by poets in Italy and Spain during the Middle Ages. Together with his teacher Joseph Roumanille and another student, Mistral formed the Félibrige movement, which sought to revitalize the Provençal language. Mistral's first major work, *Mirèio,* a poem in twelve cantos, was published in 1859, translated into English in 1872, and adapted by composer Charles Gounod for his opera *Mireille,* which was performed in Paris in 1864. The epic poem *Calendau* followed in 1867, and his last long narrative poem, *Lou Pauèmo Jóu Rose* (*The Song of the Rhone*), was published in 1897. Mistral also spent twenty years preparing a Provençal dictionary, which was published between 1878 and 1886.

Awarded the Nobel Prize in literature in 1904, Mistral used the prize money to establish the Museon Arlaten, a museum of Provençal culture.

Möbius strip A long, flat, two-dimensional surface that has only one edge and one side. Introduced in 1865 by German mathematician August Ferdinand Möbius when he took a strip of paper, gave it a half-twist (180 degrees) and attached the two ends to create a closed circular figure. Möbius and his work led to the founding of the mathematical field of topology, the study of geometric figures unaltered by continuous transformation.

Molly Maguires Secret militant labor organization. It was comprised of Irish-American miners in the anthracite coal mines of northeastern Pennsylvania from the 1850s to the 1870s. Angered by the oppressive conditions but forbidden to unionize, the Molly Maguires organized in 1854 to pursue any means necessary to fight the mine owners. They took their name from a similar organization in Ireland aimed at oppressive landlords. Their alleged tactics included blackmail, intimidation, sabotage, and murder.

In 1875 the Molly Maguires succeeded in forming a union and calling a strike. But James McParlan, a spy from the agency of ALLAN PINKERTON who was working for the owners, infiltrated the group. Testimony by McParlan and other agents led to the conviction and hanging of twenty Molly Maguires. A number of other members were imprisoned, and the organization was destroyed.

Mommsen, [Christian Matthias] Theodor (1817–1903) German historian. Born in Garding, he was the son of a Protestant minister. He studied law at the University of Kiel, where he earned his Ph.D. in 1842. A traveling scholarship to Italy developed an interest in inscriptions and a study of the classics. In 1848, Mommsen returned to Leipzig where he became professor of Roman law but was dismissed a year later because of his sympathies with the revolutionaries involved in the REVOLUTIONS OF 1848.

He then taught law at Zurich until 1854 when he transferred to Breslau. There he completed the first three volumes of the *History of Rome,* and in 1858 he moved to Berlin in order to supervise the publication of *Corpus inscriptionum Latinarum* for the Prussian Academy of Sciences.

Mommsen devoted the rest of his life to the discovery, collection, and interpretation of Latin inscriptions, providing the most accurate reconstruction of Roman history. He was awarded the Nobel Prize in 1902 for his scholarly writing. He died in Berlin.

Monet, Claude (1840–1926) French painter. An artist of tremendous influence and a pioneer of IMPRESSIONISM, Monet was born in Paris but educated at Le Havre where in 1858 he met the artist EUGÈNE BOUDIN, who first encouraged Monet to paint nature on the spot. To study nature the two went on trips to the open country and to the coast in France.

Monet painted at the Atelier Suisse in Paris in 1859 where he met CAMILLE PISSARRO and PAUL CÉZANNE. After two years of military service in Algeria, he returned to Paris in 1862. He immediately entered Gabriel-Charles Gleyre's studio and painted with PIERRE-AUGUSTE RENOIR, ALFRED SISLEY, and Jean-Frédéric Bazille.

Monet grew unhappy with Gleyre's teaching and frequently went back to Le Havre throughout the mid-1860s to create a number of marine paintings, including *The Coastline of Ste-Adresse* (1864). His paintings of the Seine estuary were well received at the 1865 Salon and revealed Monet's attraction for the wide canvas format, quick brushstrokes, and an eye for capturing subtle tonal values.

Between 1865 and 1867, Monet worked on a huge updating of EDOUARD MANET's scandalous *Le Déjeuner sur l'herbe* as an attempt to paint the subject without any studio artificiality. Monet's version was almost twenty feet wide, never completed, and preserved only in fragments. However, his studies do depict figures outdoors with the sunlight filtering onto them. This portrayal was amplified into life-size figures in his painting *Women in the Garden* (1866–67), which he had prepared for the Salon of 1867 where it was rejected.

In the late 1860s, Monet and Renoir worked in partnership and produced the first pure Impressionist paintings. At first Monet adopted Manet's concept of painting by focusing strictly on the painting's surface as patches of color. Monet's *The River* (1868) is flooded with sunlight while forms are spontaneously created through flickering dashes of color. Monet perpetuated his on-the-spot immediacy and fresh perception of painting in *La Grenouillere* (1869) where he began to break up local color into abbreviated strokes of pure color.

The word "IMPRESSIONISM" had been coined in 1874 after a critic looked at Monet's painting entitled *Impression Sunrise.* Monet contributed to five of the eight Impressionist exhibitions while working mostly at Argenteuil with Manet, BERTHE MORISOT, Renoir, and Sisley. Throughout the 1870s, Monet remained dedicated to the study of light and its changing effect on nature.

In 1876 he began the first of his series of paintings on a single subject: *Gare St. Lazare* (1876–78), followed by *Haystacks* (1890–92), *Poplars* (1890–92), and *Rouen Cathedral* (1892–94). Monet's object was to observe the transformation of a particular motif under changing light and atmosphere.

In 1883, Monet settled in Giverny where he spent the rest of his life. He built elaborate water gardens and painted numerous *Nympheas,* or water-lily paintings, through the beginning of the twentieth century. It was not until 1889 that Monet enjoyed his first big public success at an exhibition with AUGUSTE RODIN.

Monet's approach to painting signaled revolutionary changes for modern artists. He asserted the actual physical texture of paint while completely avoiding blacks and dark browns. Monet's concentrated studies of light and color as subject matter serve as precedents for most abstract painting in the twentieth century.

Moore, George Augustus (1852–1933) Irish writer. Educated at Oscott College, Birmingham, he studied painting in Paris before settling in London in 1880. After publishing two books of poetry, *Flowers of Passion* (1878) and *Pagan Poems* (1881), he published a popular study of art, *Modern Painting* (1893). His fiction invited controversy by flouting convention: His first novel, *A Modern Lover* (1883), was banned by MUDIE'S LIBRARY, and his highly successful novel *Esther Waters* (1894) was the realistic, sympathetic story of an unwed mother. He also wrote plays, including *A Drama in Muslin* (1886), which criticized genteel marriage customs in Ireland.

In 1899, Moore returned to Ireland where he participated in the Irish cultural revival. Raised Catholic, he now converted to Protestantism. His collection of short fiction, *The Untilled Field* (1903), was an important influence on James Joyce's *Dubliners* (1914). Moore's three-part *Hail and Farewell*

(1911–14), an account of the literary circle that included WILLIAM BUTLER YEATS and Lady GREGORY, is considered a classic of modern autobiography. He returned to London in 1911, where he gained recognition as a seasoned literary figure, straddling the Victorian and modern eras. He continued writing into his last years. His later works included *The Brooke Kerith* (1916), a novel about Jesus; *Conversations in Ebury Street* (1924), named for the street where he lived; and the play *The Passing of the Essenes* (1930).

Morgan, John Pierpont (1837–1913) American financier and philanthropist. Born in Hartford, Connecticut, the son of financier Junius Spencer Morgan, he made his first significant move in financial circles when he helped to form the investment banking firm Drexel, Morgan and Company, which in 1895 became J. P. Morgan and Company. He gained even greater influence by selling government securities and consolidating corporations, particularly railroads; in the process he battled with other leading financiers, such as JAY GOULD.

Morgan accumulated major financial stakes in banking, mining, manufacturing, shipping, insurance, and other business domains. At the turn of the century he purchased the Carnegie steel interests and founded the United States Steel Corporation in 1901. It was the first billion-dollar corporation in the world. An active philanthropist for most of his life, he is perhaps best known for founding the Pierpont Morgan Library in New York City and for the donation of his massive art collection to the Metropolitan Museum of Art, also in New York City.

Morgan, Junius Spencer (1813–1890) American financier. The originator of the Morgan family banking dynasty, Junius Spencer Morgan was born in West Springfield, Massachusetts, and began working in U.S. mercantile operations before joining the London banking house of George Peabody and Company, which specialized in British investments in the United States. On the death of the firm's founder, Morgan assumed control and changed the company's name to J. S. Morgan and Company. Among his many high-powered transactions was a $50 million loan to France during the 1870–71 FRANCO-PRUSSIAN WAR. Morgan's son, JOHN PIERPONT MORGAN, and grandson, John Pierpont Morgan, Jr., were also noted U.S. investment bankers.

Morisot, Berthe (1841–1895) French painter. The first female to be accepted to the all-male circle of French IMPRESSIONISM and the granddaughter of painter Jean-Honoré Fragonard, Morisot studied painting as part of her cultural upbringing, then pursued her artistic development as a pupil of CAMILLE COROT from 1862 to 1868. She became the pupil of EDOUARD MANET in 1868; it is said he was her greatest artistic influence. For her part, she led him to experiment with the Impressionist rainbow palette. In 1874, Morisot married Manet's brother Eugène. After Manet's death she was influenced by RENOIR. Beginning with the first Impressionist exhibition in Paris in 1874, Morisot's naturalistic works were exhibited in all but one Impressionist exhibition.

morphine See NARCOTICS.

Morris, William (1834–1896) English painter, decorator, designer, manufacturer, printer, poet, and Socialist leader. Morris was one of the founders of England's revolutionary ARTS AND CRAFTS MOVEMENT. While a student at Oxford, he cofounded *Oxford and Cambridge Magazine,* to which he contributed poems, stories, and essays, and began a lifelong acquaintance with fellow student

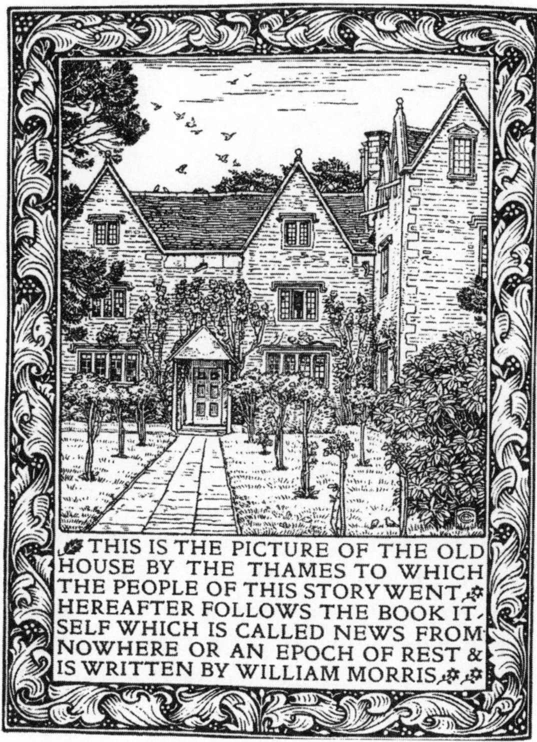

William Morris, artist and theorist, was the leader of the Arts and Crafts Movement in nineteenth-century England.

EDWARD BURNE-JONES. An admirer of the great cathedrals of the Middle Ages, Morris at first worked in an architect's office. He eventually turned to painting and studied with DANTE GABRIEL ROSSETTI. By 1857 he set up a studio in London with Burne-Jones and began a career as a PRE-RAPHAELITE painter.

Morris's interests later shifted to domestic architecture and interior decoration. Influenced by the writings of JOHN RUSKIN, Morris wanted to displace the inferior products of the machine age by reviving the beautiful and useful handicrafts of the pre-industrial past. In 1861, with the assistance of Burne-Jones, Rossetti, FORD MADOX BROWN, and PHILIP WEBB, Morris established the manufacturing and decorating firm known as Morris, Marshall, Faulkner and Company which later became simply Morris and Company. His firm activated an interest in textiles, wallpapers, and stained glass that spread throughout England and eventually influenced decorative arts in the United States.

From 1876, Morris became increasingly involved in political activities. He believed that a move toward the rebirth of art and design meant raising the condition of the workers, that art and decorative expression came from content workplaces. Morris found that the shoddy products of industrialism and ugliness around him resulted from unsound social conditions. In 1883 he joined the Socialist Democratic Federation. He later withdrew from that organization to form the Socialist League in 1885 before becoming a member of the Hammersmith Socialist Society.

In 1890, Morris revived typographical art, founding KELMSCOTT PRESS at Hammersmith for which he designed typefaces, ornamental initials, and borders. He continued to write numerous poems and songs inspired by medieval legends while arguing either allegorically or directly for Socialism in writings such as in *News from Nowhere* (1891) and *Socialism: Its Growth and Outcome* (1893).

Morris's concern that the artist understand his craft processes and materials would later be reflected in the principles of the Bauhaus. Most important, his desire to reform the arts was a catalyst to reform modern society as a whole.

Morse, Samuel Finley Breese (1791–1872) American painter and inventor. Morse was born in Charlestown, Massachusetts, and graduated from Yale in 1810. He studied painting in England from 1811 to 1815. Back in the United States he achieved substantial success as a portrait painter in Boston, Charleston, S.C., and New York City. In New York he helped found the National Academy of Design in 1826 and was its president until 1842. He was also a professor of sculpture and painting at New York University.

Morse had a lifelong interest in electricity; in 1832 he became aware of the theories of electrical telegraphy by French physicist André-Marie Ampère (1775–1836). By 1835 Morse had developed a model TELEGRAPH system that included Morse code, a way of translating electrical impulses into language. He and American physicist Joseph Henry (1797–1878) continued to perfect the model. The most important improvement was the development of a system of relays that boosted weak signals and allowed for communication over long distances by a lone operator.

In 1844, Morse sent the first public telegraph message, "What hath God wrought," over a line between Baltimore and Washington, D.C. When the federal government refused to buy Morse's invention, he founded his own company and made a fortune.

Because his work had paralleled the labors of Continental inventors, his claim to being the inventor of the telegraph has been questioned. He found himself faced with acrimonious lawsuits, and his friendship with Henry ended. Despite questions about the originality of his invention, he is recognized as the foremost pioneer in the field of telegraphy.

motion pictures Art form, technology, and industry. Motion pictures are created by using a series of still photographs projected at a rapid rate to create the illusion of movement. A number of inventors experimented with the technology throughout the latter years of the Victorian era, including English photographer EADWEARD MUYBRIDGE, who invented a multi-camera apparatus and a projecting device called the Zoopraxiscope in the 1880s; French physician Etienne-Jules Marey (1830–1904), who invented a "photographic gun" capable of shooting twelve pictures per second in 1882; and English inventor William Friese-Greene (1855–1921), who invented a motion picture camera in 1889. However, American THOMAS ALVA EDISON and his assistant W. K. L. Dickson (1860–1935) and French brothers LOUIS AND AUGUSTE LUMIÈRE are credited with inventing the first viable filming and viewing systems capable of producing a credible illusion of movement. Edison and assistant Dickson invented the Kinetograph, a motion picture camera, in 1888, and the KINETOSCOPE, a peepshow-style viewer, in 1889. The devices made use of the perforated celluloid film invented by American GEORGE EASTMAN in 1889. The Lumière brothers invented the CINEMATOGRAPH (*CINÉMATOGRAPHE*), a combination camera and projector that projected movies on a screen, in 1895.

Edison soon began looking for a projection system that would compete with that of the Lumières. In 1896 he found it in the Vitascope, a projector to which Edison bought the rights from its inventors Charles Francis Jenkins and Thomas Armat.

For the next few years the films of Dickson, the Lumières, and other early filmmakers were mostly shorts restricted to news events, stage acts, dramatic or comic episodes, fantastic illusions—in the case of Frenchman GEORGES MÉLIÈS—and items of sheer kinetic interest, such as waves breaking on a pier. Not until after 1903—the year American director Edwin S. Porter (1869–1941) premiered *The Life of an American Fireman* and *The Great Train Robbery*—did longer narrative films begin to exercise their lasting hold on world audiences.

Mott, Lucretia Coffin (1793–1880) American reformer and feminist. A Quaker lecturer for peace, temperance, workers' rights, and the abolition of slavery, she helped to found the Philadelphia Female Anti-Slavery Society in 1833, and in 1848, with ELIZABETH CADY STANTON, she organized the first woman's rights convention in Seneca Falls, New York. She was active in the UNDERGROUND RAILROAD from 1850.

Mozambique Country in southeast AFRICA. It is bounded by the Indian Ocean to the east, South Africa and Swaziland to the south, Zimbabwe, Zambia, and Malawi to the west, and Tanzania to the north. Arabs visited here as early as the tenth century and established sultanates on the coast. The Portuguese established a colony in 1505; for nearly five centuries afterward it remained under Portuguese rule. From the mid-eighteenth to the mid-nineteenth centuries, it was the site of a bustling slave trade. In the 1880s, fearing British expansion in southern Africa, the Portuguese sought to expand the western frontier of Mozambique in the hope of forging a territorial link to its colony ANGOLA, on Africa's southwest coast. The British in neighboring NYASALAND (Malawi) and ZIMBABWE countered these advances, and in 1891 Great Britain forced Portugal to sign a treaty defining the boundaries between their colonies. For most of the rest of the decade, Portugal was busy suppressing armed resistance by Mozambique's Shangana and Nyanja people.

In 1975, after a decade of civil war by black African guerrillas against Portuguese troops, the People's Republic of Mozambique gained independence.

Mudie's library Commercial circulating library. Founded in London in 1842 by Charles Edward Mudie (1818–1890), with several branches across England, Mudie's Select Library became the best known institution of this sort, charging fees for the privilege of borrowing books. Mudie specialized in offering popular three-volume novels that were much cheaper to borrow than to buy. The library remained open until 1937. A movement for tax-supported free public libraries began in Britain in the 1830s and the 1840s but did not gain widespread support until the end of the century. See also BOSTON PUBLIC LIBRARY.

mugwumps Political slang. Mugwumps is an American term for the REPUBLICANS who deserted their party's 1884 presidential nominee, James G. Blaine, to vote for Democratic candidate GROVER CLEVELAND.

Muhammad Ali (1769–1849) Also known as Muhammad Ali Pasha and Mehemet Ali. Egyptian ruler. A Turk from Macedonia, he arrived in Egypt to fight on the Ottoman side against Napoleon during the French invasion of EGYPT, 1798–1801. He stayed in Egypt after Napoleon was expelled, leading a revolt against the Ottomans and forcing them to recognize him as viceroy of Egypt in 1805. Virtually an independent ruler, he reformed Egypt's administration, centralized control of land and tax collection, expanded cultivation of cotton, and attempted without much success to manufacture textiles. He sponsored the training of a new governing class of officials, engineers, and military officers who pursued their studies in schools and in visits to Europe. Through a massacre in 1811, he broke the power of the rival military elite known as the Mamluks who to varying degrees had held power in Egypt since the thirteenth century.

Ali's armies fought on many fronts, conquering the northern SUDAN in 1820–21 and fighting on the Ottoman side in Greece in

1825–28. From 1831 to 1840 the Egyptians occupied Syria, an Ottoman possession, withdrawing only under pressure from the European nations, who considered a weak OTTOMAN EMPIRE a threat to the balance of power. In return for Egypt's withdrawal, Ali won from the Ottomans in 1841 recognition of his family's right to rule Egypt under nominal Ottoman suzerainty. His successors would be known by the special title of KHEDIVE. Abbas I (reigned 1848–54) succeeded Muhammad Ali as ruler of Egypt. The last khedive, ABBAS II (reigned 1892–1914), was deposed by the British at the start of World War I.

Muir, John (1838–1914) Explorer, naturalist, and writer. Muir was born in Scotland and emigrated to Wisconsin in 1849 with his father. Despite a lack of formal education he attended the University of Wisconsin where he studied geology, botany, and chemistry. He planned to become an inventor, but an eye accident in 1867 changed his career goals. He traveled to the Gulf of Mexico that year, and his journal was later published as *A Thousand Mile Walk to the Gulf* (1916).

He moved to California in 1868 and spent the next several years studying the geology and wildlife of the Yosemite area. Financial success in the horticultural business supported further studies and writing. He became a leader of the conservation movement, helping to persuade Congress to establish Yosemite National Park in 1890 and to create the National Forest Service. He also influenced THEODORE ROOSEVELT to protect more lands from development. His works include *The Mountains of California* (1894), *Our National Parks* (1901), and *The Yosemite* (1912). Muir Woods National Monument in California was named for him.

Mulock, Dinah Maria See CRAIK, DINAH MARIA MULOCK.

Munch, Edvard (1863–1944) Norwegian painter. Munch began to paint in Oslo around 1880 and produced a number of works rooted in the tradition of the Romantic BARBIZON SCHOOL. He befriended the Social Realist artist Christian Krohg who had a great influence on much of Munch's early work.

In 1885, Munch traveled abroad to Belgium and Paris, and studied the old masters of the Louvre as well as visited that year's Salon. Despite academic training, he developed his own approach to painting out of the examples of IMPRESSIONISM and SYMBOLISM he observed. Munch elaborated on the themes of sickness and death, common in the art and literature of the time, to create a deeply psychological manner of Expressionism drawn from personal tragedies. Both *The Sick Child* (1885–86) and *The Death Chamber* (1894) were inspired by the deaths of his brother and sister from TUBERCULOSIS.

The awakening of sexual desire was another subject treated by Munch. In the *Mystic Shore* (1892), the moon and its long reflection in the water are transformed into a phallic symbol. This motif recurs with more explicit implications in painting after painting, such as *The Dance of Life* (1899–1900).

Munch's work became widely known through periodicals in Paris and Berlin. In 1892 he was invited to exhibit at the Society of Berlin Artists. Munch's controversial exhibition caused a public sensation and encouraged painter Max Lieberman to form the Berlin Secession. Munch soon settled in Germany where he spent most of his time until 1908.

Munch's own inner fears and panics were sources for his most expressive and disturbing paintings. *The Scream* (1893) depicts an agonized shriek translated into visible vibrations while *The Red Vine* (1898) illustrates a figure fleeing in terror from a house painted blood red. Stylistically, these paintings are Munch's most characteristic work derived from the swirling lines and rhythms of VINCENT VAN GOGH and the brilliant colors of NEO-IMPRESSIONISM.

Munch was also a major graphic artist. He began making etchings and lithographs around 1894 and reworked his fascination with sex, violence, and death in drypoint, woodcut, and lithography.

Murchison, Sir Roderick Impey (1792–1871) British geologist. Known as the "King of Siluria," he did much to popularize and professionalize his discipline. Born in Scotland, Murchison fought in the Napoleonic Wars before turning to geology. In 1835, while investigating the rocks of the Welsh borderlands, he identified a system of fossil-bearing strata that he named "Silurian" for the Silures, an ancient Celtic tribe that once inhabited the region. It is now recognized that these rocks date from 395 to 440 million years ago, a period characterized mostly by invertebrate marine life.

In 1839, with ADAM SEDGWICK, he also identified the Devonian system above the Silurian strata; these rocks date from 345 to 395 million years ago. However, he and Sedgwick fell into disagreement over the base of the Silurian and Sedgwick's identification of the Cambrian system below the Silurian. The Cambrian identification is now recognized, as is the Ordovician strata between the Cambrian and Silurian, identified by British geologist Charles Lapworth in 1879. In 1841, Murchison also identified the Permian system, dating from 225 to 280 million years ago, named for its discovery in the Perm province of Russia.

An expert administrator, Murchison served at various times as president of the Geological Society, director general of the Geological Survey, director of the Royal School of Mines, and president of the Royal Geographical Society. He founded the chair of geology and mineralogy at Edinburgh (1871). A vigorous promoter of imperial exploration, trade, and expansion, his geological nomenclature was linked to his interest in increasing British influence abroad. Murchison was the author of *The Silurian System* (1839) and *Geology of Russia* (1845). Murchison Falls, Uganda, and Murchison River, Australia, were named for him.

music box Container with a mechanism that reproduces music. Early in the nineteenth century, Swiss watchmakers invented the cylinder music box in which pins arranged on a rotating cylinder strike the teeth of a metal comb, producing musical tones in a repetitive melody. This allowed people to have music in the home without having to play it themselves on a musical instrument. By 1835–45, cylinder music boxes were widely available; the craft had become so advanced that six or seven tunes could be set on one cylinder. Some music boxes had interchangeable cylinders and could produce a wide array of instrumental effects—bells, chimes, drums, and others. In 1886, German inventor Paul Lochmann developed a music box with interchangeable disks that were less cumbersome than cylinders. Listeners collected disks with favorite tunes and played them in any order they pleased. Even as Thomas Edison's PHONOGRAPH, invented in 1877, became more well known, disk music boxes remained popular into the early twentieth century.

Whether the mechanism was a cylinder or a disk, it was encased in a cabinet that at its peak of craftsmanship was often very beautiful—composed of fine woods and inlaid with materials such as brass or mother of pearl.

Some music boxes had ebonized finishes and linings of chromolithographic prints. Music boxes varied in size: Some were tabletop models, some freestanding pieces of furniture up to six feet high.

music hall a form of British entertainment and the place where the entertainment occurred. Similar to VAUDEVILLE, music hall combined musical acts, popular song, and drinking.

The Theatre Act of 1843 established the lord chamberlain as censor and controller of all legitimate plays, but music halls were responsible only to the local magistrates. Thus, the rise of the music hall as a separate place of variety entertainment was rapid. Music halls flourished in the last half of the nineteenth century, producing such stars as Joseph Grimaldi, Albert Chevalier, and Dan Leno. The music hall went into a decline at the turn of the century with the growing popularity of the radio and motion pictures.

Mussorgsky, Modest Petrovich (1835–1881) Russian composer. Born to a wealthy family, Mussorgsky served in the army for several years before resigning in 1859 to study music. Known for his naturalism and avoidance of self-conscious, calculated orchestrations, he planned much more than he completed. His greatest finished work was the opera *Boris Godunov,* based on the play by ALEKSANDR PUSHKIN. It was produced in 1874 but was later revised by NIKOLAY RIMSKY-KORSAKOV.

Mussorgsky left another opera incomplete and wrote fragments of three more as well as a number of songs, piano compositions, and orchestral works. Much of his music was edited after his death by Rimsky-Korsakov, who completed his unfinished *Khovanshchina.* Among Mussorgsky's other well-known compositions are *Night on Bald Mountain, Songs and Dances of Death, The Nursery,* and *Pictures at an Exhibition,* orchestrated by Maurice Ravel, originally for piano.

He died of epilepsy after spending much of his life in poverty and alcohol dependent.

Muybridge, Eadweard James (1830–1904) English photographer. His work with sequential photographs helped to inaugurate the development of MOTION PICTURES. Born Edward James Muggeridge in Kingston-on-Thames, England, he moved to the United States in his youth. Inspired by the work of French researcher Etienne-Jules Marey, he set up a series of twenty-four cameras on a track that captured in photographs a succession of images of a horse in motion. The still photograph experiments would be recorded in Muybridge's book *Animal Locomotion: An Electro-photographic Investigation of Consecutive Phases of Animal Movements;* the book and the experiments would come to spur film pioneers such as THOMAS ALVA EDISON and others.

Mycenae Ancient Greek city. The legendary home of the Greek prince Agamemnon in Homer's *Iliad* was excavated by German archaeologist HEINRICH SCHLIEMANN in 1876–78. Situated on a hill dominating the plain of Argos and the pass to Corinth in the eastern Peloponnesus, Mycenae became a rich and powerful walled city in the late Bronze Age (c. 1600–1100 B.C.). Its walls and Lion Gate, with a monumental relief sculpture of lions, have been visible since antiquity. In 1876, digging near the Lion Gate, Schliemann found gold treasures in royal shaft graves of the sixteenth century B.C.

Namibia Country on the west coast of southern AFRICA. It is bounded by Angola and Zambia to the north, Botswana to the east, and South Africa to the south. Its coastal regions were explored by the Portuguese and Dutch beginning in the fifteenth century. German missionaries came in the 1840s; in 1878 the British annexed Walvis Bay, making this Namibian settlement part of the Cape Colony (see SOUTH AFRICA). In 1884, Germany declared a protectorate over part of Namibia, then known as South West Africa. Swift occupation of the rest of the region followed. In 1892, Windhoek was made the capital. From the 1890s to the early 1900s Germany mercilessly suppressed uprisings by Namibia's indigenous peoples. The colony was annexed by South Africa in 1915; it remained under South African rule until 1990 when, after years of civil war and international pressure, the republic of Namibia became independent.

Napoleon III (Louis Napoleon) (1808–1873) President of the SECOND REPUBLIC (1848–52) and emperor of FRANCE as Napoleon III (1852–71). Louis Napoleon was the nephew of Emperor Napoleon I, the son of Napoleon's younger brother Louis Bonaparte and Napoleon's stepdaughter Hortense de Beauharnais. His reign as emperor, the SECOND EMPIRE, saw France achieve new status as a European power but ultimately suffer a major decline.

Louis spent his early years in France and the Netherlands, which his father ruled as king under his brother. Following the fall of Napoleon in 1815, he moved with his mother, who had separated from Louis, to Switzerland. In 1831 he became involved in an abortive revolutionary movement in the Papal States. The subsequent death of his older brother and Napoleon's son left Louis Napoleon the putative heir to the Bonaparte legacy.

In 1836 he attempted to overthrow the July Monarchy of LOUIS-PHILIPPE by suborning the garrison of Strasbourg. The coup collapsed in a few hours, and Louis Napoleon was exiled to America. In 1840 he made another attempt to spark a revolt by landing at

Boulogne. Again, the insurrection was quickly crushed, and he was sentenced to life imprisonment in the fortress of Ham in northern France. While in prison he studied various subjects and wrote several articles and pamphlets. In 1846 he escaped and fled to England, where he mixed in high society and made further plans.

The REVOLUTIONS OF 1848 in France, toppled Louis-Philippe and seemed to offer Louis Napoleon a new opportunity. He returned to Paris. Bonapartist agitation alarmed the provisional government of the Second Republic, and he was asked to withdraw. Louis Napoleon did so, and thus avoided being associated with the disorders of the new regime. A few months later, he returned to run for president. With lavish spending and skillful use of propaganda, he won a landslide victory in December 1848.

In his three years as president, Louis Napoleon worked to build support for the establishment of a new empire. To court Catholic support, he sent French troops to reinstall the Pope in Rome. Finally, in December 1851, with the support of the army, he staged a coup and declared himself Emperor Napoleon III, counting Napoleon I's son who reigned for a few days after his father's abdication as Napoleon II. In January 1853 he married EUGÉNIE de Montijo, a Spanish noblewoman. She bore him a son, Napoleon Eugène Louis Bonaparte, in 1855. Empress Eugénie played an active role in shaping the Second Empire's foreign policy.

The court life of the Second Empire was famous for brilliant display and loose morality. The Emperor himself had a long succession of mistresses. Under his rule, Paris was transformed into a modern city, with wide boulevards, parks, lighting, and sewer systems. The capital became the European center for fashion, culture, and the *demi-monde*—a term invented in the period for a class of women supported by wealthy lovers.

Economically, Louis Napoleon's rule was largely a success. By loosening credit and subsidizing large public works projects, in particular RAILROADS, the government spurred a burst of economic growth and INDUSTRIALIZATION. He also eased restrictions on trade union activity.

Politically, Louis Napoleon kept tight control over France. The police force, with its networks of informers, was expanded. The press was controlled through official censors and informal pressure. The two-chambered legislative body was elected by universal male suffrage, but manipulation of elections and extensive use of patronage ensured that only a small minority of opposition candidates were ever seated. Toward the end of his reign, Louis Napoleon loosened his political controls somewhat and was moving toward the establishment of a constitutional monarchy, but his sudden fall interrupted the process.

Foreign policy ultimately proved to be Louis Napoleon's downfall. The support of the army was crucial for the stability of the empire, and Louis felt the need to provide the army with opportunities for glory, although he lacked his uncle's military brilliance. He allied with the Ottoman Empire, Great Britain, and Sardinia against Russia in the CRIMEAN WAR (1853–56). An attempt on his life by the Italian radical Orsini reawakened his earlier enthusiasm for Italian unification, and he joined Piedmont-Sardinia in a war with Austria-Hungary (1859), in which he himself commanded the French army. The Italian war was extremely bloody and only partially successful, but Louis Napoleon was able to parade his victorious troops through Paris. French troops joined

British forces in the second of the OPIUM WARS (1856–60) against China and began the conquest of French Indochina in 1859 (see SOUTHEAST ASIA). French troops also expanded their control of Algeria.

Napoleon's later wars were less successful. He attempted to establish Maximilian of Austria as emperor of Mexico, committing a large army there from 1863 to 1866. Mexican guerrillas caused the French heavy losses, and Louis Napoleon was forced to withdraw. Meanwhile, the Emperor was disturbed by the growing power of Prussia. He attempted to intervene diplomatically during the SEVEN WEEKS' WAR between Prussia and Austria (1866) but was brushed aside by the victorious Prussians. Feeling that a showdown with Prussia was inevitable, he allowed a dispute over the placement of a Prussian prince on the Spanish throne to escalate into war.

Louis Napoleon, though old and ill, again took the field as commander. The FRANCO-PRUSSIAN WAR (1870–71) was a disaster for France. The army of the Second Empire proved to be ill-armed, badly organized, and poorly led. The Emperor allowed himself to be trapped at Sedan, where he and his large force were made to surrender. He was placed under guard in Germany while a provisional government in Paris abolished the Second Empire.

Following the end of hostilities, Louis Napoleon was allowed to settle in England where he lived out his few remaining years in the vain hope that the empire might be restored.

narcotics Pain-relieving, mood-altering, addictive drugs. In nineteenth-century Britain, opium and the popular medication LAUDANUM, opium mixed with alcohol, were administered by doctors, stirred into patent medicines, and sold over the counter as home remedies for numerous ailments. Eaten or smoked, opium was part of Victorian culture and became part of Victorian military history when Great Britain fought the OPIUM WAR with China to force it to allow the importation of opium from British India.

As the addictive consequences of narcotics began to be known, social reformers and physicians increasingly turned against them. It was determined that lawbreakers under the influence of narcotics were legally responsible for their actions. In 1861 an Englishwoman from Chelmsford was found guilty of strangling her child even though the defense claimed she was almost unconscious from an overdose of laudanum.

Some physicians hoped that the opium derivatives morphine and heroin, developed in 1805 and 1898, respectively, and administered as painkillers by hypodermic needle, would be less addictive than their parent drug, but this proved not to be the case. It was also hoped that cocaine, developed as a local anesthetic by Czech-American surgeon Carl Koller in 1884, would be safe, but that drug, too, proved addictive. By the early twentieth century, narcotics use was associated in the popular mind with crime and immorality, and access to the drugs was increasingly controlled.

Nast, Thomas (1840–1902) German-born American illustrator and caricaturist. After arriving in New York City with his family in 1846, he left school at fifteen to work as an illustrator at *Leslie's Weekly*. He traveled to Europe where he sketched GIUSEPPE GARIBALDI's military campaign in Italy for European and American newspapers. He then joined the staff of *Harpers Weekly* as a war correspondent to cover the CIVIL WAR. His battlefield sketches and illustrations attacking northern defeatists were so popular that by the end of the war he was nationally known. ULYSSES S. GRANT said he had done as much as any individual to save the Union. ABRAHAM LINCOLN called him his "best recruiting sergeant."

Nast's long-term fame rested on his campaign against "BOSS" TWEED, the corrupt leader of New York City's political organization TAMMANY HALL. Nast's 1871 cartoon in *Harper's* depicted Tweed as a grossly fat thief with the city under his thumb. Public response to the drawings was so intense that Tweed tried to bribe Nast and to have the Board of Education remove *Harper's* from the schools. Nast's most famous cartoon—a sketch of a Roman arena in which a Tammany tiger feasts on a woman symbolizing the Republic while an imperious Tweed looks on—helped defeat the Tweed organization in the 1871 municipal elections.

Nast also turned his caustic pen to presidential campaigns. No candidate he opposed won the presidency from 1864 to 1884. A staunch REPUBLICAN, he drew scathing caricatures of Democratic hopefuls HORACE GREELEY, Horatio Seymour, Samuel Tilden, and others. He invented the GOP elephant and Democratic donkey, which to this day symbolize those political parties. Nast's drawing of Santa Claus, inspired by Clement Moore's 1823 poem "A Visit from St. Nicholas," fixed the image of the jolly bearded man in America's consciousness.

The illustrator Thomas Nast was the most notorious political satirist of his day.

Natal See SOUTH AFRICA.

National League of Professional Base Ball Clubs Sport organization. Established in 1876, the "Senior Circuit" originally consisted of eight teams and was organized by a Chicago promoter, William A. Hulbert, who changed American BASEBALL from a player-dominated sport to an owner-controlled business.

In 1858 the National Association of Base Ball Players (NABBP) was created, and by 1860, sixty teams were enrolled as members. Baseball's popularity continued to spread during the Civil War, and by 1867 the NABBP consisted of three hundred teams, the box score had been developed, and a history of the game had been published.

While originally conceived as an amateur association, players were soon compensated for their efforts. In 1869 the Cincinnati Red Stockings fielded an all-salaried team and finished the season undefeated. Despite the fact that the club failed to see a profit, other teams began hiring more ballplayers, fomenting conflict between amateurs and professionals. The amateurs demonstrated their disapproval by walking out of the association's annual meeting in 1870, and in March 1871 the professionals formed their own league, the National Association of Professional Base Ball Players (NAPBBP), marking the beginning of major-league baseball in America.

The NABBP was controlled by the players, who demanded high salaries, freedom of contracts, and a powerful voice in all club decisions. The association lasted five seasons and drew large crowds before the well-financed joint-stock companies of the National League of Professional Base Ball Clubs gained control of the game.

In the 1870s a competing league, the National League (NL), headed by Hulbert and Albert G. Spalding, enforced strict rules and regulations on the players, including the banning of liquor and Sunday games. The players were restricted by rigid contracts and were forbidden to associate with gamblers. The league suffered early setbacks; in 1877, for instance, a scandal erupted when it was discovered that four Louisville players had been bribed to throw the pennant.

During the 1880s, as the popularity of the game increased, profits for the owners also increased. In 1882 the American Association (AA) was formed, and with liquor sales, Sunday games, and cheaper admission, it became a serious threat to the National League. The National Agreement of 1883 recognized the AA as a major league and imposed stricter guidelines on the second league. The AA broke with the agreement in 1891 but soon collapsed. From 1892 until 1899 the twelve-team National League dominated major league baseball.

In 1900 the president of the Western League, Byron "Ban" Johnson, began a successful challenge to the National League, occupying some of the cities that had lost teams when the NL returned to an eight-team division and enticing players to leave the NL, which had a salary cap of $2,400 and rules that forbade swearing and fighting. The newly named American League (AL) prospered, and after two years of struggle, the National League owners accepted the National Agreement of 1903, which recognized the AL and established the separate but equal major leagues.

naturalism Literary movement. In the late nineteenth and early twentieth centuries, naturalism emerged in reaction to the emotional escapism of romantic literature. Naturalists argued that the role of the fiction writer is to represent faithfully the forces of heredity and social environment that determine human destinies. It was believed that the writer should aim for an almost scientific detachment and objectivity. Founded in France, the movement saw its principles most clearly articulated by novelist ÉMILE ZOLA; other French naturalists included GUY DE MAUPASSANT and the brothers Edmond de Goncourt (1822–1896) and Jules de Goncourt (1830–1870). In Britain the works of THOMAS HARDY, GEORGE GISSING, and SAMUEL BUTLER exhibited naturalist traits. American naturalist writers included STEPHEN CRANE, THEODORE DREISER, FRANK NORRIS, and JACK LONDON. Naturalism also influenced such dramatists as Norwegian HENRIK IBSEN and Russian Maxim Gorky (1868–1936).

Ndebele See MATABELE.

Neanderthal man Hominid subspecies (*Homo sapiens neanderthalensis.*) Neanderthal man inhabited Europe and parts of North Africa and Asia from about 125,000 to 35,000 years ago. The first known skull and bones of this subspecies were discovered in 1856 by quarry workers in a cave in the Neander Valley near Düsseldorf, Germany. The fossil remains were clearly human but with differences—a heavy brow ridge, a receding forehead and chin, and large teeth. A controversy arose as to whether these features represented an early, different form of human or an ordinary but diseased individual. The publication of *THE ORIGIN OF SPECIES* by CHARLES DARWIN three years later, with its exposition of the theory of evolution, intensified the debate. German pathologist RUDOLF VIRCHOW argued on the "human but diseased" side; English biologist THOMAS HUXLEY and French anthropologist PIERRE-PAUL BROCA argued on the "early form of human" side. The latter side eventually prevailed as more fossils of early humans were discovered.

The first early-human fossil type to be discovered, Neanderthal man has remained controversial. Scientists still debate how the subspecies became extinct, whether Neanderthal genes are carried by modern humans or whether they were an evolutionary dead end, and how culturally advanced the subspecies was. Their tools were not as sophisticated as those of later CRO-MAGNON MAN—anatomically modern humans who may have driven the Neanderthals to extinction—and they have left no record of artistic or computational ability. But there is evidence that they were the first hominids to bury their dead with ritual ceremonies.

needle gun FIREARM. The first breech-loading rifle, it was completed by German inventor Johann Nikolaus von Dreyse (1787–1867) in 1841. Formerly, all military small arms had been muzzle-loaded. In contrast, the needle gun—so-called for its needlelike firing pin—was loaded at the rear of the muzzle and could therefore be reloaded much more quickly. By 1870 practical breech-loading rifles had become widespread.

needlework See EMBROIDERY.

Nègre, Charles (1820–1879) French painter and photographer. A pupil of JEAN-AUGUSTE-DOMINIQUE INGRES, he was one of the better known artists using PHOTOGRAPHY as a basis for painting. His halftone photographs, executed with the calotype process invented by WILLIAM HENRY FOX TALBOT, were popular in the 1850s.

Neo-Impressionism Artistic movement. Also known as Divisionism, Neo-Impressionism was an offshoot of IMPRESSIONISM that subjected Impressionist techniques to rigorous intellectual analysis.

Instead of mixing pigments on the palette, Neo-Impressionists created strictly formal compositions through a method known as POINTILLISM. Artists applied small dots or dashes of pure color to the canvas in order to produce fragmented areas of color. Seen at the proper distance, the fragmented areas blended together to create subtle and rich color patterns.

The movement was led by GEORGES SEURAT. He built on the closely placed color patterns of Impressionism and scientific studies of optical phenomena to construct painstakingly detailed mosaics of painted color. The term "Neo-Impressionism" was coined by Seurat's friend, critic Felix Feneon, after seeing the painter's Divisionist masterpiece *A Sunday on the Grande Jatte,* in the last Impressionist group show of 1886. Neo-Impressionism was also practiced by CAMILLE PISSARRO, Henri-Edmond Cross, and Paul Signac, who after Seurat became the style's leading exponent and helped work out the movement's theoretical principles.

Neo-Impressionism's ordered and geometric compositions anticipated the genuine abstract art of the Fauves, Cubists, and Futurists in the twentieth century.

Neptune Eighth planet from the sun. The existence of an eighth planet had been suggested ever since scientists worked out the orbit of the seventh planet, Uranus, discovered in 1781. The observed orbit of Uranus did not match the orbit predicted by Newton's gravitational theory even after allowance was made for the perturbing effects of Jupiter and Saturn. It was evident that either the theory was wrong or an unknown planet was perturbing Uranus.

In 1845, English mathematician JOHN COUCH ADAMS worked out a solution predicting where a new planet would be found. Adams sent his calculations to Sir George Airy (1801–1892), the Astronomer Royal, in October 1845, but Airy did not immediately accept the calculations and the matter was dropped.

In June 1846, French mathematician URBAIN-JEAN-JOSEPH LEVERRIER published calculations predicting virtually the same result. Leverrier convinced German astronomer Johann Gottfried Galle to look for the planet. At the Berlin Observatory on the night of September 23, 1846, Galle and his assistant Heinrich d'Arrest trained the nine-inch Fraunhofer reflecting telescope on the region of the sky in the constellation Aquarius where the planet was supposed to be. They found a previously uncharted point of light less than one degree of arc from the position Leverrier predicted. A new planet had been discovered.

Greenish in color, the planet was named after Neptune, the Roman god of the sea. The largest of its moons, Triton, was discovered on October 10, 1846, less than three weeks after the planet was first seen.

The discovery of Neptune, now jointly credited to Adams and Leverrier, was a triumph for gravitational theory, representing the first instance of a planet being discovered solely on the basis of theoretical calculations. No other planets were discovered until Pluto, the ninth planet, was found in 1930.

Netherlands Small country in northwest Europe. It is bounded by Belgium, Luxembourg, and Germany. The country is generally flat and low, much of it lying below sea level and protected by dikes. The population is ethnically homogenous, largely Dutch-speaking. Members of the Reformed (Calvinist) Church form the largest religious group, with a significant Roman Catholic minority.

At the end of the Napoleonic Wars, the Netherlands was made part of the Dutch-Belgian kingdom, ruled by a Dutch monarchy.

King William I actively tried to enforce his rule in Belgium while leaving Dutch institutions more or less intact. Belgian resentment flared into revolt in 1830. French intervention secured Belgian independence. Faced with a protracted stalemate and little Dutch support for trying to retain the south, William abandoned the war and his claims to Belgium in 1839.

William found himself isolated abroad and facing a growing criticism at home. In 1840 his proposed marriage to a Belgian Catholic caused a furor, and the king abdicated in favor of his son William II (1792–1849). Politically, liberalism developed more slowly in the Netherlands than elsewhere in Europe and did not become a force until the 1840s. Economically, the Netherlands also remained somewhat backward depending heavily on shipping and trade generated by its posts in the Dutch East Indies (modern Indonesia).

Fearful of the revolutions sweeping Europe in 1848, the king issued a constitution featuring a strong two-chambered legislature and limited male suffrage. Domestic politics in the Netherlands thereafter were comparatively peaceful. The main areas of contention were over state promotion of religious education and the extension of the franchise. INDUSTRIALIZATION began in earnest in the later nineteenth century and caused some dislocations, but the Netherlands were generally prosperous.

In foreign policy, the Netherlands was generally neutral and stayed out of major European conflicts. In the 1860s the Dutch began an aggressive campaign to expand their possessions in the East Indies beyond the trading posts. By the end of the nineteenth century they controlled Java and large portions of Borneo and Sumatra as well as several smaller islands.

New Guinea See OCEANIA.

New York Times, The American newspaper. Founded in 1851, the ailing paper was acquired by publisher ADOLPH S. OCHS in 1896; under him it gained a worldwide circulation. At a time of sensationalistic and politically slanted reporting, the *Times* set new standards for journalistic seriousness and impartiality. See also PERIODICALS.

New Zealand Country in the South Pacific Ocean, southeast of Australia. It is comprised mainly of North Island and South Island, with many outlying islands. The capital is Wellington, on North Island. The islands were occupied by the Maori since before 1400; Dutch navigator Abel Tasman in 1642 was the first European to reach them. British navigator James Cook later explored the islands (1769–77); he was followed by whalers, merchants, and missionaries. British colonizer EDWARD GIBBON WAKEFIELD established the first lasting European settlement there in 1840, the same year the Maori signed the Treaty of Waitangi in which they recognized British sovereignty while the British guaranteed Maori possession of the land. However, colonial and indigenous inhabitants soon clashed in the Maori Wars (1843–48, 1860–72), resulting in the colonists' acquisition of much Maori land. Though originally part of the colony of New South Wales, AUSTRALIA, New Zealand gained separate status in 1841 and was made a self-governing collection of six provinces in 1852. It was granted dominion status in 1907 and full independence in 1931, the latter ratified by New Zealand in 1947. In the late nineteenth century, New Zealand became a pioneer in reform legislation, passing WOMAN SUFFRAGE in 1893 and social security in 1898.

Newgate Calendar Series of collected biographies. Focusing on notorious inmates of NEWGATE PRISON and sensational in appeal, the works usually claimed a noble purpose having to do with public morality or criminal law reform. The first *Newgate Calendar* was published in five volumes in 1774; subsequent editions appeared throughout the nineteenth century, culminating in *Chronicles of Crime, or, The New Newgate Calendar* by C. Pelham. Writers of NEWGATE NOVELS frequently took inspiration from these biographical works.

Newgate novel School of crime fiction. Popular in Britain and the United States in the 1830s, the novels were named for the notorious inhabitants of NEWGATE PRISON. Also called "rogue novels" and often based on actual cases taken from the *NEWGATE CALENDAR,* these works portrayed criminals sympathetically, romanticizing their exploits and sometimes critiquing the society that led them to crime. EDWARD BULWER-LYTTON's *Paul Clifford* (1830) and *Eugene Aram* (1832) are both examples of the genre, as are WILLIAM HARRISON AINSWORTH's *Rookwood* (1834) and *Jack Sheppard* (1839). Critics complained that the novels condoned crime and endangered public morality. WILLIAM MAKEPEACE THACKERAY satirized the genre in *Catherine* (1839–40). CHARLES DICKENS offered a more realistic view of crime, the legal system, and related social issues in *Oliver Twist* (1837–38), *Barnaby Rudge* (1841), and *Bleak House* (1852–53). Though in fashion only briefly, the Newgate novel had a lasting influence on the development of crime and detective fiction.

Newgate Prison London penal institution. The principal prison in London in the nineteenth century, it was housed in a building erected in 1782, after the original had been destroyed by fire. A passageway connected the prison to the Old Bailey, site of London's main criminal court. Public hangings, typically attended by great crowds, were conducted outside the prison until 1868 when public executions came to an end. Conditions were notoriously grim inside, as described in the novels *Oliver Twist* and *GREAT EXPECTATIONS* by CHARLES DICKENS. In an effort to keep prisoners from being idle, inmates were forced to spend several hours a day walking on a treadmill or picking oakum—a rope that, when laboriously unwound by hand, would yield strands to be used in caulking ships. The prison was demolished in 1902. See also NEWGATE CALENDAR and NEWGATE NOVEL.

Newlands, John Alexander Reina (1837–1898) English chemist. Newlands developed the "law of octaves" in 1863, an early attempt at organizing chemical elements; it was superseded in 1869 by the PERIODIC TABLE OF ELEMENTS of DMITRY IVANOVICH MENDELEYEV.

Newman, John Henry Cardinal (1801–1890) English cleric and theologian. Born in London, he attended Trinity College, Oxford, and in 1822 became a fellow at Oriel College, Oxford. He was ordained by the Church of England in 1824 and named vicar of University Church–St. Mary's in 1827. While at Oriel, Newman befriended Richard Hurrel Froude (1803–1836), also a fellow there. Froude's hatred of the Protestant Reformation, which had led to the establishment of the Church of England, influenced Newman's thinking about the role of the Anglican establishment. They traveled together to Rome in 1833 where Newman was taken with the grandeur of the city and found himself more and more drawn to Catholicism.

Back in England, Newman joined the discussions that had been set off by the sermon on "National Apostasy" by JOHN KEBLE in 1833. Newman believed that this sermon marked the birth of the OXFORD MOVEMENT, which sought the return to the tenets and practices of the early Church that had been forsaken by the Anglicans since the Reformation.

Newman was the main contributor to *Tracts for the Times,* a series of publications that addressed a wide range of religious issues. The writers of the tracts, known as TRACTARIANS, questioned the historical legitimacy of the Church of England as well as its theological underpinnings. They asked if the break from the Roman Catholic Church, a church founded by God according to Protestants and Catholics alike, had been justified.

Tract No. 90, authored by Newman in 1841, brought these controversies to a head. It argued that the Church of England's fundamental doctrines as expressed in the Thirty-Nine Articles did not contradict Roman Catholic beliefs. Anglicans protested vehemently. The bishop of Oxford banned the *Tracts* but refused to dismiss Newman. He retired from his active duties as vicar of St. Mary's and resigned his position in 1843. In 1845 he became a Roman Catholic. Because of his intellectual stature, Newman's conversion prompted many other Anglicans to join the Catholic Church. HENRY MANNING, the archdeacon of Chichester and a leading figure of the Protestant hierarchy, followed Newman's path.

Newman was ordained a Catholic priest in 1846 and entered the order of Oratarians dedicated to educating the faithful. He established an oratory in Edgbaston just outside Birmingham, where he remained for most of the rest of his life. He helped found the new Catholic University in Dublin in the 1850s and served as its first rector. His lectures there were published as *The Idea of a University* (1852). Newman argued that moral instruction should be incorporated into a university education.

Newman published his most famous work, *APOLOGIA PRO VITA SUA,* or *Defense of His Own Life,* in 1864. The work was a response to the assertion by popular writer CHARLES KINGSLEY that Newman and indeed all Catholic clergy did not value truth for its own sake. The autobiography describes his spiritual journey from Anglicanism to Roman Catholicism. Newman's *The Grammar of Assent* (1870) examined the reasons for believing in God. Newman is also known as the author of the hymn "Lead Kindly Light" (1833). His most famous poem is "The Dream of Gerontius" (1866), which relates the story of a dying man facing God. Newman was made a cardinal in 1879.

news agencies Organizations that supply news reports to newspapers and other publishers. The first news agency was founded in Paris by the translator Charles-Louis Havas in 1835. He received foreign newspapers, selected and translated important items, then distributed them to his subscribers. Originally using couriers and carrier pigeons for distribution, Havas switched to the telegraph after its introduction in France in 1840.

In 1848 six daily newspapers in New York formed the New York Associated Press; it withstood competition, scandal, and a change of control, and finally became the Associated Press in 1892. In 1882 the rival United Press was formed, but this privately owned agency went bankrupt in 1897. The REUTERS NEWS SERVICE was formed in London in 1851 by the German-born book publisher Paul Julius Reuter, who saw the opportunities offered by the telegraph to establish correspondences across the globe. Reuters provided the first international service and remained under private ownership until 1925.

Nicaragua See CENTRAL AMERICA.

Nicholas I (1796–1855) Czar of Russia (1825–55). The third son of Czar Paul I, who reigned from 1796 to 1801, he was the brother and successor of Alexander I, whose twenty-four-year reign began upon their father's death. A leading force in the autocratic reaction that followed the Napoleonic era, Nicholas crushed a Polish uprising (1830–31) and helped Austria suppress a Hungarian revolt (1849). His aggressive policy toward the Ottoman Empire helped bring on the CRIMEAN WAR (1854–56), during which he died. He was succeeded by his son ALEXANDER II.

Nicholas II (1868–1918) Czar of Russia (1894–1917). The eldest son of Czar ALEXANDER III, he perpetuated his father's policies of political repression and persecution of minorities. Radical revolutionary and liberal reformist groups continued to press for change, and in 1898 Nicholas's peace proposals helped bring about the International Peace Conference at the Hague (1899). Following the Victorian era, his principal role in world history was as Russia's last czar. He was deposed by the Russian revolution in 1917, and he and his family, including his wife, ALEXANDRA, were killed by the Bolsheviks in 1918.

Nietzsche, Friedrich Wilhelm (1844–1900) German philosopher. Educated at the grammar school of Schulforta, he was influenced early in his career by ARTHUR SCHOPENHAUER. Named professor of classical philology at Basel (1869–79), he was forced to resign because of ill health. His first work, *The Birth of Tragedy from the Spirit of Music* (1872), was a revolutionary challenge to prevailing classical scholarship. It argued against the "Apollonian" perspective emphasizing reason and stasis in Greek culture, associated with eighteenth-century German classical scholar Johann Winckelman, on behalf of a "Dionysian" perspective of dynamic, tragic passion. Nietzsche championed composer RICHARD WAGNER as the embodiment of a new Dionysian blend of music and theater, though he broke with Wagner in 1876.

His later philosophical views were encapsulated most fully in *Thus Spake Zarathustra* (1883–92), which affirmed his rejection of Christian morality and the importance of the figure of the *Übermensch* (superman) throughout history. Like the ideas of CHARLES DARWIN, Nietzsche's philosophical premises profoundly undermined Victorian values of selfless Christian devotion, but unlike Darwinian thought, his insights could not be assimilated into a Victorian schema. Other works include *Human, All Too Human* (1878), *Daybreak* (1881), *Beyond Good and Evil* (1886), *On the Genealogy of Morals* (1887), and *Ecce Homo* (1888). Having spent many years in solitary thought, Nietzsche suffered a major mental breakdown in 1889 that left him insane for the rest of his life.

Nightingale, Florence (1820–1910) English nurse. The founder of modern nursing and advocate for sanitation and hygiene, she was named for the place of her birth, Florence, Italy, where she was born to a prosperous business family. She entered nursing in the

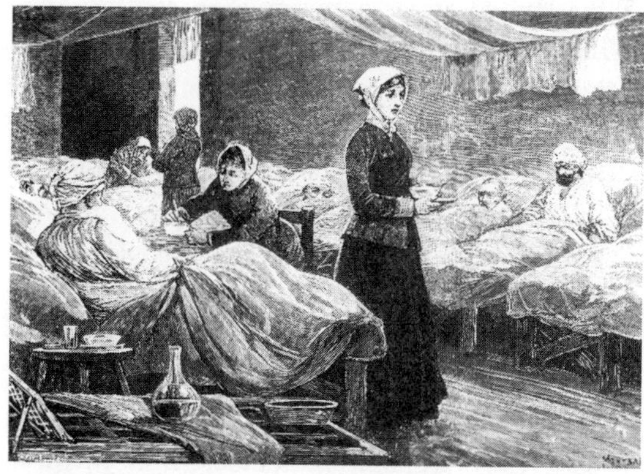

Florence Nightingale, English nurse, is considered the founder of modern nursing. Photo courtesy of Topham/ Image Works.

early 1850s and in 1853 was named superintendent of the Establishment for Gentlewomen During Illness in London. During the CRIMEAN WAR (1853–56) she became supervisor of nursing at British army hospitals. She applied stringent sanitary and dietary regulations to reduce death rates in hospitals, which had been as high as 42 percent, primarily due to infection and disease contracted in the hospital, such as cholera, dysentery, and typhus. Her experiences led her to write *Notes on Matters Affecting the Health, Efficiency, and Hospital Administration of the British Army* in 1858. In 1860 she established a modern training school for nurses, and until her death she campaigned for nursing reforms. In 1907 she became the first female to receive the British Order of British Merit. She was immortalized as the "lady with a lamp" in "Santa Filomena," a 1856 poem by HENRY WADSWORTH LONGFELLOW.

NINA Acronym. Signs were often hung in front of nineteenth-century factories in the United States, with the acronym NINA, meaning "No Irish Need Apply." It expressed the prejudice of many native-born Americans for the millions who emigrated from IRELAND to the United States between 1830 and 1860.

Niños Héroes, Los Mexican cadets. The "boy heroes" defended the fortress of Chapultepec in Mexico City in 1847 during a key battle of the MEXICAN WAR. The boys, young cadets of the military school at Chapultepec, withstood a bombardment by U.S. artillery beginning on September 12, 1847. On September 13, after the Americans had scaled the fortress walls, the Mexican cadets battled them hand to hand. Many fought to the death rather than surrender. They are still remembered in Mexican history as *Los Niños Héroes.*

nitroglycerine See DYNAMITE.

Nobel, Alfred Bernhard (1833–1896) Swedish chemist. Born in Stockholm, he moved as a child with his family to Russia where Nobel's father manufactured submarine mines and torpedoes. He was educated by private tutors and traveled abroad for two years after 1850, part of the time in the United States. After his return to Russia, he worked in his father's factory and began studying explosives, especially nitroglycerine.

In 1863, Nobel invented the blasting cap and established a small factory near Stockholm, which was destroyed in an explosion in 1864, killing Nobel's younger brother. Nobel then became concerned with creating a more manageable explosive and combined nitroglycerine with an inert substance and called the mixture "dynamite." In 1867 he was granted a British patent for dynamite and a year later obtained a U.S. patent. His patent for blasting gelatin, a jellylike combination of nitroglycerine and guncotton, was awarded in 1876. In 1888 he obtained a patent for ballistite, a smokeless powder.

While Nobel's fortune was amassed primarily through his invention of explosive materials, he obtained 355 patents in a variety of endeavors, including the production of synthetic rubber and artificial silk.

At his death, Nobel left the major portion of his fortune in trust to establish five prizes in peace, physics, chemistry, medicine, and literature. The first Nobel Prize was awarded in 1901.

noble gases See INERT GASES.

nocturne Musical nocturne. The nocturne is an instrumental piece for piano popular in the nineteenth century. The genre is marked by slow tempo, extended melody over a chordal accompaniment, and a quiet, reflective mood.

Its roots may lie in eighteenth-century *notturno, nachtmusik,* or serenade. Irish composer John Field (1782–1837) wrote the first examples; Polish composer FRÉDÉRIC CHOPIN brought the form to perfection with his nineteen nocturnes.

Norris, Frank (1870–1902) American journalist and novelist. Along with JACK LONDON and STEPHEN CRANE, Norris was a leading figure of naturalism in American literature. Born Benjamin Franklin Norris in Chicago, he moved to San Francisco with his parents in 1884 and studied art in Paris. Back in America, he attended the University of California (1890–94) where he wrote for student publications and came under the influence of EMILE ZOLA, whose novels made him reexamine his early penchant for writing romance novels. He began writing *McTeague* (1899), a novel relating how greed destroys a middle-class San Francisco family.

He reported on the BOER WAR for *Collier's* and the *San Francisco Chronicle* in 1895 and 1896, and traveled to Cuba in 1898 to write about the SPANISH-AMERICAN WAR. In 1900 he published *A Man's Woman,* a story of a love triangle between two Arctic explorers and a nurse; it exhibited some of his early romantic tendencies.

At this time he began writing his most renowned work, the "epic of the wheat." This planned trilogy was to examine the social forces and institutions that affected the growth, marketing, and consumption of wheat. *The Octopus* (1901) details the struggle between California wheat farmers and the fictional Pacific and Southwestern Railroad. The railroad dominates the state legislature, fixes freight rates and wheat prices, and ultimately evicts the farmers from their land despite armed opposition. *The Pit,* published posthumously in 1903, is about a corrupt commodities speculator at the Chicago wheat exchange who tries unsuccessfully to corner part of the wheat market. The consumption of wheat in a famine-plagued village in Europe was to have completed the trilogy, but Norris's sudden death after an appendix operation left *The Wolf* unwritten.

Northcote, Stafford Henry, 1st Earl of Iddesleigh (1818–1887) English statesman. The Oxford-educated Northcote became the personal secretary of WILLIAM GLADSTONE in 1842 and served in Parliament from 1855 to 1885. He was secretary for India (1867–78) and helped negotiate the United States's *ALABAMA* claims in 1871. The NORTHCOTE-TREVELYAN CIVIL SERVICE REPORT of 1855 helped reform the British CIVIL SERVICE. He was also chair of the Hudson Bay Company (1869–74). BENJAMIN DISRAELI made him chancellor of the Exchequer (1874–80), and he briefly served as foreign secretary in 1886.

Northcote-Trevelyan Civil Service Report (1854) British government statement. The administrative failures that plagued British operations during the CRIMEAN WAR along with continuing problems in the administration of India stoked an already high interest in CIVIL SERVICE reform. By 1853 eleven government reports had been submitted, and groups such as the Administrative Reform Association clamored for an end to patronage and the appointment of unqualified candidates.

Prime Minister WILLIAM GLADSTONE charged Sir STAFFORD NORTHCOTE and Sir Charles Trevelyan with developing reform suggestions. Their 1854 report resulted in wide-ranging changes in the British civil service. A Civil Service Commission was formed to administer competitive exams and to screen applicants.

The loss of patronage and decreased flexibility in making appointments was opposed by government departments, but by the end of the century almost all positions were being filled by examination.

Northern Rhodesia See ZAMBIA and RHODESIA.

Northwest Passage Water route along the northern coast of North America connecting the Atlantic and Pacific oceans. Sought since the sixteenth century as a possible short route from Europe to China and India, it spurred exploration of Canada by Martin Frobisher, Henry Hudson, William Baffin, and others. In 1845–47, English explorer Sir JOHN FRANKLIN found the passage but died trying; his entire expedition was lost. In 1850–54, English explorer Sir Robert John Le Mesurier McClure (1807–1873), one of the rescuers sent out to the Arctic archipelago to search for Franklin, discovered the McClure Strait and proved the existence of the Northwest Passage. It was not until 1903–6, however, that the passage was first navigated by Norwegian explorer Roald Amundsen (1872–1928), who a few years later (1911) was the first man to reach the South Pole.

Norton, Charles Eliot (1827–1908) American scholar and educator. The son of Andrews Norton, a renowned biblical scholar, Charles Norton was born in Cambridge, Massachusetts. He graduated from Harvard in 1846 and then worked for an importing firm from Boston for several years. He traveled extensively, making journeys to India, Egypt, and Europe, where he became friends with CHARLES DARWIN, THOMAS CARLYLE, JOHN RUSKIN, and JAMES RUSSELL LOWELL.

From 1864 to 1868, Norton edited the *North American Review* and was one of the founders of *The Nation* in 1865. From 1873 to 1897 he was a professor of art at Harvard and quickly became one of its most popular lecturers. An edition of his lectures was published in 1891. Norton also published the letters of Carlyle, Ruskin, and RALPH WALDO EMERSON, and a prose translation of *The Divine Comedy* (1891–92). He edited *The Poems of John Donne* (1895) and wrote a number of books, including *Consideration of Some Recent Social Theories* (1853) and *Historical Studies of Church Building in the Middle Ages* (1880). He founded the Dante Society and the Archaeological Institute of America.

Nyasaland British colony in southeast central Africa, now the independent republic of Malawi. Present-day Malawi is a tiny landlocked country about the size of Pennsylvania, bordered by Mozambique to the east, south, and southwest, Zambia to the west, and Tanzania to the north. In 1859, Scottish explorer DAVID LIVINGSTONE became the first European to venture into the mountainous country, bordered on the east by the vast Lake Nyasa, which runs north to south through Africa's Great Rift Valley. In 1889 the British South Africa Company of CECIL RHODES received a charter to develop the country. Poor in mineral resources, it became the site of large coffee plantations, and its principal exports are still such agricultural products as tobacco, sugar, and tea.

Great Britain's rivals in Nyasaland included Arab slave traders, expelled militarily in the 1890s, and the Portuguese in neighboring Mozambique. Fearing annexation of Nyasaland by Portugal, Britain itself annexed the territory in 1891. In 1953, it became part of the Federation of Rhodesia and Nyasaland. It became the independent nation of Malawi in 1964.

Obaysch Hippopotamus. Obaysch was captured in infancy in 1849 by Abbas Pasha, viceroy of Egypt, and presented as a gift to the Zoological Society of London. Described as "tame and playful as a Newfoundland puppy," Obaysch was transported in 1850 to the zoological gardens in Regent's Park where he became a popular sensation. Queen Victoria brought her children to visit him, the humor magazine *Punch* chronicled his activities, and silver models of Obaysch were offered for sale. Inspired by the animal, LEWIS CARROLL wrote a poem about a hippo riding a London bus, and a song called the "Hippopotamus Polka" became the rage. In 1854 a mate, Adhela or Dil, was acquired for Obaysch; the pair produced a daughter, Miss Guy. Obaysch died on March 20, 1878, at age twenty-nine.

Oceania Collective term for about twenty-five thousand small tropical islands in the central and south Pacific Ocean. All but a few thousand of these volcanic peaks and coral atolls are uninhabited. Also called the South Sea islands, the term sometimes includes AUSTRALIA and NEW ZEALAND as well. The islands are divided into three major groups: Melanesia, to the north and east of Australia; Micronesia in the western Pacific; and Polynesia in the central Pacific.

First settled by Asians in prehistoric times, Oceania was reached by Europeans in the sixteenth century and was later explored by Englishman James Cook (1728–1779) and Frenchman Jules Dumont d'Urville (1790–1842). In the nineteenth century, missionary activity, mostly from Great Britain and France, became intense, leading to the establishment of western colonies between 1842 and 1900. France, for example, acquired the Wallis and Futuna Islands in 1842, Tahiti in 1843, and New Caledonia in 1853; Britain annexed Fiji in 1874; and the United States obtained Hawaii in 1900. New Guinea was divided in three, with the west ruled by the Dutch (see INDONESIA), the northeast by the Germans, and the southeast by the British. Because of the Western presence in Oceania, South Sea art forms and cultural practices became known in Europe and America, transmitted, for example, by the novels of former seaman JOSEPH CONRAD, the folklore reported by Sir JAMES GEORGE FRAZER, and the Tahitian paintings of French expatriate PAUL GAUGUIN.

Independence for many of the island groups came in the 1960s and later, though some islands remain under European or American control.

Ochs, Adolph Simon (1858–1935) American newspaper publisher. Born in Cincinnati, Ohio, he founded the *Chattanooga Times* in 1878 and acquired the financially ailing *NEW YORK TIMES* in 1896 for $75,000. By eliminating light fiction, increasing coverage of financial news and war coverage, and creating a Sunday magazine and book review section, he turned the newspaper into the most widely respected American newspaper. Ochs adopted the slogan, "All the News That's Fit to Print" in 1896.

O'Connell, Daniel (1775–1847) Irish politician. Known as the "Liberator," O'Connell was the leading Irish politician of the first half of the nineteenth century. Born to a prosperous Catholic family, he established a thriving law practice before turning to politics in the 1820s. By that decade some of the harsher anti-Catholic laws passed in the centuries of Protestant English rule of IRELAND had been repealed. However, Catholics still could not take a seat in Parliament without swearing an oath that was odious to their religious principles. No Catholic had sat in Parliament for some 150 years even though they had been granted the right to vote in 1793. They were also forced to pay a tithe to support the Protestant church.

In 1823, O'Connell formed the Catholic Association dedicated to peaceful and constitutional repeal of the oath and to enactment of other reforms. Between 1826 and 1828 the association elected several Protestants who favored repeal of the oath. The group's success shocked English landlords used to commanding their tenants' votes. The association was banned, but O'Connell formed a new entity to continue the struggle. He then decided to force the issue by running for a parliamentary seat, which he easily won in 1828. The massive crowds organized for this campaign heightened English fears that violence would erupt if O'Connell was denied his seat because he could not take the oath. In 1829 a Catholic Emancipation Bill ended the oath. The bill was not made retroactive, however, and did not apply to O'Connell. He refused to swear the oath and had to run again for the same seat, which he then won unopposed.

In the 1830s, O'Connell's parliamentary faction of about thirty-nine legislators aligned itself with the Whig Party. Additional reforms were won, but O'Connell could not win parliamentary support for his main political objective: the repeal of the Act of Union of 1800. That act had dissolved the Irish Parliament, ending Irish control of their domestic affairs. O'Connell thought that only repeal of the act would substantially change landlord-tenant relations, the main cause of the Irish peasants' extreme poverty.

Parliamentary opposition hardened when the Tories swept the Whigs out of office in 1841. O'Connell continued to agitate for repeal despite this setback. Under his leadership the Repeal Association, founded in 1840, mounted vast demonstrations that *The Times* of London dubbed "monster meetings." An 1843 meeting in Cork drew half a million people; one in Tara attracted some 750,000 Irish. The disciplined ranks of Irish demonstrators and O'Connell's readiness to use military allusions while calling for peaceful change convinced many in England. Prime Minister ROBERT PEEL banned a meeting scheduled in October 1843 at Clontarf. O'Connell bowed to the order but a few weeks later found himself under arrest for conspiracy. Convicted, he was pardoned by the House of Lords after several months of imprisonment.

O'Connell continued to organize monster meetings. Meanwhile, younger members of the Repeal Association began to grow restless at his pacifism, especially when the first of a series of potato blights devastated Ireland in 1845. His health failing, O'Connell could not prevent advocates of physical force from splitting the association. His death in 1847, the horrible IRISH POTATO FAMINE of the 1840s, and the collapse of the repeal movement crippled Irish resistance to English rule for the next thirty years.

Octopus, The: A Story of California (1901) Novel by American writer FRANK NORRIS. First part of a planned but never completed "epic of the wheat" trilogy. Considered a prime example of American naturalism, it depicts the struggles between California farmers in the San Joaquin Valley and the railroad that commands the state government and slowly draws other industries into its monopolistic tentacles. Farmers organize against the railroad's control of freight prices, interest rates, and land ownership. They manage to place the son of a leading farmer on the state board that fixes rates, but the railroad bribes him. When the railroads dispossess the farmers, a bloody revolt erupts in which many farmers are killed. The railroad's triumph brings poverty and misery to the farmers.

oil (petroleum) Natural resource. A flammable, naturally occurring oil consisting chiefly of hydrocarbons, petroleum first came into commercial use in the Victorian era. Known as "crude oil" in its unrefined state, petroleum is thought to have been formed from the remains of living organisms deposited with rock particles and buried under thick layers of rock. Petroleum was known in China and Burma as early as two thousand years earlier, but its potential was not appreciated. In the 1850s an American railway conductor named Edwin L. Drake decided it might have some commercial value since animal and plant oils were widely used as lamp fuels. In 1859, he drilled sixty-nine feet under the ground in Titusville, Pennsylvania, and "struck oil," creating the first oil well.

Kerosene for lighting lamps was the first valuable product refined from oil. It quickly destroyed the already faltering whaling industry, which until then had produced most of the world's lamp oil. By 1870, JOHN D. ROCKEFELLER had established the Standard Oil Company, which came to dominate the oil refining industry. The 1880s and 1890s saw the development of the INTERNAL COMBUSTION ENGINE, which relied on gasoline and diesel oil, formerly useless byproducts of the kerosene refining process. In the twentieth century, gasoline and diesel oil became the fuels that powered industrial civilization, as coal for steam engines had powered it in the nineteenth century.

Old Bailey See NEWGATE PRISON.

Old Vic See VICTORIA THEATRE.

Olmsted, Frederick Law (1822–1903) American landscape architect. He created American public parks on massive scales that reflected the Victorian enthusiasm for nature. In 1857 he was appointed superintendent for the creation of New York's Central Park in an area far north of what was then the city. Following plans he had developed with Calvert Vaux, he transformed the acres of hog farms, bone-boiling works, and squatters' shacks into one of the most glorious, varied, and beloved parks in the world, creating a public refuge for generations of city dwellers. He gave a similar gift to Boston when in 1879 he completed the park system that formed "an emerald necklace" around the city. His advocacy helped influence Congress in 1864 to protect California's Yosemite Valley. Among Olmsted's other works were Prospect Park in Brooklyn and the grounds for the 1893 Columbia Exposition in Chicago (now Jackson Park).

omnibus Large horse-drawn vehicle for mass transportation. The ancestor of the modern bus, these conveyances were introduced to London in 1829. By 1850 their number had increased to about fifteen hundred. By the 1880s some had a circular staircase and two decks, carrying up to twenty-eight passengers. They were cramped and ran fixed routes under the eye of a conductor known as a "cad."

opium See NARCOTICS.

Opium Wars (1839–42 and 1856–60) Two international conflicts. The opium wars were fought on the Chinese coast primarily to ensure greater Western access to Chinese markets. Before the wars, the MANCHU DYNASTY restricted foreign traders to the port of Canton and imposed heavy tariffs. British and American traders began importing opium which was illegal in CHINA, to pay for their large exports of Chinese goods. Widespread opium addiction caused severe social disruption, and the Manchu government responded in 1839 by destroying the merchants' stores of opium and closing Canton.

In the First Opium War (1839–42), Great Britain launched naval attacks on the south China coast and up the Yangtze River, easily overcoming feeble Chinese resistance. China was forced to conclude treaties with Britain, France, and the United States that lowered tariffs and granted foreign merchants immunity from Chinese law in five "treaty ports." The Chinese also ceded HONG KONG to Britain.

Frictions continued between Chinese and foreigners over the sale of opium and Chinese treatment of missionaries. In 1856, Britain and France began another round of military attacks, eventually moving on Peking (Beijing). Again the Chinese were defeated. This Second Opium War (1856–60) was also known as the Arrow War because it began with the Chinese government seizure of a Chinese ship, the *Arrow,* flying a British flag and engaged in the opium trade. The war, in which British general CHARLES GORDON saw action, culminated in the burning of the imperial Summer Palace. China was forced to open more treaty ports and to legalize the opium trade.

Orange Free State See SOUTH AFRICA.

Oregon Treaty (1846) Agreement between the United States and Great Britain. The treaty partitioned the disputed Oregon territory, the land south of Alaska and north of California from the Pacific Ocean to the continental divide. Jointly occupied by Britain and the United States since 1818, by the 1840s the land had become the focus of a heated disagreement that threatened war. American expansionists, including President JAMES K. POLK, laid claim to the entire territory up to 54° 40′ north latitude, the southern end of Alaska, while Britain argued that the United States had no claim north of the Columbia River, the northern end of the modern state of Oregon. Despite the blustery slogan "Fifty-four Forty or Fight!" that signaled some Americans' determination to go to war rather than concede on the issue, a compromise was reached, extending the boundary between the United States and Canada along latitude 49° to the Pacific.

Orient Express Luxury rail line. Running between Paris and Constantinople (Istanbul) in the late nineteenth and early twentieth centuries, the Orient Express was legendary for its luxurious accommodations and exotic itinerary. When the first-class rail service was founded in 1883, transfer to a steamship across the Black Sea to Constantinople was originally part of the trip, but by 1889 the entire voyage was by rail. Stops included Munich, Vienna, and Budapest. By the mid-twentieth century the service was no longer entirely first class.

Origin of Species, The (1859) Seminal work of natural history. Written by CHARLES DARWIN, its full title is *On the Origin of Species by Means of Natural Selection, or the Preservation of Favored Races in the Struggle for Life.* Darwin's theory is that "natural selection" is chiefly responsible for the EVOLUTION of species. In natural selection, individuals best adapted to their environment survive and reproduce. Their variations are thus "selected" by nature, while individuals less well adapted are more likely to die without issue. Over time, the action of natural selection modifies and creates species, producing entirely new forms out of preexisting ones.

As Darwin expected, *The Origin of Species* provoked outrage when people realized its implications for religious belief. It undermined "natural theology," which was founded on the premise that nature was a reflection of the Creator's design; further served to unseat humanity from its central place in nature; and contradicted the biblical account of creation. Darwin's book was promptly attacked by publications from *Punch* to the *Methodist Recorder.* Bishop SAMUEL WILBERFORCE was one of the chief opponents of *The Origin of Species;* scientist T. H. HUXLEY was one of its strongest supporters. The book went through six editions between 1859 and 1872 as Darwin revised it in order to respond to objections. In the next decades Darwin's theory of evolution became widely accepted. Misapplied to the realm of human social relations, it became the basis for doctrines of SOCIAL DARWINISM.

Considered the world's most luxurious train, the Orient Express traveled from Paris to Constantinople.

O'Shea, Katharine "Kitty" (1845–1921) Mistress and wife of CHARLES STEWART PARNELL. The most famous woman of Victorian England aside from the Queen, Katharine O'Shea was the thirteenth child of Emma and Sir John Page Wood. She grew up in comfortable circumstances in the countryside outside London where her father was an Anglican vicar. The family had good political connections; Katharine's uncle was to become WILLIAM GLADSTONE's Lord Chancellor.

In 1867, Katharine Wood married Irishman Captain William O'Shea who had left the army two years earlier. The marriage quickly became strained, and by 1875, Katharine and their three children were living apart from him. In 1880, O'Shea was elected to the House of Commons from County Clare, Ireland, and that same year Charles Stewart Parnell was elected to head the IRISH PARTY. The O'Sheas invited him to a dinner party in July 1880. By the end of the year, Parnell and Mrs. O'Shea had begun a passionate love affair.

The relationship lasted until Parnell's death in 1891. The couple had three children and lived as man and wife for long periods of time. She acted as Parnell's political confidante and advisor. Her political connections often allowed her to act as intermediary between Parnell and Gladstone.

This affair was an open secret among the Irish and English political elite but did not harm Parnell's political career until 1889 when Captain O'Shea named him as correspondent in a divorce suit. O'Shea had undoubtedly known about the affair but had maintained a public silence until the divorce. He feared that a scandal would ruin his wife's chance of inheriting her aunt's large fortune. His acceptance of his cuckoldry had also given him influence with Parnell.

Katharine's aunt died in 1889, but the will, which left the estate to her, was contested by the Wood family. O'Shea's divorce suit followed after this action, an indication that the Wood family had persuaded him that the legacy was in real jeopardy and that his cooperation in the probate proceedings would be rewarded; however, the final settlement yielded him no great fortune. The subsequent trial led to a public uproar and to Gladstone's demand that Parnell step down as party chief. Parnell was ousted from his post. He and Katharine married in 1890.

The anti-Parnellite faction of the party used the divorce and the issue of Katharine's character to defeat Parnell's candidates in several elections. The press called her the "were-wolf woman of Irish politics." Parnell's political enemies never stopped referring to her as Mrs. O'Shea or "Kitty," a feline diminutive she had never been called before and by which she is now best known.

Parnell died in 1891. Katharine Parnell suffered mental breakdowns and periods of delusion. She was cared for by a daughter until a series of heart attacks led to her death.

Otis, Elisha Graves (1811–1861) American inventor. Born in Halifax, Vermont, and a mechanic by trade, he introduced the safety ELEVATOR in 1852 at the Yonkers Bedstead Manufacturing Company in Yonkers, New York. There he demonstrated a safety device that kept the elevator cage in place even if the cable was broken. In 1857 the first commercial passenger elevator began operation in the E. G. Haughwout Store in New York City. In 1861 Otis patented a steam-powered elevator. The first electric Otis elevators were installed in the Demarest Building in New York City in 1889. The elevator was a major factor in the development of urban high-rise buildings in the late nineteenth century.

Otto engine See INTERNAL COMBUSTION ENGINE.

Ottoman Empire Large multi-ethnic state. At the beginning of the Victorian era, the Ottoman Empire controlled much of the BALKANS, the Middle East, and North Africa. It was ruled from Constantinople (modern Istanbul) by the Ottoman sultan, a member of a Turkish dynasty. As *caliph,* the sultan claimed leadership of all Muslims, but the empire also had a large Christian population. From the fourteenth to the sixteenth centuries the empire had expanded from its small beginnings in western Anatolia to the gates of Vienna. But the expansion halted, and a long series of wars with Russia and other European powers from the seventeenth through the eighteenth centuries were generally favorable. By the nineteenth century the empire was long past its heyday and was known as the "sick man of Europe." Ottoman history of the nineteenth century is one of political decline punctuated by attempts at reform.

Sultan Mahmud II (reigned from 1808 to 1839) attempted major reforms. In 1826 he destroyed the Jannisaries, the traditional sultan's bodyguard, which had often dominated palace politics. Mahmud brought large areas of the empire under his direct control and began to build a European-style army. He also attempted to separate civil from religious authority. In 1840, Mahmud's successor, Abdul-Mejid (reigned from 1839 to 1861) issued a decree abolishing all legal distinctions between Muslim and non-Muslim subjects of the sultan, but the decree was never fully implemented.

These reforms strengthened the empire, but it was still dependent on outside help for continued stability. In general, Great Britain and France acted to preserve the integrity of the empire while seeking economic and political concessions. Russia generally sought to gain control of Ottoman possessions in the Balkans.

In the Greek War of Independence (1821–31), the Ottoman Empire lost its Greek domains. In 1840 rebel MUHAMMAD ALI forced the empire to recognize him as heredity ruler of Egypt, under nominal Ottoman suzerainty.

The empire allied with France, Great Britain, and Sardinia in 1853 to fight Russia in the CRIMEAN WAR (1853–56). Victory gained the empire a twenty-year respite from Russian aggression.

In the 1870s the empire suffered from famine and financial instability caused by heavy foreign debt. In 1875 revolts broke out in the Balkans; Serbia attacked the empire the following year. Russia intervened, and when the RUSSO-TURKISH WARS (1877–78) were over, the Ottoman Empire had lost all its European possessions except Macedonia and Thrace.

Faced with the loss of many of his Christian subjects, Sultan Abdul Hamid (reigned from 1876 to 1909) sought to bolster his position as leader of the Muslim world, but the empire continued to unravel. British troops intervened during nationalist agitation in Egypt in 1882 and gained effective control of that country. In the 1890s the savage repression of Armenian revolts further discredited the empire. Disgust with the empire's declining fortunes led the Young Turks, a group of nationalistic army officers, to revolt in 1908. The Sultan became a constitutional monarch. Reform came too late to save the empire, however. Nearly all remaining Balkan territory was lost in 1913, and in 1914 the Ottoman Empire joined the Central Powers in World War I. The strain of war caused its collapse.

Owen, Robert (1771–1858) Welsh industrialist, social reformer, and planner. He began working in the textile industry at the age of ten and thirteen years later had become a prosperous cotton manufacturer in Manchester, England. He moved his operations to New Lanark, Scotland, where he developed a socially advanced and economically profitable industrial community. The town featured decent housing, a ban on child labor, schools, cooperative stores, and relatively good working conditions.

Based on this experience and his extensive reading, Owen tried to spread his visions of a humane industrialism founded on common ownership of property, equality of opportunity, and shared labor. Believing that people are formed by their environment and not by inherent tendencies, he argued for the establishment of cooperative communities. In 1825 he established the New Harmony settlement in Indiana. The community was planned to run on his socialistic theories but soon suffered from a lack of skilled craftsmen and from factionalism among the one thousand inhabitants. Owen proved an ineffectual leader, and he dissolved New Harmony in 1827 after spending most of his fortune on it.

The indefatigable Owen and his followers continued to sponsor cooperative communities in America and in England, none of which survived very long. He also participated in the trade union movement. His major works include an autobiography (1857–1858) and *A New View of Society* (three volumes, 1813–1814). His theories have been lumped together under the rubric of Owenism.

Oxford Movement Religious movement. It began in 1833 with a series of sermons and meetings among students and clergy at Oriel College, Oxford. Its adherents sought to revive the Church of England by rooting its beliefs and rituals more securely in the doctrine of early Christianity. Its most famous leader, JOHN HENRY NEWMAN, began writing a series of pamphlets called *Tracts for the Times* in 1833. Other contributors to the series, along with Newman, became known as TRACTARIANS. The *Tracts* called for a restoration of Christian rituals that had been renounced since the Reformation. They also sought to strengthen the legitimacy of the Church of England by linking its history and doctrine with the original apostles while minimizing its ties to the state.

Controversy over the movement developed as some members began contemplating conversion to Roman Catholicism. *Tract No. 90* added to the contention by arguing that the basic tenets of the Church of England did not conflict with Catholicism. Newman himself converted in 1845. Those who remained in the Church continued to press for changes in rituals, including chanting of services, wearing of vestments, and redecoration of churches. These "ritualists" stressed the importance of living in spiritual fellowships and established many monastic communities that ministered to the spiritual and social needs of their flocks.

The movement gradually exerted great influence in England and abroad but not without resistance. Rioting broke out over liturgical changes, and in 1874 the Public Worship Regulation Act was passed but failed to repress the ritualists. Later in the century, movement followers increasingly stressed the importance of the Church's role in social reform, with many participating in the Christian Social Union.

Paddington Station British railway depot. Connecting London with the west of England, it was originally opened in 1838 and brought to full architectural splendor by British engineer ISAMBARD K. BRUNEL in 1854. The great station represented pride in the speed and efficiency of the new trains and faith in Victorian technology. Queen VICTORIA arrived there after her first railway journey, taken at "a terrifying" forty-four miles per hour, in 1842. Placed in a historic area, the station helped bring it a cosmopolitan flavor. Its ornate design consists of three stories of wrought iron and glass and cast-iron pillars.

Paderewski, Ignacy Jan (1860–1941) Polish composer, pianist, and statesman. A student of renowned pianist and teacher Theodor Leschetizky (1830–1915), Paderewski won a reputation as a great performer of piano works, particularly those of FRÉDÉRIC CHOPIN. He also composed numerous works, including the Minuet in G for piano and the opera *Manru.* As important as his music was his devotion to Polish independence. He became prime minister in 1919 and headed the government in exile in 1940–41.

Palmerston, Henry John Temple, 3rd Viscount (1784–1865) English statesman. He entered Parliament in 1807 as a Tory and served as secretary of war from 1809 to 1828 and was twice prime minister (1855–58 and 1859–65). He slowly turned away from the Tories for supporting conservative monarchies abroad and opposing extension of suffrage at home. He joined the Whig Party in 1830 and became foreign secretary under Earl Grey, a position he held during 1830–34, 1835–41, and 1846–51.

Domestically, Palmerston only reluctantly supported the REFORM BILL OF 1832, arguing that it went too far in enlarging the electorate. He was to oppose extension of suffrage to workers throughout his career.

As foreign secretary and prime minister he sought to conserve a balance of power in Europe, support self-determination for many smaller European states, protect the OTTOMAN EMPIRE against foreign encroachment, and preserve Great Britain's naval supremacy.

In line with those aims, he helped Greece and Belgium win their independence, even threatening France with war if its troops did not leave Belgium. He also supported the Italian unification movement and the withdrawal of Austrian troops from northern Italy. Palmerston joined France and the liberal parties of Spain and Portugal in the Quadruple Alliance to counter the coalition of Austria, Prussia, and Russia. However, he organized international resistance to France when he feared Paris would gain control of the Ottoman Empire following the invasion of Syria by MUHAMMAD ALI, pasha of Egypt, in 1839. Palmerston's government also waged the first of the OPIUM WARS against China (1839–42) and added HONG KONG and Aden (see YEMEN) to the empire.

His support for Italian unification and some of the REVOLUTIONS OF 1848 alienated the crown and many Cabinet members. He also stirred anger in 1850 when he ordered the seizure of Greek ships in the harbor of Piraeus after the claims of British subject David Pacifico for property damage went unheeded by Athens. Known as the Don Pacifico affair, this controversial incident raised protests from the French and Russians, and forced Palmerston to promise to keep Queen VICTORIA informed about his actions. However, his vigorous foreign policy won him great popularity among the British. His last tenure as foreign secretary ended in 1851 when Lord JOHN RUSSELL dismissed him for supporting the takeover by NAPOLEON III of the French SECOND REPUBLIC.

Palmerston first became prime minister (1855–58) after the government resigned over mismanagement of the CRIMEAN WAR. He negotiated an end to that war and suppressed the INDIAN MUTINY (Sepoy Rebellion) in India. His second prime ministry (1859–65) was noted for his maintenance of British neutrality during the U.S. Civil War and his support of Italian unification. He intervened on behalf of Denmark in its dispute with Prussia over the duchies of Schleswig and Holstein, but OTTO VON BISMARCK invaded Denmark in 1864. Palmerston, facing public opposition to a war, abandoned his pledge to aid Denmark. He died the following year.

Panama See CENTRAL AMERICA.

Panama Canal See CENTRAL AMERICA and LESSEPS, FERDINAND-MARIE, VICOMTE DE.

Pankhurst, Emmeline Goulden (1858–1928) British social reformer and woman suffragist. She was the author of the first WOMAN SUFFRAGE bill in Great Britain in the late 1860s and of the Married Women's Property Acts in 1870 and 1882. In 1889, she founded the Women's Franchise League, an organization that succeeded five years later in obtaining for married women the right to vote for local government positions. After the Victorian era she founded the Women's Social and Political Union (1903) and advocated extreme militancy in pursuit of woman's rights.

papacy Office of the Pope. As the head of the Roman Catholic Church and bishop of Rome, the Pope is considered by Catholics the successor to the apostle St. Peter, whom Jesus Christ appointed visible head of the Church. From 756 to the late eighteenth century, the Pope had also been a temporal ruler, the sovereign of the Papal States. Conquered by Napoleon in 1796, the Papal States were restored to papal rule in 1815; by 1859 they comprised about 16,000 square miles (41,440 square kilometers). In 1860 most of the Papal States joined Sardinia and were incorporated into the new kingdom of

ITALY. In 1870, Italy annexed the remainder, including Rome, leaving the Pope a spiritual ruler only. The "Roman question"—the question of the papacy's status vis-à-vis other nations—was not resolved until 1929 when the Lateran Treaty made the Pope the sovereign ruler of the tiny independent state of Vatican City, comprising the papal palace called the Vatican and a group of other historic buildings in Rome.

The elimination of papal territory in the nineteenth century was the culmination of centuries of attrition in the institution's temporal power. Once the seat of enormous political power in Europe, the papacy had been weakened by the Reformation and the rise of nation-states. As a spiritual institution commanding the loyalty of adherents around the world, however, the Roman Catholic Church remained a vital force in the Victorian era, inspiring the devotion of such renowned individuals as English essayist JOHN HENRY CARDINAL NEWMAN, English poet GERARD MANLEY HOPKINS, French visionary Bernadette Soubirous, whose visions of the Virgin Mary led to the founding of the pilgrimage site at LOURDES, France, and French contemplative THÉRÈSE DE LISIEUX. The papacy's central control over the Roman Catholic Church was strengthened in the nineteenth century, particularly as a result of the VATICAN COUNCIL, which was convened by Pius IX in 1869–70 and promulgated the dogma of papal infallibility.

Three popes reigned during the Victorian era: GREGORY XVI (1831–46), PIUS IX (1846–78), LEO XIII (1878–1903).

papal infallibility See PAPACY and VATICAN COUNCIL.

Papua New Guinea See OCEANIA.

Paris, Congress of (1856) Diplomatic conference. The Congress of Paris produced a peace settlement after the CRIMEAN WAR. Delegations from Russia, the allied powers of Great Britain, France, and Sardinia, and the neutrals Prussia and Austria negotiated the Treaty of PARIS. The countries also agreed to the principles of naval warfare outlined in the DECLARATION OF PARIS.

Paris, Declaration of (1856) Diplomatic accord. Reached at the CONGRESS OF PARIS, the declaration attempted to codify the law of the sea during wartime. Prior attempts had been rejected by Great Britain, but the declaration proposed by France after the CRIMEAN WAR was not; other signatories included Austria, France, Prussia, Russia, Turkey, and Sardinia. The declaration embodied four principles: neutral flags would convey safe passage of an enemy's goods except for contraband of war; privateering was outlawed; neutral goods, excepting contraband, could not be seized from a ship flying an enemy's flag; and blockades required sufficient forces to prevent access to the coast and could not exist by mere fiat.

At first the United States refused to accept the declaration, arguing that countries without strong navies needed to enlist privateers, but it had accepted its provisions by the time of the Civil War. Though theoretically in force during the world wars, the declaration was undermined by submarine warfare and artificially expanded lists of contraband.

Paris, Treaty of (1856) Agreement that ended the CRIMEAN WAR. In general it checked Russian designs to acquire power in the BALKANS at the expense of the OTTOMAN EMPIRE. The terms were negotiated by delegations from France, Great Britain, Russia, Turkey, Sardinia, Prussia, and Austria at the Congress of PARIS. Russia ceded the left bank of the lower Danube River to Moldavia and surrendered its claims as protector of Christian rights in the Ottoman Empire. The Czar also agreed to the military neutralization of the Black Sea and its opening to international commerce. The Danube was declared an international waterway.

Moldavia, Wallachia, and Serbia were established as autonomous principalities under European protection. The prewar borders of Turkey and Russia in Asia were restored. The European powers guaranteed the integrity of the Ottoman Empire while the empire agreed to improve the legal status of Christians within its borders. The Treaty of San Stefano and the Congress of BERLIN altered some of the treaty's provisions.

Paris Commune (March–May 1871) Revolutionary uprising. In the wake of France's defeat in the FRANCO-PRUSSIAN WAR, resentment over the harsh terms of peace and the repressive measures of the provisional government of the THIRD REPUBLIC led to an uprising in Paris. The Commune was created by an alliance of radical republicans (Jacobins) and utopian socialists, but it had little time to develop a clear ideology or effective institutions. The provisional government led by LOUIS-ADOLPHE THIERS organized an army and moved into Paris. Resistance was fierce, but the Communards were defeated and thousands were summarily executed. The Commune was called a proletarian revolution by Marxists but probably had more in common with Parisian uprisings going back to the French Revolution. The Commune sparked similar uprisings in other French cities. The memory of its brutal suppression fanned political hatred for years afterward.

Parkes, Bessie Raynor (1829–1925) English feminist activist, writer, and editor. Born in Birmingham, the daughter of radical politician Joseph Parkes, she published two volumes of poetry in her youth before turning to prose works on women's issues, including *Remarks on the Education of Girls* (1854) and *Essays on Woman's Work* (1865). With other British feminists of the 1850s and 1860s, such as Barbara Leigh Smith Bodichon, Mary Howitt, and Anna Jameson, she struggled to change married women's property laws, campaigned to elect JOHN STUART MILL to Parliament, and cofounded the LANGHAM PLACE CIRCLE, a group dedicated to advancing women's rights in education, employment, and other areas. She was cofounder and editor of the *English Woman's Journal* (1858–64). Conversion to Roman Catholicism, disillusionment about the movement, and marriage to Frenchman Louis Belloc combined to motivate her withdrawal from feminist activism by the end of the 1860s.

Parkman, Francis (1823–1893) American historian. Born into a well-to-do family in Boston, he followed his education at Harvard with the first of many journeys into the wilderness. With cousin Quincy Adams Shaw he lived with the Sioux Indians in Wyoming in 1846. His experiences resulted in his first book, *The Oregon Trail* (1847; rereleased as *The California and Oregon Trail* in 1849 and later named *The Oregon Trail*). Following his return from the West he experienced physical and mental debilitation, which along with limited eyesight plagued him for the rest of his life. Nonetheless he traveled the West to research his books, which include *History of the Conspiracy of the Pontiac* (1851; retitled *The Conspiracy of Pontiac and the Indian War After the Conquest of Canada* in 1870), *France and England in North America: Pioneers of France in the New World* (seven volumes, 1865), *Jesuits in North America in the Seventeenth Century* (1867), *The Discovery of the Great West* (1869; revised in 1878 as

LaSalle and the Discovery of the Great West), *The Old Regime in Canada* (1874), *Count Frontenac and New France Under Louis XIV* (1877), *Montcalm and Wolfe* (1884), and *A Half-Century of Conflict* (1892). The final two volumes represent strongly written, highly respected studies of the French and Indian war. His works are considered historical standards, although anti-French bias and racism toward Native Americans has diminished their luster. His only novel was *Vassall Morton* (1856).

Parnell, Charles Stewart (1846–1891) Irish politician. Parnell was the son of an American woman and a Protestant landlord from IRELAND. He attended Cambridge but did not earn a degree. For a while he enjoyed the pleasures of a country gentleman before standing for Parliament in 1875.

Parnell entered Parliament when ISAAC BUTT organized most of the Irish members around the HOME RULE issue. However, Butt and his followers failed to advance the cause against the opposition of the LIBERAL PARTY and the CONSERVATIVE PARTY. Parnell's charisma, iron will, and disdain for the tradition of parliamentary procedures attracted a small number of supporters. They set about holding up government business through filibusters and other delaying tactics. Parnell's strategy and leadership transformed the Irish question into the dominant issue in Parliament.

By the time Butt died in 1879, Parnell dominated the Irish members. This status was ratified in 1880 when he was elected head of the IRISH PARTY. In 1880 he also began a passionate love affair with KATHARINE "KITTY" O'SHEA, the wife of a fellow Irish member of Parliament.

Unlike Butt, Parnell realized that parliamentary politics alone would not make Home Rule a reality. He held discussions with the militant FENIANS, or Irish Republican Brotherhood (IRB) during the late 1870s. Parnell won their substantial financial support and several IRB members in Parliament helped him win the party leadership. In winning this support, Parnell gave the impression that he supported not merely Home Rule and Irish control of domestic affairs but complete independence from Great Britain. His talks with the Fenians also caused apprehension among Home Rule foes regarding his commitment to peaceful and parliamentary change.

Parnell also saw the value of supporting agrarian agitation and became the president of MICHAEL DAVITT'S newly formed LAND LEAGUE in 1879. Though officially opposed to violence, the league supported force against landlords, their agents, and tenant farmers who flouted its wishes. Parnell had begun the delicate balancing act of trying to accommodate both the violent and parliamentary factions of the Irish nationalist movement.

Parnell was jailed in 1881 by the Liberal government of WILLIAM GLADSTONE for supporting the league. The league itself was outlawed the same year. He was released after he agreed to temper violence in the countryside in exchange for protection from eviction for tenants in arrears and repeal of the COERCION ACTS, under which other league leaders had been arrested. This informal and undocumented agreement came to be known as the "Kilmainham Treaty," named after the jail where Parnell had been held.

Relations between Parnell and Gladstone were strained by the murder of two English officials in Dublin in 1882—the infamous PHOENIX PARK MURDERS. Parnell denounced the murders, which had been committed by a splinter group of the IRB, but the IRB refused to condemn the act. Parliament passed another Coercion Bill, which Parnell felt compelled to oppose.

In October 1882, Parnell founded the Irish National League, which gave the Irish Party a national structure and enforced discipline over nominees. In 1885, Parnell pressured Gladstone to act on Home Rule by voting with the Conservatives to end the Gladstone government. The Conservatives found themselves dependent on Parnell's Irish members for their majority but would not come to terms with him.

The election later that year was the first one held after the enlargement of the electorate by the REFORM BILL OF 1884. The election gave Parnell control of an Irish Party swing vote with which he could exploit the conflict between the Liberal and Conservative parties. Bolstering this strong hand was the impression that Parnell was restraining the more radical elements of the agrarian and nationalist movements.

Gladstone quickly introduced the first Home Rule Bill, but his control over the Liberal Party was not as complete as Parnell's over the Irish Party: The bill, which would have given Ireland its own legislative and executive departments, albeit still subject to the English Parliament, was defeated 341–311. Many Liberals opposed it because they believed that Parnell wanted Irish independence and would not accept anything less. Parnell denied dissatisfaction with the bill, but his association with the IRB and earlier speeches alluding to Irish independence gave many pause. Gladstone's government fell on this vote. A new coalition of Conservatives and those Liberals dedicated to maintaining the union between Ireland and Britain controlled the government for the next six years. Parnell's ultimate intentions never became known because he did not live to see another Home Rule vote.

Parnell had continued his affair with Katharine O'Shea, who had borne him three children and who had stopped living with her husband. Their relationship was an open secret among Irish and English political leaders. Her husband, Captain William O'Shea, had closed his eyes to the affair until 1886 when he unsuccessfully tried to convince his wife to end the relationship. It is characteristic of Parnell's arrogance that he feared no fallout from his actions. O'Shea sued for divorce in 1889, naming Parnell as correspondent. Parnell assured Party members that his political stature would be untouched by the divorce suit. Having just survived a clumsy forgery scheme that linked him to the Phoenix Park murders, he was at the height of his popularity. The court granted a divorce in 1890 after a highly publicized trial, and Parnell married Katharine soon after. The party still gave Parnell a unanimous vote of confidence, but Gladstone insisted that Parnell be removed from his leadership post. If not, the alliance between the Home Rulers and the Liberals would end.

Faced with this ultimatum the party rescinded its earlier support of Parnell and voted him out of power. The party became bitterly split between his supporters and the "anti-Parnellites," with opposition to Parnell encouraged by Ireland's Roman Catholic hierarchy. He ran his own candidates against the official party nominees in a series of elections, losing all of them by wide margins. Ten years would pass before the party healed its wounds and once again held the balance of power in the House of Commons.

Parry, Sir [Charles] Hubert [Hastings] (1848–1918) English composer and musical historian. With Irish-born composer CHARLES VILLIERS STANFORD, he was one of the leaders of the English Musical Renaissance. Specializing in choral works, his compositions included several settings of Milton poems, including *Blest Pair of Sirens* (1887), *Ode to St. Cecilia's Day* (1889), and *L'Allegro ed il Penseroso* (1890). He also set the Blake poem *Jerusalem* to music and composed *The Pied Piper of Hamelin* (1905). He directed the Royal College of Music from 1894, was knighted in 1898, and was made a baronet in 1903. He was professor of music at Oxford from 1900 to 1908.

passementerie Decorative items. These trimmings and cosmetic attachments, such as tassels, lace, and fringes, were used in Victorian home decor. The word is derived from the French word *passement,* which means "lace."

Pasteur, Louis (1822–1895) French chemist and bacteriologist. Pasteur formulated the GERM THEORY OF DISEASE, developed the modern technique of immunization, and produced numerous vaccines. He is also credited as the founder of the science of microbiology. Though best known for his work with microorganisms, he was educated in Paris in physics and chemistry, and made his first major discovery of optical activity in the field of stereochemistry, the branch of chemistry concerned with the structure of molecules, by identifying optical isomers, asymmetric forms of a substance that can rotate the plane of polarized light.

While a chemistry professor and dean of sciences at the University of Lille (1854–57), Pasteur began investigating the problem of souring in wine. His studies established the role of microorganisms in fermentation and led him to develop the technique of pasteurization, heating at high temperatures to destroy bacteria. The technique helped rescue France's wine and beer industries, and Pasteur on a lifelong course of studying microorganisms.

Through his studies of microorganisms, Louis Pasteur established the basis for immunization against contagious diseases. Painting by Albert Edelfelt.

In 1860, Pasteur demonstrated conclusively that microorganisms were not created by spontaneous generation but by transmission from the environment. In 1862 he developed the germ theory of disease, the view that contagious and infectious diseases are caused by microorganisms.

The remainder of Pasteur's life was spent researching the causes of diseases, such as pebrine in silkworms, anthrax, CHOLERA, diphtheria, fowl cholera, TUBERCULOSIS, and rabies, and developing vaccines to immunize people and animals against them. He drew on his knowledge of the work of English physician Edward Jenner (1749–1823), who developed a smallpox vaccine in the late 1790s, and his observations that recovery from an infectious disease gave immunity against further infection. His best known vaccines, against anthrax and rabies, were developed in 1881 and 1885, respectively.

From 1888 until his death Pasteur was the director of the Institut Pasteur in Paris, which still thrives as an international focal point for the study of infectious diseases and other disciplines related to microorganisms.

Pater, Walter Horatio (1839–1894) English critic and essayist. Born in London, he was educated at King's School, Canterbury, and at Queen's College, Oxford, where he lived for the rest of his life. After becoming a fellow of Brasenose College, Oxford, in 1864, Pater began writing essays on Leonardo da Vinci, Michelangelo, and other Renaissance figures; these were later collected in *Studies in the History of the Renaissance* (1873). Through his essays Pater developed a personal aesthetic embodied in the frequently misunderstood quote: "burn always with . . . [a] hard, gem-like flame."

Pater's emphasis on the appreciation of beauty and *carpe diem* philosophy brought him a small but devoted following, including OSCAR WILDE, and greatly influenced the ART-FOR-ART'S SAKE movement of the late nineteenth century.

In 1885, Pater provided further detail to his philosophy in *Marius the Epicurean,* in which he chronicled the spiritual growth of a young Roman who adopts the Epicurean and Stoic philosophies before opting for the Christian ideal.

Pater's critical essays differed greatly from his contemporaries because he concentrated solely on an artwork's essential quality, disavowing moral or utilitarian considerations. These essays were later collected and published in 1889 as *Appreciations.*

Pathé, Charles (1863–1957) French film pioneer. Born in Chevry-Cossigny, Pathé achieved his first industrial business success demonstrating and selling the PHONOGRAPHS of THOMAS ALVA EDISON across France. By 1897 he had extended his commitment to new technology by directing films, selling MOTION PICTURE projectors, and forming a business partnership with his brothers called Pathé Frères. Not until the first decade of the twentieth century did Pathé become known as a major European film company. In the years before World War I it was the largest film company in the world, known particularly for its comedies and its Pathé-Journal newsreels. By the middle of World War I, Pathé lost his world monopoly; by 1929 he had divested his interests and retired.

patience Card game. The British synonym for the card game solitaire, it was very popular in the Victorian era.

Patmore, Coventry Kersey Dighton (1823–1896) English poet and critic. Born at Woodford, Essex, he was the son of a critic and journalist. Educated privately at home and in Paris, he became an assistant librarian at the BRITISH MUSEUM in 1846 and worked there for nearly two decades. During that time he became associated with the PRE-RAPHAELITES. His works included *Poems* (1844) and *The Angel in the House* (1854–63), a popular four-part sequence of poems celebrating married love.

In 1862 his wife Emily died. Two years later he underwent a significant spiritual change when he visited Rome and met the woman who was to become his second wife, a convert to Roman Catholicism. Patmore was received into the Roman Catholic Church shortly before the marriage. He resigned from the British Museum and devoted himself to a new literary view of earthly love as a sign of divine love, notably in *The Unknown Eros* (1877). In addition to poems such as "Amelia," he also wrote critical and philosophical prose, including *Principle in Art* (1879) and *The Rod, the Root, and the Flower* (1895). Often experimenting with meter and language, he corresponded on these subjects with fellow Roman Catholic poet GERARD MANLEY HOPKINS.

Patti, Adelina [Adela Juana Maria] (1843–1919) Italian coloratura soprano. Born in Spain of Italian parents, Patti spent her childhood in New York City, where she trained in voice and made her operatic debut. Known for her wide range and great beauty, she spent the next four decades appearing in operas throughout the world, particularly at London's COVENT GARDEN. She made her last public appearance in 1914.

Pavlov, Ivan Petrovich (1849–1936) Russian physiologist. The son of a priest, Pavlov studied at his local seminary but was strongly influenced by the scientific writings of the day, particularly I. M. Sechenov's *Reflexes of the Brain,* which inspired Pavlov to leave his theological study, enter the University of St. Petersburg, and take classes in the natural sciences.

Pavlov received his doctorate in medicine in 1883, and his research on blood circulation earned him a two-year scholarship to study in Germany. After his return he was appointed professor of physiology at the Military Medical Academy in St. Petersburg, and in 1891 he was named director of the new Institute of Experimental Medicine, a post he maintained until his death.

At the institute Pavlov began his study of the digestive processes, which led to his discovery of the enzyme enterokinase, an explanation of the role of enzymes, and a new theory of digestion. For his efforts Pavlov was awarded the Nobel Prize for physiology in 1904. His study of digestion also led to his famous theories of behavior. In 1901, Pavlov began demonstrating that if he rang a bell each time a dog was fed, the dog would salivate at the sound of the bell even if no food was present. Pavlov's demonstration of this "conditioned reflex" led to his further study of animal behavior, applying his theories to human behavior, and the treatment of mental illness. His studies and theories had a profound impact in the fields of physiology, psychiatry, and psychotherapy, evidenced by the number of Pavlovian institutes, laboratories, and societies established around the globe.

Paxton, Sir Joseph (1801–1865) English architect and horticulturist. Paxton had a successful career as a gardener at Chatsworth and ultimately became superintendent of the Duke of Devonshire's garden, which he remodeled in 1836 with a great conservatory (see also GREENHOUSE). The conservatory led to his commission to design a similar but larger glass and iron structure known as the CRYSTAL PALACE for the GREAT EXHIBITION OF 1851 at London; the Crystal Palace was erected again at Sydenham, mainly from the same materials. He was knighted for his work.

Paxton also designed the mansion of Baron James de Rothschild at Ferrieres, France, and organized the army work corps in Crimea. He published the *Pocket Botanical Dictionary* in 1840 and was a member of Parliament from 1854.

Peach Melba Dessert. Made of vanilla ice cream layered with peaches cooked in vanilla syrup and topped with raspberry puree, the dessert was created by French chef Auguste Escoffier for Australian opera singer NELLIE MELBA following a performance at COVENT

GARDEN in 1894. Originally comprised of only peaches and ice cream, the raspberry puree was added by Escoffier in 1900 when the dessert was added to the menu of London's Carlton Hotel where he was chef.

Peel, Sir Robert (1788–1850) English politician. The son of a successful cotton manufacturer, he graduated from Oxford and became a Tory member of Parliament in 1809. As chief secretary for Ireland (1812–18) he organized a police force and opposed ending discriminatory laws against Irish Catholics. In 1819 he ushered a law through Parliament that reinstated the gold standard and stabilized the currency.

As home secretary (1822–27) he organized a sweeping reform of the criminal code. He established the London POLICE force in 1829, and its members became known as "peelers" or "bobbies." He resigned in 1827 in opposition to greater civil and political rights for Irish Catholics. Reappointed home secretary in 1828, he dropped his aversion to Catholic emancipation when DANIEL O'CONNELL, head of the movement, was elected to Parliament. He helped repeal some of the laws regarding Catholic rights but lost his seat as a result.

Peel opposed the REFORM BILL OF 1832, but his refusal to establish a Tory ministry to stop its passage alienated him from the party. Other disaffected Tories such as BENJAMIN DISRAELI and WILLIAM GLADSTONE, later the LIBERAL PARTY leader, began forming the CONSERVATIVE PARTY with Peel as its leader. He was prime minister briefly (1834–35) but resigned after an altercation with Queen VICTORIA over the BEDCHAMBER CRISIS. Six years later the Conservatives gained a majority in the House of Commons, and Peel again became prime minister (1841–46).

Peel's government reestablished the income tax, passed the BANK CHARTER ACT OF 1844, and fostered free trade by radically reducing tariffs. His foreign office improved relations with France and settled border disputes with the United States (see Lord ASHBURTON). His recall of the Earl of AUCKLAND, governor-general of India, helped temporarily to stabilize the empire's position in Afghanistan after some military reversals. Peel commissioned a study of landlord-tenant relations in Ireland and increased government contributions to the Irish Catholic Church.

Peel's government is best known for its repeal of the CORN LAWS. After he had already reduced some duties, the misery resulting from the IRISH POTATO FAMINE helped convince him that the tariffs on grain imports could not be maintained. His push for repeal split the party and forced him to resign in 1845. When the Whigs failed to form a government, he returned to office, and the Corn Laws were repealed over the bitter opposition of the gentry. Forced to resign again, he spent the rest of his life campaigning for free trade. His memoirs were published in 1856.

Peirce, Charles Sanders (1839–1914) American mathematician and philosopher. Born in Cambridge, Massachusetts, the son of mathematician Benjamin Peirce, he attended Harvard. It was Peirce who along with WILLIAM JAMES, developed the term "pragmatism" to refer to a school of philosophy which holds that the meaning and truth of ideas is to be sought in their practical consequences and that the purpose of thought is to guide action. Working as an astronomer, physicist, and professor at Harvard and Johns Hopkins University, Peirce published on such diverse topics as logic, epistemology, and mathematics. He did not become widely known until the posthumous publication in 1923 of *Chance, Love, and Logic,* a collection of his essays. Among those influenced by his work was educator and philosopher John Dewey.

pelerine Ladies' collar. Usually made of crochet, lace, or linen, it was capelike in appearance and had hanging ends in front. For the early years of the Victorian era, blouses and shirts did not have collars sewn in place.

Pendleton Civil Service Act U.S. law. Enacted on January 16, 1883, to combat political corruption in the hiring of federal employees, the bill was sponsored by Senator George H. Pendleton (1825–1889) in the wake of the assassination of President JAMES GARFIELD by a disappointed office seeker (1881). The act created the Civil Service Commission, established CIVIL SERVICE examinations, and required hiring by merit.

penny post See POSTAL SERVICES.

penny press See PERIODICALS.

penny theater Popular form of entertainment. Also known as a "gaff," the penny theater began in London in the 1830s. It was typically erected in converted shops or sheds; the audience was mostly boys, ranging in age from eight to the mid-teens. The shows, about forty-five minutes long, consisted of melodramas, burlesques, and humorous songs. Under pressure from social reformers who believed that penny theaters were a bad influence on youth, they were closed down in the 1850s and 1860s.

periodic table of elements System of organizing chemical components. First published by Russian chemist DMITRY MENDELEYEV in 1869, the system is based on the periodic law discovered by Mendeleyev and, independently, by German chemist Lothar Meyer. The principle states that the properties of ELEMENTS are a periodic function of their atomic weight or the relative mass of the atom. The horizontal rows, or periods, of the table were arranged by atomic weight and by valence, or the number of single bonds an atom can form with other atoms. In addition, each vertical column of the table represented a family of elements with similar properties.

Attempts had previously been made to bring order to the mass of known facts about the elements. English chemist JOHN ALEXANDER REINA NEWLANDS had suggested in 1863 that elements follow a "law of octaves." He arranged the elements in groups of eight in order of increasing atomic mass; on the analogy of musical octaves, he proposed that every element in the series repeated the properties of the element eight places away from it. The table did not account for many of the observed facts about elements and was rejected.

Mendeleyev's table was a vast improvement, allowing chemists to study the elements in a more systematic fashion. Moreover, Mendeleyev predicted that unknown elements with specific properties would be discovered to fill the spaces left blank in his table. He detailed three of these in particular: eka-boron, eka-aluminum, and eka-silicon. Within the next twenty years his predictions were borne out as scandium, gallium, and germanium respectively, were discovered.

The periodic table was revised in 1894 with the discovery of argon by British scientists Lord RAYLEIGH and Sir William Ramsay (1852–1916). Argon was placed alone in a new column, which Mendeleyev predicted would contain other INERT GASES, or unreactive elements, as yet unknown. These were soon discovered.

The periodic table was still flawed by the fact that certain elements had to be placed out of order to fit in their appropriate families. These discrepancies were resolved in 1914 when English physicist Henry G. J. Moseley

(1887–1915) completed the task of deriving the atomic numbers of elements—the quantity of positive charge on an atomic nucleus, corresponding to the number of protons. Moseley revised the periodic table in order of increasing atomic number rather than atomic weight, thus eliminating the discrepancies.

periodicals Regularly issued publications. Nineteenth-century technical innovations such as rotary printing presses, steam power, and cheap wood-pulp newsprint facilitated the mass production of newspapers, magazines, and journals. The availability of the telegraph for transmitting dispatches enabled rapid reporting from distant places. The one-pence cost of many periodicals in Great Britain and the United States gave rise to the term "penny press."

In England, journalists were aided by the abolition of TAXES ON KNOWLEDGE. Beginning in the 1840s such popular British newspapers as the *DAILY TELEGRAPH, Weekly Times, LONDON DAILY NEWS,* and *Lloyd's Weekly Newspaper* were printed and distributed at a low cost inconceivable in an earlier era.

Miscellanies such as *Fraser's* and *MACMILLAN'S* (1859) were a popular magazine format. One of the best of this breed was *Household Words,* a weekly magazine owned and edited by novelist CHARLES DICKENS from 1850 until 1859 in an attempt to capitalize on his growing literary fame. Printed on twenty-four double-column pages, *Household Words* ran a medley of light features, such as "Valentine's Day at the Post-Office," whimsical "think pieces," such as the novelist ELIZABETH GASKELL on the difficulties of disappearing, and popular verse, as well as "investigative stories." In one celebrated series, Dickens himself reported on having accompanied a police detective on his investigations into the criminal underground.

Some one hundred thousand copies of the first issue of *Household Words* were reportedly sold, and the success of the venture led to the production of a supplement, *The Household Narrative of Current Events.* In some ways a precursor of today's large metropolitan dailies, this periodical presented, without editorial comment, a skillfully condensed summary of all important news under the headings of Parliament and Politics, Law and Crime, Accident and Disaster, and Social, Sanitary, and Emigration Figures.

Newspaper formats changed rapidly in the 1880s; papers such as *The Pall Mall Gazette* and *The Star* added interviews, sports coverage, gossip, and sensational crime reporting. A leading publisher of the "new journalism" was George Newnes, who founded *Tit-Bits* in 1881. The higher end of the business also underwent change: Respected quarterly journals such as *Edinburgh Review* (1802) and *Quarterly Review* (1809) lost ground to monthlies such as *Westminster Review* (1824) and *THE FORTNIGHTLY REVIEW* (1865). The Victorian Age also saw new weeklies such as *Saturday Review* (1855) and *Academy* (1869).

Similar variety presented itself in American periodicals. Controlled for much of the Victorian era by the New England nexus of intellectuals, the more serious journals included *Harper's Magazine* (1850), edited for a time by WILLIAM DEAN HOWELLS, and *Atlantic Monthly* (1858), whose first editor was JAMES RUSSELL LOWELL. Short-lived but influential was the transcendentalist magazine *The Dial* (1840–44). Founded by RALPH WALDO EMERSON and MARGARET FULLER, among others, it was responsible for publishing the early works of HENRY DAVID THOREAU and other transcendentalists.

By the end of the century, magazines representing other geographical areas, intellectual communities, and public interests were becoming known. The *Overland Monthly,* notable for publishing the ribald tales of BRET HARTE, originated in California in 1868. Based in New York, Irish-born American Samuel McClure's MCCLURE'S MAGAZINE became known for its investigative works on business and government corruption, commonly known after the turn of the century as muckraking. Its reporters included IDA TARBELL and Lincoln Steffens. Some general magazines were linked to book publishers, as with *Scribner's Magazine* and Charles Scribner's Sons, and HARPER'S MAGAZINES. Other magazines took a new lease on life during the Victorian era. The venerable but struggling *Saturday Evening Post,* founded in 1821, gained a wide new readership when it was purchased for $1,000, revamped, and reduced in price by American businessman Cyrus Curtis in 1897.

Ladies' magazines, including the *Ladies' Home Journal* (1883) and *Godey's Lady's Book* (1830), particularly under the editorship of SARAH JOSEPHA HALE, were important arbiters of social correctness and good taste. As ADVERTISING came to be more commonly accepted in periodicals, women's magazines became a direct link to the consumers who purchased most of the country's household goods.

Of the many dozens of newspapers originating during the Victorian era, three New York newspapers define the medium's range: *THE NEW YORK TIMES* (1851), which aimed at comprehensive reporting of national and international news, and news of the arts; the influential *New York Tribune* (1841), driven by the literary and political force of its founder HORACE GREELEY; and the tabloid *New York Herald* (1835), which provided sensationalistic coverage of public sensation and scandal (and always led in circulation). Other highly popular tabloid-style periodicals included the inventive *Frank Leslie's Illustrated Newspaper* (1855) and the flashy, graphic *Police Gazette* (1845).

In addition to Horace Greeley, other influential newspaper publishers included Americans WILLIAM RANDOLPH HEARST and JOSEPH PULITZER. In 1887 Hearst began his vast publishing empire when he took over the *San Francisco Examiner;* seven years later he purchased the New York *Morning Journal.* With both he instituted the inflammatory reporting and presentation known as yellow journalism, which would set the tone for newspaper publishing over the next few decades.

In light of Hearst's publishing style, the Hungarian-born Pulitzer also engaged in the news stunts of yellow journalism on his papers, the *St. Louis Post-Dispatch* and the *New York World* and *Evening World.* The wars between the New York daily papers raged in the 1890s, ending with Hearst becoming the dominant publisher as the new century dawned.

In the early twentieth century, Pulitzer returned to respectable newspaper publishing, transforming his newspapers. Upon his death in 1911 he endowed the Pulitzer Prize for excellence in journalism.

Perry, Matthew Calbraith (1794–1858) American naval officer. Perry was born in Rhode Island and served in the Navy during the War of 1812. He transported freed slaves to Liberia in Africa before being assigned to the Brooklyn Navy Yard, where he helped develop the Navy's first steam vessel, which he later commanded. He commanded the U.S. squadron that helped suppress the slave trade (1843–44). During the MEXICAN WAR he headed U.S. naval forces in the Gulf of Mexico.

Perry's most famous expedition occurred in 1853–54 when he led American vessels into Edo Bay in JAPAN to open negotiations with the reluctant Japanese. Perry, through veiled threats and diplomacy, persuaded the isolationist government to sign the Treaty of Kanagawa that opened two ports to U.S. traders and provided protection for shipwrecked U.S. sailors.

Philippines Tropical archipelago of over seven thousand islands off southeast Asia. The largest islands of the Philippines are Luzon, with the capital Manila, and Mindanao. Most of the people are ethnic Malays called Filipinos. Spanish explorer Ferdinand Magellan first visited the island chain in 1521. It was a Spanish colony named for Philip II from 1542 until 1898. In 1896, EMILIO AGUINALDO led a revolt against Spanish rule; aided by the UNITED STATES, and the SPANISH-AMERICAN WAR, the rebels succeeded in 1898. Aguinaldo's forces then turned against the United States, which had taken possession of the Philippines. The United States won and maintained colonial rule until the mid-twentieth century. The Philippines gained full independence in 1946.

Phoenix Park murders Politically charged crime in IRELAND. In 1882, British prime minister WILLIAM GLADSTONE appointed Lord Frederick Cavendish, his nephew by marriage, to the important post of chief secretary of Ireland. On arriving on May 6, Cavendish was hacked to death outside the vice-regal lodge in Dublin's Phoenix Park. Thomas Burke, the undersecretary, was found dead alongside him. Both had been murdered with foot-long surgical knives.

The assassinations were the work of the Irish National Invincibles, a splinter group of the Irish Republican Brotherhood, or FENIANS. The crimes led Gladstone to impose a new round of coercion measures in Ireland. CHARLES STEWART PARNELL, the leader of the IRISH PARTY in Parliament, denounced the murders but also objected to Gladstone's Crime Act. This disagreement delayed the introduction of the first HOME RULE bill in the House of Commons.

phonograph Device for reproducing sound. The phonograph was developed by U.S. inventor THOMAS ALVA EDISON in 1877. Originally the sound was recorded on tinfoil-coated cylinders and was transmitted through a needle or stylus. Edison substituted wax for the tinfoil and added a loudspeaker in 1889–90. About

The invention of the phonograph in 1877 revolutionized the concept of entertainment in homes around the world.

1890, German-born American inventor Emile Berliner (1851–1929) improved the device by substituting flat disks for the cylinders. Records using Berliner's format displaced MUSIC BOX technology and remained the favorite vehicle for home and radio music until the 1980s.

photoelectric effect Emission of electrons by substances, particularly metals, when struck by light. German physicist Heinrich Rudolph Hertz, who discovered RADIO WAVES, discovered the effect in 1887 when he noted that electric current flowed more easily across a gap when the negative terminal, the one issuing the spark, was struck by ultraviolet light. The effect went unexplained until 1905 when German physicist Albert Einstein used it as evidence for quantum theory—the theory that light is composed of discrete packets of energy, or quanta, called photons. According to Einstein, photons of sufficient energy striking a surface liberate electrons, resulting in a flow of electric current.

photography Process of mechanically reproducing a permanent image on paper. Photography had its beginnings in the late 1820s with the development by Frenchman Joseph-Nicéphore Niepce (1765–1833) of a heliograph, the direct positive image on a pewter plate that was exposed in a camera obscura for several hours. In 1839 his business partner LOUIS-JACQUES DAGUERRE created the daguerreotype, an image made from copper plates treated with silver and exposed in a camera. Daguerre's process came into greater prominence when the rights to it were purchased by the French government and the process was made available to the public. Scores of daguerreotype portrait studios thrived during the middle of the century, making the once exclusive human portrait available to the average citizen.

The modern system of positive-negative photography was begun with the 1841 patent by English inventor WILLIAM HENRY FOX TALBOT for the calotype, a process for printing negatives on silver chloride paper. A further refinement was the development in 1851 by English photographer Frederick Scott Archer of the wet-collodion process, which employed a glass negative that was exposed in the camera. The unwieldy process remained in use until 1880 when the dry-plate glass negative was developed. Much easier for photographers to use, it popularized photography for the amateur. Along with the development in 1888 of roll film by American inventor George Eastman (1854–1932), it helped to account for the huge rise in camera use in the last decade of the nineteenth century.

Notable photographers of the Victorian era include pioneering war photographers ROGER FENTON, who shot the Crimean War, and MATHEW BRADY who shot the U.S. Civil War, French photographic stylist EUGÈNE ATGET, U.S. photojournalist JACOB RIIS, and U.S. exhibitor ALFRED STIEGLITZ.

pi (π) Ratio of the circumference of a circle to its diameter. A nonrepeating decimal, it has an approximate value of 3.14159265. Although it cannot be known exactly, it has been calculated approximately since antiquity. In 1853, English mathematician William Shanks calculated pi to 707 decimal places, further than anyone before him. The advent of computers in the twentieth century showed, however, that Shanks had made a mistake in the 528th place, causing every number thereafter to be wrong.

It had been known since the eighteenth century that pi is an irrational number, a real number that cannot be expressed as the quotient of two integers. In 1882, German mathematician Ferdinand von Lindemann (1852–1939) showed that it is a TRANSCENDENTAL NUMBER: It cannot serve as a solution to an algebraic equation with integer coefficients. This had implications for the famous problem of "squaring the circle," first posed by the ancient Greeks: Given a circle of any area, construct a square of the same area, using only a straightedge and a compass in a finite number of steps. Because pi is transcendental, that problem is impossible to solve in principle.

Pierce, Franklin (1804–1869) Fourteenth president of the UNITED STATES (1853–57). Born in Hillsboro, New Hampshire, Pierce graduated from Bowdoin College and practiced law in his hometown. After serving in the state legislature, Pierce, a DEMOCRAT, was elected to Congress in 1833 and then to the Senate in 1837. He resigned his Senate seat in 1842 to return to his law practice, which was briefly interrupted by service in the MEXICAN WAR (1847–48).

He was nominated as his state's favorite son candidate at the 1852 presidential convention. Forty-eight ballots later he was chosen as a compromise candidate by a party driven by the SLAVERY issue. He defeated Whig Winfield Scott.

Pierce achieved some foreign policy successes, including the GADSDEN PURCHASE and a trade treaty with Japan; however, his plans to annex Hawaii, Alaska, and Cuba failed. Domestically, he tried to reconcile the South and North by supporting the Kansas-Nebraska Act, which allowed settlers in those territories to admit or ban slavery. This alienated northern Democrats, while the defeat of slavery in Kansas disappointed southern Democrats. The party denied him the 1856 nomination, and he returned to New Hampshire.

piezoelectricity Electric phenomenon. Discovered in 1880 by French chemist PIERRE CURIE, piezoelectricity is an electric potential generated across the opposite faces of certain nonconducting crystals, such as quartz, by the application of pressure (Greek *pieza*) between the faces. Conversely, subjecting the crystal to an electric potential causes it to compress as though under pressure. Curie noted that if the electric potential is changed rapidly, the crystal compresses and expands in harmony with the change, and the vibrating crystal emanates ultrasonic waves, or waves above the range of human hearing. This phenomenon became essential to the invention of the microphone, record player, and quartz watch.

Pinero, Sir Arthur Wing (1855–1934) English playwright. Known both for his comedies and social dramas, Pinero was originally a character actor. He first achieved fame as a dramatist for his farces, which included *The Magistrate* (produced in 1885), *The Schoolmistress* (1886), *Dandy Dick* (1887), and *The Cabinet Minister* (1890). He then wrote a number of "problem" plays dealing with the plight of women in a conservative society. *The Second Mrs. Tanqueray* (1893) was a great success; subsequent works, such as *The Notorious Mrs. Ebbsmith* (1895), and *Mid-Channel* (1909), were also popular. *Trelawny of the "Wells"* (1898), a nostalgic comedy set in the mid-Victorian theater world, is considered by many his finest play.

Pinero provided a rare example of a Victorian playwright whose serious works were commercial successes. After the turn of the century his popularity waned, though he continued to write. By the end of his life he had completed more than fifty plays.

Pinkerton, Allan (1819–1884) American detective. Born in Scotland, he came to the

United States in 1842. He founded the country's first private detective agency in Chicago in 1850. Having won fame for solving the Adams Express robberies, he guarded Abraham Lincoln on his journey to Washington, D.C., for his 1861 inauguration and directed an espionage system in 1861–62 behind Confederate lines during the CIVIL WAR. His agency later gathered the evidence that broke up the radical labor group the MOLLY MAGUIRES in 1875 and gained notoriety as a private security force hired by management to intimidate unionizing workers and break strikes, as was the case in the HOMESTEAD STRIKE.

Pissarro, Camille (1830–1903) French painter, teacher, and one of the founders of IMPRESSIONISM. Born in the Danish West Indies, Pissarro began studies at the Ecole des Beaux-Arts in 1855 and became a student of CAMILLE COROT. He came to know and be influenced by EDOUARD MANET, adopting the more naturalistic palette of the Impressionists. He became a member of the Impressionist group and was the only member to have his work represented at all eight of its exhibitions from 1874 to 1886. Influenced by the landscapes of English painter J. M. W. TURNER, he lightened his palette again and attempted light-producing techniques. After experimenting with POINTILLISM, he returned to his Impressionist beginnings for his final paintings at the end of the nineteenth century. Over the years he influenced many artists, including GEORGES SEURAT, PAUL GAUGUIN, and PAUL CÉZANNE.

Pius IX, Pope (1792–1878) Head of the Roman Catholic Church from 1846 to 1878. Born Giovanni Maria Mastai-Ferretti, his pontificate was the longest in the Church's history. He was driven from Rome by the REVOLUTIONS OF 1848 but returned in 1850 and ruled with military support from French leader NAPOLEON III. In 1854 he proclaimed the dogma of the IMMACULATE CONCEPTION, the belief that Mary, the mother of Jesus, was preserved from the effects of original sin from the moment of her conception. Pius IX witnessed the loss of the Papal States and the annexation of Rome by ITALY in 1870, thereafter considering himself a "prisoner of the Vatican" (see PAPACY). A dedicated opponent of religious liberalism and materialism, he expressed his conservative views in the encyclical *Quanta cura* (1864) and its attached *Syllabus of Errors.* He strengthened the central authority of his office by convening the VATICAN COUNCIL and persuading it to define the dogma of papal infallibility in 1870. The declaration fostered conflict between church and state governments across Europe, most notably in GERMANY where the unsuccessful struggle of Chancellor OTTO VON BISMARCK to assert control over the Church was known as *Kulturkampf* (1871–83) and outlasted Pius IX's reign.

Plessy v. Ferguson (1896) U.S. Supreme Court decision. The case concerned Louisiana's right to segregate railway carriages by race. The Court upheld the legality of "separate but equal" public facilities, leading to the expansion and entrenchment of southern segregation laws. The 1954 *Brown v. Board of Education* decision, overturned *Plessy v. Ferguson* and marked the beginning of the end of legalized segregation.

pneumatic tire Rubber tread over an air-filled tube and mounted on a rim. Invented by Englishman John Boyd Dunlop (1840–1921) in 1888, it drastically cut down on the noise and recoil of the wooden and metal wheels that had prevailed since the wheel's invention about 3000 B.C. The pneumatic tire became indispensable to the emerging AUTOMOBILE industry.

Poe, Edgar Allan (1809–1849) American poet and short-story writer. Through his reinvention and elevation of the short story, Poe helped to establish the United States as a nineteenth-century literary force. Born to traveling actors who died when he was three years old, Poe was raised by Virginia businessman John Allan and attended the University of Virginia until gambling debts led Allan to withdraw financial support. He entered the army and later West Point; during this period, he published his first collections of poems, *Tamerlane and Other Poems* (1827), *Tamerlane and Al Aaraaf, Tamerlane and Minor Poems* (1829), and *Poems by Edgar A. Poe, Second Edition* (1831). Following his time in the army, Poe lived with his aunt Maria Clemm and her daughter Virginia, and began to support himself as a journalist, critic, and short-story writer. After winning a prize for his story "AMS. Found in a Bottle," Poe was named editor of the *Southern Literary Messenger*. Around that time he also married his thirteen-year-old cousin Virginia.

Poe's drinking led to his removal as editor of the magazine. He then spent the next decade pursuing journalistic careers in New York City and Philadelphia. He published several influential essays of literary theory as well as stories, including "Ligeia" (1838), "The Fall of the House of Usher" (1839), and the detective story "The Murders in the Rue Morgue" (1841), often said to have invented the genre (see also HOLMES, SHERLOCK). Poe's poem "The Raven" established him as a popular and important poet.

Although strongly affected by the 1847 death of his wife Virginia, to whom he had been devoted, he continued writing and traveling, revisiting Richmond, the town of his youth. On his return home from Richmond, he died under mysterious circumstances in Baltimore.

pointillism Artistic style. A technique of painting in which optical mixtures are formed by placing small dots or points of pure primary color in close juxtaposition to another so that they seem to merge, pointillism was exploited in NEO-IMPRESSIONISM, notably under GEORGES SEURAT who created larger units of color within a composition or entire pointillist compositions.

poker-work Decorative craft. Poker-work is a type of decoration in which patterns are burned onto a wooden surface with a hot metal tool, such as a poker, and then smoothed with sandpaper. It was practiced as a home craft as early as the eighteenth century. Like other home crafts, it gained renewed interest during the Victorian Age in the ARTS AND CRAFTS MOVEMENT.

police, English Civil protection force. The first modern police force in England was the Metropolitan Police Force, established in London in 1829 by Home Secretary Sir ROBERT PEEL. Before that, police work in Britain was largely an ad hoc matter, carried out by unpaid, poorly trained parish constables. Having established the Irish constabulary in 1814 when he was chief secretary for Ireland, Peel remodeled the London police force, making the constables full-time, salaried personnel within a systematic hierarchy. Constables answered to sergeants, who answered to inspectors, who answered to a superintendent, who answered to the home secretary. Their headquarters were at Scotland Yard, and like their Irish counterparts, they were nicknamed "peelers" in honor of Peel. By 1851 they were also called "roberts" and the more familiar "bobbies." In 1856 an act of Parliament established similar police forces in rural areas of England.

Polish rebellion (1863) Last and largest of a series of nationalist uprisings in Poland. Poland had been partitioned by RUSSIA, PRUSSIA, and AUSTRIA in 1792, with Russia taking the largest share. Discrimination and assimilationist policies of the controlling powers fueled nationalist agitation, particularly among students, wage earners, and the minor gentry. Revolts broke out in 1830 in Warsaw against the Russians in the "November Insurrection," in 1846 against the Russians and Austrians, and in 1848 against the Prussians in the "Ponzan uprising."

In the 1850s and 1860s an extensive radical nationalist underground developed with links to a similar Russian movement, the Land and Freedom Movement. In January 1863 a Polish national state was declared in Warsaw and a program of land redistribution was promised, to secure the support of the peasants. Guerrilla warfare began in Russian Poland, simultaneous with Land and Freedom attacks in Russia. Heavily outnumbered and outgunned, the Polish rebels hoped for foreign intervention. Austria and France expressed sympathy for the revolt but declined to support it, while Prussia actively cooperated with the Russians. Fighting lasted until early 1864 when the last guerrilla bands were dispersed. In response to the rebellion, the Russian government abolished serfdom in Russian Poland, as it had in Russia in 1861, but otherwise followed a policy of severe repression and Russification. The collapse of the rebellion of 1863 put hopes of Polish independence in abeyance until the chaos of World War I and the Russian Revolution.

Polk, James Knox (1795–1849) Eleventh president of the UNITED STATES (1845–49). Born in North Carolina, he practiced law in Tennessee until 1825 when he began a fourteen-year career in Congress that included four years as Speaker of the House (1835–39). A strong supporter of President ANDREW JACKSON, he favored territorial expansion and lower tariffs.

Governor of Tennessee from 1839 to 1841, Polk was nominated for president at the 1844 DEMOCRATIC PARTY convention after front runner MARTIN VAN BUREN alienated Jacksonians by opposing the annexation of Texas. Polk emerged from the ensuing deadlock as the country's first "dark horse" candidate.

As president, Polk settled the Oregon border dispute with England by signing the OREGON TREATY. When boundary talks with Mexico faltered and his offer to buy California was rebuffed, Polk arranged to provoke a Mexican attack that brought about war. The MEXICAN WAR and the Oregon settlement added about one million square miles to the country. The question of allowing SLAVERY in the Mexican territories became a prime cause of the CIVIL WAR.

Polk declined to run for reelection in 1848 and died three months after leaving office.

polonaise Polish national dance. Written in triple meter and moderate tempo, the polonaise is marked by sharply articulated rhythms. Originally a folk genre, the polonaise developed into a stylized courtly dance by the eighteenth century. It reached its highest expression in the nineteenth century in the thirteen examples by FRÉDÉRIC CHOPIN, which were heroic in form and nationalistic in theme.

Pony Express U.S. rapid mail delivery system. Developed by William Hepburn Russell and his express company, Russell, Majors, and Waddell, it employed several dozen riders and fast Indian horses to carry mail between 190 way stations linking Saint Joseph, Missouri, and Sacramento, California. A revenue-losing venture from the start, the Pony Express charged $2 to $10 per ounce depending on distance. The Pony Express ran for only eighteen months, from April 1860 to October 1861, before it was supplanted by the completion of the transcontinental TELEGRAPH line. See POSTAL SERVICES and WESTERN UNION.

Poor Law of 1834 British legislation. The law aimed at deterring poverty by making relief more oppressive than the lowest-paying job. The product of a royal commission report, the new poor law assumed that unemployment—which had risen massively in recent decades as a result of the dislocations caused by INDUSTRIALIZATION—was primarily due to the laziness of the poor who needed to be frightened into getting jobs rather than applying for relief. Since Elizabethan times, poor relief had been the responsibility of each parish, which appointed overseers for the task and often provided aid in the form of "outdoor allowances" to people living in their own homes. The Poor Law of 1834 shifted responsibility to a central board of commissioners in London who would oversee the work of local elected boards of guardians. Outdoor relief to the able-bodied was prohibited; the poor were to be forced to enter workhouses where the sexes were kept apart, children were separated from their parents, food and heat were scarce, and tedious and meaningless work was required.

The poor bitterly resented the law, and disturbances broke out against its enforcement. THOMAS CARLYLE attacked the bill, calling workhouses "Poor Law Bastilles." CHARLES DICKENS depicted the awful conditions of the workhouses in many of his writings. It soon became clear, however, that the law could not be completely enforced. Because outdoor relief to the able-bodied was cheaper than workhouses, it continued, eased by various loopholes in the law. No more than a third of able-bodied poor people on relief were ever actually in the workhouses. Nor was there a system of inspection to ensure that unpleasant workhouse conditions were uniformly maintained; they therefore varied widely from the relatively humane to the negligent and cruel. By century's end the workhouses were primarily institutions aimed at caring for the indigent sick, disabled, orphaned, and elderly rather than punitive institutions for the able-bodied.

poorhouse Publicly supported institution for the destitute. Distinguished from an almshouse, which was funded by private charity, in Great Britain the term "poorhouse" was gradually superseded by WORKHOUSE, which denoted the more regimented, punitive institutions mandated by the POOR LAW OF 1834.

In the United States, poorhouses existed as early as the mid-eighteenth century. Like their British counterparts, they were generally degrading, unpleasant places intended to discourage those seeking relief. Poorhouse inmates greatly outnumbered the staff, who had little authority over the noisy, rowdy squalor. The institutions were crowded and lacked adequate health care and food. The influx of millions of immigrants to the United States between 1820 and 1860 exacerbated the problem of poverty and added to the overcrowded conditions. Reform occurred when it became clear that it was far cheaper to put the poor on relief than to care for them in poorhouses, though vestiges of the system remained in the United States and Great Britain until the early twentieth century.

Pope See PAPACY.

Populist Party U.S. political party. During the late nineteenth century, falling commodity prices, climbing interest rates, severe drought conditions, and exorbitant railroad rates put tremendous pressure on American farmers. Mortgage foreclosures soared, and many independent farmers were forced to become tenants. Many of them blamed eastern bankers, railroad owners, and politicians for their declining fortunes.

Agrarian leaders met in Omaha, Nebraska, in July 1892 to form the National People's Party, commonly known as the Populist Party. Its platform called for free coinage of silver, government ownership of railroads, low-interest government loans, a graduated income tax, and other demands. Its presidential candidate, James Weaver, polled over a million votes and twenty-two electoral votes, the best third-party showing since the REPUBLICAN PARTY campaign in 1856. The Panic of 1893 worsened conditions, and the party won six Senate and seven House seats in 1894.

The DEMOCRATIC PARTY incorporated many Populist demands into its 1896 presidential platform, and Populist leaders decided to back the Democratic candidate, WILLIAM JENNINGS BRYAN. The victory of Republican WILLIAM MCKINLEY in the 1896 election, combined with rising prices and the inability of the Populists to forge an alliance with eastern workers, doomed the party. Despite its failures, many of its ideas influenced later Progressive Party politics and the policies of the New Deal.

pornography Sexually explicit material. The most common form of pornographic literature in Victorian England was a brown-paper-wrapped novel printed in Brussels or Paris and imported secretly under a false imprint. It cost about twenty guineas, which was expensive enough to keep it out of the hands of the working class. Pornographic magazines such as *The Boudoir,* first published in 1860, cost an expensive fifteen shillings for thirty-two pages of illustrations, a serial, and jokes. Pornographic photographs could be purchased for around a guinea each. The Obscene Publications Act of 1857 attempted to decrease the influx of pornographic material, but it had little effect.

The contents of the novels usually depicted a male protagonist controlling the object or objects of his desire, often through force, violence, and rape. Homosexual incidents were rare in Victorian literature, but a few homosexual novels were published, including the erotically titled *The Sins of the Cities of the Plain, or the Recollections of a Mary-Ann with Short Essays on Sodomy and Tribalism* (1881).

porridge Food. A staple food of nineteenth-century England, porridge is made of oatmeal or other types of meal boiled in milk or water.

Portugal Country in southwest Europe. It is bordered by Spain and the Atlantic Ocean. A great maritime power in the fifteenth and sixteenth centuries, with an overseas empire reaching to Asia, Africa, and the Americas, Portugal had long been in decline by the time of the Victorian era. Scattered colonies such as Brazil in SOUTH AMERICA, ANGOLA and MOZAMBIQUE in Africa, and Portuguese Timor (now part of INDONESIA) were all that remained of its empire. Under pressure from liberal opponents, Louis I (reigned from 1861 to 1889) instituted reforms, including abolition of slavery in the colonies, but the monarchy remained unpopular and was replaced by a republic in 1910.

Post, Charles Williams (1854–1914) American health food advocate. The creator of Post Cereals was born in Illinois, and worked in hardware and real estate before illness led him to devote his life to developing health foods for himself and later for a national audience. His first health food, a hot cereal called Postum, was developed in Battle Creek, Michigan, in 1895. In 1897 he developed his first cold cereal, a wheat and barley mixture called Grape-Nuts. Before his death in 1914 he had also developed Post Corn Flakes. (See also WILL KEITH KELLOGG and FOOD, PROCESSED.)

postal services Mail delivery services. Victorian postal services improved dramatically as a result of the recommendations of English educator Rowland Hill (1795–1879), who argued in 1837 against the long-standing practice of calculating domestic postage based on distance traveled. He suggested that a low uniform postage rate, prepaid through the sale of adhesive-backed stamps purchased by consumers at post offices, would raise postal volume and revenue. Parliament implemented his reforms in 1840, with a domestic rate of one penny for a half-ounce letter. The reforms were highly successful and were gradually adopted in other countries as well—including the United States, beginning in 1847. Other British innovations included a book post rate (1848), a halfpenny rate for postcards and printed papers (1870), and a parcel post rate (1883).

Post-Impressionism Artistic movement. Propelled by a group of painters who became dissatisfied with the limitations of IMPRESSIONISM by the late 1880s, the four chief exponents of Post-Impressionism were GEORGES SEURAT, PAUL GAUGUIN, VINCENT VAN GOGH, and PAUL CÉZANNE. Although they were not closely linked stylistically, these artists all shared a reaction against Impressionism's preoccupation with observed reality.

Cézanne underscored the cone, the sphere, and the cylinder as the basic qualities of his compositions while Seurat created Neo-Impressionist paintings from combinations of microscopic dots of pure color. Gauguin formulated his theories of Symbolism to render his interpretations of spirituality, while Van Gogh experimented with dramatic styles of restless expressionism. Other notable Post-Impressionists were HENRI DE TOULOUSE-LAUTREC and HENRI ROUSSEAU.

The term "Post-Impressionism" was not coined until 1910, when critic and artist Roger Fry was asked to describe the artists showing in an exhibition at the Grafton Galleries in England.

potato chips Snack food. The thinly sliced, fried potatoes were first developed in the nineteenth century by American George Crum who was working as a chef at a resort in Saratoga Springs, New York. Upset at having his thick-cut French-fried potatoes returned by a customer wanting thinner fries, he created these crisp potatoes. Eventually known as Saratoga Chips, the food became popular along the East Coast of the United States. See also FOOD, PROCESSED.

Potter, [Martha] Beatrice See WEBB, SIDNEY JAMES, AND [MARTHA] BEATRICE POTTER.

Pre-Raphaelites Group of English painters and sculptors. In September 1848, JOHN EVERETT MILLAIS, WILLIAM HOLMAN HUNT, and DANTE GABRIEL ROSSETTI formed the Pre-Raphaelite Brotherhood (PRB) in London. They wanted to revive in British painting the purity of Italian art before Raphael's move to Rome and hoped to achieve their aim through clarity of color and line and simple subjects.

The movement was a blend of romantic MEDIEVALISM and the desire to return to a realistic depiction of nature, ignoring what they considered the rules of academic art. Their preoccupation was to turn painting into a moral as well as an aesthetic act.

The PRB first issued a long list of "immortals" in history, from Jesus Christ and Job to George Washington and Edgar Allan Poe, whom they graded by a star system. As artists, they burst upon the scene at the Free Society and Royal Academy exhibitions of 1849 with a trio of works by Millais, Hunt, and Rossetti. The PRB revived, as a shared secret, the techniques of early Flemish painters, meticulously painting layer after layer of their translucent colors to capture every detail in a brilliant light. Their realistic treatment of biblical subjects provoked widespread anger and criticism, but they were defended by JOHN RUSKIN.

The artists remained as a group through the early 1850s, sometimes signing their work with the initials P.R.B., evoking suspicion of a subversive, secret society. Its identity and that of its members were made public in January 1850 when the PRB published the first of four issues of its magazine, *The Germ.*

The group also had an impact on the decorative arts through painted furniture, tapestries, stained glass, and designs for fabric and wallpaper. A number of members worked for WILLIAM MORRIS's firm and were thus instrumental in creating the ARTS AND CRAFTS MOVEMENT. The Pre-Raphaelites affected several succeeding painters, including FORD MADOX BROWN and EDWARD BURNE-JONES.

Prescott, William H[ickling] (1796–1859) American historian. Born in Salem, Massachusetts, he endured a problem with his eyesight all his life. Still, he was a prolific author who became known for his scientific technique and devotion to research in his multivolume works specializing in Spanish involvement in the Americas. They include the three-volume *The History of the Reign of Ferdinand and Isabella* (1838), the three-volume *A History of the Conquest of Mexico* (1843)—a book whose popular success was tied to interest in the MEXICAN WAR (1846–48)—and the three-volume *A History of the Conquest of Peru* (1847). Several of his books remain standards in their field.

presidents, U.S. See U.S. PRESIDENTS AND VICE PRESIDENTS.

prime ministers, British See BRITISH PRIME MINISTERS.

processed food See FOOD, PROCESSED.

prostitution Solicitation of sex acts. Prostitution was not a crime in England until 1839, after which a "common prostitute" could be arrested for soliciting, but even then public sympathy aided the large numbers of men and women working the streets. Depending on who was doing the counting, there were between 10,000 and 120,000 prostitutes working in London in the 1800s. A large number of full-time prostitutes were orphans or working-class youngsters, and the majority of their customers were working men, despite the popular notion of aristocratic men preying on "fallen women." Pimps were a rarity, but the husbands of prostitutes had a legal right to all of their wives' earnings.

In the first half of the century, prostitutes openly solicited customers in the theaters of London, including COVENT GARDEN; there were nearly one thousand brothels in the city in 1841.

The 1836 publication of *De la prostitution dans la ville de Paris,* a demographic study of twelve thousand prostitutes written by A. J. B. Parent-Duchatelet, brought a heightened sense of awareness to prostitution and served as the basis for the British social investigation of the problem for the next forty years. After a rise in venereal disease among the military, Parliament passed the first of three Contagious Disease Acts in 1864, which provided for the sanitary inspection of prostitutes. FLORENCE NIGHTINGALE officially objected to the action, however, claiming that it sanctioned "vice." Enforcing the act allowed police to subject any woman to a medical examination based solely on their personal "suspicions"; any woman who refused to submit to an examination could be charged and brought to court, where she had to prove her virtue. After much public outcry, the acts were repealed between 1870 and 1886.

Social purity leagues formed around 1873 and became somewhat effective in stigmatizing prostitutes as moral pariahs. The Criminal Law Amendment Act of 1885 reflected the changing moral attitudes and raised the age of consent for girls from thirteen to sixteen. A number of sensationalized accounts of white slavery appeared in newspapers near the end of the century and contributed to the decline of prostitution, at least as an open and unabashed Victorian profession.

protoplasm Granular colloidal material that constitutes the living portion of a cell. It was first noted and named in 1846 by German botanist HUGO VON MOHL (1805–1872) in his study of plant cells. The term derives from Greek, "first formed." A cell's protoplasm comprises its nucleus and the surrounding cytoplasm but not the vacuoles and contents waiting to be excreted or digested.

Prussia German-speaking political state. At the height of its power the former state of Prussia dominated central Europe and occupied more than half of modern GERMANY. It stretched from the Netherlands in the west to Poland in the east. Its north-south expanse ran from Denmark and the North and Baltic seas south to the Main River and Thuringean Forest.

Prussia's rise began in 1618. The ruler of Brandenburg, one of the many small German states that emerged from the fragmentation of the Holy Roman Empire, inherited the duchy of Prussia. Prussia was then a stretch of territory bordering the Baltic Sea and surrounded on its land borders by POLAND. The Brandenburg-Prussian state, led by the Hohenzollerns—Frederick William (1640–1688) and Frederick the Great (1740–1786)—expanded its borders at the expense of Poland, AUSTRIA, and other smaller German states.

By the Victorian era, Prussia and Austria vied for dominance of the German-speaking states. Prussia, under OTTO VON BISMARCK, defeated its rival in the SEVEN WEEKS' WAR of 1866. This victory ensured Prussia's dominance of central Europe. The defeat of France in the FRANCO-PRUSSIAN WAR of 1870–71 led to the declaration of the German Empire. Prussia remained the dominant state within the empire. The coming of the Third Reich ended any practical differentiation between Germany and Prussia. The Allies formally abolished Prussia as a political entity in 1947.

Puccini, Giacomo Antonio Domenico Michele Secondo Maria (1858–1924) Italian composer. He was born at Lucca into a family of musicians who had held the position of *maestro di cappella* at the Cathedral of S. Martino at Lucca for four generations. He was expected to follow the tradition, but after experiencing a performance of Verdi's *Aida* in 1876, he decided to pursue opera.

In 1880, Puccini entered the Milan Conservatory, where he studied for three years. For his graduation he wrote *Capriccio sin fonico,* an instrumental piece that attracted the attention of influential people in the music world of Milan.

A year later Puccini's one-act opera *Le Villi* was staged with great success, and the composer was quickly commissioned to write another by Italy's foremost music publisher Giulo Ricordi. The resulting opera, *Edgar* (1889), was a failure, but Puccini followed with *Manon Lescaut* (1893), which brought him international success.

His next three operas—*La Bohème (1896),* Tosca (1900), and *Madame Butterfly* (1904)—remain among the most popular operas in the world. With librettos written by Luigi Ilica and Giusseppe Giasco, all three epitomize Puccini's predominant theme of "one who has lived for love, has died for love."

Puccini's last opera, *Turnadot,* was left unfinished when Puccini died of a heart attack. The last two scenes of the opera were completed by Franco Alfano, and *Turnadot* premiered in 1926.

Pugin, August Welby Northmore (1812–1852) English architect and writer. Though he erected numerous buildings, including churches, monasteries, and convents, Pugin is best known for his influential published writings. His detailing of the form and function of Gothic architecture in *The True Principles of Pointed or Christian Architecture* (1841) made the book instrumental in England's GOTHIC REVIVAL. Pugin believed the beauty of Gothic architecture reflected the moral and spiritual superiority of medieval society.

In 1836–43, Pugin worked under Sir CHARLES BARRY on the Houses of Parliament (see WESTMINSTER PALACE), primarily in directing the execution of fittings and ornamental details. Of the sixty-five churches he executed, Pugin is best known for his cathedral in London's St. George's Fields. Among his other publications are *Gothic Furniture in the Style of the 15th Century* (1835), *Contrasts* (1836), and *Glossary of Ecclesiastical Ornament and Costume* (1844).

Pulitzer, Joseph (1847–1911) U.S. newspaper publisher. Born in Hungary, he immigrated to the United States in 1864 and enlisted in the Union Army during the U.S. CIVIL WAR. After the war he settled in St. Louis, where he became a reporter for a German-language paper. Pulitzer launched several campaigns against municipal corruption and became prominent in the reform wing of the REPUBLICAN PARTY. Following the defeat of HORACE GREELEY in the 1872 presidential election, he joined the DEMOCRATIC PARTY.

In 1878, Pulitzer bought the *St. Louis Dispatch* and merged it with the *Evening Post* to form the city's leading daily, the *Post-Dispatch.* He purchased the *New York World* from JAY GOULD in 1883 and within a year had increased its circulation from twenty thousand to one hundred thousand. After 1895, WILLIAM RANDOLPH HEARST challenged the *World* with his *New York Morning Journal.* The circulation war included all the elements of yellow journalism: irresponsible reporting, sensational headlines, and garish illustrations. The struggle reached its height during the Spanish-American War, after which the Pulitzer paper resumed its former sober reporting of the news and became the leading journal of the Democratic Party. Pulitzer's will left funds to establish the Columbia University Graduate School of Journalism and the Pulitzer Prizes. See PERIODICALS.

Pullman, Charles Mortimer (1831–1897) American industrialist and inventor. Born in Brocton, New York, Pullman worked as a cabinetmaker before moving to Chicago and experimenting with railroad car remodeling. He developed the first sleeping car, the Pullman, in 1863. It used movable seat cushions to create a sleeping berth. Through his company, the Pullman Palace Car Company, founded in 1867, he also created other specialty cars such as the dining car. He founded Pullman, Illinois, as a company town to house its employees, but his refusal to negotiate with the American Railway Union over cuts in wages led to the PULLMAN STRIKE of 1894.

Pullman Strike Labor dispute. The nationwide work interruption in 1894 by the American Railway Union against Pullman car inventor George Pullman crystallized the century's conflict between labor and business, the partnership of government and business against labor, and the rise of American socialism.

To protest Pullman's firing of one-third of his workers and slashing by 30 percent the wages of his remaining employees while maintaining all prices at his company town of Pullman, Illinois, socialist leader EUGENE V. DEBS organized a strike in which American Railway Union members refused to work on trains with Pullman cars. Pullman would not negotiate with workers, and citing the need to fight an interruption in the mails, President GROVER CLEVELAND brought a federal injunction against Debs. When Debs defied the court order, federal troops were ordered in to quell the strike. The strike was broken, and Debs was given a six-month jail sentence. The strike and its aftermath brought Debs prominence in the socialist movement, seen then by some as a necessary alternative to rapacious business leaders and the powerful public servants who supported them.

Punch Weekly comic magazine. Subtitled "The London Charivari," in reference to the French periodical *Le Charivari, Punch* was founded in 1841 by journalist Henry Mayhew and others. Blending humor, serious comment, and satirical illustrations, *Punch* was a British institution until its demise in 1992.

Punjab Region of Pakistan and northwest INDIA. It was bounded in the west by the Indus River and in the east by the Jumna River. Since the founding of Sikhism in about 1500, the Punjab had been home to a large population of Sikhs, who established their own state there in 1799 under Ranjit Singh (1780–1839). After Singh's death the Sikhs fought the British in two Sikh Wars (1845–46, 1848–49), after which the British annexed the Punjab.

A semiarid region, it was economically developed by the British, who began founding wheat-producing colonies there in 1897, watered by a network of canals. In 1947 the Punjab was divided between the newly independent countries of India and Pakistan.

Pusey, Edward Bouverie (1800–1882) English theologian. A leading member of the OXFORD MOVEMENT, Pusey was educated at Eton and Christ College, Oxford, and was Regius Professor of Hebrew at Oxford. Along with JOHN HENRY NEWMAN and JOHN KEBLE, fellow Tractarian Pusey helped in the production of *Tracts for the Times.* Alarmed that the Church of England was becoming overwhelmed by unchecked rationalist impulses, Pusey aimed to promulgate a sense of the Church's divine mission. He was continually attacked for his views by bishops and the liberal clergy. After supporting Newman's explanation of the "Thirty-Nine Articles" in the controversial *Tract No. 90,* which found the articles compatible with Catholic theology, he was suspended from the university, accused of preaching heretical views (1843). Hoping to prevent conversions to Rome, he strove to bring about a union of the English and Roman churches as well as an alliance of the English

Church, the Wesleyans, and the Eastern Church.

Pushkin, Aleksandr Sergeyevich (1799–1837) Russian writer. He is widely regarded as his country's greatest poet and the founder of modern Russian literature, strongly influencing the work of later nineteenth-century Russian writers LEO TOLSTOY, FYODOR DOSTOYEVSKY, and NIKOLAY GOGOL, among others. A child of noble parentage, he attended the Lyceum and gained a position in the foreign ministry of St. Petersburg before publishing his first important work, *Ruslan and Ludmila,* in 1820. In it and subsequent works Pushkin displayed a high regard for common people. They also featured a simple, spontaneous, and vigorous language and reflected an antiauthoritarianism that made him an enemy of the czarist government. Among his major poems are *The Robber Brothers* (1821–22), *The Gypsies* (1824), and *The Bronze Horseman* (1833). The poem often considered his masterpiece, *Eugene Onegin,* was written between 1823 and 1831. Works in other genres include the play *Boris Godunov* (1825), a political tragedy that was censored and kept from production until 1870, and the historical novel *The Captain's Daughter* (1836).

Queensberry, 8th Marquis of, Sir John Sholto (1844–1900) Scottish aristocrat. Great patron of BOXING, he supervised the formulation by John Graham Chambers of the boxing regulations known as the "Marquis of Queensberry rules" (1867). The father of Lord Alfred Bruce Douglas (1870–1945), friend of Irish playwright and poet OSCAR WILDE, Sir John publicly accused Wilde of sodomy in 1895. Sued for libel by Wilde, Sir John was acquitted while Wilde was prosecuted and imprisoned for homosexual acts.

radio waves Electromagnetic undulations. Having the longest wavelengths in the spectrum, radiowaves were predicted in 1873 in *Electricity and Magnetism* by Scottish physicist JAMES CLERK MAXWELL. They were discovered in 1888 by German physicist Heinrich Rudolph Hertz (1857–1894), who generated the waves with an oscillating electrical circuit and detected them with a loop of wire containing an air gap. Realizing that radio waves could be used to carry long-distance messages without the need for TELEGRAPH wires, physicists worked to improve the detecting devices. In 1894, English physicist Sir Oliver Joseph Lodge (1851–1940) developed a device called a coherer that could detect radio waves half a mile from the source. He also succeeded in sending and receiving messages in Morse code (see SAMUEL F. B. MORSE). In 1895, radio antennae were invented by Russian physicist Aleksandr Stepanovich Popov (1859–1905) and Italian electrical engineer Guglielmo Marconi (1874–1937). A few years later, on December 12, 1901, Marconi succeeded in broadcasting radio waves from England to Newfoundland, an event that traditionally marks the invention of radio. In time, the Victorian-era concept revolutionized twentieth-century communication.

radioactivity Spontaneous disintegration of an atomic nucleus. Several elements, including uranium and radium, are naturally radioactive. The phenomenon of spontaneous emission of radiation from uranium was discovered in 1896 by French physicist Antoine-Henri Becquerel (1852–1908), and scientists immediately began analyzing the phenomenon. In 1897, Polish-born French chemist MARIE SKLODOWSKA CURIE showed that the radiation was atomic, not molecular, in nature, while British physicist Ernest Rutherford (1871–1937) showed that it contained both positively charged particles, ALPHA PARTICLES, and negatively charged ones, BETA PARTICLES. In 1898, Curie coined the term "radioactivity" for the phenomenon and discovered that the element thorium was also radioactive. That same year she and her husband, French physicist PIERRE

CURIE, discovered the radioactive elements polonium and radium.

In 1900, Becquerel determined that beta rays were ELECTRONS, then previously known only as fundamental units of electric charge. That same year French physicist Paul Ulrich Villard (1860–1934) discovered another component of radioactivity: gamma rays, a high-energy form of electromagnetic radiation with the highest frequency and shortest wavelength in the spectrum. Also that year, German physicist Friedrich Ernst Dorn (1848–1916) discovered the radioactive radon, one of the INERT (NOBLE) GASES.

By the first decade of the twentieth century, scientists including the Curies, Rutherford, and English physicist Sir WILLIAM CROOKES showed that radioactivity resulted from the spontaneous breakdown of atoms into the atoms of other elements. Atomic disintegration was inconceivable by the framework of nineteenth-century physical principles, and some Victorian scientists, notably British physicist Lord KELVIN, were never able to accept it. It was soon established beyond a doubt, however, and this led to a reconceptualization of the atom, the discovery of atomic fission and fusion, and the invention of nuclear weapons and nuclear power.

For their discovery of radioactivity, Becquerel and the Curies shared the 1903 Nobel Prize in physics.

ragged schools English learning institutions. Ragged schools were established by private charities to provide basic education, vocational training, and religious instruction to poor, "ragged," children. The Ragged School Union, which brought the schools together in a loose confederation, was founded in 1844 and headed by Lord SHAFTESBURY. By 1852 there some three hundred thousand children in the schools; there were 110 ragged schools in London alone. The schools quickly disbanded after the EDUCATION ACT of 1870 started England on the road to universal compulsory education.

Raglan, FitzRoy James Henry Somerset, 1st Baron (1788–1855) English soldier. He served on the Duke of Wellington's staff during the Peninsular War against Napoleon's France and later lost an arm at Waterloo. During the CRIMEAN WAR he was promoted to field general and became the first British commander-in-chief of the war. After an initial victory at the Battle of the Alma River in 1854, the allies—British, French, and Turkish troops—bogged down in front of Sebastopol. Raglan, who was handicapped by his joint command with a French general and an inefficient supply system, was severely criticized for this stalemate and for the misery of his ill-equipped troops. His reputation also suffered when an inexact order from him resulted in the calamitous "CHARGE OF THE LIGHT BRIGADE." He died of disease after another allied failure to take Sebastopol. He gave his name to the raglan sleeve, which extends directly to the neckline.

railroads Form of transportation in which powered locomotives propel cars along steel rails. Invented in Great Britain in the early nineteenth century, railroads were already beginning to change the nation's transportation industry when Victoria came to the throne. The periods 1836–37 and 1844–47 were especially successful ones for railroad construction. By 1848 about five thousand miles of railway stretched across the United Kingdom, with new bridges and tunnels to ease the way and ever more powerful steam locomotives to pull the trains. By 1900 the total miles of railway had grown to more than fifteen thousand.

Among the most renowned of British lines was the elegant GREAT WESTERN RAILWAY, opened in 1838. On the continent, British talent contributed to the opening in 1883 of the opulent ORIENT EXPRESS, linking Paris and Constantinople.

Although British engineers were in high demand around the world, American inventors introduced innovations, such as the sleeping cars designed by GEORGE PULLMAN (1856) and the AIR BRAKE invented by George Westinghouse (1868). The climax of American railroad building came with the completion of the first transcontinental rail line on May 10, 1869—the date when the Union Pacific, extending westward from Nebraska, and the Central Pacific, extending eastward from California, were joined at Promontory Point, Utah.

The Victorian era also saw the introduction of streetcars or trolleys, which ran along rails sunk into city streets. At first drawn by horses, streetcars began to be powered by electricity in the 1880s in Britain and the United States. Steam-powered subways were first introduced in London in 1863; the first electric-powered subway line followed in 1890. The first American subway was built in Boston in 1898.

By shrinking travel time both within cities and across great distances, railroad technology helped to increase the pace and possibilities of Victorian life. Commerce and commuting were speeded; vacations to faraway places became more feasible. The railroad industry had other effects as well. It used prodigious amounts of natural resources—principally iron, steel, and coal—and employed large numbers of people, 440,000 in Britain alone in 1900. It made fortunes for its owners, who, especially in the United States, were often famous for corrupt and monopolistic practices. The Interstate Commerce Commission was formed in the United States in 1887 largely to curb such abuses. Railroads prompted many responses—ranging from those who decried their noise and smoke to toy train collectors who were charmed by their beauty (see DRIBBLER). Everywhere in the Victorian world, the railroad was a symbol of the modern age.

Rand (or Witwatersrand) Region in SOUTH AFRICA. In 1886, when gold was discovered here, enticing a rush of British miners, it was part of the BOER-governed republic of the TRANSVAAL. Today the Witwatersrand region continues to produce much of the world's gold and is South Africa's principal industrial region. Located between the Vaal and Olifants rivers, it is the site of South Africa's capital, Johannesburg, and of Soweto township.

Rauch, Christian Daniel (1777–1857) German sculptor. Working in the neoclassical tradition, Rauch had among his works a statue of Queen Louise for the mausoleum at Charlottenburg Palace in Berlin (1811) and a companion statue of Frederick II (1846). He also executed six *Victories* (1829–33) for the Valhalla near Regensburg and a monument to Frederick the Great in Berlin (1840–51).

Rayleigh, John William Strutt, Lord (1842–1919) English physicist. Born near Maldon, Essex, he graduated from Cambridge in 1865 and established a laboratory at his family's estate. His researches ranged over the entire field of physics, and in the late 1860s and early 1870s he published important work on the subject of optics, explaining that the short wavelength component of sunlight is scattered more than the long wavelength component, which results in a predominantly blue sky.

In 1879, Rayleigh succeeded JAMES CLERK MAXWELL as head of the Cavendish Laboratory at Cambridge, and while there he helped redetermine the ohm, ampere, and volt. He left Cavendish in 1884 and returned to his private laboratory where he devoted the next decade to the discovery of argon, for which he was awarded the Nobel Prize in 1904.

Rayleigh was elected a fellow of the Royal Society in 1873 and served as the society's president from 1905 to 1908.

rayon Synthetic fiber. Rayon was first produced in 1883 by French scientist Louis-Marie-Hilaire-Bernigaud de Chardonnet (1839–1924). The shiny silklike fiber is made primarily from cellulose that has been dissolved through chemical treatment and then forced through tiny holes, where it reconfigures as filaments. The name comes from the French word *rayon,* meaning ray or beam of light.

Realism Artistic movement. Used to describe the nineteenth-century movement in painting, literature, and drama that rejected the idealistic notions of ROMANTICISM, Realism was first proposed as a program for art in France. Painters and writers insisted on the portrayal of ordinary contemporary life and its problems. The first painter to proclaim himself a realist was GUSTAVE COURBET. He demanded that painting operate toward social change. Another realist painter, JEAN-FRANÇOIS MILLET, was one of the first artists to portray peasant laborers and rural life in a heroic manner. HONORÉ DAUMIER, on the other hand, depicted working-class people in the slums of Paris. These artists' tendency toward detached, accurate representations was also encouraged by the impact of photography.

In literature, the novel became the predominant form of Realism. Early literary exponents were HONORÉ DE BALZAC in his multivolume series *The Human Comedy* and GUSTAVE FLAUBERT and EMILE ZOLA, who vividly examined sex and violence in their novels *Madame Bovary* (1857) and *Nana* (1880), respectively. These authors claimed to observe life scientifically and described what they saw in a straightforward fashion.

In England, CHARLES DICKENS and ANTHONY TROLLOPE used realistic literary descriptions to promote social change, while GEORGE ELIOT and THOMAS HARDY took a dim view of modern life to write pessimistic novels. In the United States, Theodore Dreiser wrote dark novels of American life, such as *Sister Carrie* (1900); STEPHEN CRANE wrote a grim tale of poverty, *Maggie, a Girl of the Streets* (1896).

In drama, the Norwegian HENRIK IBSEN created a theatrical revolution by presenting contemporary social problems in such plays as *A Doll's House* (1879) and *Ghosts* (1881), while in England, GEORGE BERNARD SHAW studied subjects of social concern in *Mrs. Warren's Profession* (1893) and *Major Barbara* (1905).

Reconstruction Post–U.S. CIVIL WAR period. After the Civil War the defeated CONFEDERACY had to be readmitted to the Union, and the status of the former slaves had to be determined. ABRAHAM LINCOLN wanted to readmit state governments if they pledged to support the Union, ended slavery, and were supported by 10 percent of their voters. Congress pressed for harsher terms, and a showdown was averted only by Lincoln's assassination in 1865.

ANDREW JOHNSON succeeded Lincoln and admitted states generally along Lincoln's guidelines. The reconstructed states passed the "Black Codes," which restricted the former slaves' political and civil rights. Congressional Republicans responded by winning passage of the Fourteenth Amendment, which guaranteed the civil rights of all citizens, and by passing Reconstruction Acts over Johnson's opposition. These acts abolished the state governments, reinstituted military rule, and forced the states to give suffrage to African Americans. By 1870 all eleven states were readmitted to the Union.

These state governments are noted for their corruption and the nefarious influence of carpetbaggers, northerners who controlled parts of the state governments, and scalawags, southerners who cooperated with the new regimes. However, the governments were often no more corrupt than their northern counterparts. The period also saw the rise of the KU KLUX KLAN, a white terrorist organization that aimed to intimidate African Americans and undermine the REPUBLICAN PARTY through fear and violence. The klan was suppressed by the early 1870s, only to reemerge in the twentieth century.

The DEMOCRATIC PARTY soon reconstituted itself in the South, and by 1876 the Republicans controlled only three states. President RUTHERFORD B. HAYES withdrew federal troops in the late 1870s. African Americans soon lost their political and civil rights in the South, and southern resentment over the Union occupation helped perpetuate sectional animosity into the next century.

Red Cross International health and service organization. Dedicated to relieving suffering and improving public health the Red Cross was formed in 1863, with the original aim of bringing medical aid to wounded soldiers. It was conceived by Swiss philanthropist JEAN-HENRI DUNANT, who had been inspired by the suffering of wounded soldiers at the Battle of Solferino (1859). The sixteen countries participating in the GENEVA CONVENTION of 1864 agreed to allow passage of medical personnel bearing the organization's red cross as an emblem of neutrality. The American Red Cross was founded by CLARA BARTON in 1881. Red Cross societies have been founded in many other nations, with the organization's aims broadened to disaster relief and aid to refugees.

Redmond, John Edward (1856–1918) Irish politician. Elected to Parliament in 1881, he became a devoted follower of CHARLES STEWART PARNELL, who made him the IRISH PARTY whip. When the party split in the 1890s after Parnell's divorce scandal (see KATHERINE O'SHEA), Redmond headed the minority Parnellite faction. He became chairman of a reunited party in 1900 and led it in a fight for Home Rule. The party won passage of a Home Rule bill after World War I broke out. It was never enforced because the Easter Rebellion of 1916 spurred demands for complete national sovereignty for Ireland. His Home Rule policy passed over, Redmond resigned the party leadership in 1918 and died shortly after.

Reform Bill of 1832 British electoral law. Although it predated Queen Victoria's reign, this bill opened a process of parliamentary reform that would continue throughout the Victorian Age and mirror the changes in society during that period. Over the centuries the House of Commons failed to reflect the demographic changes brought about by INDUSTRIALIZATION. The new factory towns of the north and west, including MANCHESTER and Bristol, had no representation in Parliament. No new borough—the name given to an urban center that had parliamentary representation—had been created since the end of the seventeenth century. Some of the urban centers that sent members to Parliament had become virtually uninhabited; one was under the ocean. Elections in these so-called rotten boroughs were controlled by town corporations or large landowners. Bribery and influence peddling were common. The rural districts continued to send a disproportionate number of members to London. No provisions were made to represent the growing commercial and professional classes.

Over twenty reform bills were introduced between 1780 and 1830. All failed to pass. Continuing reform agitation, coupled with the several uprisings on the Continent in 1830 and riots in southern England, prompted the Whigs to raise the reform issue again. The Duke of Wellington, then the Tory prime minister, denounced the reformers and defended the status quo so vehemently that many of his followers abandoned him. The new Whig government of Prime Minister Lord Grey introduced a reform bill that the House of Commons rejected.

Grey resigned, but the Tories refused to form a cabinet and the Whigs returned to power. By this time riots had broken out in Bristol and other cities, and a widespread uprising seemed possible. A reform bill was introduced again, and this time the House of Commons passed it. The House of Lords, however, voted it down. When King William IV rejected the Whig request to create enough peers to pass the bill, Grey resigned again. Wellington's inability to form a government forced the King to reappoint Grey and promise to create enough peers to pass the law. The lords capitulated to prevent the expansion of the peerage, and the Reform Bill was enacted in 1832.

The bill increased the number of eligible voters from about five hundred thousand to eight hundred thousand males. Most of the new voters were lawyers, factory owners, merchants, and other members of the growing middle class. Eligibility still depended on a complicated set of property or rental qualifications.

Fifty-six boroughs, all with fewer than two thousand people, were abolished; their inhabitants could vote on a county basis instead. Boroughs with fewer than four thousand people could send only one member to London. Sixty-five seats were created for new boroughs, and sixty-five others were awarded to counties. A system of voter registration was initiated to fight fraud.

The Reform Bill did not radically democratize the electoral system. Only one of seven adult males could vote; workers and the poor remained disenfranchised. The first House of Commons elected after the bill included more than two hundred sons of lords; however, the bill did recognize England's changing demographics and the growing influence of the middle class. It also unfroze an institution that had seemed invulnerable to change and paved the way for future Victorian reform bills.

Reform Bill of 1867 Second British electoral law. In 1865, WILLIAM GLADSTONE, then a LIBERAL Cabinet member, proposed the bill against a background of mass meetings and workers' demands for an expanded electorate. A coalition from left and right defeated the bill, and the government fell. A minority CONSERVATIVE PARTY government, led by Lord DERBY and BENJAMIN DISRAELI, was faced with rioting in Hyde Park over reform and by a need to increase its numbers in Parliament. Disraeli and Derby proposed another bill in 1867 that passed.

The bill extended the franchise in the boroughs and towns by reducing various property qualifications. The electorate more than doubled, and many workers in towns could vote for the first time. Popular approval of the bill allowed the conservative government to survive another eighteen months.

Reform Bill of 1884 Third British electoral law. In 1884 the government, headed by WILLIAM GLADSTONE, passed the third reform bill of the century. It continued the work of the laws of 1832 and 1867 by further extending suffrage. Reduction in property qualifications for voting created almost 2 million more eligible voters. However, British women could not vote until 1918.

Reform League English political organization. Dedicated to extending the franchise to the working class by passing a second reform bill, which became the REFORM BILL OF 1867, the league was organized into local societies and drew its main strength from London and the industrial north. Led by lawyer Edmund Beales and braced by the oratory of JOHN BRIGHT and others, the league organized mass demonstrations in favor of franchise extension. One demonstration led to the Hyde Park Riot of 1866. The league also worked to elect sympathetic parliamentary candidates.

Renan, [Joseph-] Ernest (1823–1892) French historian and philosopher. Born in Tréguier, he was educated at an ecclesiastical college and began to study for the priesthood, but in 1845 he suffered a crisis of faith and left the Catholic Church. After the REVOLUTIONS OF 1848, he wrote *L'Avenir de la science* (*The Future of Science*) in which he posited that human science was equal to the science of nature, and he wrote, "Science is a religion. . . . Science alone is able to solve all problems and will someday displace religion." The work remained unpublished until 1890.

After a brief scholarly job in Rome, Renan returned to Paris in 1850 and lived with his sister while working as a librarian and publishing essays on religion. In 1856 he married Cornélie Scheffer, but he continued to live with his sister who supported the struggling newlyweds. In 1860, Renan visited Israel, and the following year he made another excursion with his sister and wife. His sister contracted malaria during the trip and died.

Upon his return to France in 1862, Renan was elected chair of Hebrew at the Collège de France. He was suspended after his inaugural lecture, however, when the college clerics objected to his "blasphemous" description of Jesus as "an incomparable man." After the fall of the SECOND EMPIRE in the Franco-German War of 1870–71, Renan was reappointed chair at the Collège de France. The bitterness of defeat, had changed Renan's views, however, and in *La Réforme intellectuelle et morale de la France* (1872) he argued in favor of the monarchy and against universal suffrage. His disillusionment continued to grow, and the 1885 drama *Le Prêtre de Nemi* depicted a skeptic looking for faith. Renan's final work, *Histoire du peuple d'Israël* (1887–93), revealed his hope that Judaism would disappear so that "without a compensatory Heaven justice will really exist on Earth."

Renoir, Pierre-Auguste (1841–1919) French painter. A pioneer of IMPRESSIONISM, Renoir became known as one of the nineteenth-century's greatest colorists in a wide range of portraits and genre paintings. Born in Limoges, he trained and worked as a porcelain painter in Paris from 1856 to 1859. In 1862 he entered the Ecole des Beaux-Arts and became a pupil of Gabriel-Charles Gleyre with CLAUDE MONET, Jean-Frédéric Bazille, and ALFRED SISLEY, the founders of Impressionism. Renoir eventually exhibited in four of the eight Impressionist exhibitions.

In the summer of 1869, Monet and Renoir together explored spontaneous on-the-spot paintings in their representations of *La Grenouillere, or* "the Frog Pond." Although they are paintings of the same scene, the formal results are entirely subjective. Ultimately, the general character of Impressionism emerged from Monet's and Renoir's paintings through the early 1870s.

Renoir's most important contributions to Impressionism came in 1876 with such paintings as *The Swing* and *Le Moulin de la Galette,* where he illustrated Paris's animated café life with flickering brushstrokes and patchworks of vibrant color. Renoir also turned to paintings of beautiful women: *Nude in the Sunlight* (1876) is a celebration of female sensuality rendered in free brushstrokes, soft colors, and blurring contours. Renoir had a great Salon success with his sentimental *Mme Charpentier and Daughters* (1878) toward the end of his Impressionist phase.

In 1881, Renoir visited Italy where he admired the works of Raphael, JEAN-AUGUSTE-DOMINIQUE INGRES, and French Renaissance sculpture. Throughout the 1880s, in paintings such as *Dance at Bougival* (1883) and *Les Parapluies* (1883), Renoir attempted to organize his forms with more sculptural clarity.

Renoir's greatest work during his classical period was *Les Grandes Baigneues,* begun in 1884. In a subject inspired by the paintings of Adolphe-William Bouguereau, Renoir displayed female nudes frolicking in and out of the water in a forest. This painting was well received by the public and the critics as a triumphant union of the modern and the traditional when it was exhibited in Paris at Georges Petit's gallery in 1887. In the twentieth century, Renoir returned to a more Impressionistic mode. Primarily painting interiors and female nudes, he once again composed with free brushstrokes but this time with strong reds and oranges. Throughout his entire career Renoir never developed the contemplative seriousness of EDOUARD MANET or PAUL CÉZANNE but instead dwelled on the pleasing aspects of life.

Renwick, James (1818–1895) American architect. After graduation from Columbia University in 1836 at the age of eighteen, Renwick worked as an engineer on the Erie Railroad and on the distributing reservoir for the Croton Aqueduct in New York. Renwick's national reputation was secured at the age of twenty-four when he was chosen the winner in the competition for the design of Grace Church (1843–46) in New York. Although he did not visit Europe until the 1850s, Grace Church was one of the first correctly executed GOTHIC REVIVAL designs in America. In 1849, Renwick won the commission to design the SMITHSONIAN INSTITUTION in Washington. The Smithsonian, however, demonstrated a more awkward blend of Romanesque motifs.

Renwick was chosen architect for New York's St. Patrick's Cathedral in 1859, and this became the most ambitious product of Gothic Revival. By the time of St. Patrick's dedication, the completion of Renwick's plan for the original Corcoran Gallery (1859–61, 1870–71) was well under way in Washington. Renwick's other memorable construction is the first building for Vassar College (1865), freely designed in Renaissance motifs.

Republican Party U.S. political party. Founded in 1854 by those opposed to the extension of SLAVERY into newly acquired territories, it became with the DEMOCRATIC PARTY one of the country's two major political parties. The first Republican presidential candidate, JOHN FRÉMONT, was defeated in 1856, but the second, ABRAHAM LINCOLN, won in 1860, precipitating the secession of the slave-owning South and the start of the CIVIL WAR. After the war, during the RECONSTRUCTION period, a faction known as the radical Republicans dominated the party and instituted punitive measures against the South. Though differing little from the Democrats on major issues, the Republicans dominated the White House for much of the late nineteenth century; its presidents included ULYSSES S. GRANT, RUTHERFORD B. HAYES, JAMES A. GARFIELD, CHESTER A. ARTHUR, BENJAMIN HARRISON, and WILLIAM MCKINLEY. During this period the party lost the White House only in 1885–89 and 1893–97 to Democratic president GROVER CLEVELAND, who was supported by the Republican faction known as the MUGWUMPS.

restaurant Establishment where prepared meals are served to customers. The restaurant evolved in the nineteenth century from inns, taverns, and private clubs where meals were served and from COOKSHOPS where people brought their own food to be cooked. By the century's end, dining out was fashionable, and Victorian London became home to a number of well-known restaurants, such as the Café Royale, Kettner's, and Simpson's on the Strand. Publications such as *London at Dinner; or, Where to Dine* (1858) helped people find the best places.

Return of the Native, The (1878) English novel. Written by THOMAS HARDY *The Return of the Native* is one of the great novels of the late Victorian era. It combines the structure of classical tragedy with the homely particulars and social tensions of mid-nineteenth-century rural England. Idealistic Clym Yeobright wearies of life in Paris and returns to his native Egdon Heath in England with the intention of becoming a schoolmaster. Damon Wildeve, proprietor of the tavern The Quiet Woman, has married Clym's cousin Thomasin Yeobright to spite the woman he actually loves, the passionate Eustacia Vye. Against his mother's wishes, Clym marries Eustacia, who hopes that Clym will take her with him to an exciting life in Paris. But Clym stays where he is and because his failing eyesight makes his academic dreams impossible, becomes a lowly furze cutter. In despair, Eustacia begins to dally again with Wildeve and becomes indirectly and unwittingly responsible for the death of Clym's mother from an adder bite. After being confronted by Clym, Eustacia drowns herself, and Wildeve drowns trying to save her. Later, Clym becomes a wandering preacher and Thomasin marries Diggory Venn, a reddleman, who sold red chalk used for identification markings on sheep.

Reuters News Service Information agency. The service was founded by German businessman Paul Julius Reuter. After experimenting with carrier pigeons to transmit information, Reuter moved to London in 1851 and used telegraph cables to send financial and other news across the Continent. Before long, Reuters was a worldwide news service. See also NEWS AGENCIES.

revolutions of 1848 Series of uprisings that swept Continental Europe. The three most important centers of revolt were Paris, Vienna, and Berlin.

Paris: The July Monarchy that had ruled FRANCE since 1830 had become so corrupt and hidebound that it refused to consider even the most basic political reforms. When King LOUIS-PHILIPPE balked at extending suffrage and banned demonstrations in February 1848, the working class section of Paris erupted. In three days the February Revolution had deposed the monarch. The SECOND REPUBLIC was born.

Gustave Doré's illustration, "Death of the Archbishop of Paris," depicts the emotional and physical upheaval that occurred throughout Europe during the revolutions of 1848. Photo courtesy of Max A. Polster Archive.

A Constituent Assembly was elected in April through universal male suffrage. The Assembly represented the more moderate reformers, who found themselves pitted against Louis Blanc and other radical and socialist leaders who drew their support from the Paris workers. On May 15, workers stormed the Assembly but were driven back by the national guard. When the government tried to break up the national workshops that employed many of the May 15 rebels, the workers of Paris revolted again.

Warfare raged for three days in June in the streets of Paris, the so-called June days. The government triumphed in the end, but ten thousand people were killed or wounded, and eleven thousand rebels were deported to the colonies. The intensity of this class warfare shook not only France but other countries where revolts were also taking place.

After the June days, the Constituent Assembly voted to create a strong presidency elected by universal male suffrage. The first and only president elected was Louis Napoleon Bonaparte, the nephew of Napoleon. He won the office in a landslide in December 1848. Three years later he dissolved the legislature, quelled armed resistance to this coup, and held an election that extended his term for ten years. In 1852 he declared the creation of the French Empire and proclaimed himself NAPOLEON III, the emperor of the French, thus ushering in the SECOND EMPIRE.

Vienna: Within weeks of the February 1848 revolt in Paris, rebellions broke out in AUSTRIA and PRUSSIA. Workers and students attacked the imperial palace in Vienna, capital of the Austrian Empire. The government fell quickly, and Prince KLEMENS VON METTERNICH fled to England. Rebellion spread to outlying areas of the suddenly paralyzed empire: Hungary, northern Italy, Venice, Czechoslovakia. Local leaders demanded national autonomy, constitutional and representational government, expanded suffrage, and other liberal reforms.

Despite these upheavals, the imperial army, led by old-line aristocrats, remained loyal to Emperor Ferdinand of Austria. The army crushed an insurrection in June and later defeated rebels in northern Italy and Hungary. When rebellion broke out in Vienna again in October and the emperor fled the city, the army successfully besieged the city. Emperor Ferdinand abdicated and was succeeded by FRANZ JOSEPH. Some revolts continued into 1849, particularly in Hungary where Louis Kossuth led a movement for national independence. When the army failed to quash the revolt, Czar Nicholas of Russia invaded Hungary and ended the resistance.

Berlin: Berlin, the capital of Prussia, saw its streets erupt in rebellion on March 15. King FREDERICK WILLIAM IV stopped his army from completely crushing the revolt and permitted the election of a legislative assembly based on universal suffrage. This assembly met in May to draft a constitution. The King, under the influence of the reactionary Junker landowners, changed his mind about the assembly. By the end of the year he had dissolved the body and presented his subjects with a very conservative constitution.

The lesser German states also experienced upheavals in 1848. Voters throughout the states sent representatives to Frankfurt in an effort to forge a unified Germany. Called the Frankfurt Parliament, this assembly convened in May and spent the rest of the year hammering out a constitution. King Frederick refused the offer to rule over a unified Germany because it came from a popularly elected Parliament. Most of the assembly disbanded. A few scattered revolts broke out in Saxony and Bavaria, and were quelled by the Prussian army.

Rhodes, Cecil John (1853–1902) British empire builder, industrialist, and statesman. The son of the vicar of Bishop's Stortford, Hertfordshire, he traveled to Natal in what is now SOUTH AFRICA in 1870 to work on his brother Herbert's cotton farm. The brothers found farming unprofitable but discovered large profits in the newly opened diamond fields of Kimberley, located in the Orange Free State (now also part of South Africa), then an independent republic governed by the BOERS, or Afrikaners. Cecil Rhodes stayed in Kimberley from 1871 to 1888, cofounding De Beers Consolidated Mines, Ltd., and making a vast fortune. By the 1890s he controlled 90 percent of the world's diamond production and had acquired a large interest in the gold mines of the TRANSVAAL (now also part of South Africa).

Rhodes's industries were only a stepping stone to his imperial ambitions. He dreamed of a British Empire that would stretch through the African interior from CAPE TO CAIRO, from the Cape of Good Hope to the sands of Egypt. He also hoped, through diplomacy, good government, and force when needed, to make the Boers of southern Africa willing and equal subjects under British rule. Spurred by these ambitions, he entered the Parliament of Cape Colony in 1881, a position he held for the rest of his life, and became the colony's prime minister in 1890.

Rhodes persuaded the British government to annex BECHUANALAND (now Botswana) in 1884. In 1889 he made his greatest mark on the map of Africa when he convinced the crown to grant a charter to his BRITISH SOUTH AFRICA COMPANY to colonize the region north of the Transvaal. This region became RHODESIA (now Zimbabwe). Pressing north through the interior, employees of Rhodes's company gained control of northern Rhodesia (now ZAMBIA) and NYASALAND (now Malawi). The Cape-to-Cairo route was never realized, but Rhodes managed to drive a British wedge in the African interior between the Portuguese in the west and the Germans in the east. Rhodes's influence was felt throughout the region, nowhere more so than in Rhodesia, which he governed as a virtual dictator, and Cape Colony, where he was an active and lordly prime minister.

Self-driven as Rhodes was, it was fitting that he administer the most damaging blow to his own power. In 1895 he secretly authorized LEANDER STARR JAMESON to invade the Transvaal to try to overthrow the Boer government. An utter failure, the Jameson Raid deepened hostilities between Boer and British colonists and in 1896 forced Rhodes to resign the prime ministry of Cape Colony and his role in the British South Africa Company. Even so, "Mr.

Rhodes," as he was known to his de facto subjects, continued to enjoy wide influence in Rhodesia and to work on its development.

Rhodes was an extravagant, dominating man, given to grandness in his actions, whether it was building a railway bridge across the chasm of VICTORIA FALLS or entertaining international guests at Groote Schuur, the personal palace he renovated in Dutch colonial style in Cape Town. Convinced of the racial superiority of Europeans, he dispossessed vast numbers of black Africans and contributed to generations of racial conflict in southern Africa. But he is also remembered for the program of scholarships at Oxford that he founded in his will which forbade disqualification on the basis of race.

Rhodes's reputation in his last years was marred by a scandal concerning an acquaintance named Princess Radziwill who was forging letters and bills of exchange in his name. But his funeral was as grand as his life had been: a spectacular procession to his burial site in the granite heights of the Matopo Hills in Rhodesia.

Rhodesia British colony in southern Africa, now the independent republic of Zimbabwe. Most of it is savanna raised on a high plateau, the *highveld,* north of what are now SOUTH AFRICA and Botswana (then called BECHUANALAND). On its southern border is the Limpopo River, on the northern border the ZAMBESI RIVER, site of the spectacular VICTORIA FALLS.

BANTU-speaking, Iron Age people arrived in the region between A.D. 500 and 1000. The MASHONA arrived between 1000 and 1400. In the 1830s the MATABELE, another Bantu group, conquered the Mashona and dominated the region from their base in Bulawayo, an area known as Matabeleland.

In 1889, British colonizer CECIL RHODES obtained a charter giving his British South Africa Company the right to colonize the region as Rhodesia. With a column of settlers and soldiers, Rhodes founded SALISBURY in 1890 in what was known as Mashonaland. After war broke out with King Lobengula of the Matabele in 1893, the British also conquered Matabeleland. The Mashona and Matabele rebelled several times more, but by 1900 the British were in control.

The colony was governed by the British South Africa Company until 1923, when it voted to become a self-governing British colony, named Southern Rhodesia to distinguish it from Northern Rhodesia (now ZAMBIA). In 1965, Southern Rhodesia unilaterally, declared its independence from Britain, becoming the white-ruled republic of Rhodesia. Years of guerrilla warfare with black African nationalists and economic sanctions from western nations followed. Multiracial elections were held in 1980, and Rhodesia became the modern state of Zimbabwe, a name that comes from a complex of stone ruins dating mainly to the eleventh to seventeenth centuries. The royal temple-fort complex was built by Bantu-speaking Africans who established an inland empire in the region; it was rediscovered in 1867.

Rhymers' Club Informal association of poets. Gathering at the Cheshire Cheese in Fleet Street, London, from 1891 to 1894, the group, founded by Ernest Rhys (1859–1946), included Ernest Dowson (1867–1900), Lionel Johnson (1867–1902), ARTHUR SYMONS, and WILLIAM BUTLER YEATS; it published two collections of poetry (1892 and 1894).

Richardson, Henry Hobson (1838–1886) American architect. After a year at the University of Louisiana, Richardson attended Harvard where he studied civil engineering. Upon graduation he traveled to Europe, eventually attending the Grande Ecole des Beaux-Arts in Paris.

Richardson returned to the United States in 1865 and worked with the architect Emlin J. Littell on his first three buildings: the Church of the Unity, the Boston and Albany Railroad offices, and Grace Church in New York City. In 1867 he entered into partnership with the well-established architect Charles Gambrill. One of his first great works was Trinity Church in Boston (1873–77), inspired by the Romanesque churches of southern France. The Winn Memorial Library at Woburn near Boston, commissioned in 1877, was the first of many public libraries for small towns to illustrate Richardson's picturesque tendencies. Sever Hall, commissioned for Harvard University in 1878, was Richardson's first work after his partnership with Gambrill was dissolved in 1878. The building flaunts Richardson's Romanesque leanings, with its soft, deep red brickwork accented by bright red tiles. He looked to the simplicity and clarity of proportion of eighteenth-century English town houses in his own designs for American domestic architecture, which include The Stoughton House in Cambridge, Massachusetts (1883).

Like many other architects from Boston and New York, Richardson took advantage of the CHICAGO FIRE of 1871 to create vast building projects. Richardson's last major building for Chicago, the Marshall Field Wholesale Store designed in 1885, filled an entire city block; it was demolished in 1930. Although Romanesque in their representation of mass and stability, Richardson's later buildings, particularly the Marshall Field Store, were prototypes of and direct influences on the CHICAGO SCHOOL of modern architecture.

Riel, Louis (1844–1885) Canadian insurgent leader. In Riel's first rebellion (1869–70), he led the Indians and Métis, or half-breeds, of Manitoba's Red River Settlement to oppose the transfer of their land from the Hudson's Bay Company to CANADA. The government of Canada put down the uprising but gave Red River its own provincial government. After fleeing to the United States, Riel returned to lead Métis who were trying to secure land claims in Saskatchewan (1884–85). After a showdown at Batoche, Riel was captured, tried, and hanged.

Riis, Jacob [August] (1849–1914) Danish-born American photographer and social reformer. Riis's unsparing works prompted improvements in late-nineteenth-century urban planning and enriched the photo-documentary tradition begun with *John Thomson's Street Life in London* (1877). Acquainted with the social iniquities of New York through his experiences as an immigrant and police reporter for the *New York Tribune,* he became a voice for reform with his book about the city's Lower East Side life, *How the Other Half Lives* (1890). The photographic inquiry into the tenements, flophouses, workhouses, and street life led THEODORE ROOSEVELT and other New York politicians to reform housing and child labor laws. Similar exposés by muckraking journalists continued the trend to reform into the early twentieth century. Riis's memoir, *The Making of an American,* was published in 1901; he founded a New York City settlement house the same year.

Rimbaud, [Jean-Nicolas-] Arthur (1854–1891) French poet. He was born in Charleville; his father abandoned the family in 1860, leaving Rimbaud and his three siblings in the care of their "cantankerous and vindictive" mother. Rimbaud began writing verse at age eight, and his first published poem appeared in January 1870. After earning first prize at the Concours Académique for a Latin poem in August 1870, he ran away to Paris but was arrested for riding a train without a ticket and spent ten days in jail. His schoolmaster, Georges Izambard, paid Rimbaud's fine and sent him to Douai to live with Izambard's aunts. Rimbaud fled, however, only to return two weeks later with poems he had written about his experiences with hunger, struggle, and freedom.

Rimbaud's mother had him returned home with the help of the police, but Rimbaud sold his watch in early 1871 and left for Paris. He then rejected his early poems, expressing a disgust for them and life in general. He began to develop a personal aesthetic, and in letters to Izambard and a few other friends Rimbaud expressed his belief that the poet must be a seer, a "*voyant,*" who is an instrument of a higher force.

Writing with a new purpose, Rimbaud sent copies of his poems to Paul Verlaine, who was immediately impressed with the young poet and sent for him. Rimbaud moved in with the older poet and his wife, which quickly became a scandal. Rimbaud returned to Charleville in March 1872 in order for Verlaine to reconcile with his wife, but Verlaine quickly begged for Rimbaud's return. Together they moved to London in July 1872, where Rimbaud began writing prose poems.

Rimbaud's relationship with Verlaine lasted almost a year, and then a bitter argument ended with Verlaine shooting Rimbaud and hitting him in the wrist. Verlaine was arrested and sentenced to two years in prison. Rimbaud wrote *Une Saison en Enfer* (A Season in Hell). Discouraged by the book's reception in Paris, Rimbaud abandoned the edition, burned his manuscript, and left bales of copies in the attic of the printer, where they were not discovered until 1901.

In 1875, Rimbaud traveled to Germany to learn the language and was visited there by Verlaine. Their meeting ended in another quarrel, but it is believed that during this meeting Rimbaud gave Verlaine the manuscript of prose poems that Verlaine later published as *Les Illuminations.* Rimbaud left Europe for Egypt in 1880.

Verlaine and Rimbaud never met again, but other writers pleaded with him to return to France and lead a new literary movement. Their invitations were ignored.

In 1891 Rimbaud developed a tumor on his right leg and traveled to Marseilles, where the leg was amputated. His health continued to deteriorate, and he died in Marseilles.

Rimsky-Korsakov, Nikolay Andreyevich (1844–1908) Russian composer. Born in Tikhvin, he received his first piano lesson at age six and began to reveal his talent as a composer as early as age nine. Following family tradition, he was enrolled in a military school in St. Petersburg and entered the navy at twelve. In 1861, however, Rimsky-Korsakov met the composer M. A. Balakirev, leader of the group of Russian nationalist composers known later as THE FIVE, with Rimsky-Korsakov as one of its members. Balakirev inspired the seventeen-year-old to compose his Symphony No. 1, which was successfully performed, with Balakirev as conductor, in 1865. Although he did not leave the navy until 1873, Rimsky-Korsakov was appointed professor of composition and instrumentation at the St. Petersburg

Conservatory in 1871. The self-taught instructor studied secretly in order to provide his students with the training he lacked.

Upon his retirement from the navy, Rimsky-Korsakov was named the inspector of naval bands and took the opportunity to learn how to play every instrument. In 1878 he composed the world's first trombone concerto. In 1873 he completed his first opera, *The Maid of Pskov* (revised 1892), and the following year he married pianist Nadezhda Purgold. From 1874 to 1881, Rimsky-Korsakov served as director of the Free School of Music concerts, and from 1886 to 1900 he served as conductor of the Russian Symphony concerts. His best known orchestral works were written during this period, in 1887–88: *Spanish Capriccio, Scheherezade,* and the *Russian Easter Festival* overture. His book *Principles of Orchestration* expressed his ideas on the subject. His operas included *The Snow Maiden* (1881) and *Mlada* (1890). He also edited and arranged operas by such Russian composers as Mikhail Glinka, ALEKSANDR BORODIN, and MODEST MUSSORGSKY.

Rimsky-Korsakov suffered a period of self-doubt from 1891 to 1893 when he was unable to compose and felt a profound distaste for all music. After his recovery, however, he created some of his finest works, including the operas *Sadko* (1895) and *Tsar Sultan* (1900); these compositions contain the popular themes "Song of India" and "Flight of the Bumblebee," respectively.

A nationalistic composer, Rimsky-Korsakov drew frequently on Russian history, legend, and folk music. He was also skilled in orchestral clarity and color. His pupils included twentieth-century Russian composer Igor Stravinsky (1882–1971), on whom he had a lasting influence.

For his sympathies with the Russian Revolution of 1905, Rimsky-Korsakov was dismissed from the St. Petersburg Conservatory, with a two-month ban placed on the performance of all his works. After the ban was lifted, his music became increasingly popular. The composer used the imposed retirement to write his memoirs, *My Musical Life,* first published in 1909. Because of its elements of political satire, his opera *The Golden Cockerel* was not permitted to be performed until 1909, after his death.

Ring des Nibelungen, Der (*The Ring of the Nibelung*) Opera cycle. The four operas were written by RICHARD WAGNER and based on the Nordic Nibelung saga, in which a magic ring gives the bearer power to dominate the world but only by giving up love. The complete cycle of what many consider Wagner's greatest work was first performed in Bayreuth on August 13–17, 1876. Wagner described the cycle, dedicated to Ludwig II of Bavaria, as a "festival drama for three days and a preliminary evening." The cycle comprises *Das Rheingold* (*The Rhine Gold,* 1869), *Die Walküre* (*The Valkyrie,* 1870), *Siegfried* (1876), and *Götterdämmerung* (*Twilight of the Gods,* 1876).

Risorgimento Italian political movement. It was originally the name of a nationalist Italian newspaper, first published by COUNT CAMILLO DI CAVOUR in 1847, the term *risorgimento* (resurgence) eventually was applied to the entire movement of Italian political, literary, and cultural revival in the early nineteenth century. The primary aim of most of the participants, including GUISEPPE GARIBALDI and GIUSEPPE MAZZINI, in the Risorgimento was the creation of a unified Italian state, achieved in 1861.

Ritschl, Albrecht (1822–1889) German theologian. Ritschl emphasized ethics and the human community rather than metaphysics. He opposed rationalistic theology, arguing that God can be known only as revealed in the person and activities of Jesus Christ.

Roberts, Frederick Sleigh, 1st Earl Roberts (1832–1914) British soldier. The son of a general, he was educated at Eton and Sandhurst. He saw service during the INDIAN MUTINY (1857–58) and became a national hero with his battlefield successes during the second of the ANGLO-AFGHAN WARS (1878–80), including his intrepid relief march from KABUL TO KANDAHAR, which he led astride his white Arab horse Vonolel. He went on to serve as commander in chief in India (1885–93). After becoming a field marshal in 1895 and serving as commander in chief in Ireland, he was commander in chief in South Africa from 1899 to 1900, winning several important battles of the BOER WAR. Perhaps the most popular British general of the Victorian Age, the small, good-natured officer was known affectionately as "Bobs" to his troops, a moniker commemorated in the poem of the same name by RUDYARD KIPLING. In 1901 he was made an earl and became the last commander in chief of the British army until the abolition of that post in 1904. His last years were spent campaigning for compulsory military service. Roberts was the author of *Forty-one Years in India* (1897).

Rockefeller, John Davison (1839–1937) American industrialist. Born in upstate New York, he was the son of a lumber trader who moved his family to Ohio where he sold patent medicines. He worked as a clerk in a shipping office before joining with Maurice Clark to start a produce-shipping business. The enterprise prospered during the Civil War and began to boom when it added OIL (PETROLEUM) to its list of merchandise. Located in the prime oil-producing region in the United States, Rockefeller and Clark built a refinery in Cleveland in 1863. Two years later Rockefeller bought Clark out.

The rapidly growing markets caused by the opening of the West and the influx of immigrants fed Rockefeller's enterprises. He opened another refinery and in 1870 formed the Standard Oil Company of Ohio with the help of his close friend Henry Flagler. The company's large regular shipments of oil enabled him to wring discounted rates from the railroads and to undercut his competitor's prices.

By the spring of 1872 he held sway over most of Cleveland's refineries and controlled some large ones in New York City. He and Flagler then began a ruthless buyout and price-undercutting campaign, which by 1879 had given him control of 90 percent of U.S. refining capacity. In 1882 he established the Standard Oil Trust, which consolidated his holdings in other industries under one corporate roof.

Not content with controlling most of the refining end of the oil business, Standard Oil also stepped into the sales end with the same fierce underpricing and buyout tactics. By the mid-1880s the company controlled about 80 percent of the business. Extending its reach into the production area, Standard acquired control of 25 percent of U.S. crude oil products by 1891. These monopolistic practices led to the dissolving of the trust by the Ohio Supreme Court; it was promptly replaced by the Standard Oil Company of New Jersey, which was then abolished by the U.S. Supreme Court in 1911.

Rockefeller had withdrawn from active control of his empire by 1897. His name had become synonymous with fabulous wealth, and much of his next four decades was spent in philanthropic pursuits, including the bankrolling of the University of Chicago and the founding of the Rockefeller Foundation in 1913.

Rodin, Auguste [Francois-Auguste-René] (1840–1917) French sculptor. He was born on the Left Bank of Paris, the son of a police official. He left school at thirteen and the following year entered the Petit Ecole, a government vocational school for draftsmen and stonecutters. Three years at the school introduced him to sculpture and clay modeling. He applied to the Grande Ecole des Beaux-Arts, the traditional gateway to government commissions and artistic fame. Admitted as a drawing student, he failed three times to win a place as a sculpture student.

Rodin began to earn a living by sculpting ornamental masonry and bric-a-brac. He entered a religious order in 1862 after the death of his sister but left within a year. In 1864 he began working for Carrier-Belleuse, France's largest producer of statuettes. In that year he sculpted what is considered his first major work, *The Man with the Broken Nose,* which was rejected by the staid Académie des Beaux-Arts. The roughly hewn clay statue of an ordinary man did not conform to the Académie's taste for heroic monuments. Rodin continued to work in clay that was then cast in plaster. The plaster cast served as a base for a bronze casting.

He lived in Brussels from 1870 to 1875, and in 1875 journeyed to Florence where he came under the influence of Renaissance artist Michelangelo. Back in Brussels he sculpted *The Age of Bronze.* The plaster cast of this statue was so realistic he was accused of casting it from a live model. Like his previous work, this statue defied the static, monumental style favored by most of the Paris art establishment. Edmund Turguet, the undersecretary of the Ministry of Fine Arts, admired the statue and bought it on behalf of the government in 1880.

Rodin returned to Paris in 1877. He won his first major public commission from Turguet. Hired to execute a portal for a proposed museum of decorative arts in Paris, Rodin worked at it until his death thirty-seven years later. The portal, called *The Gates of Hell,* was inspired by Dante's Inferno. It was 21 feet high, 13 feet wide, and 3 feet deep, and it contained 180 figures. Some of his most famous works were designed for the portal: *The Kiss, The Prodigal, Eternal Springtime,* and *The Thinker.* The museum was never built, and the gates are now at the Rodin Museum in Paris.

His fame grew steadily, though his commitment to REALISM and to the human aspects of his subject matter continued to incite controversy. His famous group statue, *The Burghers of Calais,* unveiled in 1895, enraged its sponsors who wanted a monument to their heroic ancestors and got instead a realistic vision of brave men facing death. Likewise his renowned statue of Balzac—brooding and massive—caused such an uproar that he withdrew it from an exhibition.

Rodin's presentation of more than 150 works at the 1900 Paris Exhibition won him an international reputation. Orders poured in from everywhere for bronze casts and marble replicas. He commanded 40,000 francs for a sitting as he produced busts of GEORGE BERNARD SHAW, JOSEPH PULITZER, GUSTAV MAHLER, Georges Clemenceau, and others. He was named commander in the Legion of Honor and was elected president of the International Society of Painters, Sculptors, and Engravers. After suffering a stroke in 1916, Rodin died quietly the following year.

Roman Catholic Church See PAPACY.

Romania (Rumania) Country bordering on RUSSIA, AUSTRIA-Hungary, SERBIA, and BULGARIA. It consists of the former Moldavia and Wallachia, the "Danubian Principalities," which at the beginning of the Victorian era were autonomous regions within the OTTOMAN EMPIRE and under Russian protection.

Following the CRIMEAN WAR, France supported the unification of Wallachia and Moldavia, and plebiscites were held in which Alexander Cuza was elected governor of both provinces. In 1861 the two were officially united as Romania with Russian and French approval. Cuza introduced political and agrarian reforms. In 1866 he was ousted by conservatives and replaced by Charles Hohenzollern-Sigmaringen. Following the RUSSO-TURKISH WAR (1877–78), Romania was granted full independence.

In the years after independence, Romania's economy developed slowly. The country managed to avoid involvement in disputes with other states of the BALKANS, but the large Romanian populations in Austria-Hungary and Russia were a source of continued tension. As a reward for joining the victorious Entente Powers in World War I, Romania received Transylvania and Bessarabia.

Romanticism Artistic movement. A term used to describe a revolution in the visual arts, literature, and music from the mid-eighteenth century through the nineteenth century, Romanticism rejected the ideas of the Enlightenment that life could be understood on the basis of reason alone. Instead, it emphasized emotion, passion, self-expression, and individuality through optimistic interpretations of the world. The celebration of nature, nostalgia for the past, and the search for an ideal, nonexistent world were other key ingredients of Romanticism. It was believed possible through Romanticism to make the world over and even to change human nature for the better.

All of the arts were affected by Romanticism. Authors began to take an interest in old legends, folk ballads, antiquities, ruins, and rustic characters. The word "Romanticism" derives from the late-eighteenth-century taste for romances, medieval tales of adventure so-called because they were written in Romance languages.

Many writers relied heavily on their imagination to describe idealistic pictures of nature. The English poets William Blake, Samuel Taylor Coleridge, and William Wordsworth exemplified the Romantic preoccupation with individualism, with nature, and with the supernatural. Sir Walter Scott took an optimistic approach in his historical novels. In *Waverly* (1814) he presented the past motivated by idealism, chivalry, love, and devotion. Romantic literature also tended to include trivial and sentimental love stories as well as some powerfully dramatic novels. Among the best known Romantic novels are CHARLOTTE BRONTË's *JANE EYRE* (1847), EMILY BRONTË's *WUTHERING HEIGHTS* (1847), HERMAN MELVILLE's *Moby-Dick* (1851), and Mary Shelley's *Frankenstein* (1818).

In the visual arts, Romanticism stressed a feeling for nature and an expression of emotion and imagination. The Romantic artist worshiped power, love, violence, the Greeks, and the Middle Ages, leading to the GOTHIC REVIVAL and MEDIEVALISM movements. Romanticism favored the revival not of one style but of an unlimited number of styles. Romanticism in painting began in England in the works of John Constable and J. M. W. TURNER that demonstrated a new awareness of landscape. American THOMAS COLE also specialized in landscapes. Typical manifestations of Romanticism in German painting are the medieval townscapes of Karl Friedrich Schinkel and Moritz von Schwind as well as the mysterious landscapes of Caspar David Friedrich. In France, EUGÈNE DELACROIX and Theodore Gericault became Romanticism's leading exponents.

Influenced by the literature and painting of the time, nineteenth-century music became Romantic through intensely personal expressions of emotion. Composers rejected the limitations of set forms and wrote music that was more pictorial in their attempts to imitate nature. The great German Romantic composers, sometimes called Romantic classicists, were Franz Schubert, Felix Mendelssohn, and ROBERT SCHUMANN. In France, innovations in Romantic style and form were further developed by HECTOR BERLIOZ, FRÉDÉRIC CHOPIN, and FRANZ LISZT.

Although Romanticism declined toward the latter part of the nineteenth century with the growth of REALISM, its influential assertion of the artist's imagination and individuality can be seen in the diverse works of TRANSCENDENTALISM, IMPRESSIONISM, and POST-IMPRESSIONISM.

Röntgen, Wilhelm Conrad See X RAYS.

Roosevelt, Theodore (1858–1919) Twenty-sixth president of the UNITED STATES (1901–9). Born in New York City to a socially prominent family, Roosevelt was elected to the state assembly (1882–84). Defeated in the 1886 New York City mayoralty race, he was appointed to the U.S. Civil Service Commission (1889–95). He won recognition for his crusade against corruption as New York City's Police Commissioner (1895–97). Named assistant secretary of the Navy in 1897, he resigned in 1898 to fight in the SPANISH-AMERICAN WAR. His war exploits helped him become New York's governor (1898–1900). His reform politics dismayed many political bosses who had him removed from New York by convincing President WILLIAM MCKINLEY to choose him as his vice-presidential running mate in 1900. Roosevelt became president after McKinley's assassination in 1901.

Roosevelt supported stricter enforcement of antitrust laws, reinvigorated the Interstate Commerce Commission, and championed the Pure Food and Drug Act, which protected consumers from unsanitary food processors. He established the U.S Park Service and set aside 150 million acres of government land as forest preserves.

Internationally, he sent Marines to Central America to establish Panama's independence from Colombia, leading to the building of the Panama Canal. He won the Nobel Peace Prize in 1906 for mediating the end of the Russo-Japanese War. He retired after his second term but mounted an unsuccessful third-party candidacy in 1912 after becoming disappointed with his successor, William H. Taft. His most famous book is the four-volume *The Winning of the West* (1889–96).

Rosebery, Archibald Philip, Primrose, 5th Earl of (1847–1929) British politician. Rosebery was born in London and assumed the title of earl upon his grandfather's death in 1868. He assisted WILLIAM GLADSTONE in his MIDLOTHIAN CAMPAIGNS of 1879 and 1880 for the LIBERAL PARTY and later served as foreign secretary under Gladstone (1886 and 1892–94).

As foreign secretary Rosebery followed his strong imperialist leanings, which contrasted sharply with Gladstone's beliefs. He established a protectorate in Uganda in 1894, an area Gladstone wanted to abandon. Rosebery succeeded Gladstone as prime minister (1894–95) after Gladstone resigned over increased spending on the Navy, a measure Rosebery favored.

Rosebery led a largely ineffective government. His aristocratic ways, including a great fondness for race horses and yachts, alienated many Liberals, as did his imperialist beliefs. The House of Lords led by the CONSERVATIVE PARTY also opposed him and would pass no laws except the budget. He resigned in 1895 and gave up the leadership of the Liberals in 1896. He continued to support strong imperialist policies, including England's stance in the FASHODA CRISIS and the prosecution of the BOER WAR. His final split with the Liberals came in 1905 when he opposed Irish HOME RULE and retired from politics.

Ross, Sir James Clark (1800–1862) Scottish explorer. After several voyages to the Arctic, he explored ANTARCTICA in 1839–43, discovering the Ross Sea and Victoria Land and following the Ross ice shelf for many miles. He was among those who searched the waters of northern Canada for lost explorer SIR JOHN FRANKLIN (1848–49). He is the author of *Voyage of Discovery* (1847).

Rossetti, Christina Georgina (1830–1894) English poet. The sister of artist and poet DANTE GABRIEL ROSSETTI and editor WILLIAM MICHAEL ROSSETTI, she shared their involvement in the PRE-RAPHAELITE artistic movement. In 1850 she published poems in the first issue of the Pre-Raphaelite Brotherhood's literary journal, *The Germ*. A devout Christian, she was also influenced by the Anglo-Catholicism of the OXFORD MOVEMENT and reportedly rejected two marriage proposals because of religious differences with her suitors. Her poetry is marked not only by the pictorial vividness and luxurious sensuality of Pre-Raphaelite art but by a spirit of renunciation, loss, and frustrated desire. It is also praised for its metrical inventiveness and clear, lucid style. Her best known collection is her first, *Goblin Market and Other Poems* (1862). *The Prince's Progress and Other Poems* (1866) also contained much of lasting value. Active until near the end of her life, she also wrote books of nursery rhymes and religious verse. Her last work was *The Face of the Deep: A Devotional Commentary on the Apocalypse* (1892).

Rossetti, Dante Gabriel [Gabriel Charles Dante] (1828–1882) English poet and painter. The son of Gabriele Rossetti, the Italian poet and professor of languages, Rossetti was a founder with JOHN EVERETT MILLAIS and WILLIAM HOLMAN HUNT, of the Pre-Raphaelite Brotherhood.

Rossetti began studying art at the age of fourteen but had been writing verses as a

Dante Gabriel Rossetti exemplified the stylistic qualities of the Pre-Raphaelites in his painting La Ghirlandata.

child. In 1850 the Pre-Raphaelite Brotherhood published a magazine, *The Germ,* edited by Rossetti's brother WILLIAM MICHAEL ROSSETTI. With his sister CHRISTINA GEORGINA ROSSETTI, Dante contributed poems to the publication, including "The Blessed Damozel" written when he was nineteen.

An adherent of Romanticism, Rossetti echoed his efforts as a poet in his paintings. Rossetti found poetry and art interrelated forms of expression and saturated his words and images with passion and anxiety. Through 1860, Rossetti worked chiefly in watercolor. By means of rejuvenating Christian painting, he painted his famous *Ecce Ancilla Domini* (*The Annunciation*) in 1850. His interpretation of the Annunciation is without traditional Christian attributes and introduces a complex emotional intensity that is both sexual and enigmatic.

In 1860, Rossetti married his model Elizabeth Siddal and focused his art on more sensual, personal fantasies. When his young wife died from a drug overdose, Rossetti buried with her the manuscripts of his poems and painted an idealized portrait of her entitled *Beata Beatrix* (1863). He depicted his wife in a trancelike state as she moves from earth to heaven. Like the paintings of Gustave Moreau, Rossetti evokes a mysterious mixture of experiences ranging from love to death.

Rossetti's late paintings were chiefly on Arthurian and Dantesque themes. His writings include translations from the Italian versions of *The Early Italian Poets* (1861) and *Dante and His Circle* (1874). Rossetti's own *Ballads and Sonnets* (1881) includes the great sonnet sequence "The House of Life" and the ballads "Sister Helen" and "The White Ship."

Rossetti, William Michael (1829–1919) English editor. Brother of CHRISTINA ROSSETTI and DANTE GABRIEL ROSSETTI, he was a founder of the Pre-Raphaelite Brotherhood and editor of its short-lived literary journal *The Germ* (1850). His works about the artistic movement include *Ruskin, Rossetti, Praeraphaelitism* (1899) and *Praeraphaelite Diaries and Letters* (1900). His other works include a translation of Dante's *Inferno,* editions of his brother's and sister's collected works, and editions of William Blake, Percy B. Shelley, and WALT WHITMAN.

Rostand, Edmond-Eugène-Alexis (1868–1918) French playwright and poet. Rostand's romantic verse plays set him apart from prevailing nineteenth-century naturalist writers. Rejecting as his subjects the social issues popular in turn-of-the-century French theater, he wrote instead of the unconsummated love and patriotic duty of quixotic heroes who lived in exotic locales in the distant past.

Rostand's early works, which include *Les Romanesques* (*The Romantics*), produced in 1894; *La Princesse Lointaine* (*The Faraway Princess*), produced in 1895; and *La Samaritaine* (*The Women of Samaria*) (1897), met with some success. However, it was his comedy *Cyrano de Bergerac,* which premiered in December 1897, that secured his fame. It tells the tale of soldier-poet Cyrano who, believing his huge nose makes him an unworthy suitor of his beloved Roxanne, courts her through love letters written in the name of Christian.

Later notable works include the historical drama *L'Aiglon* (*The Eaglet*) (1900), the allegorical comedy *Chantecler* (1910), and the posthumously produced *La Dernière Nuit de Don Juan* (*The Last Night of Don Juan*) (1922). In 1901, at the unusually young age of thirty-three, Rostand was elected by the Académie Française.

Rothschild, Lionel Nathan (1808–1879) English banker. The son of Sir Nathan Mayer Rothschild (1777–1836) who founded the

London branch of the Rothschild banking empire and who helped bankroll the armies that defeated Napoleon, Lionel Rothschild dominated the family business after his father's death and floated huge international loans that helped support IRISH POTATO FAMINE relief in 1847 and the CRIMEAN WAR in 1856. Another loan in 1875 made the British government the chief stockholder in the Suez Canal Company. In 1858 he became the first Jewish member of the House of Commons.

Rouault, Georges [-Henri] (1871–1958) French painter. Born in Paris, Rouault apprenticed as a draftsman in stained glass. In 1892 he studied painting in the studio of Gustave Moreau where he met Henri Matisse. He became curator of the Musée Moreau upon Moreau's death in 1898. Moreau greatly influenced Rouault's early paintings, particularly his religious works. Rouault's *The Child Jesus Among the Doctors* (1894) reflects both his own taste for medieval art as well as Moreau's paintings.

Religious subject matter came easily to Rouault who was deeply religious himself and profoundly moralistic. His intense religiosity was heightened by his contacts with the novelist Joris-Karl Huysmans, who nearly talked Rouault into joining a monastery, and with the Catholic writer Léon Bloy.

At the turn of the century, Rouault's art displayed a radical change as he sought subjects appropriate to his anger and disgust over what he perceived as a rotting modern society. He in turn perpetuated the concern of VINCENT VAN GOGH and PAUL GAUGUIN for the corrupt state of the world.

Stylistically, Rouault's violent slashing brushstrokes, glowing colors, and thickly applied paint placed him with the Fauves at the 1905 Salon d'Automne, but his emphasis on the direct expression of emotion was more in common with the tenets of contemporary German Expressionism.

Rousseau, Henri [-Julien-Félix] (1844–1910) French painter. After serving in the army and as a customs official, Rousseau retired in 1886 to begin painting full time. He was an untrained artist who made copies in the Louvre and exhibited regularly at the Salon des Independants. His art bridged nineteenth-century ROMANTICISM and twentieth-century fantasy.

The still lifes and landscapes he created throughout his career recall the work of amateur or folk artists. His rather direct style was a mixture of naïveté, innocence, and insight. He combined his strange imagination with a sharp way of seeing in *Carnival Evening* (1886), his first painting exhibited in the Salon des Independants. The composition, characteristic of most of his work, includes deep space with all of the formal elements treated frontally and flatly.

By 1890, Rousseau had exhibited twenty paintings at the Salon des Independants. He continually painted and drew scenes of Paris, still lifes, portraits of his friends, and details of plants, leaves, and animals. Although consistently ridiculed by the public and the critics, Rousseau had his admirers, including Odilon Redon, EDGAR DEGAS, HENRI DE TOULOUSE-LAUTREC, and PIERRE-AUGUSTE RENOIR.

Rousseau later developed a romantic passion for the terror and beauty of faraway jungles that would last until his death. His visionary quality first appeared in *Storm in the Jungle* (1891) and recurred in a series of canvases of North Africa, like *The Sleeping Gypsy* (1897). In these dreamy compositions Rousseau displayed a simplicity of form and color and imaginativeness of subject. His work came as a revelation to modern artists seeking new means of expression. In his last paintings, Rousseau transformed the leaves he picked up and the animals and plants he observed in the Paris Zoo and Botanical Garden into scenes of tropical mystery. *The Dream* (1910), featuring a bizarre setting of lions, birds, and bison for a reclining female nude, is a masterpiece of fantasy that influenced twentieth-century surrealism.

Rousseau, [Pierre-Etienne-] Théodore (1812–1867) French painter. Rousseau's maternal uncle, Gabriel Colombet, was a portrait painter and pupil of Jacques-Louis David. Rousseau himself began to paint at a very young age, making copies of Claude Lorrain at the Louvre. At the age of nineteen he contributed *A View in Auvergne* to the Salon of 1831. His personal revolt against formalism in 1832 led to a series of Salon refusals, which included *Descent of Cattle from the Jura* in 1836 and *Avenue of Chestnuts* in 1837. No painting of his appeared at the Salon until 1849.

In 1842, Rousseau left for a seven-month sojourn in the Berry, a province recommended to him for its quiet character by another Barbizon painter, Jules Dupré. There Rousseau painted *Under the Birches* (1842–43) and established the main features that would be practiced by the BARBIZON SCHOOL. Strongly influenced by John Constable and seventeenth-century Dutch landscapists, Rousseau captured the distinct elements of a particular time of day, combining the effects of changing light with closely observed details of trees, rocks, and leaves.

Rousseau often visited the tiny village of Barbizon in the forest of Fontainebleau, where he painted a number of Romantic pictures. In 1846 he established a studio in Paris before settling permanently in Barbizon in 1848.

Royal Albert Hall See ALBERT HALL, ROYAL.

Royal Exchange London financial center. Founded in the Elizabethan Age and known familiarly as "'Change," it burned down in 1838 and was rebuilt in 1844. The new building was designed by William Tite and featured a neoclassical pediment inset with Richard Westmacott's sculpture of *Commerce*. The building is now the headquarters of the London International Financial Futures Exchange.

Royal Opera House See COVENT GARDEN.

roystering Musical revelry occurring at social gatherings where oysters were served. Roystering was all the rage in America in the 1880s. Originally a delicacy for aristocrats, oysters—scalloped, stewed, and raw—became a favorite food of the masses as well.

Rubáiyát of Omar Khayyám Poem. One of the most popular poems in the English language, it was adapted from the Persian by EDWARD FITZGERALD. The first edition, published anonymously in 1859, consisted of seventy-five quatrains—*rubáiyát* is the Persian word for quatrains. FitzGerald translated it very loosely from the work of Omar Khayyám, an eleventh-century Persian mathematician and poet. FitzGerald molded the verse into four-line stanzas and unified Khayyám's poetry into connected themes. It is more of an adaptation than a translation, and it is difficult to separate the Englishman from the Persian.

Although the book was at first a commercial failure, it caught the attention of DANTE GABRIEL ROSSETTI and other artists and writers of the day. Its popularity then spread, and FitzGerald changed and expanded the poem in three other editions in 1868, 1872, and 1879. The last edition contained 101 quatrains.

The poem's popularity rests partly on its insouciant, even cheerful cynicism. The world-weary poet makes light of human preoccupations with material things as well as honor, love, knowledge, and other virtues. At the same time he merrily casts doubt on the role of supernatural agency in human affairs. The swift march of time and the nothingness waiting for us after death should inspire us to seize the day and live for the moment's delight. We should make the most of our "one moment in annihilation's waste," ideally sipping wine as we do.

G. K. Chesterton called it "one of the most remarkable achievements of that age." Its weary, sensual agnosticism was echoed by Ernest Dowson and other English poets toward the end of the century. Its phrases were incorporated into popular songs and some remain popular, including perhaps the most famous quatrain:

A book of verses underneath the bough,
A jug of wine, a loaf of bread—and thou
Beside me singing in the wilderness—
Oh, wilderness were paradise enow!

rubber Naturally occurring compound of carbon and hydrogen. Found in the form of globule clusters called latex in rubber trees, rubber is indigenous to tropical and subtropical countries. Rubber was used by Indians in South America and Central America as early as the sixteenth century and was introduced to Europe by Columbus. With the exception of its use in fabric for the waterproof Macintosh raincoat in 1823, rubber was not employed for large-scale practical purposes because of its instability under varying temperatures. It became sticky in the heat, brittle in the cold. Then in 1839 inventor CHARLES GOODYEAR discovered a method for VULCANIZING or temporizing rubber, making it resistant to heat and cold. Among those who capitalized on Goodyear's discovery was U.S. businessman BENJAMIN FRANKLIN GOODRICH, who developed the first rubber firehose. By the end of the century, rubber was used in a variety of commercial products, such as gaskets and bottle plugs. Synthetic rubber was not developed until 1909, by German scientist Karl Hoffman.

rugby Sport. The kicking, passing, and tackling game originated at RUGBY SCHOOL in England in the early nineteenth century and was the basis for American FOOTBALL. It still exists today in two forms: rugby union and rugby league. In the amateur version called rugby union (developed at Rugby around 1840), two teams of fifteen players compete on a grass field 110 yards by 75 yards. The ball may be kicked, carried, or passed. Tackling is permitted, but not blocking. Points are scored when the ball is carried across the goal line or kicked between the goal posts.

In the professional version called rugby league, introduced in 1895, teams consist of thirteen players, and the rules encourage passing and running.

Rugby School Preparatory educational institution for boys. The school was founded in 1567 in Rugby, Warwickshire, England. Under the headmastership of THOMAS ARNOLD, the school became a model for Victorian secondary schools for gentlemen. Alumnus MATTHEW ARNOLD, son of Thomas, wrote about the school, as did alumnus THOMAS HUGHES in *TOM BROWN'S SCHOOL DAYS*. The game of RUGBY originated here.

Ruskin, John (1819–1900) English writer and critic on art, economics, and social reform. With THOMAS CARLYLE, Ruskin is considered one of the "prophets" of the Victorian Age.

As a young boy Ruskin ardently studied nature and painting. From 1836 to 1840 he stayed at Oxford where he won the Newdigate Prize for poetry. He collected the work of JOSEPH MALLORD WILLIAM TURNER at an early age and began his meditations on art.

The first volume of his *Modern Painters* appeared in 1843 and started as a defense of Turner but developed into a treatise elaborating the principle that art is based on national and individual morality. He applied his theory to architecture in *The Seven Lamps of Architecture* (1849) before finishing the five volumes of *Modern Painters* in 1860.

Ruskin was also a passionate defender of the PRE-RAPHAELITES and attempted to interpret the meticulous details in the paintings of JOHN EVERETT MILLAIS and WILLIAM HOLMAN HUNT. In *The Stones of Venice* (1851–53), Ruskin maintained that the excellence of art is independent of representation, citing that the Gothic architecture of Venice reflected national and domestic virtue whereas Venetian Renaissance architecture reflected corruption.

In 1860, Ruskin turned his attention from art to theories of political economy. He wrote *Unto this Last* (1860–62) and *Munera Pulveris* (1862–63), which attacked the foundations of mercantile England, finding that modern art reflected the ugliness of modern industry. Ruskin's program for social reconstruction appeared in *Sesame and Lilies* (1865), *The Crown of Wild Olive* (1866), and *Time and Tide* (1867). He used his own money to carry out experiments based on his programs.

He was made the first professor of art in England as Slade Professor at Oxford in 1870. His health gradually deteriorated, and he suffered from several periods of insanity. Ruskin did manage, however, to write some of his greatest prose during that meantime, including his classic autobiography *Praeterita* (1885–89).

Russell, George William (AE) (1867–1935) Irish poet. An integral part of the Irish Literary Renaissance, Russell was born in Lurgan, County Armagh, Ireland. He met WILLIAM BUTLER YEATS at a Dublin art school and became interested in theosophy. In 1886 the two were among the founding members of the Dublin lodge of the Theosophical Society. Russell published *Homeward: Songs by the Way*, his first collection of poems, in 1894, and a printer's error on the title page in the word AEON (an eternal being in Gnostic belief) provided Russell with his pseudonym. In 1901, Russell was one of the founders of the Abbey Theatre, home of the Irish National Theatre Society.

Russell, John Russell, 1st Earl of (1792–1878) British politician. One of the foremost voices of liberal reform in Victorian England, Russell entered Parliament as a Whig in 1813, and in 1819 he began the long fight for the extension of suffrage that culminated in the passage of the REFORM BILL OF 1832. As a Cabinet minister in several administrations he continued to sponsor reform causes, including religious freedom for Irish Catholics, educational reforms, and the reduction in the number of crimes that carried the death penalty.

In 1845 his support of repealing the CORN LAWS helped influence Prime Minister ROBERT PEEL to end the import duties. Peel's decision split the CONSERVATIVE PARTY, and Russell became prime minister in 1846.

As head of what many consider the first LIBERAL PARTY government, Russell remained true to his liberal impulses. He helped establish the ten-hour day in many factories, set up a national board of health, and reformed the Australian government. He failed, however, to further extend the franchise or abolish the laws that limited the civil rights of Jews.

After his first administration he represented England at an unsuccessful conference in 1855 to end the CRIMEAN WAR. Made foreign secretary to Viscount PALMERSTON (1860–65), he helped ensure English neutrality during the U.S. CIVIL WAR. His second administration (1865–66) collapsed when he again tried to extend suffrage.

Russell was a prolific writer. His works include biographies of Lord William Russell and Charles James Fox, and an autobiography, *Recollections and Suggestions, 1813–1873* (1875).

Russia Country in Victorian era bordering Prussia, the Austrian Empire, and the Ottoman Empire to the south. To the east lay vast tracts of central Asia that would come under Russian domination by century's end.

NICHOLAS I became czar in 1825; he died 1855. Serfdom still persisted, and Russia lagged behind the rapidly industrializing European nations. The Russian elite was divided into two broad camps: Westernizers who wanted to reform Russian political and economic institutions, and the Slavophiles who favored some reform but idealized the Russian past and wanted to protect Russian culture from western European liberalism.

Nicholas I presided over a despotic regime that allowed little political change and continued to expand Russia's borders. The numerous ethnic and national groups that came under Moscow's rule proved hostile at various times throughout the century. POLAND revolted in 1830 but suffered defeat in the Russian-Polish War of 1831. Russian expansionism focused on the OTTOMAN EMPIRE to the south, with its warm weather ports and access to the Black Sea. Moscow assisted various internal rebellions against the Ottomans and negotiated treaties in the 1830s and 1840s that permitted the passage of Russian warships into the Black Sea. Nicholas also helped Austria quell the Hungarian revolt of 1848–49. His willingness to dispatch troops to crush rebellions against European autocrats earned Russia the nickname of "policeman of Europe."

Russia's southern ambitions helped spark the CRIMEAN WAR (1853–56) in which Russia was defeated by Great Britain, France, and the Ottomans. The war revealed Russia's industrial and military deficiencies. The new czar, ALEXANDER II, instituted several reforms, including the ending of serfdom in 1861, the establishment of county and provincial elected assemblies, and major changes in the judicial system, but he refused to approve an elected national assembly.

Under Alexander, Russian expansion continued to the borders of Afghanistan and China, and to the Pacific Ocean. Russia won the RUSSO-TURKISH WAR of 1878 while suppressing nationalist movements in Poland and the Ukraine. English fear of a Russian invasion of Afghanistan led to one of the ANGLO-AFGHAN WARS (1878–80). Fighting broke out between Russian and Afghan troops in 1884, but agreements between Russia and Britain settled the Russian-Afghan frontier questions into the twentieth century. Fearing the rise of Prussia, and countering its TRIPLE ALLIANCE with Italy and Austria-Hungary, Russia entered into an alliance with France in the 1890s. By 1907 that alliance would evolve into the Triple Entente among Russia, France, and Britain.

Growing discontent with czarist rule led to the formation of secret revolutionary groups in the 1860s and 1870s, one of which assassinated Alexander in 1881. His successor, ALEXANDER III, tried to stamp out the groups by sending many into exile. National groups within the empire, including Poles and Lithuanians, were subjected to a campaign of cultural assimilation while Jews suffered the worst pogroms yet inflicted on them. The revolutionary groups persisted, however, and produced some of the leaders of the future Soviet Union, including Vladimir Lenin, Joseph Stalin, and Leon Trotsky.

NICHOLAS II, the last czar, succeeded Alexander III in 1894. Under his incompetent rule the disastrous Russo-Japanese War of 1905 led to the revolution of 1905, which moved Russia toward adopting a parliamentary system. The Russian Revolution of 1917 finally ended czarist rule.

Russia produced some of the world's greatest writers during this period, including LEO TOLSTOY, IVAN TURGENEV, ANTON CHEKHOV, and FYODOR DOSTOYEVSKY. Notable composers include PYOTR TCHAIKOVSKY and NICOLAY RIMSKY-KORSAKOV.

Russo-Turkish War (1877–78) Last of a long series of wars fought between RUSSIA and the OTTOMAN EMPIRE in the BALKANS and the Caucasus. The war was precipitated by Russian intervention in support of the Balkan uprisings that began in 1875. The Turks resisted fiercely, particularly at the siege of Plevna, but the Russians eventually marched on Constantinople and compelled the Sultan to accept the Treaty of San Stefano. The treaty called for an expanded Montenegro and an independent BULGARIA ruled by a king chosen with Russian approval. The other European powers objected to this drastic expansion of Russian influence. Great Britain dispatched a fleet to the Bosporus, and diplomacy followed. Eventually the treaty signed at the Congress of BERLIN (1878) superseded San Stefano. By this treaty Bulgaria and ROMANIA gained independence and RUSSIA gained some territory, but the Ottoman Empire was allowed to keep Macedonia and Thrace. The war was also notable for the first appearance of the term JINGOISM in England.

Rutherford, Ernest See RADIOACTIVITY.

Rwanda See GERMAN EAST AFRICA.

saccharin First commercial artificial sweetener. The popular name for orthobenzoyl sulfimide, it was discovered in 1879 at Johns Hopkins University by U.S. scientist Ira Remsen (1846–1927) and his German student Constantine Fahlberg while they were testing coal tar derivatives. An accidental taste of the compound by Fahlberg alerted them to its sweetness. It was named for the Latin word *saccharum,* meaning "sugar." A scientific paper in 1880 introduced the compound, noting its sweetness. Without consulting Remsen, Fahlberg gained financial backing and began to produce it for commercial use. As early as 1907, the safety of saccharin for human use was being questioned.

sachet Small bag or packet containing perfumed powder or dried flowers used to scent clothes or household linen. Derived from the French for "a small bag," the diminutive of *sac,* the sachet has been used since ancient times and was a common personal article for women in the Victorian Age. It is assembled by wrapping dried FLOWERS in a lace handkerchief or a bit of fine lawn or silk, and then tucking the packet into the folds of a skirt.

safety razor Shaving tool. The precursor of the modern safety razor used a guard along one edge of the blade to prevent accidental cuts. The earliest version appeared in France in 1762, but a less cumbersome one was produced in Sheffield, England, in 1828. Concurrently, a hoe-shaped safety razor was made in the United States. In 1895, King Camp Gillette began developing a double-edged disposable blade with the hoe-shaped razor. The design was complete in 1901, but the manufacturing technology took longer to perfect. The first Gillette razor went on sale in 1903 and was an immediate success.

sahib Hindi term of address. Meaning "sir, master," it was used by Indians in British India to address a European man of high status or rank. "MEMSAHIB" was the term for a European woman of high status.

Saint-Gaudens, Augustus (1848–1907) Irish-born American sculptor. He studied sculpture at the Ecole des Beaux-Arts while carving cameos for a living. With the outbreak of the Franco-Prussian War, Saint-Gaudens went to Rome where he spent two years and received his first commissions for large-scale sculpture. Saint-Gaudens greatly admired the extremely shallow reliefs of the fifteenth-century Italian sculptors as a point of departure for his own "Neo-Florentine" carved portrait panels. The best known example is his portrait of ROBERT LOUIS STEVENSON (1887), which blends his experience in carving cameos with the immediacy and freshness of a sketch.

The largest body of work by Saint-Gaudens consists of public monuments relating to the U.S. Civil War. In these, Saint-Gaudens underscored his strength for realism but with a feeling of sentimentality. In his first public monument, the FARRAGUT *Monument* (1876–81), Saint-Gaudens designed the pedestal with the help of Stanford White to be an integral part of the monument rather than a mere support. In the *Shaw Monument* for Boston (1884–97), he carved a meticulously detailed, larger-than-life-size relief of Colonel *Robert Shaw* leading the first all-black volunteer regiment of the Civil War.

In 1888, Saint-Gaudens carved an impressive bust of General WILLIAM TECUMSEH SHERMAN based on eighteen sittings. In 1891, Saint-Gaudens was chosen by the Sherman Monument Committee to create an equestrian monument. Completed in 1900 for the Paris Universal Exposition, the *General Sherman Monument* is a neoclassical masterpiece depicting a Winged Victory preceding General Sherman, who is seated like a Roman equestrian emperor. By the end of the century he had become North America's leading sculptor.

Saint-Saëns, [Charles-] Camille (1835–1921) French composer. The music of Saint-Saëns is characterized by elegant, clearly articulated lines and ordered musical style. Rejecting trends toward modern music, Saint-Saëns based much of his work on earlier composers, including ROBERT SCHUMANN, Felix Mendelssohn, Ludwig von Beethoven, and Johann Sebastian Bach.

A child prodigy, Saint-Saëns composed a piano piece soon after his third birthday and gave a full debut concert at the age of eleven before entering the Paris Conservatoire in 1847. He was a pupil of Fromental Halévy and Charles Gounod, and composed his first symphony in 1851. He was the organist at the church of Saint-Merri in 1853 and at the Madeleine from 1857 to 1876 where FRANZ LISZT called him the world's greatest organist. During this time Saint-Saëns rediscovered the music of Bach, Wolfgang Amadeus Mozart, and George Handel. He taught from 1861 to 1865 at the Ecole Niedermeyer and cofounded La Société Nationale de Musique in 1871 to promote and perform new music by French composers.

In 1875 he composed one of his most successful works, the symphonic poem *Danse Macabre.* He composed several operas, including the popular *Samson et Dalila* (1877), but his instrumental music and orchestration brought him fame. His works include chamber music, concertos for piano, violin, and cello, and such orchestral works as the renowned *Third Symphony* (1886) that was dedicated to Liszt and is scored for orchestra with organ and two pianos.

Saint-Saëns's musical criticism was collected and published in 1885 as *Harmonie et Melodie.* After 1888 his extensive travels in Europe, the Middle East, and eastern Asia were reflected in his music, such as in *Africa* (1891) for piano and orchestra. He traveled in the U.S. in 1915 before spending the rest of his life in Algeria.

Saintsbury, George Edward Bateman (1845–1933) English literary critic and historian. Saintsbury graduated from Merton College, Oxford University, in 1867 and became a classical master at Elizabeth College, Guernsey, from 1868 to 1874 and headmaster of the Elgin Educational Institute from 1874 to 1876. He established himself at London in 1876 and contributed to the *Saturday Review* and other periodicals. Saintsbury became an authority on French literature and was professor of rhetoric and English literature at Edinburgh from 1895 to 1915. There he edited a series of volumes, *Periods of English Literature.* Some of his other writings include *A Primer of French Literature* (1880), *A Short History of French Literature* (1882), *A History of Elizabethan Literature* (1887), *Nineteenth Century Literature* (1896), biographies of John Dryden (1881), Sir Walter Scott (1897), and MATTHEW ARNOLD (1899), and several collections of essays.

Salisbury African city. The capital of the British colony of RHODESIA in southern Africa, now renamed Harare, it is the capital of the independent nation of ZIMBABWE. It was founded by British explorer CECIL RHODES in 1890 to serve as a center for gold-mining operations in his new colony. Named for Prime Minister Lord SALISBURY, it was originally settled by a few hundred single men, including farmers, miners, artisans, and engineers. After 1891, British women emigrated there; by 1900 the town combined the roughness of a colonial outpost with the rudiments of European manners, commerce, and class structure. Salisbury was dominated by Government House, a large, Indian-style bungalow where the chief administrator Lord Grey lived and polite dances were held. A few French, Germans, and Indians also lived in Salisbury—traders, prospectors, and miscellaneous thieves and adventurers—along with British troops to do battle with the neighboring MATABELE and MASHONA tribes.

In 1982, after white-ruled Rhodesia had become the black-ruled Zimbabwe (1980), Salisbury was renamed Harare in honor of a nineteenth-century African chief.

Salisbury, Robert (Arthur Talbot Gascoyne) Cecil, 3rd Marquess of (1830–1903) English statesman. The last prime minister to sit in the House of Lords, Salisbury was born to the aristocracy, making his home at the ancestral seat of the Cecils at Hatfield. Elected to Parliament as a CONSERVATIVE in 1853, he was a foe of democratization. He resigned in 1867 to protest his party's support for the REFORM BILL OF 1867 that enfranchised about two million members of the working class. In 1874, Salisbury returned to government as Secretary of State for INDIA under BENJAMIN DISRAELI. In 1878, Salisbury became foreign secretary, a position he was to hold for most of the rest of his life.

As foreign secretary, Salisbury was instrumental in helping Britain expand its empire. He made his mark first at the Congress of BERLIN in 1878 when his shrewd diplomacy assisted in rolling back Russian power in the Balkans and put Cyprus under British occupation. He also managed foreign policy during the ANGLO-AFGHAN WARS of 1878–79 and the ZULU WAR of 1879.

When Disraeli died in 1881, Salisbury became the leader of the CONSERVATIVE PARTY. A moody, scholarly man with a long beard and disheveled attire, Salisbury had little taste for courting the electorate. He preferred religious and scientific pursuits, which he carried out in his private chapel and private laboratory at

Hatfield. Even more, however, he had patrician dedication to what he saw as the duty of government. He served a short term as prime minister, from June 1885 to January 1886. He served again from 1886 to 1892, winning the support of liberals. His last ministries were in 1895–1900 and 1900–2 when he led a Conservative-Liberal Unionist coalition.

As an M.P. and prime minister, Salisbury promoted several social reforms, including slum clearance (1884), free public education (1891), and workmen's compensation (1897). He was aided by his nephew ARTHUR BALFOUR, who acted as government leader in the House of Commons in 1891–92 and 1895–1902 and who succeeded Salisbury as prime minister(1902–5). However, domestic legislation was not Salisbury's principal interest; foreign policy was. He remained foreign secretary during most of his time as prime minister, basing his pragmatic, conciliatory, reserved style on Lord Castlereagh, foreign secretary (1812–22) during the defeat of Napoleon.

Salisbury expanded the British Empire while avoiding a European war and staying out of alliances with other great powers. He expanded British power in Africa through the Conference of BERLIN (1884–85) and presided over the reconquest of the SUDAN (1896–99) and the BOER WAR (1899–1902).

Despite his central role in the expansion and consolidation of GREAT BRITAIN's empire, Salisbury did not believe in empire for its own sake. For him the empire was a tool to serve traditional British interests, such as maintaining balance of power in Europe and securing eastern trade routes. Salisbury disdained the more strident and belligerent imperialism of his colonial secretary JOSEPH CHAMBERLAIN (1895–1903), although the two worked together to protect the empire.

salon Literary or artistic center or exhibition. During the Victorian era there were a number of meanings for the word "salon." To serious artists, the salon referred to an annual exhibition in Paris of artworks selected by a jury and sponsored by the French Royal Academy. By the mid-nineteenth century the Salon, which began in 1737, had come to represent conservative artistic tastes. In the 1860s artists whose works were rejected by the Salon jury assembled a number of renegade salons. By the end of the century these salons offered a substantial alternative to the Academy Salon.

Most notable of these salons was the SALON DES REFUSÉS, an exhibition held in Paris in 1863 that showcased the works of EDOUARD MANET, PAUL CÉZANNE, JAMES WHISTLER, and others. In 1890 the Society Nationale des Beaux-Arts (later the salon de la Nationale) was founded by AUGUSTE RODIN and others. The Salon des Independants was founded in 1884 by GEORGES SEURAT and others.

The term "salon" also referred to the regular association of writers and thinkers who were usually sponsored by a patron of the arts. The practice dates back at least as far as the eighteenth century and the intellectual salon of French-Swiss woman of letters Germaine de Stael.

In its most mundane sense, a salon referred to a large public room in the private home of a well-to-do family.

Salon des Refusés French art exhibit. A special exhibition was held in Paris on May 15, 1863, two weeks after the official one, showing the works refused by the Salon of that year. The exhibition was ordered by Napoleon III after the discontent caused by the number of rejections. The Salon had refused more than half of the five thousand submissions and excluded twenty-eight hundred artists. The government offered an exhibition space in the Palais des Champs-Elysées where the public and critics could examine the work. The counter-Salon immediately attracted hordes of Parisians. One of the principal exhibits was EDOUARD MANET's *Le Dejeuner sur l'herbe* (1863). Other exhibiting artists were EUGÈNE BOUDIN, PAUL CÉZANNE, CAMILLE PISSARRO, and JAMES ABBOTT MCNEILL WHISTLER. Nevertheless, the paintings exhibited were attacked by critics and public alike.

saltcellar Small dishes. Saltcellars were usually glass or silver, with perforated lids, used to hold table salt. A valuable commodity in the nineteenth century, salt was scooped from the dishes with tiny spoons.

Salvation Army Christian social service organization. Founded in 1865 in London by English minister WILLIAM BOOTH and his wife Catherine, the institution is based on Booth's belief that "a man may be down but he's never out." Originally known as the East London Revival Society, it adopted its name in 1878 and has consistently operated under a military structure, employing the terms ministers and soldiers for members as well as a standard army uniform. A branch opened in the United States in 1880.

San See BUSHMEN.

Sand, George [Amandine-Aurore-Lucile Dupin Dudevant] (1804–1876) French novelist. Born in Paris, she was educated near her grandmother's estate at Nohant. Her grandmother died in 1821, and a year later Dupin married Baron Casimir Dudevant. Although the couple had two children, Aurore Dudevant soon began an affair with Stephane de Grandsagne, a neighbor whose freethinking life-style changed Dudevant's thinking about her genteel attitudes and morals. It has been suggested that Grandsagne was the father of Dudevant's second child, Solange, born in 1828.

Dudevant separated from her husband in 1831 and moved to Paris in order to be with her lover Jules Sandeau. The couple began publishing a few stories in collaboration under the name Jules Sand. Dudevant published her first novel *Indiana* in 1832 under the name George Sand. The novel's critique of marriage and protest against the social conventions of the time brought her immediate fame.

After leaving Sandeau in 1833, Sand traveled to Italy with the poet and playwright Alfred de Musset. The emotionally stormy excursion became the basis for *Elle et lui* (1859) and inspired novels and stories by a number of friends and relatives. In 1838, Sand began an eight-year relationship with composer FRÉDÉRIC CHOPIN; her time spent attending to the tubercular Chopin on the island of Majorca was chronicled in *Un Hiver à Majorque,* published in 1841.

While Sand spent her early career publishing "socialistic" novels such as *Mauprat* (1837) and *Consuelo* (1842), the revolution of 1848 and its disappointing aftermath returned her to Nohant and more conservative themes. *Constance Verrier* (1860) advocates a traditional marriage, and *Valvedre* (1861) criticizes romantic passion. Sand's later writing also produced sentimental sketches of country life, such as *La petite Fadette,* which did little for her literary legacy but sealed her reputation as the "good lady of Nohant."

Sargent, John Singer (1856–1925) American painter. The prolific and fashionable portraitist began his career as an artist in Paris, studying under the classically academic painter Carolus Duran. Sargent's earliest works resulted from European influence, particularly the masterpieces of Frans Hals and Diego Velázquez, whose subtle control of values within an atmospheric space informed the development of his own unique painterly style. In 1878 he received an honorable mention at the Paris Salon and in 1881 a second-class medal.

With MARY CASSATT, Sargent was part of a cosmopolitan society of Americans in Paris who painted a world of elegant aristocrats. Sargent was best known for painting his sitters with complete accuracy while flattering them at the same time, as in an early portrait of *Mrs. Charles Gifford Dyer* (1880). Yet as a society portraitist, Sargent chose to explore the mysterious psychological realms of his subjects. In his seven-foot-square group portrait of *The Daughters of Edward Darley Boit,* executed in Paris in 1882 for exhibition at the following year's Salon, Sargent probed beneath formal appearances to evoke a quiet psychological drama of domestic life.

In 1884, Sargent arrived in London and adapted his painting style to a more accepted variant of IMPRESSIONISM in a series of watercolors and drawings. The watercolors best display Sargent's technical brilliance. The handling of informal subject matter, in paintings such as *Portrait of Paul Helleu Sketching* (1889) and *Simplon Pass: The Lesson* (1911), is more delicate and intimate than the still posturings of his academically inspired portraits. Here, Sargent revealed an American attempt at French Impressionism by emphasizing local color and off-center, on-the-spot points of view.

Technically, Sargent was a virtuoso painter who gave way to quick, sharp brushstrokes as if he had flung his paint onto the canvas. Critics saw his expressive painting style as a degradation of Impressionism and dubbed Sargent and his followers "the Slashing School."

Satsuma Revolt (1877) Japanese uprising. The revolt by a group of samurai, JAPAN's hereditary warrior class, was aimed against Emperor Meiji's reforms. Led by Saigo Takamori (1827–1877), forty thousand warriors in Satsuma in the south rebelled against decrees commuting samurai pensions and prohibiting the wearing of swords except by men in the newly formed army. For eight months, beginning on January 29, 1877, the aristocratic samurai engaged the citizen army fielded by the Emperor. The new army prevailed. Saigo was killed during a final battle near Kagoshima on September 24, 1877; many of his defeated followers committed suicide.

Saturn Planet. Saturn, the sixth planet from the sun, has been known since antiquity. Italian scientist Galileo Galilei (1564–1642), the first person to make astronomical observations through a telescope, noticed in 1612 that Saturn had an odd, bulging appearance. Dutch astronomer Christiaan Huygens (1629–1695), working with a better telescope, determined in 1656 that what Galileo had seen was a ring around Saturn; it is now known to be a complex system of rings composed of rock and ice particles. Huygens also discovered that Saturn had at least one satellite, called Titan. By the end of the eighteenth century, seven satellites of Saturn had been discovered.

The Victorian era saw the discovery of two more satellites of Saturn: In 1848, English astronomer William Lassell (1799–1880) and, independently, American astronomer George Phillips Bond (1825–1865) discovered an eighth moon of Saturn, Hyperion. In 1898, American astronomer William Henry Pickering discovered a ninth Saturnian moon, Phoebe. No more were discovered until the 1980s. Saturn is now known to have at least seventeen satellites and probably four to six more.

In addition, Saturn's ring system was studied in the 1840s by French astronomer Edouard

Albert Roche, who showed mathematically that tidal effects would break up a smaller body orbiting a larger one if the smaller body came within 2.5 times the radius of the larger one. Conversely, an orbiting cloud of particles within that limit, called the Roche limit, would be prevented from coalescing into a body. This hypothesis explained the existence of Saturn's rings, which were within 2.5 times the radius of Saturn: Saturn's tidal force prevented the particles in the rings from coalescing into a satellite. The calculations of Scottish mathematician JAMES CLERK MAXWELL in 1857 confirmed Roche's hypothesis.

Scandinavia Region consisting of the northernmost parts of Europe. Definitions of the region vary; the most inclusive embraces the modern countries of Denmark, Sweden, Norway, Finland, and Iceland. The geography of this region is varied: Norway and northern Sweden feature rugged mountains. Southern Sweden and Finland are generally flat forest and lake country. Denmark consists mostly of coastal plains and islands. Iceland is rugged and treeless, with glaciers and active volcanoes. The Scandinavian climate is moist, ranging from cool temperate in the south to full arctic in the north. Ethnically, the population can be divided into three linguistic or cultural groups: the Nordic group, including Danes, Swedes, Norwegians, and Icelanders; the Finns; and the Lapps or Saami, an indigenous people living mostly on the northern tundra. Lutheranism is the dominant faith, with a significant minority of Russian Orthodox in Finland. Many of the Lapps practice their traditional shamanistic beliefs.

At the beginning of the Victorian era, Scandinavia was dominated by Sweden and Denmark, both constitutional monarchies with limited suffrage. The king of Sweden was also king of Norway, though Norway had its own legislature. Denmark ruled Iceland and also Greenland. The Russian czar was grand duke of Finland. As a whole, the region was poor and economically backward, with a population that was largely rural and self-sufficient.

Each region had its own nationalist movement, although some intellectuals espoused "Scandinavianism" and envisioned a unified region consisting of Sweden, Norway, and Denmark.

Denmark's politics in the early Victorian era were affected by uncertainty over the status of Schleswig-Holstein, predominantly German regions held by the Danish crown. In the midst of the REVOLUTIONS OF 1898 in Europe, war broke out with PRUSSIA over the Danish attempt to impose a uniform constitution on the region. Denmark retained the area but was unable to fully incorporate it. At the same time, the Danish king renounced absolute rule and issued a liberal constitution with a representative assembly. AUSTRIA and Prussia joined in a second war over Schleswig-Holstein in 1864, and Denmark lost the region entirely. Following this, Denmark experienced peace and political stability for the remainder of the century.

Sweden, too, was peaceful in the Victorian era, although it aided Denmark in the first war over Schleswig-Holstein. In 1866 a bicameral legislature was established, superseding the old assembly. The last years of the century saw increasingly strained relations with Norway, but conflict was avoided.

Norway also managed to avoid serious conflict, but the Norwegians found Swedish rule increasingly irksome. In 1884 the Norwegian Assembly gained the right to elect its own ministers, but friction with the Swedish crown continued over foreign policy. In 1905, Norway declared itself independent and invited

Prince Carl of Denmark to take the throne as Haakon VII. Sweden was reluctant to begin a war, and the separation was carried out peacefully.

Finland continued under Russian rule for the entire period, with special status and privileges, such as exemption from Russian military service. Nevertheless, Finnish nationalism grew, and when the Russian government collapsed during World War I, Finland declared its independence.

Economically, the region as a whole developed quickly, thanks in part to its abundant natural resources. Norway was particularly active in shipping; Sweden in iron, copper, and wood; Denmark in agricultural products; Finland in wood. A period of hardship in the 1870s and 1880s caused significant emigration to North America, but prosperity generally returned in the 1890s. Culturally, Scandinavia was noted for producing a great number of outstanding artists, writers—including HENRIK IBSEN—, scientists, and explorers for the small size of its population.

Schiaparelli, Giovanni Virginio (1835–1910) Italian astronomer. A graduate of Turin University (1854), he is best known for his 1877 observation of narrow markings on Mars that he believed were channels of water, or *canali.* Mistranslated into English as "canals," this term became the basis for the widespread belief, advocated by American astronomer Percival Lowell, that there was a system of artificial canals on Mars by an advanced race to transport water from the polar ice caps to the dry equatorial region. Space probes to Mars have shown that markings of the sort Schiaparelli described would not have been visible at the resolution of his telescope and that his sighting was most likely an illusion. Schiaparelli's finding in 1889 that the planet Mercury always presents the same side to the sun has also been disproved.

One finding of Schiaparelli's that has withstood scrutiny was that meteor swarms move in cometary or bits and probably result from the breakup of comets. In 1861 he discovered an asteroid, Hespera. From 1862 to 1900 he was the director of Brera Observatory in Milan.

Schleiden, Matthias Jakob (1804–1881) German botanist. Best known for the microscopic study of plant growth and structure, Schleiden postulated in 1838 that cells are the fundamental unit of plant tissues. With biologist THEODOR SCHWANN, who concluded the same about animal tissues, he advanced the CELL THEORY (1839), which states that cells are the basic unit of all living tissue. Schleiden also noted the importance of the cell nucleus, particularly in relation to cell division.

Schleimann, Heinrich (1822–1890) German archaeologist. He is known for discovering the ruins of TROY, site of Homer's *Iliad.* The son of a German pastor, Schliemann grew up poor but with a hunger for knowledge. As a child he was mesmerized by a picture of Troy in flames and vowed to find the ruins despite the common belief that Troy existed only in legend. Starting out as a grocery clerk, Schliemann made a large fortune in trade on such commodities as saltpeter during the Crimean War and gold nuggets during the California gold rush. He also educated himself, learning ancient Greek and Latin and about a dozen modern languages.

At the age of forty-one, Schliemann retired and set out to find Troy. Relying on details from the *Iliad,* he began digging in 1871 at the hill called Hissarlik in Turkey near the entrance to the Dardanelles. In 1873 he found a treasure of vases, jewelry, and golden cups that he concluded was the treasure of Priam, the Trojan king at the time in which the *Iliad* is set. Schliemann's announcement of his find thrilled many of his contemporaries, connecting as it did modern exploration, commercial success, and the classical European heritage.

Schliemann's discoveries did not stop with Troy. In 1876–78 he excavated Mycenae, legendary city of the Greek leader Agamemnon. In 1878 he discovered ancient Ithaca, described in Homer's *Odyssey* as the home of Odysseus. In 1884–85 he excavated Tiryns. Schliemann's work, described in his voluminous writings, gave historical basis to the civilization of pre-classical Greece (6000 to 1000 B.C.) previously known only in legend. Archaeologists today are still building on his discoveries.

Schliemann's reception among subsequent archaeologists has been mixed. His makeshift methods, such as digging a crude trench straight down, have created havoc for future archaeologists. Some of his conclusions rested on shaky ground: The stratum of Troy that he called "Priam's city" later turned out to be the ruins of a city destroyed long before the period Homer wrote about. Even so, Schliemann's basic conclusion that Hissarlik was the site of ancient Troy was verified by later excavators, and he is regarded by many as the father of modern archaeology.

Schopenhauer, Arthur (1788–1860) German philosopher. Born in Danzig to a merchant family, he studied medicine and natural science at Göttingen, then switched to philosophy and philology. He befriended Johann Wolfgang von Goethe, the Romantic poet and novelist, and became interested in Indian mysticism and its commonalities with the Western tradition. In 1819 he published *The World as Will and Idea,* which contains the basic expression of his ideas; the remainder of his life was spent perfecting them. In 1820 he qualified as a lecturer in philosophy in Berlin, but he found himself competing unsuccessfully with Georg Hegel for students. From 1825 until his death he lived in semiretirement. His works began to attract attention in the last decade of his life.

In contrast to Hegel, who imagined that a universal idea or spirit guided men's thoughts and historical events, Schopenhauer argued that the individual creative will projected itself onto the world and organized knowledge and experience, often in irrational, intuitive ways. Schopenhauer's philosophy influenced such diverse thinkers as FRIEDRICH NIETZSCHE and the Existentialists.

Schumann, Clara Josephine Wieck (1819–1896) German pianist and composer. She was the daughter and pupil of piano teacher Friedrich Wieck (1785–1873), who initially opposed her marriage to another of his pupils, ROBERT SCHUMANN, in 1840. After her first recital in Leipzig in 1830, Clara became a renowned concert pianist, playing in Paris, Vienna, and Britain as well as Germany. She was a major interpreter of her husband's music. She also taught and composed piano music and songs.

Schumann, Robert Alexander (1810–1856) German composer. Schumann became the leader of German ROMANTICISM in music. He is best known for writing beautiful mood pieces and musical portraits with descriptive titles.

From 1828 to 1830, Schumann studied law at Heidelberg before pursuing a career in music at Leipzig. He trained as a pianist under Friedrich Wieck but turned to composition after crippling one of his fingers.

In 1834 he founded the musical journal *Die Neue Zeitschrift für Musik* and remained its editor until 1844. Through his criticism, Schumann encouraged new music and was among the first to recognize the genius of JOHANNES BRAHMS, FRÉDÉRIC CHOPIN, and HECTOR BERLIOZ.

He married pianist CLARA WIECK SCHUMANN in 1840, the same year he composed more than one hundred songs. Aggravated by the onset of a neurological illness, Schumann attempted to drown himself in the Rhine River in 1854. He was rescued but died in an asylum near Bonn.

Although many works were left unfinished, he wrote several piano pieces, the opera *Genoveva,* four symphonies, chamber music, and about 250 songs. He often gave the piano accompaniment more importance than the melody. Among his chief works are *Das Paradies und die Peri,* the song cycles *Liederkreis* and *Spanisches Liederspiel,* as well as incidental music to Byron's *Manfred* and Goethe's *Faust.*

Schwann, Theodor Ambrose Hubert (1810–1882) German physiologist. Born near Dusseldorf to Catholic parents who initially wanted their son to be a Jesuit priest, Schwann attended the University of Bonn, where he met the renowned physiologist and anatomist Johannes Muller (1801–1858). After obtaining his medical degree in 1834 at the University of Berlin, Schwann served for five years as an experimental assistant under Muller at the Anatomical Museum of Berlin. During this time he discovered the sheath surrounding nerve fibers and the digestive enzyme pepsin. In 1839 he argued that the cell was the basic unit of all animal tissues; with MATTHIAS JAKOB SCHLEIDEN, who argued the same for plants in 1838, he became the cofounder of the CELL THEORY and of modern histology, the microscopic study of living tissues.

Schwann's contributions to biology were manifold. He was the first to investigate the laws of muscular contraction, demonstrating that the tension of contracting muscles varies with their length. His research on the role of microorganisms in putrefaction and fermentation laid some of the groundwork for the discoveries of LOUIS PASTEUR. He developed basic principles of embryology, showing that the tissues of all animals develop from embryonic cells. He is also credited with coining the term "metabolism" for the sum of the chemical reactions occurring within an organism.

Scotland Yard Headquarters of the Metropolitan Police Force in Westminster, London, from 1829 until 1967 (see POLICE, BRITISH).

Scott, Sir George Gilbert (1811–1878) English architect. A leader of GOTHIC REVIVAL, he restored such buildings as Ely and Salisbury cathedrals and Westminster Abbey and designed numerous others, including the ALBERT MEMORIAL (1863–72) and the Midland Hotel at St. Pancras Station (1867–74).

screw thread The projecting spiral rib of a screw. In 1841, English inventor Sir JOSEPH WHITWORTH proposed that the pitch, or distance, between screw threads be standardized for ease of use in industrial mass production. The proposal was gradually adopted.

scrimshaw American term for the craft of hand-engraving an artistic design into an aesthetically pleasing surface. Scrimshaw objects, often made from ivory or whale bone in which a design had been pounded and colored with lampblack or India ink, were used as household, desk, and boudoir items. Larger pieces of scrimshaw could be used as freestanding ornaments. During the Victorian Age, creating scrimshaw was especially popular among sailors.

Second Empire (1852–70) Period in French history. Following the SECOND REPUBLIC and after a coup the previous year, Louis Napoleon

(NAPOLEON III), nephew of Napoleon I, had himself crowned emperor on December 2, 1852. In theory he ruled as a constitutional monarch, but he freely manipulated elections and in practice had nearly absolute power.

The period was generally prosperous for FRANCE. Napoleon initiated large public works projects, in particular the reconstruction of Paris and the building of railroads. France also engaged in successful foreign wars in CRIMEA (1853–56) and ITALY (1859) that boosted national pride.

Napoleon's ambitions caused the empire's eventual downfall. The continued campaigns to subdue Algeria were costly. Napoleon also supported the coronation of Archduke Maximilian of Austria as emperor of Mexico, which involved him in a futile war in that country (1861–66). Finally, Napoleon was maneuvered into a war with PRUSSIA in 1870. As commander of the French armies, he was defeated and captured at the battle of Sedan in September 1870, bringing the empire to an end.

Second Republic (1848–52) Period in French history. Occurring after the July Monarchy of LOUIS-PHILIPPE, the Republic was declared in February 1848 following an insurrection in Paris. Universal male suffrage was decreed and a coalition formed between liberals and socialists. A conservative group called the Party of Order gained power by stirring up fears of socialism. In the "June Days," large numbers of socialists and other suspected radicals were massacred in Paris. Louis Napoleon, nephew of Napoleon I, was elected president against a divided opposition in November 1848. In December 1851 he seized power in a coup, and on December 2, 1852, he was crowned Emperor NAPOLEON III, thus beginning the SECOND EMPIRE.

Sedgwick, Adam (1785–1873) English geologist. He studied the geology of Cornwall, Devon, northern England, the Lake District, and Wales. He identified the Cambrian period and, with Sir RODERICK I. MURCHISON, the Devonian period. He is the author of *A Synopsis of the Classification of the British Palaeozoic Rocks* (1855).

Seeley, Sir John Robert (1834–1895) English historian. He was educated at Cambridge, where he was appointed professor of modern history in 1869. His account of the life of Christ, *Ecce Homo,* published anonymously in 1865, was controversial for not acknowledging the divinity of its subject. He was also known as a defender of British imperialism in such works as *The Expansion of England in the Eighteenth Century* (1883) and *The Growth of British Policy* (1895). He helped develop history as a discipline, encouraging the teaching of modern political history with works such as *The Life and Times of Stein, or, Germany and Prussia in the Napoleonic Age* (1878).

Semmelweis, Ignaz Phillipp (1818–1865) Hungarian obstetrician. Born in Buda and educated at universities in Pest and Vienna, he became an assistant in the first obstetric unit of Vienna's General Hospital. While there, he discovered that the bacterial infection of the genital tract known as puerperal, or childbed fever, which during the 1840s killed over 30 percent of women giving birth in European obstetrical wards, was more likely to strike women attended by medical students than those attended by midwives. After a colleague died of septicemia, a blood infection, as a result of a scalpel cut sustained during an autopsy, Semmelweis hypothesized that puerperal fever was acquired in the same way—by transmission from external sources. Medical students attended autopsies and dissections immediately before their clinical rotation in the obstetrical ward, while the midwives worked exclusively within the ward. By applying ANTISEPTIC prophylaxis—ordering students to wash their hands with chlorinated lime before examining patients—Semmelweis reduced the maternal mortality rate in the hospital to less than 1 percent.

Semmelweis published his findings in 1860 in the revolutionary treatise *The Etiology, Concept, and Prophylaxis of Childbed Fever*; however, his findings were rejected for years by hospital officials and other medical professionals, both in Europe and abroad. Frustrated, Semmelweis developed mental illness and was placed in a Viennese insane asylum, where he died, ironically, of septicemia at age forty-seven. His views on ANTISEPSIS did not gain acceptance until after research by JOSEPH LISTER in the 1870s.

Seneca Falls Convention U.S. woman's rights meeting. The July 19–20, 1848, meeting in Seneca Falls, New York, was conceived and organized by ELIZABETH CADY STANTON and LUCRETIA COFFIN MOTT. Among the accomplishments of the convention were a sixteen-point Declaration of Sentiments and the passage of twelve resolutions, including one calling for WOMAN SUFFRAGE. Attending the convention were sixty-eight women and thirty-two men. It is often considered to mark the start of the women's rights movement.

sepoy Indian soldier. Trained, equipped, and led by the British army in India, anger among the sepoys sparked the INDIAN MUTINY, also called the Sepoy mutiny.

Sepoy Mutiny See INDIAN MUTINY.

Serbia Country in southeast Europe. It borders on Hungary, Montenegro, BULGARIA, and ROMANIA. Serbia was the first region to free itself from the OTTOMAN EMPIRE without outside help. In 1830 Sultan Mahmud II recognized Serbian autonomy after protracted guerrilla warfare. Turkish garrisons remained in Serbia until 1861. Serbian politics was marked by constant feuding between the Obrenovic and Karadjorjevic families, the main leaders of resistance against the Turks. Serbia was declared a kingdom in 1882. IRREDENTISM was the main feature of Serbia's foreign policy, as politicians agitated for the amalgamation of the Serb populations in Bosnia, Macedonia, and Croatia into a "Greater Serbia." Irredentism was the motive for unsuccessful wars against the Ottoman Empire (1876) and Bulgaria (1885). Serbia's main success came in Macedonia, a large portion of which was seized from the Ottoman Empire in 1912.

Seurat, Georges [-Pierre] (1859–1891) French painter. Born in Paris, he studied at the Ecole des Beaux-Arts from 1878 to 1879 with Henry Lehmann, a disciple of JEAN-AUGUSTE-DOMINIQUE INGRES. Seurat's early drawings show a complete absorption of Ingres's classical tradition, as do the careful sketches and color studies he made for each of his seven large paintings. Seurat was also an admirer of ancient Greek sculpture and of such classical masters as Piero della Francesca and Nicolas Poussin. He studied the drawings of Hans Holbein, Rembrandt, and JEAN-FRANÇOIS MILLET, and learned the structure of mural design from the academic symbolist Puvis de Chavannes.

Seurat became obsessed with theories and principles of color organization. He studied the paintings of EUGÈNE DELACROIX and read Ogden Rood's *Modern Chromatics* as well as treatises by Charles Blanc and Michel-Eugène Chevreul that treated the question of how light could be broken down into component colors. From these texts, Seurat worked with his younger artist friend Paul Signac to create a system of painting composed of calculated and intense optical sensations. In his theory of Divisionism, later called NEO-IMPRESSIONISM, Seurat found that each local color is made up of tiny particles of pure color to represent both the color of an object and the color of light. Seen at a distance, these colors are blended by the eye.

Seurat devoted his efforts to a few very large paintings, spending a year or more on each of them. His first large-scale painting, *A Bathing Place* (*Asnieres*), recalls popular Impressionist subject matter but is composed in calculated color geometries and systematic, impersonal dabs of paint. The 1884 Salon rejected his canvas, forcing Seurat and other rejected artists to form the Société des Artistes Independants. It sponsored regular exhibitions, uncensored by a jury, known as the Salon des Independants.

Seurat's greatest work, *A Sunday on the Grande Jatte* (1884–86) is an experiment in the illusion of perspective depth by flattening the planes of color, light, and shadow. Most of all, however, it is a masterpiece of POINTILLISM where brushstrokes have been replaced by tiny dots of brilliant color that seem to merge in the spectator's eye. Seurat built his composition out of thousands of minute color dots. The painting is Seurat's Neo-Impressionist translation of nature that attempts to unite the tradition of Renaissance perspective painting with the modern interest in scientific color theories.

Seurat's later works, which include *Poseuses* (1866–67), *Le Chahut* (1889–90), and *Le Cirque* (1890), became increasingly linear and decorative, reflecting the curvilinear swirls of ART NOUVEAU. He succeeded in liberating pure color as a reaction against the formlessness of IMPRESSIONISM. His paintings and influential theories had a tremendous impact on almost all abstract art of the twentieth century.

Seven Weeks' War (Austro-Prussian War) Conflict between AUSTRIA and PRUSSIA. Prussia's premier, OTTO VON BISMARCK, provoked war by occupying the duchy of Holstein, which had been administered by Austria since the Danish-Prussian War. Bismarck's motive was to force Austria out of the GERMAN CONFEDERATION, which would allow Prussia to dominate GERMANY. In the brief war that followed, several German states allied with Austria; ITALY allied with Prussia. Prussia quickly overran the states of Saxony, Hanover, Bohemia, and Electoral Hesse. Austria won a sea battle near Lissa that saw the first combat use of armored ships in Europe. The Treaty of Prague on August 23, 1866, ended the war. As Bismarck wished, Austria was excluded from the administration of Germany; Italy gained Venetia; and Prussia gained control of Schleswig-Holstein, Hanover, Nassau, Frankfurt, and Hesse. The German Confederation was replaced by the North German Confederation, a precursor of the Prussian-dominated German Empire in 1871.

sewing machine Device for stitching cloth. The first sewing machine, a single-thread device, was invented by Barthelemy Thimmonier, a French tailor, in 1830. The French government commissioned Thimmonier to make military uniforms, but after a mob of tailors destroyed his factory, he never tried mass-production techniques again.

The modern sewing machine, with its double-thread, lock-stitch system, was developed some years later in Boston. Elias Howe, a Boston machinist, patented his version in 1846. Powered by a hand-driven wheel, its curved, horizontally moving needle made 250 stitches a minute, as compared to the human speed of about 30 stitches a minute. But the high price of the invention and threats by American tailors made garment manufacturers reluctant to invest in the new technology.

In 1850, Boston machinist Isaac Singer patented his own design, with a foot-operated treadle, a straight needle that bobbed up and down, and an adjustable lever to keep the cloth in place. The machine, priced at about $100, a third the price of Howe's, was widely successful. Singer's successful marketing of the invention, including the introduction of the installment plan, helped create the ready-made clothing industry.

When Howe sued Singer for patent infringement, a court ruled that Singer had to share the wealth with him. Howe received a royalty for every machine sold until his death in 1867.

Seychelles Archipelago of about one hundred islands and islets in the Indian Ocean east of Kenya. The total land area of the subtropical islands is about 110 square miles; the largest island is Mahé (55 square miles), where most of the population lives. Other major islands are Praslin and La Digue.

Portuguese explorer Vasco da Gama discovered the Seychelles in 1502. Beginning in 1768, French planters and their African slaves settled there. The British took over the Seychelles in 1794 and later administered it as part of Mauritius. After abolishing slavery in 1833, the British brought to the Seychelles many liberated African slaves and gave the name of Great Britain's queen to the capital, Victoria. The French influence remained, however, and most inhabitants still speak a Creole patois, though both English and French are the official languages. The Seychelles became a British crown colony, separate from Mauritius, in 1903 and acquired independent status as a nation in 1976.

Shaftesbury, Anthony Ashley Cooper, 7th Earl (1801–1885) English politician. Shaftesbury entered the House of Commons in 1826. He supported the end of the CORN LAWS and the repeal of laws that discriminated against Roman Catholics. However, he opposed the REFORM BILL OF 1832's extension of suffrage.

Shaftesbury is best known for his social reform efforts. He helped pass the Lunacy Act of 1845, which pioneered the humane treatment of INSANITY. His Mine Act of 1842 banned all females and boys under thirteen years of age from the pits. He also became a leader of the factory reform movement, and the Ten Hours Acts of 1847 was popularly known as "Lord Ashley's Act," as he was known until 1851. He helped guide the FACTORY ACTS through Parliament. His work to shorten the workday for children earned him the title of "the children's friend."

Shaftesbury also championed the building and inspection of workers' housing. He was president of the Ragged Schools Union, which presided over RAGGED SCHOOLS for some three hundred thousand impoverished children. He founded many YOUNG MEN'S CHRISTIAN ASSOCIATIONS, was president of the British and Foreign Bible Society, and financed several missionary societies.

Sharps rifle FIREARM. The breech-loading rifle was patented by American inventor Christian Sharps in 1848. Powerful and accurate at long range, the weapons were used by Union "sharpshooters," or snipers, during the U.S. CIVIL WAR. Forty different models were made by the Sharps Company from 1840 to 1880.

Shaw, George Bernard (1856–1950) Irish playwright and critic. Shaw transformed the stagnant theater of late-Victorian Britain with his candor, wit, and exploration of social and political issues. Many of Shaw's dramas are "discussion" plays in which the characters talk through or argue about the issues at hand. He usually sought to convey messages through his plays and often made them explicit in lengthy prefaces.

Born in Dublin into genteel poverty, Shaw received little public education but studied art, music, and literature on his own. In 1876 he decided to become a writer and moved to London; he remained in England for most of his long life. After five unsuccessful novels and many reviews of books, art, music, and theater, he concentrated on playwrighting. He also became involved in politics, becoming a Fabian socialist in 1884 and serving for a time as spokesperson for the FABIAN SOCIETY.

George Bernard Shaw, Irish playwright and critic, transformed the traditional Victorian melodrama into an open, witty exploration of political and social ideas. Photo by Josef Karsh, courtesy of Topham/The Image Works.

In 1898 he married Charlotte Payne-Townshend, a wealthy woman who shared his progressive views. He also carried on lengthy, intimate correspondences with actresses ELLEN TERRY and MRS. PATRICK CAMPBELL.

His first professionally produced play was *Widowers' Houses* (1892), an indictment of contemporary London slumlords; it was heavily influenced by HENRIK IBSEN. It was followed by *Arms and the Man* (1894), *Candida* (1895), *The Devil's Disciple* (1897), and *You Never Can Tell* (1899). Often revived, *Candida* tells the story of a morally ambiguous woman who must choose between her minister husband and a young poet who loves her passionately.

Shaw's greatest and most popular works premiered in the first decades of the twentieth century. They include *Man and Superman* (1905), *Major Barbara* (1905), *Caesar and Cleopatra* (1906), *Pygmalion* (1913), and *Saint Joan* (1923).

Sherman, William Tecumseh (1820–1891) U.S. army commander. Born in Ohio, he graduated from West Point in 1840 and served in the MEXICAN WAR. He left the army in 1853 to join a bank in San Francisco that failed four years later. Moving to Louisiana, he headed a military academy but resigned when the CIVIL WAR started.

Sherman was commissioned a colonel and commanded a brigade at the Union's defeat at Bull Run early in the war. He held commands in Kentucky and Missouri before serving with distinction under General ULYSSES S. GRANT at the battle of Shiloh. Made a brigadier general in 1863, he commanded the western theater after Grant assumed command of the Union Army in 1864.

Sherman's troops invaded Georgia in May 1864 and captured Atlanta in September. Seeing modern warfare as a struggle between entire nation-states and not just between armies in the field, Sherman commenced his famous "march to the sea" in November. His sixty thousand troops devastated a sixty-mile-wide swath from Atlanta to Savannah in twenty-four days, destroying the South's last important supply area. Sherman later accepted the surrender of the last major Confederate army on April 26, 1865.

When Grant became president in 1869, he made Sherman commanding general of the United States Army, a post he held until 1883. He declined to be considered for a presidential nomination in 1884.

Sherman Anti-Trust Act U.S. legislation. Public outcry against huge corporations or "trusts" that had established monopolies led to the passing of the law in 1890. Named after Senator John Sherman, it prohibited "conspiracy in restraint of trade," but its vague provisions led to its weakening by the Supreme Court, which issued a series of rulings effectively preventing the government from enforcing the law.

"Trust buster" THEODORE ROOSEVELT used the bill with more success in dissolving the Northern Securities Company, a railroad monopoly, in 1904. The Standard Oil Trust and American Tobacco Company were prosecuted under the act in 1911. The Clayton Anti-Trust Act of 1914 bolstered the Sherman Act by proscribing various business practices that restricted competition.

ships Large seagoing vessels. Ships were the lifeblood of the world economy of the Victorian Age, the essential means of transporting trade goods, laborers, equipment, and imperial troops. All the trading nations of Europe and North America depended on ships, but no power rivaled Great Britain in its naval and merchant marine capabilities. By century's end, more than half the world's merchant shipping—amounting to 13.5 million tons in 1897—was British. Major shipping lines included the Peninsular and Oriental, Elder Dempster, British India, the Royal Mail Steam Packet Company, and the CUNARD LINE. They served not only trade needs but passenger travel for business, pleasure, and migration.

Packet ships had begun sailing on regular schedules across the Atlantic in 1818. The CLIPPER SHIP, a sailing ship designed for speed, was introduced by the United States in the 1840s. Clippers soon lost ground to steamships, which had been under development since the late eighteenth century. In 1838 the British steamship *Sirius,* a side-wheeler—that is, it was propelled by side paddlewheels—became the first to offer regularly scheduled service across the Atlantic under steam power alone. The introduction of the screw propeller in the 1840s was a substantial improvement over the paddlewheel design. Favored for greater strength and lightness, iron steamships began to replace wooden ones in mid-century, and steel ships began to replace iron ones for the same reasons in the late nineteenth century. Compound steam engines with two cylinders rather than one and steam turbines with more powerful and efficient engines were other important innovations of the late nineteenth century. The diesel-powered INTERNAL COMBUSTION ENGINE, invented in the 1890s, rivaled steamship engines in the twentieth century.

Steamships required prodigious amounts of fuel, which was supplied by networks of coaling stations. At harbors and islands maintained around the world by Britain, coal was plentifully stocked, along with food provisions and repair supplies. Despite the dominance of steam power, sailing ships continued to operate, particularly in areas where coaling depots were scarce.

Three of the most famous steamships of the era—the *GREAT WESTERN,* the *GREAT BRITAIN,* and the *GREAT EASTERN,* were built by British engineer ISAMBARD KINGDOM BRUNEL.

shipwreck Sea disasters. Among the most famous shipwrecks of the Victorian era were the following:

- The schooner *Hesperus,* wrecked off the coast of Gloucester, Massachusetts, in December 1837 and commemorated in HENRY WADSWORTH LONGFELLOW's ballad "The Wreck of the Hesperus" (1841).
- The side-wheeler *SULTANA,* wrecked as a result of a boiler explosion on the Mississippi River near Memphis, Tennessee, on April 27, 1865, with 1,547 killed.
- The emigrant ship *Annie Jane,* wrecked off the coast of Scotland on September 29, 1853, with 348 killed.
- The German ship *Deutschland,* wrecked off the coast of Wales on December 7, 1875. The death of five nuns seeking refuge in the U.S. from religious persecution in Germany was commemorated in GERARD MANLEY HOPKINS's poem "The Wreck of the *Deutschland*" (1875).
- The *City of Portland,* wrecked off Cape Cod, Massachusetts, on November 26, 1898, with 157 killed.

Shona See MASHONA.

showboat Floating theater. Showboats were popular in the United States from the 1830s to the 1940s. The *Floating Theatre,* built in 1831 in Pittsburgh, Pennsylvania, by William Chapman, a British actor, is considered the first showboat. Chapman and his family floated down the Ohio and Mississippi rivers, stopping periodically to perform plays by Shakespeare and other dramas. Chapman's success spawned a number of other showboats on midwestern rivers, offering entertainment ranging from drama and VAUDEVILLE to museums, lectures, and gambling. The Civil War effectively brought an end to the showboats, at least for a time.

In 1878, Augustus Byron French of Palmyra, Missouri, built *The New Sensation* and led the showboat revival. Three more French-owned showboats toured the rivers, and French's wife became the first licensed woman pilot on the Mississippi River in 1883. French established many of the operating methods that became standard, including advance advertising, the calliope, and a band that paraded through town on the day of the showboat's arrival.

The eccentric American Edwin A. Price owned eight showboats between 1887 and 1928, and is reputed to have been the inspiration for Captain Andy Hawks in Edna Ferber's novel *Showboat* (1926).

The advent of talking movies and other landlocked entertainment ended the reign of floating theaters.

Siam See SOUTHEAST ASIA.

Sidgwick, Henry (1838–1900) English philosopher. Born in Yorkshire and educated at Trinity College, Cambridge, where he became a fellow, Sidgwick was an early supporter of equal education for women. He was a follower of JOHN STUART MILL; his area of expertise was the political implications of ethical conduct, a subject he explored in such works as *The Ethics* *of Conformity and Subscription* (1870) and *The Principles of Political Economy* (1883). He was appointed Knightsbridge Professor of Moral Philosophy at Cambridge in 1883.

Sienkiewicz, Henryk [Adam Aleksandr Pius] (1846–1916) Polish writer. Born in Wola Odrzejska, he studied at the University of Warsaw but left in 1871 without a degree and became a journalist. His first work of fiction, *No Marne* (In Vain), was published in 1872. In 1876 he traveled to Anaheim, California, to live as a member of a socialist colony started by the actress Helena Modjeska. He returned to Poland two years later and began work on a trilogy dealing with Poland's struggle for freedom in the seventeenth century: *With Fire and Sword,* 1883; *The Deluge,* 1886; *Pan Micahel,* 1888.

Quo Vadis?, a novel about Roman life under Nero, was published in 1895 and quickly became the author's most popular work. He was awarded the Nobel Prize in literature in 1905.

Sierra Leone Republic on the west coast of Africa. Bordered by Guinea and Liberia, the nation has its capital at Freetown.

Sierra Leone was founded by British abolitionists in 1787 as a home for freed African slaves; in 1792 freed slaves from Nova Scotia, Canada, founded Freetown, which was under the control of a private company until the British took over in 1808. Tens of thousands of freed slaves settled in Sierra Leone in the nineteenth century. Fearing French expansion in West Africa, Great Britain established a protectorate in the interior of Sierra Leone in 1896. The nation gained independence in 1961.

Sikh Wars See PUNJAB.

Singapore See SOUTHEAST ASIA.

Sino-French War (1883–85) Conflict between FRANCE and CHINA. It began when Annam, in what is now central Vietnam, asked China for help in stopping French expansion in the kingdom, which was nominally part of the Chinese Empire. In 1883, France seized Hanoi, the chief city of Tonkin, in what is now northern Vietnam, and forced a treaty making Annam a French protectorate. Chinese troops then forced the French to withdraw from Tonkin, but the French successfully attacked the Chinese port of Foochow (Minhow) and the island of Formosa (Taiwan). The war ended with the Treaty of Tientsin (June 9, 1885) in which China evacuated from Tonkin and recognized the French claim to Annam, while France returned Formosa and the Pescadores Islands to China.

Sino-Japanese War (1894–95) Conflict between CHINA and JAPAN. It began when both China and Japan intervened in Korea to help stop a revolt against the government. Japan installed a new government and in the war that followed forced the Chinese from the Korean peninsula. On September 17, 1894, the opposing navies met in the Battle of the Yalu River, a Japanese victory followed by more successes at Port Arthur (Lu-shun) and Weihaiwei in Shantung. The defeated Chinese were forced to submit to a harsh peace in the Treaty of Shimonoseki (1895), ceding Formosa (Taiwan) and the Pescadores Islands to Japan, recognizing Korea's independence, paying a large indemnity, and opening four more ports to Japanese trade. Territorial concessions on the Chinese mainland were avoided due to the intervention of Russia, Germany, and France.

Sisley, Alfred (1839–1899) French painter of English descent. While a student of Gabriel-Charles Gleyre from 1863 to 1864, Sisley met CLAUDE MONET, PIERRE-AUGUSTE RENOIR, and Jean-Frédéric Bazille. He painted with them near Fontainebleau and created some of the first paintings of IMPRESSIONISM. Sisley became a central figure of the Impressionist group, exhibiting in the first Impressionist show and three others.

Sisley was influenced at first by the paintings of CAMILLE COROT whose serenity he admired. Once Sisley discovered the Impressionist palette and technique, his style changed very little throughout his career. Sisley's interpretation of Impressionism can be seen as more relaxed than the passion of Monet. His canvases are painted with great deliberation and are always complete, without any of the fragmentary sensibility characteristic of the genre. Sisley's paintings of the floods at Marly are masterpieces of Impressionism.

Sitting Bull (1831?–1890) Sioux chief and medicine man. Born Tatanka Iyotake in what is now South Dakota, he became the leader of the Sioux nation in 1867. In the 1870s he joined with Chief CRAZY HORSE to lead Sioux resistance to white encroachment into the Black Hills that culminated in the Battle of Little Big Horn and the death of General GEORGE ARMSTRONG CUSTER in 1876. Afterward, Sitting Bull was chased to Canada by U.S. troops, but he returned in 1881 to settle on a reservation. He toured with the Wild West Show of Buffalo Bill CODY in 1885. Five years later he was one of the leaders of the "ghost dance" agitation among the Sioux and was killed by Indian police while allegedly resisting arrest. Many of his followers were massacred by U.S. troops at WOUNDED KNEE later that year.

sitting room Casual area in a residence. Commonly used in the Victorian Age for personal or family activities. Not used for the formal entertaining of a DRAWING ROOM.

skyscraper Building of great height constructed on a steel skeleton. The many mechanical developments of the last quarter of the nineteenth century contributed to the skyscraper's evolution and made it an almost exclusively American type of building. The development of the hydraulic passenger ELEVATOR made it possible for a building to reach a height of eighteen to twenty stories. The earliest tall buildings were of solid masonry construction with thick walls on the lower stories. The elevator revealed the need for a form of construction that would permit thinner walls throughout the entire height of a building. Architects began to use cast iron with masonry followed by cage construction, in which the iron frame supported the floors and the masonry walls carried their own weight.

Widespread skyscraper construction began with the innovative CHICAGO SCHOOL. Architect William Le Baron Jenney (1832–1907) invented a system in which the metal framework supported not only the floors but also the walls. This appeared in his Home Insurance Building (1883) in Chicago, which became the first in the world to embody steel skeleton construction. Many similar buildings appeared in Chicago, including Holabird and Roche's Tacoma Building (1889) and Burnham and Root's Reliance Building (1894).

Throughout the 1890s the steel frame was developed into its final form, that of a completely riveted skeleton bearing all the structural weight. LOUIS SULLIVAN organized the exterior of his first skyscraper, the Wainwright Building in St. Louis (1890–91), to reflect and express the strong verticals of the steel skeleton.

With the growth of the skyscraper also came the need to solve urban planning problems of transit and hygiene. Height regulations and a steady recession of the exterior walls gave rise to the setback buildings that came to profile American cityscapes.

slavery Forced servitude. International trade in African slaves to supply cheap labor for European plantations in the Americas began to flourish in the late sixteenth century. At first a Portuguese and Spanish enterprise, aided by Africans who participated in capturing slaves, it attracted merchants of other nations by the seventeenth century, including Great Britain, France, the Netherlands, and Denmark. In the coming centuries, more than 10 million Africans were captured and transported as slaves to the New World. Many more died in wars between African states that resulted from the slave trade or died while being transported from the interior to the ports of West Africa or died on the deadly "Middle Passage" across the Atlantic Ocean. In the eighteenth century, moral opposition to slavery grew in Europe and the American colonies. Britain outlawed the slave trade in 1807 and outlawed slavery itself in 1833. By 1840, Spain and Portugal also outlawed commerce in slaves, although slave smuggling continued for years, and slavery was not abolished in Portugal's colonies until later in the nineteenth century. In the southern UNITED STATES, slave labor was considered essential to the cotton-based economy. It became the focus of tension between the antislavery states of the North and the proslavery states of the South. The antislavery side included those who supported abolitionism, such as WILLIAM LLOYD GARRISON and JOHN BROWN, and those who were merely opposed to the extension of slavery into newly acquired territories, such as ABRAHAM LINCOLN. The election of the latter as president precipitated the secession of the southern states and the U.S. CIVIL WAR (1861–65). Although slavery had long been undermined by such means as the UNDERGROUND RAILROAD, by which fugitive slaves were secretly helped to escape to freedom in the North or Canada, complete abolition of slavery did not take place until the South was defeated in the Civil War and the Thirteenth Amendment was passed.

Smedley, Frank [Francis Edward] (1818–1864) English novelist. Smedley's novels blended romance, adventure, and sport. His works included *Frank Fairleigh, or Scenes from the Life of a Private Pupil* (1850) and *Lewis Arundel* (1852).

Smiles, Samuel (1812–1904) Scottish doctor, writer, and social reformer. Educated at Edinburgh University, he practiced medicine but became known for his social crusading and belief in self-improvement, which he successfully conveyed in one of the earliest works on the subject, *Self-Help: With Illustrations of Character and Conduct* (1859). Other popular self-betterment books followed: *Character* (1871), *Thrift* (1875), and *Duty* (1880). He also wrote several biographies of industrial leaders, all informed by Smiles's moral outlook, including *The Lives of the Engineers* (1867, rev. 1874).

Smith, Joseph (1805–1844) American religious leader and founder of Mormonism. In the 1820s Smith experienced visions commanding him to restore the church of Christ. A vision in 1827 revealed to him a sacred scripture written on golden tablets; he translated and published this text as *The Book of Mormon* in 1830. That year he founded the Church of Jesus Christ of Latter-day Saints in Fayette, New York. Other revelations recorded by Smith include *A Book of Commandments* (1833) and *Doctrine and Covenants* (1835). Persecuted for their unorthodox views, the Mormons moved to Kirtland, Ohio, then to Missouri, then to Nauvoo, Illinois. There Smith and his brother Hyrum were arrested on charges of treason; in 1844 the two brothers were murdered by a mob in Carthage, Illinois. Following their death, the Mormons moved to Utah under the leadership of BRIGHAM YOUNG.

Smithsonian Institution Group of U.S. cultural and scientific centers. Located in Washington, D.C., it was established by an act of the U.S. Congress in 1846 following the £100,000 bequest in 1829 by British chemist and metallurgist James Smithson to create "an establishment for the increase and diffusion of knowledge among men." The original Smithsonian Institution was a single museum; it is now a group of museums in Washington, D.C., and New York City. The original museum mounted significant exhibits for the 1876 U.S. Centennial, including an American Indian exhibition for the Centennial Exposition in Philadelphia.

Snow, John (1813–1858) English physician. Born in York, a farmer's son, he studied medicine at the Newcastle Infirmary and the University of London, receiving his medical degree in 1844. He was the first to deliver research data in support of the water-borne theory of the spread of some diseases. In 1849 he published his influential article "On the Mode of Communication of Cholera" on the transmission of one of the deadliest diseases of the nineteenth century. He became famous for reducing mortality from CHOLERA in the Broad Street area of the London neighborhood of Soho by controlling the water source.

Snow also gained renown for his refinements in the developing field of ANESTHESIA. Although he experimented with ETHER, his greatest contributions were related to CHLOROFORM. He designed an improved inhaler for chloroform administration, studied the pharmacological properties of anesthetics, and warned against the dangers of improper use of chloroform. An accomplished anesthetist, he successfully administered chloroform to several thousand patients. His competence led to his selection as the physician who administered chloroform to Queen Victoria in April 1853 during the birth of her son Prince Leopold.

soccer Sport. The world's most popular sport, antecedents of this ball and goal game were played in classical antiquity and the Middle Ages, but the modern sport was codified and established in Britain from the 1840s to the 1860s. Known also as football, it was popular in Victorian Britain at both the amateur and professional level. It is distinguished from the related sports of American FOOTBALL and RUGBY.

Social Darwinism Sociological theory. Although it took its name and inspiration from the biological theory of EVOLUTION proposed by English naturalist CHARLES DARWIN, this theory did not represent the views of Darwin himself. Originating in the late nineteenth century in the works of English social philosopher HERBERT SPENCER, Social Darwinism was taken up in England by WALTER BAGEHOT, in Austria by Ludwig Gumplowicz (1838–1909), and in the United States by William Graham Sumner (1840–1910). The theory argued that human groups and individuals competed for advancement in human society in the same way that Darwin described organisms competing for survival in nature. "Survival of the fittest"—a phrase introduced not by Darwin but by Spencer—was seen as a positive good, a way of ensuring social progress and the distribution of wealth, power, and status to those most deserving. The doctrine gained popularity as a way of justifying laissez-faire capitalism, the existing class structure, racist segregation, and IMPERIALISM, and as a weapon against social programs that were seen as aiding the weak.

Social Democratic Party of Germany Political group. Germany's socialist party was founded as the Socialist Workers' Party in 1875 at the Gotha conference; it was renamed the Social Democratic Party of Germany in 1890. At the conference, the revolutionary socialists who followed KARL MARX and FRIEDRICH ENGELS joined forces with the more reformist and gradualist adherents of Ferdinand LaSalle to form what would be the largest socialist party in the world. The party's official ideology was implacable opposition to the Kaiser and the German state, but by the 1890s it had adopted a parliamentary rather than a revolutionary stance.

German Chancellor OTTO VON BISMARCK reacted strongly to the formation of the party. Antisocialist legislation passed between 1878 and 1890 banned socialist newspapers and meetings, and restricted the activities of trade unions linked to the party. He also tried to woo workers away from socialism by establishing old age pensions, disability insurance, factory inspections, and sickness and accident insurance.

This carrot-and-stick approach did little to deter the growth of the party. The antisocialist laws never interfered with the right to vote, and when the antisocialist program ended in 1890, there were more socialist members in the Reichstag than in 1878. The party won forty-four seats in the 1893 elections, making it the fourth largest party in the Reichstag. The party continued to grow in the early twentieth century.

social problem novel British fictional narrative focusing on the exploitation and abuse of industrial workers. Examples included CHARLOTTE BRONTË's *Shirley* (1849), CHARLES DICKENS's *Hard Times* (1854), BENJAMIN DISRAELI's *Coningsby* (1844), GEORGE ELIOT's *Felix Holt, the Radical* (1866), and ELIZABETH GASKELL's *North and South* (1855).

socialism Political and economic theory. Although the term encompasses a variety of views, socialism is generally characterized by a belief in collective or state ownership of the means of production of goods. Among the many distinct forms in Victorian Britain were Owenite socialism, founded by philanthropist ROBERT OWEN and advocating cooperative communities; Christian socialism, espoused by FREDERICK D. MAURICE; FABIAN socialism, founded in 1884 and advocating gradual, evolutionary change; the socialism of WILLIAM MORRIS, based on medieval ethical and aesthetic ideals; and, most influential of all, the revolutionary communism espoused in *THE COMMUNIST MANIFESTO* of KARL MARX and FRIEDRICH ENGELS (1848), who advocated violent overthrow of the capitalist system and establishment of a workers' state. Although not English, Marx and Engels were influenced by living in England and witnessing the social consequences of industrial capitalism firsthand. In the United States, the nation's most prominent socialist was EUGENE V. DEBS, who first ran for president as the Socialist Party candidate in 1900. The SOCIAL DEMOCRATIC PARTY OF GERMANY, founded in 1875, espoused Marxist principles.

Socialist thinking influenced many labor organizers and social reformers in nineteenth-century Europe and America. In its more gradualist and utopian forms, socialism attracted widespread interest, as indicated by the commercial success of *Looking Backward* (1888), a hopeful account of a future socialist society by American writer Edward Bellamy (1850–1898). But revolutionary Marxist socialism—associated as it was with atheism, rejection of bourgeois morality, and the threat of force—frightened many people and met with stiff opposition from business and government leaders.

sociology Field of scientific study. Sociology focuses on the collective behavior in human societies. The term was coined in 1838 by French philosopher AUGUSTE COMTE, considered the father of the discipline. Among those who made important contributions to Victorian-era sociology were KARL MARX, HERBERT SPENCER, and French scholar EMILE DURKHEIM, whose research helped give the discipline a rigorous theoretical and methodological foundation.

Solomon Islands Island chain in OCEANIA, east of New Guinea; also, the modern nation that consists of the southern islands in this chain. The chain stretches nine hundred miles from Buka and Bougainville in the northwest to Guadalcanal and San Cristobal (Makira) in the southeast. In 1567, the Spanish became the first Europeans to visit the islands, but full-scale colonization did not take place until the nineteenth century when traders and missionaries came in larger numbers. Germany claimed the northern islands in 1885; Great Britain created a protectorate in the southern islands in 1893. In 1900, Germany gave up control of all its islands except Buka and Bougainville. The latter two became part of Papua New Guinea in 1975. All the other islands in the chain gained independence as the Solomon Islands in 1978. See also OCEANIA.

Somerville, Mary Fairfax Greig (1780–1872) Scottish writer on science and mathematics. Born Mary Fairfax, she married Samuel Greig in 1804 and, following Greig's death, William Somerville in 1812. In addition to publishing four scientific papers, she wrote popular works that disseminated scientific and mathematical ideas to a wide audience. These included *Celestial Mechanism of the Heavens* (1831), a version of *Mécanique céleste* by French astronomer Pierre de Laplace (1799–1825); *The Connection of the Physical Sciences* (1834); *Physical Geography* (1848); and *On Molecular and Microscopic Science* (1868). Known as the queen of nineteenth-century science, she was honored in the naming of Somerville College, Oxford.

"The Song of Hiawatha" (1855) Popular narrative poem by American poet HENRY WADSWORTH LONGFELLOW. It tells the story of Hiawatha an Ojibway Indian reared by his grandmother Nokomis, daughter of the moon. He seeks to avenge his mother Wenonah against his father, the West Wind, then becomes leader of his people and advises them to accept the coming of the white man. When his wife Minnehaha dies, he follows her to the land of the Northwest Wind. Written in a meter based on the Finnish epic *THE KALEVALA,* the poem was hugely popular in its day. In decades after it will often be parodied.

Sousa, John Philip (1854–1932) Composer and bandmaster. Sousa was born in Washington, D.C., and at a young age became conductor of the Marine Corps Band (1880–92). Under his leadership the band earned an international reputation for its renditions of traditional marches and ones written by Sousa. Sousa left the service in 1892 to organize his own band and lead it on successful tours at home and abroad. His most famous compositions include "The Stars and Stripes Forever" (1897) and the "Washington Post March" (1889). He was called the March King, and his autobiography is *Marching Along* (1928).

sousaphone Musical instrument. This type of tuba was invented in 1899 for the band of JOHN PHILIP SOUSA. The tubing encircles the musician's body, terminating in a large forward-facing bell above the head.

South Africa Country in southern AFRICA. It is bordered on the east by the Indian Ocean and Mozambique, on the north by Zimbabwe, Botswana, and NAMIBIA, and on the west by the Atlantic Ocean. The Atlantic and Indian oceans meet to its south.

The history of the area during Victoria's reign is one of British expansion at the expense of African natives and Dutch settlers, or BOERS, who had preceded the British.

The British occupied the thriving Dutch colony along the Cape of Good Hope (established 1652) in 1806. Settlement began in earnest in the 1820s. Expansion eastward touched off a series of frontier wars, the KAFFIR WARS, with the Xhosa tribe, whom the British referred to as KAFFIRS, between 1811 and 1851. The last resistance was broken in the 1870s, and the British annexation of the lands between the Cape Colony and Natal, an area bordering the Indian Ocean, was ensured.

Meanwhile, the Boers grew increasingly restless under British rule. They were particularly troubled by English laws that regulated master-slave relations and that tried to improve the lot of native workers. The ending of slavery in 1833 also prompted many Boers to move north in the GREAT TREK migrations of the 1830s. The Trekkers defeated the African tribes to the north, including the ZULUS, and established the republics of TRANSVAAL, the Orange Free State, and Natal. Natal was annexed by the British in 1843 to protect its trade routes to India. The other Boer republics formed the South African Republic, but its central authority remained weak and the Boer states maintained an uneasy existence among hostile tribes.

The British colonies gradually incorporated more land but could not solve a chronic labor shortage. Large numbers of indentured servants were brought from India to work on the sugar plantations. More and more Africans were assigned to reservations that could barely support them.

The discovery of diamonds in the Orange River in 1868 and of vast gold fields in the Witwatersrand area in 1886 turned the economically backward region into a boom area. British emigrated there in great numbers and put additional pressure on the Boers and Africans. Great Britain annexed Transvaal in 1877, but a successful Boer uprising in 1881 resulted in Boer control of Transvaal internal affairs. The German colonization of what came to be known as German South West Africa and the possibility of German alliances with the Boers worsened relations between the English and the Boers.

The British South Africa Company of CECIL RHODES (established 1889), in conjunction with the British government, extended British power into the hinterlands through wars and negotiations with African tribes. The unsuccessful invasion of Transvaal by LEANDER STAR JAMESON in 1895 further exacerbated tensions in the region. The BOER WAR, a bitter and expensive conflict, finally erupted in 1899 and ended three years later with a British victory. The Union of South Africa was formed in 1910, incorporating Natal, Cape Colony, the Orange Free State, and Transvaal.

South America Continent. South America in the Victorian Age was the home of a number of newly independent states. From 1813 to 1828, Paraguay, Argentina, Chile, Peru, Gran Colombia, Bolivia, and Uruguay became independent of SPAIN. In 1830, Gran Colombia broke up into Colombia, Venezuela, and Ecuador; Panama became independent in 1903, with support from the United States, which intended to build a canal there. Throughout the nineteenth century, many of the states underwent chronic internal turmoil, with frequent revolutions, coups, and civil wars, often ending in military dictatorships. In Colombia, for example, a series of civil wars between liberal and conservative factions racked the nation from 1867 to 1880, and more than one hundred thousand people were killed in another civil war at century's end (1899–1902). The states also fought frequently over boundary disputes and in unsuccessful attempts to build larger states or federations. From 1879 to 1884, Chile fought and won a territory-related war against Peru and Bolivia in the War of the Pacific. In the War of the Triple Alliance (1865–70), the bloodiest conflict in Latin American history, Paraguay lost nearly its entire male population in an unsuccessful struggle for dominance over Argentina, Brazil, and Uruguay.

Occupying nearly half the continent, Brazil remained a colony of PORTUGAL until 1889 when a republic was established, precipitated by the crown's abolition of slavery in Brazil the year before. In the late nineteenth and early twentieth centuries, Brazil's economy developed rapidly with the growth of coffee and RUBBER industries and massive immigration from Europe. Elsewhere on the continent, notably in Argentina and Chile, U.S. and European—primarily British—capitalists invested heavily in the late nineteenth century, spurring the development of railways, raw material industries, such as tin, copper, and saltpeter, and large-scale plantations.

The discovery of gold in British Guiana in 1879 intensified a long-standing boundary dispute between Great Britain and Venezuela, ultimately settled by arbitration in 1899 at the insistence of the United States. British Guiana, organized as a colony in 1831, gained independence as Guyana in 1966, but French Guiana, settled by the French in 1604, remains a French possession. It was notable in the Victorian Age for its offshore penal colony Devil's Island, established by NAPOLEON III in 1852. Notorious for its brutality and squalor, the colony was used mainly for political prisoners, such as ALFRED DREYFUS.

South Sea Islands See OCEANIA.

Southeast Asia Region including the modern nations of Thailand (formerly Siam), Vietnam, Cambodia, Laos, Myanmar (Burma), INDONESIA (formerly Dutch East Indies), Malaysia, Brunei, the PHILIPPINES, and Singapore. The region was colonized by Europeans beginning in the sixteenth century. Located on the sea route between the riches of India and China, these peninsular and island areas were valuable as trading posts, markets, and supply stops. By the Victorian era, all of Southeast Asia except Thailand was under European control.

Thailand, then known as Siam, used skillful diplomacy to keep its independence. King Mongkut (who reigned from 1851 to 1868) pursued a program of westernization, described in the memoirs of his children's Welsh governess ANNA LEONOWENS; King Chulalongkorn (who reigned from 1868 to 1910) continued to modernize the country.

Vietnam began the Victorian era as the three kingdoms of Tonkin, Annam, and Cochin China. France captured the city of Saigon in 1859 and made Cochin China a colony in 1867; Tonkin and Annam were made protectorates in 1884. In 1887, France merged its Vietnam holdings with Cambodia, a French protectorate since 1863, forming French Indochina. Laos, formerly a Thai possession, was made a French protectorate and incorporated into French Indochina in 1893. France was driven out of Indochina in 1954.

Myanmar, known in Victorian times as Burma, had been the site of British East India trading posts since 1612. As a result of three Anglo-Burmese Wars (1824–26, 1852, 1885–86), Burma came completely under the domination of the BRITISH EMPIRE by the late Victorian Age. Annexed to India in 1886, it gained independence in 1948.

Indonesia, known in the nineteenth century as the Dutch East Indies, had been under the control of the Netherlands since 1595. It won its independence in 1949.

The republic now known as Malaysia was formerly a collection of British colonies. Modern-day West Malaysia is located on the Malay Peninsula of the Asian mainland; East Malaysia is on the island of Borneo. In the nineteenth century, what is now West Malaysia came gradually under British control. Penang, Malacca, and Wellesley had been acquired by the dawn of the Victorian Age; the states of Malay followed, beginning in 1874. In 1894 the British reorganized several Malaysian colonies into the Malay Federated States. By that time what is now East Malaysia had also come under British control—Sarawak since 1841, Sabah since 1881. Another part of Borneo, Brunei, had been under British rule since 1888. West Malaysia gained its independence in 1957; East Malaysia joined it in 1963.

The city of Singapore, at the tip of the Malay Peninsula, was founded by the British in 1819. Governed by the BRITISH EAST INDIA COMPANY, it flourished and became a major world port, a base for British trade in South Asia and along the coast of China. By the Victorian era, Singapore was considered part of the Straits Settlement colony, which also included Penang and Malacca. Singapore became an independent republic in 1965.

Southern Rhodesia See ZIMBABWE and RHODESIA.

Spain Country in southwest Europe. Spain suffered political instability in the years leading up to the Victorian era. Napoleon I's occupation and the long Peninsular War (1808–14) against him left the country politically divided and economically ruined. Revolution in the 1820s and the breaking away of nearly all Spain's colonies in the Americas further weakened the country.

Spain was ruled by the Bourbon dynasty. The Cortes, a representative assembly elected by limited suffrage, was often able to resist the king, but constitutional arrangements were vague. In 1833, Don Carlos, the brother of King Ferdinand VII, launched a civil war against Maria Christina, who was acting as regent to the ailing monarch. The Carlists were supported by Basque separatists and members of the clerical party who feared Maria Christina's liberal tendencies. The First Carlist War dragged on until 1840, and the government was forced to rely increasingly on generals as political leaders. A new constitution was issued in 1837, clarifying the powers of the Cortes. In the same year Maria Christina abdicated in favor of her daughter Isabella II.

Isabella's court soon gained a reputation for immorality and corruption. Leopold O'Donnell, a general in the Carlist War, led a coup against Isabella in 1854 but then joined the Queen's party. The following years were relatively peaceful, marked by the beginnings of industrialization and foreign adventures in Morocco, Chile, and Indochina.

Revolution broke out again in 1868, and Isabella was deposed. Amadeus I, son of VICTOR EMMANUEL II of Italy, was chosen by the Cortes as the new king in 1870. A new Carlist uprising broke out in 1872 in support of Don Carlos's grandson. Amadeus, finding the Cortes too radical for him, abdicated in 1873. The country was convulsed with regional revolts and rural socialist uprisings.

In 1875, Isabella's son Alfonso XII returned to Spain and was proclaimed king. The Carlists and other rebels were defeated by 1876, and peace was restored. Alfonso XII ruled as a constitutional monarch. He reasserted press controls and close ties between Church and state, but introduced universal male suffrage. When he died in 1885, he was succeeded by his infant son Alfonso XIII.

The remnants of Spain's overseas empire were a further source of trouble. A ten-year revolt in the sugar-producing island of Cuba (1868–78) ended with Spanish promises of reform, which were not honored. Another revolt broke out in Cuba in 1894. The UNITED STATES intervened in 1898. The SPANISH-AMERICAN WAR was a debacle for Spain, resulting in the loss of Cuba, Puerto Rico, and the PHILIPPINES.

Spanish-American War (1898) Conflict between SPAIN and the UNITED STATES. Revolts against Spanish colonial rule in Cuba in 1895 attracted many U.S. sympathizers, especially after its brutal repression and sensationalistic reporting by the American press about events there. Many Americans also believed that the United States should expand beyond its continental borders, and Cuba had been an object of imperialist interest throughout the nineteenth century.

In 1898, after riots broke out in Havana, Cuba, the U.S. battleship *Maine* was sent there to protect resident Americans. The ship exploded on February 15, killing 260 sailors. Spain argued that an accident was responsible, while the U.S. Navy claimed an underwater mine caused the explosion. After Spain refused to accept responsibility, President WILLIAM MCKINLEY declared war on April 26.

American victory was swift and complete. The Asiatic Squadron, commanded by Admiral George Dewey, destroyed the Spanish fleet in Manila Bay in the PHILIPPINES on May 1 without losing a single American. Manila fell on August 19. U.S. troops landed in Cuba in June and took control of key fortifications near Santiago. The troops of the First Volunteer Cavalry, or "Rough Riders," distinguished themselves in this fighting, as did Lieutenant Colonel THEODORE ROOSEVELT. A Spanish Caribbean fleet was demolished on July 3, and Santiago fell two weeks later.

The peace treaty provided for Cuban self-government starting in 1902. Spain ceded the Philippines, Guam, and Puerto Rico to the victors. Overnight the United States had gained a colonial empire with over 8 million inhabitants. The sudden emergence of the two-ocean responsibilities for the United States also spurred the building of the Panama Canal.

spectacles Victorian term for eyeglasses. Spectacles in the Victorian era usually had wire frames and octagonal, oval, or round frames. One-handed spectacles, also popular at the time, were known as lorgnettes. Handles and frames were often made of exotic material such as mother-of-pearl or gold.

Speke, John Hanning (1827–1864) English explorer. Born in Jordans, Ilminster, he was the son of a captain in the dragoons. After service in the Indian army, he joined RICHARD FRANCIS BURTON in a hazardous expedition to Somaliland, after which the Royal Geographic Society sent the pair out on a search in 1857 for the equatorial lakes of Africa. Possessed of a keen knowledge of natural history, Speke, with Burton, discovered Lake TANGANYIKA (1858). While traveling alone, he also discovered Lake VICTORIA NYANZA (1858) and in it the headwaters of the Nile. In 1860, Speke returned with Captain James Grant and explored the lake, tracing the Nile's outflow.

He was set to defend himself against Burton's public doubts at the British Association meeting at Bath when he accidentally shot himself while partridge shooting.

Speke's discoveries were important in the expansion of European geographic consciousness. He and Grant were the first Europeans to cross Equatorial Eastern Africa, thereby gaining knowledge of a vast region until then uncharted. He was the author of *Journal of the Discovery of the Source of the Nile* (1863).

Spencer, Herbert (1820–1903) English philosopher. One of the leading thinkers and writers of the Victorian period, Spencer declined a chance to attend Cambridge and educated himself in the natural sciences. He was a railroad engineer (1837–41) before becoming a journalist and then an editor at the *Economist* in 1848. He resigned from the magazine in 1853 after receiving a bequest from an uncle that enabled him to pursue his ambitious scholarly projects.

Spencer developed a vast system of social and scientific theory based on the unifying principle of evolutionary progress. This progress, present in both society and nature, was driven by an unknowable force that transformed homogeneous entities—whether in society, the solar system, or animal species—into more differentiated structures. For example, this "law of the multiplication of effects" explained the evolution of despotic, collective societies into more pluralistic, individualistic ones, just as it explained the evolution of simple organisms into more complicated, differentiated ones.

Spencer's theories, which he presented in the ten-volume *The Synthetic Philosophy* as well as in other works, influenced many areas of thought even though they lacked the scientific validity he claimed for them. His published theories on EVOLUTION predate those of CHARLES DARWIN and ALFRED RUSSEL WALLACE, and his work helped the public understand this controversial subject. He coined the phrase "survival of the fittest" to describe the effects of natural selection on evolutionary change.

Spencer's theories on the continual development of individualism led him to champion a radical form of laissez-faire economics and politics that condemned the regulation of work conditions and other social reform legislation. His work in this area contributed to the body of thought that became known as SOCIAL DARWINISM. His insistence on applying what he considered scientific principles to the examination of human society helped establish SOCIOLOGY as a field of study. He also promulgated an ethical system that was based on the individual's need to respond to environmental changes and that linked right behavior to survival.

Spencer's major work, *The Synthetic Philosophy,* consists of *First Principles* (1862); *The Principles of Biology* (1864–67); *The Principles of Psychology* (1855); *The Principles of Sociology* (1876–96); and *The Principles of Ethics* (1892–93). Other major works include *Social Statics* (1851); *The Study of Sociology* (1872); and *Autobiography* (1904).

spiritualism Religious movement. Centering on the view that communication between the living and the spirits of the dead is possible, channeled through individuals called mediums, modern spiritualism began in the United States with Andrew Jackson Davis's book *Nature's Divine Revelations* (1847) and the activities of medium Margaret Fox and her sisters in 1848. Fox claimed that the dead communicated with her through strange "rappings," though she later admitted that these were produced by trickery. Still, by the 1850s, claims of communication with the spirit world were common in Great Britain and America. Among those who supported spiritualism were British scientists ALFRED RUSSEL WALLACE and Sir WILLIAM CROOKES, American journalist HORACE GREELEY, and British author Sir ARTHUR CONAN DOYLE.

Sri Lanka See CEYLON.

Stanford, Charles Villiers (1852–1924) Irish composer and teacher. With CHARLES HUBERT HASTINGS PARRY, Stanford was one of the leaders of the "English Musical Renaissance." Some of his works, such as *Irish Rhapsodies* and his Third Symphony (the *Irish,* 1887), bore the influence of Irish folk songs. But he also incorporated continental influences, as in his *Requiem* (1897). His operas included *Shamus O'Brien* (1896) and *The Veiled Prophet of Khorassan* (1881). He taught at the Royal College of Music from 1883 and was a professor at Cambridge from 1887 to 1924. He was knighted in 1901. His pupils included composer Ralph Vaughan Williams (1872–1958).

Stanley, Sir Henry Morton (1841–1904) British explorer and journalist. Born John Rowlands in Denbigh, Wales, he was left fatherless as a child and spent several years in a workhouse. As a teenager he sailed as a cabin boy to New Orleans, where an English cotton broker adopted him, giving him his own name, Henry Stanley. He lived through many adventures—as a soldier on both sides of the U.S. Civil War and against American Indians in the West; as a journalist in Abyssinia and Spain—before undertaking his most famous assignment. In 1871 the *New York Herald* commissioned him to find Scottish missionary and explorer DAVID LIVINGSTONE in central AFRICA. Stanley found him in November 1871, reputedly greeting him with the phrase, "Dr. Livingstone, I presume?" Stanley went on to explore the length of the Congo River (1874–79) and, on a Belgian-sponsored journey (1879–84), to help found what became the independent state of the Congo. He was repatriated as a British subject in 1892, served as a member of Parliament (1895–1900), and was knighted. His books include *Through the Dark Continent* (1878) and *In Darkest Africa* (1890).

Stanton, Elizabeth Cady (1815–1902) American social reformer and a founder of the woman's rights movement. Born Elizabeth Cady in Johnstown, New York, she attended the Troy Female Seminary. Partly influenced by her father, who through his work as a lawyer uncovered existing legal barriers to women, Cady decided to devote part of her life to women's issues. At her 1840 wedding to abolitionist Henry B. Stanton, she insisted that the vows not contain the word "obey." In 1848 she and Lucretia Coffin Mott organized the SENECA FALLS CONVENTION, the first woman's rights convention, which put forth several calls for equality under the law, including WOMAN SUFFRAGE. Starting in 1851, Stanton worked with activist SUSAN B. ANTHONY to effect such changes as joint guardianship of children, property rights, and the right to sue in court. She was the first president of the National Woman Suffrage Association (1869–90) and the National American Woman Suffrage Association (1890–92). Among the books she helped compile are the first three volumes of the six-volume *History of Woman Suffrage, 1881–1922*. Her autobiography is *Eighty Years and More* (1898).

Starr, Belle (1848?–1889) U.S. outlaw. Born near Carthage, Missouri, she gave information about Union forces to Confederate fighters during the Civil War. After the war she became an outlaw, joining the William C. Quantrill gang. She married Sam Starr in 1880, and she and her husband turned their home in Oklahoma Territory into a haven for outlaws. She was jailed for horse theft two days before her forty-first birthday. In 1889 she was shot to death by an unidentified gunman.

Statue of Liberty U.S. monument. The 151-foot high, 225-ton monument, one of the engineering marvels of the Victorian Age, was first proposed by Edouard-René de Laboulaye, a French historian and author of a three-volume history of the United States. The approaching centennial of the Declaration of Independence prompted him to broach the idea to sculptor Frédéric-Auguste Bartholdi in 1865. It was not until 1874 that Bartholdi was sent to the United States to design a memorial. New York Harbor struck him as the perfect site for the statue, and he sketched out a plan for a monument to be called "Liberty Enlightening the World."

Funds were raised for the project through subscriptions to the French people and donations from New York's leading citizens. Alexandre-Gustave Eiffel, designer of the EIFFEL TOWER, designed the iron framework that supports the statue. The statue itself was made from copper sheets hammered into shape on wooden molds.

The French did not meet the 1876 deadline. The statue was shipped in parts to New York after a ceremony in Paris on July 4, 1884, and was reassembled on Bedloe's Island, which was renamed Liberty Island in 1956. The pedestal on which the statue stands, 154 feet high, was designed by architect Richard Morris Hunt. President GROVER CLEVELAND dedicated it on October 28, 1886.

Although originally built to commemorate American independence and French-American friendship, the statue became associated with the millions of immigrants who landed in the harbor at the end of the nineteenth century. The famous poem by EMMA LAZARUS, "The New Colossus," was added to the monument in 1903. The statue became a national monument in 1924 and was refurbished in 1986 for its centennial celebration.

steam power Primary motive force for Victorian heavy machinery. Conceived by Scottish inventor James Watt in 1769, the steam engine worked by converting heat energy—typically from the burning of coal or wood—into mechanical energy, with steam as the medium of conversion. Although steam power dominated until the end of the nineteenth century, powering railroad locomotives, steamships, and industrial equipment, the invention of ELECTRIC POWER and the INTERNAL COMBUSTION ENGINE during that same period brought about its rapid obsolescence in the twentieth century.

Stendhal [Marie-Henri Beyle] (1783–1842) French novelist and critic. A writer of psychological novels, he was the western European counterpart of FYODOR DOSTOYEVSKY. With a heavy focus on the inner lives of his characters, he probed into unconscious motivation decades before SIGMUND FREUD. He was a political writer as well, vividly recording the fear and disillusionment in France and Italy in the early nineteenth century. Born at Grenoble into an aristocratic but not wealthy family, he supported himself in his youth by serving as an army officer. He later worked for the French foreign service in Italy, drawing on that experience in writing the novel *The Charterhouse of Parma* (1839). That work and the novel *The Red and the Black* (1830) are considered his masterpieces, although he also wrote short stories, travel journals, biographies, criticism, and two unfinished novels. His work gained in reputation after his death, becoming popular in the mid and late Victorian Age, especially among the young.

Stephen, Sir Leslie (1832–1904) English biographer and critic. Born in London, he was educated at home, then furthered his studies at Eton, King's College, and Trinity Hall, Cambridge, where he became a fellow in 1854. He earned a reputation as an excellent rowing coach and inaugurated the Oxford and Cambridge athletic contests.

Stephen was ordained in 1855, but after the publication of *THE ORIGIN OF SPECIES* (1859) by CHARLES DARWIN, he began to doubt his faith; in 1862 he resigned his position at Cambridge and moved to London. He started writing and contributing to a number of periodicals. His essays on agnosticism were collected in *Essays on Freethinking and Plainspeaking* (1873) and *An Agnostic's Apology* (1893), and his literary criticism was collected in *Hours in a Library* (1874–79). In 1876 he published *A History of English Thought in the Eighteenth Century*. During his eleven-year tenure as editor of the *Cornhill* (1871–82), Stephen published and encouraged a number of writers, including THOMAS HARDY, HENRY JAMES, and ROBERT LOUIS STEVENSON.

In 1878 he married Julia Jackson, and two of their children, Vanessa Bell and Virginia Woolf, became important artists and intellectuals. From 1882 until 1891, Stephen edited the first twenty-six volumes of the *Dictionary of National Biography,* to which he contributed numerous biographical entries. He was knighted for his work in 1902.

stereograph (also called stereo cards or stereo views) Double-image photograph created by a binocular (two-lens) camera. Stereographs became popular in the 1850s when photographers were attempting to create three-dimensional images from two-dimensional ones.

Stevenson, Robert Louis [Balfour] (1850–1894) Scottish novelist, essayist, and poet. Stevenson is best known for his adventure stories *TREASURE ISLAND* (1883) and *Kidnapped* (1886), and the eerie novella *THE STRANGE CASE OF DR. JEKYLL AND MR. HYDE* (1886). His book *A Child's Garden of Verses* (1885) is considered a masterpiece of children's literature. His essays and travel books earned him a reputation as an acclaimed stylist of English prose. HENRY JAMES once praised Stevenson as "the only man in England who can write a decent English sentence." Many critics have since discounted Stevenson's melodramatic plots and stagy characters, although he has never lacked enthusiastic readers.

Born in Edinburgh, Scotland, he was, in his own words, "an only child and, it may be in consequence, both intelligent and sickly." He developed tuberculosis, which was to trouble him his whole life; he nevertheless traveled extensively and loved the open air. Although he studied engineering and law, and passed the bar, he never practiced. In Paris, at the age of twenty-six, he fell in love with Fanny Osbourne, an older married art student and mother of two; he followed her to San Francisco. They married in 1880, after her divorce. Their scandalous union caused financial difficulties because Stevenson's family opposed it. They moved often, seeking to improve his health, trekking through resorts in Europe, with a long stay in a sanitarium at Saranac Lake, New York.

Stevenson's most celebrated works date from this period. *Treasure Island* originated as a pirate adventure told to amuse his stepson.

The Strange Case of Dr. Jekyll and Mr. Hyde, a horror story, arose through a dream. It is a powerful psychological study that can be interpreted as emblematic of the conflicts of civilization, modernity, and science. *Kidnapped* tells of David Balfour, a lowland Scottish boy; it incorporates an actual Scottish murder committed in 1745 and depicts the political tensions in eighteenth-century Scotland.

Stevenson traveled through the South Seas, settling in Samoa in 1890. He built a large house for his family, his widowed mother, and his stepson Lloyd Osbourne. The Samoans honored him with the title "Tusitala" (the Tale-teller), and built a road to his house that they called "The Road of the Loving Heart." After his wife partially recovered from a nervous collapse, Stevenson died of a brain hemorrhage at the age of forty-four. He was buried on Mount Vaea near Apia, Samoa.

Stevenson counted among his many friends the writers HENRY JAMES and MARK TWAIN. Two famous portraits were painted by JOHN SINGER SARGENT. His output was prodigious and included thirteen novels, three books of short stories, six travel books, four books of essays, and two books of poetry. He collaborated on some with his stepson Lloyd Osbourne; he wrote several unsuccessful plays in collaboration with others, including the poet William Ernest Henley.

Stieglitz, Alfred (1864–1946) American photographer. His promotion of a modernist aesthetic in photography moved the art from the Victorian Age into the twentieth century. Born in Hoboken, New Jersey, he studied and practiced his craft in Berlin in the 1880s. Returning to New York, he launched his career as a promoter of photography through his editorship of *American Amateur Photographer* (1893–96), *Camera Notes* (1897–1902), and *Camera Work* (1902–17), which provided a forum for introducing new photographers such as Edward Steichen and Clarence White. By the early twentieth century Stieglitz had cofounded the Photo-Secessionists, an association of photographers devoted to the artistic possibilities of the medium rather than its technical abilities to reproduce images. In various ways the dichotomy between the artistic and more documentary-style photography formed the basis of a central debate among photographers and critics during the twentieth century. Stieglitz later became known for the groundbreaking photographic portraits of his wife, American painter Georgia O'Keeffe.

Stoker, [Abraham] Bram (1847–1912) Irish writer. Born in Dublin and educated at Trinity College, he worked as a civil servant, a drama critic, editor, and business manager for the celebrated actor Sir HENRY IRVING. The author of fifteen works of fiction, he gained lasting fame for one, *DRACULA* (1897). Much adapted, phenomenally popular, and highly influential, the novel about the king of vampires is a carefully wrought narrative intermixing diaries, letters, journals, and newspaper extracts. From 1878, Stoker was married to Florence Balcombe, a renowned beauty whose suitors included OSCAR WILDE and who was painted by Irish artist Walter Frederick Osborne. Stoker's other works included the story collection *Under the Sunset* (1882) and the novel *The Mystery of the Sea* (1902).

Stone, Lucy See BLACKWELL, ELIZABETH.

Stowe, Harriet [Elizabeth] Beecher (1811–1896) American writer. Born in Litchfield, Connecticut, to clergyman LYMAN BEECHER, she studied and later taught at her sister Catherine's Hartford Female Seminary. In her young adulthood she accompanied her family to Cincinnati, Ohio, when her father was named president of Lane Theological Seminary; there she began her writing career and married scholar Calvin Ellis Stowe, with whom she moved to Maine in 1850. Early life in New England informed her first book, *The Mayflower; or, Sketches of Scenes and Characters Among the Descendants of the Pilgrims* (1843); later life on the border of the South gave force to her 1852 novel *UNCLE TOM'S CABIN.* The story of the slave Uncle Tom, the owner's young daughter Little Eva, and the driving owner Simon Legree was born of her long-standing opposition to slavery and, more immediately, of the passage of the Fugitive Slave Law. The book became one of the best-selling novels in U.S. history, galvanized forces behind the CIVIL WAR, and led to related works, including *The Key to Uncle Tom's Cabin* (1853) and *Dred: A Tale of the Great Dismal Swamp* (1856). Stowe also penned a variety of domestic, theological, and children's novels, and wrote with her sister Catherine Beecher the popular women's sourcebook *The American Woman's Home* (1869).

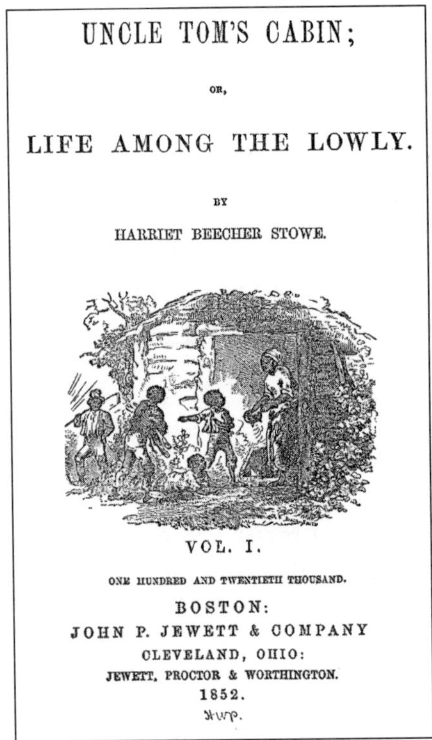

UNCLE TOM'S CABIN;

OR,

LIFE AMONG THE LOWLY.

BY

HARRIET BEECHER STOWE.

VOL. I.

ONE HUNDRED AND TWENTIETH THOUSAND.

BOSTON:

JOHN P. JEWETT & COMPANY

CLEVELAND, OHIO:

JEWETT, PROCTOR & WORTHINGTON.

1852.

Through her 1852 novel Uncle Tom's Cabin, *Harriet Beecher Stowe helped stimulate support in the North for the anti-slavery movement. Private collection.*

Strange Case of Dr. Jekyll and Mr. Hyde, The (1886) British novel. A classic horror story and a suggestive psychological parable, the novel by ROBERT LOUIS STEVENSON proceeds through a series of narratives told by the characters Enfield, Utterson, Lanyon, and Poole. The philanthropic, highly regarded Dr. Henry Jekyll is obsessed with the nature of good and evil. He develops a drug that allows him to separate his good and evil tendencies by transforming him for short periods into Mr. Edward Hyde, a repulsive figure who is free to satisfy all of Jekyll's evil desires. For a time Jekyll lives a double life, turning into the hedonistic Hyde and returning to his respectable identity as Jekyll simply by drinking a potion. But he finds it increasingly harder to prevent himself from turning into Hyde, and his supplies of the antidote are running low. Wanted for a murder committed by Hyde and unable to reconstruct the formula that will restore him as Jekyll, he kills himself.

As a psychological study, the novel prefigures SIGMUND FREUD's theory of the unconscious and twentieth-century studies of multiple personality disorder. Like OSCAR WILDE's *The Picture of Dorian Gray* (1890), the novel speaks of the conflict between Victorian ideals of virtue and the pull of sensuality and vice. It is a story with perennial appeal.

Strauss, Johann Sebastian (1825–1899) Austrian composer, conductor, and violinist. He won fame as the "waltz king" by dominating the world of European ballroom dance with his music. Child of a popular conductor and composer, Johann Strauss, Sr. (1804–1849), young Johann also wanted to be a musician and wrote his first waltz at the age of six. At his father's urging, however, Johann became a bank clerk before studying the violin with Joseph Drechsler and Anton Kohlmann. In 1844 he formed an orchestra and played his first concert with his own and his father's compositions. After his father's death, Strauss combined his father's orchestra with his and gave concerts throughout Europe. He toured extensively between 1850 and 1890, traveling as far as Boston and New York City in 1872.

In addition to more than four hundred dance compositions, Strauss wrote sixteen operettas, including *Der Karneval in Rom* (1873), *Die Fledermaus* (1874), *Prinz Methusalem* (1877), and *Der Zigeunerbaron* (1885). Among his most famous waltzes are *The Blue Danube, Tales from the Vienna Woods, The Emperor Waltz,* and *Wine, Women, and Song.*

Strauss, Richard [Georg] (1864–1949) German conductor and composer. Strauss injected unusual realism into his music, often employing discordant tone combinations and unique sound effects. Born in Munich, Strauss showed signs of musical talent at an early age: He played the piano at four and began composing at six. A student of Friedrich Wilhelm Meyer in Munich, Strauss wrote his *Serenade for 13 Winds* when he was seventeen. In 1885, Strauss became conductor Hans von Bulow's assistant to the Meiningen Orchestra before becoming third conductor of the Royal Opera at Munich. There he began to introduce radical and controversial orchestral innovations. Each new work met sharp criticism. In 1898 he settled in Berlin as conductor of the Royal Opera, a post he held until 1918.

His symphonic poems include *Don Juan* (1888), *Aus Italien* (1889), *Macbeth* (1891), *Also Sprach Zarathustra* (1896), *Don Quixote* (1897), and *Ein Heldenleben* (1898). Of Strauss's operas, *Salome* (1905) was his most innovative and greatest success and *Der Rosenkavalier* (1911) his most popular.

Street, George Edmund See GOTHIC REVIVAL.

street arabs Victorian slang. Children who, lacking homes, lived on the street were called street arabs, referring to their nomadic quality.

Strindberg, [Johan] August (1849–1912) Swedish playwright, novelist, poet, and essayist. Over the course of his long but troubled career, Strindberg moved from naturalism to REALISM to Expressionism, reflecting the movement of drama during and just after the Victorian Age and ultimately influencing later playwrights.

The son of a servant and an ex-gentlemen, he worked at various jobs, including a position at the Royal Library. His first major work, *Master Olof* (produced in 1881), marked the beginning of a number of historical plays that decades later still have importance in their native country. Of his naturalist works, *The Father* (1887) and *Miss Julie* (1889) are considered his greatest offerings. *The Dance of Death* (1905), a two-part work, is believed by some to be Strindberg's strongest example of Realism. His later works, *A Dream Play* (1907) and *The Ghost Sonata* (1908), are considered his finest experimental, expressionistic plays.

In his writing, Strindberg searched for the origin and meaning of suffering, particularly his own. The deprivations of his youth and the psychosis and paranoia of his adult years, which culminated in his "Inferno Crisis," a two-year period (1894–96) of severe mental illness, both hampered and fueled his creative efforts. His strong interest in religion, philosophy, science, and the occult also influenced his work. His major themes included the inherently combative relationship between men and women—reflecting his marriages, which ended unhappily—intergenerational and class conflict, and the alienation of the artist from society.

Sudan Country in northeast AFRICA. The Sudan was bordered on the west by the Central African Republic, Chad, and Libya; on the east by the Red Sea and Ethiopia; on the north by EGYPT; and on the south by Kenya, Uganda, and Zaire. It was strategically important in the Victorian era because a great stretch of the Nile runs through it, making control of the country essential to British domination of Egypt and its plans of building a railroad the length of the continent, the so-called CAPE TO CAIRO link.

Arabs subdued the native peoples in the fifteenth and sixteenth centuries, and converted the bulk of the population to Islam. In the 1820s, Egypt, then a part of the OTTOMAN EMPIRE, conquered most of the country and established a government center at Khartoum. In 1869, Ismail Pasha, the viceroy of Egypt, hired the Englishman Samuel Baker to conquer the southern reaches of the region and to suppress the huge slave trade there. CHARLES GORDON continued this work as governor and governor-general of Sudan in the 1870s but resigned in 1881 when Ismail went bankrupt. In the 1880s the MAHDI led a successful revolt against Egyptian rule of Sudan. The Mahdist state tried to expand its borders but met with little long-term success.

Great Britain, which had occupied Egypt since 1882, invaded the Sudan to counter French attempts to win a foothold in the area, resulting in the FASHODA CRISIS. Lord KITCHENER crushed Mahdist forces at Omdurman in 1898 and recaptured Khartoum. Sudan came under the nominal control of an Anglo-Egyptian administration but in effect became a British possession. Sudan became independent in 1956.

Suez Canal Artificial waterway in Egypt. It links the Mediterranean Sea and the Red Sea. About 100 miles (160 kilometers) long, the canal was built by a private French company in 1859–69 under the supervision of French engineer FERDINAND DE LESSEPS. By eliminating the need to travel around the tip of Africa, the canal greatly reduced the travel time between Europe and south and east Asia. It was therefore an essential link between Great Britain and its possessions and trading partners in the East, particularly India. The British acquired control of the canal in 1875, and the Suez Canal Convention was signed by European powers in 1888 to guarantee the waterway's neutrality. In 1956 control of the canal passed from Britain to Egypt.

Sullivan, John Lawrence (1858–1918) American pugilist. The last bare-knuckle world heavyweight champion was born in Roxbury, Massachusetts. The right-handed fighter was known as the "Great John L" and the "Boston Strong Boy." He won his first bare-knuckle championship in 1882, defeating Paddy Ryan for the London Prize Ring. In 1889 he won the final major bare-knuckle world heavyweight championship in a seventy-five-round fight against Mississippi-born Jake Kilrain. He lost his 1892 defense of his title to James John "Gentleman Jim" Corbett in the first title match in which the fighters wore boxing gloves and followed the MARQUIS OF QUEENSBURY rules.

Sullivan, Louis Henry (1856–1924) American architect. Considered the father of modern architecture in the United States, Sullivan developed a personal style of architecture that was distinct from historic models. In his use of ornament, Sullivan also created a parallel to ART NOUVEAU decoration. Born in Boston, Sullivan studied architecture briefly at the Massachusetts Institute of Technology and the Ecole des Beaux-Arts in Paris. In 1879 he joined Dankmar Adler's firm and became his partner two years later. The firm of Adler and Sullivan produced more than one hundred buildings during its fourteen-year existence.

As part of the growing CHICAGO SCHOOL, the firm's first masterpiece was Chicago's Auditorium Building (1887–89), an unusual combination of a hotel and office building that wrapped around a 3,982-seat auditorium. The exterior was strongly influenced by H. H. RICHARDSON's Marshall Field Wholesale Store, but the interior was lavishly decorated with Sullivan's unique style of ornamentation.

Adler and Sullivan entered the field of SKYSCRAPER construction in 1890 with their Wainwright Building in St. Louis, Missouri. Sullivan approached the architectural problems of skyscraper design by emphasizing verticality. He accentuated the tall building's individual layers with ornamental bands under the windows and crowned the building with a projecting cornice. He continued his skyscraper innovations in the Guaranty Trust Building, now the Prudential Building, in Buffalo, New York, begun in 1894. The last of Sullivan's great commercial buildings was the Carson Pirie Scott Department Store in Chicago, built in two stages, 1899–1901 and 1903–4. The ornament of white terra-cotta sheathing follows the grid of the steel frame to give the building a lightly elegant appearance in the fashion of Art Nouveau. This time Sullivan turned to horizontal lines and employed Chicago windows, which featured large fixed panes with narrower movable windows on either side, to help wrap the horizontal layers around the facade.

Sullivan's famous opinion that "form follows function" is from a magazine article he wrote in 1896, "The Tall Office Building Artistically Considered." Sullivan believed that architecture must evolve from the environment as well as express its function and structural basis. Just before his death he published *The Autobiography of an Idea.*

Sultana Mississippi riverboat. It was destroyed in the worst SHIPWRECK in U.S. history, on April 27, 1865. The side-wheeler was carrying about 2,400 Union solders, prisoners-of-war who were recently liberated from the Confederate camps; about 100 civilians; and an assortment of livestock, including hogs, mules, horses, and a captive alligator. A few miles from Memphis, Tennessee, the ship was destroyed by a boiler explosion; at least 1,547 people drowned or were burned to death in the flaming wreckage. One passenger saved his life by killing the alligator and floating away in the remains of the crate that had contained it.

Sunday, Billy [William Ashley] (1862–1935) American evangelist. Born William Ashley Sunday in Ames, Iowa, Sunday played professional baseball for the Chicago White Stockings from 1883 to 1891. That year he experienced a conversion and began to work for the YOUNG MEN'S CHRISTIAN ASSOCIATION. He became a full-time evangelist in 1896, although he was not ordained a Presbyterian minister until 1903. Using theatricality and high emotion, he became one of the most popular preachers of the early twentieth century. Among the beliefs he promoted were prohibition and the restriction of immigration.

Supreme Court See U.S. SUPREME COURT, CHIEF JUSTICES.

surgery Medical procedure. The Victorian era was a watershed period in surgical history. The introduction of ANESTHESIA in the 1840s and the use of ANTISEPSIS in the 1870s and 1880s changed the face of operative surgery. Previously, surgery was a fast, desperate emergency measure limited to such procedures as amputation and gross tumor removals. Because surgery itself often resulted in fatal infection, it was undertaken only when the patient's death was otherwise almost certain. By reducing or eliminating pain, anesthesia provided calmer conditions and the opportunity for longer operating times, which permitted the development of complex procedures and elective surgeries. Speed and strength no longer had to be a surgeon's foremost skills.

Although anesthetic agents such as ETHER, nitrous oxide, and CHLOROFORM made more complicated procedures possible, mortality rates from postoperative infection remained high. Much of the problem was due to the state of the typical early-nineteenth-century operating theater. It often consisted of a single, poorly lit room that reeked of years of past surgeries. Surgeons wore everyday suits, only occasionally removing their jackets and rolling up their sleeves to work. Masks and gloves were not used. To provide heat in cold weather, an open fire was often burning. The theater was crowded as well: Anyone could watch an operation, so the room was often filled with a crowd of medical students, other physicians, and curious onlookers.

These conditions were radically altered by British physician JOSEPH LISTER, who recognized the validity of the GERM THEORY OF DISEASE of LOUIS PASTEUR and in 1867 published his first articles on antisepsis, the destruction or suppression of agents of wound infection by disinfectants. His use of phenol, or carbolic acid, as an antiseptic agent in the operating room resulted in a dramatic drop in mortality rates. By the 1880s the basic elements of Lister's approach were in wide use. By the 1890s linens were steam sterilized, instruments were boiled, hands were scrubbed, and modern surgical garb—masks, gloves, caps, and gowns—was worn.

The combination of anesthesia and antisepsis gave surgeons new confidence. Abdominal surgeries, usually fatal in the 1830s, were done successfully. Chest cavities were opened. Cesarean sections became more common and less deadly. Brain surgery, though still dangerous, was done more often. After German physicist Wilhelm Conrad Röntgen discovered X RAYS in 1895, surgeons began using the new technology as a diagnostic tool.

New techniques gave the surgeon greater power to save lives, and the term "surgeon" became specialized and respected. Before the nineteenth century, the term referred to almost any medical practitioner; by century's end, surgeons were highly qualified specialists.

suttee Indian Hindu funeral custom. Suttee consisted of self-immolation by a widow on the grave of her husband. Originating in the Sanskrit word *sati,* meaning "faithful wife," suttee was prohibited in 1829 by British leaders in India, but it continued sporadically throughout the Victorian era. Ostensibly meant to unite the separated pair for eternity, suttee actually served to eliminate marital claimants to the husband's estate. The banishment of suttee was so disliked by Indian traditionalists that it served as a stimulus for the INDIAN MUTINY.

Swaziland Independent kingdom in southeast AFRICA. Formerly a British protectorate, the tiny, mountainous country is surrounded on three sides by SOUTH AFRICA and to the east by Mozambique. The Bantu-speaking Swazi people first migrated to this area from Mozambique in the early nineteenth century, under pressure from Zulu attacks. Later in the century, the Swazis granted concessions to Europeans. The British colony of South Africa administered Swaziland as a protectorate from 1894 to 1899; in 1902, after the BOER WAR, the British crown took direct control. Swaziland gained its independence in 1968.

Sweet, Henry (1845–1912) English phonetician. Educated at Heidelberg and Balliol College, Oxford, he published such influential works as *History of English Sounds* (1874), *Handbook of Phonetics* (1877), *The History of Language* (1900), and *The Sounds of English: An Introduction to Phonetics* (1908). He was also a leading scholar of Old English, compiling the *Anglo-Saxon Reader* (1876) and publishing an edition of King Alfred's translation of Gregory the Great's *Cura Pastoralis,* dating from the ninth century. Sweet gained indirect fame after his death when he became the basis for the insufferable phonetician Henry Higgins in the 1913 play *Pygmalion* by GEORGE BERNARD SHAW.

Swinburne, Algernon Charles (1837–1909) English poet, playwright, novelist, and critic. Scion of an aristocratic naval family, he was brought up largely on the Isle of Wight. After leaving Oxford without a degree, Swinburne established a reputation as a brilliant *enfant terrible* of Victorian poetry.

With exceptional productivity, Swinburne published a diverse variety of works, beginning with *Poems and Ballads* (1866), which brought him instant notoriety for its defiance of Victorian subject matter; the politically charged *A Song of Italy* (1867); the comic novel *Love-Cross Currents: A Year's Letters* (1877); and a body of criticism on such diverse figures as William Blake, CHARLES BAUDELAIRE, Lord Byron, and CHARLES DICKENS.

The English writer Algernon Swinburne was a prolific poet, playwright, novelist, and critic, a forerunner of English aestheticism. Photo courtesy of Max A. Polster Archive.

Inspired by ROMANTICISM, Swinburne was an energetic refashioner of old literary forms, a bold innovator, and a precursor of English aestheticism. His poetry is notable for its daring subject matter, verbal cascades, expressive imagery, and metrical pyrotechnics.

Symbolism Artistic movement. Symbolism's rejection of objectivity in favor of the subjective was a direct descendant of ROMANTICISM. The prime concern of art was not to depict an exact representation of reality but to suggest ideas through symbols. Symbolism combined religious mysticism with an interest in the decadent and the erotic.

To describe what was happening in the arts, the word "Symbolism" was coined from writer

Jean Moréas's "Symbolist Manifesto," published in 1886 in *Figaro Littéraire.* The Symbolist literary movement reacted against earlier schools of naturalism and REALISM. Designed to convey impressions, Symbolism found its first expression in poetry. Moréas claimed CHARLES BAUDELAIRE as the precursor to the movement and the greatest influence on Symbolist poets PAUL VERLAINE, STÉPHANE MALLARMÉ, and ARTHUR RIMBAUD. These writers experimented with forms of free verse and were accused of writing with a perverse morbidity. The movement was continued in drama by MAURICE MAETERLINCK and in criticism by Rémy de Gourmont. The influence of the French Symbolists not only gave rise to similar schools in England, Germany, and other countries but encouraged the development of the Imagists and Decadents as well as the twentieth-century work of T. S. Eliot, James Joyce, and Gertrude Stein.

In the visual arts, Symbolism took the style of painting known as Synthetism, pioneered by PAUL GAUGUIN and Emile Bernard. Their technique, called Cloissonism, was characterized by flat areas of color and heavy outlines. Gauguin's Symbolist followers believed that an artist must synthesize his impressions and paint from memory rather than make direct recordings. The Symbolist artists organized an exhibition under the title "Synthetisme" during the International Exhibition of 1889, and in 1891 they formed the Groupe Synthetiste. Among the artists associated with the movement were Odilon Redon, Gustave Moreau, and Puvis de Chavannes in France, Ferdinand Hodler in Switzerland, and GUSTAV KLIMT in Austria.

Symbolism also influenced the group of French artists called the Nabis in 1888. They turned to Gauguin's flat pattern compositions to derive a common style and borrowed the expressive doctrines of Symbolism as their own philosophy. The Symbolist search for a new context based on emotion rather than intellect or objective observation reappeared in the works of twentieth-century Expressionists, Dadaists, and Surrealists.

Symons, Arthur William (1865–1945) English poet and critic. In the 1890s he was a member of the group of poets known as the RHYMERS' CLUB. A friend of OSCAR WILDE, WILLIAM BUTLER YEATS, and Ernest Dowson, he contributed to the decadent periodical *THE YELLOW BOOK* and became editor of the *Savoy* in 1896. His poetry was published in such works as *Days and Nights* (1889) and *Images of Good and Evil* (1899). He is best remembered now for his translations of the works of French SYMBOLISM and his critical study *The Symbolist Movement in Literature* (1899), which introduced English readers to this literary movement and influenced poets such as Yeats. Symons's other critical works included studies of ROBERT BROWNING and CHARLES BAUDELAIRE.

Tahiti See OCEANIA.

Taine, Hippolyte-Adolphe (1828–1893) French critic, philosopher, and historian. Educated at home until the age of fourteen, he attended college in Paris, earning a doctorate in 1853. For much of the rest of his life he combined teaching with prolific writing. Taine supported a scientific approach to the study of art, literature, and psychology. A strong critic of the French Revolution and of strong central government, he developed a philosophy that combined French positivism with German idealism. His works included *Les Philosophes français du XIX*[e] *siècle* (1857), an attack on contemporary French philosophy, and *Histoire de la littérature anglaise* (1863–64), a four-volume study of English literature. His other works include the psychological treatise *De l'Intelligence* (1870), the unfinished historical work *Les Origines de la France contemporaine,* and many essays and lectures.

Talbot, William Henry Fox (1800–1877) English inventor and author. As a scholar of calculus, astronomy, and optics, he became interested in photography. Through experimentation he created the calotype/Talbotype process for making paper negatives that yielded relatively permanent positive prints. Although his findings became popular at the same time as those of LOUIS DAGUERRE, they soon dimmed in importance. Among Talbot's other accomplishments was the 1844 book *The Pencil of Nature,* the first work with photographs to be sold commerically. His scholarly books include *The Antiquity of the Book of Genesis* (1839) and *English Etymologies* (1847).

Tammany Hall Headquarters for New York political group. The term is also used to refer to the group itself. The Tammany Society was founded in 1789 in New York City. Other branches emerged in Philadelphia and other cities, but the New York branch was by far the most long-lived and prosperous. The organization was named after the Delaware Indian chief Tamanend, the supposed welcomer of William Penn. Initially a social and patriotic body replete with pseudo-Indian rituals, the New York organization turned to Democratic politics early in its history. It backed the candidacies of Thomas Jefferson and ANDREW JACKSON, and in 1855 elected its first mayor, Fernando Wood. Tammany Hall consolidated its power by providing successive waves of immigrants with jobs and other services in exchange for votes and turning a blind eye to corruption. In pursuit of its own interests, the organization corrupted judges, dictated the nominating process for all important positions, controlled patronage, and awarded city contracts.

Tammany's most infamous leader, WILLIAM MARCY "BOSS" TWEED, became a national symbol of the corrupt municipal official. His downfall in 1871 came after he and his cohorts robbed the city of over $30 million. A brief period of reform followed, but Tammany returned to power in the 1870s under John Kelly and a succession of bosses. After 1886, Tammany controlled city politics except for brief revivals of reform.

Tanganyika, Lake Freshwater lake in east Africa. It is one of the largest lakes in the world and the second deepest—420 miles (676 kilometers) long, 12,700 square miles (32,893 sq km) in area, and reaching a maximum depth of 4,708 feet (1,435 meters). Situated in Africa's Great Rift Valley, it marks the border between Zaire and Tanzania. Known to Arab slave traders since the early nineteenth century, the lake received its first European visitors in 1858: British explorers RICHARD BURTON and JOHN SPEKE. Burton wrote of the experience: "Nothing . . . could be more picturesque than this first view of the Tanganyika Lake, as it lay in the lap of the mountains, basking in the gorgeous tropical sunshine."

Tanner, Henry Ossawa (1859–1937) African-American painter. Tanner was a leading representative of the journeyman period of African-American art. Born in Pittsburgh, Pennsylvania, Tanner chose painting over the ministry, despite the objections of his father, an African Methodist Episcopal bishop. He attended the Pennsylvania Academy of Fine Arts and taught at Clark University in Atlanta, Georgia, working part-time as a photographer. His work in this period concentrated on black subject matter and included *The Banjo Lesson* (1890).

In 1891, Tanner left the United States for Paris, where he took up religious themes. His symbolic *Daniel in the Lion's Den* (1896) won honorable mention at the Paris Salon. In 1897 the French government purchased his *Resurrection of Lazarus.* In 1900, Tanner won the Medal of Honor at the Paris Exposition and the Lippincott Prize.

Tanzania See GERMAN EAST AFRICA.

tapestry Decorative fabric. In a tapestry, a pictorial or ornamental design is created by weaving colored weft threads alternately over and under the warps. It differs from EMBROIDERY, in which patterns are formed by needlework on fabric. Tapestry-making was a widespread craft in Arab countries in the early Middle Ages and in northern Europe in the later Middle Ages. By the nineteenth century it was almost obsolete. It was revived in England as part of the ARTS AND CRAFTS MOVEMENT in the late nineteenth century at two important workshops: Windsor, where M. Henri directed French emigrant weavers, and Merton Abbey, where WILLIAM MORRIS sought to revive the high standards of medieval masters of the craft. EDWARD BURNE-JONES designed tapestry scenes. By 1893 tapestry looms were set up in New York City and Edgewater, New Jersey.

Tarbell, Ida Minerva (1857–1944) American writer. Born in Hatch Hollow, near

Wattsburgh in Erie County, Pennsylvania, Tarbell graduated from Allegheny College in 1880 and worked as a preceptress at an Ohio seminary before she began her life as a journalist for *Chautauquan* in 1882. From 1891 to 1894 she studied at the Sorbonne and the Collège de France, researching the role of women in the French Revolution at the Bibliothèque Nationale. In 1894 she was hired by editor Samuel Sidney McClure to write a biography of Napoleon Bonaparte for the socially forward-thinking *McClure's Magazine.* During her twelve years with *McClure's,* Tarbell wrote her best known work, *The History of the Standard Oil Company,* which revealed that JOHN D. ROCKEFELLER controlled 90 percent of U.S. oil-refining capabilities. First serialized in 1901, it was published in a two-volume book form in 1904. Her work led to Federal antitrust action against the Standard Oil Company. Tarbell continued her reformist journalism in writing for the *American Magazine.* She aligned herself with the work of JANE ADDAMS and the welfare capitalism of Henry Ford but resisted the WOMAN SUFFRAGE movement because of its dependence on social laws and systems. Her autobiography is *All in a Day's Work* (1939).

Tate Gallery London art exhibition site. Originally called the National Gallery of British Art, it opened in 1897. The building and original collection were the gift of sugar refiner and philanthropist Sir Henry Tate (1819–1899). Its current collections include important works by J. M. W. TURNER and the PRE-RAPHAELITES.

taxes on knowledge British taxes and duties imposed on paper, printing, publications, and advertisements. Such taxes dated from 1712 and included the "stamp tax" on newspapers that amounted to four pence per copy from 1815 to 1836, making newspapers unaffordable to the poor. These "taxes on knowledge" raised revenue and controlled circulation. In the 1830s, popular agitation against taxes on knowledge grew heated, and several radical publishers flouted the law, sometimes at the cost of going to prison, by publishing unstamped newspapers. The advertisement duty and newspaper tax were reduced in the 1830s, but not enough to satisfy opponents of taxes on knowledge. From 1853 to 1861 the advertisement duty, the newspaper stamp, and the excise duty on paper were all repealed. The repeals spurred the growth of a popular press and of mass PERIODICALS supported chiefly by advertising.

Taylor, Zachary (1784–1850) Twelfth president of the UNITED STATES. Born in Virginia, he made his mark as a soldier in the War of 1812, the Black Hawk War (1832), and the Seminole War (1835–42). He commanded the U.S. Army in northern Mexico during the MEXICAN WAR, scoring impressive victories at the battles of Palo Alto, Monterrey, and Buena Vista.

Taylor's success led to his victory in the 1848 presidential election on the Whig ticket. He fought the COMPROMISE OF 1850, insisting that California be admitted to the Union with no concessions to the South. He threatened to invade the area if rebellion erupted. This stand by the slave-owner president greatly increased tensions between North and South.

Taylor died suddenly in July 1850, a victim of cholera morbus. His successor, MILLARD FILLMORE, backed the compromise legislation enacted in September 1850.

Tchaikovsky, Pyotr Ilich (1840–1893) Russian composer. Tchaikovsky's music is renowned for its melodic harmonies and orchestration, and the use of Russian folk tunes. He began taking piano lessons at the age of seven but enrolled in the School of Laws when his family moved to St. Petersburg in 1850. In 1859, Tchaikovsky obtained a position in the ministry of justice, but after a trip to western Europe, he turned to music. He began to study under Anton Rubinstein at the St. Petersburg Conservatory of Music in 1863. After graduation he became a teacher at the Moscow Conservatory, where he composed some of his most famous works, including the ballet *Swan Lake,* the overture *Romeo and Juliet,* and the popular *First Piano Concerto.*

In 1877, Tchaikovsky began a correspondence with Nadezhda von Meck, a wealthy widow who gave him encouragement and money. Supported entirely by von Meck, he resigned his teaching position to devote himself to composition. By 1880, Tchaikovsky was the most popular composer in Russia.

In 1887, Tchaikovsky conducted publicly for the first time and began a series of concert tours. He went to New York in 1891 at the invitation of the New York Symphony Society and conducted a number of his own compositions, appearing at the opening of the Music Hall, now Carnegie Hall.

Upon his return to Russia, he completed the *Nutcracker Suite.* While in St. Petersburg, Tchaikovsky died of cholera soon after conducting the first performance of his Sixth Symphony, usually called the *Pathétique.* Tchaikovsky's other orchestral works include *Marche Slave,* the *1812 Overture,* and *Capriccio italien.*

teapoy Small table. Used to display and serve a tea set and made of wood, it had four legs and was 20 inches to 30 inches in size. It was stored in the dining room or kitchen. "Teapoy" comes from a Hindi term for "three-foot."

telegraph Communication technology. Although the American artist and scientist SAMUEL F. B. MORSE is often considered the inventor of the telegraph in 1837, methods of transmitting messages via an electromagnetic medium had been developed as early as 1774.

William F. Cooke, an English medical officer in the Indian Army, had used a primitive form of telegraph, and upon his return to England in 1837, he and physicist Charles Wheatstone applied for the first patent for a telegraphic signal. A year later the first electric telegraph linked Paddington Station in London with West Dayton Station, a distance of thirteen miles.

In America, Morse was busy trying to convince the U.S. government to give him funds, and after a narrow victory he was appropriated $30,000, which he used to establish a telegraph line between Washington, D.C., and Baltimore, Maryland, in 1844. Although it became known as Morse code, it was actually Morse's partner, Alfred Vail, who devised the system of long and short signals, dots and dashes, that became the standard mode of communication on the telegraph.

On January 1, 1845, a telegraphic message sent to Paddington Station was instrumental in arresting a murderer. After the criminal was hanged, many newspapers hailed the advantages of telegraph technology. The Electric Telegraph Company was formed the same year, and by the end of the century nearly 400 million telegrams were sent annually across the 15,500 miles of telegraph wire that spanned England.

In 1856 the American businessman Hiram Silbey began the Western Union Telegraph Company, and within a decade more than four thousand offices were in operation.

With the completion of the first transcontinental telegraph line in 1861, the world seemed smaller, and by the 1890s the entire British Empire could be covered in an instant with the aid of the telegraph. (See CABLE.)

Telegraph Plateau Central level surface at the bottom of the Atlantic Ocean. It was discovered in 1854 by American oceanographer MATTHEW FONTAINE MAURY, who was preparing a chart of the ocean depths in preparation for the laying of the transatlantic CABLE. It was the first significant physical discovery about the ocean floor.

telephone Communications device. The telephone was invented by Scottish-born American inventor ALEXANDER GRAHAM BELL in 1876. He registered his patent just ahead of competing American inventor Elisha Gray (1835–1901). It was improved in 1877 by American inventor THOMAS ALVA EDISON's addition of a mouthpiece containing carbon powder. Earlier contributors to the technology included Philip Reis of Germany (1861) and Antonio Meucci of Italy (1857). In 1878 the first commercial telephone exchange was established in New Haven, Connecticut. The device went on to revolutionize twentieth-century communication.

Temple Bar London gate dividing the Strand on the west from Fleet Street on the east. It marks the formal entrance to the City of London (on the east). It stood north of the Temple, an area that in Victorian times contained two of the four Inns of Court, the Inner Temple and Middle Temple.

Tenniel, Sir John (1820–1914) English illustrator. Born in London, he received his first art training at the Royal Academy but soon left, dissatisfied at the lack of knowledge he attained. In 1836 he sent his first picture to an exhibition of the Society of British Artists, and in 1845 he received a commission to illustrate Dryden's *St. Cecilia* in the "Hall of Poets" of the House of Lords.

Five years later, Tenniel joined the staff of *PUNCH,* where he was quickly appreciated for his humor and political satire. He contributed more than two thousand drawings and cartoons to *PUNCH,* and illustrated more than thirty books, including *ALICE'S ADVENTURES IN WONDERLAND* (1866) and *Through the Looking Glass* (1870), which made him world-famous. He was knighted in 1893.

tennis Sport. While the indoor sport of court tennis dates to before the twelfth century, the outdoor game of lawn tennis—or simply "tennis" in the United States—was developed in England in 1874. That year, Major Walter C. Wingfield patented an outdoor game played on an hour-glass-shaped grass court with a net, rubber balls, and rackets. Originally called "Sphairistikè," the game was quickly renamed "tennis-on-the-lawn" and, later, "lawn tennis."

By 1875 the dimensions of the court had been changed to a rectangle, and the Marylebone Cricket Club of London devised a set of rules that have since been virtually unchanged, although the height of the net fluctuated several times before being standardized at 3 feet in 1884.

The first championship tournament was held in 1877 at the All England Croquet Club, which was renamed the All England Lawn Tennis and Croquet Club, at Wimbledon. Spencer W. Gore won the first tournament in the only event played, men's singles. Men's doubles matches were added to Wimbledon in 1879, and women's singles and doubles followed in 1884 and 1913, respectively. The Lawn Tennis Association was founded in 1888.

Tennis was played in the United States and Canada as early as 1874. The first U.S. tournament, which was little more than a social event, was held in Nahant, Massachusetts, in 1876. Confusion and inconsistencies in the sport prevailed until 1881 when the U.S. National Lawn Tennis Association was organized to regulate the sport. The first recognized U.S. men's singles championship was played at Newport, Rhode Island, in 1881; Richard D. Sears won the first title and retained it for the next seven years.

As the sport spread across the globe, so did the desire for international competition, and in 1900, Harvard student Dwight F. Davis donated a trophy to a tournament consisting of four singles matches and one doubles match. Named the Davis Cup, it was won in its first year by the U.S. team, which defeated the British players in Boston.

Tennyson, Alfred, Lord (1809–1902) English poet. Born in Somersby, Lincolnshire, he was one of eight children and was educated at a local grammar school and by his father, a local vicar.

With his first poetic work, "The Devil and the Lady," a fragment in Elizabethan style, written in 1823 and published in 1930, he declared his precocity in verse. He attended Trinity College, Cambridge, where he became a member of the Apostles, an established social and discussion group, and formed a close friendship with Arthur Henry Hallam. After Tennyson's father died following a mental and physical breakdown, the poet left the university without a degree. More ill luck came when his *Poems* (1832) received a brutal review in the influential *Quarterly Review,* after which Tennyson refused to publish his work for a decade. The shock of Hallam's sudden death in 1833 prompted him to compose what most consider his greatest work, "In Memoriam A.H.H.," an elegy for his friend, published in 1859 but begun as early as 1834. After a brief infatuation with Rosa Baring in 1833, he married Emily Sellwood in 1850, the same year that he succeeded William Wordsworth as poet laureate.

The success of English poet Alfred, Lord Tennyson during the Victorian era is partially attributed to the politically conservative tone of his poems. Photo courtesy of Topham/The Image Works.

Tennyson moved with his wife to the Isle of Wight, where he entered a period of extraordinary productivity. He published *Maud and Other Poems* (1855), which included "THE CHARGE OF THE LIGHT BRIGADE" and "The Ode on the Death of the Duke of Wellington," and *The Idylls of the King* (1859), his ambitious extended narrative in the form of an Arthurian romance. His poem "Enoch Arden" (1865) was one of his most popular works; it detailed a man's return to his family after having been presumed lost in a shipwreck, only to discover that his beloved wife has married a rival. "The Princess" (1847) was a poetic "medley" permeated with scientific and social issues and imbued with a sustained lyricism; it told the story of a prince, subject to "weird seizures," who pursues a recalcitrant, solitary princess.

Esteemed by the public and Queen VICTORIA herself, who found particular comfort in "IN MEMORIAM" following the death of Prince ALBERT, Tennyson lost critical standing after the Victorian era. His characteristically high moral tone and his endorsement of imperialist aims did not appeal to twentieth-century readers. Still, he is remembered for his technical acumen and his ability to capture the sensibilities of an entire nation.

Terry, [Dame] Ellen Alice (1848–1928) English actress. Born to an acting family, she became one of the foremost English performers of her generation, appearing in lead roles on the London stage, often Shakespearean productions. She was married several times, to painter George Frederic Watts, Charles Kelly, and James Carew. She also lived for a time with architect and designer Edward Goodwin. From the age of thirty-one her primary acting partner was English actor Sir HENRY IRVING, whose magnetic power kept her in his professional and emotional control. She was made a dame in 1925, and her correspondence with GEORGE BERNARD SHAW was published in 1931.

Thackeray, William Makepeace (1811–1863) English novelist, critic, and editor. Born in Calcutta of Anglo-Indian parents, Thackeray went to England in 1817 and a decade later spent two unfruitful years at Cambridge, never acquiring a degree. He lost most of his patrimony in the Indian bank failures of 1833 and married a woman who subsequently became mentally unsound. In 1857 he ran unsuccessfully for Parliament as an Independent Liberal.

Beginning in the 1830s, Thackeray wrote regularly for periodicals, including *Fraser's Magazine* and *PUNCH*. Among his contributions were *The Yellowplush Papers* (1837–38) and *Catherine* (1839–40). In 1844 he published his first full-length novel, *Barry Lyndon*.

Although his work in periodicals afforded him some literary recognition, his reputation was not consolidated until the publication of *The Book of Snobs* (1846–47), a searing taxonomy of Victorian class consciousness, serialized in *Punch*. With *VANITY FAIR* (1847–48), published in monthly installments, he found a large readership and critical acclaim for his ironic depiction of English social life during the Napoleonic era. It was followed by a number of major works: *The History of Pendennis* (1848–50); a semiautobiographical novel, *The History of Henry Esmond* (1852); *The Newcomes* (1853–55); *The Rose and the Ring* (1855); and *The Virginians* (1857–59). In 1859 he became the first editor of the literary periodical *The Cornhill Magazine*.

A pivotal figure in the development of literary REALISM, Thackeray's fiction, indebted to eighteenth-century satire, provides thoughtful contemporary commentary on the themes of imposture, performance, and hypocrisy.

Thailand See SOUTHEAST ASIA.

Theed, William (1804–1891) English sculptor. The son of a painter and sculptor of the same name (1764–1817), he trained under sculptor EDWARD HODGES BAILY and at the Royal Academy Schools. After working in Rome, he returned to London in 1848 to become a prolific sculptor whose works included the colossal group of *Africa* for the ALBERT MEMORIAL.

Theosophical Society Religious philosophical organization. Founded in New York in 1875 by MADAME [HELENA PETROVNA] BLAVATSKY, Henry Steel Olcott, and William Q. Judge, the group later established a temple at Adyar near Madras, India, as their center of operation. From the Greek for "divine wisdom," the term "theosophy" encompasses a number of traditions of philosophical and religious thought about the nature of God, the soul, and the universe based on direct mystical insight and/or philosophical speculation. Elements of theosophy are found in the Hindu Vedas, the Chinese *I Ching* and *Tao Te Ching,* the Judaic kabbala, and Platonism, Neoplatonism, and Gnosticism. German mystic Jakob Böhme (1575–1624) and Swedish philosopher Emanuel Swedenborg (1688–1772) were important theosophists.

Theosophical doctrine as defined by the Theosophical Society stated that God is the source of all spirit and matter, that humans have souls, and that humans can attain insight into the nature of God and the spiritual nature of the universe. Drawing on Buddhism and Brahmanism, and sharing much in common with SPIRITUALISM, the Theosophists believed in reincarnation, occult knowledge and powers, and the practice of Yoga. Among the disciples of the Theosophical Society were English author ANNIE BESANT and Irish poet WILLIAM BUTLER YEATS.

Thérèse de Lisieux (1873–1897) French contemplative. Born Marie-Françoise-Thérèse Martin, she became a Carmelite nun at Lisieux at age fifteen and lived in seclusion until dying of tuberculosis nine years later. She developed the doctrine of the "Little Way," achieving spiritual growth through humble, everyday tasks. Her posthumously published book *Histoire d'une âme* (1898) became one of the best known spiritual autobiographies of the era. She was canonized as a Roman Catholic saint in 1925.

thermodynamics Scientific study of the interrelation of energy, heat, and work. The field developed in response to the need to improve the efficiency of STEAM POWER, specifically the steam engine. In *Reflections on the Motive Power of Heat* (1824), French physicist Sadi Carnot (1796–1832) studied the interconnection between heat and work as applied to steam engines. The first law of thermodynamics, the law of conservation of energy, was articulated by German physicist Hermann von Helmholtz (1821–1894) in 1847: The total amount of energy in an isolated system does not change. Energy cannot be created or destroyed but only converted from one form to another.

The second law, the law of ENTROPY, was articulated by German physicist Rudolf Clausius (1822–1888) in 1850: The disorder of an isolated system increases with time or, at best, remains constant. Clausius later coined the term entropy as a measure of a system's disorder or the unavailability of energy to do work.

The third law, the law of absolute zero, was discovered by German physical chemist Walther H. Nernst (1864–1941) in 1906: All bodies at absolute zero would have the same entropy; however, absolute zero, the state of zero energy, can never be perfectly reached. The law provides an absolute scale of values for measuring entropy.

Though the third law postdated Victoria's reign, the first two laws revolutionized nineteenth-century physics. They also found their way into social, philosophical, and artistic thought. Writers such as JOHN TYNDALL used conservation of energy to support a materialistic philosophy. In support of the concept of

SOCIAL DARWINISM, Balfour Stewart adopted systems of energy as a model for society in which social superiors are seen as possessing greater energy than their inferiors. Other writers, such as AGERNON CHARLES SWINBURNE, HENRY ADAMS, and Gustav LeBon, employed entropy as a metaphor for growing social disorder and irreversible decline.

Thiers, Louis-Adolphe (1797–1877) French politician and historian. Before the THIRD REPUBLIC (1870–1940), Thiers had a distinguished career as a journalist, publicist, and historian. He wrote multivolume histories of the French Revolution and the reign of Napoleon I, which are widely regarded as the classic liberal view of the period. He held political office under the Restoration, the July Monarchy, the SECOND REPUBLIC, and the SECOND EMPIRE. He was critical of the government of NAPOLEON III and the conduct of the FRANCO-PRUSSIAN WAR (1870–71).

In 1871, after an armistice with Germany had been signed, he was elected the first president of the Third Republic. He urged all parties to suspend their struggle over the constitution until France was secure. He authorized the suppression of the Paris Commune and negotiated the peace settlement with Germany. He engineered a rapid payment of reparations and the quick withdrawal of German troops. He resisted a Bourbon restoration, although he also tried to stop what he regarded as democratic excesses. He was voted out of office by disgruntled royalists in 1873, but he had seen the Third Republic through its weakest period.

Third Republic (1870–1940) Period in French history. The Third Republic was declared in the midst of the FRANCO-PRUSSIAN WAR (1870–71) after NAPOLEON III's capture and the fall of the SECOND EMPIRE. The first years of the republic were tumultuous. The people of Paris established the radical revolutionary PARIS COMMUNE, which was brutally suppressed. Monarchists threatened a Bourbon restoration. Nevertheless, France recovered quickly from the effects of the war.

Throughout the republic there was continual struggle over the form the government should take and frequent alternation between liberal and conservative governments. France was ruled by a two-chamber Parliament—with the lower house elected by universal male suffrage—which together elected the president. The Third Republic saw the secularization of French education in the 1880s. It also saw the expansion of French colonies in Africa and Indochina. The Dreyfus affair (1894–1906), a controversy over the rigged conviction of ALFRED DREYFUS, a Jewish army officer, as a German spy, was divisive. But the most significant feature of the Third Republic was the fact that all the controversies were fought out within the political sphere without recourse to insurrection or coup. France's economy also expanded fairly rapidly throughout the Third Republic, and preparations for revenge against Germany for its victory in the Franco-Prussian War were a priority of all governments. The Third Republic ended with the fall of France to Germany in 1940, in the midst of World War II (1939–45).

Thomson, Sir Joseph John See ELECTRON.

Thoreau, Henry David (1817–1862) American transcendentalist writer and thinker. Born in Concord, Massachusetts, he attended Harvard, where he first became acquainted with the writings of RALPH WALDO EMERSON, the dean of American TRANSCENDENTALISM. Soon after hearing Emerson present "The Divinity School Address" at Harvard's 1841 commencement exercises, the newly graduated Thoreau began a close association with him. Over the next few years Thoreau lived with and worked at a variety of jobs for Emerson, including the tutoring of his nephew. During this time Thoreau also began to publish poems and the essay "Natural History of Massachusetts" in the transcendentalist journal *The Dial.*

For two years beginning in 1845, Thoreau lived in a hut by Walden Pond near Concord, on property owned by Emerson, and devoted himself to writing. He produced two major works, one that was to define him. In 1849 his first book, based on his "fluvial excursion" with his brother, *A Week on the Concord and Merrimack Rivers,* was published. It was a publishing failure. In 1854, *Walden* appeared; it was his account of his experiment in unfettered living, epitomized by his call to "simplify, simplify." The book was a moderate success in its day, leading nineteenth-century audiences to acknowledge him as a transcendentalist writer, albeit in the shadow of Emerson.

In July 1846, as a statement against the MEXICAN WAR, Thoreau refused to pay his poll tax and was imprisoned. Although his stay lasted only one night and his aunt paid the tax, the experience served as the basis for the essay "Resistance to Civil Government," later renamed "Civil Disobedience." The essay stresses the need to refuse cooperation with unjust laws: "Let your life be a counterfriction to stop the machine," he wrote. In the twentieth century, the essay served as a founding document for civil disobedience movements, including those of Mahatma Gandhi and Martin Luther King.

Thoreau continued his individual moral crusade by speaking against the Fugitive Slave Law and defending JOHN BROWN after his attack on Harpers Ferry in 1859. His later work life included several nonwriting jobs as a laborer and a member of his family's pencil business. Following a trip to Minnesota to treat his TUBERCULOSIS, he died of the disease and was buried in Sleepy Hollow Cemetery in Massachusetts, along with fellow literary contemporaries NATHANIEL HAWTHORNE, Emerson, and BRONSON ALCOTT. Among Thoreau's posthumously published writings are the naturalist works *The Maine Woods* (1864) and *Cape Cod* (1865).

Three Emperors League Political alliance. Part of OTTO VON BISMARCK's alliance system to maintain European stability, the league was formed by an agreement of emperors WILLIAM I of GERMANY, Alexander II of RUSSIA, and FRANZ JOSEPH of AUSTRIA in 1873 and revived in 1881. The first agreement called for each member of the league to go to the defense of any member that was attacked and to support one another against the threat of revolution. The second agreement in 1881 guaranteed that each party would remain neutral in the event of a war involving another member and divided the BALKANS into Russian and Austrian spheres of influence. The league's major effect was to lessen tensions between Russia and Austria-Hungary in the Balkans. The league lapsed following Bismarck's dismissal by WILLIAM II. Germany and Austria-Hungary continued their close alliance, but Russia drew closer to France, setting the stage for World War I.

Tiffany, Louis Comfort (1848–1933) Painter, decorator, stained-glass artist. This leader in the ART NOUVEAU movement was born in New York City, the son of jeweler and entrepreneur Charles Lewis Tiffany, who founded the jewelry store Tiffany & Company.

The younger Tiffany first established himself as an oil and watercolorist in Europe and Morocco, making a specialty of Oriental scenes. Among his major paintings are *Street Scene in Tangiers* (1876), *Duane Street, New York* (1878), *Feeding the Flamingoes* (1888), and *Market Day at Nuremberg* (1892).

In the 1870s, Tiffany established an interior decorating firm in New York, under the name Tiffany Studios. He and his staff of designers specialized in church work, including stained-glass windows and mosaics. He discovered the formula for making an iridescent decorative glass known as Tiffany *favrile;* it became his trademark. He also established the Tiffany Furnaces in Corona, New York, which produced lamp shades, vases, and other small forms, and won many awards for beauty and craftsmanship.

Tiffany's creations as a decorator and stained-glass artist include the Tiffany Chapel, which was exhibited at the World's Columbian Exposition in Chicago in 1893 and later became part of the crypt of New York's Cathedral of St. John the Divine; and the electric fountain in the Grand Court of the Manufactures and Fine Arts Building at the Pan-American Exposition in Buffalo in 1901.

Time Machine, The (1895) English novella. Written by H. G. WELLS, it was the first of his "scientific romances." Developed from a series of speculative articles he wrote in 1888 for *The Science Schools Journal,* the novella appeared in two serial versions before being published as a book in 1895.

In the novella, a group of friends listens to the "Time Traveller" as he tells how he built a time machine and rode it into the future. Most of the action takes place in the year A.D. 802,701, a period when humans have evolved into two separate species: the frail, beautiful Eloi and the monstrous, apelike Morlocks. The Eloi live lives of empty pleasure and leisure on the earth's surface. The Morlocks live underground, laboring to provide for the Eloi's needs. At night the Morlocks come out and feed on the Eloi.

The Time Traveller's machine is stolen by the Morlocks, and he has to battle them to get back home. Along the way he befriends a childlike female Eloi named Weena, who is killed when the Time Traveller recklessly lights a fire that burns down the forest where they are sleeping.

After recovering his machine, the Time Traveller goes even further into the future, when the landscape is deserted except for giant crabs, and reaches the period 30 million years from now when the sun is red, swollen, and cooling, and the earth is dying. He returns to contemporary England to tell the story of his adventures to his friends, only to depart on his machine the next day for points unknown, never to return.

The Time Machine is a classic of science fiction, the progenitor of a rich subgenre of time travel novels, stories, and movies in the twentieth century. It also expresses Wells's concerns about the dark side of nineteenth-century progress and warns about the dangerous division between capitalists and laborers represented by the Eloi and Morlocks.

Tocqueville, [Count] Alexis [-Charles-Henri-Clérel] de (1805–1859) French politician and historian. A child of aristocrats, he trained as a lawyer and worked for the government, which in 1831 sent him to the United States to study its penal system. His observations of the country informed his *Democracy in America* (1835, 1840), considered the first complete study of the workings of American democracy. In the introduction to the work he says he means to portray "the image of democracy itself, with its inclinations, its character, its prejudices, and its passions, in order to learn what we have to fear or to hope from its progress." A member of the Chamber of Deputies while writing *Democracy in America,* he also served as a minister of foreign affairs under Louis Napoleon, later NAPOLEON III, in the late 1840s. His book *The Old Regime and the French Revolution* (1856) was meant to be the first of a multivolume history on the revolution.

toilet Apparatus for human waste disposal. Although the water closet with a bowl and one-way valve was developed in 1775 and 1778 by Alexander Cumming and Joseph Bramah, it saw several modernizations during the nineteenth century. These included changing the bowl from cast iron to ceramic for easier cleaning, creating vents for traps that held standing water, and developing the "washdown closet" in 1890, in which the water tank is placed behind the toilet. The term also indicated the various activities that were part of grooming and dressing.

Tolstoy, [Count] Leo [Nikolayevich] (1828–1910) Russian novelist, philosopher, and social reformer. Though he wrote short stories, plays, and religious and philosophical works, he reached the height of his powers in two epic novels, *War and Peace* and *Anna Karenina,* recognized as world masterpieces. In these works he succeeded in providing a panoramic view of Russian society, creating dozens of richly drawn and psychologically complex characters, and presenting his ideas about the human search for meaning and fulfillment.

Born into nobility, Tolstoy was educated at home and at the University of Kazan. He served in the Russian army during the Crimean War and began his literary career in his spare time. He completed a trilogy of autobiographical fiction—*Childhood* (1852), *Boyhood* (1854), and *Youth* (1856)—and several short stories. In the late 1850s he became interested in progressive education, publishing a magazine and textbooks on the subject and starting a school for peasant children. Following his 1862 marriage to the much younger Sonya Anreevna Bers, he shifted his focus to managing his estate and writing novels.

War and Peace (1864–69) is set in the early 1800s during Russia's war with Napoleon. Following the fortunes of several families on the battlefield and back home, it includes such memorable characters as the passionate Natasha, the proud and aristocratic Andrei, and the ever-searching Pierre. Despite the suffering it depicts, the novel is essentially optimistic, with principal characters who are morally strong and ultimately happy.

By contrast, *Anna Karenina* (1873–76) is largely pessimistic. The affair of married woman Anna with Count Vronsky leads to tragedy, and few of the book's other characters fare well. Human weakness and social hypocrisy are highlighted. Its opening line is one of the most famous in all literature: "All happy families are similar, but each unhappy family is unhappy in its own way."

After completing *Anna Karenina,* Tolstoy became increasingly depressed. In *A Confession* (1879–81) he discusses his anguished quest for meaning and spiritual conversion. He ultimately embraced Christian anarchism, seeking to follow the teachings of Christ but rejecting the authority of church and state. Following his conversion he sought to live more simply and self-sufficiently and wrote books, pamphlets, and articles promulgating his new views on religion and social reform. These include *What I Believe* (1883) and *What Then Must We Do?* (1886).

In *What Is Art?* (1897), Tolstoy applied his religious beliefs to aesthetics. He argued that for art to be valuable, it must be simple and accessible, and must convey the feelings of its creator to the audience. He believed religious art was the highest form and rejected complex, stylized works, including his own novels.

During his post-conversion years, he wrote several pieces of short fiction, including *Two Old Men* (1885) and *The Death of Ivan Ilyich* (1886), and the novel *Resurrection* (1899). In addition, he completed the tragedy *The Power of Darkness* (1887) and the satirical comedy *The Fruits of Enlightenment* (1889).

Tolstoy's religious ideas brought him both followers and opponents. The Russian holy synod excommunicated him in 1901, and his own family grew increasingly alienated, put off by the burdens of his asceticism and the frequent visits of his converts. Tolstoy fled his home late one night in 1910 and died of pneumonia a few days later at the railway station of Astapovo.

Tom Brown's School Days (1857) English novel. An affectionate remembrance of life at the RUGBY SCHOOL, this children's novel by Rugby alumnus THOMAS HUGHES set the pattern for future public school stories. In the novel, young Tom Brown enters boarding school shy, homesick, and teased by older boys but learns to like it as he takes on manly characteristics. The tale ends with Tom chosen "Head Boy" under the mentorship of real-life Rugby headmaster THOMAS ARNOLD. A model of the "character formation" public schools were meant to nurture, Tom Brown appeared again in a sequel, *Tom Brown at Oxford* (1861).

Tom Sawyer, The Adventures of (1876) See *ADVENTURES OF TOM SAWYER, THE*

Toulouse-Lautrec, Henri [-Marie-Raymond] de (1864–1901) French painter and graphic artist. Toulouse-Lautrec's reactions to IMPRESSIONISM helped revolutionize the arts of poster design and lithography. His brief but intense career was an important manifestation of the *FIN DE SIÈCLE* spirit that swept Europe. Born into an aristocratic family, Lautrec broke both his legs as a child, which left him dwarfish and crippled. From 1882 to 1885 he studied in Paris with Emile Bernard and met VINCENT VAN GOGH in 1886. Early on, Lautrec tried to adapt Impressionism's pastel color palette and hatched brushstroke technique, but for most of his career he remained a draftsman who used color in long, clearly defined brushstrokes. Lautrec's method is evident in his first important work, *Le Cirque Fernando* (1888), which is reminiscent of the flat patterns of color of EDOUARD MANET and the tilted perspective of EDGAR DEGAS.

Like Degas, Lautrec studied aspects of contemporary life. His greatest single source of material was the dance hall and cabaret called the Moulin Rouge. He also painted the world of the theater, cafés, restaurants, and brothels. Lautrec was a central figure of the society he depicted and a personal friend of the singers, dancers, and prostitutes. He primarily captured his favorite subjects, the dancers Louise Weber, known as La Goulue, and the anonymous woman who chose the name Jane Avril. Lautrec's posters called for a new simplification and reduction of design in order to create an immediate visual effect. *La Goulue at the Moulin Rouge* (1891) is typical in its strong color, theatrical lighting, and masterful silhouettes.

By 1896, Lautrec's prolific output declined with his deteriorating health. Lautrec's work inspired GEORGES ROUAULT, GEORGES SEURAT, and Vincent Van Gogh, and bridged many of the formative tendencies of Pablo Picasso and HENRI MATISSE in the twentieth century.

Tractarians A group of English religious thinkers. The Tractarians led the OXFORD

MOVEMENT, which supported spiritual and liturgical changes in the Church of England. Their name refers to a series of influential pamphlets they wrote, "Tracts of the Times," between 1833 and 1841. The most famous Tractarian was JOHN HENRY NEWMAN; others included JOHN KEBLE and EDWARD B. PUSEY.

Trafalgar Square Plaza in London. Laid out in 1829 and adjacent to Charing Cross at the traditional central point of London, it is centered around a monument to Admiral Horatio Nelson, hero of the Battle of Trafalgar in 1805, in which Napoleon's navy was defeated off the coast of Spain. It is flanked by the National Gallery, the Church of St. Martin-in-the-Fields, and the National Portrait Gallery. It was the site of BLOODY SUNDAY, or the Trafalgar Square Riots.

Trafalgar Square Riots See BLOODY SUNDAY.

Trail of Tears Path taken by Cherokee Indians during their forced removal. The Cherokee Indians had been ordered to leave the southeastern United States by 1837 under the provisions of the Treaty of Echota forced on them by the U.S. government after the discovery of gold in Cherokee territory in Georgia. They fought the treaty in the courts, but Washington refused to adhere to a Supreme Court ruling in the Cherokees' favor. During the fall and winter of 1838–39, between fifteen thousand and eighteen thousand Cherokees were expelled and four thousand died on the journey to the Oklahoma Territory from disease and exposure. The route became known to the tribe as "The Trail Where They Cried."

transcendental number Mathematical term. A transcendental number is not algebraic, that is, it cannot serve as a solution to an algebraic equation with rational coefficients. The first number to be identified as transcendental was *e,* the base of the system of natural logarithms having the approximate value 2.71828 . . . ; it was identified as such by French mathematician Charles Hermite (1822–1901) in 1873. In 1882, German mathematician Ferdinand von Lindemann (1852–1939) showed that *PI,* the ratio of the circumference of a circle to its diameter, is also transcendental.

transcendentalism Philosophical, literary, and religious movement. It was active in the United States from the 1830s to the 1850s. Transcendentalism asserted the intuitively known nature of reality and the unity of the world as created by the Over-Soul. Humans and nature were part of the Over-Soul and as such could embody divinity. Originating in New England and led by RALPH WALDO EMERSON, the movement attracted several of the leading minds of the day, including MARGARET FULLER, BRONSON ALCOTT, and HENRY DAVID THOREAU. The movement's philosophy was first made popular with the publication of Thoreau's essay "Nature" in 1836; the influential periodical *The Dial* served as its organ from 1840 to 1844. A response to the rationalism of the day, transcendentalism had roots in the ideas of Plato and drew on the idealism of Immanuel Kant, the ROMANTICISM of Johann W. Goethe and William Wordsworth, and the mysticism of Emanuel Swedenborg. It championed the direct experience of the individual rather than external forms of reason or authority as a code of conduct and in some circles was considered a radical ideology.

Transvaal African region. Now a province of northeast SOUTH AFRICA, the Transvaal was in Victorian times an independent republic. Located at an elevation of 3,000 to 6,000 feet in the grassy plateau of the African veld, it was one of the regions settled by Dutch-descended

Afrikaners, or BOERS, in 1838 during their GREAT TREK from the Cape Colony. It became the South African Republic in 1856.

Britain annexed the Transvaal in 1877. The Boers regained self-rule in a war in 1881, although the republic stayed nominally under British suzerainty. Gold was discovered in the RAND region in 1886, leading to an influx of gold-mining UITLANDERS, or foreigners. Most of them were British, and all of them were denied political rights by the government of Transvaal—that is, its cofounder and president Paul Kruger (1825–1904; president from 1883 to 1900). In 1895, CECIL RHODES, prime minister of the neighboring Cape Colony, authorized the unsuccessful raid by LEANDER STARR JAMESON to attempt to annex the Transvaal for Great Britain. The raid was defeated by the South African Republic and disowned by the British crown, but it intensified the republic's distrust of Britain. That distrust led the Transvaal to launch the first attack of the BOER WAR (1899–1902), in which Britain conquered and annexed the Transvaal and the other Afrikaner republic, the Orange Free State. The Transvaal became a province of the Union of South Africa in 1910.

Travels in Arabia Deserta (1888) British travel narrative. Written by CHARLES MONTAGU DOUGHTY, it recounts his two years of wandering with the Bedouins in Arabia in the 1870s, including his pilgrimage to Mecca. The odd, deliberately archaic style combines elements of Elizabethan travel literature with Arabic expressions.

Trent affair Diplomatic incident. In 1861, during the early days of the U.S. CIVIL WAR, Union captain Charles Wilkes halted the British vessel *Trent* and took prisoner the Confederate commissioners John Slidell and J. M. Mason. Hostilities between the United States and Britain seemed imminent, until diplomacy by British prince ALBERT and American secretary of state William H. Seward led to the release of the commissioners and averted war.

Triple Alliance International agreement. The Alliance was forged in 1882 among GERMANY, Austria-Hungary (see AUSTRIA), and ITALY, with SERBIA also joining that year and ROMANIA joining in 1883. After Germany defeated France in the FRANCO-PRUSSIAN WAR, its leader, OTTO VON BISMARCK, feared that France would try to regain the lost provinces of Alsace and Lorraine. He also feared that Germany could not survive a general European war. In 1879 he formed the secret Dual Alliance with Austria-Hungary. Italy joined after France thwarted Italian colonial plans in Tunisia. The basic agreement stated that if any member of the Alliance went to war with two or more nations, the others would aid it militarily.

In 1890, France and Russia entered into a secret pact that became an open alliance in 1895. Great Britain officially joined that alliance in 1907, forming the Triple Entente. Its primary reason for existence was to stand guard against the Triple Alliance. The two opposing coalitions finally clashed militarily in World War I.

Triple Entente See TRIPLE ALLIANCE.

Trochu, Louis-Jules (1815–1896) French general and politician. Trochu served in the CRIMEAN WAR (1853–56) and the war in Italy against Austria-Hungary. At the outbreak of the FRANCO-PRUSSIAN WAR (1870–71) he was appointed military governor of Paris and directed the defense of the city until its capitulation in January 1871. He commanded troops of the provisional government in the suppression of the PARIS COMMUNE. He served briefly in the Chamber of Deputies of the new THIRD REPUBLIC before retiring.

Trollope, Anthony (1815–1882) English novelist. Born in London and educated at Harrow and Winchester, he grew up in considerable poverty owing to his father's disastrous business failures. His family fled temporarily to Belgium, where his mother, Frances Milton Trollope, supported her husband and children through her writings, which came to include the popular *Domestic Manners of the Americans* (1832). A ferociously productive author who typically produced ten pages each morning before leaving for his job as a postal official, Trollope aimed, as he wrote of the novelist generally in his *Autobiography* (1883), "to make his readers so intimately acquainted with his characters that the creations of his brain should be to them speaking, moving, living human creatures." This was accomplished, he said, only after the novelist lived with his characters in the "full reality of established intimacy."

Public recognition for Trollope came with his fourth novel, *The Warden* (1855), which was followed by *Barchester Towers* (1857), *Doctor Thorne* (1858), and *Framley Parsonage* (1860). But it was with the series of works comprising the Barsetshire novels that the "regional novel" took a resonance previously unknown in English fiction. Its realistically rendered depiction of an intimate, middle-class community brought Trollope a loyal audience. The Palliser novels, Trollope's other significant extended sequence, were more political in theme. Beginning with *Can You Forgive Her?* (1864–65) and concluding with *The Duke's Children* (1879–80), the works focus on parliamentary activity as it affects the fortunes of Plantagenet Palliser and his wife Glencora. In addition to his fiction, Trollope published a monograph on WILLIAM MAKEPEACE THACKERAY, travel books on the West Indies, Australia, and North America, as well as biographies of Cicero and politician Lord Palmerston.

Trollope himself was an unsuccessful Liberal candidate in 1868, a bitter experience he recounted in *Phineas Redux* (1873–74). One of his darkest works of fiction, it is matched only by *The Way We Live Now* (1874–75), a panoramic satire often regarded as his masterpiece. Although formally conventional and frequently reliant on elaborate plots, Trollope's novels together present one of the most vividly detailed perspectives on the Victorian period.

Troy Archaeological site. The setting of Homer's *Iliad,* Troy became a historical fact in the 1870s with the excavations of German archaeologist HEINRICH SCHLIEMANN. The site is located at the hill called Hissarlik in Turkey, near the modern city of Canakkale and the entrance to the Dardanelles. In ancient times its strategic position, controlling trade routes between Asia and Europe, made it a place of wealth and frequent warfare. It is composed of nine principal strata representing nine different fortified settlements, successively raised and destroyed over the course of thirty-five hundred years. The strata range from Troy I at the oldest and deepest level to Troy IX at the newest and shallowest level. Troy I (c. 3000–2400 B.C.) was an Early Bronze Age citadel. Troy II (c. 2400–2200 B.C.), with its imposing palace, gold and silver, and fine artifacts, was mistakenly identified by Schliemann as the site of King Priam's Troy. Later study has made it more probable that Homeric Troy was located in a higher stratum dating from about 1250 B.C. After Schliemann's death, Troy was excavated by his colleague Wilhelm Dorpfeld in 1893–94.

Truth, Sojourner (1797–1883) African-American abolitionist, woman's rights advocate, and evangelist. Born Isabella Van Wagener in New York State, she was a slave until she was freed in 1827. At that point she worked as a domestic in New York City. Throughout her life she claimed to have divine visions, and she preached on the streets of New York under the auspices of a missionary society. She left the city in 1843 and forsook her given name in favor of Sojourner Truth. She preached at camp meetings and churches, and embraced abolitionism. Her fiery eloquence drew huge crowds to hear her denunciation of SLAVERY. In the early 1850s she also became an eloquent speaker for woman's rights. Truth, who never learned to read, told her life story to Olive Gilbert and published it as *The Narrative of Sojourner Truth.*

When the U.S. CIVIL WAR began, she helped supply black regiments. In 1864 she helped integrate Washington, D.C., streetcars and met with President ABRAHAM LINCOLN. She was appointed to the Freedmen's Relief Association where she helped resettle former slaves.

tuberculosis Chronic or acute infectious disease. Popularly known as consumption, it was the leading cause of death in the nineteenth century and was most prevalent in conditions of urban poverty, overcrowding, and malnutrition. In the Victorian mind, it was also associated with creative genius; artists, poets, and other romantic types were considered more susceptible to the wasting away caused by the disease.

The forms and stages of tuberculosis were identified early in the nineteenth century by French physicians Gaspard Laurent Bayle (1774–1816) and René Laënnec (1781–1826), both of whom died from the disease. Considered incurable, its cause was a mystery until 1882 when German microbiologist ROBERT KOCH discovered *Mycobacterium tuberculosis,* the bacillus that causes tuberculosis. Koch went on to develop in 1890 the tuberculin test that became a primary tool in diagnosing the disease. Effective drugs against tuberculosis were not developed until the twentieth century, though improvements in sanitation, housing, and diet helped reduce the spread of the disease by the end of the Victorian era. For the upper classes, the favored treatment for the disease was rest and relaxation at winter resorts, on sea voyages, or at sanatoriums in the mountains. Edward Livingston Trudeau (1848–1915) established the first tuberculosis sanatorium in 1874 in upstate New York. It became a model for similar institutions in Europe and the United States well into the twentieth century.

tulle Net material. The stiff silk net much used in the nineteenth century for ladies' hats, gowns, and ballet costumes was named for its city of origin in southern France.

Turgenev, Ivan Sergeyvich (1818–1883) Russian novelist and playwright. Turgenev's work evolved from early-nineteenth-century European ROMANTICISM to late-century naturalism. His 1862 novel *Fathers and Sons* helped him become the first Russian writer known in the West. Born into an unhappy family in Orel, Russia, he attended the University of St. Petersburg and pursued graduate studies at the University of Berlin, planning to become a philosopher. He turned to writing after philosophy was forbidden as an academic subject in Russian schools. He published several plays over the next few years, including *A Month in the Country* (1850; original title *The Student*), generally considered the first Russian psychological drama. He also published his collection of stories about the suffering of the serfs, *Sportsman's Sketches,* in 1852, along with poetry and essays. In all his fictional works, Turgenev created realistic characters and situations, focusing on internal as well as external conflict and dealing with the major issues of the day—the institution of serfdom, the status of the nobility, and the clash of liberal and conservative political ideologies. His political and literary opinions often antagonized leading writers of his day, including LEO TOLSTOY and FYODOR DOSTOYEVSKY.

During the latter part of his career, Turgenev wrote highly acclaimed novels, including *Rudin* (1856), *A Nest of Gentlefolk* (1859), and *Virgin Soil* (1877).

Turkey See OTTOMAN EMPIRE.

Turner, Frederick Jackson (1861–1932) American historian and teacher. He was born in Wisconsin and began teaching at the state university in 1885. Turner electrified his profession in 1893 when he read his essay "The Significance of the Frontier in American History" before the American Historical Association in Chicago. He argued in it that the history of the United States and the uniquely democratic nature of its institutions and political ideas could be understood by considering the continuous advance of settlers into vast areas of free land. The availability of land acted as an "escape valve" for workers who would otherwise be subject to the class inequities and resentments of Europe. Frontier conditions, whether on the Atlantic Coast for the early colonists or in the Rocky Mountains for settlers in the 1880s, promoted democratic institutions. These conditions also helped form the American character, marked by pragmatism, optimism, materialism, and an almost anarchic individualism. For Turner the announcement of the 1890 census that a frontier line of open land and new settlements no longer existed was a momentous occasion in American history.

The study of American history changed radically under the influence of Turner's thesis, which he published in 1894. Almost an entire generation of scholars turned away from New England and the eastern seaboard as keys to understanding the United States. The frontier dominated the field for the next thirty years. Turner helped cultivate this focus through his tenure at Harvard (1910–24), where he became the most famous professor of American history of his time.

For all his renown as a scholar, Turner published little. His landmark article was included in *The Frontier in American History,* a collection of short essays published in 1920. His other major work, *The Significance of Sections in American History,* was published in 1932, the year he died. It received the 1933 Pulitzer Prize for history.

Turner's argument was not seriously challenged until the 1920s when some scholars began to accuse him of ignoring economic factors and class antagonisms in American history. Others deemed the argument oversimplified, short on evidence, and overly optimistic about the frontier's impact on democracy. However, no one after Turner could ignore the importance of the frontier in the country's past.

Turner, Joseph Mallord William (1775–1851) English painter. Turner was a leading exponent of ROMANTICISM; his full-scale, expressive pictures of nature satisfied the Romantic taste for the picturesque. At the beginning of the nineteenth century, Turner was already established as a prolific academic painter. He made studies in the Louvre and traveled extensively through Switzerland, North Wales, and Scotland to produce a large number of scenic and historical works, such as *Falls of the Rhine at Schaffhausen* (1806) and *Hannibal Crossing the Alps* (1812). Turner frequently turned to the French landscapist Claude Lorraine, whose influence is seen in several idyllic landscapes, including *Dido Building Carthage* (1815).

Throughout the 1840s, Turner was obsessed with the sublime power of nature, as were many of his Romantic contemporaries. He adopted an increasingly free painting technique where forms and details were suggested only by broad areas of color. *The Slave Ship* (1840) and *Steamer in a Snowstorm* (1842) are masterpieces of Turner's vision of an apocalyptic nature; each composition is a mass of swirling activity.

Turner's priority was the painting of light by concentrating on loose areas of yellows, whites, blues, and cool grays. He is often thought of as a proto-Impressionist even though color and light for Turner were ingredients for abstraction, not description. Turner's approach to light influenced IMPRESSIONISM, especially CLAUDE MONET and CAMILLE PISSARRO who saw his work in London in 1870 while taking refuge during the German occupation.

Twain, Mark [Samuel Langhorne Clemens] (1835–1910) American humorist, newspaperman, novelist, short story writer, and lecturer. His experiences growing up in Hannibal, Missouri, were transformed into the archetypal lives of Tom Sawyer and Huck Finn in *THE ADVENTURES OF TOM SAWYER* (1876) and *The Adventures of Huckleberry Finn* (1884).

Born in Florida, Missouri, Mark Twain was twelve years old when his father died, forcing the boy to go to work as a printer. He also began writing occasionally for the Hannibal *Journal.* In 1853 and for the next four years Twain worked as a printer around the country. In 1857 he became a cub pilot on the Mississippi River, learning the river so well that "the face of the water, in time, became a wonderful book—a book that . . . told its mind to me without reserve, delivering its most cherished secrets as clearly as if it uttered them with a voice."

American writer Mark Twain satirized contemporary American culture in his classics The Adventures of Tom Sawyer *and* The Adventures of Huckleberry Finn. *Photo courtesy of Topham/The Image Works.*

The Civil War put an end to steamboat traffic and to Twain's career. After two weeks of military service for the Confederacy, he set out for Nevada where he began using the pen name Mark Twain (meaning "two fathoms deep"). Soon he moved to San Francisco, where he published "The Celebrated Jumping Frog of Calaveras County" (1865), which was reprinted in newspapers all over the country.

In 1866 he began publishing accounts of his travels and building a lucrative lecture career. *The Innocents Abroad* (1869), humorous accounts of his travels in Europe and Palestine, was wildly successful. Financially secure, Twain married Olivia Langdon in 1870.

His reputation grew steadily. He made an odd figure, with his trademark white suits and billowing hair, and spoke with a deliberately quaint drawl. He loved to shock his conservative wife and friends. He was appreciated during his lifetime as a humorist and speaker rather than the great lyrical writer and social critic he is now considered to be.

Twain's children were born over the ten years from 1870 to 1880. Unfortunately Twain was extravagant and fond of gadgets and schemes, and in 1894 he went bankrupt. After repaying all his debts with the income from an around-the-world lecture tour and after the death of his wife and beloved daughter Susy, Twain's vision became darker and darker. In 1909 he wrote, "I came in with Halley's comet in 1835. . . . It will be the greatest disappointment of my life if I don't go out with Halley's comet. The Almighty has said, no doubt: 'Now here are these two unaccountable freaks; they came in together, they must go out together.' " His daughter Clara married in 1909; his daughter Jean, who had been acting as his secretary, died on Christmas Eve that year. Twain was desolate and alone. In April 1910, Halley's comet appeared. The next day Twain died.

His works include the novels *The Prince and the Pauper* (1882), *A Connecticut Yankee in King Arthur's Court* (1889), and *The Tragedy of Pudd'nhead Wilson* (1894); the autobiographical *Roughing It* (1872) and *Life on the Mississippi* (1883); the travel accounts *The Innocents Abroad* (1869), *A Tramp Abroad* (1880), and *Following the Equator* (1897); and the stories "The Man Who Corrupted Hadleyburg" (1900) and "The Mysterious Stranger" (1916).

Tweed, William Marcy "Boss" (1823–1878) The most infamous of TAMMANY HALL's corrupt and corrupting leaders was born in New York City. As a young man Tweed worked as a bookkeeper and became known in his political ward through his volunteer fireman activities. The Democrat was elected alderman in 1851 and was a congressman from 1853 to 1855. He also served as school commissioner, chairman of the board of supervisors, and state senator (1867–71).

But Tweed's real power base and the source of his enormous fortune was the leadership of Tammany Hall, the Democratic political organization in New York City through which he controlled patronage and government contacts. The Tweed Ring—himself, the mayor, the comptroller, and the city chamberlain—defrauded the city of over $30 million through inflated and imaginary bills. Judges were bribed, nominations bought and sold, votes purchased, and the voter placated with jobs and charity.

Attempts within Tammany to oust Tweed were unsuccessful. However, a series of exposés in the *NEW YORK TIMES* and the biting political cartoons of THOMAS NAST in *Harper's Weekly* stirred the public against him. The Tammany slate lost the 1871 municipal elections, although Tweed was returned to the state Senate.

Samuel Tilden, the state Democratic chairman, helped collect damaging evidence against

Tweed, who was convicted of fraud in 1873. He served one year in jail but was immediately arrested on other charges after his release. He escaped to Cuba and then to Spain, but was brought back to the United States in 1876. He died in prison two years later.

Tyler, John (1790–1862) Tenth president of the UNITED STATES (1841–45). Tyler was born in Charles City, Virginia. He served in Congress (1817–21) and was governor of Virginia (1825–27). The staunch defender of states' rights was elected to the Senate (1827–36) but resigned, leaving the Jacksonian Democrats over the nullification issue (see JOHN CALHOUN) and the economic policies of ANDREW JACKSON. He joined the Whigs and became vice president in 1841 as the running mate of WILLIAM HENRY HARRISON.

Tyler became president after Harrison died one month into his term. Tyler and Whig leaders clashed over whether Tyler would be a caretaker president or an independent executive. He vetoed several Whig measures and his whole Cabinet, except DANIEL WEBSTER, resigned in 1841. An impeachment resolution was issued in 1843, but the House of Representatives defeated it.

Without party support Tyler still managed to settle border questions with Canada, authorize the annexation of Texas, and reorganize the navy. He did not run in 1848. In 1861 he led an unsuccessful conference of southerners that tried to stop secession. He was elected to the Confederate House of Representatives but died before taking office.

Tyndall, John (1820–1893) Irish physicist. From 1853 to 1867 he was professor of natural history at the Royal Institution; he also served as its superintendent from 1867 to 1887. Omnivorous in his interests, he wrote more than 180 research papers on many subjects, including light, heat, sound, glaciers, and the atmosphere. Among his most important discoveries was the identification in 1863 of the GREENHOUSE EFFECT—the tendency of atmospheric constituents such as carbon dioxide and water vapor to keep in INFRARED RADIATION, thus raising the earth's surface temperature. He also discovered the Tyndall effect, the scattering of light, particularly at shorter wavelengths, by particles in a colloid—an effect that explains the blueness of the sky and the redness of sunrise and sunset, as light is scattered by atmospheric dust.

In addition to his serious research, Tyndall was a dedicated popularizer of science. His lectures at the Royal Institution drew large crowds; his addresses, articles, and books, such as *Heat as a Mode of Motion* (1855), made the latest concepts of physics accessible to a wide audience. Tyndall used his popularity to urge public support for scientific research and to advocate the naturalistic views he called scientific materialism—though the latter made him anathema to the religious establishment.

Tz'u-hsi, Empress (1835–1908) Dowager Empress (also called Ci Xi). The mother of MANCHU (Qing) emperor T' ung Chi (also called Deng Ji; he reigned from 1862 to 1875), she began to rule CHINA from behind the scenes when he took the throne as a child. She initially favored a policy of accommodation with the Western powers in return for helping to subdue the Taiping Rebellion (1848–64). She also allowed minor reforms of the Chinese government but resisted more radical changes. After the death of her son, she was temporarily out of power. When the new emperor attempted major reforms in 1898, she had him imprisoned in the Imperial Palace and ruled on his behalf. When the BOXER REBELLION, an anti-Manchu, anti-European movement, broke out in 1900, she negotiated an alliance with the rebels against the Europeans. Following the defeat of the Boxers, she again tried minor reforms. On her deathbed she had the captive emperor murdered and named two-year-old Pu Yi to succeed him.

Uganda Republic in east central AFRICA. It is bounded by Sudan on the north, Kenya in the east, Tanzania and Rwanda in the south, and Zaire in the west. Despite its small size (91,133 square miles), the equatorial country contains fertile plateaus, swampy lowlands, a desert region, lakes, and several mountain ranges. Deep in the African interior, it was the site of several BANTU-speaking kingdoms as early as the fourteenth century; by the nineteenth century the most powerful kingdom was Buganda. Europeans and Arabs first reached the region in the 1840s, and it was opened to British interests in the 1860s by explorers JOHN HANNING SPEKE and HENRY MORTON STANLEY. By agreement between Great Britain and Germany in 1890, the region was declared a British sphere of influence. In 1894 the kingdom of Buganda became a British protectorate, a designation later extended to the rest of what is now Uganda. The country did not gain independence until 1962.

uitlander Afrikaner term for foreigner. The Afrikaners, or BOERS, people of Dutch descent living in South Africa, used the term to describe the outsiders, mostly British, who flocked to the TRANSVAAL after gold was discovered there in 1886. Concentrating in Johannesburg, these miners and adventurers were regarded as a wild, unscrupulous lot, contrasting with the pastoral Afrikaners. One observer wrote of the uitlanders: "They bribed, they lied, they swindled. They lived at the best hotels and drank champagne at eleven o'clock in the morning." Denied political rights by the Afrikaner government of the Transvaal, uitlanders were expected to rise up against the government to support LEANDER STARR JAMESON's raid, an unofficial British invasion, in 1895, but the uprising never took place and the raid was defeated.

umbrella Shield for sun or rain. The umbrella was introduced in Europe and North America in the late eighteenth century but was popularized during the Victorian Age. Of particular importance were the handles, which were often made of distinctive material such as GUTTA-PERCHA or ivory and carved with intri-

The umbrella represented the height of fashion during the Victorian era. Photo courtesy of the Max A. Polster Archive.

cate markings. Some umbrella handles could be screwed open to provide storage for money or liquor. An umbrella for women to use in the sun was known as a parasol or sunshade.

Uncle Tom's Cabin, or Life Among the Lowly U.S. novel. Written by HARRIET BEECHER STOWE, it was published serially in the abolitionist newspaper *National Era* from June 5, 1851, to April 1, 1852, and in book form in March 1852. Written to protest SLAVERY in general, and the Fugitive Slave Act of 1850 in particular, it became America's most popular novel, with more than three hundred thousand copies sold within a year of publication. It was translated into twenty languages.

The plot centers on Uncle Tom, a slave who is sold by the Shelbys, a family in financial trouble. Tom saves the life of a little girl on his trip down the Mississippi River and is bought by the girl's father. Two years later Tom's new master dies, and he is sold to Simon Legree, a sadistic planter who has Tom flogged to death after his refusal to reveal the whereabouts of two slaves who had staged a fake escape. George Shelby, one of Tom's original owners, appears as the slave dies. He then swears allegiance to the abolition of slavery.

The novel, along with unauthorized dramatizations of it, raised antislavery sentiments in the North. The validity of the book was attacked, and Stowe published *A Key to Uncle Tom's Cabin* in 1853 to answer her critics. The propaganda value of the book was recognized by Abraham Lincoln, who on meeting Stowe was supposed to have said, "So you're the little woman who wrote the book that made this great war."

underground railroad Antislavery operation. The underground railroad was an informal network of white sympathizers and free blacks in the United States who helped runaway slaves escape to Canada or to havens in the North. At least one thousand slaves a year received food, clothing, shelter, and other help in the 1840s and 1850s as they journeyed northward. The railroad was more organized in some places than others. Regular members of the railroad operated in and around Philadelphia, for example, while most of the help in other sections was offered spontaneously by different individuals.

The network developed sometime after 1812, and by the 1840s the railroad metaphor was fully established. Fugitive slaves were "passengers," safe places "stations," and helpers "conductors." One of the most famous conductors was Harriet Tubman, a former slave.

Many slaves and conductors were captured. The runaways were taken back to the South, and their helpers were fined or imprisoned under the Fugitive Slave Act of 1793. Congress passed a new fugitive act in 1850 that raised the penalties for helping fugitives and made it easier for southern pursuers to establish ownership claims on northern blacks.

United Kingdom See GREAT BRITAIN.

United States Country. The United States stretches from the Atlantic Ocean westward to the Pacific Ocean, with Canada forming its northern border and Mexico its southern one. The United States underwent a remarkable territorial expansion during the Victorian era, fulfilling the belief of many Americans in MANIFEST DESTINY. Texas was annexed in 1845; Mexico surrendered California and most of the rest of its vast southwest holdings after losing the MEXICAN WAR; and the Northwest, consisting of the modern states Oregon, Washington, and Idaho, was secured through negotiations with the British. Lured by cheap land, settlers spread into the new territories west of the Mississippi River while continuing to settle the older territories. A huge system of roads, canals, and railroads developed. European immigrants, mostly German and Irish, flocked to the country in the 1840s and 1850s. They helped populate the hinterlands and also swelled the populations of the eastern coastal cities. The Native American Indians were slowly pushed off their land through a series of INDIAN WARS and through forced migrations such as that across the TRAIL OF TEARS.

The politics of the 1830s and 1840s became increasingly more democratic as more white men gained suffrage and local appointed offices were opened to elections. ANDREW JACKSON, MARTIN VAN BUREN, and the DEMOCRATIC PARTY dominated presidential politics in the 1830s but were challenged by the Whig Party in the 1840s, led by DANIEL WEBSTER and HENRY CLAY.

The question of SLAVERY and continuing sectional conflicts dominated the 1840s and 1850s. Four million African-American slaves lived in the South, which remained an agricultural region producing cotton, rice, sugar, and other cash crops. Many southerners favored the extension of slavery into the territories acquired in the Mexican War and opposed high tariffs that raised the price of imported goods. Many in the North, while believing that African Americans were inferior to Europeans, feared that the extension of slavery would undermine the status of free white laborers throughout the country. Those who supported the abolition opposed slavery on moral grounds.

The COMPROMISE OF 1850 temporarily eased tensions between North and South, but the Kansas-Nebraska Act, which allowed slavery into areas where it had been banned, spurred antislavery activity, including the formation of the REPUBLICAN PARTY which took a strong stand against the spread of slavery. The Supreme Court's DRED SCOTT DECISION (1857) and the raid by JOHN BROWN on Harper's Ferry (1859) further polarized the nation. After Republican ABRAHAM LINCOLN was elected president in 1860, eleven southern states left the Union to form the CONFEDERACY. The Union won the ensuing CIVIL WAR at great cost to both sides. Slavery ended, but the RECONSTRUCTION period after the war failed to ensure the political and civil rights of the former slaves.

The nation's population boomed in the decades after the war. Nine million immigrants, mostly from southern and eastern Europe, came to the U.S. between 1880 and 1900. The westward migration continued, as did the growth of cities. The lure of gold and silver, the growth of the cattle industry, and the expansion of the railroads led to the opening of new areas in the West.

American industry also developed rapidly and by 1900 was producing more steel and iron than Great Britain. The oil industry boomed, as did coal mining, meat packing, shipbuilding, the mass production of consumer goods, public utilities, and other industries. INDUSTRIALIZATION was accompanied by the consolidation of businesses into trusts, which dominated entire industries, the most famous example being JOHN D. ROCKEFELLER's Standard Oil Trust. He and other "captains of industry," such as ANDREW CARNEGIE, CORNELIUS VANDERBILT, and JAY GOULD, became fabulously wealthy during this GILDED AGE.

This growth of industry heightened tensions between workers and owners. The LABOR MOVEMENT began, and national labor unions were formed, most notably the Knights of Labor. A national railroad strike in the 1870s led to widespread violence, as did other work stoppages. EUGENE V. DEBS and other organizers tried to steer labor into taking more radical, socialist stances, but that approach gave way to the more pragmatic and nonideological strategies of SAMUEL GOMPERS and the American Federation of Labor.

Widespread crop failures and rising debt in the 1880s and 1890s led farmers to organize against rate fixing by RAILROADS and to support unlimited coinage of silver. The POPULIST PARTY was formed in 1891; it won some local elections and supported the bid by WILLIAM JENNINGS BRYAN for the presidency in 1896.

Few divisive issues marked national politics after the Civil War. The DEMOCRATIC PARTY was generally more sympathetic to farmers' demands for unlimited coinage of silver, while Republicans backed business's demands to restrain inflation by backing currency with gold. Republicans won all but two presidential elections between 1868 and 1912, and dominated Congress as well. This was despite the widespread corruption associated with Republican president ULYSSES S. GRANT. The SHERMAN ANTI-TRUST ACT and the Interstate Commerce Act did little to control the trusts and railroad, but did set a precedent for more effective laws in the future. The assassination of President JAMES GARFIELD in 1881 led to the establishment of the Civil Service Commission, which redressed some of the worst abuses of the federal patronage system.

Local politics saw the rise of political machines in the larger cities such as New York City's TAMMANY HALL, which controlled votes by doling out jobs and contracts but did little to address the growth of slums and other urban ills. Municipal corruption spurred the Progressive movement, which toppled some city machines and fought for social and political reform both locally and nationally.

Foreign policy was dominated by the SPANISH-AMERICAN WAR in 1898, which made the United States an imperial power in the Pacific. The Hawaiian Islands were annexed in 1898. The United States supported a Panamanian revolt against Colombia, which laid the groundwork for the building of the Panama Canal.

American literature flourished throughout the century. WALT WHITMAN and EMILY DICKINSON were major poets. NATHANIEL HAWTHORNE, HERMAN MELVILLE, HENRY DAVID THOREAU, and RALPH WALDO EMERSON are the most famous writers of the antebellum and Civil War era. MARK TWAIN, THEODORE DREISER, HENRY JAMES, and JACK LONDON are some major figures of the postwar period. Artists from the HUDSON RIVER SCHOOL, WINSLOW HOMER and THOMAS EAKINS, dominated the art scene. JOHN PHILIP SOUSA was its most famous composer.

Universal Postal Union (UPU) Worldwide mail agency. The UPU provides nations with general and technical advice on bettering postal services. Begun in 1875 under the Universal Postal Convention of 1874, the UPU is also involved in setting charges for the transport of international mail. Headquartered in Bern, Switzerland, the UPU has been an agency of the United Nations since 1948. In 1990 it had 169 members.

Uranus Planet. Uranus, seventh planet from the sun and the first one discovered since antiquity, was first detected in 1781 by British astronomer Sir William Herschel. A few years later Herschel discovered two satellites of the planet, Titania and Oberon (1787). These were the only Uranian moons known until 1851 when British astronomer William Lassell discovered two more moons of Uranus, Ariel and Umbriel. Fifteen satellites of Uranus are now known.

U.S. Constitution, amendments Three amendments to the U.S. Constitution were ratified during the Victorian era, all adopted as a consequence of the U.S. CIVIL WAR. The Thirteenth Amendment, ratified in 1865, abolished SLAVERY. The Fourteenth Amendment, ratified in 1868, granted citizenship to former slaves and prohibited state governments from abridging citizens' rights, violating due process of law, or denying equal protection of the laws. Intended to protect former slaves from discrimination by states, these clauses were later used by the Supreme Court to strike down a variety of state laws deemed to interfere with citizens' rights. The equal protection clause became one of the most important legal weapons available to African Americans during the civil rights movement of the 1950s and 1960s. Other provisions of the Fourteenth Amendment barred former officials of the CONFEDERACY from holding office and repudiated government responsibility for losses incurred by the freeing of slaves. The amendment also affirmed that former slaves counted as whole persons, not "three-fifths" of a person. Although this provision tended to increase southern representation, another clause reduced representation for states that prevented citizens from voting.

The Fifteenth Amendment, ratified in 1870, prohibited federal or state infringement on citizens' rights on the basis of race, color, or previous servitude.

U.S. presidents and vice presidents The following served as president and vice president of the UNITED STATES during the reign of British monarch Queen Victoria:

In addition, the United States acquired several territories. The Oregon territory (1845), the Mexican Cession (1848), and the Gadsden Purchase (1853) were acquired and parti-

DATES	PRESIDENT (PARTY)	VICE PRESIDENT
1837–41	MARTIN VAN BUREN (Dem.)	Richard M. Johnson
1841	WILLIAM HENRY HARRISON (Whig)	JOHN TYLER
1841–45	John Tyler (Whig)	(no vice president)
1845–49	JAMES KNOX POLK (Dem.)	George M. Dallas
1849–50	ZACHARY TAYLOR (Whig)	MILLARD FILLMORE
1850–53	Millard Fillmore (Whig)	(no vice president)
1853–57	FRANKLIN PIERCE (Dem.)	William R. King (1853 only; afterward no vice president)
1857–61	JAMES BUCHANAN (Dem.)	John C. Breckinridge
1861–65	ABRAHAM LINCOLN (Rep.)	Hannibal Hamlin, 1861–65; ANDREW JOHNSON, 1865
1865–69	Andrew Johnson (Dem., National Union)	(no vice president)
1869–77	ULYSSES SIMPSON GRANT (Rep.)	Schuyler Colfax, 1869–73; Henry Wilson, 1873–75; no vice president, 1875–77
1877–81	RUTHERFORD B. HAYES (Rep.)	William A. Wheeler
1881	JAMES A. GARFIELD (Rep.)	CHESTER A. ARTHUR
1881–85	Chester A. Arthur (Rep.)	(no vice president)
1885–89	GROVER CLEVELAND (Dem.)	Thomas A. Hendricks, 1885 (afterward no vice president)
1889–93	BENJAMIN HARRISON (Rep.)	Levi P. Morton
1893–97	Grover Cleveland (Dem.)	Adlai E. Stevenson
1897–1901	WILLIAM MCKINLEY (Rep.)	Garret A. Hobart, 1897–99; no vice president, 1899–1901; THEODORE ROOSEVELT, 1901

U.S. states admitted and territories acquired Nineteen states entered the UNITED STATES during Queen Victoria's reign (see next page).

tioned into states during this period. Alaska (1867) and Hawaii (1898) were acquired but did not become states until the twentieth century. The PHILIPPINES were acquired (1899)

State	Date Admitted
Florida	1845
Texas	1845
Iowa	1846
Wisconsin	1848
California	1850
Minnesota	1858
Oregon	1859
Kansas	1861
West Virginia	1863
Nevada	1864
Nebraska	1867
Colorado	1876
North Dakota	1889
South Dakota	1889
Montana	1889
Washington	1889
Idaho	1890
Wyoming	1890
Utah	1896

and were granted independence in the twentieth century.

U.S. Supreme Court, chief justices Four individuals served as chief justice of the UNITED STATES Supreme Court during the Victorian era (see chart below).

utilitarianism Philosophical school. Utilitarianism argued that right and wrong are determined by the goodness or badness of an action's consequences and that the greatest happiness of the greatest number of people is the foundation of morality. Founded by English philosopher Jeremy Bentham (1748–1832), the school became highly influential in the Victorian era and was often associated with advocacy of political and social reforms. Its greatest spokesperson of the period was JOHN STUART MILL. CHARLES DICKENS was a critic.

Name	Birth–Death	Served
Roger B. Taney	1777–1864	1836–64
Salmon P. Chase	1808–1873	1864–73
MORRISON R. WAITE	1816–1888	1874–88
MELVILLE W. FULLER	1833–1910	1888–1910

V

vaccination Medical procedure. It is the process of rendering humans immune to an infectious organism by inoculating them with a weakened form of the organism that stimulates production of antibodies. Although invented and given its name in 1796 by British physician Edward Jenner, who used vaccinia, or cowpox, virus to produce protection against smallpox, vaccination received its greatest refinements during the Victorian Age. In the 1880s, French bacteriologist LOUIS PASTEUR introduced several vaccines, most notably those for anthrax and rabies. A vaccine against typhoid fever was developed in En-gland in 1897, but deaths from the disease did not drop dramatically until the isolation of the first antibiotic effective against the typhoid bacilli in the mid-twentieth century.

valence See FRANKLAND, Sir EDWARD.

Valentine cards Greeting on St. Valentine's Day. The feast is celebrated on February 14 and has its origins in the ancient Roman Lupercalia, a festival associated with fertility. The Christian church turned it into the feast day of

The Victorian era popularized the tradition of sending romantic valentine cards on February 14th.

the martyr St. Valentine, who died around 270 and became known as the patron saint of lovers. The practice of sending Valentine cards to lovers, friends, and family was popularized during the Victorian era. One reason may have been the development of inexpensive printing techniques such as chromolithography, which allowed for the low-cost reproduction of color. Mass-production machinery also allowed for complexity of card design, making possible such intricacies as embossing and machine-cut pop-ups.

Van Buren, Martin (1782–1862) Eighth president of the UNITED STATES (1837–41). He was elected state senator in 1812 and became state attorney general in 1816. His adept use of patronage helped make him a U.S. senator (1821–28). In Washington he supported the policies of President ANDREW JACKSON and became his closest advisor, helping him build a political organization that later developed into the DEMOCRATIC PARTY. In 1828 he abandoned the Senate to run successfully for governor of New York. Jackson appointed him Secretary of State (1829–31) and chose him as his running mate in the 1832 election.

With Jackson's blessing, Van Buren won the 1836 presidential nomination and a substantial popular victory in the election. However, his popularity faltered in the face of the Panic of 1837 and its lingering economic effects. He also angered people by opposing the annexation of Texas and by refusing to help a Canadian revolt against Great Britain in 1837. He lost the 1840 election to Whig WILLIAM HENRY HARRISON. Failing to win the nomination in 1844, he broke with the Democrats over the extension of slavery into the territories. He was the Free Soil Party's unsuccessful candidate for president in 1848.

van Gogh, Vincent [Willem] (1853–1890) Dutch painter. Van Gogh, whose father was a clergyman of the Dutch Reformed Church, was born in the Dutch village of Groot Zundert near the Belgian border. He left school at sixteen, perhaps for financial reasons, and worked for an art dealer in the Hague. He spent six years at the firm, including assignments in London and Paris, but his increasing interest in spiritual matters led him to neglect his work, and he was fired in 1875. He held a variety of jobs for the next two years, including teaching at an English boarding school and selling books in the Netherlands.

Van Gogh began studying for the clergy in 1877 but abandoned this quest a year later. He enrolled in a school for lay preachers in 1878, but after his training the school did not offer him a formal assignment. He began preaching informally in Belgium and, in 1880, began to sketch and paint the people and landscape of the country. This was the start of one of the most prolific decades in painting history. Some seventeen hundred drawings and paintings survive from his brief artistic career, which ended with his death ten years later at the age of thirty-seven.

From 1880 to 1886, Van Gogh painted in Belgium and Holland, never achieving any commercial success and sometimes receiving material help from his brother Theo, an art dealer in Paris. In 1886 he moved to Paris where he met other painters of POST-IMPRESSIONISM, including HENRI DE TOULOUSE-LAUTREC, PAUL GAUGUIN and EDGAR DEGAS. Under their influence his palette brightened until his paintings became known for their vivid colors, although he still failed to realize any financial gain from his art.

Drinking heavily and increasingly on edge, he left Paris in 1888 for the light and warmth of southern France. For a time he lived with Gauguin in the town of Arles, where he began to have extreme bouts of depression and hallucinatory episodes. Toward the end of 1888 he was hospitalized after cutting off one of his earlobes and presenting it to a prostitute at a local brothel. He was released in January 1889 but committed again in May of that year, this time to an asylum of Saint-Rémy where he continued to suffer mental breakdowns and severe depression.

Released again, he returned to Paris in 1890 and then moved to Auvers, a small town outside the French capital. On July 27 he shot himself in the stomach and died one and a half days later.

Van Gogh's work was sold publicly only once during his lifetime—in 1890, the year of his death, when a collector bought "The Red Vineyard" for the equivalent of $80. Today his paintings sell for millions of dollars. His best known works include *The Potato Eaters, Sunflowers, Night Café, Self-Portrait with Bandaged Ear, Yellow Cornfield,* and *Starry Night.*

Vanderbilt, Cornelius (1794–1877) American shipping and RAILROAD tycoon. Born on Staten Island, New York, to a poor father who commanded small boats in New York Harbor, Vanderbilt bought his own ship on borrowed money and soon controlled most ferry lines in the harbor. By the 1840s he owned a fleet that operated along the Atlantic seaboard. After the CALIFORNIA GOLD RUSH he established a sea-land route to the West Coast by way of Nicaragua. He had amassed a huge fortune and became known as "Commodore."

In the 1860s, Vanderbilt sold his shipping businesses and began buying railroads. By the 1870s he had consolidated the New York and Harlem, Hudson River, and New York Central lines into one of the largest railroad systems in the country, despite losing a bitter fight against JAY GOULD for control of the Erie Railroad. When he died in 1877 he was worth over $100 million.

Vanity Fair (1847–48) British novel. Subtitled "A Novel Without a Hero," WILLIAM MAKEPEACE THACKERAY's first popular success in fiction originally appeared accompanied by the novelist's own drawings in serial monthly installments. The novel concerns the fortunes of Becky Sharp, the orphan daughter of a penniless artist who flirts her way into the hearts of men, and Amelia Sedley, her slow-witted but virtuous friend. After a failed attempt at securing Amelia's brother Joseph Sedley as a husband, Becky becomes a governess at the Hampshire home of the Crawley family, where Sir Pitt falls in love with her and proposes marriage. Becky, however, is already married to Rawdon Crawley, whose family disowns him, requiring the couple to live by their wits. Although she is secretly loved by the officer William Dobbin, Amelia marries Dobbin's friend George Osborne, the dashing, selfish son of a wealthy merchant. The novel traces the entangled fates of these characters as played out in urban and rural England up until and beyond the disaster at Waterloo.

A panoramic novel targeting the crass opportunism of European high society, *Vanity Fair* is one of the greatest social-satirical works, and Becky Sharp one of the most colorful heroines, in English literature.

variety, palaces of See VAUDEVILLE.

Vatican Council (1869–70) The twentieth ecumenical meeting of the Roman Catholic Church. Convened by Pope Pius IX (see PAPACY), it strengthened the Pope's authority over the Church by defining his primacy as successor to St. Peter. On July 18, 1870, it promulgated the dogma of papal infallibility: the supreme apostolic authority of the Pope when speaking *ex cathedra,* or as head of the Church, on faith or morals. This event represented the triumph of ultramontanism: the previously controversial view that papal jurisdiction over the Church is supreme. Most of the nearly eight hundred church leaders in attendance supported the Pope on papal infallibility, although a vocal minority opposed it on grounds of theology, history, and prudence. About sixty participants essentially abstained by leaving Rome the day before the vote. The Vatican Council came to a sudden end when Italian troops captured Rome for the new kingdom of ITALY. The second Vatican Council, known as Vatican II, took place in 1962–65.

vaudeville Type of popular American public entertainment. Vaudeville featured a variety of independent acts, including song, dance, comedy skits, acrobatics, and magic acts. A successor to minstrel shows (see EDWIN P. CHRISTY), which featured performers in blackface acting in parodies and doing specialty acts, it was also related to burlesque, which focused on broad comedy and, as the century progressed, scantily clad women. Vaudeville originated in the off-color men-only variety show and was born in spirit in 1865 with the opening of a New York variety theater by former circus clown Tony Pastor. He offered family entertainment and offered giveaways to attract female patrons. Although Pastor is acknowledged as the "father of American vaudeville," the term was not used until the 1880s when American businessmen Edward Albee and Benjamin Keith opened a string of vaudeville theaters that offered wholesome round-the-clock entertainment. The phenomenon that came to be known as "the Sunday School circuit" was popular well into the twentieth century and launched the careers of many comics and performers, such as Will Rogers and Jack Benny. In Great Britain, the equivalent of vaudeville were the palaces of variety. The successor to the MUSIC HALL, these offered as wide a variety of acts as vaudeville and also launched a number of careers. Vaudeville is named for the French town Vau-de-Vire, the site where a type of song known as a vaudeville originated.

Veblen, Thorstein Bunde (1857–1929) American economist. Born in Wisconsin of Norwegian parents, he graduated from Carleton College in 1880 and received a Ph.D. from Yale in 1884. He taught at several universities, including the University of Chicago and the New School in New York City. Veblen attacked the notion that people are naturally acquisitive and competitive, arguing that capitalism had prevented the more benign and cooperative aspects of human nature from developing. His most famous work, *The Theory of the Leisure Class* (1899), argued that goods produced under capitalism were not valued for their utility but for the status they conferred on the consumer. In this work he coined the phrase "conspicuous consumption."

Veblen became more radical in his later years, attacking private property and business influence over universities. Other works include *The Theory of Business Enterprise* (1904) and *The Vested Interests and the Common Man* (1919).

veld (veldt) Grassy plateau of SOUTH AFRICA and Zimbabwe. They are usually filled with scattered trees and shrubs and occur at elevations from 500 to 6,000 feet. In the late nineteenth century, the veld became the site of diamond and gold mining by Afrikaners (BOERS) and the British.

Verdi, Giuseppe [Fortunino Francesco] (1813–1901) Italian composer. In his nearly thirty operas, Verdi often linked musical themes and motifs with specific characters and events. Born in Le Roncole, Verdi showed unusual musical talent at an early age; he was appointed organist of his hometown when he was only ten. A local musician named Antonio Barezzi helped Verdi with his education and sent him to Milan when he was eighteen. He stayed in Milan for three years, then served as musical director for secular music in Busetto for two years before returning to Milan where his first opera, *Oberto,* had a moderate success. His second *Un giorno di regno,* a comedy, failed, but the third, *Nabucco* (1842), was a triumph that helped launch his career. Verdi's fame and fortune were secured with his opera *Ernani* in 1844.

Verdi's opera production has been divided into four periods. The first period, strongly influenced by Gioacchino Rossini, ended in 1849 with *La Battaglia di Legnano.* The second, which concentrated on character development, culminated in *La Traviata* in 1853. Verdi's third period, inspired by Giacomo Meyerbeer's Germanic interpretations of Italian opera, ended with *Aida* in 1871, and the fourth comprised his last two operatic masterpieces, *Otello* (1887) and *Falstaff* (1893).

Verdi was also a member of the Italian Parliament for a short time in 1860 and was even chosen a senator in 1875. His works include *Rigoletto* (1851), *Un Ballo in maschera* (1859), *Don Carlos* (1867), and other choral works, songs, and chamber music pieces.

Verlaine, Paul (1844–1896) French poet. Born at Metz, he moved with his family to Paris in 1851. Verlaine began writing at an early age, and at fourteen he sent a poem to VICTOR HUGO. In 1862 he was employed as an insurance clerk but continued writing, and by the next year his poems began to appear in literary magazines.

His first collection of verse, *Poemes saturniens,* was published in 1866 and was largely ignored. Verlaine published two more collections, one of which, *La Bonne Chanson* (1870), was inspired by his wife Mathilde Mauté. He became infatuated with a visitor in his home, the young poet ARTHUR RIMBAUD, and in 1872 abandoned his wife and infant son in order to travel with Rimbaud throughout Europe.

After arriving in London, Verlaine began work on the poems that would form *Romances sans paroles* (Songs Without words), the 1874 work that would became the seminal doctrine of SYMBOLISM. Verlaine's poems now sought to establish music as the essence of poetry, supplanting literal sense with sound in an attempt to articulate the ineffable.

Verlaine's relationship with Rimbaud was volatile and erratic, and in Brussels in July 1873, after Rimbaud announced his intentions of leaving Verlaine, a drunken Verlaine produced a pistol and shot Rimbaud in the wrist. Rimbaud pressed charges, and Verlaine was sentenced to two years in prison.

Verlaine returned to France in 1877 and three years later published *Sagesse,* a collection of poems recounting his religious conversion in prison as well as other personal and emotional verses. The collection made him famous and was followed by "Art poetique" in 1882, which clarified his poetic theories and became the credo of the younger poets following in the symbolist tradition. He tried his hand at farming, but after the death of his mother in 1886, he spent much of his time drinking. His uncompromising, decadent life-style made him notorious, and his legacy of poems made him a revered literary figure. He died in the home of an aging prostitute.

Verne, Jules (1828–1905) French novelist. Credited as the father of modern science fiction and educated in law, Verne wrote for the stage before gaining his greatest fame for his romances that combined scientific fact, speculation, and adventure. These included *Five Weeks in a Balloon* (1863), *Voyage to the Center of the Earth* (1864), *From the Earth to the Moon* (1865), *20,000 Leagues Under the Sea* (1870), and *The Mysterious Island* (1874). Grounding his fantastic tales in the science of his day, he popularized such areas of emerging knowledge as geology and electricity and predicted such latter-day marvels as the SUBMARINE and space travel. His novel *Around the World in Eighty Days* (1873) celebrated the swift, worldwide travel made possible by nineteenth-century technology, colonialism, and trade. It also introduced Phileas Fogg, the British gentleman who, as the archetype of Victorian assurance and punctuality, undertakes a wager to circle the globe in what was then an unbelievably short time. A previously undiscovered novel, *Paris in the 20th Century* (written in 1863), was attributed to him and first published in 1994.

Victor Emmanuel II (1820–1878) King of Piedmont-Sardinia (1849–61) and first king of ITALY (1861–78). Born in Turin, he became king after his father King Charles Albert abdicated in disappointment when the Piedmontese troops failed to liberate Lombardy from the Austrians in 1849. He benefited from the guidance of COUNT CAMILLO DI CAVOUR, his first minister, and presided over a program of liberalization in Piedmont. This program convinced most Italian nationalists to support the unification of Italy under the Piedmontese monarchy. Piedmont also participated in the CRIMEAN WAR (1853–56), which garnered the goodwill of Great Britain and France.

In 1859 a secret agreement with NAPOLEON III gave Piedmont the necessary strength to challenge Austria again. The subsequent war was a partial success: Austria ceded Lombardy but kept Venice. The following year, GIUSEPPE GARIBALDI, on his own initiative, invaded and conquered Sicily and Naples. The Piedmontese army intervened late in the campaign to prevent Garibaldi from attacking the Pope in Rome. The king and Garibaldi met, and Garibaldi turned over the conquered territories to the monarchy. Victor Emmanuel was declared king of Italy in 1861.

The next decade was spent securing the remaining important Italian territories, organizing the new government, and putting down a serious revolt in the south. In 1866, Italy gained Venice as payment for helping Prussia in the SEVEN WEEKS' WAR. In 1870 the MARCH ON ROME took the city from the Pope.

Victor Emmanuel's last years revealed the difficulties of ruling the newly united kingdom. The nobility was uncooperative, and the king was forced to rely on shifting coalitions in the lower chamber. Ambitious plans for social reforms and economic development proved difficult to implement.

victoria CARRIAGE. The open-top, low-built, four-wheeled carriage was popular among the well-to-do as a vehicle for ladies.

Victoria, children of Queen Victoria's nine children in order of birth were as follows:

Victoria (1840–1901) Princess royal. She married Prussian crown prince Frederick William (later German Emperor or Kaiser FREDERICK III) in 1858. In 1859 she became the mother of the future Kaiser William II, who, during World War I, would become the bitter enemy of his mother's and grandmother's homeland.

Edward (1841–1910) Prince of Wales. He succeeded his mother as EDWARD VII. In

1863 he married Princess Alexandra, eldest daughter of the future King Christian IX of Denmark.

Alice (1843–1878) Duchess of Saxony. In 1862 she married Frederick William Louis of Hesse, who became Grand Duke Louis IV of Hesse-Darmstadt. Her fourth daughter, Alix, became Czarina Alexandra, the wife of Czar NICHOLAS II of Russia, who, along with her husband and children, was murdered by the Bolsheviks in 1918.

Alfred (1844–1900) Duke of Edinburgh and of Saxe-Coburg-Gotha. He rose through the British navy to become admiral of the fleet in 1893. He married the daughter of Russian czar ALEXANDER II.

Helena (1846–1923) In 1866 she married Prince Christian of Schleswig-Holstein-Sonderburg-Augustenburg.

Louise (1848–1939) In 1871 she married the marquess of Lorne, who afterward became duke of Argyll.

Arthur (1850–1942) Duke of Connaught and Strathearn. Made a general in 1893, he later served as governor general of Canada (1911–16).

Leopold (1853–1884) Duke of Albany. In 1882 he married Princess Helena of Waldeck.

Beatrice (1857–1944) In 1885 she married Prince Henry of Battenberg.

Victoria, places named It is possible that no monarch in the history of the world has had more places named for her than Queen VICTORIA. Her name was spread to locations throughout the British Empire and many other places that wanted to honor her. Towns, lakes, mountains, capes, bays, straits, valleys, peaks, counties, harbors, and hills took her name. Here are some of the most important geographical sites named around the world for Britain's Queen Victoria. (See also ALBERT, PLACES NAMED).

- Towns named Victoria in Grenada; Guinea; Honduras; Malaysia; Mindoro, Philippines; Newfoundland, Canada; Nigeria; Tarlac, Philippines; Seychelles; Illinois, Kansas, and Texas in the United States; Vancouver Island, Canada.
- Victoria, Australia (state)
- Victoria River, Australia
- Victoria Nile River, Uganda
- Grand Lake Victoria, Canada
- Lake VICTORIA NYANZA, Africa
- Mount Victoria, Burma
- Mount Victoria, Papua New Guinea
- Victoria Beach, Canada
- VICTORIA FALLS, Zimbabwe
- Victoria Harbour, Canada
- Victoria Island, Canada
- Victoria Land, Antarctica
- Victoria Peaks, Philippines
- Victoria Range, New Zealand
- Victoria Reservation, Canada
- Victoria River Downs, Australia
- Victoria West, South Africa
- Victoriaville, Quebec, Canada

Victoria, Queen (1819–1901) Monarch of the United Kingdom of GREAT BRITAIN and IRELAND (1837–1901) and empress of INDIA (1876–1901). During her reign, the longest in British history, she influenced the character of the monarchy, the political life of the nation, and the moral life of the age. Born Alexandrina Victoria on May 24, 1819, she was the only child of Edward, Duke of Kent, fourth son of King George III, and of Mary Louisa Victoria of Saxe-Coburg-Gotha. Raised principally at her birthplace of Kensington Palace,

This pacific portrait of Queen Victoria suggests the impeccably moral character that set the tone for the era. Photo courtesy of Topham/Image Works.

London, her father died when she was eight months old. She was tutored privately and had a sheltered childhood, with her mother and governess Louise (later Baroness) Lehzen as her main influences. On June 20, 1837, at the age of eighteen, she succeeded her uncle William IV as British monarch, though as a woman she could not succeed to the throne of Hanover, thus ending the link between those two monarchies. Her coronation took place on June 28, 1838.

Graceful but inexperienced, the young monarch depended on her close friend and Whig Prime Minister Lord MELBOURNE for counsel. She soon fell into a minor scandal (1839) however, when rumors spread that her lady-in-waiting Flora Hastings was pregnant; it was later discovered that Hastings was ill with a fatal tumor. That same year, when Melbourne resigned the ministry and Tory leader Sir ROBERT PEEL prepared to take his place, Victoria exhibited the first sign of the political steel that would make her legendary for stubbornness. In what was called the BEDCHAMBER CRISIS, she refused Peel's request to dismiss the Whig ladies of the bedchamber, whom Peel believed were exerting a partisan influence on her. Peel responded by declining to take office as prime minister, prompting Melbourne to return for two more years.

Victoria and her court changed greatly when she married her first cousin ALBERT OF SAXE-COBURG-GOTHA on February 10, 1840. Their loving marriage transformed Victoria from an independent monarch into a devoted wife and mother, while her willingness to heed Albert's advice allowed him to exert considerable influence on the shape of the court. Albert took seriously the monarchy's consulting role under the British constitution and urged Victoria to work methodically and dutifully at shaping the Cabinet, keeping up with dispatches, and advising her ministers. He also swayed her political views, which had previously been Whiggish, to become more conservative. Scrupulously moral to the point of being straitlaced, and greatly concerned with court decorum, Albert influenced Victoria to become more like himself. The concern with spotless character that is usually called "Victorian" was more "Albertine" in its origins, though Victoria herself came to adopt it.

Their union produced nine children: Victoria (1840), Edward, Prince of Wales, later

King EDWARD VII (1841), Alice (1843), Alfred (1844), Helena (1846), Louise (1848), Arthur (1850), Leopold (1853), and Beatrice (1857). (See VICTORIA, CHILDREN OF.) Their marriages and those of their grandchildren linked the British royal house to those of Russia, Germany, Denmark, Greece, and other nations, earning Victoria the name "grandmother of Europe." Literally a grandmother since 1859, she had thirty-seven great-grandchildren alive at the time of her death.

Meanwhile, with Albert's guidance, Victoria continued to exercise political influence. She played an important role in forming coalition cabinets during the period 1846–59 when no single party could command a clear majority in the House of Commons. In 1851 she helped bring about the dismissal of foreign secretary Lord PALMERSTON, with whom she strongly disagreed. During the CRIMEAN WAR, she established the Victoria Cross, an honor first conferred in 1857.

Albert's death on December 14, 1861, devastated Victoria, sending her into lifelong mourning. One of her few consolations was the poem "IN MEMORIAM A.H.H." by poet laureate ALFRED, Lord TENNYSON, to whom she granted the first of several audiences in 1862. For years she declined to perform most ceremonial functions other than dedicating monuments to Albert, including the ALBERT MEMORIAL. Her absence from the public eye caused her popularity to wane, and it was exacerbated by unsubstantiated rumors of a romantic liaison with her Scottish servant John Brown. Republican feeling appeared in the late 1860s, briefly threatening the existence of the monarchy. But by the end of her reign her popularity had been restored, as was demonstrated by the public celebrations of her Golden Jubilee (1887) and DIAMOND JUBILEE (1897).

Despite her period of seclusion, she continued to follow Albert's wishes in keeping up with her ministers' dispatches and making recommendations. The warm, considerate attention of Conservative leader BENJAMIN DISRAELI, who became prime minister briefly in 1868 and again from 1874 to 1880, helped bring her out of seclusion. He recognized her support for his policies of IMPERIALISM by securing for her the title "Empress of India" in 1876. She sided with him on most matters and disagreed often with his longtime rival, Liberal Prime Minister WILLIAM GLADSTONE. Although an advocate of constitutional government and religious toleration, Victoria was conservative on most matters, opposing democratization, WOMAN SUFFRAGE, and HOME RULE for Ireland. However, the REFORM BILL OF 1867, by greatly increasing the electorate and encouraging stronger party organization, weakened her political influence, marking a transition to the largely ceremonial and symbolic form the monarchy would take in the twentieth century.

Although not always in touch with current trends, Victoria reflected and influenced Victorian culture. From her first railroad journey in 1842, Victoria made train travel part of her life, using it to journey frequently among her favorite residences, including Windsor Castle, Osborne House on the Isle of Wight in the winters, and Balmoral in the Scottish Highlands in the summers. Her use of ANESTHESIA in the birth of her last two children made that medical practice more acceptable and popular. Although noble-born, she seemed in sympathy with the moral and political views of the middle classes. She eschewed the aristocratic vices and extravagance of her royal predecessors, favoring instead moral propriety and domesticity. As head of the Church of England, she took a middle position between High Church and Low Church, often preferring to attend Presbyterian services in Scotland. Having kept a journal since her adolescence, she expressed her views in *Leaves from the Journal of Our Life in the Highlands* (1868) and *More Leaves* (1883).

Victoria died at Osborne on January 22, 1901, and was succeeded by her son Edward VII (1841–1910). She was buried beside Albert in Frogmore mausoleum near Windsor. Her longevity and moral steadiness during a time of rapid transformation had helped to unify the nation, the empire, and the age. Her death was mourned throughout Britain and its colonies, but her name lived on in towns, train stations, public buildings, rivers, waterfalls, and hills (see VICTORIA, PLACES NAMED). When she died, HENRY JAMES wrote, "We all feel a bit motherless today."

Victoria and Albert Museum Exhibition place in South Kensington, London. One of the world's great collections of fine and decorative art, it began as the Museum of Manufacturers in Marlborough House in 1852 and was moved to the South Kensington site as the Museum of Ornamental Art in 1857. Conceived by Prince ALBERT, it was endowed with profits from the GREAT EXHIBITION OF 1851 and contained objects of applied art from that exhibition; it was intended to provide models for improving the design of functional objects. In 1899, Queen VICTORIA laid the foundation stone for a new building on the same site, designed by Sir Aston Webb (1849–1930) and opened in 1909.

The rich, lively collection now includes examples of medieval, Asian, Middle Eastern, and contemporary art and design. It has the greatest collection of Indian art outside of India and the most complete collection of English painter John Constable's work. It includes fine collections of Italian Renaissance sculpture, portrait miniatures, furniture, musical instruments, and such assorted treasures as the tapestry cartoons painted in 1516 by Italian artist Raphael.

Victoria Falls African waterfall. Located in south central Africa on the ZAMBESI RIVER on the border between Zimbabwe and ZAMBIA, the falls are among the world's highest, ranking thirty-fourth, with a drop of 355 feet. The first European to see them was Scottish explorer DAVID LIVINGSTONE in 1855. As the region was developed, Victoria Falls became a tourist site for adventurous travelers. A railway bridge across the chasm, first conceived by British empire-builder CECIL RHODES, was completed in 1905.

Victoria Nyanza, Lake (or Lake Victoria) Body of water in east Africa. It is the largest freshwater lake in Africa and the third largest in the world. Its area is 26,828 square miles (69,485 square kilometers) and its length 200 miles (322 kilometers). Located on the border between Uganda and Tanzania, it is one of the principal sources of the Nile River. The first European to visit it was English explorer JOHN HANNING SPEKE in 1858. Explaining his naming of the lake, he wrote, "This magnificent sheet of water I have ventured to name *Victoria* after our gracious sovereign." In 1862, Speke discovered the Victoria Nile River, which issues from the lake's north end and feeds into the White Nile River.

Victoria Theatre London building for theatrical performances. Originally called the Coburg Theatre when built in 1817, it was renamed in 1833 for the princess who became Queen VICTORIA; the theater is now known as the Old Vic. CHARLES DICKENS described it in the essay "The Streets-Night" in *Sketches by Boz* (1836–37).

Victorian style General term for the eclectic, revivalist tendencies in British architecture and design during Queen Victoria's reign. The most significant aspect was the GOTHIC REVIVAL, which produced such achievements as WESTMINSTER PALACE. But other styles were also revived, combined, and reimagined: Elizabethan, Italianate, classical, French Empire. St. Pancras Station (1867–74) by Sir George Gilbert Scott and the Royal Courts of Law (1874–82) by George Edmund Street are esteemed examples of eclectic architecture.

Vienna Secession Avant-garde art movement. The Vienna Secession was founded by painter GUSTAVE KLIMT (1862–1918) in 1897. Klimt acted in response to his dislike for the naturalistic academic style of the day and the classical and allegorical subjects favored by its adherents. He and other painters began instead to paint in a flat, highly decorative style reminiscent of Art Deco. Their paintings often had erotic overtones and were frequently considered controversial.

vinaigrette Container. This small Victorian vessel held perfume, scented vinegars, or smelling salts, and was carried by women to treat fainting spells.

Virchow, Rudolf Ludwig Carl (1821–1902) German pathologist. Born in what is now Poland and educated at the University of Berlin, he filled many medical posts, including director of the University of Berlin's pathological institute. The founder of cellular pathology, he introduced the concepts of *pyemia,* a form of septicemia, or blood infection, caused by the presence of pus-forming organisms in the blood, and *embolism,* the obstruction of a blood vessel by foreign substances or a blood clot. He was also the first to show that the cell theory applies to pathological tissue as well as healthy tissue. He is best known for his 1858

A group of Austrian artists withdrew from the conservative Viennese Academy, initiating a design movement called the Vienna Secession, typified by this piece by Koloman Moser. Private collection, courtesy of Barry Friedman Ltd., New York.

treatise on cells, *Cellular Pathology as Based on Histology*.

Active in the fields of anthropology and archaeology, Virchow founded the Berlin Society of Anthropology, Ethnology, and Prehistory as well as the Pathological Institute and Museum in Berlin.

vulcanization RUBBER-treating process. In this process, named after Vulcan, Roman god of fire, rubber is combined with sulfur, making it resistant to heat and cold. Vulcanization was discovered by CHARLES GOODYEAR in 1839, and utilized effectively by BENJAMIN FRANKLIN GOODRICH.

Wagner, Otto (1841–1918) Austrian architect. Born in Vienna, he began his professional architectural career in the late 1860s, at a time when Vienna needed public and private buildings. By 1894 he had been appointed a chair in the Austrian Academy of Fine Arts. Because of his involvement in city planning and the building of Vienna's municipal railway system, Wagner was regarded as a pioneer of modern urban architecture. His iron-and-concrete bridges, tunnels, and dams combined modern building materials with classical ornamental flourishes. Wagner recommended the use of new principles of construction and materials in the book *Moderne Architektur* in 1896; it was translated into English as *The Brickbuilder* in 1901.

From 1899 until 1905, Wagner was a member of the VIENNA SECESSION group led by artist GUSTAV KLIMT; it emphasized the dynamic use of line and two-dimensionality typical of the ART NOUVEAU style. He is best known for the Postal Savings Bank in Vienna (1904–6), which is considered a landmark in modern architecture for its curving glass roof, foreshadowing the glass-and-steel construction later in the century.

Wagner, [Wilhelm] Richard (1813–1883) German composer. Wagner's works represent the culmination of German musical ROMANTICISM. He was born in Leipzig, Saxony, but the identity of his natural father is uncertain. At the age of sixteen Wagner was determined to become a composer, unaware of the fact that no major composer in history had started so late in life.

Wagner's early career was marked by unsuccessful compositions and mounting debts. In 1839 he and his wife Minna fled to France in an attempt to escape those debts. He was unable to do so, however, and *Rienzi* (1840), his first success, was completed during a several week stay in debtor's prison in Paris. The Wagners returned to Germany, where he began studying the legends of his homeland. The subsequent *Der fliegende Hollander* (The Flying Dutchman) lasted only four performances in early 1843.

In February 1843, Wagner was appointed director of the court opera; his *Tannhäuser* was produced in 1845. He was dismissed from his position for espousing republican principles shortly after the failed REVOLUTION OF 1848. A warrant for Wagner's arrest on charges of treason was issued in 1849, and the composer immediately fled to Zurich, leaving his wife and new debts behind.

While he was in exile in Switzerland, his opera *Lohengrin* was produced at Weimar (1850). Wagner also wrote four essays that became the subject of great scrutiny and controversy. *Die Kunst die Revolution* (Art and Revolution, 1849), *Das Kuntswerk der Zukunft* (The Art-Work of the Future, 1849), *Oper and Drama* (Opera and Drama, 1851), and *Das Judenthum in Musik* (Jews in Music, 1850) advocated socialist revolution and advanced anti-Semitic ideas, attacking the Jewish composers Moses Mendelssohn and Giacomo Meyerbeer. More important for musical history, Wagner recommended the creation of a new art form, "music dramas," that would differ from conventional opera by fusing music, drama, and spectacle in an aesthetic balance. To achieve dramatic unity, he developed the idea of maintaining a continuous symphonic flow, and leitmotif, the reiterated musical phrases associated with characters, emotions, or events. He also argued that texts should be drawn from legend.

Wagner's innovative ideas were embodied in his masterpiece, *DER RING DES NIBELUNGEN* (The Ring of the Nibelung), a four-part opera begun in 1854 and not completed for two decades. As with all his operas, both music and libretto were by the composer. The *Ring's* four parts, with dates of first performance, were *Das Rheingold (The Rhine Gold,* 1869), *Die Walküre (The Valkyrie,* 1870), *Siegfried* (1876), and *Götterdämmerung (Twilight of the Gods,* 1876).

Work on the *Ring* was interrupted for nearly two years as Wagner completed *Tristan und Isolde* in 1858 (first performed in 1865). *The Mastersingers* was completed in 1867 and first performed in 1868.

During this period, Wagner once again faced imprisonment for his large debts but was granted amnesty in Germany by one of his most faithful admirers, Ludwig II of Bavaria, who offered Wagner a royal patronage to finish the *Ring* in Munich. Wagner accepted but spent little time on his grand opera, devoting himself to political essays, his autobiography, and his friend FRANZ LISZT's married daughter Cosima. Wagner had been separated from Minna for some time, and her death in 1866 gave him greater freedom in his pursuit of Cosima. In 1870, a year after the birth of their son Siegfried, Cosima and Wagner were married. Because of the scandal, Wagner was forced once again to relocate, this time to Bayreuth. Ludwig II remained loyal to Wagner's music, however, and provided funding for an opera house in Bayreuth, which was completed in August 1876. The same month the complete *Ring* was performed in Ludwig's presence.

Wagner influenced individuals in many artistic and intellectual fields, including French poet CHARLES BAUDELAIRE, German novelist Thomas Mann, and German philosopher FRIEDRICH NIETZSCHE, who long championed Wagner before finally breaking with him.

Waite, Morrison Remick (1816–1888) American lawyer. He was born in Lyme, Connecticut, the son of Henry Matson Waite, a chief justice of Connecticut. After graduating from Yale College in 1837, he moved to Maumee, Ohio, where he was admitted to the bar and entered the law office of Samuel M. Young. In 1849 he was elected for one term in the Ohio legislature. His efforts on behalf of the Union cause during the CIVIL WAR earned him an appointment to the Ohio Supreme Court in 1863, which he rejected in order to serve as an unofficial advisor to the governor of Ohio.

In 1871, President ULYSSES S. GRANT appointed Waite to serve on the American council in the Geneva Arbitration, in which the U.S. government sought damages from England for its participation in the Civil War. Waite contributed five of the thirteen chapters of the American argument, known as the *ALABAMA* claims. In 1874, Grant appointed him chief justice of the Supreme Court.

He was chief justice until 1888 and adopted a limited interpretation of the Constitution, deferring many decisions to states' rights, especially in the area of civil rights. Waite did not consider it the responsibility of the federal government to protect African-American citizens but deemed it the duty of each state to protect its own people. However, he did protect the rights of blacks to serve on juries (*Strauder v. West Virginia,* 1880). Waite also upheld the criminal status of bigamy even when it was permitted by religious beliefs, as with the Mormons. He also upheld the right of a state to deny the vote to women.

Wakefield, Edward Gibbon (1796–1862) English colonial theorist. The cofounder of colonies in AUSTRALIA and NEW ZEALAND was born in London and named for his distant relative Edward Gibbon, the eighteenth-century author of *The Decline and Fall of the Roman Empire.* After an early diplomatic career, Wakefield achieved notoriety when he tricked young heiress Ellen Turner, daughter of Cheshire manufacturer William Turner, into marrying him. Before consummation could take place, Ellen's angry relative caught up with the couple at Calais. By act of Parliament the marriage was dissolved; Wakefield was convicted of abduction and sentenced to three years in prison.

While in NEWGATE PRISON, Wakefield had occasion to meditate on poverty, crime, and punishment. His *Facts Relating Punishment of Death in the Metropolis* (1831) influenced reform of English criminal law. The thoughts expressed in *A Letter from Sydney* (1829) and *England and America* (1833) influenced colonial policy. In these works Wakefield argued that the policy of populating Australia with convicts and offering free land grants would not result in an orderly, prosperous colony. Instead, Wakefield proposed that Britain sell crown lands in small units at a fixed, modest price and that the proceeds be used to finance more emigration. The emigrants should be evenly divided between both sexes and represent a cross-section of trades and professions.

Wakefield's ideas were taken seriously by British empire builders. In 1831, regulations along Wakefield's lines were applied to New South Wales, Australia, and the Cape Colony, South Africa. The South Australian Act of 1834 laid the grounds for a new colony in Australia following Wakefield's principles; their South Australian colony was formally constituted in December 1836. In 1837, Wakefield founded the New Zealand Association for the purpose of encouraging annexation and colonization of New Zealand. The company was unable at first to get British government permission to found a colony but went ahead anyway, precipitating the government's decision to annex New Zealand in 1840 just before an anticipated move by France.

In 1838, Wakefield expanded his colonial interests by visiting CANADA and serving as colonial advisor to governor-general Lord DURHAM. Wakefield's advice influenced the Durham report, which advocated the union of Upper Canada (Ontario) and Lower Canada (Quebec) under a single legislature. From 1842 to 1844, Wakefield represented Beauharnois, Quebec, in the Canadian legislative assembly.

In 1846, Wakefield suffered a breakdown due to overwork; after his recovery he cofounded the Church of England settlement of Canterbury on the North Island of New Zealand. In 1853, Wakefield himself arrived in New Zealand, where he became a member of the General Assembly. In 1854 he suffered a complete breakdown and spent the rest of his life in retirement. His bust was placed in the colonial office in 1875.

Walker, Frederick (1840–1875) British illustrator and painter. Although trained as a wood engraver, Walker became a prominent illustrator in the 1860s. He later turned to painting, in which he became highly influential for his scenes of peasants in a rural landscape. His oil paintings include *The Wayfarers* (1866) and *The Bathers* (1867); his watercolors include *Strange Faces* (1862).

Walker, William (1824–1860) American adventurer and despot. Born in Nashville, Tennessee, he graduated from the University of Nashville in 1838 and received his M.D. from the University of Pennsylvania in 1843.

After a year of postgraduate study in France, Walker moved to New Orleans, where he practiced law for a brief time before working as editor of the *Daily Crescent* newspaper in 1848. Two years later he moved to California and continued his work as a journalist and sometime lawyer until 1853 when he led an expedition to Baja California, Mexico, and proclaimed it an independent state with himself as president. Walker was arrested by U.S. authorities for violation of neutrality laws, but he was acquitted by a sympathetic jury in 1854.

With the support of shipping magnate CORNELIUS VANDERBILT, Walker organized another expedition, this time to Nicaragua. He arrived there in 1855 with fifty-seven followers and immediately captured the capital city of Grenada. By 1856, Walker had himself inaugurated as president. He intended to extend his designs of MANIFEST DESTINY throughout much of CENTRAL AMERICA, angering the British and French governments, who also had interests in the area. When he angered Vanderbilt by presuming to take control of a Vanderbilt-owned supply route, Vanderbilt turned against him, cutting Walker's supply lines and aiding the other forces against him. In 1857, Walker surrendered to the U.S. Navy and returned to the United States.

In 1860, Walker led another expedition to Nicaragua in hopes of reclaiming his presidency, but he was shipwrecked and spent his time writing *The War in Nicaragua* (1860). Walker finally made his way to Honduras and tried to reach Nicaragua by land, but he was arrested by British authorities and executed by a Honduran firing squad.

Wall Street Journal, The U.S. newspaper. The national daily financial-centered newspaper was established in 1889. Originating from the daily financial reports of Dow Jones and Company, the *Journal* grew to one of the largest newspapers in the United States, with a circulation of approximately 2 million.

Wallace, Alfred Russel (1823–1913) English naturalist. His biological studies in the Amazon region of South America (1848–52) and the Malay archipelago (1854–62) led him to develop a theory of EVOLUTION by natural selection that was essentially the same as that derived independently by English naturalist CHARLES DARWIN. They both published their ideas in 1858, but Darwin received lasting fame for his systematic exposition in *THE ORIGIN OF SPECIES* (1859). Considered the founder of biogeography, Wallace identified Wallace's line in 1869: an imaginary line indicating the general differences of Australian species from those of Asia, a phenomenon presumed to result from long geographical separation. His books included *Travels on the Amazon and Rio Negro* (1853), *The Malay Archipelago* (1869), *The Geographical Distribution of Animals* (1876), *Darwinism* (1889), and *Man's Place in the Universe* (1903).

Wallace, Lew[is] (1827–1905) American writer and soldier. Born in Brookville, Indiana, he was an officer in the Mexican War and earned the rank of major general on the Union side of the Civil War. Between the wars he practiced law and served in politics. After the Civil War he served as governor of the New Mexico territory, where he administered an amnesty to participants in the range conflict called the Lincoln County War (see BILLY THE KID). In 1881 he was sent to Turkey as U.S. minister. He is best remembered, however, not for his political or military exploits but as the author of *Ben-Hur* (1880). Subtitled "A Tale of the Christ," this novel was a great commercial success and is still known to millions, either in book form or in its two movie versions. It tells the story of the impact of Christ's life and death on Judah Ben-Hur, a Judean sentenced to the galleys when his Roman friend Messala betrays him. Wallace wrote several other works of fiction, nonfiction, and poetry, including *The Boyhood of Christ* (1888) and an autobiography.

wallpaper Wall decoration. Machine-made in 1841, wallpaper was first made accessible in price and quantity to middle-class consumers during the Victorian era. English manufacturers produced more rolls in an hour than an artisan could make by hand in a day. Their rich color, pattern, and design covered the walls of many homes by the 1850s. Realistic copies of flowers, trailing vines, gathered fabric, and architectural details were prevalent until about 1870. From 1870 to 1880 the tripartite wall prevailed; it included a detail at the bottom, a major pattern in the middle, and a frieze pattern at the top. The end of the century brought an enthusiasm for pattern, expressed in many forms: heavily embossed paper painted to resemble wood, leather, or metal; WILLIAM MORRIS designs; exotic patterns imported from Japan and Turkey; and as many as four or five patterns on walls and ceilings.

Walpole, Sir Spencer (1839–1907) English historian. He is primarily remembered for his five-volume *History of England from 1815*, published from 1878 to 1886, and its four-volume sequel, *History of Twenty-five Years* (1904–1908), which covered the period from 1856 to 1880. Walpole was regarded as an excellent historian and was knighted in 1898.

Walter, Thomas Ustick (1804–1887) American architect. Born in Philadelphia, Pennsylvania, Walter was apprenticed to his father, a bricklayer, as a boy and became a master bricklayer in 1825. Three years later he entered the office of architect William Strickland and in 1830 began his own practice. Walter's first important commission was for the Philadelphia County Prison in 1831, and two years later he received the commission for Girard College. In 1851 he was appointed by President Millard Fillmore as architect of the

Capitol building. During his tenure (1851–65) Walter added the House and Senate wings as well as the dome to the existing building, which had been completed in 1830. Walter also helped found the American Institute of Architects in 1857; he served as its president from 1876 until his death.

"Waltzing Matilda" (1895) Australian song. Now Australia's unofficial national anthem, this ballad was composed by Australia's most popular *FIN-DE-SIÈCLE* poet Andrew Barton "Banjo" Paterson. In the ballad, a "swagman," or hobo, leaps to his death in a "billabong," or pond, when chased by police for stealing a "jumbuck," or sheep. The ballad's title refers to the bouncing of the swagman's pack as he walks.

War of the Pacific (1879–1884) Conflict in SOUTH AMERICA. In 1878, Bolivia, in violation of an 1874 treaty, levied a tax on nitrate exported from Antofagasta, an area claimed by both Chile and Bolivia. A year later Chilean troops entered Bolivia and claimed Antofagasta, citing the treaty violation as its justification. After Peru refused to renounce its loyalties to Bolivia, Chile declared war on both nations in April 1879.

Within a month of the first invasion, Chile had conquered Bolivian territory as far as the border of Peru and turned its attention to a naval conflict. Two wooden Chilean ships established a blockade in the port of Iquique in the disputed territory and unsuccessfully battled two ironclad Peruvian cruisers in May 1879. Despite losing the battle, Chilean commander Arturo Prat became a national hero for his valor, and the Chilean navy dispatched its own ironclads, defeating Peru's navy in October 1879.

At the beginning of 1880, Chile invaded Peru, and within a year troops had occupied Lima, essentially securing a victory. In the peace treaty ratified in 1883, Chile increased its territory by a third, retaining Antofagasta and a monopoly on the valuable nitrate supply.

Warren, Henry Clarke (1854–1899) American scholar. A fall as a child resulted in a spinal lesion, causing Warren to appear "humpbacked," and due to his physical disability, he was educated at home. Warren graduated from Harvard in 1879 and continued his studies at Johns Hopkins University. On a trip to England in 1884, he became interested in Buddhism, to which he devoted the rest of his scholarly life. He spent time studying the ancient sacred writings at the Pali Text Society and became the first American to attain distinction there.

After his father's death in 1888, Warren returned to the family home in Massachusetts and used his inheritance to publish the thirty-one-volume *Harvard Oriental Series* (1891–1932). At the time of his death, Warren was working on a four-volume translation of Buddhaghosa's *Visuddhimagga* (Way of Purity), a seminal Pali text circa 400.

washing machine Box-shaped mechanical implement for laundering clothes. The washing machine was first introduced in the 1870s. Made of enamel, tin, or wood, it was fitted with wooden paddles and a hand crank, and was used in conjunction with a wringer, which extracted excess water from clothes. It was one of the first of many mechanical implements aimed primarily at women, whose importance as consumers was to grow in importance.

Washington, Booker Taliaferro (1856–1915) American educator. Born a slave in Franklin County, Virginia, to an African-American slave and a white man, he spent a hardscrabble youth working in the coal and salt mines, and continued to work while attending

Hampton Normal and Agricultural Institute. After establishing himself as a teacher and scholar at Hampton, he was invited to organize Tuskegee Institute in Alabama. Through his efforts it became a leading educational facility for blacks. A noted speaker who stressed education as a tool to gain economic freedom and hence parity with whites, he was also a prolific author. His works include *Sowing and Reaping* (1900), *Character Building* (1902), and his autobiography *Up from Slavery* (1901). He founded the National Negro Business League in 1901. In the twentieth century his ideas about black equality were challenged by more radical thinkers, such as W. E. B. DU BOIS.

Washington Monument World's tallest masonry structure. Built in Washington, D.C., in commemoration of the first U.S. president, George Washington, the monument rises 555 feet into the air. Designed by Robert Mills, it was completed in 1888 after forty years of erratic construction. Because the stone for the monument was mined from various quarries, its color changes partway up. The stone for the lower part came from quarries in the south, a region that chose not to contribute more of its resources once the Civil War began. The building was completed with stone from other quarries, resulting in the two-tone effect.

Waterhouse, Alfred See GOTHIC REVIVAL.

Waterloo Bridge Structure in London. It was designed by John Rennie and completed in 1817. Its name commemorates the defeat of Napoleon at Waterloo in 1815. It figured as a landmark in several works by CHARLES DICKENS, including *Sketches by Boz* (1836, 1839), in which "Drunkard's Death" tells the story of suicide from the steps of the bridge. Despite strong protests, the bridge was demolished in 1934. The new bridge was designed by Sir Giles Gilbert Scott and officially completed in 1945.

Wayland, Francis (1796–1865) American clergyman and educator. Born in New York City, Wayland graduated from Union College in Schenectady, New York, in 1813 and attended Andover Theological Seminary, but he returned to Union College in 1817 in order to earn money as a tutor. He remained there until 1821 when he was selected as pastor of the First Baptist Church in Boston. His published sermons earned him an honored reputation, and in 1827 he was named president of Brown University, a position he held until 1855. Under his guidance, Brown grew in reputation and enrollment, and Wayland was recognized as the leading figure in education. Much of his educational philosophy can be found in *Thoughts on the Present Collegiate System in the United States* (1842), in which he contended that colleges did not successfully meet the needs of their students, who had an increasing diversity of backgrounds and interests. He urged an expanded curriculum, with more electives and better facilities. After resigning from Brown, he devoted himself to religious and philanthropic pursuits, serving as pastor of the First Baptist Church in Providence, Rhode Island. His books include *Elements of Moral Science* (1835) and *Elements of Political Economy* (1837).

Weaver, James Baird (1833–1912) American politician. Born in Dayton, Ohio, Weaver became a Union general and a U.S. Iowa congressman (1879–81, 1885–89). An advocate of the free coinage of silver, he ran unsuccessfully as the presidential candidate of the Greenback Party in 1880. He helped to found the POPULIST PARTY in 1892 and was nominated as its first presidential candidate the same year; his running mate was James C.

Field, a Confederate general from Virginia. Weaver lost that election, too, but won over a million votes, setting the stage for WILLIAM JENNINGS BRYAN to run on the Populist ticket in 1896.

Webb, Philip Speakman (1831–1915) English architect. Webb completed his training in G. E. Street's Oxford office, where he became friends with WILLIAM MORRIS. His first commission was the historic Red House in Bexley Heath, built in 1859 for Morris. That project led to the founding of Morris, Marshall, Faulkner, and Company, which became a driving force in the ARTS AND CRAFTS MOVEMENT. Webb was one of six members of the firm, and he became well known for his designs of glassware, stained glass, jewelry, and furniture.

In 1877, Webb founded the Society for the Protection of Ancient Buildings, although his own architectural style looked toward the functional architecture of the twentieth century. Webb's buildings were characterized by sparse design and often left the structural elements of the building exposed.

Webb, Sidney James (1859–1947), and **[Martha] Beatrice Potter** (1858–1943) English socialist reformers and thinkers. Both were accomplished social activists when they married in 1892. During the 1880s, Sidney Webb was active in the FABIAN SOCIETY; Beatrice Potter had written a work of social history, *The Co-operative Movement in Great Britain* (1891). Together they promoted social and educational reform through writing, educational vision, and political force. They wrote several works on trade unionism and socialism, including *The History of Trade Unionism* (1894), *Industrial Democracy* (1897), and the multivolume *English Local Government* (1906–29). In 1913 they also founded the progressive periodical *The New Statesman*. Instrumental in the founding of the London School of Economics in 1895, they also championed the passage of the Educational Acts of 1902 and 1903. An active holder of political office for much of his life, Sidney Webb held positions in the London County Council, the Labour Party, and the House of Commons. He also served as president of the Board of Trade and colonial secretary in the first and second Labour governments, respectively. Although he was granted the name Baron Passfield in his later years, his wife Beatrice did not accept the corresponding title of Lady Passfield.

Webster, Daniel (1782–1852) American politician, orator, and lawyer. Born in New Hampshire, the son of a poor farmer, Webster graduated from Dartmouth College and was admitted to the Massachusetts bar in 1805. He was a New Hampshire congressman from 1813 to 1817. He left politics temporarily to practice law and won two famous Supreme Court cases: *Dartmouth College v. Woodward* and *McCullough v. Maryland.*

Webster was elected a senator from Massachusetts in 1826 and became a leading statesman. A strong nationalist, he backed the stand of Democratic president ANDREW JACKSON against JOHN C. CALHOUN's theories of nullification and states' rights. He split with Jackson, however, over fiscal policies and joined the Whig Party in 1834. He was the unsuccessful presidential candidate of the northern wing of the Whigs in 1836.

As Secretary of State (1841–43) Webster negotiated the WEBSTER-ASHBURTON TREATY, which lessened tensions between the United States and Great Britain. Reelected to the Senate in 1846, he condemned the MEXICAN WAR and supported the antislavery WILMOT PROVISO. He angered many abolitionists, Whigs, and other antislavery groups, when he supported the COMPROMISE OF 1850 in order to stave off the collapse of the Union and to keep his 1852 presidential hopes alive. Webster was reappointed Secretary of State in 1850 and supported American recognition of emerging European republics resulting from the REVOLUTIONS OF 1848. Ill health caused him to retire in 1852, and he died the same year.

Webster, Thomas (1800–1886) British genre painter. Webster was at the center of a group of artists known as the Cranbrook Colony, named for the village in Kent that served as their base. Influenced by Scottish artist David Wilkie (1785–1841), these artists painted rustic scenes of daily life, often set in cottage interiors. Webster specialized in scenes of childhood.

Webster-Ashburton Treaty (1842) Agreement between the UNITED STATES and GREAT BRITAIN. Negotiated by U.S. Secretary of State DANIEL WEBSTER and Alexander Baring, 1st Baron ASHBURTON, of Great Britain, the treaty settled the northeastern boundary between the United States and CANADA. It also provided for suppression of the African slave trade. By averting a potential war, it set a precedent for future peaceful settlements of disputes between the United States and Canada. See also AROOSTOOK WAR.

Wedekind, Frank (1864–1918) German dramatist and actor. Born in Germany, he grew up in Switzerland and then returned to Germany after an argument with his father. He worked as a journalist, advertising manager, secretary in a circus, and actor before writing and producing his own plays. Government displeasure over his satirical essays in the humor magazine *Simplicissimus* led him into exile in Paris; when he tried to reenter Germany, he was imprisoned for six months.

Upon his release from prison, Wedekind became a popular cabaret performer, reciting monologues, singing, and performing in a group known as the Eleven Hangmen. The publication of *Fruhlings Erwachen* (The Awakening of Spring) in 1891 caused a scandal due to the play's theme of teen sex, and the play was suppressed by censorship for nearly fifteen years.

Wedekind is best remembered for his "monster tragedy," a drama in two parts; *Erdgeist* (Earth Spirit, 1895) and *Die Büchse der Pandora* (Pandora's Box, 1902), which portrayed the rise and fall of a prostitute, Lulu, who is eventually murdered by JACK THE RIPPER, originally played by Wedekind. His later plays became more autobiographical, especially *Zensur* (Censorship, 1907), in which a true moralist battles hypocritical religious authorities.

Wedekind treated his themes of sex and crime realistically, but his plays also contain elements of Expressionism and often employ exaggerated language.

Weld, Theodore Dwight (1803–1895) American abolitionist. Born in Hampton, Connecticut, Weld studied with evangelist Charles G. Finney and helped to form the American Anti-Slavery Society. In 1838 he published *American Slavery as It Is,* a highly influential antislavery work that was a source for the novel *UNCLE TOM'S CABIN* by HARRIET BEECHER STOWE. He was coeditor of the antislavery periodical *Emancipator.*

Wells, Henry (1805–1878) American businessman. Apprenticed as a tanner and shoemaker, Wells became an agent for Harnden's Express in 1841, running between Albany and New York City. Within two years he had established Livingston, Wells & Pomeroy's Express from Albany to Buffalo. Wells worked as the messenger, carrying letters for six cents each, one-fourth of the government rate at the time.

Wells's services expanded rapidly, and by 1844 he had opened a line to Detroit and had hired William E. Fargo as a messenger; Fargo later continued service to Chicago, Cincinnati, and St. Louis.

In 1850, Wells merged several lines into the American Express Company and served as its president for eighteen years. In 1852 he organized WELLS FARGO AND COMPANY to serve California and Oregon with mail, courier, and banking services. In 1861 he purchased the PONY EXPRESS and operated it in the final months before the completion of the telegraph made the service obsolete.

A lifelong stammerer, Wells established several schools for others afflicted, and in 1868 he founded Wells Seminary, later Wells College for Women, in Aurora, New York.

Wells, H. G. [Herbert George] (1866–1946) English writer. He was born in Bromley, Kent; his father was an unsuccessful shopkeeper, and his mother a servant on a large estate. In his teens he tried working as a draper's apprentice, but he left that line of work to become a student assistant at Midhurst Grammar School. In 1884 he won a scholarship to the Normal School of Science, now Imperial College, London, where he studied under biologist THOMAS HUXLEY, who was an important source of Wells's faith in EVOLUTION and science. Wells won another scholarship to London University, from which he graduated in 1890. He became a schoolteacher but suffered serious kidney damage from an accident and decided to devote himself to writing.

After writing textbooks on biology and geography, he published his first major novel, *THE TIME MACHINE* (1895). With this and several subsequent novels, Wells cofounded with contemporary JULES VERNE the modern literary field of science fiction. His "scientific romances" from this period helped to establish many common motifs of science fiction, including time travel; biological manipulation, in *The Island of Dr. Moreau* (1896); chemical-induced metamorphosis, in *The Invisible Man* (1897); extraterrestrial invasion, in *The War of the Worlds* (1898); and space travel, in *The First Men in the Moon* (1901). The outlandish subject matter gave Wells the opportunity not only to build exciting narratives but to speculate on humanity's future and to reflect satirically on social and political issues.

Wells developed his social and political ideas in later works of fiction and nonfiction that were more expressly didactic. He was a socialist, a feminist, an internationalist, an evolutionist, a supporter of science, and an advocate of free love. He was also a member of the FABIAN SOCIETY, although he argued often with fellow members, most notably GEORGE BERNARD SHAW.

Wells married his cousin Isabel in 1891, but the marriage was short-lived. He married Amy Robbins in 1895; it lasted until her death in 1927. His most famous liaison was with English writer Rebecca West, from 1913 to 1923.

Throughout his long life Wells was a prolific, popular, and sometimes controversial writer, but he is best remembered today for the scientific romances he wrote at the outset of his career. His later works included the novels *Kipps: The Story of a Simple Soul* (1905) and *The History of Mr. Polly* (1910) and the nonfiction work *The Outline of History* (1920).

Wells Fargo and Company U.S. overland freight or transport service. Founded by entrepreneurs William George Fargo and HENRY WELLS in 1852, the company originated in 1843 as an express service that eventually connected Buffalo, Detroit, Cincinnati, Chicago, and St. Louis. It established itself as a nationwide service in 1852 and became known for providing mail and financial services to the Pacific coast. An 1866 consolidation with the Overland Mail Company, among other stage companies, guaranteed its preeminence in the business. In 1918 it joined the American Railway Express system. The Wells Fargo Bank, separated from the transport part of the company, remains an active California-based bank.

Welsbach mantle Lighting device. Invented in 1885 by Austrian chemist Carl Auer von Welsbach (1858–1929), it consisted of a wad of cotton soaked in a thorium nitrate and cerium nitrate mixture. When burned, it provided a brighter and cleaner light than the smoky and noxious gas burners prevalent at the time. The Welsbach mantle is still used in outdoor kerosene lanterns.

West Indies Archipelago between North America and South America on the eastern edge of the Caribbean Sea. The four main island groups are the Greater Antilles,—Cuba, Jamaica, Hispaniola, and Puerto Rico; the Lesser Antilles,—Leeward and Windward Islands, Barbados, and Trinidad and Tobago; the Bahamas; and the Dutch West Indies or Netherlands Antilles—Aruba, Curaçao, and Bonaire. While geographically a part of the Americas, the West Indies have been associated with Europe as colonies longer than any other part of the New World.

The Spanish were the first to explore and colonize the twenty-five-hundred-mile-long island chain, settling soon after Christopher Columbus mistakenly proclaimed the islands to be off the coast of India. The Spanish colonized the Greater Antilles, and in 1624, English settlers landed on St. Kitts in the Lesser Antilles, where they planted tobacco and eventually established colonies throughout the island group known as the Virgin Islands.

In the 1630s the Dutch claimed their three islands, while the French settled in Martinique and Guadeloupe. In 1655, Jamaica was forcibly taken from Spain by Great Britain; competition for more colonies led to heavier fighting, and Great Britain emerged victorious. By Victorian times, British possessions in the West Indies included the Bahamas, Barbados, the British Virgin Islands, Jamaica, the Leeward Islands, Tobago, Trinidad, Turks and Caicos Islands, and Windward Islands.

Until the early nineteenth century, the West Indies were the site of plantations owned by a wealthy few and worked by African slaves. The abolition of SLAVERY in the British Empire in 1833 led to economic changes and turmoil in its West Indian possessions. In Jamaica, where a decline in the sugar-export economy led to increased poverty, colonial governor EDWARD EYRE brutally suppressed an African-American revolt in 1865. The result was heated controversy in Britain, including failed attempts to prosecute Eyre on criminal charges.

The island Hispaniola in the Greater Antilles had two distinct histories. The western part passed from Spanish to French hands in the late seventeenth century and gained independence as Haiti in 1804. The eastern part gained independence from Haiti in 1844, becoming the Dominican Republic. During the SPANISH-AMERICAN WAR (1898), Spain lost its last two colonies, with Cuba gaining independence and Puerto Rico becoming a U.S. territory.

Cuba, Haiti, and the Dominican Republic were the only independent countries until 1962, but Jamaica, Trinidad, Barbados, the Bahamas, Grenada, and others soon became independent nations.

Western Union U.S. telegraph company. The first major U.S. industrial monopoly was chartered in 1856 from a number of smaller telegraph companies by financiers Hiram Gibley and Ezra Cornell, the pair who had supported SAMUEL F. B. MORSE in his 1844 development of telegraph service. In 1866, Western Union Telegraph bought two smaller companies, giving it control of seventy-five thousand miles of wire and creating a monopoly over U.S. telegraph service. JAY GOULD and WILLIAM VANDERBILT provided financing for the company. The monopoly was broken in 1886 with the formation of Postal Telegraph by J. W. Mackay.

In an attempt to surpass the work of ALEXANDER GRAHAM BELL on the telephone, which it considered a scientific curiosity, Western Union hired THOMAS EDISON in 1876 to create a more useful model. Western Union's Speaking-Telephone Company provided only short-lived competition with Bell in the late 1870s.

Westinghouse, George (1846–1914) American manufacturer and inventor. Born in Central Bridge, New York, Westinghouse acquired over four hundred patents. In 1868 he developed the air brake, a device that uses compressed air to stop a train, and the frog, which allows train wheels to cross an intersecting track. One year later he founded the first of his three companies, the Westinghouse Air Brake Company. The second, the Union Switch and Signal Company, followed in 1882 with his development of a railroad signal system. The third, the Westinghouse Electric Company, was founded in 1886 to systematize and spread the use of alternating current for appliances and electrical transmission.

Westminster Bridge Structure over the Thames River in London. The second bridge to span the Thames, after the Roman-built London Bridge sixteen hundred years earlier, Westminster Bridge was designed by Charles Labelye in 1738–50. The construction was beset by problems, and no sooner was Westminster Bridge completed than a parliamentary committee agreed to rebuild it. The new bridge also took a long time. Designed in 1854 by Thomas Page and Sir Charles Barry, it was completed in 1862.

Westminster Cathedral London church. When Herbert Vaughan became archbishop of Westminster in 1892, he appointed John Francis Bentley as the architect to design a cathedral with a budget of £45,000. Bentley rejected the popular Gothic style in favor of an early Christian Byzantine design, characterized by the use of brick and a predilection for circular shapes. In order to meet the restrictions of the budget, Bentley left the interior design for future generations, and it remains unfinished. Both Bentley and Vaughan died shortly before the completion of the horizontally striped red-and-gray-brick cathedral, which was finished in 1903.

Westminster Conference (1866–67) Political meeting. Also called the London Conference, it was attended by delegates from CANADA, Nova Scotia, and New Brunswick. They met with the British government to debate the plan for confederation of the Canadian provinces; the plan had been adopted by the provinces at the Quebec Conference in October 1864. The resolutions from the Westminster Conference led to the British North America Act of 1867, in which the dominion of Canada was ratified.

Westminster Palace Seat of the Houses of Parliament. The largest Gothic building in England, it covers eight acres in the heart of London. Originally built in 1035 and used as the royal home, the palace was destroyed by fire in 1053 and on various occasions over the years.

After a fire in 1834 consumed most of the interior, a competition was held for a new design, and Sir CHARLES BARRY emerged as the winner, with help from AUGUSTUS PUGIN. Barry was responsible for the Gothic exterior, while Pugin designed the interior, complete with paneled ceilings, tiled floors, stained glass, fireplaces, wallpaper, umbrella stands, and inkwells. Pugin's work was marked by a keen eye for detail and lavish intricacy.

Construction began in 1837, with Barry's wife given the honor of placing the first stone. The House of Commons and House of Lords were completed in the 1840s, BIG BEN in 1858, and Victoria Tower in 1860. Both architects suffered nervous breakdowns brought on by overwork during the construction, and neither lived to see the structure completed.

Wharton, Edith [Newbold Jones] (1862–1937) American writer. Born into the upper echelons of New York society, she traveled widely in Europe and began publishing poetry while still in her teens. Her first book, *The Decoration of Houses* (1897), was a collaborative effort with architect Ogden Codman about new psychologically oriented trends in home design and decoration. By the late 1890s she moved to Lenox, Massachusetts, and published her first effort at fiction, the short-story collection *The Greater Inclination* (1899); the short novel *The Touchstone* (1900) followed. In these works she began to develop the social and ethical conflicts that would motivate her strongest offerings. Informing all these works were the novels and short stories of her friend HENRY JAMES, whose influence she acknowledged in her treatise *The Writing of Fiction.*

American author Edith Wharton portrayed high society in her intense novels, which include The House of Mirth *and* The Age of Innocence. *Photo courtesy of Beinecke Library, Yale University.*

The twentieth century saw the flowering of Wharton's literary talents, most of it in works that commented on late-nineteenth- and early-twentieth-century society. Among her novels are *The Age of Innocence* (1920), *Ethan Frome* (1911), and *The House of Mirth* (1905).

Wheatstone, Sir Charles (1802–1875) English scientist and inventor. Wheatstone began his own business making musical instruments at the age of twenty-one, and in 1834 he became an experimental physicist at Kings College. A year later he demonstrated that electrical sparks from different metals produced different spectra. He also conducted experiments measuring the speed of light with rotating mirrors.

In 1837 he patented an electrical telegraph that used copper wire, but a practical application of his device was not made until after the successful use of SAMUEL F. B. MORSE's invention. In 1843, Wheatstone popularized, though he did not invent, the Wheatstone bridge, a device for measuring electrical resistance. He became a fellow of the Royal Society in 1836 and was knighted in 1868.

Whewell, William (1794–1866) English philosopher and mathematician. Highly influential in the philosophy of science, he served at Cambridge from 1828 to 1866, at various times as professor, master of Trinity College, and vice chancellor. There he instituted the tripos, or final honors examination, of moral science and natural science. His works included *History of the Inductive Sciences* (1837), *Philosophy of the Inductive Sciences* (1840), and *On the Philosophy of Discovery* (1860).

whist Card game. Whist was very popular in nineteenth-century England. A precursor to bridge, it was played by two couples, with the partners seated opposite each other. Each player was dealt thirteen cards, and the game was won by scoring five or ten points, depending on whether it was "short" or "long" whist. The best two out of three games was called a "rubber." Whist was considered a sober and reflective game.

Whistler, James Abbott McNeill (1834–1903) American painter. Born in Lowell, Massachusetts, he received his first art training at the Imperial Academy of Fine Arts in St. Petersburg, Russia, where his father, a West Point graduate, was overseeing the building of railroads. Whistler himself entered West Point at seventeen, but he left in his third year after accumulating numerous demerits and flunking a chemistry exam. He worked for a year for the U.S. Coast and Geodetic Survey. His family then subsidized his move to Paris in 1855 to study art. Whistler would never return to the United States.

In France, Whistler came under the influence of the realist painter GUSTAVE COURBET. In 1859, Whistler moved to London to take advantage of its growing art market.

Whistler encountered controversy throughout his career, beginning with the painting *The Woman in White,* which was refused by the Paris Salon and the Royal Academy of Art. It was shown at the SALON DES REFUSÉS in Paris, a consolation exhibit of rejected works. Critics attacked the full-length portrait of a young woman against a plain background for its lack of a story line and its failure to make a moral point. A French critic referred to it as a "symphonie du blanc." Whistler was so delighted by this comment that he renamed it *Symphony in White No. 1: The White Girl.* This was the first of many paintings of his with musical names such as nocturnes, harmonies, arrangements, and variations.

Whistler's atrocious temper, flamboyant antics, sharp wit, and disregard for most social and artistic conventions attracted as much attention as his paintings. His fierce defense of ART FOR ART'S SAKE also won him a reputation as something of a crank.

During the 1860s he befriended DANTE GABRIEL ROSSETTI and other members of the PRE-RAPHAELITES. During this time he also became interested in Asian art and its more abstract style. The Asian influence on his art found its greatest expression in *Harmony in Blue and Gold: The Peacock Room* (1876–77).

In 1872 he submitted his most famous work, *Arrangement in Grey and Black, No. 1: The Artist's Mother,* to the Royal Academy. What became known as "Whistler's Mother" was refused and ignominiously stored with other rejected paintings before its rescue by a member of the academy.

By the end of the 1870s, Whistler had rejected Courbet's realism in favor of IMPRESSIONISM. This shift in style led him into one of the most famous legal trials in the history of art. When his very impressionistic *Nocturne in Black and Gold: The Falling Rocket* was displayed in 1877, England's preeminent art critic JOHN RUSKIN accused him of "flinging a pot of paint in the public's face." Ruskin also sneered at the price of 200 guineas. Whistler responded with a £1000 libel suit. Although Ruskin suffered a mental collapse and was unable to attend the trial, his representatives berated the painting while Whistler took the stand to defend his art. One memorable moment of the trial occurred when *The Falling Rocket* was displayed to the jury—upside down.

Whistler won the case, but the jury awarded him only one farthing, and the judge ordered him to pay his half of the court costs. Ruskin's criticism hurt Whistler in the marketplace, and he declared bankruptcy in 1879. His situation improved when the Fine Arts Society commissioned him to do twelve etchings of Venice scenes. These works, together with pastels also done in Venice, restored him to solvency.

The last two decades of his life saw his reputation climb. He garnered medals and positions, saw his work displayed across Europe, and heard himself declared a genius. His artistic theories and flouting of social conventions are thought to have influenced OSCAR WILDE, a friend, and the movement known as AESTHETICISM. He wrote a book of critical essays, *Ten O'Clock* (1888), and *The Gentle Art of Making Enemies* (1890), a collection of essays damning his work, accompanied by his acerbic rejoinders.

"White Man's Burden, The" English poem. Although it is unclear whether RUDYARD KIPLING coined the term, he is responsible for its popularity in the poem of the same name, published in 1899. Kipling's lines, "Take up the white man's burden/Send forth the best you breed,/Go bind your sons to exile/To serve the captive's need," capture the condescending attitude prevailing among Victorian imperialists toward the people of their colonies who comprised the BRITISH EMPIRE.

Whitechapel Bell Foundry English casting company. Established in 1420, the foundry cast many of the world's most famous bells, including those for Westminster Abbey (1540), America's original Liberty Bell (1752), and the thirteen-ton BIG BEN (1858). After the first bell for Big Ben cracked, architect Sir CHARLES BARRY had it recast at Whitechapel. The bell was drawn through the crowded streets of London by sixteen horses on a flat cart; with teams of eight men using a winch, it took thirty hours to raise it to the bell tower.

The bell began to toll in July 1859, but in September it, too, cracked because the striking hammer was too heavy. It was repaired and modified at Whitechapel and still tolls as a symbol of England.

Whitman, Walt[er] (1819–1892) American poet. Son of a carpenter and occasional farmer, he was born in West Hills, Long Island, New York, but moved with his family to Brooklyn when their farm was sold. After attending public schools until age eleven, he learned the printing trade and worked in it through much of his young adulthood. He was also a newspaper reporter and editor, and aside from a year (1838–39) as a schoolteacher, he continued to work as a journalist throughout his life on a variety of newspapers, including the *Huntington Long Islander,* the *Brooklyn Star, Brooklyn Times,* and *Brooklyn Daily Eagle.* His tenure was often tied to the owner's disagreement with Whitman's liberal Democratic political views.

In 1849, after an unsuccessful attempt to sustain *The Freeman,* the Free Soil newspaper he founded the previous year, Whitman began work on the poems for *LEAVES OF GRASS.* The collection of twelve untitled poems, which began with what became known as "Song of Myself," was self-printed and published in 1855. Distributed in New York and Brooklyn, it sold few copies but disturbed many of its readers with its freedom of imagery and verse structure. His lone literary champion was American essayist RALPH WALDO EMERSON, whose letter of congratulations welcomed him at "the beginning of a great career."

By the time of the CIVIL WAR, Whitman had self-published two revised editions of *LEAVES OF GRASS,* which included the poems "Children of Adam" and "Calamus." During the Civil War, Whitman was employed in Washington, D.C., in various army or government posts and was a military hospital volunteer, assisting doctors and providing temporary companionship and assistance to wounded soldiers. His experiences of the war informed the collection *Drum-Taps* (1865); a later edition included his elegy to slain President ABRAHAM LINCOLN, "When Lilacs Last in the Dooryard Bloom'd."

In the late 1860s, a Whitman collection was published in England and helped to establish him there as a poet. A new U.S. edition of *Leaves of Grass* appeared in 1870–71; it contained the essay "Democratic Vistas" in which he discussed the strengths of American democracy.

In 1873 a stroke led Whitman back to his family, now in Camden, New Jersey. Known by this time to the literary and art worlds, he was visited regularly by leading figures of the day. Royalties on *Leaves of Grass,* despite its banning in Boston, allowed him to buy a small house in Camden. With the help of American editor Horace Traubel, Whitman published a final edition of *Leaves of Grass* before his death.

The decades following his death saw massive growth in Whitman's stature, both as a poet and as a celebrant of the United States. His personal imagery and frank championship of the physical has invited literary imitation and won a diverse readership.

Whittier, John Greenleaf (1807–1892) American poet. Best known for rural New England works and patriotic verse, Whittier was born in East Haverhill, Massachusetts. He was raised a Quaker and was largely self-educated. His early poems were published by abolitionist WILLIAM LLOYD GARRISON, who helped him gain a job on a Boston newspaper. His first book, *Legends of New England in Prose and Verse,* was published in 1831, and although he continued to write poetry over the next several years, he devoted the bulk of his efforts to the abolition of SLAVERY. Among the works he produced were the pamphlet *Justice and Expediency* (1833), *Poems Written During the*

Progress of the Abolition Question (1838), and *Songs of Labor* (1850).

During the U.S. CIVIL WAR he wrote many patriotic poems, notably "Barbara Frietchie" (1863) and the collection *In War Time and Other Poems* (1864). Yet these and the years just before the war were also fertile grounds for Whittier's development as a rural poet. Using the people and way of life of New England for artistic grounding, he wrote several of his most well remembered works, including "Snow-Bound" (1866), "Telling the Bees" (1858), "The Barefoot Boy" (1855), and "Maud Muller" (1854). These evocative, nostalgic verses made him a beloved poet. His final years, spent writing many religious poems, resulted in verses used in hymns today.

Whitworth, Sir Joseph (1803–1887) English mechanical engineer. Whitworth left school at fourteen in order to work for an uncle in the cotton business. In 1833 he started his own business in MANCHESTER as a toolmaker; he was one of the first manufacturers to recognize the practicality of standardized parts, and in the 1840s he developed a system of uniform measures and gauges.

The Whitworth SCREW THREAD, which revolutionized screws, was introduced in 1841, and by 1851, Whitworth's machine tools had become internationally known for their quality and accuracy. In 1857, Whitworth introduced the Whitworth gun, a FIREARM that had an improved range and accuracy, and in 1862 he demonstrated a new armor-piercing shell.

Whitworth later helped found the chair of engineering and laboratories at Owens College in Manchester, and in 1868 he established the Whitworth scholarships, given to students pursuing studies in mechanical engineering.

Wilberforce, Samuel (1805–1873) English prelate. Born in London, he was the son of William Wilberforce, politician and antislavery philanthropist. Educated privately, Samuel was directed into a life in the church by his father. He took his deacon's orders in 1828, and in 1830 he began a ten-year tenure in the rectory at Brightstone on the Isle of Wight, where he immediately received attention for the eloquence of his sermons, though his detractors dubbed him "Soapy Sam."

In 1838, Wilberforce published a five-volume biography of his father, *Life of William Wilberforce,* and in 1844 he wrote *History of the Protestant Episcopal Church in America.* In 1843 he was appointed dean of Westminster but stayed only a few months. He left for Oxford where he remained as bishop for nearly twenty-five years. Wilberforce is often cited as a major figure in the preservation of the OXFORD MOVEMENT, which sought to reintroduce certain Roman Catholic ideas and practices into the Church of England, and while Wilberforce agreed with many of the aims of the movement, he also tried to reconcile the differences between factions.

From 1847 to 1869, Wilberforce served as the lord high almoner, the royal dispenser of alms, to Queen Victoria, and in 1869 he was appointed bishop of Winchester. Bishop Wilberforce was generally opposed to novelty, preferring conventional orthodoxy, but in 1870 he initiated the movement to modernize the language of the King James Bible, which was published in three parts from 1881 to 1895. A detractor of *THE ORIGIN OF SPECIES* by CHARLES DARWIN (1859), Wilberforce gained attention in 1860 in a publicized debate with biologist THOMAS HUXLEY at the British Association meeting in Oxford, where the bishop attacked Darwin's theory of EVOLUTION.

Wild Duck, The (1884) Norwegian play. In the drama HENRIK IBSEN depicts the value of lies and ignorance, the dangers of truth, and the tragedies of life through satire and symbolism.

Gregers Werle, "suffering from an acute attack of integrity," insists on telling his friend Hjalmar Ekdal the truth about Gregers's father, an unscrupulous merchant. Gregers alleges that the older Werle was once the lover of Hjalmar's wife and may be the true father of Hjalmar's fourteen-year-old daughter Hedvig. Upon learning that the older Werle has been providing Hedvig with a small allowance, Hjalmar disowns the child. Gregers tries to mend the family differences by advising Hedvig to prove her love for her father by killing her most prized possession, a wild duck she nursed back to health after it had been shot by the older Werle. Hedvig kills herself instead.

Considered one of Ibsen's finest play, *The Wild Duck* has had considerable influence on twentieth-century drama.

Wilde, Oscar Fingall O'Flahertie Wills (1854–1900) Irish writer. He was born in Dublin, Ireland, where his father, Sir William Wilde, was a famous surgeon and his mother, Jane Francesca Elgee, wrote inflammatory prose for the YOUNG IRELAND movement under the pen name "Speranza."

Wilde was awarded a scholarship to Magdalen College, Oxford, in 1874. He studied there for four years and became influenced by JOHN RUSKIN and WALTER PATER. He was determined to follow Pater's advice to "burn always with a hard gemlike flame."

In 1878, Wilde was awarded the prestigious Newdigate prize for his poem "Ravenna," and later the same year he toured Greece before settling in London. Wilde quickly became part of the movement known as ART FOR ART'S SAKE, which included his friend and foil, painter JAMES MCNEILL WHISTLER. Wilde gained a reputation as an

Satirist Oscar Wilde, author of The Importance of Being Earnest, *was convicted of homosexual conduct, for which he served two years in jail. Courtesy of the Mary Evans Picture Library.*

aesthete and a dandy, dressing in silk breeches and capes, carrying lilies, and wearing long hair. He became so well known that GILBERT AND SULLIVAN lampooned him in their comic opera *Patience* in the character of the "fleshy poet" Bunthorne.

Wilde published his mostly derivative and widely popular *Poems* in 1881, and the next year he embarked on a successful lecture tour of the United States and Canada, creating headlines with his witty epigrams and controversial statements on the function of art.

In 1884, Wilde and Constance Lloyd were married and quickly had two sons, Cyril (born in 1885) and Vyvyan (born in 1886). Wilde spent the next few years as editor of *The Woman's World* magazine before publishing *The Happy Prince and Other Tales* in 1888; it marked the beginning of a productive writing period.

Wilde's only novel, *The Picture of Dorian Gray* (1891), caused a scandal for the perceived immorality of the young man who pursues a decadent life-style and remains young and beautiful while his portrait bears the scars of his debauchery. As in much of Wilde's writing, *The Picture of Dorian Gray* attempts to reveal the hypocrisy and duplicity of the Victorian Age, but with his usual wit and style. "Death and vulgarity are the only two facts in the nineteenth century that one cannot explain away," the novel's narrator states.

Salome (1892) was written in French and designed to shock its audience with its depiction of unnatural passion. The play was banned for a time before being published in 1893, and was finally translated into English in 1894, with illustrations by AUBREY BEARDSLEY.

Wilde then concentrated on writing for the stage. *Lady Windermere's Fan* premiered in 1892 and introduced a new kind of English comedy, with unconventional plot and stylized, epigrammatic dialogue. *A Woman of No Importance* (1893) and *An Ideal Husband* (1895) continued in the same style; then Wilde created his masterpiece, *The Importance of Being Earnest* (1895), in which he subsumes plot and logic to language. The stylized comedy explores the virtues of role-playing and the paradoxes of truth, sincerity, and language in a Wildean tour de force. It was to be Wilde's final public triumph.

Wilde had begun his relationship with Alfred Douglas in 1891, but Douglas's father, Sir JOHN SHOLTO DOUGLAS, the MARQUIS OF QUEENSBERRY, disapproved of the relationship and accused Wilde of homosexual practices. Wilde, at the urging of Alfred Douglas, prosecuted Queensberry for libel, but Wilde lost the case and was subsequently arrested and charged with homosexual offenses under the Criminal Law Amendment Act of 1885. After two trials, Wilde was found guilty and sentenced to two years in prison at Reading Gaol.

While in prison, Wilde wrote a letter to Douglas, published posthumously as the personal essay *De Profundis* (1905), and the long poem, *The Ballad of Reading Gaol* (1898). After his release, Wilde traveled through Italy and France, using the name Sebastian Melmoth which had poignant literary allusions. Sebastian not only referred to the martyr saint shot with arrows but also to the arrows on Wilde's prison uniform. Melmoth was taken from the Charles Robert Maturin novel *Melmoth the Wanderer* (1820); the title character, who has sold his soul to the devil in exchange for everlasting life, can regain it if he can convince another to take the bargain. Despite their own sufferings, no one trades with the doomed Melmoth.

Plagued by ill health and bankruptcy, Wilde roamed Europe with his characteristic charm and wit; he died in Paris.

Wilhelmina [Helena Pauline Maria] (1880–1962) Queen of the NETHERLANDS, 1890–1948. Born at the Hague, Wilhelmina was the only daughter of King William III and his second wife, Emma of Waldeck-Pyrmont. Upon her father's death on November 23, 1890, Wilhelmina became queen under the regency of her mother and was enthroned shortly after her eighteenth birthday.

In 1901, Wilhelmina married Henry Wladimir Albert Ernst, Duke of Mecklenburg-Schwerin, and in 1909 she gave birth to Princess Juliana, to whom she would abdicate her throne soon after World War II.

Wilkes, Charles (1798–1877) American naval officer and explorer. Wilkes entered the navy in 1818 and became a lieutenant in 1826; in 1830 he was appointed head of a depot of charts and instruments in Washington, D.C., that eventually became the U.S. Naval Observatory.

In 1838, President Martin Van Buren authorized the U.S. Exploring Expedition, and Wilkes was selected to command six ships that would explore several island groups in the South Pacific and Australia, and areas in ANTARCTICA now called Wilkes Land. Wilkes also traveled to Fiji, Hawaii, the Pacific northwest, and the Philippines before returning to New York in June 1842. Wilkes was promoted to the rank of commander and spent the next nineteen years preparing the nineteen-volume account of his round-the-world expedition. He was awarded the founder's medal of the Royal Geographical Society of London in 1847 for his explorations.

During the CIVIL WAR, Wilkes was given orders to command the ironclad *Merrimac* in April 1861, but by the time he arrived in Norfolk where the ship was docked, it had been scuttled. He was then assigned to command the *San Jacinto,* with which he stopped the British steamer *Trent* and unlawfully removed the Confederate commissioners James M. Mason and John Slidell. The incident strained Union relations with Great Britain, and President Abraham Lincoln publicly apologized for Wilkes's actions.

In 1862, Wilkes was sent to the West Indies to protect Union commerce in the region, but the commander offended several foreign governments as well as the Secretary of the Navy in his attempts to capture Confederate soldiers. Wilkes was eventually suspended from duty and court-martialed for insubordination in 1864. Two years later he was promoted to the rank of rear admiral and retired.

William I [Wilhelm Friedrich Ludwig] (1797–1888) King of PRUSSIA (1861–71) and first modern emperor of GERMANY (1871–88). His reign saw the unification of Germany under Prussian leadership and its arrival as a great power. William served in the Prussian army and government before taking over as regent in 1858 for his brother FREDERICK WILLIAM IV after he suffered a stroke. William succeeded his brother to the throne in 1861. Although he had taken a strongly reactionary position during the REVOLUTIONS OF 1848, as king he eased many of the speech and press restrictions of his brother's reign. He faced a constitutional crisis when the *Landstag,* the national legislative assembly, refused to pass increased military budgets. After considering abdication, he appointed OTTO VON BISMARCK his first minister. The policies of the rest of William's reign were almost entirely dictated by Bismarck.

Guided by Bismarck, Prussia reformed its constitution and defeated AUSTRIA in the SEVEN WEEKS' WAR (1866), ending its influence in Germany. Then Prussia headed a coalition of German states that defeated France in the FRANCO-PRUSSIAN WAR (1870–71). At the conclusion of this conflict, German unification was declared, and William was crowned kaiser, or emperor, at Versailles on January 18, 1871.

Following his coronation, William presided over Bismarck's social welfare policies, establishing a complex system of European alliances.

William II [Friedrich Wilhelm Viktor Albert] (1859–1941) Emperor of GERMANY (1888–1918). William's reign saw Germany take its "place in the sun" as a world power, then collapse in World War I. Born in Berlin, he faced an early bout with polio that left him with a crippled arm. Nonetheless he received a military education and served in the Prussian army. In 1888, following the brief reign of his brother FREDERICK III, who died after three months as emperor, William took the throne. Like his brother, he disliked the cautious policies of OTTO VON BISMARCK, the chancellor and chief statesman of Germany. Following several disputes, William dismissed Bismarck in 1890.

Although political arrangements remained the same under William, the new emperor reversed many of Bismarck's policies. Domestically, he pressed for broader social welfare legislation and workplace regulation. In foreign affairs he allowed diplomatic relationships with Russia and France to deteriorate. He supported an aggressive drive for colonies in Africa and the Pacific. Perhaps most seriously, he became involved in a naval arms race with Great Britain.

William's reign saw Germany continue its rapid economic expansion and INDUSTRIALIZATION. Working conditions showed some improvements, but despite William's welfare policies, SOCIALISM continued to grow. The Social Democrats also gained in voting strength but were refused any significant government posts. Ultimately, William's foreign policy contributed to an escalation of European tensions. The overconfidence of William and his generals in power in the German military led the Emperor into a series of greater provocations, culminating in the outbreak of World War I.

Wilmot Proviso U.S. political issue. In 1846, American Democratic congressman David Wilmot of Pennsylvania introduced an amendment to an appropriations bill. The bill set aside $2 million to buy lands from Mexico as part of negotiating an end to the Mexican War. The amendment or proviso stipulated that SLAVERY could not be introduced into any territory acquired from Mexico. The House of Representatives passed the amended bill twice during the Mexican War, but southern senators defeated it. The proviso was submitted unsuccessfully to Congress many times after that and helped illustrate the growing conflict over slavery between the North and South. The COMPROMISE OF 1850 ultimately laid it to rest.

Witwatersrand See RAND.

woman suffrage Political movement. Although women did not gain full voting rights in Great Britain and the United States until the twentieth century, the groundwork was laid by a wide variety of women's rights groups throughout the nineteenth century. In Britain, after being excluded from the franchise by the REFORM BILL OF 1832, woman suffrage groups gathered force. Attempts to grant suffrage in bills in 1867, 1870, 1883, and 1892 were rejected. However, the support of JOHN STUART MILL in 1867 granted the issue new gravity. Before the end of the nineteenth century, partial suffrage was granted. An 1888 decision allowed women to vote in county and municipal races; the Local Government Act of 1894 permitted women to vote and be elected to office. It took twenty-four years before passage of a law allowing women aged thirty and over to vote (1918) and ten more years for females aged twenty-one and over (1928). Central leaders in the suffrage movement in Britain included Dame MILLICENT GARRETT FAWCETT and EMMELINE

British women fought for a century to reverse the Repeal Bill of 1832, which denied them the right to vote. Photo courtesy of Mary Evans Picture Library.

PANKHURST; their central organization until after the turn of the century was the National Union of Women's Suffrage Societies.

In the United States, the suffrage movement began in earnest in 1848 when women's rights activists SUSAN B. ANTHONY, ELIZABETH CADY STANTON, and others gathered at the SENECA FALLS CONVENTION in New York, and called for the right of women to vote. Before national suffrage was granted, some U.S. territories granted women the right to vote. In 1918, the Nineteenth Amendment to the Constitution granted American women the right to vote. Important women's rights groups during the nineteenth century included the National American Woman Suffrage Association.

Woolworth, Frank Winfield (1852–1919) American businessman. He is the founder of F. W. Woolworth Company, purveyors of low-cost merchandise in stores commonly known as five-and-ten-cents stores. Born in Rodman, New York, he began his experiments in low-cost retail when, as a store clerk, he borrowed $400 to open a store in Utica, New York, that offered only five-cent items. Although it failed, a similar store that year in Lancaster, Pennsylvania, was a success. That led to more stores in cities across Pennsylvania, New Jersey, and New York. By 1900 the Woolworth chain included fifty-nine stores that showed sales of over $5 million. By the time of Woolworth's death in 1919, there were more than one thousand F. W. Woolworth stores in the United States. It was not until 1932 that the store began to sell items that cost more than five and ten cents.

Wordsworth, William (1770–1850) English poet. During a sojourn in France between 1791 and 1792, at the height of the French Revolution, he developed a passion for radical politics. In 1793 he published his first poetic collections, *An Evening Walk* and *Descriptive Sketches.* In 1798 he and Samuel Taylor Coleridge became the founding poets of English ROMANTICISM with their collection *Lyrical Ballads.* In a second edition in 1800 Wordsworth included a preface declaring his aesthetic principles, notably his view that poetry should be based on everyday speech and experience. Precise observation and love of nature are also characteristic of his works. Poems published in his lifetime included "Tintern Abbey," "Simon Lee," "Alice Fell," the *Lucy* poems, "Resolution and Independence," "I Wandered Lonely as a Cloud," "Ode: Intimations of Immortality," and the long philosophical poem *The Excursion.*

By the 1830s Wordsworth's greatest poetic achievements were in the past, and he had turned from the revolutionary fervor of his youth to become a staunch conservative. A nationally esteemed figure, he was named poet laureate in 1843, and his awe-struck followers were known as "Wordsworthians." His reputation increased with the posthumous publication in 1850 of his most important work, *The Prelude.* Begun in 1798 and worked on throughout most of his life, the fourteen-book autobiographical poem is a reflection on poetry, memory, nature, and society. In the 1870s and 1880s Wordsworth's poetry and philosophy experienced a revival, notably through the publications of the Wordsworth Society (founded in 1880).

Wordsworth was survived by his wife, Mary (*née* Hutchinson), whom he married in 1802, and his sister Dorothy Wordsworth (1771–1855). A close companion to her brother, Dorothy inspired much of his poetry through her thoughtful, expressive journal writings and conversation.

workhouse British institution for relief of the destitute. As conceived by the POOR LAW OF 1834, workhouses were supposed to deter poverty by making relief more oppressive than the lowest-paying job. The new law prohibited outdoor, or at home, relief to the able-bodied poor and required recipients of state aid to live in workhouses where the sexes were kept apart and, until 1842, children were separated from their parents. Hunger, cold, and tedious and useless work were to be maintained as incentives for people to stay off the dole. Despite the harsh conditions mandated by the Poor Law and decried by writers such as THOMAS CARLYLE and CHARLES DICKENS, workhouse conditions actually varied greatly, with no system for enforcing their punitive aspects. Because of loopholes in the law, most of the able-bodied poor were able to continue getting outdoor relief, and by century's end the workhouses were primarily institutions aimed at caring for the needs of the indigent sick, disabled, orphaned, and aged.

Workingmen's Party of America (WPA) Political organization. The WPA had its roots in Philadelphia, Pennsylvania, in 1828 and in New York City in 1829. It was founded to protest unemployment, defend the ten-hour workday, and emphasize mass education. Under the leadership of Fanny Wright and Robert Dale Owen, the movement spread quickly but soon stalled due to political infighting. In 1830, Evastus Root, speaker of the New York State Assembly, packed conventions of the "Workies" with his own supporters, thereby securing his nomination for governor. The nomination was denounced by Wright and Owen, but the WPA's influence had already waned. The formation of the Whig Workingmen's Party in New York City brought an end to the WPA.

The WPA proved to be a model for other labor parties, however. The second Workingmen's Party, formed in Boston, Massachusetts, in 1834, was another short-lived organization under the leadership of Samuel Clesson Allen, who steered the party toward the policies of Andrew Jackson.

The Social Democratic Workingmen's Party, formed by a small trade union in 1874 in New York City, officially changed its name to the Workingmen's Party of America in 1876. A year later the name was again changed, to the Socialist Labor Party, which eventually nominated Simon Wing and Charles H. Matchet as presidential and vice presidential candidates in 1892. With little more than twenty-one thousand voting members, the party failed to have much of an impact on the national election.

World's Parliament of Religions Meeting of delegates of varied faiths. It was held in conjunction with the Columbian Exposition in Chicago, Illinois, September 11–18, 1893. A prominent Chicago Presbyterian minister, John Henry Barrows, presided over the parliament, which promoted dialogue between Western and Eastern religious leaders, including several delegates from Asia who were among the first representatives of their respective religions to travel to America. The Roman Catholic Church disapproved of participation by its members, as did many conservative Protestants. But the international meeting created a larger interest in the world's religions, and the number of college courses in comparative religion increased as a result. A second parliament was held in Chicago in August 1993.

Worth, Charles Frederick (1825–1895) English clothing designer. Worth was the developer of the first haute couture "collection" of original clothing designs. After working in a Paris apparel shop in the mid-1840s and early 1850s, he opened his own shop in 1858, offering a line of clothing rather than creating individual designs for each client. By the end of the nineteenth century Maison Worth was the ruling design force in Europe, clothing the courts of Great Britain, France, and Austria. Among Worth's design contributions is the predecessor to the ready-made suit; he also established Paris as the world's fashion center. Maison Worth went out of business in 1956.

Wounded Knee, Battle of (1890) U.S. conflict with American Indians. The last major conflict between the UNITED STATES military and American Indians was more accurately a massacre than a battle.

On December 15, 1890, Sioux chief SITTING BULL, long a leader of Native American resistance against U.S. claims on the West, was shot dead in a skirmish as U.S. troops attempted to arrest him. Many of his followers fled west to join Chief Big Foot, a leader, along with WOVOKA, in the Ghost Dance Religion, which promised restoration of the continent to Native Americans. On December 28 the Seventh Cavalry, commanded by Colonel James W. Forsyth, intercepted Big Foot and nearly 350 other Native Americans and returned them to Wounded Knee. The next morning, while soldiers were disarming the captives, an indiscriminate shot was fired. The 500 soldiers panicked and began shooting wildly. Three hundred Native Americans were killed, more than half of them women and children. Those who survived were pursued and butchered. Losses among the cavalry numbered about 25, as well as 33 wounded. Most of the cavalry casualties resulted from "friendly fire."

In response to the massacre, 4,000 American Indians barricaded themselves in a large camp of the Pine Ridge Agency, but within three weeks General Nelson A. Miles was able to end the violence through diplomacy. He also brought charges against Colonel Forsyth for the officer's role in the Wounded Knee massacre, but a court of inquiry absolved Forsyth of any wrongdoing.

Wovoka (1858–1932) Native American religious leader. Born near Walker Lake, Nevada, around 1856, Wovoka meaning "the Cutter," was the son of a Paiute mystic, Tavibo. After his father's death, the fourteen-year-old Wovoka was adopted by a white rancher, David Wilson.

Wovoka changed his name to Jack Wilson and worked on the Wilson farm until he was almost thirty years old. While working in the mountains, the Paiute had a religious vision in which God revealed to him that the earth would one day be returned to the American Indians and the whites would disappear. God also told him to return to the American Indians and preach peace and pacifism.

The Ghost Dance Religion, which Wovoka founded after his vision, was embodied in symbolic dances, songs, and clothing that were supposed to protect the members of the religion from the white man's weapons. It was followed by most of the American Indian tribes from the Plains to the Rockies as they prepared for the new era. As time passed, however, anxiety and apprehension grew, resulting in the Ghost Dance War of 1890.

After the killing of Chief SITTING BULL and the American Indian defeat in the Battle of WOUNDED KNEE, the Ghost Dance Religion faded, and Wovoka spent his remaining years in comfortable obscurity.

Wright, Chauncey (1830–1875) American philosopher. Born in Northampton, Massachusetts, Wright entered Harvard in 1848 and studied mathematics and philosophy. From 1863 to 1870 he edited the annual proceedings of the American Academy of Arts and Sciences. In 1864 he began a series of philosophical essays in the *North American Review* and contributed to the *Mathematical Monthly*. Wright was also interested in natural history, and his article proposing an evolutionary explanation for "The Uses and Origin of the Arrangements of Leaves in Plants" received praise from CHARLES DARWIN. He was noted for helping to introduce British empiricism to the United States.

In 1870, Wright delivered a series of lectures at Harvard on the principles of psychology and produced a number of important essays on the subject. "Evolution of Self-Consciousness" anticipated later philosophical trends, especially the ideas of WILLIAM JAMES, whose writings and popularity quickly overshadowed Wright's reputation.

Wright, Frank Lloyd (1867–1959) American architect. Born in Richland Center, Wisconsin, Frank Lloyd Wright spent many summers on his uncle's farm in Spring Green, Wisconsin. In 1886, J. L. Silsbee built a small chapel on the farm, and early the next year Wright, who had dropped out of high school, was hired by Silsbee to work in his office in Chicago, Illinois.

By the end of the year, Wright worked with Dankmar Adler and LOUIS SULLIVAN, who ran one of the most influential architectural firms in the United States at the time. In his spare time, Wright began to design houses for his own clients, which was a violation of his contract with Sullivan. Wright left Sullivan's firm in 1893 and began his own practice, creating the "prairie style" house, characterized by low horizontal lines that reflect the landscape.

Most of Wright's accomplishments took place after the Victorian Age; throughout his career Wright strived to make his work simpler, employing fewer lines and fewer forms, which led to his dramatic use of basic geometrical shapes in his later work.

Wright's work forms the foundation on which most of twentieth-century architectural thought resides.

Wundt, Wilhelm (1832–1920) German psychologist and physiologist. For seventeen years Wundt lecturered at the University of Heidelberg, where he had earned his Ph.D. and M.D. In 1867 he began teaching the first formal academic course in psychology. Until that time psychology had been considered a branch of philosophy, but Wundt showed that psychology could be an experimental science.

The two volumes of Wundt's lecture notes, *Grundzüge der physiologischen Psychologie* (Fundamentals of Physiological Psychology, 1896), became one of the most important works in the history of psychology. The publication led to a faculty position for Wundt at the University of Leipzig in 1875, where he established the first psychological laboratory in the world.

Wundt was a highly prolific writer, and in 1881 he established the first journal solely devoted to psychology, *Philosophische Studien*. He continued his lectures and studies, concentrating on the customs, behavior, and language systems of various ethnic groups, until his retirement in 1917.

Wuthering Heights (1847) English novel. EMILY BRONTË's only novel was first published under the pen name Ellis Bell. "Wuthering" is a Yorkshire word that refers to turbulent weather. The powerful tale of the undying and ferocious love of Heathcliff and Catherine Earnshaw shocked contemporaries. It is famed for its emotional intensity, moral ambiguity, and precisely realized Yorkshire settings. It is also respected for its shifting narrative viewpoints, being largely told to a visitor named Lockwood by Mrs. Dean, a servant to the Earnshaw family.

An orphan named Heathcliff is raised by Mr. Earnshaw at Wuthering Heights, a lonely estate on the moors, along with Earnshaw's natural children, Catherine and Hindley. Catherine and Heathcliff become fiercely attached, while Hindley hates and bullies Heathcliff. Feeling despised but determined to prove himself, Heathcliff runs away and returns a wealthy man. By that time Catherine has married the rich Edgar Linton of Thrushcross Grange.

Heathcliff takes vengeance for Catherine's rejection of him, doing his best to ruin the lives of Hindley, Hindley's son Hareton, Edgar Linton's sister Isabella, and Catherine's daughter Cathy. Even so, he and Catherine remain passionately connected. After Catherine dies, Heathcliff longs for death and supernatural reconciliation with her. Once he is dead, Catherine's daughter Cathy and Hindley's neglected son Hareton are free to nurture their own love for each other.

X rays Electromagnetic radiation. Of much shorter wavelength and higher frequency than visible light, the invisible and strongly penetrating X rays were discovered in 1895 by German physicist Wilhelm Conrad Röntgen (1845–1923) using a CATHODE-RAY tube and phosphorescent paper. Because X rays permitted the study of internal structure, they became important in the twentieth century in medicine, industry, security, and other fields. For his discovery, Röntgen won the first Nobel Prize in physics in 1901.

yachting Sport or pastime. "Yacht" dates back to the late 1600s when Charles II introduced the word and the sport to England. The world's first yachting club, the Water Club of Cork Harbour, was formed in Ireland in 1720.

John and Edwin Stevens organized the New York Yacht Club in 1844, and in 1851 their schooner *America* defeated a fleet of British yachts in a fifty-three-mile race around the Isle of Wight, off the southern coast of England. In 1857 the New York Yacht Club offered the trophy known as the "America's Cup" as a perpetual challenge for international yacht racing.

The Yacht Racing Association was founded in 1875 in Great Britain—with Edward VII, the Prince of Wales, as its president—in order to provide rules and regulations for sailing. It was followed by the International Yacht Racing Union, founded in 1906.

Yale, Linus (1821–1868) American inventor and manufacturer. The son of a distinguished locksmith and inventor, Yale began working on locks in Shelburne Falls, Massachusetts, around 1851. In 1862, he developed the "Monitor Bank Lock," which became the first dial or combination lock. The dial lock moved away from the necessity of a key; the dial was turned to a series of designated positions, which in turn lifted levers that released the catches of the lock. In 1865, Yale patented his design, including a cylinder lock with pin tumblers. This particular type of lock dated back to ancient Egypt, but Yale had simplified the construction, making it suitable for mass production. The inventor lacked the necessary funds for a manufacturing plant, but with the help of John Henry Towne, the Yale Lock Manufacturing Company was founded in 1868. Shortly thereafter Yale died of a heart attack.

Yeats, William Butler (1865–1939) Irish poet and playwright. One of the greatest poets of the twentieth century, Yeats was a leading figure in the Irish Renaissance that began in the late nineteenth century. Born in Dublin, he was the son of a Protestant painter. He was raised partly in his mother's home county of Sligo, where he grew attached

William Butler Yeats, Irish poet and playwright, is regarded as one of the greatest writers of the twentieth century. Born near the end of the Victorian era, Yeats was already an important poet by the turn of the century. Photo courtesy of Topham/The Image Works.

to the countryside's natural beauty and discovered the Irish legends he would incorporate in his work, and in London, where he attended high school. While he is best known for his poetry collections published in the 1920s and 1930s, such as *The Tower* (1928) and *The Winding Stair* (1933), which include "Sailing to Byzantium," "Leda and the Swan," "Among School Children," and others, his youth in the 1890s demonstrated a keen interest in Irish folkloric traditions, the composition of poetic drama, and Irish politics.

The reception of his first book of poems, *The Wanderings of Oisin* (1889), persuaded him to leave art school and pursue literary endeavors. The tales gathered in *The Celtic Twilight* (1893) and the verse in *Poems* (1895) and *The Wind Among the Reeds* (1899) demonstrate his intense interest in Irish themes. With Ernest Rhys he founded the RHYMERS' CLUB in 1890. As a young man Yeats became absorbed in the Irish Republican movement and the FENIANS, and in 1889 he fell in love with Irish patriot MAUD GONNE, who became the inspiration for his love poetry. By 1897, with Lady GREGORY, GEORGE MOORE, and Edward Martyn, he helped establish an Irish national theater. Known as the Irish Literary Theatre, it opened in 1899 with a production of Yeats's 1892 play *The Countess Kathleen;* it was soon reestablished as the Abbey Theatre (1904).

A disciple of occult movements such as the THEOSOPHICAL SOCIETY of MADAME BLAVATSKY, the Rosicrucian Society, and the Hermetic Order of the Golden Dawn, he later developed a philosophical system of his own that provided a coherent network of symbols for his poetry.

Yellow Book, The (1894–97) English illustrated quarterly. Published in book form and edited by the novelist Henry Harland and the illustrator AUBREY BEARDSLEY, it was financed by John Lane, one of London's leading publishers of the avant-garde. The publication contained short stories, poetry, articles, and illustrations, with an emphasis on the exotic and the "modern," including works by OSCAR WILDE, WILLIAM BUTLER YEATS, HENRY JAMES, and H. G. WELLS.

The first issue, which proclaimed "no prejudice against anything except dullness and incapacity," was published on April 15, 1894, and was harshly criticized by the English press. The publication made headlines a year later when Oscar Wilde was arrested on morals charges and was described as having a copy of the yellow-bound periodical under his arm. Although he was actually holding a copy of *Aphrodite* by Pierre Louys, the publishers of *The Yellow Book* saw fit to change the binding to a dull gray, which it remained until the publication's demise in April 1897.

yellow fever Infectious disease. Caused by a virus transmitted by the bite of the female *aedes aegypti* mosquito, it is endemic to many tropical and subtropical regions. In 1900 the U.S. Army Yellow Fever Commission, headed by Walter Reed who worked with the Cuban physician Carlos J. Finley, proved Finley's theory of mosquito transmission. A vaccine was developed in the early 1940s, and immunization became an effective prevention.

Yellowstone National Park U.S. recreational grounds. President ULYSSES S. GRANT signed an act of Congress on March 1, 1872, establishing the world's first national park. The Yellowstone National Park Act was written by William H. Clagett, Jr., from a proposal by David E. Folsom, a Montana surveyor, and Cornelius Hedges, a Montana judge. Yellowstone National Park covers more than 2 million acres in Montana, Idaho, and Wyoming. It also contains the world's largest concentration of thermal features, including three thousand hot springs and two hundred geysers, of which Old Faithful remains one of the most popular tourist attractions. Yellowstone Lake is the largest mountain lake in North America, covering 137 square miles.

Yemen Middle Eastern country. It extends nearly seven hundred miles along the southern coast of the Arabian Peninsula, with Saudi Arabia to the north and Oman to the east. An Islamic region since 628, it was occupied by the Ottoman Turkish Empire in 1538 and remained nominally under Ottoman suzerainty until 1918. In 1839 the British seized the port of Aden, of strategic importance in protecting their sea route to INDIA. After the opening of the SUEZ CANAL in 1869, Aden's importance increased, and until 1914, Great Britain gradually expanded the colony through purchases and treaties with surrounding rulers. It gained its independence in 1967 as the People's Republic of Southern Yemen. The rest of Yemen had gained independence from the Ottoman Empire in 1918 and was recognized by other nations as Yemen. It merged with Southern Yemen in 1990, forming the unified republic of Yemen.

Yonge, Charlotte Mary (1823–1901) English writer. Born in Otterbourne, Hampshire, England, Yonge was influenced by the vicar in a neighboring village and began to associate herself with the High Church faction, or OXFORD MOVEMENT, in the Church of England. Her books are infused with her religious views. She was a popular author from her first success in 1853, *The Heir of Redclyffe;* among her later novels were *Heartsease* (1854), *The Daisy Chain* (1856), and *The Young Stepmother* (1861). A diverse and prolific writer, Yonge published biographies, popular history, historical romances, and scripture interpretations. She also edited the girl's magazine *Monthly Packet* from 1851 to 1899.

Young, Brigham (1801–1877) Mormon leader. He was born in Whitingham, Vermont, but reared in the region of New York State known as the "burnt-over district" due to the religious fervor of many of the area's citizens. Young worked as a farmer, carpenter, and painter before moving to Mendon, New York, in 1829 where, a year later, Joseph Smith founded the Mormon faith with the publication of the *Book of Mormon*. Young left the Methodists and joined the Mormon Church after his first wife's death in 1832. He then led a group of converts to Kirtland, Ohio, where he began his rise in the Church. By 1835, Brigham Young was named third in seniority in the newly organized Quorum of the Twelve Apostles, a group that ranked just below Joseph Smith in the government of the Mormon Church.

When the Mormons were driven from Missouri in 1839, Young organized the move to Nauvoo, Illinois, where he became senior member of the Twelve Apostles. Young was campaigning in Boston on behalf of Smith's run for the presidency in 1844 when he was notified of the leader's murder. Young quickly returned to Nauvoo and in 1847 led a group of 148 followers to the Great Salt Lake in Utah, which he named Deseret.

The Great Salt Lake was claimed by Mexico at the time, but Young appointed himself governor of the territory, which he used as the base of his Mormon colony. He developed church-owned businesses, established the University of Deseret, now the University of Utah, in 1850, and enticed more than seventy thousand people to join him at Deseret. After the MEXICAN WAR, an act of Congress changed Deseret into the Utah Territory in 1850, and Young was retained as governor, until friction between the Mormons and the federal judiciary led President JAMES BUCHANAN to replace Young in 1857.

Brigham Young continued to build the Mormon Church, transforming the loose organization into a powerful social and economic force in the American West. He is reputed to have had more than twenty wives and over fifty children.

Young England Informal British political group. Made up of four Tory politicians who opposed the policies of party leader ROBERT PEEL and tried to stamp the party with their own philosophy, the group rejected what it considered Peel's middle-class, "shop-owner" conservatism in favor of a nostalgic attachment to aristocratic rule. BENJAMIN DISRAELI led the quartet, which also included Alexander Baillie-Cochrane, Lord John Manners, and George Smythe. The group, which was firmly established by 1843, formed a voting bloc in Parliament that opposed free trade and Peel's various Irish policies. The four men wielded influence beyond their numbers, almost completely because of Disraeli's stature. Its opposition to the repeal of the CORN LAWS helped bring down Peel's government in 1846. Disraeli's novel, *Coningsby; or, the New Generation* (1844), is a portrayal of the band.

Young Ireland Irish revolutionary group. Active between 1840 and 1850, Young Ireland served as a political counter to DANIEL O'CONNELL. Extreme in their opinions, the young Irish radicals advocated a violent revolution but received little support from the Irish people who had been suffering through famine.

Among the party leaders were John Mitchel, William Smith O'Brien, poet Thomas Davis, and John Blake Dillon, whose journal *Nation* promoted a political insurrection and the use of physical force. In 1848 the thirty-three-year-old Mitchel was arrested for treason, along with other members, and sent to Tasmania while O'Brien led a failed rebellion. Mitchel escaped to the United States with other Young Irelanders in 1853 and tried to organize Irish resistance there. O'Brien was pardoned in 1854.

Young Men's Christian Association (YMCA) International social and instructional organization for young men. The YMCA was founded in London, England, in 1844 by George Williams, a twenty-two-year-old dry goods clerk who had formed a club with twelve young men in order to improve "the spiritual condition of young men in the drapery and other trades." The first meetings were held in a reading room, but the size and scope of the association quickly grew, and religious meetings and assistance to young men entering London soon became the organization's primary activities.

The first YMCA in the United States was formed in Boston, Massachusetts, by T. V. Sullivan in 1851, the same year as the founding of the YMCA in Montreal. Both were based on the Williams model. An international convention was held in Buffalo, New York, in 1854, and a year later the World Alliance of YMCAs was created, with its headquarters in Geneva, Switzerland. By the late 1880s missionaries had introduced the YMCA into Japan and China; in 1892 the London staff helped organize a YMCA in Cairo, Egypt.

Athletics and physical activity played an important role in the YMCAs, and in 1891 staff member James Naismith invented the game of BASKETBALL at the YMCA training school at Springfield College in Massachusetts. Volleyball was invented in 1895 by the YMCA physical director, William G. Morgan, at Holyoke, Massachusetts.

Younger Brothers American outlaws. Born near Lee's Summit, Missouri, Thomas Coleman "Cole" Younger (1844–1916) and his brothers Jim (1848–1901) and John (1853–1874) joined a band of marauding criminals during the CIVIL WAR, led by William Quantrill. They traveled the Missouri countryside, robbing and murdering for personal gain while aligning themselves with the Confederate cause. John Younger is reputed to have killed four Union soldiers by age ten.

Frank and JESSE JAMES were also members of Quantrill's guerrillas, and on February 13, 1866, Frank James joined the Younger brothers. It was the beginning of a spree of robberies throughout the Midwest and extending into Texas, Arkansas, and Colorado. Jesse James joined the gang in October 1866, and eighteen-year-old Robert Younger began his involvement in 1872.

John Younger was killed on March 16, 1874, during a shootout with lawmen near Morgan Springs, Missouri. In September 1876 the Younger-James gang was dissolved after a failed robbery attempt in Northfield, Minnesota.

In November, Cole, Jim, and Robert Younger pleaded guilty to two murder charges and were sentenced to life imprisonment in the Minnesota State Penitentiary. Robert Younger died in the Stillwater Penitentiary from tuberculosis in 1889. Cole and Jim were paroled in July 1901 after serving twenty-five years; Jim Younger committed suicide in a St. Paul hotel room in October.

Cole Younger worked as a tombstone salesman in St. Paul before receiving a full pardon in 1903. He returned to Missouri and reunited with his old partner in the short-lived "Cole Younger–Frank James Wild West Show." He then joined the Lew Nichols Carnival Company, where he continued to present his past exploits as a sideshow attraction.

Youth's Companion, The (1827–1929) The U.S. children's weekly magazine. One of the most significant of all American PERIODICALS, it was founded in June 1827 by a political journalist and publisher, Nathaniel Willis. *The Youth's Companion* grew out of the popularity of the children's section in another of Willis's publications, *Recorder,* an important religious newspaper of the time.

The publication was dominated by religious and instructional material until the 1840s when Willis began to include biographies and nature articles. In 1857 the magazine was sold to Daniel Sharp Ford, a Baptist newspaper owner, and while Willis was retained as "senior editor," he was rarely involved with the publication. Ford lessened the religious overtones of *The Youth's Companion* and gave fiction dominance, especially adventure tales.

Under Ford's direction the magazine's circulation grew from five thousand in 1857 to more than five hundred thousand in the late 1890s, becoming the highest circulated magazine in the United States. HARRIET BEECHER STOWE, LOUISA MAY ALCOTT, L. FRANK BAUM, JACK LONDON, and Woodrow Wilson contributed to the publication, which after the Civil War offered lanterns, chemistry sets, and other prizes to readers who sold subscriptions.

Following Ford's death in 1899, the magazine was guided by editors who lacked Ford's ability to gauge and meet the desires of the publication's audience, and in 1929 *The Youth's Companion* merged with *American Boy.*

Yukon gold rush Alaskan pursuit for minerals and riches. The search for fortune near the junction of the Yukon and Klondike rivers in Canada, near the turn of the nineteenth century, began in August 1896 when George W. Carmach and two American Indian companions discovered gold in Bonanza Creek, a tributary of the Klondike River. The discovery precipitated an influx of thousands of people to the region. The city of Dawson was named capital of the newly created Yukon Territory and swelled to twenty-five thousand residents in 1898, eventually becoming known as the "Paris of the North." Within a year the richest gold deposits had been emptied, few new lodes had been discovered, and the territory quickly fell into decline, with only four thousand residents left in Dawson by 1921. It is estimated that between 1897 and 1904 more than $100 million worth of gold was extracted from the Yukon.

The gold rush years were popularized in the writings of Robert Service and JACK LONDON.

Zambezi River Waterway in south central Africa. One of the world's longest rivers (ranking thirtieth), it flows about seventeen hundred miles from its source in Zambia to the Mozambique Channel, interrupted along the way by VICTORIA FALLS. In 1851, Scottish explorer DAVID LIVINGSTONE became the first European to lay eyes on the Zambezi.

Zambia (Republic of Zambia) Landlocked country in south central AFRICA. Clockwise from the north, it is surrounded by Zaire, Tanzania, Malawi, Mozambique, Zimbabwe, Botswana, Namibia, and Angola. Its capital is Lusaka; its principal export since Victorian times has been copper. In 1889, British colonizer CECIL RHODES gained mining concessions in the region from King Lewanika of the Barotse. Settlement followed, and Rhodes's British South Africa Company ruled the territory as Northern Rhodesia until 1924. In 1924, Northern Rhodesia became a British protectorate administered by the crown. On October 24, 1964, it became the independent nation of Zambia.

Zanzibar Island and name of city in the Indian Ocean off the East African coast. Now part of Tanzania. Arab traders settled the island of Zanzibar by the tenth century or earlier. The first European to visit Zanzibar was Portuguese explorer Vasco da Gama, en route to India, in 1499. The island, valuable for its Indian Ocean trade, fell under Portuguese control for about two hundred years until the Arabs from Oman gained power in 1698. In the 1860s, the sultan of Zanzibar became independent of the sultan of Oman. Zanzibar's sultan controlled a flourishing trade in slaves and ivory, along with the island's trade in cloves, of which Zanzibar is the world's largest producer. In the 1860s the sultan established Dar es Salaam, now Tanzania's capital, as a summer residence on the mainland in the region known as Tanganyika.

Zanzibar's rich trade attracted the interest of European powers. While Germany took over the mainland region of Tanganyika, making it German East Africa in 1885, the British made Zanzibar a protectorate in 1890, but the sultan remained the nominal head of government.

After the Germans were defeated in World War I, Tanganyika was made a British mandate. In 1963, Zanzibar gained political independence, and in 1964 it merged with Tanganyika to become Tanzania.

Zeeman, Pieter (1865–1943) Dutch physicist. Born at Zonnemaire, Zeeland, on May 25, 1865, Zeeman studied at the University of Leiden, where he taught from 1890 until 1900 when he was appointed professor of physics at the University of Amsterdam. His doctoral dissertation on the influence of magnetism on polarized light earned a gold medal from the Netherlands Scientific Society of Haarlem in 1892. The effects of magnetism on light, resulting in the splitting of spectral lines, became known as the ZEEMAN EFFECT. It has been applied to quantum mechanics and to determining the magnetic fields of stars.

Zeeman's later work included precise measurements of the speed of light through glass. His results agreed with Albert Einstein's newly proposed theory of relativity. He was awarded the Nobel Prize in 1902.

Zeeman effect Scientific influence. The effect of a magnetic field on a light source was discovered in 1896 by Dutch physicist PIETER ZEEMAN, who was awarded the Nobel Prize in 1902 for his work.

Zeppelin, Ferdinand Adolf August Heinrich von, Count (1838–1917) German soldier and aeronaut. Zeppelin attended the Ludwigsburg Military Academy and the University of Tübingen before receiving an army commission in 1859. In 1863 he acquired permission to act as a military observer with the Army of the Potomac during the U.S. Civil War. He later joined an expedition to the source of the Mississippi River, where in St. Paul, Minnesota, he made his first ascent in a BALLOON.

Returning to Germany, Zeppelin fought against Prussia in the SEVEN WEEKS' WAR in 1866 and was a cavalry officer in the FRANCO-PRUSSIAN WAR of 1870–71. He was promoted to the rank of general before retiring in 1891 to devote his attention to experiments with the dirigible or airship, a power-driven steerable balloon. Although his interest in airship travel left Zeppelin nearly bankrupt, he was able to fly the first airship with a rigid frame in 1900, and by 1914 several of the "zeppelins" had flown more than one thousand miles.

The explosion of the Hindenburg in 1937 brought an abrupt end to the popularity of rigid airships.

Zetkin, Clara Eissner (1857–1933) German political leader. Clara Eissner became a socialist under the influence of Russian revolutionary Osip Zetkin, whom she later married. She joined the German SOCIAL DEMOCRATIC PARTY in 1881 and became an outspoken champion of woman's rights, serving as a representative of women workers at the 1889 meeting of the Second Socialist International. She argued that SOCIALISM and feminism were connected in the pamphlet *The Question of Women Workers and Women at the Present Time* (1889). In the 1890s, Zetkin helped found a women's bureau in Germany and edited the newspaper that she renamed *Equality* (*Gleichheit*) instead of *The Working Woman*. She cofounded the International Socialist Women's Congress in 1907. She moved to Moscow in 1921 and remained there for the rest of her life; three volumes of her speeches and writings were published in East Germany in the late 1950s.

Zimbabwe See RHODESIA.

Zionism Jewish political movement. Coined by the Austrian writer Nathan Birnbaum in 1893, the term describes the movement and aspiration of the Jewish people to return to

Zionism, the modern political movement dedicated to reestablishing the Jewish nation state in Palestine, began to attract settlers in the 1880's. Photo courtesy of the Zionist Archives and Library.

their ancient homeland. In 1825 an American surveyor, Mordecai Manuel Noah (1785–1851), suggested Grand Island in the Niagara River as a Jewish state; then in 1844 he pleaded for support of Jewish resettlement in Palestine. His cause was taken up by Sir Laurence Oliphant (1829–1888) in Great Britain, who wanted to fulfill ancient prophecies and "bring about the end of the world." Oliphant made a number of visits to the Middle East and traveled with the Hebrew poet Naftali Herz Imber (1856–1909), whose "Hatikwa" became the Zionist national anthem.

The First Aliya—Hebrew for "going up"—to Palestine occurred in 1882, with members of the Hoveve Zion migrating from Russia and Romania. The settlements in Palestine quickly gained the support of the French Jewish financier Baron Edmond de Rothschild, and by 1897 the World Zionist Organization was formed by the Austrian newspaper correspondent Theodor Herzl (1860–1904). The same year, the First Zionist Congress met in Switzerland, which solidified Zionism as a political force.

Asher Ginzberg (1856–1927), writing under the pen name Ahad Haam (One of the People), argued that a Jewish state in Palestine could not succeed due to the small size of the country and the existence of a large native population. Instead, Ginzberg advocated the formation of a Jewish cultural center in Palestine. The idea of Zionism prevailed, however, with the formation of Israel in 1948.

zipper Clothing fastener. The forerunner of the modern zipper was invented in 1893 by Whitcomb Judson, an inventor and engineer who lived in Chicago, Illinois. The "clasp-locker," as it was called, was invented to replace shoelaces on boots. Judson's invention consisted of two rows of parallel hook-and-eye

Through his novels and essays, Emile Zola stressed the importance of realism. He was a leader in the French Naturalist Movement. Private collection.

locks that were brought together by the upward motion of a metal tab. Judson's brainchild jammed too often to be a commercial success, and he died in 1909 thinking his invention would never find a market.

A more dependable and easier-to-use version was developed in 1913, and it was first ordered by the U.S. Army during World War I. The term "zipper" did not come into use until 1923 when rubber magnate B. F. GOODRICH started producing galoshes with the new fasteners.

Zola, Emile [-Edouard-Charles-Antoine] (1840–1902) French novelist. Zola was a proponent of the naturalist technique of writing, which argued that literature must be scientific in its approach, not imaginative. His twenty-novel series *Les Rougon-Macquart,* published between 1871 and 1893, was the landmark of Zola's career and the French Naturalism movement.

Born in Paris, Zola saw his father, a civil engineer, die suddenly in 1847, leaving the family in poverty. Zola struggled as a writer while working in the sales department of a publishing house. An autobiographical novel, *La Confession de Claude,* was published in 1865. He courted notoriety with his defense of the paintings of EDOUARD MANET, who was generally condemned at the time. Zola's support won him the immediate friendship of Manet and other artists who became important figures in IMPRESSIONISM a decade later.

After his second novel, *Thérèse Raquin* (1867), the writer began work on *Les Rougon-Macquart,* subtitled "the natural and social history of a family under the Second Empire." Zola conceived of the series as an exhaustive study of the period, one that allowed him to test his theories of fiction and also press for social reform. *L'Assommoir* (1877), one of the novels in the series, made Zola a best-selling author. As in the other Rougon-Macquart novels, Zola employed brutal, sordid detail to tell the story of the Paris slums. Other important novels in the series included *Nana* (1880), *The Soil* (1887), and *The Human Animal* (1890). *Germinal* (1885), widely considered the best of these works, expressed great sympathy for the suffering of the poor in the story of an unsuccessful miners' strike.

In 1880, Zola published *Le Roman experimental,* in which he formally advocated the naturalist technique and likened the writer to a surgeon or scientist, able to impartially observe his subjects and establish a rational cause and effect in the characters. Despite his pronouncements of distance and impartiality,

Zola's novels are characterized by a subtle understanding of emotion.

In his last novels—the trilogy *Les Trois Villes* (1894–98) and the unfinished series *Les Quatre Evangiles* (1899–1903)—Zola advocated a variety of Christian SOCIALISM that would alleviate the public evils he had thoroughly documented in his earlier works. Zola achieved his greatest fame from the January 13, 1898, publication of his letter (beginning "J'accuse") in which he defended Captain ALFRED DREYFUS and pointed out irregularities in the trial. Prosecuted for libel and found guilty, Zola escaped to England until a general amnesty permitted his safe return. He died in Paris due to an accidental asphyxiation caused by a blocked chimney in his bedroom.

Zorrilla y Moral, José (1817–1893) Spanish dramatist and poet. Born in Valladolid, Spain, and educated at the Seminario de Nobles in Madrid, Zorrilla studied law in Toledo and Vallodolid. Zorrilla left the university in 1836 and devoted himself to literature. He achieved fame a year later when he leaped into the grave of the romantic writer and critic Mariano José de Larra and recited an emotional eulogy. Zorrilla's subsequent collection *Poesías* (1837) became an immediate popular success, as did the later collection *Cantos del trovador* (1840–41) based largely on Spanish legends. The works brought him to the forefront of Spanish ROMANTICISM.

Zorrilla's success as a poet was quickly eclipsed by the fame of his play *Don Juan Tenorio* (1844), which became the most popular play of nineteenth-century Spain and is still regularly performed. Zorrilla deprecated the drama, however, and embarked on an ambitious effort to retell the history of Grenada in three volumes. Only two volumes were completed, published as *Grenada* in 1852.

Zorrilla moved to Mexico in 1855, where the emperor Maximilian commissioned him to found a national theater. When Maximilian was removed from power, Zorrilla returned to Spain and lived in poverty, despite the popularity of his writing, until he was named poet laureate in 1889 and received a pension from the Spanish government. He published his autobiography *Recuerdos del tiempo viejo* in 1880; like most of his writing, the work is based loosely on fact, steeped in legend, and retold in a fanciful and exaggerated style.

Zulu Name applied to an African tribe. Residing in SOUTH AFRICA, the tribe became internationally known for its resistance to BOER settlers in the Natal and TRANSVAAL regions of South Africa and the defeat of British forces in 1878 before the capture of the chief, Cetewayo, in the ZULU WAR. Its historic home of Zululand was annexed by the British in 1887.

Zulu War (1879) Violent conflict between GREAT BRITAIN and the ZULU tribe.

After the discovery of diamonds in 1871, Great Britain was determined to maintain control of the southern African coastline, and by April 1877 the TRANSVAAL region had become a British colony. Great Britain believed that no stability could be possible in South Africa with the existence of the independent Zulu kingdom. Sir Bartle Frere, the high commissioner, dispatched an ultimatum to Cetewayo (1836?–1884) to disband his army within thirty days and accept a British resident as "the eyes, ears, and mouth of Queen Victoria's government." Cetewayo refused, and his country was invaded by British forces on January 11, 1879.

On January 22, the Zulu army engaged the British troops at Isandhlwana, killing sixteen hundred British soldiers in the worst British defeat since the CRIMEAN WAR. The British sent reinforcements, but Zulu resistance continued to be strong, and the war gained international notice with the killing of Louis J. J. Bonaparte (1856–1879), son of former French emperor NAPOLEON III. On July 4, 1879, British troops under the command of General Garnet J. Wolseley (1833–1913) finally defeated the Zulu army. Cetewayo was captured in August and forced to make peace.

After Cetewayo's capture, the land was divided into thirteen separate territories, each governed by its own chief. Few of the appointed chiefs were able to govern the territories, however, and in 1882, Cetewayo visited Queen Victoria and was subsequently allowed to regain control of some of Zululand. During a civil war in 1884, Cetewayo was forced to flee and relinquish his power; the British government again intervened and appointed its own magistrates, leaving only about one-third of the territories under Zulu control. The British formally annexed Zululand in 1887.

Bibliography

Abrams, M. H., ed. *The Norton Anthology of English Literature,* rev. ed. New York: W. W. Norton, 1968.

Adams, James Truslow. *The British Empire 1784–1939.* New York: Dorset Press, 1940.

Ammer, Christine. *Harper's Dictionary of Music.* New York: Harper and Row, 1972.

Anderson, Bonnie S., and Judith P. Zinsser. *A History of Their Own: Women in Europe from Prehistory to the Present,* 2 vols. New York: Harper and Row, 1988.

Arnason, H. H. *History of Modern Art.* Englewood Cliffs, N.J.: Prentice-Hall; New York: Harry N. Abrams, 1979.

Aronson, Joseph. *The Encyclopedia of Furniture.* New York: Crown, 1966.

Asimov, Issac. *Asimov's Biographical Encyclopedia of Science and Technology,* 2d ed. Garden City, N.Y.: Doubleday, 1982.

———. *Asimov's Chronology of Science and Discovery.* New York: Harper and Row, 1989.

———. *Asimov's New Guide to Science.* New York: Basic Books, 1984.

Barker, Felix, and Peter Jackson. *London: 2,000 Years of a City and Its People.* New York: Macmillan, 1973.

Barnhart, Clarence L., ed. *New Century Cyclopedia of Names.* New York: Appleton-Century-Crofts, 1954.

Benét, William Rose, ed. *Benét's Reader's Encyclopedia.* New York: Harper and Row, 1987.

Bindman, David, ed. *The Thames and Hudson Encyclopedia of British Art.* London: Thames and Hudson, 1985.

Blackburn, David, and Geoffrey Holister. *Encyclopedia of Modern Technology.* New York: G. K. Hall, 1987.

Blake, Robert. *Disraeli.* New York: St. Martin's Press, 1967.

Bordman, Gerald. *The Oxford Companion to American Theatre.* Oxford: Oxford University Press, 1984.

Braden, Donna. *Leisure and Entertainment in America.* Dearborn, Mich.: Henry Ford Museum and Greenfield Village, 1988.

Bradley, Ian. *William Morris and His World.* New York: Charles Scribner's Sons, 1978.

Brantlinger, Patrick, ed. *Energy and Entropy: Science and Culture in Victorian Britain.* Bloomington: Indiana University Press, 1989.

Bridgwater, William, and Elizabeth J. Sherwood. *The Columbia Encyclopedia,* 2d ed. New York: Columbia University Press, 1950.

Briggs, Asa. *A Social History of England.* New York: Viking, 1983.

———. *Victorian People: A Reassessment of Persons and Themes, 1851–67.* New York: Harper Colophon, 1963.

Bynum, W. F., and Roy Porter, eds. *Companion Encyclopedia of the History of Medicine.* London: Routledge, 1993.

Canaday, John. *Mainstreams of Modern Art.* New York: Holt, Rinehart and Winston, 1959.

Carpenter, Humphrey, and Mari Prichard. *The Oxford Companion to Children's Literature.* Oxford: Oxford University Press, 1984.

Chilvers, Ian, Harold Osborne, and Dennis Farr, eds. *The Oxford Dictionary of Art.* Oxford: Oxford University Press, 1988.

Colbert, Edwin H. *The Great Dinosaur Hunters and Their Discoveries.* New York: Dover, 1984.

Collier's Encyclopedia. New York: Macmillan, 1992.

Concise Science Dictionary, 2d ed. Oxford: Oxford University Press, 1991.

Crowley, David. *Introduction to Victorian Style.* New York: Mallard Press, 1990.

Curtis, Edmund. *A History of Ireland.* London: Methuen, 1965.

Dangerfield, George. *The Damnable Question: A Study in Anglo-Irish Relations.* Boston: Little, Brown, 1976.

Dictionary of American History. New York: Charles Scribner's Sons, 1976.

Drabble, Margaret, ed. *The Oxford Companion to English Literature,* 5th ed. Oxford: Oxford University Press, 1985.

Dyos, H. J., and Michael Wolff, eds. *The Victorian City.* London: Routledge & Kegan Paul, 1973.

Encyclopedia Americana. Danbury, Conn.: Grolier, 1994.

Encyclopedia of Collectibles. Alexandria, Va: Time-Life Books, 1979.

Ensor, Sir Robert. *England 1870–1914.* Oxford: Oxford University Press, 1966.

Eyewitness Travel Guides: London. New York: Dorling Kindersley, 1993.

Farwell, Byron. *Queen Victoria's Little Wars.* New York: W. W. Norton, 1972.

Faust, Patricia L., ed. *Historical Times Illustrated Encyclopedia of the Civil War.* New York: HarperPerennial, 1991.

Foner, Eric, and John A. Garraty, eds. *The Reader's Companion to American History.* Boston: Houghton Mifflin, 1991.

Garraty, John A., and Peter Gay, eds. *The Columbia History of the World.* New York: Harper and Row, 1972.

Gassner, John, and Edward Quinn, eds. *The Reader's Encyclopedia of World Drama.* New York: Thomas Y. Crowell, 1969.

Gloag, John. *A Short Dictionary of Furniture.* New York: Bonanza, 1965.

Greene, David Mason. *Greene's Biographical Encyclopedia of Composers.* Garden City, N.Y.: Doubleday, 1985.

Grolier's Academic American Encyclopedia, online. Danbury, Conn.: Grolier Electronic Publishing, 1994.

Grolier's: The New Book of Knowledge. Danbury, Conn.: Grolier, 1980.

Grun, Bernard. *The Timetables of History,* rev. ed. New York: Touchstone, 1982.

Gutman, Herbert G., et al. *Who Built America?,* 2 vols. New York: Pantheon, 1989, 1992.

Hardwick, Michael and Mollie. *The Charles Dickens Encyclopedia.* Ware, Hertfordshire, England: Wordsworth Editions, 1992.

Hart, James D., ed. *The Oxford Companion to American Literature,* 5th ed. Oxford: Oxford University Press, 1983.

Hartnoll, Phyllis, ed. *The Oxford Companion to the Theatre,* 4th ed. Oxford: Oxford University Press, 1993.

Hendrickson, Robert. *The Henry Holt Encyclopedia of Word and Phrase Origins.* New York: Henry Holt, 1987.

Hibbert, Christopher. *London: The Biography of a City.* New York: William Morrow, 1969.

Hickok, Ralph. *New Encyclopedia of Sports.* New York: McGraw-Hill, 1977.

Hinsley, F. H. *The New Cambridge Modern History.* Cambridge: Cambridge University Press, 1962.

Hourani, Albert. *A History of the Arab Peoples.* Cambridge, Mass.: Belknap Press/ Harvard University Press, 1991.

Huggett, Frank E. *A Dictionary of British History, 1815–1973.* London: Basil Blackwell, 1974.

The Information Please Almanac, 1990, 1993. Boston: Houghton Mifflin, 1989, 1992.

Janson, H. W. *History of Art.* New York: Harry N. Abrams, 1986.

Jelavich, Charles and Barbara. *The Balkans.* Englewood Cliffs, N.J.: Prentice-Hall, 1970.

Johnson, Allen. *Dictionary of American Biography.* New York: Charles Scribner's Sons, 1964.

Katz, Ephraim. *The Film Encyclopedia,* 2nd ed. New York: HarperCollins, 1994.

Kee, Robert. *The Green Flag: The Turbulent History of the Irish Nationalist Movement.* New York: Delacorte Press, 1972.

Kinder, Hermann, and Werner Hilgemann. Trans. Ernest A. Menze. *The Anchor Atlas of World History,* vol. II. New York: Anchor Books, 1978.

Kohn, George C. *Dictionary of Wars.* New York: Anchor Books, 1987.

Levey, Judith S., and Agnes Greenhall, eds. *The Concise Columbia Encyclopedia.* New York: Columbia University Press, 1983.

Lucie-Smith, Edward. *The Thames and Hudson Dictionary of Art Terms.* London: Thames and Hudson, 1988.

MacDonagh, Oliver. *Ireland.* Englewood Cliffs, N.J.: Prentice-Hall, 1968.

Mace, O. Henry. *Collector's Guide to Victoriana.* Radnor, Pa.: Wallace-Homestead, 1991.

The McGraw-Hill Encyclopedia of World Biography. New York: McGraw-Hill, 1973.

McNeil, William. *History of Western Civilization,* rev. ed. Chicago: University of Chicago Press, 1969.

Magill, Frank N., ed. *Cyclopedia of World Authors.* New York: Harper and Bros., 1958.

———. *Masterpieces of World Literature in Digest Form.* New York: Harper and Row, 1952.

Michels, Robert. *Political Parties.* New York: Macmillan, 1962.

Mitchell, Sally, ed. *Victorian Britain.* New York: Garland, 1988.

Morehead, Philip D. *The New International Dictionary of Music.* New York: Meridian, 1992.

Morgan, Kenneth O., ed. *The Oxford History of Britain.* Oxford, England: Oxford University Press, 1988.

Morison, Samuel Eliot. *The Oxford History of the American People,* vol. 2. New York: New American Library, 1972.

Morris, James. *Pax Britannica: The Climax of an Empire.* San Diego: Harvest/Harcourt Brace Jovanovich, 1968.

Natural History (magazine). New York: American Museum of Natural History.

The New Columbia Encyclopedia. New York: Columbia University Press, 1975.

The New Encyclopedia Britannica, 15th ed. Chicago: Encyclopaedia Britannica, 1992.

Newman, Peter. *A Companion to Irish History.* New York: Facts on File, 1991.

Novak, Barbara. *American Painting of the Nineteenth Century.* New York: Harper and Row, 1979.

Osborne, Harold, ed. *An Illustrated Companion to the Decorative Arts.* London: Wordsworth Editions, 1989.

Ousby, Ian, ed. *The Cambridge Guide to Literature in English.* Cambridge: Cambridge University Press, 1988.

Palmer, R. R., and Joel Cotton. *A History of the Modern World Since 1815,* 5th ed. New York: Alfred A. Knopf, 1978.

Panati, Charles. *Extraordinary Origins of Everyday Things.* New York: Harper and Row, 1987.

Perkins, George, Barbara Perkins, and Phillip Leininger. *Benét's Reader's Encyclopedia of American Literature.* New York: HarperCollins, 1991.

Peterson, Jeanne M. *The Medical Profession in Mid-Victorian London.* Berkeley: University of California Press, 1978.

Petrie, Sir Charles. *The Victorians.* New York: David McKay, 1962.

Placzek, Adolf K., ed. *Macmillan Encyclopedia of Architects.* New York: Free Press, 1982.

Pool, Daniel. *What Jane Austen Ate and Charles Dickens Knew.* New York: Simon and Schuster, 1993.

Porter, Darwin, and Danforth Price. *Frommer's London '93.* New York: Prentice Hall Travel, 1992.

Potter, E. B., ed. *The United States and World Sea Power.* Englewood Cliffs, N.J.: Prentice-Hall, 1955.

Priestly, J. B. *Victoria's Heyday.* New York: Harper and Row, 1972.

Random House Encyclopedia, online. New York: Random House, 1994.

Read, Herbert, ed. *The Thames and Hudson Dictionary of Art and Artists.* London: Thames and Hudson, 1985.

Reader's Digest Family Encyclopedia of American History. Pleasantville, N.Y.: Reader's Digest Association, 1975.

Rosenblum, Robert, and H. W. Janson. *19th-Century Art.* New York: Harry N. Abrams, 1984.

Sadie, Stanley, ed. *The New Grove Dictionary of Music and Musicians.* New York: Macmillan, 1980.

Schlereth, Thomas J. *Victorian America: Transformations in Everyday Life, 1876–1915.* New York: HarperPerennial, 1991.

Showalter, Elaine. *A Literature of Their Own: British Women Novelists from Brontë to Lessing.* Princeton, N.J.: Princeton University Press, 1977.

Sifakis, Carl. *The Encyclopedia of American Crime,* rev. ed. New York: Smithmark, 1992.

Smith, Carter, exec. ed. *American Historical Images on File: The Civil War.* New York: Facts on File, 1989.

Smith, Goldwin. *A History of England,* 4th ed. New York: Charles Scribner's Sons, 1974.

Smithsonian (magazine). Washington: Smithsonian Institution.

Stephen, Sir Leslie, and Sir Sidney Lee, eds. *The Dictionary of National Biography.* London: Oxford University Press, 1917.

Strasser, Susan. *Never Done: A History of American Housework.* New York: Pantheon, 1982.

Talbott, John H. *A Biographical History of Medicine.* New York: Grune and Stratton, 1970.

Trager, James. *The People's Chronology,* rev. ed. New York: Henry Holt, 1992.

Uglow, Jennifer S., ed. *The Continuum Dictionary of Women's Biography.* New York: Continuum Publishing, 1989.

Varnedoe, Kirk, and Adam Gopnik. *High and Low: Modern Art and Popular Culture.* New York: Museum of Modern Art, 1990.

Victorian Studies (journal). Bloomington: Indiana University Press.

Wasson, Tyler, ed. *Nobel Prize Winners.* New York: H. W. Wilson, 1987.

Webb, R. K. *Modern England from the 18th Century to the Present.* New York: Dodd, Mead, 1968.

Webster's Biographical Dictionary. Springfield, Mass.: Merriam-Webster, 1988.

Weinreb, Ben, and Christopher Hibbert. *The London Encyclopedia.* New York: St. Martin's Press, 1983.

Wetterau, Bruce. *Macmillan Concise Dictionary of World History.* New York: Macmillan, 1983.

———. *The New York Public Library Book of Chronologies.* New York: Prentice Hall Press, 1990.

Williamson, Roxanne Kuter. *American Architects and the Mechanics of Fame.* Austin: University of Texas Press, 1991.

Wintle, Justin, ed. *Makers of Nineteenth-Century Culture, 1800–1914.* London: Routledge and Kegan Paul, 1982.

Woodham-Smith, Cecil. *Victoria.* New York: Alfred A. Knopf, 1927.

The World Book Encyclopedia. Chicago: World Book, 1992.

Youngson, A. J. *The Scientific Revolution in Victorian Medicine.* London: Croom Helm, 1979.

Zinn, Howard. *A People's History of the United States.* New York: Harper and Row, 1980.